The Business Environment

Visit the *The Business Environment*, *sixth edition*, Companion Website at **www.pearsoned.co.uk/worthington** to find valuable **student** learning material including:

- Self-assessment questions to check your understanding
- Links to articles and resources on the Internet
- Searchable online glossary

The Business Environment

Sixth edition

Ian Worthington and Chris Britton

Leicester Business School, De Monfort University, Leicester

Prentice Hall
FINANCIAL TIMES

An imprint of **Pearson Education**

Harlow, England • London • New York • Boston • San Francisco • Toronto • Sydney • Singapore • Hong Kong
Tokyo • Seoul • Taipei • New Delhi • Cape Town • Madrid • Mexico City • Amsterdam • Munich • Paris • Milan

Pearson Education Limited

Edinburgh Gate
Harlow
Essex CM20 2JE
United Kingdom

and Associated Companies around the world

Visit us on the World Wide Web at:
www.pearsoned.co.uk

First published in Great Britain in 1994
Second edition 1997
Third edition 2000
Fourth edition 2003
Fifth edition 2006
Sixth edition 2009

© Ian Worthington and Chris Britton 1994, 1997, 2000, 2003, 2006, 2009

ISBN-13: 978-0-27371-675-4

British Library Cataloguing-in-Publication Data
Worthington, Ian, 1946-
  The business environment / Ian Worthington and Chris Britton. -- 6th
ed.
        p. cm.
  Includes bibliographical references and index.
  ISBN 978-0-273-71675-4 (pbk. : alk. paper) 1. Industrial
management--Great Britain. 2. Great Britain--Commerce. 3. European
Union countries--Commerce. 4. Industrial policy--Great Britain. 5.
Industrial policy--European Union countries. 6. International economic
relations. 7. Business. I. Britton, Chris. II. Title.
  HD70.G7W64 2009
  658--dc22
                                                    2009012758

Library of Congress Cataloging-in-Publication Data
A catalog record for this book is available from the Library of Congress.

10 9 8 7 6 5 4 3 2
13 12 11 10

Typeset in 9.5/13 pt Stone Serif by 30.
Printed and bound by Graficas Estella, Spain.

The publisher's policy is to use paper manufactured from sustainable forests.

For Lindsey, Tom and Georgina and for
Rachael, Philip, Nick and Megan, with our love

Brief contents

Contents

Part One INTRODUCTION

Part Two CONTEXTS

5 The macroeconomic environment   96

Ian Worthington

6 The demographic, social and cultural context of business   135

Ian Worthington

Part Three FIRMS

10 Legal structures   237

Ian Worthington

11 Size structure of firms   268

Chris Britton

12 Industrial structure   295

Chris Britton

13 Government and business   321

Ian Worthington

Part Four MARKETS

Part Five CONCLUSION

Supporting resources

Visit **www.pearsoned.co.uk/worthington** to find valuable online resources

Companion Website for students
- Self-assessment questions to check your understanding
- Links to articles and resources on the web
- Searchable online glossary

For instructors
- Complete, downloadable Instructor's Manual
- PowerPoint slides that can be downloaded and used for presentations
- Testbank of question material

Also: The Companion Website provides the following features:
- Search tool to help locate specific items of content
- Online help and support to assist with website usage and troubleshooting

For more information please contact your local Pearson Education sales representative or visit **www.pearsoned.co.uk/worthington**

Contributors

Authors

Ian Worthington, BA (Hons), PhD, is Professor of Corporate Sustainability in the Department of Strategy and Management, Leicester Business School, De Montfort University, where he specialises in business environment and greening business. He has published both in Britain and the USA and is co-author of a recent book on economics.

Chris Britton, BA (Hons), MSc, is Principal Lecturer in the Department of Strategy and Management, Leicester Business School, De Montfort University. Her teaching and research interests lie in the field of industrial economics and labour markets, where she has contributed to several publications, including co-authorship of a book on executive recruitment for *The Economist*. With Ian Worthington and Andy Rees she has recently completed a book on Business Economics.

Contributors

Diane Belfitt, BA (Hons), Diploma in Welfare Law, has taught law at a number of institutions, including Leicester Polytechnic, Leicester University and Charles Keene College in Leicester. She has examined for a number of Examination Boards.

Zena Cumberpatch, BA (Hons), MSc, is Senior Lecturer at Nene College, Northampton. Her main research interests include teaching and learning strategies and gender issues; she has given conference papers on these topics.

Martyn Kendrick, BA (Hons), FCII, Chartered Insurance Practitioner, is Principal Lecturer and Deputy Head in the Department of Strategy and Management, Leicester Business School, De Montfort University. His main teaching and research interests lie in the fields of business ethics, corporate responsibility and E-Business.

Martin Morgan-Taylor, LLB, LLM, FRAS I, LTM, is a Senior Lecturer in the School of Law at De Montfort University, Leicester, where he teaches business and commercial law on a range of undergraduate and postgraduate courses. His research interests include online trading, consumer protection, and light pollution and nuisance. He is a legal advisor on the latter to the Campaign for Dark Skies and the British Astronomical Association.

David Orton, BA (HOns) is a Senior Lecturer in the Department of Strategy and Management, Leicester Business School, De Montfort Universtiy. His teaching and research interests lie in the fields of Strategic Management and Crisis and Business Continuity Management.

Dean Patton, BA (Hons), PhD, PGCE, is a Senior Research Fellow in the School of Management at Southampton University. His teaching and research interests centre on small firms and environmental policies within business. He has published in both these areas.

Preface to the first edition

Interest in business studies has never been greater; witness, for example, the spectacular growth in the number of business schools in British universities and institutes of higher education over the last ten years and the rapidly increasing number of courses at degree and sub-degree level in which business is an important, and frequently dominant, element. Accompanying this growth in institutional provision has been an equally impressive growth in the number of books and journals devoted to the various aspects of business – including texts on management principles and practice, organisation theory, strategic management, marketing, human resource management, business economics, accounting and finance, and so on. While such contributions have invariably been welcomed and have augmented our knowledge of the business world, the overwhelming preoccupation of scholars with the internal aspects of organisational life has tended to mean that the external influences on business activity have received little attention. This book is an attempt to redress the balance.

It should be stated at the outset that our central aim is to provide a study of business, rather than a study for business – a text for students rather than practitioners, although hopefully the latter will find much of the material useful and informative. In embarking on this study, we recognise that our perspective has been conditioned by years of teaching students on business studies courses in a variety of institutions, as well as our own interests and specialisms, and consequently the choice of subject matter and the ordering of material will not suit all tutors teaching on Business Environment courses. We have, however, attempted to discuss all the mainstream areas found on degree and HND level courses in the large number of institutions with which we are familiar, as well as exploring some newer topics which are beginning to receive prominence in a growing number of business schools (e.g. corporate responsibility). In addition, whilst adopting a UK perspective, we have also drawn a substantial amount of our material from European and international sources – something often promised but not always delivered!

Each chapter in the book follows a common format, which includes objectives, a case study, review questions and assignments, and a guide to further reading. A comprehensive review of data and information sources is included in Chapter 16 (now Chapter 18) and we would strongly encourage students to make regular use of these sources, particularly the quality newspapers and journals which contain a wealth of information and analysis on the changing business environment.

In carrying out this study, we have received considerable help from numerous organisations to whom we extend our thanks. These have included the Department of Trade and Industry, the Department of the Environment, the Cabinet Office, the Monopolies and Mergers Commission, the European Commission, the European Information Centre (Leicester City Council), Business in the Community, and the Confederation of British Industry.

Our gratitude also goes to the students and staff of Leicester Business School who have unwittingly helped us to gather information and to formulate our ideas over more years than we would care to mention. In particular we would like to acknowledge the considerable help and encouragement given to us by Gary Cook, Andy Rees, Professor Derrick Ball, Professor John Coyne and the staff of De Montfort University Library. To Janice Cox, who typed the majority of the script under demanding circumstances, goes our special thanks and admiration – she never once complained and always met the deadlines.

We would also like to acknowledge the considerable help, support and encouragement given to us by Dr Penelope Woolf of Pitman Publishing who has retained faith in us throughout the project. To her go our special thanks.

Our greatest debt, however, is owed to our families who have paid the highest price in terms of lost time, boring conversations, tetchiness and a general lack of consideration. Despite all this they have remained encouraging, supportive and loving. It is to them that we rightly dedicate this book.

Preface to the sixth edition

As with previous editions, we continue to be guided by the very helpful and constructive comments of our reviewers and by our own refections on how we could improve on the text and presentation of the material. For this edition we have added a new chapter on 'The global context of business' and have revised and repositioned the material on corporate social responsibility which now becomes a chapter on the ethical and ecological environment. All other chapters have been revised and updated and many contain new, internationally focused cases and/or mini cases. To emphasise the international/global aspects of business, we have introduced on 'International business in action' feature at the end of each of the four main sections of the book. We have also moved the chapter on 'The Technological environment: e-business' (Chapter 16 in the fifth edition) to the website where it becomes on additional chapter that can be downloaded for those readers who want more detail on this topic.

As ever, we are indebted to all those colleagues and past students who have supported us in this project over many years. Special thanks go to them and to the team at Pearson Education for their continued help and advice. We would also like to thank Nathan Rush in the De Montfort University library for his invaluable assistance.

Ian Worthington
Chris Britton
April 2009

Acknowledgements

We are grateful to the following for permission to reproduce copyright material:

Figure 18.3 Copyright © 2005, by The Regents of the University of California. Reprinted from the California Management Review, Vol. 48, No. 1. By permission of The Regents.

In some instances we have been unable to trace the owners of copyright material, and we would appreciate any information that would enable us to do so.

Guided tour

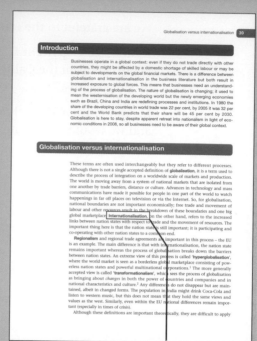

Learning Outcomes highlight core coverage in terms of expected learning outcomes after completing each chapter, to help students focus their learning and evaluate their progress.

Key Terms are drawn out at the start of every chapter and are emboldened the first time they appear in the text to enable students to locate information quickly. A full **Glossary** appears at the end of the book.

Links to relevant web pages are highlighted throughout the text and repeated on the website *www.pearsoned.co.uk/worthington* to help direct students' research.

Case studies of varying complexity relate the theory represented in the chapter to real life situations in a range of diverse organisations.

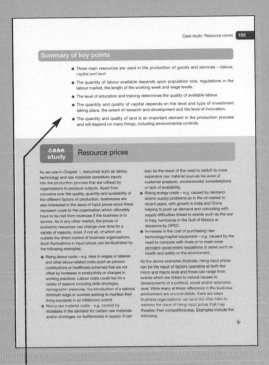

Summary of key points provide the student with a useful revision aid.

Questions and **assignments** provide engaging activities for students and lecturers in and out of the classroom situation. Further questions on the website help to evaluate their progress.

Part One

INTRODUCTION

1 Business organisations: the external environment

Ian Worthington

Business organisations differ in many ways, but they also have a common feature: the transformation of inputs into output. This transformation process takes place against a background of external influences which affect the firm and its activities. This external environment is complex, volatile and interactive, but it cannot be ignored in any meaningful analysis of business activity.

Learning outcomes

Having read this chapter you should be able to:

- indicate the basic features of business activity
- portray the business organisation as a system interacting with its environment
- demonstrate the range and complexity of the external influences on business activity
- identify the central themes inherent in the study of the business environment

Key terms

Environmental change
External environment
General (or contextual) environment

Immediate (or operational) environment
Inputs
Open system

Outputs
PESTLE analysis
Transformation system

Introduction

Business activity is a fundamental and universal feature of human existence and yet the concept of 'business' is difficult to define with any degree of precision. Dictionary definitions tend to describe it as being concerned with buying and selling or with trade and commerce, or the concern of profit-making organisations, and clearly all of these would come within the accepted view of business. Such a restricted view, however, would exclude large parts of the work of government and its agencies and the activities of non-profit-making organisations – a perspective it would be hard to sustain in a climate in which business methods, skills, attitudes and objectives are being increasingly adopted by these organisations. It is this broader view of business and its activities which is adopted below and which forms the focus of an investigation into the business environment.

The business organisation and its environment

A model of business activity

Most business activity takes place within an organisational context and even a cursory investigation of the business world reveals the wide variety of organisations involved, ranging from the small local supplier of a single good or service to the multibillion dollar international or multinational corporation producing and trading on a global scale. Given this rich organisational diversity, most observers of the business scene tend to differentiate between organisations in terms of their size, type of product and/or market, methods of finance, scale of operations, legal status and so on. Nissan, for example, would be characterised as a major multinational car producer and distributor trading on world markets, while a local builder is likely to be seen as a small business operating at a local level with a limited market and relatively restricted turnover.

> **web link**
>
> Further information on Nissan is available at *www.nissan-global.com*
> The Nissan UK website address is *www.nissan.co.uk*

While such distinctions are both legitimate and informative, they can conceal the fact that all business organisations are ultimately involved in the same basic activity, namely, the transformation of **inputs** (resources) into **outputs** (goods or services). This process is illustrated in Figure 1.1.

In essence, all organisations acquire resources – including labour, premises, technology, finance, materials – and transform these resources into the goods or services required by their customers. While the type, amount and combination of resources will vary according to the needs of each organisation and may also vary over time, the simple process described above is common to all types of business organisation and provides a useful starting-point for investigating business activity and the environment in which it takes place.

A more detailed analysis of business resources and those internal aspects of organisations which help to transform inputs into output can be found in Chapters 2 and 7 below. The need, here, is simply to appreciate the idea of the firm as a **transformation**

Figure 1.1   The business organisation as a transformation system

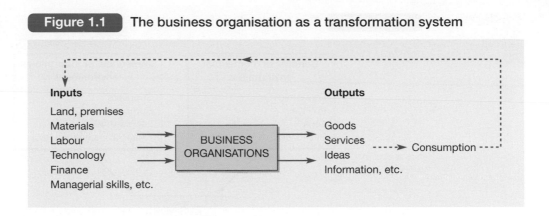

system and to recognise that in producing and selling output most organisations hope to earn sufficient revenue to allow them to maintain and replenish their resources, thus permitting them to produce further output which in turn produces further inputs. In short, inputs help to create output and output creates inputs. Moreover, the output of one organisation may represent an input for another, as in the case of the firm producing capital equipment or basic materials or information or ideas. This interrelationship between business organisations is just one example of the complex and integrated nature of business activity and it helps to highlight the fact that the fortunes of any single business organisation are invariably linked with those of another or others – a point clearly illustrated in many of the examples cited in the text.

The firm in its environment

The simple model of business activity described above is based on the systems approach to management (see Chapter 2). One of the benefits of this approach is that it stresses that organisations are entities made up of interrelated parts which are intertwined with the outside world – the **external environment** in systems language. This environment comprises a wide range of influences – economic, demographic, social, political, legal, technological, etc. – which affect business activity in a variety of ways and which can impinge not only on the transformation process itself, but also on the process of resource acquisition and on the creation and consumption of output. This idea of the firm in its environment is illustrated in Figure 1.2.

Figure 1.2   The firm in its environment

Figure 1.3 Two levels of environment

In examining the business environment, a useful distinction can be made between those external factors which tend to have a more immediate effect on the day-to-day operations of a firm and those which tend to have a more general influence. Figure 1.3 makes this distinction.

The **immediate** or **operational environment** for most firms includes suppliers, competitors, labour markets, financial institutions and customers, and may also include trading organisations, trade unions and possibly a parent company. In contrast the **general** or **contextual environment** comprises those macroenvironmental factors such as economic, political, socio-cultural, technological, legal and ethical influences on business which affect a wide variety of businesses and which can emanate not only from local and national sources but also from international and supranational developments.

This type of analysis can also be extended to the different functional areas of an organisation's activities such as marketing or personnel or production or finance, as illustrated in Figure 1.4. Such an analysis can be seen to be useful in at least two ways. First, it emphasises the influence of external factors on specific activities within the firm and in doing so underlines the importance of the interface between the internal and external environments. Second, by drawing attention to this interface, it highlights the fact that, while business organisations are often able to exercise some degree of control over their internal activities and processes, it is often very difficult, if not impossible, to control the external environment in which they operate.

Figure 1.4 Environmental influences on a firm's marketing system

The general or contextual environment

While the external factors referred to above form the subject-matter of the rest of the book, it is useful at this point to gain an overview of the business environment by highlighting some of the key environmental influences on business activity. In keeping with the distinction made between general and more immediate influences, these are discussed separately below. In this section we examine what are frequently referred to as the 'PESTLE' factors (i.e. political, economic, socio-cultural, technological, legal and ethical influences). A **'PESTLE'** (or **'PEST'**) **analysis** can be used to analyse a firm's current and future environment as part of the strategic management process (see Chapter 18).

The political environment

A number of aspects of the political environment clearly impinge on business activity. These range from general questions concerning the nature of the political system and its institutions and processes (Chapter 4), to the more specific questions relating to government involvement in the working of the economy (Chapter 5) and its attempts to influence market structure and behaviour (Chapters 11, 15, 17). Government activities, both directly and indirectly, influence business activity and government can be seen as the biggest business enterprise at national or local level (Chapter 13). Given the trend towards the globalisation of markets (Chapters 3 and 16) and the existence of international trading organisations and blocs, international politico-economic influences on business activity represent one key feature of the business environment (Chapters 4, 7 and 16). Another is the influence of public, as well as political, opinion in areas such as environmental policy and corporate responsibility (Chapter 9).

The economic environment

The distinction made between the political and economic environment – and, for that matter, the legal environment – is somewhat arbitrary. Government, as indicated above, plays a major role in the economy at both national and local level (Chapters 5 and 13) and its activities help to influence both the demand and supply side (e.g. see Chapter 14). Nevertheless there are a number of other economic aspects related to business activity which are worthy of consideration. These include various structural aspects of both firms and markets (Chapters 10, 11, 12 and 15) and a comparison of economic theory and practice (e.g. Chapters 14, 15 and 16).

mini case   A healthy business?

Even the world's largest and most powerful business organisations are affected by a changing business environment, a point well illustrated by the problems faced by General Motors (GM), in recent years. In the first quarter of 2005, GM reported losses of over $1 billion in North America and subsequently announced its intention to close some of its plants and cut 25–30 000 jobs over the next three years from its North American operations. This plan followed in the wake of its job-cutting exercise in GM Europe which was ultimately expected to reduce its European workforce by around 12 000 jobs, most of them in Germany.

GM's decline in fortunes was attributed to a number of important developments: a falling market share, problems with its product mix, rising raw material prices and the soaring costs of providing healthcare for its US workers (see e.g. *Guardian*, 8 June 2005, p.19). According to the company's Chief Executive, the latter was the most challenging problem facing the business, with the cost of the healthcare programme estimated to account for around $1500 on the price of every vehicle sold.

By slimming down its operations and running its remaining plants at full capacity, GM hoped to address some of the demand (i.e. sales) and supply side (i.e. costs) problems it had been experiencing. The company has also taken steps to make its offering more attractive to customers by increasing its spending on new vehicles and by improving its marketing effort in the hope that this will arrest the decline in market share.

As far as the healthcare programme is concerned, this is likely to prove more of an intractable problem for the organisation's management, particularly as the unions have resisted any attempt to shift some of the burden on to the employees. It is worth noting that the burgeoning cost of healthcare provision is by no means unique to GM, but is one facing a large number of US corporations. Indeed, according to some observers, the healthcare burden faced by corporate America is so substantial that it threatens not only the future prospects of individual businesses but also the long-term strength of the American economy and its international competitiveness.

In the period since the last edition was published, GM's position does not appear to have changed significantly for the better. Talks with Nissan and Renault on forming a global manufacturing alliance – designed to drive down costs – were abandoned in late 2006. By early 2007 Toyota had overtaken GM as the world's leading supplier of cars. Like Ford, GM has continued to be affected by the switch in consumer tastes away from SUVs and pick-up trucks and towards smaller, cheaper, more environmentally friendly vehicles. Rising petrol prices, the slow-down in the US economy and unfavourable exchange rates have not helped GM and the company has found it necessary to invest in new fuel-efficient models (including hybrids) to meet the challenge from its rivals.

On the cost side, it also announced plans in mid-2008 to make savings of around $15 billion to cope with plummeting car sales which have been affected by the global financial crisis. Among the measures announced were a pay freeze for its workers, a programme of voluntary redundancies, scrapping of health insurance for many of its retired workers and a suspension of dividend payments to shareholders.

The social, cultural and demographic environment

Both demand and supply are influenced by social, cultural and demographic factors. Cultural factors, for example, may affect the type of products being produced or sold, the markets they are sold in, the price at which they are sold and a range of other variables. People are a key organisational resource and a fundamental part of the market for goods and services. Accordingly, socio-cultural influences and developments have an important effect on business operations, as do demographic changes (Chapters 6 and 7).

The technological environment

Technology is both an input and an output of business organisations as well as being an environmental influence on them. Investment in technology and innovation is frequently seen as a key to the success of an enterprise and has been used to explain differences in the relative competitiveness of different countries (Chapter 7). It has also been responsible for significant developments in the internal organisation of businesses in the markets for economic resources.

The legal environment

Businesses operate within a framework of law which has a significant impact on various aspects of their existence. Laws usually govern, among other things, the status of the organisation (Chapter 10), its relationship with its customers and suppliers and certain internal procedures and activities (Chapter 8). They may also influence market structures and behaviour (e.g. Chapters 15 and 17). Since laws emanate from government (including supranational governments) and from the judgments of the courts, some understanding of the relevant institutions and processes is desirable (e.g. Chapters 4 and 8).

The ethical and ecological environment

Ethical considerations have become an increasingly important influence on business behaviour, particularly among the larger, more high profile companies. One area where this has been manifest is in the demand for firms to act in a more socially responsible way and to consider the impact they might have on people, their communities and the natural environment (Chapter 9).

The immediate or operational environment

Resources and resource markets

An organisation's need for resources makes it dependent to a large degree on the suppliers of those resources, some of whom operate in markets which are structured to a considerable extent (e.g. Chapter 7). Some aspects of the operation of resource markets or indeed the activities of an individual supplier can have a fundamental impact on an organisation's success and upon the way in which it structures its internal procedures and processes. By the same token, the success of suppliers is often intimately connected with the decisions and/or fortunes of their customers. While some organisations may seek to gain an advantage in price, quality or delivery by purchasing resources from overseas, such a decision can engender a degree of uncertainty, particularly where exchange rates are free rather than fixed (Chapter 16). Equally, organisations may face uncertainty and change in the domestic markets for resources as a result of factors as varied as technological change, government intervention or public opinion (e.g. conservation issues).

Customers

Customers are vital to all organisations and the ability both to identify and to meet consumer needs is seen as one of the keys to organisational survival and prosperity – a point not overlooked by politicians, who are increasingly using business techniques to attract the support of the electorate. This idea of consumer sovereignty – where resources are allocated to produce output to satisfy customer demands – is a central tenet of the market economy (Chapter 5) and is part of an ideology whose influence has become all pervasive in recent years. Understanding the many factors affecting both individual and market demand, and the ways in which firms organise themselves to satisfy that demand is a vital component of a business environment that is increasingly market led.

Competitors

Competition – both direct and indirect – is an important part of the context in which many firms operate and is a factor equally applicable to the input as well as the output side of business. The effects of competition, whether from domestic organisations or from overseas firms (e.g. see Chapter 16), is significant at the macro as well as the micro level and its influence can be seen in the changing structures of many advanced industrial economies (Chapter 12). How firms respond to these competitive challenges (e.g. Chapter 11) and the attitudes of governments to anti-competitive practices (Chapter 17) is a legitimate area of concern for students of business.

Analysing the business environment

In a subject as all encompassing as the business environment it is possible to identify numerous approaches to the organisation of the material. One obvious solution would be to examine the various factors mentioned above, devoting separate chapters to each of the environmental influences and discussing their impact on business organisations. While this solution has much to recommend it – not least of which is its simplicity – the approach adopted below is based on the grouping of environmental influences into three main areas, in the belief that this helps to focus attention on key aspects of the business world, notably contexts, firms and their markets.

mini case The people's car

Changing economic circumstances (e.g. oil price rises, growth or recession) provide 'opportunities' as well as 'threats' for business organisations, a point well illustrated by the Indian car manufacturer

Tata Motors. While many of the world's leading car producers continue to face tough economic circumstances, Tata has been able to capitalise on the growth in the Indian economy and a potentially huge, untapped domestic market by producing the world's cheapest car, the Nano, which is scheduled to go on sale in 2008 with a price tag of 100,000 rupees (around £1260). The Nano is less than half the price of its rivals, making it affordable to the millions of Indian citizens who currently buy motorbikes and scooters. Its price has been kept low by replacing some of the steel parts with plastic and by swapping traditional welding technology with hi-tech glue.

Tata Motors is a subsidiary of one of India's largest conglomerates, which includes the Anglo-Dutch steelmaker Corus and Tetley Tea. In 2008, the group acquired the Land Rover and Jaguar marques from Ford as part of a longer-term plan to become an international car company. Tata also has plans to bring an upgraded version of the Nano to Europe in what some observers see as a reflection of the global shift in wealth from the developed world to the developing one.

All has not been plain sailing, however, for the Indian car producer. Violent protests by farmers in the state of West Bengal – whose land had been acquired for the Tata factory – looks likely to hold up production of the Nano. At the time of writing (September 2008), the company was threatening to move production to another state if the protests did not cease.

web link   The website for Tata Motors is *www.tatamotors.com*

Following a basic introduction to the idea of the 'business environment', in Part Two consideration is given to the political, economic, social, cultural, demographic, legal, ethical and ecological contexts within which businesses function. In addition to examining the influence of political and economic systems, institutions and processes on the conduct of business, this section focuses on the macroeconomic environment and on those broad social influences which affect both consumers and organisations alike. The legal system and the influence of law in a number of critical areas of business activity is also a primary concern and one which has links with Part Three.

In Part Three, attention is focused on three central structural aspects: legal structure, size structure and industrial structure. The chapter on legal structure examines the impact of different legal definitions on a firm's operations and considers possible variations in organisational goals based on legal and other influences. The focus then shifts to how differences in size can affect the organisation (e.g. access to capital, economies of scale) and to an examination of how changes in scale and/or direction can occur, including the role of government in assisting small-business development and growth. One of the consequences of changes in the component elements of the economy is its effect on the overall structure of industry and commerce – a subject which helps to highlight the impact of international competition on the economic structure of many advanced industrial economies. Since government is a key actor in the economy, the section concludes with an analysis of government involvement in business and in particular its influence on the supply as well as the demand side of the economy at both national and local level.

In Part Four, the aim is to compare theory with practice by examining issues such as pricing, market structure and foreign trade. The analysis of price theory illustrates the degree to which the theoretical models of economists shed light on the operation of business in the 'real' world. Similarly, by analysing basic models of market structure, it is possible to gain an understanding of the effects of competition on a firm's behaviour and to appreciate the significance of both price and non-price decisions in the operation of markets.

The analysis continues with an examination of external markets and the role of government in influencing both the structure and operation of the market-place. The chapter on international markets looks at the theoretical basis of trade and the development of overseas markets in practice, particularly in the context of recent institutional, economic and financial developments (e.g. the Single Market, globalisation, the Euro). The section concludes with an investigation of the rationale for government intervention in markets and a review of government action in three areas, namely, privatisation and deregulation, competition policy and the operation of the labour market.

To emphasise the international dimension of the study of the business environment, each of the three main parts of the book conclude with a section entitled 'International business in action' which draws together some of the key themes discussed in the previous chapters. By examining specific issues and/or organisations, the aim is to highlight linkages between the material discussed in the text and to provide an appreciation of some of the ways in which business activity reaches well beyond national boundaries.

The concluding chapter in the book stresses the continuing need for organisations to monitor change in the business environment and examines a number of frameworks through which such an analysis can take place. In seeking to make sense of their environment, businesses need access to a wide range of information, much of which is available from published material, including government sources. Some of the major types of information available to students of business and to business organisations – including statistical and other forms of information – are considered in the final part of this chapter.

Central themes

A number of themes run through the text and it is useful to draw attention to these at this point.

Interaction with the environment

Viewed as an **open system**, the business organisation is in constant interaction with its environment. Changes in the environment can cause changes in inputs, in the transformation process and in outputs and these in turn may engender further changes in the organisation's environment. The internal and external environments should be seen as interrelated and interdependent, not as separate entities.

Interaction between environmental variables

In addition to the interaction between the internal and external environments, the various external influences affecting business organisations are also frequently interrelated. Changes in interest rates, for example, may affect consumer confidence and this can have an important bearing on business activity. Subsequent attempts by government to influence the level of demand could exacerbate the situation and this may lead to changes in general economic conditions, causing further problems for firms. The combined effect of these factors could be to create a turbulent environment which could result in uncertainty in the minds of managers. Failure to respond to the challenges (or opportunities) presented by such changes could signal the demise of the organisation or at best a significant decline in its potential performance.

The complexity of the environment

The environmental factors identified above are only some of the potential variables faced by all organisations. These external influences are almost infinite in number and variety and no study could hope to consider them all. For students of business and for managers alike, the requirement is to recognise the complexity of the external environment and to pay greater attention to those influences which appear the most pertinent and pressing for the organisation in question, rather than to attempt to consider all possible contingencies.

Environmental volatility and change

The organisation's external environment is further complicated by the tendency towards **environmental change**. This volatility may be particularly prevalent in some areas (e.g. technology) or in some markets or in some types of industry or organisation. As indicated above, a highly volatile environment causes uncertainty for the organisation (or for its sub-units) and this makes decision-making more difficult (see Case study: A shock to the system).

Environmental uniqueness

Implicit in the remarks above is the notion that each organisation has to some degree a unique environment in which it operates and which will affect it in a unique way. Thus, while it is possible to make generalisations about the impact of the external environment on the firm, it is necessary to recognise the existence of this uniqueness and where appropriate to take into account exceptions to the general rule.

Different spatial levels of analysis

External influences operate at different spatial levels – local, regional, national, supranational, international/global. There are few businesses, if any, today which could justifiably claim to be unaffected by influences outside their immediate market(s).

Two-way flow of influence

As a final point, it is important to recognise that the flow of influence between the organisation and its environment operates in both directions. The external environment influences firms, but by the same token firms can influence their environment and this is an acceptable feature of business in a democratic society which is operating through a market-based economic system. This idea of democracy and its relationship with the market economy is considered in Chapters 4 and 5.

Synopsis

In the process of transforming inputs into output, business organisations operate in a multifaceted environment which affects and is affected by their activities. This environment tends to be complex and volatile and comprises influences which are of both a general and an immediate kind and which operate at different spatial levels. Understanding this environment and its effects on business operations is of vital importance to the study and practice of business.

Summary of key points

- Business activity is essentially concerned with transforming inputs into outputs for consumption purposes.

- All businesses operate within an external environment which shapes their operations and decisions.

- This environment comprises influences which are both operational and general.

- The operational environment of business is concerned with such factors as customers, suppliers, creditors and competitors.

- The general environment focuses on what are known as the PESTLE factors.

- In analysing a firm's external environment attention needs to be paid to the interaction between the different environmental variables, environmental complexity, volatility and change and to the spatial influences.

- While all firms are affected by the environment in which they exist and operate, at times they help to shape that environment by their activities and behaviour.

A shock to the system

For the most part changes in a firm's (or industry's or sector's) external environment tend to be relatively predictable and this can aid business planning. Economic indicators, for example, usually signal the onset of a recession (or recovery) well before it occurs and this provides businesses with time to consider not only how they are likely to be affected by economic change, but also what steps they can take to minimise any potential threat to the organisation (or maximise any opportunity). On occasions, however, the business environment can change dramatically and unexpectedly for the worse, leaving some firms to face rapidly deteriorating trading conditions often without any contingency plans in place.

Such a situation occurred on Tuesday 11 September 2001 when terrorist attacks on the World Trade Center and the US Department of Defense rapidly sent shock waves through the global economic system, engulfing a wide range of firms and industries in all countries. The most immediate and obvious manifestation of the crisis was seen in the airline industry where the major airline operators suddenly found people unwilling to fly, thereby significantly exacerbating the problems already being experienced as a result of increased competition and recession in some of their markets. In the United States carriers such as United, Delta and Continental announced tens of thousands of redundancies and further job losses were announced by British Airways, Virgin and Air Canada. Elsewhere in Europe both Swissair and Sabena went into receivership and other operators signalled a period of retrenchment.

The knock-on effect of the reduction in air travel also impacted on two allied industries: aircraft manufacturing and tourism. Again this found expression in falling demand and the inevitable loss of jobs. Companies such as Airbus Industrie, Boeing and Bombardier slimmed down their workforces and additional job losses occurred in supplier organisations including Rolls-Royce and in travel, tourism and allied industries such as hotels, catering and car hire. For a company such as Disney, for instance, the impact on visitor numbers at its theme parks in America and Europe was immediately felt and numerous other organisations and holiday destinations rapidly experienced the effect of the decline in overseas tourists in the immediate aftermath of the attack.

While it was suggested at the time by a number of observers that some businesses might have been taking advantage of the crisis to slim down their workforces, there seems little doubt that the attack had a significant economic as well as human and psychological impact. Mercifully such shocks to the system tend to be few and far between and even when they occur some enterprising firms will find they provide unexpected business opportunities.

Case study questions

1 Can you think of any other examples of major unanticipated events in your own country that have had a serious adverse effect on businesses?

2 Can you think of any businesses which may have benefited commercially from the events of September 11?

web link

There is a great deal of commentary on September 11 and its aftermath. You should try typing 'September 11 and Business' in *Google*. There is also an archive of material at *September11.archive.org*

Review and discussion questions

1 In what senses could a college or university be described as a business organisation? How would you characterise its 'inputs' and 'outputs'?

2 Taking examples from a range of quality newspapers, illustrate ways in which business organisations are affected by their external environment.

3 Give examples of the ways in which business organisations can affect the external environment in which they operate.

Assignments

1 Assume you are a trainee in a firm of management consultants. As part of your induction process you have been asked to collect a file of information on an organisation of your choice. This file should contain information not only on the structure of the organisation and on its products, but also on the key external influences which have affected its operations in recent years.

2 For a firm or industry of your choice, undertake a 'PESTLE' analysis indicating the likely major environmental influences to be faced by the firm/industry in the next five to ten years.

Further reading

Brooks, I., Weatherston, J. and Wilkinson, G., *The International Business Environment*, FT/Prentice Hall, 2004.

Daniels, J. D., Radebough, L. H. and Sullivan, D. P., *International Business: Environments and Operations*, 10th edition, Prentice Hall, 2004.

Morris, H. and Willey, B., *The Corporate Environment*, Financial Times/Prentice Hall, 1996.

Steiner, G. A. and Steiner, J. F., *Business, Government and Society: A Managerial Perspective*, 7th edition, McGraw-Hill, 1994.

Wetherly, P. and Otter, D. (eds) *The Business Environment: Themes and Issues*, Oxford University Press, 2008.

Worthington, I., Britton, C. and Rees, A., *Economics for Business: Blending Theory and Practice*, 2nd edition, Financial Times/Prentice Hall, 2005, Chapter 1.

Web links and further questions are available on the website at:
www.pearsoned.co.uk/worthington

2 Business organisations: the internal environment

Ian Worthington and Zena Cumberpatch

The systems approach to the study of business organisations stresses the interaction between a firm's internal and external environments. Key aspects of the internal context of business include the organisation's structure and functions and the way they are configured in pursuit of specified organisational objectives. If the enterprise is to remain successful, constant attention needs to be paid to balancing the different influences on the organisation and to the requirement to adapt to new external circumstances. This responsibility lies essentially with the organisation's management, which has the task of blending people, technologies, structures and environments.

Learning outcomes

Having read this chapter you should be able to:

- outline the broad approaches to organisational and management, paying particular attention to the systems approach
- identify alternative organisational structures used by business organisations
- discuss major aspects of the functional management of firms
- illustrate the interaction between a firm's internal and external environments

Key terms

Bureaucracy	Holding company	Organisation chart
Classical theories of organisation	Human relations approach	Profit centre
	Human resource management	Project team
Contingency approaches	Management	Re-engineering
Divisional structure	Marketing	Scientific management
Downsizing	Marketing concept	Sub-systems
Formal structures	Marketing mix	Systems approach
Functional organisation	Matrix structure	Theory X and Theory Y
Functional specialisation	Organisation by product	Theory Z
Hierarchy of needs		Virtual organisation

Introduction

The internal features of business organisations have received considerable attention from scholars of organisation and management, and a large number of texts have been devoted to this aspect of business studies.[1] In the discussion below, the aim is to focus on three areas of the internal organisation that relate directly to a study of the business environment: approaches to understanding organisations, organisational structures, and key functions within the enterprise. Further insight into these aspects and into management and organisational behaviour generally can be gained by consulting the many specialist books in this field, a number of which are mentioned at the end of this chapter. Issues relating to a firm's legal structure are examined in Chapter 10.

A central theme running through any analysis of the internal environment is the idea of **management**, which has been subjected to a wide variety of definitions. As used in this context, management is seen both as a system of roles fulfilled by individuals who manage the organisation (e.g. entrepreneur, resource manager, co-ordinator, leader, motivator, organiser) and as a process which enables an organisation to achieve its objectives. The essential point is that management should be seen as a function of organisations, rather than as a controlling element, and its task is to enable the organisation to identify and achieve its objectives and to adapt to change. Managers need to integrate the various influences on the organisation – including people, technology, systems and the environment – in a manner best designed to meet the needs of the enterprise at the time in question and be prepared to institute change as and when circumstances dictate.

Approaches to organisation and management

An important insight into the principles which are felt to underlie the process of management can be gained by a brief examination of organisational theories. These theories or approaches – some of which date back to the late nineteenth century – represent the views of both practising managers and academics as to the factors that determine organisational effectiveness and the influences on individuals and groups within the work environment. Broadly speaking, these approaches can be broken down into three main categories: the classical approach, the human relations approach, and the systems approach.[2] Since the last of these encompasses the model presented in Chapter 1, particular attention is paid to this perspective.

The classical approach

Classical theories of organisation and management mostly date from the first half of the twentieth century and are associated with the work of writers such as Taylor, Fayol, Urwick and Brech. In essence, the classicists viewed organisations as **formal structures** established to achieve a particular number of objectives under the direction of management. By identifying a set of principles to guide managers in the design of the organisational structure, the proponents of the classical view believed that organisations would be able to achieve their objectives more effectively. Fayol, for example, identified fourteen principles which included the division of work, the scalar chain, centralisation and the unity of command – features which also found expression in Weber's notion of 'bureaucracy'. Urwick's rules or principles similarly emphasised aspects of organisation structure and operations – such as specialisation, co-ordination, authority, responsibility and the span of control – and were presented essentially as a code of good management practice.

Within the classical approach special attention is often given to two important sub-groupings, known as **scientific management** and **bureaucracy**. The former is associated with the pioneering work of F. W. Taylor (1856–1915) who believed that scientific methods could be attached to the design of work so that productivity could be increased. For Taylor, the systematic analysis of jobs (e.g. using some form of work study technique) was seen as the key to finding the best way to perform a particular task and thereby of achieving significant productivity gains from individuals which would earn them increased financial rewards. In Taylor's view, the responsibility for the institution of a scientific approach lay with management, under whose control and direction the workers would operate to the mutual benefit of all concerned.

The second sub-group, bureaucracy, draws heavily on the work of Max Weber (1864–1920) whose studies of authority structures highlighted the importance of 'office' and 'rules' in the operation of organisations. According to Weber, bureaucracy – with its system of rules and procedures, specified spheres of competence, hierarchical organisation of offices, appointment based on merit, high level of specialisation and impersonality – possessed a degree of technical superiority over other forms of organisation, and this explained why an increasing number of enterprises were becoming bureaucratic in structure. Over 50 years after Weber's studies were first published in English, bureaucratic organisation remains a key feature of many enterprises throughout the world and is clearly linked to increasing organisational size and complexity. Notwithstanding the many valid criticisms of Weber's work, it is difficult to imagine how it could be otherwise.

The human relations approach

Whereas the classical approach focuses largely on structure and on the formal organisation, the **human relations approach** to management emphasises the importance of people in the work situation and the influence of social and psychological factors in shaping organisational behaviour. Human relations theorists have primarily been concerned with issues such as individual motivation, leadership, communications and group dynamics and have stressed the significance of the informal pattern of relationships which exist within the formal structure. The factors influencing human behaviour have accordingly been portrayed as a key to achieving greater organisational effectiveness, thus elevating the 'management of people' to a prime position in the determination of managerial strategies.

The early work in this field is associated with Elton Mayo (1880–1949) and with the famous Hawthorne Experiments, conducted at the Western Electric Company (USA) between 1924 and 1932. What these experiments basically showed was that individuals at work were members of informal (i.e. unofficial) as well as formal groups

Figure 2.1   A hierarchy of needs

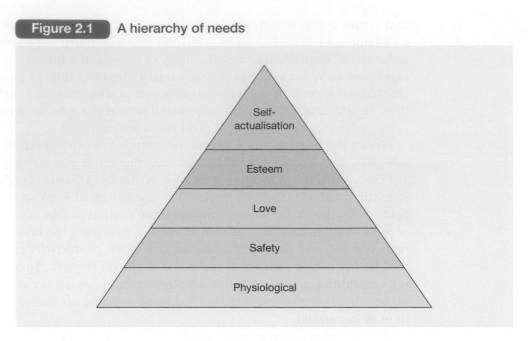

and that group influences were fundamental to explaining individual behaviour. Later work by writers such as Maslow, McGregor, Argyris, Likert and Herzberg continued to stress the importance of the human factor in determining organisational effectiveness, but tended to adopt a more psychological orientation, as exemplified by Maslow's '**hierarchy of needs**' and McGregor's '**Theory X and Theory Y**'. Maslow's central proposition was that individuals seek to satisfy specific groups of needs, ranging from basic physiological requirements (e.g. food, sleep, sex), through safety, love and esteem, to self-actualisation (i.e. self-fulfilment), progressing systematically up the hierarchy as each lower-level need is satisfied (see Figure 2.1). To McGregor individuals at work were seen by management as either inherently lazy (Theory X) or committed to the organisation's objectives and often actively seeking responsibility (Theory Y). These perceptions consequently provided the basis for different styles of management, which ranged from the coercive to the supportive.

McGregor's concern with management styles is reflected in later studies, including Ouichi's notion of **Theory Z**.[3] According to Ouichi one of the key factors in the success of Japanese manufacturing industries was their approach to the management of people. Theory Z organisations were those which offered workers long-term (often lifetime) employment, a share in decision making, opportunities for training, development and promotion, and a number of other advantages which gave them a positive orientation towards the organisation. For Ouichi, the key to organisational effectiveness lay in the development of a Japanese-style Theory Z environment, adapted to western requirements.

The systems approach

More recent approaches to organisation and management have helped to integrate previous work on structures, people and technology, by portraying organisations as socio-technical systems interacting with their environment. Under this approach –

which became popular in the 1960s – organisations were seen as complex systems of people, tasks and technologies that were part of and interacted with a larger environment, comprising a wide range of influences (see Chapter 1). This environment was frequently subject to fluctuations, which on occasions could become turbulent (i.e. involving rapid and often unpredictable change). For organisations to survive and prosper, adaptation to environmental demands was seen as a necessary requirement and one which was central to the process of management.

The essence of the **systems approach** has been described in Chapter 1, but is worth repeating here. Organisations, including those involved in business, are open systems, interacting with their environment as they convert inputs into output. Inputs include people, finance, materials and information, provided by the environment in which the organisation exists and operates. Output comprises such items as goods and services, information, ideas and waste, discharged into the environment for consumption by 'end' or 'intermediate' users and in some cases representing inputs used by other organisations.

Systems invariably comprise a number of **sub-systems** through which the process of conversion or transformation occurs. Business organisations, for example, usually have sub-systems which deal with activities such as production, marketing, accounting and human resource management and each of these in turn may involve smaller sub-systems (e.g. sales, quality control, training) which collectively constitute the whole. Just as the organisation as a system interacts with its environment, so do the sub-systems and their component elements, which also interact with each other. In the case of the latter, the boundary between sub-systems is usually known as an 'interface'.

While the obvious complexities of the systems approach need not be discussed, it is important to emphasise that most modern views of organisations draw heavily on the work in this area, paying particular attention to the interactions between people, technology, structure and environment and to the key role of management in directing the organisation's activities towards the achievement of its goals. Broadly speaking, management is seen as a critical sub-system within the total organisation, responsible for the co-ordination of the other sub-systems and for ensuring that internal and external relationships are managed effectively. As changes occur in one part of the system these will induce changes elsewhere and this will require a management response that will have implications for the organisation and for its sub-systems. Such changes may be either the cause or effect of changes in the relationship between the organisation and its environment, and the requirement for managers is to adapt to the new conditions without reducing the organisation's effectiveness.

Given the complex nature of organisations and the environments in which they operate, a number of writers have suggested a **contingency approach** to organisational design and management (e.g. Lawrence and Lorsch, Woodward, Perrow, Burns and Stalker).[4] In essence, this approach argues that there is no single form of organisation best suited to all situations and that the most appropriate organisational structure and system of management is dependent upon the contingencies of the situation (e.g. size, technology, environment) for each organisation. In some cases a bureaucratic structure might be the best way to operate, while in others much looser and more organic methods of organisation might be more effective. In short, issues of organisational design and management depend on choosing the best combination in the light of the relevant situational variables; this might mean different structures and styles coexisting within an organisation.

Organisational structures

Apart from the very simplest form of enterprise in which one individual carries out all tasks and responsibilities, business organisations are characterised by a division of labour which allows employees to specialise in particular roles and to occupy designated positions in pursuit of the organisation's objectives. The resulting pattern of relationships between individuals and roles constitutes what is known as the organisation's structure and represents the means by which the purpose and work of the enterprise is carried out. It also provides a framework through which communications can occur and within which the processes of management can be applied.

Responsibility for establishing the formal structure of the organisation lies with management and a variety of options is available. Whatever form is chosen, the basic need is to identify a structure which will best sustain the success of the enterprise and will permit the achievement of a number of important objectives. Through its structure an organisation should be able to:

● achieve efficiency in the utilisation of resources;
● provide opportunities for monitoring organisational performance;
● ensure the accountability of individuals;
● guarantee co-ordination between the different parts of the enterprise;
● provide an efficient and effective means of organisational communication;
● create job satisfaction, including opportunities for progression; and
● adapt to changing circumstances brought about by internal or external developments.

In short, structure is not an end in itself, but a means to an end and should ideally reflect the needs of the organisation within its existing context and taking into account its future requirements.

mini case   'Into the Dragon's Den'

As the chapter illustrates, the structure of an organisation is a means by which an enterprise can achieve its objectives. As the environment in which a business operates changes, firms should be willing to adapt the structure to meet the new circumstances. This might mean moving beyond the traditional models discussed below, in an effort to improve performance.

The global pharmaceutical giant GlaxoSmithKline (GSK) illustrates this idea of an evolving organisational structure. In July 2008, GSK announced that in future its scientists would have to pitch their ideas for new drugs to a development board, based essentially on the lines of the 'Dragon's Den', a popular UK television programme where would-be entrepreneurs seek to gain backing for their ideas from a group of financiers. The board will include two venture capitalists and will be a mixture of executives from inside the company and GSK outsiders. The plan is to stimulate innovation by requiring smaller teams of scientists to pitch three-year business plans to the new drug discovery investment board in an effort to secure funding for new drug treatments.

web link You can access the website for GSK at *www.gsk.com*

The essence of structure is the division of work between individuals and the formal organisational relationships that are created between them. These relationships will be reflected not only in individual job descriptions, but also in the overall **organisation chart** which designates the formal pattern of role relationships, and the interactions between roles and the individuals occupying those roles. Individual authority relationships can be classified as line, staff, functional and lateral and arise from the defined pattern of responsibilities, as follows:

● *Line relationships* occur when authority flows vertically downward through the structure from superior to subordinate (e.g. managers–section leader–staff).
● *Staff relationships* are created when senior personnel appoint assistants who normally have no authority over other staff but act as an extension of their superior.
● *Functional relationships* are those between specialists (or advisers) and line managers and their subordinates (e.g. when a specialist provides a common service throughout the organisation but has no authority over the users of the service). The personnel or computing function may be one such service that creates a functional relationship. (Note that specialists have line relationships with their own subordinates.)
● *Lateral relationships* exist across the organisation, particularly between individuals occupying equivalent positions within different departments or sections (e.g. committees, heads of departments, section leaders).

With regard to the division of work and the grouping of organisational activities, this can occur in a variety of ways. These include:

● *By function or major purpose*, associated particularly with departmental structures.
● *By product or service*, where individuals responsible for a particular product or service are grouped together.
● *By location*, based on geographical criteria.
● *By common processes* (e.g. particular skills or methods of operation).
● *By client group* (e.g. children, the disabled, the elderly).

In some organisations a particular method of grouping will predominate; in others there will tend to be a variety of types and each has its own particular advantages and disadvantages. In the discussion below, attention is focused on five main methods of grouping activities in business organisations. Students should attempt to discover what types of structure exist within their own educational institution and the logic (if any) which underlies the choices made.

Functional organisation

The functional approach to organisation is depicted in Figure 2.2. As its name indicates, in this type of structure activities are clustered together by common purpose or function. All marketing activities, for example, are grouped together as a

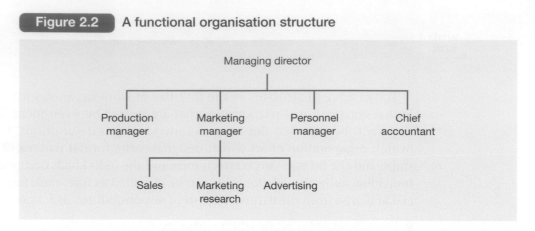

Figure 2.2   A functional organisation structure

common function, typically within a marketing department. Similarly, other areas of activity, such as production, finance, personnel and research and development, have their own specialised sections or departments, responsible for all the tasks required of that function.

Apart from its obvious simplicity, the functional organisation structure allows individuals to be grouped together on the basis of their specialisms and technical expertise, and this can facilitate the development of the function they offer as well as providing a recognised path for promotion and career development. On the downside, functional specialisation, particularly through departments, is likely to create sectional interests which may operate to the disadvantage of the organisation as a whole, particularly where inequalities in resource allocation between functions become a cause for interfunction rivalry. It could also be argued that this form of structure is most suited to single-product firms and that it becomes less appropriate as organisations diversify their products and/or markets. In such circumstances, the tendency will be for businesses to look for the benefits which can arise from specialisation by product or from the divisionalisation of the enterprise.

Organisation by product or service

In this case the division of work and the grouping of activities is dictated by the product or service provided (see Figure 2.3), such that each group responsible for a

Figure 2.3   A product-based structure

particular part of the output of the organisation may have its own specialist in the different functional areas (e.g. marketing, finance, personnel). One advantage of this type of structure is that it allows an organisation to offer a diversified range of products, as exemplified by the different services available in National Health Service hospitals (e.g. maternity, orthopaedic, geriatric, and so forth). Its main disadvantage is the danger that the separate units or divisions within the enterprise may attempt to become too autonomous, even at the expense of other parts of the organisation, and this can present management with problems of co-ordination and control.

The divisional structure

As firms diversify their products and/or markets – often as a result of merger or takeover – a structure is needed to co-ordinate and control the different parts of the organisation. This structure is likely to be the divisional (or multi-divisional) company.

A **divisionalised structure** is formed when an organisation is split up into a number of self-contained business units, each of which operates as a profit centre. Such a division may occur on the basis of product or market or a combination of the two, with each unit tending to operate along functional or product lines, but with certain key functions (e.g. finance, personnel, corporate planning) provided centrally, usually at company headquarters (see Figure 2.4).

The main benefit of the multi-divisional company is that it allows each part of what can be a very diverse organisation to operate semi-independently in producing and marketing its products, thus permitting each division to design its offering to suit local market conditions – a factor of prime importance where the firm operates on a multinational basis. The dual existence of divisional **profit centres** and a central unit responsible for establishing strategy at a global level can, however, be a source of considerable tension, particularly where the needs and aims of the centre appear to conflict with operations at the local level or to impose burdens seen to be unreasonable by divisional managers (e.g. the allocation of central overhead costs).

Figure 2.4   A divisional structure

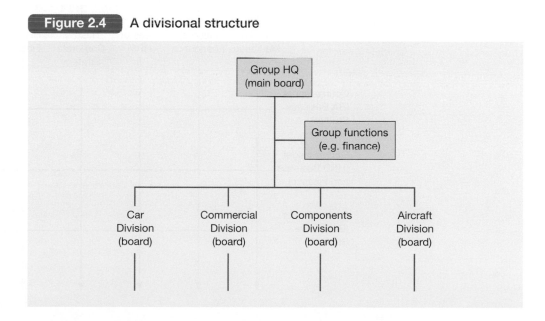

Much the same kind of arguments apply to the **holding company**, though this tends to be a much looser structure for managing diverse organisations, favoured by both UK and Japanese companies. Under this arrangement, the different elements of the organisation (usually companies) are co-ordinated and controlled by a parent body, which may be just a financial entity established to maintain or gain control of other trading companies. Holding companies are associated with the growth of firms by acquisition which gives rise to a high degree of product or market diversification. They are also a popular means of operating a multinational organisation.

Matrix structures

A **matrix** is an arrangement for combining functional specialisation (e.g. through departments) with structures built around products, projects or programmes (see Figure 2.5). The resulting grid (or matrix) has a two-way flow of authority and responsibility. Within the functional elements, the flow is vertically down the line from superior to subordinate and this creates a degree of stability and certainty for the individuals located within the department or unit. Simultaneously, as a member of a project group or product team, an individual is normally answerable horizontally to the project manager whose responsibility is to oversee the successful completion of the project, which in some cases may be of very limited duration.

Matrix structures offer various advantages, most notably flexibility, opportunities for staff development, an enhanced sense of ownership of a project or programme, customer orientation and the co-ordination of information and expertise. On the negative side, difficulties can include problems of co-ordination and control,

Figure 2.5 A matrix structure in a business school

conflicting loyalties for staff and uncertain lines of authority. It is not uncommon in an organisation designed on matrix lines for project or programme leaders to be unsure of their authority over the staff from the contributing departments. Nor is it unknown for functional managers to withdraw their co-operation and/or support for projects located outside their immediate sphere of influence.

Project teams

Despite its flexibility, the matrix often has a degree of permanence; in contrast, the project team is essentially a temporary structure established as a means of carrying out a particular task, often in a highly unstable environment. Once the task is complete, the team is disbanded and individuals return to their usual departments or are assigned to a new project.

Fashioned around technical expertise rather than managerial rank and often operating closely with clients, project teams are increasingly common in high-technology firms, construction companies and in some types of service industry, especially management consultancies and advertising. Rather than being a replacement for the existing structure, they operate alongside it and utilise in-house staff (and in some cases, outside specialists) on a project-by-project basis. While this can present logistical and scheduling problems and may involve some duplication of resources, it can assist an organisation in adapting to change and uncertainty and in providing products to the customer's specifications. Project teams tend to be at their most effective when objectives and tasks are well defined, when the client is clear as to the desired outcome and when the team is chosen with care.

mini case **Royal Dutch Shell**

In March 1995 the multinational Anglo-Dutch oil giant, Royal Dutch Shell, announced its intention to radically change its long-admired matrix organisation (see, for example, the *Financial Times*, 30 March 1995). For historical reasons, Shell had developed a structure based on geographically defined operating companies. These operating companies had executives representing national or regional units, business sectors (or divisions) and functions such as finance. Within this three-dimensional matrix, powerful individuals were able to influence the organisation's policies at regional level and a considerable bureaucracy was required to 'police' the matrix and to co-ordinate decisions between the different elements of the structure.

Faced with growing global competition and shareholder pressure for improved performance,

Shell decided to restructure the organisation by attacking problems of overstaffing and bureaucracy and by eliminating many of the regional fiefdoms through which the company had come to run its worldwide empire. Its plan involved shaping the group around five business organisations covering its main activities (e.g. exploration and production, refining and marketing, etc.), with each operating company reporting to and receiving its strategic targets from whichever of the five organisations were relevant to its activities. A new system of business committees was given responsibility for strategic and investment decisions within the different organisations, although executive authority rested with the operating companies. Through this arrangement Shell hoped to retain the sensitivity to local market needs that had traditionally been part of its organisational creed.

In a further effort to improve the company's performance, Shell indicated that more restructuring needed to take place (see, for example, the *Guardian*, 15 December 1998). Part of its blueprint for reshaping itself for the twenty-first century included additional streamlining of its management structure, away from committee-based decision making and towards a system based on American-style chief executives.

Subsequently in October 2004 the company announced the merger of its two elements – Royal Dutch and Shell Transport and Trading – into a single company, to be known as Royal Dutch Shell plc. The new entity comprises an Executive Board, a Supervisory Board, a Board of Management and a Board of Directors for Shell Transport. Members of the Executive Committee are also members of the latter two boards.

The website address for Royal Dutch Shell is *www.shell.com*

The virtual organisation

As indicated above, traditional organisations have structures which are designed to facilitate the transformation of inputs into output. Increasingly as the business environment changes, relationships both within and between organisations have needed to become more flexible and this has given rise to such developments as the growth in teleworking and the establishment of dynamic broker/agent networks involving considerable outsourcing of sub-tasks to 'agents' (e.g. manufacturing, distribution) by the core organisation (the 'broker'). It is fair to say that this demand for greater flexibility has been driven partly by the market and partly by cost considerations and the process of change has been facilitated by relatively rapid developments in information technology. One area currently exciting the interest of writers on management and organisation is the concept of the **virtual organisation**, arguably the ultimate form of organisational flexibility.

In essence a virtual organisation or firm signifies an extremely loose web of essentially freelance individuals or businesses who organise themselves to produce a specific customer product (e.g. an individual holiday package with particular features unique to the customer). Without any permanent structure or hierarchy this so-called firm can constantly change its shape and, despite existing across space and time, tends to appear edgeless, with its inputs, outputs and employees increasingly dispersed across the linked world of information systems. Given modern forms of communication, the potential exists for a totally electronic-based organisation trading in expertise and information with no real-world physical identity. This stands in stark contrast to the traditional view of the firm as an arrangement which adds value by transforming basic economic inputs (e.g. land, labour, capital) into physical outputs or services.

For a useful reading list on virtual organisations *see*
www–users.cs.york.ac.uk/~kimble/teaching/mis/Virtual_Organisations.html

Structural change

Internal change is an important feature of the modern business organisation. In order to remain competitive and meet stakeholder needs, a firm may have to find ways to restructure its organisation as the environment in which it operates changes. Solutions can range from a partial or wholesale shift in the organisation's structural form to strategies for reducing the overall size and shape of the company (e.g. **downsizing**) or a radical redesign of business processes (e.g. **re-engineering**).

Whereas business re-engineering normally connotes a root-and-branch reform of the way in which the business operates, downsizing essentially involves shrinking the organisation to make it leaner and fitter and hopefully more flexible in its response to the marketplace. For some companies this means little more than reducing the size of the workforce through natural wastage and/or redundancies, as and when opportunities arise; for others it involves delayering the organisation by removing a tier, or tiers, of management, thus effectively flattening the organisation's hierarchy and helping it to reduce its unit costs of production.

In its most systematic and long-term form, downsizing can be used as a vehicle for cultural change through which an organisation's employees are encouraged to embrace notions of continuous improvement and innovation, and to accept that structural reform is a permanent and natural state of affairs. Under such an approach, retraining and reskilling become vital tools in implementing the chosen strategy and in shaping the organisation to meet the demands of its changing environment. The danger is, however, that a firm may become too concerned with restructuring as a cure for all its problems, when the real cause of its difficulties lies in its marketplace. Cutting the number of employees, in such a situation, is unlikely to make unattractive products attractive, nor is it likely to boost morale within the organisation.

Aspects of functional management

Most organisation structures reflect a degree of **functional specialisation**, with individuals occupying roles in departments, units or sections which have titles such as Production, Finance, Marketing, Personnel, and Research and Development. These functional areas of the internal organisation, and the individuals who are allocated to them, are central to the process of transforming organisational inputs into output. The management of these functions and of the relationships between them will be a key factor in the success of the enterprise and in its ability to respond to external demands for change.

The interdependence of the internal functions can be demonstrated by a simple example. Providing goods and services to meet the market's needs often involves research and development which necessitates a financial input, usually from the capital market or the organisation's own resources. It also requires, as do all the other functions, the recruitment of staff of the right quality, a task which is more often than not the responsibility of the Personnel department. If research and development activities lead to a good idea which the Marketing department is able to sell, then the Production department is required to produce it in the right quantities, to the right specifications and at the time the market needs it. This depends not only on internal scheduling procedures within the Production department, but also on having the right kind of materials supplied on time by the Purchasing department, an appropriate system of quality control and work monitoring, machinery that is working and regularly serviced, the finished items packed, despatched and delivered and a multitude of other activities, all operating towards the same end.

The extent to which all of these requirements can be met simultaneously depends not only on internal factors, many of which are controllable, but also on a host of external influences, the majority of which tend to be beyond the organisation's control. To demonstrate this interface between the internal and external environments, two key areas of functional management are discussed briefly below – marketing and human resource management. An examination of the other functions within the organisation would yield very similar findings.

Human resource management (HRM)

People are the key organisational resource; without them organisations would not exist or function. All businesses need to plan for and manage the people they employ if they are to use this resource effectively and efficiently in pursuit of their objectives. In modern and forward-looking organisations this implies a proactive approach to the management of people which goes beyond the bounds of traditional personnel management and involves the establishment of systems for planning, monitoring, appraisal and evaluation, training and development and for integrating the internal needs of the organisation with the external demands of the marketplace. Such an approach is associated with the idea of **human resource management**.

As in other areas of management, HRM involves a wide variety of activities related to the formulation and implementation of appropriate organisational policies, the provision of opportunities for monitoring, evaluation and change, and the application of resources to the fulfilment of organisational ends. Key aspects of 'people management' include:

- recruitment and selection;
- working conditions;
- training and career development;
- job evaluation;
- employee relations;
- manpower planning; and
- legal aspects of employment.

In most, if not all, cases these will be affected by both internal and external influences (e.g. size of the firm, management style, competition, economic and political developments), some of which will vary over time as well as between organisations.

The provision of these activities within an organisation can occur in a variety of ways and to different degrees of sophistication. Some very small firms may have little in the way of a recognisable HRM function, being concerned primarily with questions of hiring and firing, pay and other working conditions, but not with notions of career development, staff appraisal or job enrichment. In contrast, very large companies may have a specialist HRM or Personnel department, often organised on functional lines and responsible for the formulation and implementation of personnel policies throughout the organisation. Such centralisation provides not only some economies of scale, but also a degree of standardisation and consistency across departments. To allow for flexibility, centralised systems are often combined with an element of decentralisation which permits individual departments or sections to exercise some influence in matters such as the recruitment and selection of staff, working conditions, training and career development.

To illustrate how the different aspects of HRM are influenced by external factors, one part of this function – recruitment and selection of staff – has been chosen. This is the activity within the organisation which seeks to ensure that it has the right quantity and quality of labour in the right place and at the right time to meet its requirements at all levels. To achieve this aim, the organisation initially needs to consider a large number of factors, including possible changes in the demand for labour, the need for new skills and likely labour turnover, before the processes of recruitment and selection can begin. These aspects in turn will be conditioned by a variety of factors such as changes in the demand for the product, the introduction of new technology and social, economic and demographic changes, some of which may not be anticipated or expected by strategic planners.

Once recruitment and selection is ready to begin, a further raft of influences will impinge upon the process, some of which emanate from external sources. In drawing up a job specification, for example, attention will normally need to be paid to the state of the local labour market, including skill availability, competition from other employers, wage rates in comparable jobs and/or organisations, and socio-demographic trends. If the quality of labour required is in short supply, an organisation may find itself having to offer improved pay and working conditions simply to attract a sufficient number of applicants to fill the vacancies on offer. Equally, in fashioning its job advertisements and in drawing up the material it sends out to potential applicants, a firm will need to pay due attention to the needs of current legislation in areas such as equal opportunities, race discrimination and employment protection, if it is not to infringe the law.

Among the other external factors the enterprise may need to take into consideration in recruiting and selecting staff will be:

● the relative cost and effectiveness of the different advertising media;
● existing relationships with external sources of recruitment (e.g. job centres, schools, colleges, universities);
● commitments to the local community;
● relationships with employee organisations (e.g. trade unions, staff associations); and
● opportunities for staff training and development in local training and educational institutions.

Ideally, it should also pay some attention to possible future changes in the technology of the workplace, in order to recruit individuals either with appropriate skills or who can be retrained relatively easily with a minimum amount of disruption and expense to the organisation.

The marketing function

The processes of human resource management provide a good illustration of the interactions between a firm's internal and external environments. An even better example is provided by an examination of its marketing activities, which are directed primarily, though not exclusively, towards what is happening outside the organisation.

Like 'management', the term **marketing** has been defined in a wide variety of ways, ranging from Kotler's essentially economic notion of an activity directed at satisfying human needs and wants through exchange processes, to the more managerial definitions associated with bodies like the Chartered Institute of Marketing.[5] A common thread running through many of these definitions is the idea that marketing is concerned with meeting the needs of the consumer in a way which is profitable to the enterprise. Hence, strategic marketing management is normally characterised as the process of ensuring a good fit between the opportunities afforded by the marketplace and the abilities and resources of an organisation operating in it.

> **web link** Information about the Chartered Institute of Marketing is available at *www.cim.co.uk*

This notion of marketing as an integrative function within the organisation – linking the needs of the consumer with the various functional areas of the firm – is central to modern definitions of the term and lies at the heart of what is known as the **marketing concept**. This is the idea that the customer is of prime importance to the organisation and that the most significant managerial task in any enterprise is first to identify the needs and wants of the consumer and then to ensure that its operations are geared to meeting these requirements profitably. Though it would be true to say that not all organisations subscribe to this view, it is generally accepted that the successful businesses are predominantly those with a customer rather than a production or sales orientation. Equally, the evidence suggests that the need to adopt such a customer-centred approach applies not only to private sector trading organisations, but also increasingly to public sector enterprises and to bodies not established for the pursuit of profits but for other purposes (e.g. charities, political parties, trade unions).

When viewed from a customer perspective, marketing can be seen to comprise a range of activities that go beyond the simple production of an item for sale. These include:

● Identifying the needs of consumers (e.g. through marketing research).
● Designing different 'offerings' to meet the needs of different types of customers (e.g. through market segmentation).
● Choosing products, prices, promotional techniques and distribution channels that are appropriate to a particular market (i.e. designing a 'marketing mix' strategy).

- Undertaking market and product planning.
- Deciding on brand names, types of packages, and methods of communicating with the customer.
- Creating a marketing information system.

As already indicated, in carrying out these activities the firm is brought into contact with a range of external influences of both an immediate and indirect kind. This external marketing environment can have a fundamental impact on the degree to which the firm is able to develop and maintain successful transactions with its customers and hence on its profitability and chances of survival.

To illustrate how a firm's marketing effort can be influenced by external factors, the following brief discussion focuses on 'pricing', which is one of the key elements of the **marketing mix**, that is, the set of controllable variables which a business can use to influence the buyer's response, namely, product, price, promotion and place – the 4Ps. Of all the mix elements, price is the only one which generates revenue, while the others result in expenditure. It is therefore a prime determinant of a firm's turnover and profitability and can have a considerable influence on the demand for its products and frequently for those of its competitors (see Chapter 14).

web link

There are lots of useful websites discussing the idea of the 'marketing mix'. Try typing the term into Google.

Leaving aside the broader question of a firm's pricing goals and the fact that prices will tend to vary according to the stage a product has reached in its life cycle, price determination can be said to be influenced by a number of factors. Of these, the costs of production, the prices charged by one's competitors and the price sensitivity of consumers tend to be the most significant.

In the case of cost-based pricing, this occurs when a firm relates its price to the cost of buying or producing the product, adding a profit margin or 'mark-up' to arrive at the final selling price. Such an approach tends to be common amongst smaller enterprises (e.g. builders, corner shops) where costs are often easier to estimate and where likely consumer reactions are given less attention than the need to make an adequate return on the effort involved. The essential point about this form of price determination is that many of the firm's costs are influenced by external organisations – including the suppliers of materials, components and energy – and hence pricing will often vary according to changes in the prices of inputs. Only larger organisations, or a group of small businesses operating together, will generally be able to exercise some influence over input prices and even then not all costs will be controllable by the enterprise.

Organisations which take an essentially cost-based approach to pricing will sometimes be influenced by the prices charged by competitors – particularly in markets where considerable competition exists and where the products are largely homogeneous and a buyer's market is evident (e.g. builders during a recession). The competitive approach to pricing, however, is also found in markets where only a few large firms operate and where the need to increase or maintain market share can give rise to virtually identical prices and to fierce non-price competition between the market leaders (see Chapter 15). In Britain, for instance, a big cross-Channel ferry operator will normally provide the service to customers at the same price as its rivals, differentiating its offering in terms of additional benefits (e.g. on-board entertainment) rather than price. Where this is the case, the external demands of the market rather than costs constitute the primary influence on a firm's decisions, and changes in market conditions (e.g. the actual or potential entry of new firms; changes in a competitor's prices; economic recession) will tend to be reflected in price changes.

This idea of market factors influencing pricing decisions also applies to situations where firms fix their prices according to the actual or anticipated reactions of consumers to the price charged for a product – known in economics as the price elasticity of demand (see Chapter 14). In this case, the customer rather than a firm's competitors is the chief influence on price determination, although the two are often interrelated in that consumers are usually more price sensitive in markets where some choice exists. Differential levels of price sensitivity between consumers of a product normally arise when a market has distinct segments based on factors such as differences in income or age or location. In such cases a firm will often fix its prices according to the segment of the market it is serving, a process known as 'price discrimination' and one which is familiar to students claiming concessionary fares on public transport.

While the above discussion has been oversimplified and does not take into account factors such as the price of other products in an organisation's product portfolio (e.g. different models of car), it illustrates quite clearly how even one of the so-called controllable variables in a firm's marketing mix is subject to a range of external influences that are often beyond its ability to control. The same argument applies to the other elements of the marketing function and students could usefully add to their understanding of the internal/external interface by examining how the external environment impinges upon such marketing activities as promotion, distribution or market research.

Synopsis

The internal dimension of business organisations constitutes an extensive field of study and one to which students of business devote a considerable amount of time. In seeking to illustrate how a firm's internal organisation is influenced by its external environment, emphasis has been placed on a selected number of aspects of a firm's internal operations. Of these, its structure and functions were seen to provide a good illustration of the interface between the internal and external environments. Appreciating the existence of this interface is facilitated by adopting a systems approach to organisational analysis.

Summary of key points

- Management is a key aspect of the internal environment of the business organisation.
- Theories of organisation and management basically fall into three categories: classical theories; human relations approaches; systems approaches.

- The systems view of organisations depicts businesses as open systems interacting with their external environment as they convert inputs into outputs.

- The external environment of the organisation affects all aspects of the business including its structures, functions and processes.

- To carry out their tasks businesses can structure themselves in a variety of ways, including functionally, by product/service, by divisions, in a matrix format or via project teams. Each has its advantages and disadvantages.

- Structural change tends to be a feature of large modern organisations.

- Within the organisation the different business functions such as marketing, production, HRM, purchasing and so on are influenced by external factors of both a general and operational kind.

- An examination of the marketing and HRM functions reveals the importance of the wide range of external influences that can impinge upon the day-to-day areas of organisational work.

- Investigations of other functional areas within the organisation would produce a similar picture.

case study   Structuring global companies

As the chapter illustrates, to carry out their activities in pursuit of their objectives, virtually all organisations adopt some form of organisational structure. One traditional method of organisation is to group individuals by function or purpose, using a departmental structure to allocate individuals to their specialist areas (e.g. Marketing, HRM and so on). Another is to group activities by product or service, with each product group normally responsible for providing its own functional requirements. A third is to combine the two in the form of a matrix structure with its vertical and horizontal flows of responsibility and authority, a method of organisation much favoured in university Business Schools.

What of companies with a global reach: how do they usually organise themselves?

Writing in the *Financial Times* in November 2000 Julian Birkinshaw, Associate Professor of Strategic and International Management at London Business School, identifies four basic models of global company structure:

- *The International Division* – an arrangement in which the company establishes a separate division to deal with business outside its own country. The International Division would typically be concerned with tariff and trade issues, foreign agents/partners and other aspects involved in selling overseas. Normally the division does not make anything itself, it is simply responsible for international sales. This arrangement tends to be found in medium-sized companies with limited international sales.

- *The Global Product Division* – a product-based structure with managers responsible for their product line globally. The company is split into a number of global businesses arranged by product (or service) and usually overseen by their own president. It has been a favoured structure among large global companies such as BP, Siemens and 3M.

- *The Area Division* – a geographically based structure in which the major line of authority lies with the country (e.g. Germany) or regional (e.g. Europe) manager who is responsible for the different product offerings within her/his geographical area.

▶

● *The Global Matrix* – as the name suggests, a hybrid of the two previous structural types. In the global matrix each business manager reports to two bosses, one responsible for the global product and one for the country/region. As we indicated in the previous edition of this book, this type of structure tends to come into and go out of fashion. Ford, for example, adopted a matrix structure in the later 1990s, while a number of other global companies were either streamlining or dismantling theirs (e.g. Shell, BP, IBM).

As Professor Birkinshaw indicates, ultimately there is no perfect structure and organisations tend to change their approach over time according to changing circumstances, fads, the perceived needs of the senior executives or the predispositions of powerful individuals. This observation is no less true of universities than it is of traditional businesses.

Case study questions

1 Professor Birkinshaw's article identifies the advantages and disadvantages of being a global business. What are his major arguments?

2 In your opinion what are likely to be the key factors determining how a global company will organise itself?

Review and discussion questions

1 In the systems approach to organisations, reference is made to 'feedback'. What is meant by this term and how can feedback influence the process of transforming 'inputs' into 'output'?

2 Should a firm's internal structure be influenced by considerations of management or by the market it serves? Are the two incompatible?

3 Examine ways in which a firm's external environment can influence one of the following functional areas: finance or production or research and development.

4 Describe the structure of an organisation with which you are familiar (e.g. through employment or work experience), indicating why the organisation is structured in the way it is. Are there any alternative forms of structure the organisation could adopt?

Assignments

1 As a student on a business studies course, you have decided to get some practical experience of the business world by running a small venture with a number of colleagues which you hope will also earn you enough income to support you during your time at college or university. Your idea involves printing and selling customised T-shirts throughout the institution and possibly to a wider market. Design an appropriate organisational structure which you feel will help you achieve your objectives, indicating your rationale for choosing such a structure and the formal pattern of relationships between individuals.

2 In self-selecting groups of three or four, identify an organisation which you feel has a bureaucratic structure. Produce a report indicating:

(a) those features of the organisation's structure, management and operations which best fit the idea of bureaucracy; and

(b) the practical consequences of these features for the working of the organisation.

Give examples to support your comments.

Notes and references

1 See, for example, Mullins, L. J., *Management and Organisational Behaviour*, 8th edition, Financial Times/Prentice Hall, 2007; Cole, G. A., *Management: Theory and Practice*, 6th edition, Thomson, 2004.

2 For a more detailed account of the three approaches see, *inter alia*, the texts referred to in n. 1.

3 Ouichi, W. G., *Theory Z: How American Business can Meet the Japanese Challenge*, Addison-Wesley, 1981.

4 The contingency approach is discussed in Cole, *op. cit.*

5 See, for example, Kotler, P. and Armstrong, G., *Principles of Marketing*, 11th edition, Prentice Hall, 2005.

Further reading

Campbell, D. J., *Organizations and the Business Environment*, Butterworth-Heinemann, 1997.

Cole, G. A., *Management: Theory and Practice*, 6th edition, Thomson, 2004.

Handy, C., *The Age of Unreason*, Arrow Books, 2nd edition, 1995.

Kotler, P., *Principles of Marketing*, 4th European edition, Prentice Hall International, 2005.

Morrison, J., *The International Business Environment: Global and Local Marketplaces in a Changing World*, 2nd revised edition, Palgrave Macmillan, 2006.

Mullins, L. J., *Management and Organisational Behaviour*, 8th edition, Financial Times/Prentice Hall, 2007.

Mullins, L. J., *Essentials of Organisational Behaviour*, FT/Prentice Hall, 2008.

Pugh, D. S. and Hickson, D. J., *Great Writers on Organizations*, 2nd Omnibus edition, Ashgate, 2007.

web link

Web links and further questions are available on the website at:
www.pearsoned.co.uk/worthington

3 The global context of business

Chris Britton

Businesses of all sizes operate in international markets – products are sold across borders; the resources used in production can come from anywhere in the world; communication is instantaneous; and financial markets are inextricably linked, as the events of 2008 demonstrate. Individual businesses operate across borders in a variety of ways – they can do this directly, through the formation of strategic alliances or through merger and takeover. It is clear then that businesses need to be aware of the global context of their markets.

Learning outcomes

Having read this chapter you should be able to:

● understand the difference between globalisation and internationalisation

● outline the main elements of globalisation

● illustrate the role of the multinational enterprise

● introduce the implications of globalisation for business

Key terms

Capital market flows
Consortium
Cross-subsidisation
Customs union
Emerging economies
Foreign direct investment (FDI)
Franchising

Free trade area
Globalisation
Hyperglobalisation
Internationalisation
International trade
Joint venture
Licensing

Multinational enterprise (MNE)
Regionalism
Regional trade agreements (RTAs)
Strategic alliance
Transfer pricing
Transformationalism

Introduction

Businesses operate in a global context: even if they do not trade directly with other countries, they might be affected by a domestic shortage of skilled labour or may be subject to developments on the global financial markets. There is a difference between globalisation and internationalisation in the business literature but both result in increased exposure to global forces. This means that businesses need an understanding of the process of globalisation. The nature of globalisation is changing; it used to mean the westernisation of the developing world but the newly emerging economies such as Brazil, China and India are redefining processes and institutions. In 1980 the share of the developing countries in world trade was 22 per cent, by 2005 it was 32 per cent and the World Bank predicts that their share will be 45 per cent by 2030. Globalisation is here to stay, despite apparent retreat into nationalism in light of economic conditions in 2008, so all businesses need to be aware of their global context.

Globalisation versus internationalisation

These terms are often used interchangeably but they refer to different processes. Although there is not a single accepted definition of **globalisation**, it is a term used to describe the process of integration on a worldwide scale of markets and production. The world is moving away from a system of national markets that are isolated from one another by trade barriers, distance or culture. Advances in technology and mass communications have made it possible for people in one part of the world to watch happenings in far off places on television or via the Internet. So, for globalisation, national boundaries are not important economically; free trade and movement of labour and other resources result in the breakdown of these boundaries and one big global marketplace. **Internationalisation**, on the other hand, refers to the increased links between nation states with respect to trade and the movement of resources. The important thing here is that the nation state is still important; it is participating and co-operating with other nation states to a common end.

Regionalism and regional trade agreements are important in this process – the EU is an example. The main difference is that with internationalisation, the nation state remains important whereas the process of globalisation breaks down the barriers between nation states. An extreme view of this process is called '**hyperglobalisation**', where the world market is seen as a borderless global marketplace consisting of powerless nation states and powerful multinational corporations.[1] The more generally accepted view is called '**transformationalism**', which sees the process of globalisation as bringing about *changes* in both the power of countries and companies and in national characteristics and culture.[2] Any differences do not disappear but are maintained, albeit in changed forms. The population in India might drink Coca-Cola and listen to western music, but this does not mean that they hold the same views and values as the west. Similarly, even within the EU national differences remain important (especially in times of crisis).

Although these definitions are important theoretically, they are difficult to apply in practice, so here the term globalisation is used to mean the process of integration of markets, however that happens. Until recently globalisation meant the westernisation (or Americanisation) of markets but the world has started to change. Companies from **emerging economies** have started to compete with the older **multinational enterprises (MNEs)** and the nature of the MNE is being redefined. Globalisation has taken place because of closer economic ties between countries and because of developments in mass communications, in transportation, electronics and the greater mobility of labour. A heated debate has taken place over the past decade between the pro- and the anti-globalisation lobbies.

The arguments put forward by the proponents of globalisation stem from the benefits brought about by increased international trade and specialisation (see Chapter 16 for a discussion). They argue that all countries open to international trade have benefited – only those that are closed to international trade (some African countries, for example) have become poorer. In the case of China, the opening up to world trade in 1978 has led to increases in GDP per capita, up from $1460 per head in 1980 to $5400 per head in 2007. The pro-globalisation arguments can be summarised as follows:

- increased globalisation leads to greater specialisation so that all countries involved benefit from the increased international trade;
- countries that are open to international trade have experienced much faster growth than countries that are not;
- barriers to trade encourage industries to be inefficient and uncompetitive;
- it is not just the large multinationals that benefit from globalisation – small and medium-sized companies are also engaged in global production and marketing.

The arguments against globalisation are just as strong. It is claimed that the benefits of higher world output and growth brought about through globalisation have not been shared equally by all countries. The main beneficiaries have been the large multinationals rather than individual countries or people. It is suggested that the international organisations that promote free trade should pay more attention to the issues of equity, human rights and environment rather than focusing simply on trade. It is also argued that increased globalisation leads to economic instability. The anti-globalisation arguments can be summarised thus:

- the benefits of globalisation have not been shared equitably throughout the world;
- globalisation undermines the power of nation states – it empowers the large multinationals at the expense of governments – many multinationals are financially bigger than nation states;
- the large organisations that promote free trade (such as the WTO and the IMF) are not democratically elected and their decisions are not made in the public eye;
- the policies of these organisations are only aimed at trade – human rights and environmental concerns are often ignored.

The main international organisations concerned with globalisation are discussed in more detail in Chapter 5. They are the World Trade Organisation (WTO), the International Monetary Fund (IMF), the World Bank and the OECD. In addition to these there is the United Nations Conference on Trade and Development (UNCTAD), which is a permanent intergovernmental body of the United Nations that aims to maximise investment to the developing nations and to help them in their integration into the world economy.

There are several key elements of economic globalisation: international trade; foreign direct investment; and capital market flows. The OECD categorises members into three bands – high income countries, which includes the EU, North America and Australasia; middle income countries, which includes East Asia and the Pacific Rim; and low income countries, which includes South Asia and Africa.

International trade

The share of international trade in goods as a percentage of GDP increased between 1990 and 2005 for all income groups and particularly for the middle income group (see Table 3.1). The same is true for services. Thus there is evidence of increased globalisation. Note that there are differences within each group; in the low income group, for example, although the share has increased overall, there are countries that have experienced negative growth (Botswana and Paraguay for instance – both of which are open to international trade). Although the share of developing countries has increased over time, world markets are still dominated by the developed world, especially in high-value, high-tech products. It is also true that increased trade does not automatically lead to increased development as in parts of sub-Saharan Africa where the products sold are basic primary products.

Table 3.1 Elements of economic globalisation

	Trade in goods as a % of GDP		Gross private capital flows as a % of GDP		Gross FDI as a % of GDP	
	1990	2005	1990	2005	1990	2005
Low income	23.6	41.1	2.4	0.7	0.4	1.5
Middle income	32.5	62.1	6.6	13.3	0.9	3.1
High income	32.3	43.9	11.0	37.2	1.0	2.1

Source: Adapted from Table 6.1, *World Development Indicators*, 2007, World Bank, *www.worldbank.org/data/wdi2007.index.html*.

Capital market flows

This refers to the flows of money from private savers wishing to include foreign assets in their portfolios. This has also increased in all income bands between 1990 and 2005 (Table 3.1). The overall figures hide a greater volatility than in international trade or **foreign direct investment** and the fact that the flows have been largely restricted to emerging economies in East Asia. **Capital market flows** occur because investors want to diversify their portfolios to include foreign assets; it is therefore aimed at bringing about short-term capital gains. Unlike foreign direct investment, there is no long-term involvement on the part of the investor.

Foreign direct investment (FDI)

This refers to the establishment of production facilities in overseas countries and therefore represents a more direct involvement in the local economy (than capital market flows) and a longer-term relationship. Between 1990 and 2000, the value of **FDI** worldwide more than doubled – the two biggest recipients and donors were the UK and the USA. Since 2000 FDI has fallen in line with world economic recession but it recovered slightly by 2004 (Table 3.1). FDI represents the largest form of private capital inflow into the developing countries. The importance of FDI is considered in the case study at the end of the chapter.

Each of the three elements of economic globalisation has a different effect and carries different consequences for countries. Capital market flows are much more volatile and therefore carry higher risk – these flows introduce the possibility of 'boom and bust' for countries where capital market flows are important. The financial crises in the emerging Asian countries in the late 1990s had a lot to do with these capital flows. Openness to trade and FDI are less volatile and it is these that are favoured by the international organisations such as the World Bank and the WTO. It is also true that the benefits of globalisation have not been shared equally between those taking part – the developed nations have reaped more benefit than the poorer nations.

The role of multinational enterprises

Substantial amounts of foreign trade and hence movements of currency result from the activities of very large multinational companies or enterprises. Multinational enterprises/companies (MNEs/MNCs), strictly defined, are enterprises operating in a number of countries and having production or service facilities outside the country of their origin. These multinationals usually have their headquarters in a developed country but this is beginning to change. At one time globalisation meant that businesses were expanding from developed to developing economies. The world is a different place now – business flows in the opposite direction and often between developing countries. One indication of this is the number of companies from the emerging nations that appear in the Fortune 500 list of the world's biggest companies. Between 2003 and 2007 it had doubled from 31 to 62. Most of these come from Brazil, Russia, India and China (the BRIC countries) and include Infosys, an Indian multinational IT services company, and Lenovo, a Chinese computer manufacturer which bought IBM's personal computer business in 2005. These companies offer a different model of an MNE from the traditional one. Lenovo, for example, does not regard itself as a Chinese company; it does not have headquarters in a particular country although its marketing department is located in Bangalore – meetings of managers rotate between countries where the company has a presence.

Multinationals can diversify their operations across different countries and many are well-known household names (see Table 3.2). The footloose nature of such companies brings with it certain benefits.

Table 3.2 The world's ten largest non-financial MNEs, ranked by foreign assets, 2006

Rank	Company	Home economy	Transnationality index %*
1	General Electric	United States	53
2	British Petroleum Company plc	UK	80
3	Toyota Motor Corporation	Japan	45
4	Royal Dutch/Shell group	UK/Netherlands	70
5	Exxon Mobil Corporation	United States	68
6	Ford Motor Company	United States	50
7	Vodafone Group plc	United Kingdom	85
8	Total	France	74
9	Electicite De France	France	35
10	Wal-Mart Stores	United States	41

Note: * Measured as the average of three ratios: foreign assets to total assets, foreign sales to total sales, and foreign employment to total employment.
Source: Adapted from Annex Table A1.15, *World Develpment Report*, UNCTAD, 2008.

1 MNEs can locate their activities in the countries which are best suited for them. For example, production planning can be carried out in the parent country, the production itself can be carried out in one of the newly industrialised countries where labour is relatively cheap and marketing can be done in the parent country where such activities are well developed. The relocation of production may go some way to explaining the decline in the manufacturing sector in the developed nations.

2 An MNE can cross-subsidise its operations. Profits from one market can be used to support operations in another one. The **cross-subsidisation** could take the form of price cutting, increasing productive capacity or heavy advertising.

3 The risk involved in production is spread, not just over different markets but also over different countries.

4 MNEs can avoid tax by negotiating special tax arrangements in one of their host countries (tax holidays) or through careful use of **transfer pricing**. Transfer prices are the prices at which internal transactions take place. These can be altered so that high profits can be shown in countries where the tax rate is lower. For example, in the USA in 1999 two-thirds of foreign-based multinationals paid no federal income tax. The loss to US taxpayers from this has been estimated as in excess of $40 billion per year in unpaid taxes.

5 MNEs can take advantage of subsidies and tax exemptions offered by governments to encourage start-ups in their country.

The very size of MNEs gives rise to concern as their operations can have a substantial impact upon the economy. For example, the activities of MNEs will affect the labour market of host countries and the balance of payments. If a subsidiary is started in one country there will be an inflow of capital to that country. Once it is up and running, however, there will be outflows of dividends and profits which will affect the invisible balance. Also, there will be flows of goods within the company, and therefore between countries, in the form of semi-finished goods and raw materials. These movements will affect the exchange rate as well as the balance of payments and it is likely that the effects will be greater for developing countries than for developed countries.

There is also the possibility of exploitation of less developed countries, and it is debatable whether such footloose industries form a viable basis for economic development. Added to this, MNEs take their decisions in terms of their overall operations rather than with any consideration of their effects on the host economy. There is therefore a loss of economic sovereignty for national governments.

The main problem with multinationals is the lack of control that can be exerted by national governments. In June 2005 the OECD updated its *Guidelines for Multinational Enterprises*, which are not legally binding but are promoted by OECD member governments. These seek to provide a balanced framework for international investment that clarifies both the rights and responsibilities of the business community. It contains guidelines on business ethics, employment relations, information disclosure and taxation, among other things. In 2008 the International Accounting Standards Board is considering a proposal which would force the world's giant oil and mining companies to reveal the amount of tax paid in each country in which they have a presence. If successful, this could be in place by 2010 but there is already high-level lobbying taking place to water down the proposal. Against all this is the fact that without the presence of MNEs, output in host countries would be lower, and there is evidence that on labour market issues the multinationals do not perform badly.

Transnationality

The transnationality index gives a measure of an MNE's involvement abroad by looking at three ratios – foreign asset/total asset, foreign sales/total sales and foreign employment/total employment. As such it captures the importance of foreign activities in its overall activities. In Table 3.2 Vodafone Group plc has the highest index – this is because in all three ratios it has a high proportion of foreign involvement. Since 1990 the average index of transnationality for the top 100 MNEs has increased from 51 per cent to 55 per cent.

These multinationals are huge organisations and their market values often exceed the GNP of many of the countries in which they operate. There are over 60 000 MNEs around the world and they are estimated to account for a quarter of the world's output. The growth in MNEs is due to relaxation of exchange controls, making it easier to move money between countries, and the improvements in communication, which makes it possible to run a worldwide business from one country. The importance of multinationals varies from country to country, as Table 3.3 shows.

Table 3.3 Share of foreign affiliates in manufacturing production and employment, 2004

Country	% share of foreign affiliates in manufacturing production	% share of foreign affiliates in manufacturing employment
Ireland	80	48
Hungary	63	42
Czech Republic	52	37
UK	41	26
Netherlands	41	25
Luxembourg	34	25
Germany	27	16
USA	21	11
Finland	16	17
Italy	15	7
Japan	3	1

Source: Adapted from OECD Science, Technology and Industry Scoreboard 2007.

As can be seen, foreign affiliates are very important for some countries and not so important for others; in the case of Japan there is hardly any foreign presence at all. For all of the countries, except Finland, foreign affiliates have a bigger impact on production than employment.

Globalisation and business

Businesses of all sizes need to have an awareness of their international context. As noted above, even if they are not directly involved in international trade, firms will be affected by international forces that lie largely outside their control. Globalisation has meant that the financial crisis of 2008, for instance, has affected virtually the whole world. Some of the issues facing businesses are discussed below in brief; many of them are discussed later in the book in more detail.

Markets

Globalisation means that firms are faced with bigger markets for their products. Many of these markets are covered by **regional trade agreements (RTAs)**, which are groupings of countries set up to facilitate world trade. All such agreements have to be notified to the World Trade Organisation and they can take a variety of forms. The most basic relationship and the most common is a **free trade area**, where trade barriers between members are abolished but where each member maintains its own national barriers with non-members. An example of this is the North American Free Trade Agreement (NAFTA). Agreements can also take the form of a **customs union** or common market, where members abolish trade barriers between themselves and adopt a common external tariff which is applied to non-members. An example of this is the EU. All of these agreements increase the size of the market-place for producers in the member countries and the enlargement of these agreements (the EU for example) means that markets are increasing all of the time.

In addition to these trade agreements, the opening up of the emerging economies (e.g. China and India) to international trade, their high growth rates and the corresponding increase in per capita income mean that there has been a massive increase in the demand for goods and services. The population in India is 1147 million, income per head has doubled since 2000 and GDP growth rate was over 9 per cent per annum between 2005 and 2008. The Chinese population stood at 1330 million in 2007, income per head has almost doubled since 2000 and the average growth rate over the 4 years up to 2008 was 11 per cent.[3] Many believe that China's high growth rate has been fuelled by exports, but recent research shows that demand is more consumption driven than previously thought.[4] It also shows that consumer demand has changed in favour of products that have a higher imported content. This is good news for the rest of the world.

Labour markets

It has been estimated that the global integration of emerging markets has doubled the supply of labour for the global production of goods. The OECD estimates that the percentage of the world population living outside their country of birth doubled between 1985 and 2005. About half of this is between the developed countries, the other half from developing to developed countries. The impact of migration is considered in more detail in the international case study at the end of Part Two ('Contexts').

International labour mobility can be used by businesses for hard to fill vacancies. Typically these are at the low-skill, high-risk and low-paid end of the spectrum and at the high-skill, high-paid end. Legal labour migration can be permanent (where migrants settle permanently) or temporary (where migrants eventually return home). The regulations pertaining to these will differ. In addition to international labour migration there are three other alternatives: outsourcing (for example, the location of US call centres in India involve the movement of jobs rather than people); cross-border commuting (for example, the commuting of Poles into western Europe); or the use of Internet trade (where the work could take place anywhere).

For businesses wishing to recruit internationally, there are practical problems including locating the necessary people and dealing with the rules and regulations involved in employing migrants, such as work permits and visas. These requirements will vary from one country to another.

Other resources

As well as labour, businesses have to source and purchase other resources such as raw materials and energy. Natural resources are differentially distributed around the world and therefore they require international trade to take place if firms are to acquire these inputs. The market for energy, for example, is a global market, with attendant concerns about the environmental impact of the methods used for its generation (see the mini case study, below). The issue of resources is further discussed in Chapter 7.

mini case   UK nuclear power industry

The market for energy is global. The European Commission adopted a policy at the end of 2007 designed to promote more competition within the EU energy market. These measures include breaking the link between production and supply of energy and the establishment of an Agency for the co-operation of National Energy Regulators to facilitate cross-border energy trade. In the UK four of the main electricity suppliers are foreign owned: EDF (French), RWE (German owners of npower), E.ON (German) and Iberdrola (Spanish owners of Scottish Power).

Because of the calls for cleaner forms of energy and the targets set for carbon emissions worldwide, there has been a search for cleaner sources of energy. One possibility is nuclear energy. The use of nuclear power in the generation of electricity in the UK is smaller than many other European countries (France, for example, generates nearly all of its electricity through nuclear power) and the UK government aims to increase this contribution and therefore reduce its reliance on fossil fuels. Of course there are arguments against this that revolve around the safety issues of nuclear power stations.

At the beginning of 2008 British Energy – which owned most of the aged British nuclear plants – was put up for sale. In September 2008 EDF, the French power giant, agreed to buy British Energy. EDF is the biggest nuclear energy producer in the world and one of the largest power suppliers. It already holds 6 per cent of the electricity industry in the UK through direct sales of electricity.

There are arguments for and against the foreign ownership of industries like energy. The main argument against is that energy is a strategic good and it is unwise to allow foreign ownership of such goods. This has been seen recently in the strategic withdrawal of gas supplies to the Ukraine by Russia. Current global economic conditions also highlight a possible problem – when times are bad, foreign-owned companies might ensure that their own consumers are supplied over those of other countries. In addition, in this case it might result in a lack of competition as British Energy owns all but two of Britain's nuclear plants and these are due to close in 2010. Of course, against this there are advantages – it is possible that a country does not have the expertise or, as in the case of building nuclear power stations, companies with the necessary capital to build them. Economies of scale mean that costs of building and maintenance can be kept low.

The proposed takeover has to be cleared by shareholders and regulators in the UK and the EU (although given EU policy it should not be a problem). EDF has plans to expand further worldwide – it already has a bid in for the US energy company Constellation Energy.

Financial markets

Businesses need to raise capital to be able to produce, trade and invest. Although much of this takes place domestically, banks operate internationally and so businesses are exposed to global forces. Never has this been seen more vividly than in the events of 2008 (see mini case study, below, and the 'International business in action' at the end of Part Four, 'The global financial crisis').

mini case   Financial markets

The speed with which the global financial crisis spread in 2008 illustrates well how interrelated financial markets are. It started in October 2007 in the USA when Citigroup announced a $6.5 billion write-off of sub-prime mortgage losses. The credit crunch worsened in the US and spread to other parts of the world but came to a head in September 2008. On 15 September Lehman Brothers was declared bankrupt – the largest in US history. That record was broken on 25 September when Washington Mutual was closed. On 29 September the House of Representatives rejected a $700 billion rescue plan for banks saddled with bad mortgage debt (although the plan was subsequently agreed). On 29 September Ireland was the first EU country to be declared officially in recession and the Irish government intervened in the financial markets to protect savers. In the UK, Bradford and Bingley was nationalised and reassurances given to savers. Similar things have been seen in other EU countries but this is not confined to the USA and Europe. In Iceland the three biggest banks have all failed. In Russia several banks have been rescued by the government and trading on the stock market temporarily suspended. The Chinese stock market values fell by 60 per cent in 2008 and the rate of interest was cut in September of that year.

At the time of writing, it is not clear where this will end. Most governments and international organisations have intervened in the markets to reassure the general public and to attempt to maintain confidence in the financial system. It is clear by the speed of all this that countries are not immune to what happens in other countries – financial markets are truly global. It is also clear that this crisis might lead to increased nationalism on the part of individual countries as they try to protect their own populations and businesses.

Globalisation and the small and medium-sized firm

There are problems for small and medium-sized enterprises (SMEs) wishing to trade internationally. They will not have the same access to resources, finance or markets as the large multinationals or even the large national companies which could either trade directly or expand internationally through mergers and takeovers. SMEs, however, have a number of options:

- **Strategic alliances** are collaborative agreements between firms to achieve a common aim, in this context a presence in other markets. These agreements can take many forms.
- **Franchising** is an arrangement where one party (the franchiser) sells the rights to another party (the franchisee) to market its product or service. There are different types of franchise relationship (see Chapter 10) and this is a possibility for international expansion. It is an attractive option for companies seeking international expansion without having to undertake substantial direct investments.
- **Licensing** is where a company (the licensor) authorises a company in another country (the licensee) to use its intellectual property in return for certain considerations, usually royalties. Licensors are usually multinationals located in developed countries (see Chapter 10).
- **Joint ventures** are usually a jointly owned and independently incorporated business venture involving two or more organisations. This is a popular method of expanding abroad as each party can diversify, with the benefit of the experience of the others involved in the venture and a reduction in the level of risk. Where a large number of members is involved in such an arrangement, this is called a **consortium**.

Synopsis

This chapter has looked at the global context of business. No business is immune from international forces no matter what it is producing or how small its markets are. The whole concept of globalisation has been discussed along with the claimed costs and benefits. The elements of globalisation have been outlined along with the impact of globalisation on businesses.

Summary of key points

- There is a difference between globalisation and internationalisation which centres on the role of national boundaries.
- There are costs and benefits associated with the process of globalisation.
- There are three main elements of globalisation – international trade, capital market flows and foreign direct investment.

- Multinational enterprises are very important in the process of globalisation.

- With the arrival of the emerging economies in the global marketplace, some changes in the nature and the process of globalisation are evident.

- Globalisation affects all firms in one way or another – either through its markets, its access to resources or finance.

- There are several different possibilities for small and medium-sized businesses wishing to expand internationally.

case study

Multinationals and FDI

FDI is not only an important element in the process of globalisation, but also in the activities of multinational enterprises. Figure 3.1 shows the patterns of world FDI flows from 1990 to 2007.

Figure 3.1 Flows of FDI, 1990–2007

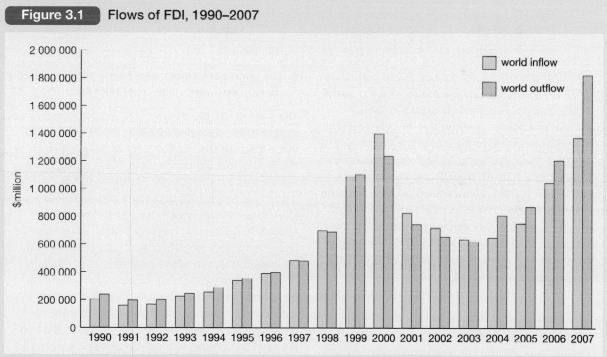

Source: Adapted from Table 1.1. *Trends and Recent Developments in FDI*, OECD, 2007.

The wave of FDI in the 1980s brought new companies and jobs – in the USA, for example, the number of Americans employed by foreign companies more than doubled between 1980 and 1990. This changed in the 1990s, when FDI was directed towards mergers and acquisitions rather than the opening of new factories or subsidiaries. In 1997, for example, it was estimated that 90 per cent of FDI took the form of mergers and acquisitions.[5] Between 2000 and 2003 both the number of cross-border mergers and acquisitions and the level of FDI flows fell dramatically. Since then there have been record increases in FDI flows. Within this average there has been great variability in the performance of individual countries as Table 3.4 shows.

The reasons put forward for the dramatic decline in total FDI flows in the early 2000s were: the sluggishness of the global economy; some uncertainty over monetary policy in some countries; and, most significantly, increasing international political instability and insecurity. The reasons put forward for the recovery in FDI flows are: the relative decline in the value of the US$ and large-value mergers and acquisitions during the period. The OECD is predicting falls in the value of FDI for 2008 and beyond because of the worsening global financial crisis.[6]

Table 3.4 Change in FDI flows between 2001 and 2006, selected countries (%)

	FDI outflow change %			FDI inflow change %		
	2001–2003	2003–2004	2005–2006	2001–2003	2003–2004	2005–2006
Total OECD members	−14	+12	+29	−18	−12	+22
USA	−2	+79	+38	−60	+60	+67
UK	−14	−2	−5	−50	+300	−28
Japan	−25	+8	+10	+2	+23	−132
Australia	+18	+16	−61	+46	+600	+70

Source: Adapted from Table 2.1, *Trends and Recent Developments in FDI*, OECD, 2007.

Table 3.5 Matrix of inward FDI performance and potential

	High FDI performance	Low FDI performance
High FDI potential	Frontrunners	Below potential
Low FDI potential	Above potential	Underperformers

Source: Adapted from Figure 1.8, *World Investment Report*, UNCTAD, 2008.

UNCTAD has combined data on FDI performance and FDI potential to draw up a matrix which is useful to policy makers. The matrix is shown in Table 3.5.

FDI performance is measured as an index number of FDI inflows relative to the size of the economy. FDI potential is measured using 12 factors which include GDP per capita, growth of GDP and the share of exports in GDP. Both are measured over a given time period (e.g. 2002–2006) to even out any short-term fluctuations and the data covers 140 countries. The top four performers were Hong Kong, China, Bulgaria and Iceland. The top three for FDI potential were the USA, Singapore and the UK.[7]

The 140 countries were then assigned to the matrix.

- **The front runners** include many industrialised nations such as Belgium, Luxembourg, the Netherlands and the UK and some advanced transitional economies such as the Czech Republic and Slovakia.
- **Above potential** include some African countries (e.g. Namibia and Zambia) and some South American countries such as Nicaragua and Colombia.
- **Below potential** include some major industrialised nations such as the USA and Japan and some newly industrialising countries including the Republic of Korea.
- **The underperformers** were mainly poor or unstable economies such as India and South Africa.

The purpose of this analysis is to aid decision makers in both those countries receiving the FDI flows and those initiating the FDI flows. It gives an indication of the factors that are important in FDI flows and looks at how they have changed. The exercise has been carried out since 1995 and some countries (the USA, for example) have moved from being front runners to performing below potential, while some underperformers (e.g. Nicaragua) have moved from underperformers to above potential.

At one time economists thought of international trade and FDI as alternatives – instead of trading with a country a company could enter that country, by opening a subsidiary. These days, however, the two are seen as complementary. A major study by the OECD[8] found that for donors of FDI, each outward investment of $1 produces additional exports of $2. For recipients of FDI, the short-term effect is an increase in imports; an increase in exports is not seen until the longer term.

Case study questions

1 Why are FDI flows cyclical in nature?

2 How might a country make itself more attractive to inward FDI?

Review and discussion questions

1 What role does the advancement of ICT have in the process of globalisation?

2 What are the arguments for and against foreign ownership of strategic industries such as energy?

3 How are multinationals changing?

4 For a business considering expansion into another country, what methods of expansion are available? What are the advantages and disadvantages of each?

5 What has been the impact of the financial crisis in 2008 on the process of globalisation? (At the time of writing it seemed that there was a movement away from global solutions towards national ones.)

Assignments

1 You work in a local office of a multinational enterprise and your line manager has been invited to take part in a discussion arranged by the local newspaper on the pros and cons of globalisation. You have been asked to provide a briefing paper outlining the arguments for your line manager.

2 You have been asked to give a presentation to students of business at a local college on regional trade agreements. Research which regional trade agreements your country is a member of and what effects membership has on labour mobility. Prepare PowerPoint slides together with notes to accompany each slide.

Notes and references

1 See Gray, J., *False Dawn: The Delusions of Global Capitalism*, Granta Books, London, 1998.

2 See Held, D., McGrew, A., Goldblatt, D. and Perraton, J., *Global Transformations: Politics, Economics and Culture*, Polity Press, Cambridge, 1999.

3 World Bank, 2008.

4 Capital Economics, 2007.

5 *Survey of Current Business*, ONS, 2004.

6 *Trends and Recent Developments in FDI*, OECD, 2007.

7 *World Investment Report*, UNCTAD, 2008.

8 Fontagne, L., *Foreign Direct Investment and International Trade: Complements or Substitutes?* OECD, 1999.

Further reading

Daniels, J. D., *International Business: Environments and Operations*, 11th edn, Financial Times/Prentice Hall, 2007.

Ellis, J. and Williams, D., *International Business Strategy*, Pitman Publishing, 1995.

Griffiths, A. and Wall, S., *Applied Economics*, 10th edn, Financial Times/Prentice Hall, 2004.

Worthington, I., Britton, C. and Rees, A., *Business Economics: Blending Theory and Practice*, 2nd edn, Financial Times/Prentice Hall, 2005.

Web links and further questions are available on the website at:

www.pearsoned.co.uk/worthington

The car industry

All businesses are affected by external factors, many of which lie outside their direct control. While some of these influences concern developments within an organisation's operational environment (e.g. a loss of a supplier), others relate to changes of a more general or contextual kind which can affect a wide variety of businesses, sometimes in different ways (e.g. fluctuations in the exchange rate). As the opening chapter of this book illustrated, these general/contextual variables include political, economic, socio-cultural, technological, legal and ethical influences that can occur at all spatial levels from the local to the global. For organisations operating in the international/global marketplace, developments at both the micro and macroenvironmental levels can represent a significant challenge (or opportunity) and can have a substantial influence on the strategic decision-making process.

To illustrate how organisations can be affected by some of the broader contextual changes discussed in Part Two, we can examine the car industry, which comprises many well-known international brands including Ford, Toyota, General Motors, Chrysler, Honda, Renault, PSA Citroen-Peugeot, Fiat, Nissan, BMW and Volkswagen. As the mini-case in Chapter 1 illustrates, even some of the world's largest and most powerful businesses in this industry have faced difficulties over recent years because of developments in their external environment and many have been forced to respond in a variety of ways.

What have some of the major challenges been and how have they affected the key players?

Rises in oil and other commodity prices

A combination of increased demand (e.g. because of growth in China and India) and tight supply has meant that oil and other commodity prices (e.g. steel) have risen quite substantially and this has meant that production costs in the industry have tended to rise. As these price rises also affect consumers, sales of vehicles in some countries have tended to decline and many consumers are switching to more economical/fuel-efficient models as petrol prices increase.

Economic downturn

The falling sales of vehicles being experienced in some parts of the world has not been helped by a general downturn in many economies as a result of the impact of the 'credit crunch'. As countries go into or face recession, consumers tend to defer spending on larger, more expensive items such as cars. This affects both the market for new vehicles and the second-hand market.

Emerging markets

While many economies are facing difficult economic circumstances, growth in some countries (e.g. China, India, Brazil, Russia) has provided an opportunity for car producers to exploit new and expanding markets. By the same token, this growth is encouraging newer companies to come into the marketplace and to increase the possibility of future competition in the traditional areas of the international car market (e.g. Europe and the US).

Environmental issues

The growing threat of climate change has meant that the environmental impact of cars and other vehicles has become a prime concern for both governments (see below) and consumers. As far as the latter are concerned, there has been a slight shift in consumer taste away from high-polluting, gas-guzzling models (e.g. SUVs, 4x4s, pick-ups) towards more fuel-efficient vehicles that have a smaller environmental impact. Rising oil prices have reinforced this trend towards smaller cars. There has also been increased investment in electric vehicles and in hybrids.

Legislative/policy developments

Governmental concerns over the contribution of cars to climate change, has resulted in threats of future national and/or international legislation and/or targets regarding vehicle CO_2 emissions. In the EU, for example, the European Commission is currently (2008) negotiating with the major car producers over the issue of emission reductions for vehicles coming on to the European market in future years.

Currency fluctuations

For firms involved in international trade, exchange rate fluctuations/volatility can sometimes be problematical (see Chapter 16). Such fluctuations in the values of the dollar, yen and euro in recent years have had a direct impact on the major car producers in the US, Japan and Europe, making prices sometimes more and sometimes less competitive. As oil is also priced in dollars, a fluctuation in the dollar exchange rate has also impacted on the industry.

How should/have the major players respond(ed)?

As the analysis above illustrates, the international car industry has faced significant changes in the external environment over recent years. While some of these changes have provided opportunities for the major players, many have been particularly challenging and have caused vehicle manufacturers to look at both the supply side (e.g. costs) and the demand side (e.g. market development) of their businesses. Some of the key questions being faced by the major brands are:

- How can costs be reduced (e.g. should the workforce be reduced)?
- What product mix should be offered to the consumers (e.g. should some of the less fuel-efficient models be phased out)?
- What markets should be targeted (e.g. should the focus shift towards the emerging markets)?

- How should the new markets be accessed (e.g. are joint ventures a better solution than direct manufacturing)?
- Where should production take place (e.g. can costs be reduced and/or new markets be exploited more effectively by manufacturing cars in the emerging countries)?
- How can the new, emerging competitors be challenged (e.g. should new models be developed)?
- How can legislative requirements be met (e.g. how and where should the industry lobby against tougher emission standards)?

For the major international players in the car industry, these are some of the important strategic issues that are currently being faced and a number of key trends appear to be emerging. For example, many car producers are looking towards Asia as a suitable place for manufacture, with India potentially becoming a global hub for small car production, thanks to its lower costs and the skills of its workforce. Added to this, the big players are being forced towards global product development (with future models likely to be based on a common platform and sold on a global basis) and/or some form of integration (e.g. GM is currently in discussions with Chrysler about a possible merger).

Part Two

CONTEXTS

4

The political environment

Ian Worthington

Politics is a universal activity which affects the business world in a variety of ways. Understanding political systems, institutions and processes provides a greater insight into business decisions and into the complexities of the business environment. Given the increasing globalisation of markets, this environment has an international as well as a domestic element and the two are closely interrelated. Appreciating some of the key aspects of this environment and its impact on business organisations is vital for students of business and for managers alike.

Learning outcomes

Having read this chapter you should be able to:

● explain the political context within which business operates

● demonstrate the relevance of political values to the organisation of business activity

● identify and discuss key political institutions and processes at a variety of spatial levels

● illustrate how business organisations can influence, as well as be influenced by, the political environment

Key terms

Authoritarianism
Backbench MPs
Bureaucrats
Cabinet
Checks and balances
Civil servants
Coalition government
Constitution
Council of Ministers
Decisions
Democracy
Direct (or pure) democracy
Directorates-General
Directives
Electoral system
European Commission
European Council
European Court of Justice
European Parliament
Federal system of government

First-past-the-post system
Government
Government departments
House of Commons
House of Lords
Judiciary
Legislature
Lobbies
Manifesto
MEPs
Ministers
MPs
Parliament
Parliamentary system of
  government
Plebiscites
Political accountability
Political executive
Political parties
Political sovereignty

Politics
Presidential system of
  government
Pressure groups
Prime Minister
Professional lobbyist
Proportional representation
Qualified majority vote (qmv)
Recommendations and
  opinions
Referendums
Regulations
Representative government
Secretary of State
Separation of powers
Sovereignty
Supreme Court
The Council of the European
  Union
Unitary system of government

Introduction

In the late 1980s, following a period of difficult negotiations, the British government entered into a collaborative agreement with the governments of Germany, Italy and Spain, to develop and produce a European fighter aircraft (EFA), due to come into service in the later 1990s. This agreement, which involved the participants jointly funding research and development costs, was greeted with delight by firms in Britain's aerospace industry and by their suppliers who welcomed the prospects of a large order of aircraft at a time when defence spending was being restrained. For firms such as GEC Ferranti, BAe, Lucas Aerospace, Rolls-Royce and Smiths Industries, the collaborative venture offered the prospects of future profits and the opportunity to retain their technological edge. For the communities in which these firms were based, it promised to sustain and possibly create employment during a period of growing economic uncertainty.

Subsequent indications (in 1992) that the German government would pull out of the venture – on the grounds of escalating costs and a reduced military threat – sent shock waves through the British aerospace industry and threatened to sour relations between the participating governments, the rest of whom wished to continue with the project. In the event, a compromise was reached under which the countries involved agreed to continue with research and development in an effort to produce a cheaper aircraft, to be known as the Eurofighter 2000. Given the problems of German reunification, the German government reserved the right to make a final decision on production at some time in the future. In late 1997 the four countries finally signed an agreement to proceed with production after years of political controversy and delay, thereby triggering a multi-billion-pound contract culminating in delivery of the first aircraft in 2002. The project, however, has continued to face a number of ongoing difficulties, as orders of the aircraft have tended to fluctuate because of political developments and there have been allegations of illegal payments to secure export contracts. As late as mid-2008, there were still questions over the commitment of some of the participating governments regarding the agreed number of planes to be purchased in the third tranche of sales. Changing defence requirements and budgeting problems have cast doubts over the willingness of some of the partners to honour the contracts (see e.g. *The Guardian*, 14 July 2008, 'Eurofighter U-turn would cost Britain billions').

What this simple example illustrates is that business activity takes place both within and across state boundaries and frequently involves governments, whether directly or indirectly. Consequently the political and economic arrangements within the state in which a business is located and/or with which it is trading can have a fundamental impact on its operations – even to the extent of determining whether it is willing or, in some cases able, to trade at all. It is this politico-economic context within which businesses function and the philosophical foundations on which it is based that are the focus of this and the following chapter.

As a prelude to a detailed analysis of the political environment, it is necessary to make a number of general observations regarding political change and uncertainty and its impact on business activity. First, the nature of a country's political system – including its governmental institutions – tends to reflect certain underlying social values and philosophies which help to determine how decisions are made, including decisions about the allocation of resources. Thus, while governments may come and go, the values on which their decisions are based tend to be more enduring and as a result disputes normally centre around 'means' (e.g. sources of revenue), rather than 'ends' (e.g.

controlling inflation). While this gives a certain degree of stability to the business environment, this stability cannot be taken for granted, as events in eastern Europe have readily demonstrated. In short, the political environment of business is a dynamic environment, containing elements of both continuity and change, and students and practitioners of business alike need to be constantly aware of developments in this area, if they are to gain a greater insight into the background of business decision-making.

Second, changes in the political environment also emanate from a country's institutional arrangements. The tendency in democratic states, for example, to have regular elections, competing political parties offering alternative policies, and a system of pressure groups, all help to generate a degree of discontinuity, which renders predictions about the future more uncertain. For a business, such uncertainty can create not only opportunities but also a degree of risk which will often be an important influence on its decisions. Moreover, given that perceptions of such risks (or opportunities) are also normally reflected in the attitudes and behaviour of a country's financial and other markets, this represents a further variable which at times can be critical for an organisation's future prospects. For many businesses, taking steps to maximise opportunities (or to minimise risk) may ultimately make the difference between short-term failure and long-term survival.

Third, it is important to emphasise that political influences are not restricted to national boundaries – a point emphasised by the increasing importance of international and supranational groupings such as the G8 nations, the European Union and the World Trade Organisation, all of which are discussed below. These external politico-economic influences form part of the environment in which a country's governmental institutions take decisions, and their impact on domestic policy and on business activity can often be fundamental. No discussion of the business environment would be complete without an analysis of their role and impact, particularly in shaping international political and economic relationships.

Fourth, the precise impact of political factors on a business tends to vary to some degree according to the type of organisation involved. Multinational corporations – operating on a global scale – will be more concerned with questions such as the stability of overseas political regimes than will the small local firm operating in a localised market, where the primary concern will be with local market conditions. That said, there will undoubtedly be occasions when even locally based enterprises will be affected either directly or indirectly by political developments in other parts of the globe – as in the case of an interruption in supplies or the cancellation of a foreign order in which a small business is involved as a subcontractor. In short, while some broad generalisations can be made about the impact of global (or domestic) political developments on an individual organisation, each case is to some extent unique in both space and time, and observers of the business scene need to be cautious and open-minded in their analysis if they are to avoid the twin dangers of over-simplification and empiricism.

Finally, it needs to be recognised that businesses are not merely reactive to changes in the political environment; they can also help to shape the political context in which they operate and can influence government decision-makers, often in a way which is beneficial to their own perceived needs. One of the hallmarks of democracy is the right of individuals and groups to seek to influence government, and businesses – both individually and collectively – have been active in this sphere for centuries. It would be a mistake to underestimate their impact on government policy or on the shaping of values in the established capitalist nations of western Europe and elsewhere.

Political systems

The nature of political activity

All social situations at certain times require decisions to be made between alternative courses of action. Parents may disagree with their offspring about the kind of clothes they wear or how late they stay out at night or how long they grow their hair. Students may challenge lecturers about a particular perspective on an issue or when they should submit a piece of work. The members of the board of directors of a company may have different views about future investment or diversification or the location of a new factory. In all these cases, some solution needs to be found, even if the eventual decision is to do nothing. It is the processes involved in arriving at a solution to a problem, where a conflict of opinion occurs, that are the very essence of political activity.

Politics, in short, is concerned with those processes which help to determine how conflicts are contained, modified, postponed or settled, and as such can be seen as a universal social activity. Hence, individuals often talk of 'office politics' or the 'politics of the board room' or the 'mediating role' played by a parent in the event of a family dispute. For most individuals, however, the term 'politics' tends to be associated with activities at state level, where the resolution of conflict often involves large numbers of people and may even involve individuals in other states. Political activity at this level is clearly qualitatively different from the other social situations mentioned, and given the scale and complexity of the modern state, the problems requiring solutions can often be acute and chronic. Solving those problems tends to be seen, at least in part, as the function of government.

Government as a process is concerned with the pursuit and exercise of power – the power to make decisions which affect the lives of substantial numbers of people, be it at local, regional, national or even international level. Government may also refer to the institutions through which power tends to be formally and legitimately exercised, whether they be cabinets, parliaments, councils, committees or congresses. Whereas the pursuit and exercise of power tends to be an enduring feature of any society, governments are normally transitory, comprising those individuals and/or groups who, at a particular time, have the responsibility for controlling the state, including making laws for 'the good of society'. How governments exercise their power and the ideological foundations on which this is based, helps to indicate the nature of the political system and its likely approaches to the resolution of conflicts.

Authoritarian political systems

Broadly speaking, political systems can be seen to range across two extremes, on the one hand **authoritarian** and on the other **democratic**. In an authoritarian political system the disposition is to settle conflicts through the enforcement of rules, regulations and orders by an established authority. This authority may be an individual (e.g. a monarch or other powerful individual) or a group of individuals (e.g. a political party or military junta) who may have assumed political power in a variety of ways (e.g. by birth, election or coup). Once in power, the individual or group will tend to act so as to limit the degree of participation by others in the process of decision making, even to the extent of monopolising the process altogether and permitting no opposition to occur. Where this is the case, a society is often described as being 'totalitarian' and is perhaps best exemplified by Nazi Germany and Stalinist Russia.

Democratic political systems

In contrast, in a democratic political system, the assumption is that as far as possible conflicts should be resolved by rational discussions between the various parties concerned, with the final solution being accepted voluntarily by all participants, even if they disagree. At one extreme, such consultation may involve all individuals, who have – in theory at least – equal influence over the final outcome (e.g. as in **referendums** or **plebiscites**). Given the scale and complexity of modern states, however, such examples of **pure** or **direct democracy** tend to be rare and it is invariably the case that the democratic solution to conflict resolution is achieved 'indirectly' through a system of political representation and responsibility. Under such a system, the wishes and views of individuals are said to be represented in an established authority (e.g. a government) that has normally been chosen by the people and which is accountable (responsible) to them at regular intervals through a variety of mechanisms, including regular and free elections (see Figure 4.1). Implicit in this, of course, is the requirement that individuals are able to change this authority and select another individual or group to represent them. Monopolisation of political power by any one individual or group can only occur, therefore, with the expressed consent of the people.

| Figure 4.1 | Representative democracy |

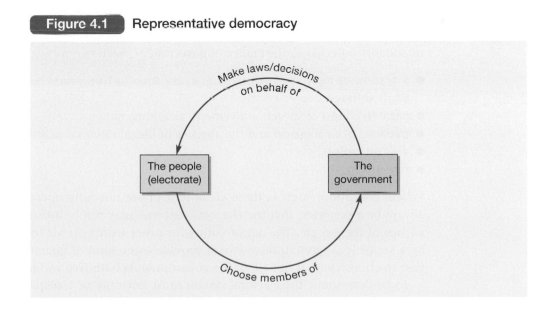

Government in democratic states

Democratic institutions and processes

Democracy means far more than just popular government or a system of regular elections; the democratic approach to government implies the existence of a complex array of institutions and processes through which the wishes of the people are articulated and carried out. While the specific institutional arrangements tend to vary between states, countries which are held to be democratic invariably have a political system which comprises four common and interlocking elements: an electoral system, a party system, a representative assembly and a system for the articulation of sectional interests. The generic roles of these major building blocks of democratic government are discussed below. Location-specific information on how the system operates in a national (i.e. United Kingdom) and a supranational (i.e. European Union) context can be found in the appendices to this chapter. Non-UK readers are encouraged to substitute their own political arrangements for those described in the appendices.

The electoral system

As indicated above, in a representative democracy the **electoral system** links the people (the electorate) with government; it is through elections that a country's citizens periodically get to choose who will exercise the power to make decisions which will ultimately shape the lives of individuals. Elections, in short, are a vital ingredient of a representative system of government. That said, the fact that elections exist in a particular country is not a sufficient guarantee that it is democratic in the accepted sense of the word.

In order to operate in a way which is normally regarded as democratic, a country's electoral system would need to exhibit a number of features which suggest that the wishes of individual citizens – as expressed through the ballot box – are reasonably reflected in the choice of government. Such features would include:

- a system of regular elections (e.g. every four to five years) based on universal adult suffrage;
- basic freedoms of speech, movement, assembly, etc.;
- freedom from coercion and the absence of illegal electoral practices;
- a secret ballot;
- free media.

Where conditions such as these are absent or are not fully operational, there will always be a suspicion that the electoral outcome may not be a true reflection of the wishes of the people. The act of voting, in other words, needs to be accompanied by a set of legal prescriptions which provide some kind of guarantee that an election to choose part, if not all, of the government is both free and fair.

To be democratic the electoral system must not only be transparent; it must also ensure that the wishes of the majority – as expressed through the number of votes cast – are reflected in the final result. In **first-past-the-post systems** (e.g. in most current UK elections) a simple majority is sufficient to ensure victory; as a consequence some winning candidates may be elected with fewer than half of the votes cast. Where a system of **proportional representation** operates (e.g. in many other European countries) a redistribution of votes occurs when there is no outright winner, resulting in a final decision which can be said to more closely represent the wishes of the whole electorate. While the intricacies of different electoral systems are beyond the scope of this book, it is worth observing that the voting system a country uses can have important ramifications for the government elected to office. On the whole, a plurality or first-past-the-post system of voting usually results in majority government, with a single party dominating the organs of decision-making and able to pursue its legislative programme relatively free from constraint by the losing side(s). In contrast, where a proportional representation system is used the resulting government is often made up of a **coalition** of different parties, some of which may hold radically different views from the largest party within the coalition. In effect, coalition government is predominantly a matter of negotiation, accommodation and compromise, an exercise in consensus building and persuasion, as commonly found in most types of organisational setting, including the business world.

The party system

While it is possible to have democratic government in a one-party state, democracy is normally taken to imply that citizens get to choose between alternative candidates when casting their vote at an election. Invariably such candidates tend to represent different **political parties** and to this extent a vote for a specific candidate can be said to equate to a vote for the party that he or she represents and which is ultimately hoping to form the government.

The existence of political parties, which compete for office at election time, is clearly a convenient – if sometimes questionable – means of organising a system of representative democracy; hence the universality of party systems in democratic states and the relative lack of candidates standing with no party tag at governmental elections at all spatial levels. Parties not only help to choose most of the candidates who compete in these elections, but usually also support and sustain them (e.g. financially) before, during and after the election campaign and help to organise a system of (largely unpaid) volunteers to work to get them elected, as well as providing candidates with a platform of policies on which to stand for office. Whereas some of these activities tend to be the responsibility of the party at national level, others are undertaken at a regional and/or local level, often in the constituency (i.e. geographical area) that a candidate represents. Since questions of organisation, policy making and finance are central to the operation and success of a political party in modern democratic states, party structures have tended to become complex, bureaucratic, multi-layered and increasingly professionalised. As in other types of organisational framework, they also provide an arena in which a substantial degree of in-fighting occurs between individuals of different temperaments, views and ambitions who are seeking to push the party in a particular direction.

From the electors' point of view, one of the primary benefits of the party system is that it provides a means of selecting political leaders and the kind of policies they are likely to pursue if the party achieves political office. Describing candidates by a party label (e.g. Democratic, Republican, Socialist, Conservative, Liberal, etc.) allows voters to choose those candidates whose views most closely represent their own, given that parties normally have an identifiable policy stance and produce some form of statement (or **manifesto**) outlining their policy preferences during an election campaign. Thus, while an individual elector is unlikely to agree with every single policy or proposed piece of legislation that a party puts forward in its attempts to gain office, he/she is at least able to express a preference between alternative approaches to government at the ballot box. To that extent it can be argued that there is likely to be a degree of congruence between the legislative programme of the party democratically elected to form the government and the wishes of the people who elected it, albeit that in some cases the government may have received less than 50 per cent of the popular vote.

It is worth remembering that party labels are not always a good guide to the policy or legislative preferences of individual candidates, since someone described as a 'Democrat' or 'Liberal' in one part of a country may hold radically different views on a range of issues from others of the same title elected to constituencies in other areas. If anything, identifying election candidates in party political terms gives voters a broad indication of the underlying values and beliefs to which an individual subscribes: parties in practice are always destined to be (sometimes fragile) coalitions of groups and individuals representing a range of opinions and preferences under a party banner.

A representative assembly

As previously indicated, one of the key features of democratic government is the existence of a representative decision-making body, a group of individuals chosen by a country's citizens to help make important decisions on their behalf. In the same way that shareholders in a public company elect directors to guide the organisation and to represent their interest, voters at election time choose individuals they wish to represent them in government in the various organs of decision making and policy implementation (see below). While not everyone chosen by the electorate becomes part of the small group of key decision makers (the government or **political executive**), all normally have some kind of role to play in the decision-making process and usually get an opportunity to scrutinise policy and legislative proposals put forward by the governing element and to vote upon them. The fact that the electorate periodically has the opportunity to express its opinion on the performance of the incumbent decision-makers – and where necessary to replace them – provides for a degree of **political accountability**, a central tenet of a democratic system of government.

As over two centuries of political theory have demonstrated, the concept of **representation** can have at least two meanings: decision-makers may represent the views of their constituents in the literal sense that they articulate them in or to government or they may simply represent them in so far as they have been elected by a majority (simple or otherwise) of voters to be the representative of a geographical area. In practice both these interpretations of representation can be seen to operate at different times, according to the predispositions of individual decision-makers and the influences emanating from the prevailing political culture in a country, region or area. For example, in a system of government where national political parties are relatively weak and where an individual's success in elections depends very much on supporting policies which are consistent with those of significant elements in one's electorate (e.g. in the United States), representation tends to be seen in the more literal sense of supporting local views and preferences. In contrast, where there is a strong party system and where individuals are held to be elected on the basis of party affiliation (e.g. the United Kingdom), elected representatives are generally expected to be loyal to the party in a policy sense, even if this results on occasions in a conflict with the views of the majority of one's constituents.

In modern democratic states the model of representative decision-making usually operates at all spatial levels. In Europe, for example, voters not only elect their own national governments but also choose decision-makers at a local and/or regional level and many European citizens are also able to vote in elections for pan-European institutions (i.e. for the European Parliament – see Appendix 4.3). One of the consequences of this arrangement is that on occasions the party (or parties) elected to office at national level may be different from that (or those) in power locally, regionally and/or supranationally. Where this occurs, clashes between decision-makers representing different geographical areas tend to be inevitable and can give rise to problems of decision-making and policy implementation, thus potentially disrupting the programme on which a government has been elected to office.

In this context a useful distinction can be drawn between **federal** and **unitary systems of government**. In the former, **sovereignty** (i.e. the legitimate power to make decisions) is divided between two levels of government (e.g. national and local/regional), each with independent powers that are usually laid down in a written constitution which is interpreted by the courts. Thus, in the United States, education is in the hands of the elected government at state (i.e. subnational) level, while defence and foreign affairs are federal (i.e. national) governmental responsibilities. In Germany, the federal government similarly has exclusive jurisdiction over foreign and defence policy and environmental protection, while the Länder (states) control such areas as education and the police.

In contrast, under a unitary system ultimate authority rests with the national government and any powers granted to subnational levels by the central sovereign authority can ultimately be rescinded, including the right of government at subnational level to exist. Under such an arrangement – particularly where it is written down in the form of a **constitution** – government at national level clearly holds the whip hand and would normally expect its view to prevail where a dispute over an issue or policy occurred between it and a subnational authority. That said, decision-makers in democratic states at all levels and under different governmental systems have, on the whole, a tendency to settle such conflicts through negotiation, bargaining and compromise rather than by exerting their power and authority, although this might be used on occasions. This predisposition goes some way to explaining why in democratic systems of government, the policies and legislative programmes of elected governments are much more likely to be incremental than they are to be radical.

mini case   The end of an era

Political developments such as a change of government can have a significant impact on the business community both at the macro and micro levels. Apart from altering the way in which the economy is managed, a new government can make changes to legislation which can affect how businesses operate, what they can and cannot do, and how they treat employees, consumers, suppliers etc.

An example of how the political environment shapes business operations can be seen in the decision by the centre-right French government of Nicholas Sarkozy to reform France's cherished 35-hour working week, which was seen as a major obstacle to the country's economic growth. In July 2008 French MPs voted to scrap the long-standing policy of previous socialist governments and replace it with a law which allows companies to decide how many hours and how much overtime their employees can clock up each week. In a move designed to make the French labour market less rigid, the new law permits employees to negotiate a working week of 48 hours, with every hour over 35 treated as overtime. While some workers may still opt to work no more than 35 hours, the new measures effectively remove the cap on the length of the working week and hold out the prospect that for some French workers the working year may increase from 218 to 235 days.

A system for articulating sectional interests

Elections and a party system provide one way in which the views of an individual can be represented in government; an alternative is via **pressure group** activity. Like competing political parties, the existence of pressure groups is usually regarded as an important indicator of a democratic system of government. For many citizens in democratic countries, joining such a group is seen as a much more effective way of influencing government than through the party system.

Whereas political parties seek influence by formally contesting political office, pressure groups seek to influence government in other ways, although this distinction is increasingly becoming blurred. In essence pressure groups (or **lobbies**) are collections of like-minded people who have voluntarily joined together to try to influence government thinking and behaviour and to represent the interest of their members. Nowadays, many of these groups are highly organised and are powerful bodies, supported by substantial funding and formidable research facilities. Such groups (frequently referred to as NGOs or non-governmental organisations) provide a vehicle through which a collective and non-party political view can be articulated in decision-making circles; as such they can be said to operate as a kind of safety-valve within a democratic system of government.

Traditionally in pressure group literature, a distinction tends to be drawn between groups which represent 'somebody' and those which represent 'something'. The former are usually referred to as 'interest groups' or 'protective groups' and would include groups representing a particular section of the community, such as trade unions or professional associations. The latter tend to be known as 'cause groups' or 'issue groups', as exemplified by Greenpeace, Amnesty International and the various animal rights groups. In practice, of course, it is often difficult to make such a clear-cut distinction, given that some interest groups such as trade unions often associate themselves with particular causes and may campaign vigorously alongside other groups in support of or against the issue concerned.

Most large pressure groups have websites which contain useful information. Greenpeace, for example, can be accessed at *www.greenpeace.org.uk*

From a governmental point of view the existence of structures for articulating sectional interests is seen as an aid to efficient and representative decision-making. Pressure groups not only provide government with detailed information on specific areas of everyday activity without which rational decision-making would be difficult; they also fulfil a number of other important functions in a democratic system. These would include:

● helping to defend minority interests;
● assisting in the implementation of government policy and legislation;
● providing for continuity in communication and consultation between the governors and the governed between elections.

The successful introduction of reforms in a country's health service, for example, is dependent upon support from the various arms of the medical profession and from organisations representing the different interests of health service workers. Similarly the effectiveness of government economic policies, and their subsequent impact on the business community, will be conditioned at least in part by the reactions of groups representing large employers, small and medium enterprises, workers, financial interests, etc., as well as by individual entrepreneurs and consumers.

This relative interdependence between government and pressure groups under a democratic system is exemplified by the practice of prior consultation; this is the arrangement whereby the elected government actively seeks the views of interested parties during the policy and/or legislative process. Such consultation may be 'formal' (e.g. where a group has representation on an advisory or executive body or where it is invited to offer its views on a proposal) or 'informal' (e.g. off-the record meetings between representatives of the group and the government) or a mixture of the two; it may also involve a group in hiring the services of a **professional lobbyist** – often an ex-politician or bureaucrat familiar with the structure of decision-making in government and with access to key decision-makers. Groups which are regularly consulted and whose opinion is readily sought by government may acquire 'insider status' and may even be incorporated into the formal decision-making process – prizes which are highly valued since they imply that the group has a legitimate right to be consulted by government prior to deciding on a particular course of action or inaction. In comparison, 'outsider groups' often find it difficult to make their voice heard in decision-making circles and for this reason may be forced to resort to different forms of direct action in order to publicise their views in the wider community in the hope of gaining influence through public sympathy and support.

As this discussion of 'insider' and 'outsider groups' illustrates, pressure groups can use a variety of methods to attract support for their cause or to protect and promote the interests of their members. These range from direct lobbying of government to marches, strikes, disruption and other forms of demonstrative action designed to attract media and hence public attention – although frequently such action can have an adverse effect. In addition, some of the larger and better-resourced groups may employ experts to advise on policy issues and/or establish their own research facilities to provide information to strengthen their case (e.g. Greenpeace).

What method(s) a group employs and where it seeks to bring its influence to bear tends to vary from issue to issue and group to group, and generally reflects not only differences in group status and resources but also the structure of decision-making within the policy community concerned. In the United States for instance, direct lobbying of Congressmen/women is a common tactic used by pressure groups, given the relative weakness of the party system and the tendency for an individual's electoral fortunes to be tied up with the views of key groups in the constituency. In contrast in the United Kingdom, the pressures of party discipline, the domination of the executive branch of government and the influence of senior civil servants tend to make direct appeals to key actors in government a more effective method of achieving political influence than operating at constituency level.

As a final comment it is worth recalling that decisions in a democracy may be made locally, nationally, supranationally or internationally and often require co-operation between different levels of government and/or between different agencies and arms of government at both the formulation and implementation stages. Accordingly, pressure groups are increasingly to be found operating at the interface between the institutions of government and across the whole range of spatial levels from the local to the global. Given the large number of pressure points where vested interests can bring their influence to bear, it tends to be easier for a group to prevent or limit government action than to persuade decision-makers to change the direction of policy. To this extent policy formulation and implementation in democratic states is perhaps best portrayed as the 'art of the possible' rather than the 'science of the desirable'.

The three branches or functions of government

In a broad sense the process of governing involves three major activities: making decisions, putting them into effect and adjudicating over them in the event of dispute or non-compliance. Each of these functions or branches of government, as they operate at a national level, is discussed in turn below. A similar form of analysis could, if necessary, be applied at other spatial levels.

The legislative function

Governing, as we have seen, is about making decisions which affect the lives of large numbers of people. Some of these decisions require new laws or changes to existing laws to bring them into effect so that the individuals and/or groups to whom they apply become aware of the government's wishes and requirements. In a democratic system of government this formal power to make the law (i.e. to legislate) is vested in a legislative body (**the legislature**) which is elected either wholly or partly by the people. As indicated above, this process of choosing a representative decision-making body by popular election is a central feature of the democratic approach to government.

Leaving aside for one moment the relative power of the legislative and executive branches of government, it is possible to identify a number of common features which apply to legislatures and the legislative function in most, if not all, democratic states. These include the following:

- *A bicameral legislature*, that is, a legislature with two chambers: an upper house and a lower house, each with specific powers and roles in the legislative process. In most countries each chamber comprises representatives chosen by a separate electoral process and hence may be dominated by the same party or different parties or by no single party, depending on the electoral outcome. For a legislative proposal to be accepted, the consent of both chambers is normally required. This is one of the many **checks and balances** normally found in democratic systems of government (see below).

- *A multi-stage legislative process* – involving the drafting of a legislative proposal, its discussion and consideration, where necessary amendment, further debate and consideration and ultimate acceptance or rejection by either or both legislative chambers. Debates on the general principles of a proposed piece of legislation would normally involve all members of each chamber, whereas detailed discussion tends to take place in smaller groups or committees.

- *An executive-led process*, that is, one in which most major legislative proposals emanate from the executive branch of government. In a **presidential system** of government (e.g. the USA) the chief executive (the President) is normally elected separately by the people and is not part of the legislature (in other words there is a **separation of powers**). In a **parliamentary system** (e.g. the UK) members of the executive may also be members of the legislative body and hence may be in a position to control the legislative process.

- *Opportunities for legislative initiatives by ordinary representatives*, that is, arrangements which permit ordinary members of the legislative assembly to propose new laws or changes to existing laws. In practice such opportunities tend to be limited and dependent to a large degree for their success on a positive response from the political executive.

- *Opportunities to criticise and censure the government and, in some cases, remove it from office* (e.g. through impeachment) – this is a vital function within a democratic system of government in that it forces decision-makers to defend their proposals, explain the logic of their actions and account for any mistakes they may have made. Opposition parties play an important role in this context within the legislative body and through media coverage can attack the government and articulate alternative views to the wider public. Specialist and Standing Committees for scrutinising legislation and the day-to-day work of the executive branch of government also usually exist in democratic regimes.

- *Control of the purse strings*, that is, the power to grant or deny government the money required to carry out its policies and legislative programme. In theory this is a formidable power, given that no government can operate without funds. In practice the power of the legislature to deny funding to a democratically elected government may be more apparent than real and, where necessary, compromise tends to occur between the executive and legislative branches of government.

As will be evident from the comments above, legislating is a complex and time-consuming process, offering numerous opportunities for individuals and groups both within and outside the legislative body (e.g. pressure groups) to delay and disrupt the passage of legislation. While no government can guarantee to achieve all its legislative aims, there is a cultural expectation in a democracy that, as far as possible, promises made before an election will be put into effect at the earliest opportunity by the democratically elected government. Such an expectation usually provides the incumbent administration with a powerful argument for legislative support on the occasions when it is confronted with intransigence within the legislative assembly or hostility from outside sectional interests.

mini case   The demise of the VW law

As the previous mini case demonstrates (see 'The end of an era'), the business community can be affected by changes in legislation brought about by a shift in political power. In democratic systems of government, changes in the law can also occur as a result of judicial decisions at different spatial levels and these too can impact upon businesses.

In October 2007, for instance, the European Court of Justice (ECJ) – the EU's highest court – ruled that the so-called Volkswagen law, which gave the German state a blocking vote on potential bids for VW from outside buyers, breached EU rules on the free movement of capital. While the court did not rule out limitations on capital movements if these were based on legitimate national interests (e.g. national security), its new ruling opened up the possibility of more pan-European mergers and acquisitions by challenging the existence of special voting rights and 'golden shares' as a mechanism to protect privatised businesses (see Chapter 17). Such obstacles to the free movement of capital still exist across the EU and it seems likely that they will become a target for the ECJ in the coming years.

The executive function

Governing is not only about making decisions, it is also about ensuring that these decisions are put into effect in order to achieve the government's objectives. Implementing governmental decisions is the responsibility of the executive branch of government.

In modern states the term 'the executive' refers to that relatively small group of individuals chosen to decide on policy and to oversee its implementation; some of these individuals will hold political office, others will be career administrators and advisers, although some of the latter may also be political appointees. Together they are part of a complex political and administrative structure designed to carry out the essential work of government and to ensure that those responsible for policy making and implementation are ultimately accountable for their actions.

The policy-making aspect of the executive function is normally the responsibility of a small political executive chosen (wholly or in part) by popular election. Under a presidential system of government, the chief executive or President is usually chosen by separate election for a given period of office and becomes both the nominal and political head of state. He/she subsequently appoints individuals to head the various government departments/ministries/bureaux which are responsible for shaping and implementing government policy. Neither the President nor the heads of departments normally sit in the legislative assembly, although there are sometimes exceptions to this rule (e.g. the Vice-President in the United States).

In contrast, in a parliamentary system the roles of head of state and head of government are separated, with the former usually largely ceremonial and carried out by either a president (e.g. Germany, India) or a monarch (e.g. UK, Japan). The head of government (e.g. Prime Minister), while officially appointed by the head of state, is an elected politician, invariably the head of the party victorious in a general election or at least seen to be capable of forming a government, possibly in coalition with other parties. Once appointed, the head of government chooses other individuals to head the different government departments/ministries and to be part of a collective decision-making body (e.g. a Cabinet) which meets to sanction policy proposals put forward through a system of executive committees and subcommittees (e.g. Cabinet Committees). These individuals, along with the head of government, are not only part of the executive machinery of the state but also usually members of the legislative assembly and both 'individually' and 'collectively' responsible to the legislature for the work of government.

The day-to-day administration of government policy is largely carried out by non-elected government officials (sometimes referred to as **civil servants** or **bureaucrats**) who work for the most part in complex, bureaucratic organisations within the state bureaucracy. Apart from their role in implementing public policy, government officials help to advise ministers on the different policy options and on the political and administrative aspects of particular courses of action. Needless to say, this gives them a potentially critical role in shaping government policy, a role which has been substantially enhanced over the years by the practice of granting officials a significant degree of discretion in deciding on the details of particular policies and/or on how they should be administered.

Whereas politicians in the executive branch of government tend to be transitory figures – who come and go at the whim of the head of government or of the electorate   most, if not all, officials are permanent, professional appointees who may serve a variety of governments of different political complexions and preferences during a long career in public administration. Whatever government is in power, officials are generally expected to operate in a non-partisan (i.e. neutral) way when advising their political masters and when overseeing the implementation of government policy. Their loyalty in short is to the current administration in office, a principle which helps to ensure a smooth transition of government and to guarantee that the upheaval caused by a general election does not prevent the business of the state from being carried out as usual.

The judicial function

Governing is not just about making and implementing laws; it is also about ensuring that they are applied and enforced. The latter is essentially the role of the third arm of government, namely the **judiciary** and the system of courts. Like political institutions, legal structures and processes tend to a degree to be country specific and vary according to a number of influences including history, culture and politics. For example, while some states have a relatively unified legal system, others organised on a federal basis usually have a system of parallel courts adjudicating on federal and state/provincial law, with a **Supreme Court** arbitrating in the event of a dispute. In some countries a proportion of the judges may be directly or indirectly elected by the public, in others they may be appointed by government and/or co-opted by fellow judges. Business students should make themselves familiar with the legal arrangements within their own country (see e.g. Chapter 8, which contains information on the legal system in England and Wales). In this section we look briefly at the judicial function as related to the concept of democracy.

Whereas in totalitarian systems of government the judiciary is essentially the servant of the ruling élite (e.g. the 'party'), in a democracy it is an accepted principle that there should be a separation between the judicial function and the other two branches of government in order to protect the citizen from a too powerful state. This notion of an impartial and independent judiciary, free to challenge the government and to review its decisions, is regarded as one of the hallmarks of a democratic system of government, a further manifestation of the doctrine of the separation of powers.

In practice of course, notions of judicial independence and role within the democratic political process tend to be the subject of certain amount of debate, particularly in countries where senior appointments to the judiciary appear to be in the gift of politicians (e.g. Supreme Court judges in the United States are nominated by the President with the consent of the Senate) or where individuals with judicial powers also have an executive and/or legislative role (e.g. the Home Secretary in Britain). Equally there are questions over the degree to which the courts should have the power to review the constitutionality of decisions made by a democratically elected government. In the United States, for example, the Supreme Court has a long-established right to declare a law void if it conflicts with its own interpretation of the American constitution. In contrast in Britain, the legal sovereignty of Parliament and the absence of a codified written constitution push the judiciary towards trying to interpret the intentions of the framers of government legislation and any legal decision unwelcomed by the government can be reversed by further legislation. That said, it is interesting to note that in recent years there has been an increased willingness on the part of the British judiciary to review administrative decisions, particularly those made by ministers.

Other aspects, too, call into question how far in modern democratic states there is a total separation between the different arms of government (e.g. increasing use of administrative courts/tribunals) and whether it makes sense to rigidly distinguish between rule making and rule adjudication. Certainly some of the past judgments by the United States Supreme Court (e.g. in the area of civil rights) demonstrate that the courts can be influential in shaping decisions on major issues of policy and suggest that the judiciary are susceptible to influences from their own values or to general societal pressures. In short it seems fair to suggest that under current legal arrangements, legal adjudication is not far removed from the world of politics; arguably we may like to perpetuate the myth of an entirely separate and independent judiciary since this is a necessary aspect of the stability of many existing political systems.

Checks and balances in democracies

As will be evident from the analysis above democracy implies the existence of a system of checks and balances, arrangements which serve to curb government action and restrict its influence on the day-to-day lives of its citizens. These restraints on the actions of the state at national level can be divided into two main types: political and social/economic.

Political checks and balances emanate primarily from three main sources:

- *the separation of powers* – particularly the notion that the three arms of government are in separate hands and that decisions require the concurrence of all branches of government;
- *a bicameral legislature* – with legislation having to be accepted by both houses and subject to scrutiny and amendment by opposition parties;
- *the territorial division of powers* – whether under a federal arrangement or through the devolution of power to regional bodies and/or local authorities. Supranationalism is a further development.

The point is not that these arrangements necessarily exist in their most complete form in democratic states, but that – however imperfect in practice – their existence helps to provide time for reflection and delay in the decision-making process and to encourage consultation, negotiation and consensus building, the essence of the democratic approach to conflict resolution.

The notion of social and economic checks and balances refers to those countervailing pressures on the activities of the state and its agencies that derive from the existence of non-state structures and processes which affect the lives of individuals and which ultimately restrict the scope of government influence. These include private business organisations, professional associations, promotional bodies, churches and other groups which help to shape our economic, social and moral environment. As subsequent chapters will demonstrate, the bulk of economic decisions in democratic states are not taken by the government but by private individuals and organisations (i.e. firms) interacting through a market system. This acts as a kind of check and balance on the free activity of the public sector and is a fundamental characteristic of democratic government.

A model of the policy process

It is appropriate to conclude this examination of the political environment with a brief discussion of the process of governmental decision making in democratic systems. Here, the basic model of the organisation in its environment introduced in Chapter 1 serves as a useful analytical tool (see Figure 4.2). Governments, like firms, are organisations which transform inputs into output and they do so in an environment largely the same as that which confronts other types of enterprise. Like other organisations, government is a user of resources, especially land, labour, capital, finance and expertise, but in addition all governments face political demands and supports when considering their policy options.

Figure 4.2	Government and its environment

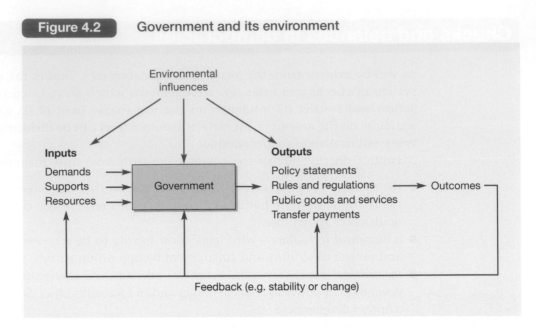

As indicated above, political demands – including those directly or indirectly impinging on business activity – become translated into action through a variety of mechanisms, including the electoral system, party activity, pressure group influence and political communication; hence a government is always keen to point out that electoral victory implies that it has a mandate for its policies. The supports of the political system are those customs, conventions, rules, assumptions and sentiments which provide a basis for the existence of the political community and its constituent parts and thus give legitimacy to the actions and existence of the incumbent government. In democratic systems, the belief in democratic principles, and the doctrines and practices emanating from that belief, are seen as central to the activities of government and its agencies.

The outputs of the political system vary considerably and range from public goods and services (e.g. healthcare) – provided predominantly from money raised through taxation – to rules and regulations (e.g. legislation, administrative procedures, directives) and transfer payments (i.e. where the government acts as a reallocator of resources, as in the case of the provision of state benefits). Taken together, the nature, range and extent of government output not only tend to make government the single biggest business in a state, they also influence the environment in which other businesses operate and increasingly in which other governments make decisions.

As far as governmental decision-making is concerned, this is clearly a highly complex process which in practice does not replicate the simple sequence of events suggested by the model. Certainly governments require 'means' (inputs) to achieve 'ends' (output), but the outputs of the political system normally only emerge after a complex, varied and ongoing process involving a wide range of individuals, groups and agencies. To add further confusion, those involved in the process tend to vary according to the decision under discussion as well as over time, making analysis fraught with difficulties. One possible solution may be to distinguish between the early development of a policy proposal ('initiation') and its subsequent 'formulation' and 'implementation', in the hope that a discernible 'policy community' can be identified at each stage. But even this approach involves a degree of guesswork and arbitrary decision-making, not least because of the difficulty of distinguishing precisely between the different stages of policy-making and of discerning the influence of individuals and groups at each phase of the process.

Notwithstanding these difficulties, it is important for students of business and for businesses themselves to have some understanding of the structure of decision-making and of the underlying values and beliefs which tend to shape governmental action, if they are to appreciate (and possibly influence) the political environment in which they exist. In short, studies of political systems, institutions and processes help to provide insight into how and why government decisions are made, who is important in shaping those decisions and how influence can be brought to bear on the decision-making process. As an increasing number of individuals and groups recognise, knowledge of this kind can prove a valuable organisational resource that on occasions is of no less significance than the other inputs into the productive process.

Synopsis

Laws and policies which influence business activity are made by politicians and bureaucrats, operating at a variety of spatial levels. In the United Kingdom, the decisions of local and central government emanate from a complex process of discussion and negotiation involving a range of formal and informal institutions, including political parties and pressure groups, and frequently involving international and supranational bodies. This process is part of the democratic approach to decision-making and provides opportunities for individuals and groups to influence government thinking on both the formulation and implementation of policy and legislation. Students of business and managers need to have a broad understanding of this political environment in order to appreciate one of the key influences on a firm's operations.

Summary of key points

- Politics is a universal activity which affects businesses of all types and sizes.

- It occurs at a variety of spatial levels from the local to the global.

- Political systems, structures and processes reflect underlying social values and philosophies and these influence the ways in which major decisions are taken.

- In any democratic system of government the key political institutions are likely to include an electoral system, a party system, a representative decision-making assembly and a system for articulating sectional interests.

- The three key functions of government are legislative, executive and judicial.

- While political institutions, practices and processes tend to vary between countries, democratic government is typified by a system of representative democracy and by political, social and economic checks and balances which act as a constraint on the actions of government.

- Such checks and balances in the system include the activities of pressure groups which seek to influence government through a variety of means, and which often play a key role in policy formulation and implementation.

- Business organisations and the bodies which represent them are key pressure groups in democratic societies and an important part of the external environment in which government and its agencies operate.

Appendix 4.1 · A democratic political system in action: UK national government

As far as the United Kingdom is concerned, the four interrelated elements of a democratic system of government are illustrated in Figure 4.3.

Through a system of regular elections British citizens (the electorate) vote for candidates of competing political parties who are seeking to form the national government (or to be members of the devolved assemblies in Northern Ireland, Scotland or Wales). Successful candidates at the national elections become Members of Parliament (MPs) and the party with the largest number of MPs is invited by the monarch to form a government, with individuals within the government being allocated specific responsibilities for particular areas of work. The work of government is scrutinised by Parliament (see below), which acts as the people's representative between elections, thereby providing for a measure of public accountability. Equally, between (or during) elections individuals are free to seek to influence government by joining pressure groups or other types of organisation (e.g. political parties) and by making their views known to their elected representatives. The media is free and therefore able to scrutinise the government's performance and to inform the public about political developments.

Figure 4.3 · The elected government at Westminster

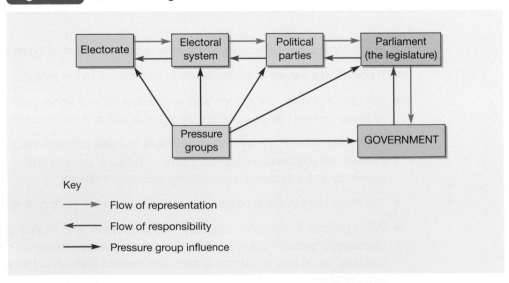

Key

→ Flow of representation

← Flow of responsibility

→ Pressure group influence

For information on the political arrangements in Northern Ireland, Scotland and Wales see e.g. *www.northernireland.gov.uk*; *www.niassembly.gov.uk*; *www.scottish.parliament.uk*; *www.scotland.gov.uk*; *www.assemblywales.org*; *http://new.wales.gov.uk*

The legislative branch of government at national level

As indicated above, a directly elected legislature – representative of the people and responsible for making laws – is an important component of a democratic system of government. In the United Kingdom as a whole this function is carried out by **Parliament**, which currently comprises a non-elected upper chamber (the **House of Lords**) and an elected lower chamber (the **House of Commons**) whose members (currently 646 **MPs**) are elected by universal suffrage by the majority of citizens aged 18 and over. While it is true to say that the Lords still retains some important powers, including the power to delay government legislation, the upper house is currently being reformed and in future is likely to contain an elected element. Whatever happens it seems likely that the House of Commons will remain the most important part of the UK legislature, particularly since it contains key members of the political executive, including the Prime Minister and most of the Cabinet. For this reason the discussion below focuses on the role of the House of Commons.

Website addresses for the UK Parliament include *www.explore.parliament.uk* and *www.parliament.uk*

Political representation and responsibility are achieved in a number of ways. For a start, Members of Parliament are directly elected by their constituents and one of the MP's main roles is to represent the constituency for the period between general elections. Apart from holding regular surgeries at which individuals (including businessmen and women) can discuss their problems and views with their representative, MPs also speak on constituency matters in Parliament, frequently raise questions which require answers from government ministers, and generally scrutinise government proposals for any potential effects they may have on the constituency, including key groups within the local electorate (e.g. local businesses). Needless to say, there will be occasions when the views of the elected member may differ from those of his or her constituents, particularly those who voted for candidates of an opposing political party, but this does not negate the idea of representation under the British system of parliamentary democracy. MPs represent their constituents first and foremost by having been elected *by them* and hence they provide a direct link between the electorate and the government of the day, which is essentially drawn from the senior members of the majority party in Parliament.

Parliament also provides opportunities for the people's representatives to scrutinise and, where necessary, to criticise and challenge the decisions of government. In addition to such parliamentary mechanisms as question time and the adjournment debate, Parliament provides for a system of Select Committees of **backbench MPs** whose primary role is to scrutinise the work of government departments and other state agencies. Such committees – chaired by both government and opposition backbenchers – are able to question ministers and civil servants, call for departmental papers, cross-examine experts from outside government, and generally investigate the work of the executive, prior to reporting to Parliament on their findings. In bringing their views before Parliament and the public generally (especially through the media), Select Committees provide a check on government activity and hence form one of the strands by which governments remain answerable to the electorate in the period between elections.

Another significant strand is provided by the Opposition which represents not only an alternative choice of government, but also a means of scrutinising and criticising the work of the incumbent administration. Fundamental to this role is the ability of opposition MPs to publicise the decisions of government and to present alternative views to the public via party political broadcasts or promotional literature or debates in parliament, or by general media coverage. Such free and open discussion of issues and policies is a necessary condition for democracy and is an important element in the political education of the nation. Even where governments have large majorities, the role of opposition parties remains a vital component of democracy and helps to provide a curb on unlimited government action.

Turning to its role as a legislative body, there is little doubt that the UK Parliament is largely a legitimising institution, giving formal authority to the wishes of the majority party. Through its control of the process of legislation, the parliamentary timetable, the flow of information and the votes of its members, the government is able to ensure that its legislative proposals not only come before Parliament, but also are almost invariably accepted, even if some delay occurs from time to time in enacting the government's programme. Opportunities for individual MPs to sponsor legislation (e.g. through private members' bills) are few and far between and the outcome of such proposals depends ultimately on government support (or reluctant acquiescence), if the legislation is to get through its various stages in Parliament. Not surprisingly, this effective stranglehold by the government on the legislative process has led some commentators to talk of an 'elective dictatorship' and to question the true extent of democratic decision making, particularly when modern governments are invariably elected by less than 50 per cent of the electorate.

The executive branch of government

Putting laws and policies into effect is formally the work of the executive. In the UK this role is carried out by a wide variety of institutions and agencies that are part of the machinery of government. These include the Cabinet, government departments, local authorities, nationalised industries and a large number of other non-departmental public bodies or quasi-autonomous national government agencies, often referred to as 'quangos'.[1] In the discussion below attention is focused initially on the key institutions at central level since these are fundamental to the process of decision making in Britain. Discussion of some of the other agencies can be found in subsequent sections of this chapter.

web link Information on non-departmental public bodies (NDPBs) is available via the Cabinet Office website at *www.cabinetoffice.gov.uk*

Under the British system of government, the core of the executive is the Cabinet, headed by the **Prime Minister**, an office of crucial importance given the absence of an elected head of state with effective political powers. British Prime Ministers not only have a number of significant political roles – including leader of the governing party, head of the government and head of the Cabinet – but also have traditionally held a formidable array of political powers, including the power to:

- choose members of the Cabinet;
- choose other non-Cabinet ministers;
- promote, demote or dismiss ministers;
- appoint individuals to chair Cabinet committees;
- appoint top civil servants;
- confer certain appointments and titles; and
- determine the date of the general election within the five-year term of office.

While the existence of such rights and responsibilities does not infer that Prime Ministers will inevitably be all-powerful, it is clear that holders of the office have a key role to play in the decision-making process and much will depend upon how an individual interprets that role, upon their personality, and upon the constraints they face (both 'real' and 'imagined') in carrying it out. As the Conservative Prime Minister Mrs Thatcher (1979–90) found to her cost, retaining the office of Prime Minister is dependent not only on the electorate, but also on maintaining the support and confidence of parliamentary colleagues in the period between elections.

As indicated above, as head of the Cabinet the Prime Minister chairs the committee of senior ministers that is the overall directing force – or board of management – within British central government. Comprising about 20 to 30 ministers who have been appointed by the Prime Minister to head the various government departments (or to fulfil some other important functions), the Cabinet is responsible for directing and co-ordinating the work of the whole executive machine. Its functions include:

- making decisions on the nature and direction of government policy, including public expenditure, economic policy, defence, foreign relations, industrial policy, and so on;
- overseeing and co-ordinating the administration of government;
- arbitrating in the event of disputes between ministers or departments;
- discussing, deciding and generally directing the government's legislative programme, including laws relating to business.

A large part of this work, of course, is carried out using a system of committees and subcommittees, which are comprised of individuals chosen by the Prime Minister (including the chairperson) and which are supported by a small but powerful secretariat, headed by the Cabinet Secretary (a civil servant). Apart from providing an opportunity for more detailed discussions of issues and policies prior to full consideration by the Cabinet, the committee system has the advantage of allowing non-members of the Cabinet (including non-Cabinet ministers and civil servants) to participate in discussions in which they may have an interest. In this way, the system helps to provide a mechanism for communication and co-ordination between government departments and serves as a training ground for junior ministers, many of whom will subsequently achieve full Cabinet responsibilities. An illustrative list of selected Cabinet committees in January 2008 is shown in Table 4.1. This list excludes the National Economic Council, set up in October 2008 to deal with pressing economic issues such as the global financial crisis, price volatility and recession.

Table 4.1 Selected Cabinet committees, 2008

Committee name	Designation
Ministerial Committee on Productivity, Skills and Employment	ED(PSE)
Ministerial Committee on Environment and Energy	ED(EE)
Ministerial Committee on Europe	NSID(EU)
Ministerial Committee on Legislation	L
Ministerial Group on Public Services and Public Expenditure	PSX
Ministerial Committee on Talent and Enterprise	LC(TE)
Ministerial Committee on Domestic Affairs	DA
Ministerial Committee on the Olympic and Paralymic Games	ED(OPG)

Source: Cabinet Office (*www.cabinetoffice.gov.uk/secretariats/committees*).

Much of the day-to-day work of central government is carried out in vast and complex administrative structures called government departments – a selected list of which is shown in Table 4.2. Most **government departments** are headed by Cabinet ministers (usually called the **Secretaries of State**) and include other ministers outside the Cabinet (e.g. Ministers of State, Parliamentary Under Secretaries of State) who have been appointed by the Prime Minister and who may include individuals drawn from the world of business. Together these ministers constitute the political executive. As the head of a department, the Secretary of State has ultimate responsibility for its work and is answerable to Parliament through the various mechanisms referred to above.[2] In addition, he or she is expected to give overall direction to the work of the department – within the policy of the government as a whole – and to represent its interest in the Cabinet (e.g. over the size and use of its budget), in Parliament (e.g. in steering through legislation) and in the outside world (e.g. in the media). Large areas of this work are delegated to the Ministers of State who assume responsibility for specific areas of departmental work and they in turn will tend to delegate some duties to the department's junior ministers. Such an arrangement not only ensures coverage of the different aspects of a department's responsibilities, but also provides invaluable experience and training for ambitious young MPs appointed to a ministerial post.

Table 4.2 Key government departments, October 2008

Cabinet Office
HM Treasury
Foreign and Commonwealth Affairs
Business, Enterprise and Regulatory Reform
Communities and Local Government
Innovation, Universities and Skills
Energy and Climate Change
Home Department
Environment, Food and Rural Affairs
Defence
Health
Work and Pensions
Culture, Media and Sport
Transport

web link

Each government department has its own website with lots of useful material.
Examples of current addresses include:
www.berr.gov.uk
www.dius.govt.uk
www.defra.gov.uk
www.hm_treasury.gov.uk

Ministers are assisted in their work by permanent officials, known as **civil servants**, many of whom have spent a large part of their working lives in the government machine and hence are familiar with how it works and how to manipulate it in order to achieve particular objectives. Whereas ministers are politicians, civil servants are administrators vested formally with the task of carrying out the policies of the incumbent government, irrespective of their own political views and preferences. Perhaps not surprisingly, as key advisers to ministers on policy formulation and implementation, senior civil servants can exercise considerable influence over the nature and shape of government policy and legislation – a point amusingly emphasised in a popular British television programme *Yes, Minister*.[3] For this reason, individuals or groups seeking to shape government thinking on an issue or piece of legislation frequently 'target' senior departmental officials in the hope of gaining influence in the policy process.

This potential for influence by senior civil servants is, of course, enhanced by the scope and complexities of modern government and by the fact that government ministers have a wide range of non departmental as well as departmental responsibilities (e.g. as constituency MPs). Ministers consequently rely heavily on their officials for information and advice and civil servants are normally entrusted, under ministers, with the conduct of the whole gamut of government activities, including filling in the details of some legislation. Added to this, the need for policy co-ordination between departments requires regular meetings between senior officials, in groups which mirror the meetings of Cabinet subcommittees. Since these meetings of officials help to provide the groundwork and briefing papers for future discussions by ministers, they permit civil servants to influence the course of events, especially when a particular line or policy option is agreed by the senior officials in a number of departments.

Criticism of the influence of the senior civil service and of its secrecy and reluctance to change has led to a number of inquiries into how to improve its efficiency and *modus operandi*. For example, in 1979, the new Conservative government appointed Sir Derek Rayner of Marks & Spencer to introduce private-sector management methods into the service and this was continued by his successor, Sir Robin Ibbs of ICI, who produced a report called *The Next Steps* (1988). This report led to many civil service responsibilities being 'hived off' to 'executive agencies', which operate semi-independently of government ministers, with their own budgets and performance targets and with a greater degree of independence over pay, financial and staffing matters, despite remaining formally part of the civil service. In the early 1990s the government under John Major introduced 'market testing', under which a proportion of the work of each department and agency had to be put out to competitive tender. More recently, the Gershon Report (2004) examined the issue of public sector efficiency and made a number of recommendations aimed at releasing resources for frontline services and cutting waste, bureaucracy and duplication in the public services.

It is perhaps worth noting at this point that, however pervasive its influence, the civil service is not the only source of policy advice for governments. Apart from traditional bureaucratic channels, ministers often turn to specially appointed bodies for help and guidance in making policy choices. Some of these sources are permanent (or relatively permanent) and would include the various advisory bodies set up by past and present governments to assist in the policy process in specific functional areas (e.g. the Arts Council). Others are temporary, having been specially constituted by government to consider a particular problem and to report on their findings prior to going out of existence (e.g. public inquiries, Royal Commissions). While the appointment of these advisory sources does not oblige the government to follow their advice, they can be regarded as useful sources of information, ideas and advice from outside the formal bureaucratic machine. Moreover the fact that they tend to have a membership representing a wide cross-section of interests (including representatives of particular pressure groups, industrialists, trade unionists, MPs, academics and others drawn from the list of 'the great and the good') helps to widen the scope of consultation and thus to enhance the democratic process.

The last generation has also seen governments turning increasingly to special advisers and policy planning units for help with policy development. Whereas advisers are individuals appointed by ministers (including the Prime Minister), usually from outside the civil service, policy planning units and/or research units are groups of individuals generally recruited from and located within the government machine, with the aim of providing a range of policy and programme advice to both policy-makers and administrators. Often comprised of young and highly qualified individuals seconded to a unit from a wide range of occupational categories and disciplines (including statisticians, social scientists, economists, and general administrators), policy units are a valuable source of information and advice, and their operation at both central and local government level provides policy-makers with detailed research and analysis with which to support their policy judgements.

A further important development has been the increased use of 'focus groups', collections of individual citizens consulted by government on policy proposals prior to legislation and/or implementation. In canvassing the views of individuals affected by government policy, the current government hopes to improve the policy process in a wide range of areas, including the delivery of public services, where it has a programme to provide round-the-clock availability and (ultimately) complete electronic access. While some see citizens' panels or focus groups as nothing more than a gimmick, others regard their use as a move towards a more modern and democratic form of government with increased levels of public accountability and access to information.

The judicial branch of government

The third arm of government, the judiciary – comprising the judges and the courts – is formally separate from and independent of Parliament and the government, despite the fact that until recently the head of the judiciary, the Lord Chancellor, was both a member of the government and a member of the House of Lords, where he or she presided as Speaker. In essence the role of the judiciary is to put into effect the laws enacted by Parliament and to keep the government within the limits of its powers as laid down in statutes and in common law, as interpreted by the judiciary. Since 1973, it has also been responsible for interpreting European Union law. Given the complexities of the legal system and its relevance to the world of business, it is important to examine this aspect of government in more detail. This is undertaken in Chapter 8.

Postscript

In Britain as elsewhere, both change and continuity are features of the political system. Apart from the developments mentioned above (e.g. reform of the House of Lords, elections to the new Scottish Parliament, Welsh Assembly and Northern Ireland Assembly, proposed reforms of the civil service), there have been proposals to introduce a new voting system (see, for example, the Jenkins Report 1998), to reform government policy-making and delivery systems (see, for example, the Wilson Report 1998) and to consider elected regional assemblies in England, though the latter still appear relatively unpopular. Various systems of proportional representation have been used for the elections to the new regional assemblies and for the European elections (in June 1999) and London elected a mayor in the year 2000 (see below). More recently, the current government has floated a number of other possible future reforms including introducing compulsory voting; giving voters a second vote; reducing some of the PM's powers and changes to party funding. Developments such as these would clearly have implications for the business environment.

Appendix 4.2 Subnational government: UK local authorities

Democratic government occurs at subnational as well as national level and takes a wide variety of forms. In addition to the local branches of central government departments and public utilities, many states have local agencies for the administration of justice, local special-purpose authorities (e.g. in the health service) and a system of regional and/or local government, whether under a federal or a unitary arrangement. Such decentralisation and deconcentration of political authority is generally seen as beneficial, since it brings the formulation and administration of policy 'nearer to the people' and is said to provide for decisions which are more sensitive to local needs and aspirations. Concomitantly, however, it can raise the question as to the degree of autonomy of local agencies within a centralised system of government and as recent history has demonstrated this is a controversial and perennial source of debate and dispute in many parts of the world.

Within the United Kingdom as a whole, political power is devolved at two main levels: regionally and locally. Scotland, Wales and Northern Ireland now have their own directly elected regional assemblies (the Scottish Parliament; the National Assembly for Wales; the Northern Ireland Assembly) and systems of executive government (the Scottish Executive; the Welsh Assembly Government; the Northern Ireland Executive), each with differing levels of devolved authority. In England (outside of London), regional government does not currently exist, although voluntary regional chambers or assemblies have been set up in the English regions to perform a number of core functions relating to regional issues such as housing development, planning, transport and strategic development.

Local government – the focus of this section – has a considerable historical pedigree and remains a key element of the country's system of institutionalised democracy and a major actor in the national as well as the local economy. Given its impact in the business environment, it deserves special attention.

As one form of local administration, local government has a number of distinctive features. For a start it involves self-government by the people of the locality as well as for them, with local authorities exercising considerable discretion in the ways they apply national laws within their areas. In addition, local decision makers (councillors) are elected to oversee multi-purpose authorities, financed by revenue raised predominantly from local sources – although the proportion from central government has risen in recent years. In short, each local authority constitutes a miniature political and administrative system: each has the institutions and processes of government – including an electoral system, a legislative body (the council), appointed officials (local government officers), party activity, and conflict between individuals and groups within the local community over the allocation of resources and the enforcement of values.

Figure 4.4 illustrates this parallel between the basic operation of government at central and local level. The electorate in each local constituency (e.g. district, county, metropolitan district) periodically choose between candidates who are mostly representing the same parties as those found at national level and the successful candidates in the election are elected to represent their constituency in the deliberating body (the council). Senior members of this body are chosen to serve on the various committees and subcommittees, with the leading party on the council having an in-built majority in the committee system, where most decisions have traditionally been made prior to being sanctioned (or not) by the full council. Since the passage of the Local Government Act (2000), councils have been allowed to adopt one of three broad categories of constitution which provide for a separate executive. These three categories are (1) a directly elected mayor with a cabinet

Figure 4.4   The local government system

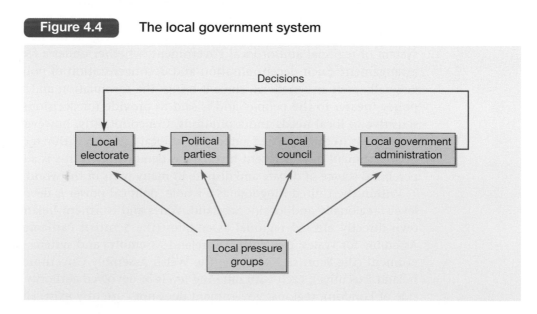

selected by the mayor, (2) a cabinet either elected by the council or appointed by its leader, and (3) a directly elected mayor and council manager.

For the most part, senior councillors are the political heads of the various local authority departments and agencies (e.g. housing, social services, education, and so on) that are responsible for providing those services within the local community which national laws require or, in some cases (e.g. sports centres), do not forbid. Much of this work is carried out by local officials who are appointed by the local authority to administer local services and to advise councillors on policy matters. As the local equivalent of civil servants, local government officers exercise considerable influence over the formulation as well as the implementation of local decisions. For this reason, they too tend to be targeted by local pressure groups which operate at all levels and stages of the political process in their attempts to influence local decision-making.

The current structure of local government in the United Kingdom is illustrated in Table 4.3. In England, outside the metropolitan areas, most 'shire' counties have a two-tier structure of county councils and district councils, with the former providing the larger services (e.g. education and social services) while the latter have responsibility for a range of other services (such as housing, leisure, refuse collection and local planning). Elsewhere (e.g. Avon, Cleveland, Humberside, Isle of Wight) new 'unitary authorities' either have taken over the functions of the former county and district councils or operate alongside them as all-purpose authorities (e.g. Leicester, York). In the metropolitan areas (including London) the single tier of district councils (or London borough councils) remains unchanged from previous years (see below).

Table 4.3 The structure of UK local government, 2008

Types of local authority

England	**Wales and Scotland**	**N. Ireland**
Non-metropolitan areas County councils District councils Unitary councils (plus joint arrangements)	*All mainland areas* Unitary councils (plus three island councils in Orkney, Shetland and the Western Isles)	For the purpose of local government Northern Ireland has 26 district councils with limited powers (e.g. collecting rubbish and providing leisure facilities)
Metropolitan areas Metropolitan district councils (plus joint boards)		
London London Borough Councils (plus Corporation of the City of London and joint boards)		

Following legislation in 1994, the two-tier structure in Wales and Scotland was abolished and was replaced (on 1 April 1996) with single-tier, all-purpose, unitary authorities which have inherited the majority of the functions of the previous councils. In Northern Ireland the system of single-tier district councils remains, although these authorities still have limited responsibility for service provision.

Like central government, UK local government has also faced pressures for reform, and a number of important developments have taken place in recent years.

- London elected its first executive mayor in 2000 and a streamlined assembly (25 members) to control its budget and appointments. The assembly of the Greater London Authority was elected by proportional representation and is responsible for major strategic issues such as transport, economic development, planning and the environment.
- Compulsory Competitive Tendering has been replaced by 'Best Value' in the delivery of local services.
- Councils have been asked to consider reform of the decision-making process and to consider alternative models (see *also* White Paper, 'Modern Local Government in Touch with the People', 1998). Some councils have implemented such changes.
- Consideration is currently being given to reform of the local government taxation system and to allowing local electors a say in how a proportion of local rates are spent.

As indicated previously, such changes in the political system have implications for the relationship between business and government.

Appendix 4.3 — Supranational government: the European Union

Decisions and law affecting business activity are increasingly being made at supranational as well as national and subnational levels. Nowhere is this more evident than in western Europe, where the influence of the European Union is profound. As a significant part of the political environment of the major world economies, the EU deserves special consideration, particularly since its decisions often have global as well as regional consequences – affecting not only firms within its member states, but also businesses and governments trading with these states both directly and indirectly. In the following analysis, attention is focused on the political institutions of the European Union and their relative importance in the process of decision making.[4] The economic significance of the EU within the international marketplace is discussed in Chapter 16.

The EU's official website called 'Europa' can be accessed at *http://europa.eu*. This provides links to lots of other very useful sites.

The European Parliament

The **European Parliament** is a directly elected body currently of 785 members (MEPs), with each member state's representation being roughly equivalent to the size of its population. The United Kingdom, for example, has 78 MEPs, elected at five-yearly intervals by UK citizens using a regional list system of proportional representation introduced for the June 1999 European elections. Since voting under a proportional system enhances the prospects of representation by smaller political parties, the European Parliament contains members representing a diversity of political parties who sit in political groups with similar affiliations. Figure 4.5 shows, for example, the number of MEPs by broad affiliation as they stood at June 2004. The next elections are due to be held in 2009.

web link

For information on the European Parliament see *www.europarl.europa.eu*

The importance of party affiliation is emphasised by the fact that Parliament's organisation is deliberately biased in favour of multinational groupings, with recognition of a political grouping entitling the group to offices, funding, representation on committees and influence in debates and legislation. In order to decide its attitude to an issue or policy proposal coming before the Parliament or one of its committees, a group would normally meet for several days in the week before each session and the issue would be discussed and an agreed line would be decided. As in the case of national parliaments, the attitudes of the political groups have a significant impact on the discussions and decisions within the European Parliament, both in committee and when the House is in full session. Given the number of party groups, however, and the fact that no single group tends to have an absolute majority – unlike in some national parliaments – there is often a need for a group to try to build a coalition of support if it is to achieve its objectives in Parliament. Understandably – and perhaps inevitably – decisions by the European Parliament thus tend to involve compromise between individuals and groups, with the final outcome frequently being a course of action which is acceptable to a majority.

In terms of its role and methods of operation, the European Parliament essentially mirrors national parliaments. Much of its detailed work is handled by specialist committees, meeting mostly in Brussels, which report on and offer recommendations to full sessions of the House which take place in Strasbourg. Membership of each committee is broadly representative of the strengths of the party groupings and the chairmen and women of the permanent committees tend to be influential figures in their own right. In addition to carrying out detailed examination and amendment of draft laws, the committees discuss issues (e.g. women's rights, consumer protection, employment), question officials, hold public

Figure 4.5   MEPs by party affiliation at June 2004 (prior to enlargement)

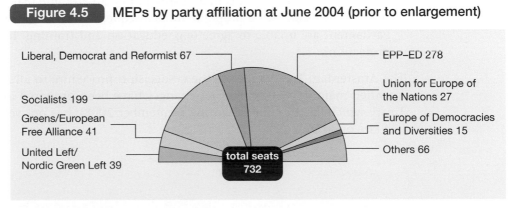

Source: Adapted from European Parliament data.

hearings at which experts and representatives of specialist organisations give evidence, and generally offer their opinion and advice on issues of concern to the EU. As in the case of national parliaments, detailed discussion in committee prior to debate and decision by the full house provides Parliament with an effective means of carrying out its duties and serves as a mechanism for scrutinising the work of both the Council and the Commission.

With regard to its functions, these predominantly fall into four main areas:

1 *Legislation*. The Parliament's formal approval is required on most proposals before they can be adopted by the Council of Ministers (see below).
2 *The budget*. Along with the Council of Ministers, the Parliament acts as the Community's 'budgetary authority' and can reject the Council's draft budget and may modify expenditure proposals on 'non-compulsory' items. It can question the Commission's management of the budget and call in the Court of Auditors.
3 *Supervision*. The Parliament supervises the Commission, which it has the power to dismiss by a vote of censure and whose work it scrutinises using a variety of mechanisms. Under the Maastricht Treaty (1992) it has the right to be consulted on the appointment of a new Commission and can veto its appointment. The power of democratic supervision has been extended to other EU institutions including the Council of Ministers.
4 *Initiative*. This includes debates on important regional and international issues and demands for changes to existing policies and/or legislation. Parliament must also approve applications from countries wishing to join the EU.

In the legislative field, authority traditionally rested with the Council of Ministers and the Commission, and Parliament's role was largely to sanction proposals put before it. Changes under the Single European Act (1986), the Maastricht Treaty (1992), the Amsterdam Treaty (1997) and the Nice Treaty (2001) have, however, helped to strengthen Parliament's position by establishing new procedures for 'assent', 'co-operating' and 'co-decision'. Thus:

● In certain fields an absolute majority of the European Parliament must vote to approve laws before they are passed (e.g. foreign treaties, accession treaties, the Common Agricultural Policy).
● In specified areas Parliament now has a second reading of proposals and its rejection of such proposals can only be overturned by a unanimous decision of the Council of Ministers (e.g. Single Market laws, trans-European networks).
● Parliament can also reject certain legislation by an absolute majority vote if, after the second reading of a proposal and subsequent conciliation, the Council and Parliament are unable to agree (e.g. education and training, health, consumer protection).

The Amsterdam Treaty extends the co-decision procedure to all areas covered by qualified majority voting. Further changes have been proposed under the Lisbon Treaty which, at the time of writing (September 2008), has not yet been fully ratified (see opposite).

The Council of The European Union (the Council of Ministers)

The Council of The European Union (the **Council of Ministers**) – the Union's ultimate decision-making body – comprises one minister from each of the 27 member states, with participants on the Council varying according to the issue under discussion (e.g. agricultural issues are discussed by Ministers of Agriculture from each state). Meetings of the Council, which are mainly held in Brussels, are chaired by the minister from the country holding the presidency, which currently rotates on a six-monthly basis (e.g. Slovenia and France held the presidency in 2008). Along with the meetings of ministers are regular meetings of officials (Council Working Groups), together with the work of the Committee of Permanent Representatives of the Member States (COREPER) whose task is to co-ordinate the groundwork for Union decisions undertaken by the numerous meetings of senior officials. In addition, the Council is serviced by a general secretariat also based in Brussels.

> **web link**
>
> The Council of Ministers website is at *www.consilium.europa.eu*. Information is also available through the EU's main website at *http://europa.eu*

In essence, the role of the Council of Ministers is to make major policy decisions and to respond to legislative proposals put forward mainly by the Commission. In general, major EU decisions require unanimity in the Council but, increasingly, many decisions (especially after the Amsterdam and Nice Treaties) are now being taken by a **qualified majority vote** (**qmv**). Member states have weighted votes in the Council that are roughly proportional to their relative population sizes, with the total number of votes now being 321. Since January 2007, a qualified majority will be reached if two conditions are met: (1) a majority of member states approve (in some cases a two-thirds majority is needed); (2) a minimum of 255 votes (i.e. 73.9 per cent) is cast in favour of the proposal. In addition, a member state can also ask for confirmation that the votes in favour represent at least 62 per cent of the total population of the EU. If not, the decision will not be adopted.

While the 'right of initiative' under the Treaties rests with the Commission, the ultimate power of decision essentially lies with the Council, which may adopt Commission proposals as drafted, amend them, reject them, or simply take no decision, having consulted the European Parliament and normally a number of other bodies (see below). If adopted, Council of Ministers' decisions have the force of law and are described as regulations, directives, decisions, or recommendations and opinions. **Regulations** apply directly to all member states and do not have to be confirmed by national parliaments to have binding legal effect. **Directives** lay down compulsory objectives, but leave it to member states to translate them into national legislation. **Decisions** are binding on those states, companies or individuals to whom they are addressed, while **recommendations and opinions** have no binding force, but merely state the view of the institution which issues them.

The Council's power to pass a law – even if the European Parliament disagrees with it – was reduced under the Maastricht Treaty. In specified policy areas, joint approval is now necessary and MEPs have an effective veto if the two sides cannot reach agreement following conciliation. Moreover, following Maastricht a Committee of the Regions has been established to advise the Commission and the Council on issues concerning the European regions – a development which should help to ensure a stronger regional voice at European level. That said, it is still the case that the Council remains responsible for setting general policy within the EU and relies on the Commission to take decisions on the detailed application of legislation or to adapt legislative details to meet changing circumstances. To this extent – and given the Commission's other responsibilities – the ultimate influence over EU decisions is, to say the very least, open to question, as is often the case at national level.

The European Council

The work of the 'specialist' Councils within the Council of Ministers (e.g. Agriculture, Economics and Finance, Employment and Social Affairs) is co-ordinated by the General Affairs Council, comprising the Foreign Ministers of the 27 member states. This Council is also responsible for preparing for the meetings of the European Council which occur two or three times each year. The **European Council** is attended by the Heads of Government/State of each member state along with their Foreign Ministers and the President of the Commission, and its work invariably attracts substantial media coverage. Under the chairmanship of the country holding the presidency, the European Council's role is to discuss important policy issues affecting the EU and to propose policy to the Council of Ministers. As the meeting at Maastricht in December 1991 indicated, these 'summits' of Heads of Governments can have a profound effect on the development of the Union and its institutions.

 web link Information on the European Council is available via the Council of Ministers website. See above.

The European Commission

The **Commission**, which has its headquarters in Brussels and Luxembourg, is the EU's bureaucratic arm, currently comprising 27 Commissioners (one from each member state) nominated by their respective governments and a staff of about 23 000 permanent civil servants drawn from all member states. Headed by a president, and organised into **Directorates-General**, each with a Commissioner responsible for its work, the European Commission's role is essentially that of initiator, supervisor and executive. More specifically its tasks are:

1 To act as guardian of the Treaties so as to ensure that EU rules and principles are respected.
2 To propose policies and legislation for the Council of Ministers to discuss and, if appropriate, adopt or amend.
3 To implement EU policies and supervise the day-to-day running of these policies, including managing the funds which account for most of the EU budget (e.g. EAGGF, ERDF, ECSC).[5]

 web link You can find further information on the Commision at *ec.europa.eu*

In carrying out these duties, the Commissioners are required to act in the interest of the EU as a whole and may not receive instructions from any national government or from any other body (Article 157 of the Treaty of Rome). Moreover, while each Commissioner is responsible for formulating proposals within his or her area of responsibility, the final decision is taken on a collegiate basis and the work is subject to the supervision of the European Parliament. As mentioned above, Parliament is the only body which can force the Commission to resign collectively; interestingly, it has no authority over individual Commissioners, although its endorsement is needed when the President of the Commission and the other Commissioners are appointed.

Much of the undoubted power and influence of the Commission stems from its central involvement in the legislative process. Proposals for consideration by the Council and the Parliament are initially drafted by the Commission, usually following consultation with the Economic and Social Committee (representing the interests of employers, trade unions, farmers, consumers, etc.) and other advisory bodies as appropriate. Moreover EU Treaties specifically give the Commission the power to make regulations, issue directives, take decisions, make recommendations and deliver opinions, as well as to implement policies based on either Council decisions or Treaty provisions. Thus, while legislative power in the EU in general rests with the Council of Ministers, the Commission is also able to legislate in order to implement earlier Council regulations, particularly where technical or routine matters are concerned – a situation which has parallels in the operation of government at national level.

Further powers with regard to specific sectors (e.g. coal and steel) or particular aspects of EU work (e.g. the budget, international agreements) serve to enhance the Commission's influence and to confirm its position as the 'driving force' of the Union. Perhaps understandably, pressure groups seeking to influence the policy process within the European Union regard the Commission as an important institution to target, together with Parliament and the Council of Ministers. Recent and proposed changes in the relationship between these three institutions will undoubtedly have an effect not only on the legislative process, but also on the practice of lobbying within the EU context.

The European Court of Justice

The **European Court of Justice**, which sits in Luxembourg, comprises 27 judges who are appointed for a six-year period by consent of the member states and eight advocates-general. The Court's role is:

1 To pass judgment, at the request of a national court, on the interpretation or validity of points of EU law.
2 To quash, at the request of an EU institution, government or individual, any measures adopted by the Commission, the Council or national governments which are judged to be incompatible with the existing treaties.

The Court can also be invited to offer an opinion, which then becomes binding, on agreements the EU proposes to undertake with third countries.

Three aspects of its work are particularly worthy of note:

1 Individuals as well as member states can bring cases to the Court, and its judgments and interpretations apply to all (i.e. EU institutions, member states, national courts and private citizens) and are backed by a system of penalties for non-compliance.
2 Its rulings on matters of European law, which has primacy over national law, are final and its decisions are binding on member countries.
3 The Court has tended to follow the principle that EU Treaties should be interpreted with a degree of flexibility so as to take account of changing conditions and circumstances. This has permitted the Community to legislate in areas where there are no specific Treaty provisions, such as the fight against pollution.

> **web link** The Court of Justice website can be accessed at *curia.europa.eu*

Current developments

With the decision to enlarge the EU, steps were taken to establish a Constitution for Europe which was designed to replace the exisiting treaties and to streamline the EU's decision-making process. The draft Constitution was ratified by Heads of Government/State in October 2005 and was subsequently subject to referendums in a number of member states. Rejection of the plans by voters in Holland and France in 2005 led to changes to the 'Constitution' which subsequently has been renamed a 'reform treaty'. It is expected that most national governments of the member states will ratify this treaty without undertaking a national referendum, with the treaty being scheduled to come into force in the middle of 2009. In June 2008, however, Irish voters rejected the reform treaty in a referendum, throwing the whole process into abeyance. While steps are being taken to overcome the problem, it is at present (September 2008) uncertain what the final outcome will be.

case study Divided we stand

As the chapter has illustrated, democratic systems of government are characterised by a separation of powers, with the three main functions of government – legislative, executive, judicial – held mostly (if not wholly) in separate hands. Such an arrangement acts as an important 'check and balance' in a democratic political system, and provides an important element of constraint on the actions and decisions of the incumbent government.

Decision-making power and authority in a democracy is also shared in other ways, as exemplified by a federal system of government where powers are divided between the federal government (i.e. national government) and the government(s) at a sub-national level (e.g. in regions or states). One of the consequences of this division of responsibilities can be that decisions affecting individuals and groups (including business organisations) in one part of a country may not always be the same as in other parts, thereby creating what is sometimes described as an 'unlevel playing field'.

To demonstrate this, it is worth examining governmental reactions in the United States to the problem of greenhouse gas emissions. In the 1990s the federal government in Washington, led by President Clinton, participated in international discussions on how to tackle the growing problem of global climate change. These discussions culminated in the Kyoto Protocol in 1997, which set limits for greenhouse gas emissions in the developed economies over the coming decade.

Although the US government initially indicated its willingness to sign up to Kyoto, a change in government in 2000/1 meant that the US ultimately failed to ratify the treaty. The new American president (George Bush) – under pressure from powerful lobby groups including the oil and car industries – argued that US businesses would be at a competitive disadvantage if the US accepted limitations on its greenhouse gas emissions when some other countries (notably India and China) were not obliged to do so under the Kyoto agreements. The US, along with a number of other countries (e.g. Australia), steadfastly refused to tackle climate change by refusing to accept the principle of agreed targets for emissions of greenhouse gases such as carbon dioxide and methane.

While the US federal government under President Bush has come in for a lot of international criticism for its stance on Kyoto, the federal system of government in America has meant that decision makers at a sub-national level (e.g. state governors and legislators; city mayors) have sometimes taken a different view on the issue of climate change. In California, for example, Governor Schwarzenegger has signed a law requiring a 25 per cent cut in greenhouse emissions in the state by 2020, with penalties available for non-compliant organisations. Other US states have taken similar stances and at a local level a growing number of city mayors have signed up to an initiative to get their cities to meet the US Kyoto environmental targets that have been rejected by the Bush administration.

It is interesting to note that developments such as these have been accompanied by other political pressures on the federal government to address the issue of climate change. For example, very large and powerful institutional investors in the US have called upon Congress to introduce a mandatory policy for greenhouse gas emissions and further lobbying has taken place by coalitions of businesses and environmental groups that want to see the cuts in emissions agreed by the government in Washington. Perhaps more significantly, the US Supreme Court in 2007 effectively overruled the president's refusal to restrict carbon dioxide emissions when it ruled that the US Environmental Protection Agency had the power to restrict exhaust emissions from vehicles on US roads. The Court's judgment was in response to a lawsuit filed by several US states and a number of environmental groups that wanted action on greenhouse gas emissions. Needless to say, the lawsuit was opposed by various business interests including car manufacturers and energy suppliers.

While President Bush had recently signed an energy bill designed to improve the efficiency level of cars and homes, the general feeling is that progress on the issue of emissions targets is unlikely without a change of government in Washington. Following such a change in Australia, the Australian government signed up to Kyoto and committed the country to meeting certain targets for cuts in greenhouse gas emissions. It remains to be seen whether the new American President is willing to do the same when the follow-up treaty to Kyoto (hopefully) is signed in the next year or so.

Case study questions

1 What factors could explain the difference in response to emission targets between the federal government in Washington and some of the governments at the state and local level?

2 Why do you think that large institutional investors are pressuring the US Congress to introduce a mandatory policy on greenhouse gas emissions in the US?

Review and discussion questions

1 To what extent do you think a change of government in your country would affect the business community?

2 Many top civil servants take directorships in large companies on retirement from government. Why should companies be keen to recruit retired bureaucrats?

3 How far is the enlargement of the European Union likely to benefit UK businesses?

4 In what ways could a business organisation seek to influence central government decision-makers on issues in which it has an interest (e.g. taxes on company profits or the level of interest rates)?

Assignments

1 You are employed as a research assistant by a group representing the interest of small and medium-size enterprises (e.g. a Chamber of Commerce). Using contemporary source material (e.g. the Internet, manifestos, etc.) produce a draft report highlighting current government policy for the SME sector.

2 Imagine you are employed as a political lobbyist, with a special interest in conservation issues. You have been approached by a local conservation group which is concerned about government plans to build a bypass round a village in its area. The government's proposals for the road would cause significant damage to a Site of Special Scientific Interest (SSSI) and the group is determined to oppose the plans. Your brief is to draft an 'action plan' for the group, indicating what forms of pressure group activity you would recommend, in what sequence and using which channels of potential influence.

Notes and references

1 See, for example, Barker, A., *Quangos in Britain*, Macmillan, 1982; Ridley, F. F. and Wilson, D. (eds), *The Quango Debate*, OUP/Hansard Society, 1995; Pollitt, C. and Talbot, C., *Unbundled Goverment*, Routledge, 2004.

2 Individual ministerial responsibility should not be confused with collective Cabinet responsibility, both of which apply to Ministers of the Crown.

3 Senior civil servants who are in a position to influence policy are sometimes called 'mandarins'. This term only applies to a very small percentage of the civil service.

4 Numerous books exist on the EU. Students can also gain information by contacting EU institutions directly, particularly through their national offices or by accessing the numerous websites.

5 European Agriculture Guarantee and Guidance Fund (EAGGF); European Regional Development Fund (ERDF); European Coal and Steel Community (ECSC). See Chapter 13 for a further discussion of EU structural funds.

Further reading

Cocker, P. and Jones, A., *Contemporary British Politics and Government*, Liverpool Academic Press, 2002.

Coxall, W. N., Robins, L. and Leach, R., *Contemporary British Politics*, 4th edition, Palgrave Macmillan, 2003.

European Commission, *The Institutions and Bodies of the European Union: Who's Who in Europe*, Office of Official Publications of the European Communities, 2001.

Greenwood, J., Pyper, R. and Wilson, D., *New Public Administration in Britain*, Routledge, 2002.

Hix, S., *The Political System of the European Union*, 2nd edition, Palgrave Macmillan, 2005.

Leach, S. and Wilson, D., *Local Political Leadership*, Policy Press, 2000.

Massey, A. and Pyper, R., *Public Management and Modernisation in Britain*, Palgrave Macmillan, 2005.

Pedler, R. H. (ed.), *European Union Lobbying*, Palgrave, 2002.

Peterson, J. and Shackleton, M. (eds), *The institutions of the European Union*, OUP, 2002.

Rose, A. and Lawton, A. (eds), *Public Services Management*, Financial Times/Prentice Hall, 1999.

Warleigh, A., *European Union: The Basics*, Routledge, 2004.

Wetherly, P. and Otter, D. (eds), *The Business Environment: Themes and Issues*, Oxford University Press, 2008, Chapters 4 and 11.

Web links and further questions are available on the website at:
www.pearsoned.co.uk/worthington

5   The macroeconomic environment

Ian Worthington

Business organisations operate in an economic environment which shapes, and is shaped by, their activities. In market-based economies this environment comprises variables which are dynamic, interactive and mobile and which, in part, are affected by government in pursuit of its various roles in the economy. As a vital component in the macroeconomy, government exercises a significant degree of influence over the flow of income and hence over the level and pattern of output by the public and private sectors. Other key influences include a country's financial institutions and the international economic organisations and groupings to which it belongs or subscribes.

Learning outcomes

Having read this chapter you should be able to:

- compare alternative economic systems and their underlying principles and discuss the problems of transition from a centrally planned to a market-based economy

- illustrate flows of income, output and expenditure in a market economy and account for changes in the level and pattern of economic activity

- analyse the role of government in the macroeconomy, including government macroeconomic policies and the objectives on which they are based

- explain the role of financial institutions

- identify the key international economic institutions and organisations which influence the business environment in open, market economies

Key terms

Accelerator effect
Aggregate monetary demand
Balance of payments
Capital market
Capitalist economy
Central bank
Centrally planned economy
Circular flow of income model
Consumer Price Index (CPI)
Consumer sovereignty
Crowding out
Cyclical unemployment
Deindustrialisation
Direct controls
Direct taxation
Economic growth
Economic scarcity
Economics
Exchange rate
Factory gate prices
Financial intermediaries

Fiscal policy
Free-market economy
Full employment
G8 nations
Government spending
Gross domestic product
Headline inflation
Income flows
Indirect taxation
Inflation
Injections
Interest rates
Leakages
Macroeconomic analysis
Macroeconomic environment
Microeconomic analysis
Monetary aggregates
Monetary policies
Money market
Money stock
Multiplier effect

National Debt
Opportunity cost
Public sector net borrowing (PSNB)
Real cost
Real flows
Real interest rates
Real national income
Recession
Retail Price Index (RPI)
State bank
Stock exchange
Structural unemployment
Technological unemployment
Underlying rate of inflation
Wages/prices inflationary spiral
Withdrawals

Introduction

By 2008 many of the world's economies were facing substantial economic problems as a result of rising oil prices, increased food and energy costs and the aftermath of the 'credit crunch' in the United States. In countries across the globe the talk was predominantly of 'recession' and the impact on the consumer, businesses and the public finances of a downturn in economic activity. In an effort to boost the US economy, the Bush administration provided a $168bn (£86bn) economic stimulus package, using tax refunds for around 130 million US households, in an effort to boost consumer spending. The evidence suggests that the US government's fiscal response had some impact on consumer behaviour, with some retailers (e.g. Wal-Mart) reporting an increase in like-for-like sales in the period after households received their refund cheques. In other areas of the US economy, however, the picture was less rosy, with many businesses experiencing extremely tough trading conditions as consumers reduced their spending to cope with higher domestic bills for food, petrol and energy and the global crisis in financial markets continued to cause considerable uncertainty about future economic prospects.

What this simple example is designed to demonstrate is the intimate relationship between business activity and the wider economic context in which it takes place, and a glance at any quality newspaper will provide a range of similar illustrations of this interface between business and economics. What is important at this point is not to understand the complexities of global economic forces or their effect on businesses, but to appreciate in broad terms the importance of the **macroeconomic environment** for business organisations and, in particular, the degree of compatibility between the preoccupations of the entrepreneur and those of the economist. To the economist, for example, a recession is generally marked by falling demand, rising unemployment, a slowing down in economic growth and a fall in investment. To the firm, it usually implies a loss of orders, a likely reduction in the workforce, a decline in output (or a growth in stocks) and a general reluctance to invest in capital equipment and/or new projects.

Much of the detailed discussion of the economic aspects of business can be found in Parts Three and Four. In this chapter the focus is on the broader question of the economic structure and processes of a market-based economy and on the macroeconomic influences affecting and being affected by business activity in this type of economic system. As suggested in the previous chapter, an understanding of the overall economic context within which businesses operate and its core values and principles is central to any meaningful analysis of the business environment.

Three further points are worth highlighting at this juncture. First, business activity not only is shaped by the economic context in which it takes place, but helps to shape that context; consequently the success or otherwise of government economic policy depends to some degree on the reactions of both the firms and the markets (e.g. the stock market) which are affected by government decisions. Second, economic influences operate at a variety of spatial levels, as illustrated by the opening paragraph, and governments can find that circumstances largely or totally beyond their control can affect businesses either favourably or adversely. Third, the economic (and for that matter, political) influence of industry and commerce can be considerable and this ensures that business organisations – both individually and collectively – usually constitute one of the chief pressure groups in democratic states. This political and economic relationship between government and business is discussed more fully in Chapter 13.

Economic systems

The concept of economic scarcity

Like politics, the term **economic** tends to be used in a variety of ways and contexts to describe certain aspects of human behaviour, ranging from activities such as producing, distributing and consuming, to the idea of frugality in the use of a resource (e.g. being 'economical' with the truth). Modern definitions stress how such behaviour, and the institutions in which it takes place (e.g. households, firms, governments, banks), are concerned with the satisfaction of human needs and wants through the transformation of resources into goods and services which are consumed by society. These processes are said to take place under conditions of **economic scarcity**.

The economist's idea of 'scarcity' centres on the relationship between a society's needs and wants and the resources available to satisfy them. In essence, economists argue that whereas needs and wants tend to be unlimited, the resources which can be used to meet those needs and wants are finite and accordingly no society at any time has the capacity to provide for all its actual or potential requirements. The assumption here is that both individual and collective needs and wants consistently outstrip the means available to satisfy them, as exemplified, for instance, by the inability of governments to provide instant health care, the best roads, education, defence, railways, and so on, at a time and place and of a quality convenient to the user. This being the case, 'choices' have to be made by both individuals and society concerning priorities in the use of resources, and every choice inevitably involves a 'sacrifice' (i.e. forgoing an alternative). Economists describe this sacrifice as the **opportunity cost** or **real cost** of the decision that is taken (e.g. every pound spent on the health service is a pound not spent on some other public service) and it is one which is faced by individuals, organisations (including firms), governments and society alike.

From a societal point of view the existence of economic scarcity poses three serious problems concerning the use of resources:

1 What to use the available resources for? That is, what goods and services should be produced (or not produced) with the resources (sometimes described as the 'guns v. butter' argument)?
2 How best to use those resources? For example, in what combinations, using what techniques and what methods?
3 How best to distribute the goods and services produced with them? That is, who gets what, how much and on what basis?

In practice, of course, these problems tend to be solved in a variety of ways, including barter (voluntary, bilateral exchange), price signals and the market, queuing and rationing, government instruction and corruption (e.g. resources allocated in exchange for personal favours), and examples of each of these solutions can be found in most, if not all, societies, at all times. Normally, however, one or other main approach to resource allocation tends to predominate and this allows analytical distinctions to be made between different types of economic system. One important distinction is between those economies which are centrally planned and those which operate predominantly through market forces, with prices forming the integrating mechanism. Understanding this distinction is fundamental to an examination of the way in which business is conducted and represents the foundation on which much of the subsequent analysis is built.

The centrally planned economy

In this type of economic system – associated with the post-Second World War socialist economies of eastern Europe, China, Cuba and elsewhere – most of the key decisions on production are taken by a central planning authority, normally the state and its agencies. Under this arrangement, the state typically:

● owns and/or controls the main economic resources;
● establishes priorities in the use of those resources;
● sets output targets for businesses which are largely under state ownership and/or control;
● directs resources in an effort to achieve these predetermined targets; and
● seeks to co-ordinate production in such a way as to ensure consistency between output and input demands.

The fact that an economy is centrally planned does not necessarily imply that all economic decisions are taken at central level; in many cases decision making may be devolved to subordinate agencies, including local committees and enterprises. Ultimately, however, these agencies are responsible to the centre and it is the latter which retains overall control of the economy and directs the use of scarce productive resources.

The problem of co-ordinating inputs and output in a modern planned economy is, of course, a daunting task and one which invariably involves an array of state planners and a central plan or blueprint normally covering a number of years (e.g. a five-year plan). Under such a plan, the state planners would establish annual output targets for each sector of the economy and for each enterprise within the sector and would identify the inputs of materials, labour and capital needed to achieve the set targets and would allocate resources accordingly. Given that the outputs of some industries (e.g. agricultural machinery) are the inputs of others (e.g. collective farms), it is not difficult to see how the overall effectiveness of the plan would depend in part on a high degree of co-operation and co-ordination between sectors and enterprises, as well as on good judgement, good decisions and a considerable element of good luck. The available evidence from planned economies suggests that none of these can be taken for granted and each is often in short supply.

Even in the most centralised of economies, state planning does not normally extend to telling individuals what they must buy in shops or how to use their labour, although an element of state direction at times may exist (e.g. conscription of the armed forces). Instead, it tends to condition *what* is available for purchase and the *prices* at which exchange takes place, and both of these are essentially the outcome of political choices, rather than a reflection of consumer demands. All too often consumers tend to be faced by queues and 'black markets' for some consumer products and overproduction of others, as state enterprises strive to meet targets frequently unrelated to the needs and wants of consumers. By the same token, businesses which make losses do not have to close down, as the state would normally make additional funds available to cover any difference between sales revenue and costs. This being the case, the emphasis at firm level tends to be more on meeting targets than on achieving efficiency in the use of resources and hence a considerable degree of duplication and wastage tends to occur.

In such an environment, the traditional entrepreneurial skills of efficient resource management, price setting and risk taking have little, if any, scope for development and managers behave essentially as technicians and bureaucrats, administering decisions largely made elsewhere. Firms, in effect, are mainly servants of the state and their activities are conditioned by social and political considerations, rather than by the needs of the market – although some market activity normally occurs in planned economies (especially in agriculture and a number of private services). Accordingly, businesses and their employees are not fully sensitised to the needs of the consumer and as a result quality and choice (where it exists) may suffer, particularly where incentives to improved efficiency and performance are negligible. Equally, the system tends to encourage bribery and corruption and the development of a substantial black market, with differences in income, status and political influence being an important determinant of individual consumption and of living standards.

The free-market economy

The **free-market** (or **capitalist**) **economy** stands in direct contrast to the centrally planned system. Whereas in the latter the state controls most economic decisions, in the former the key economic agencies are private individuals (sometimes called 'households') and firms, and these interact in free markets, through a system of prices, to determine the allocation of resources.

The key features of this type of economic system are as follows:

● Resources are in private ownership and the individuals owning them are free to use them as they wish.
● Firms, also in private ownership, are equally able to make decisions on production, free from state interference.
● No blueprint (or master plan) exists to direct production and consumption.
● Decisions on resource allocation are the result of a decentralised system of markets and prices, in which the decisions of millions of consumers and hundreds of thousands of firms are automatically co-ordinated.
● The consumer is sovereign, i.e. dictates the pattern of supply and hence the pattern of resource allocation.

In short, the three problems of what to produce, how to produce and how to distribute are solved by market forces.

The diagram in Figure 5.1 illustrates the basic operation of a market economy. In essence, individuals are owners of resources (e.g. labour) and consumers of products; firms are users of resources and producers of products. What products are produced – and hence how resources are used – depends on consumers, who indicate their demands by purchasing (i.e. paying the price) or not purchasing, and this acts as a signal to producers to acquire the resources necessary (i.e. pay the price) to meet the

Figure 5.1 The market economy

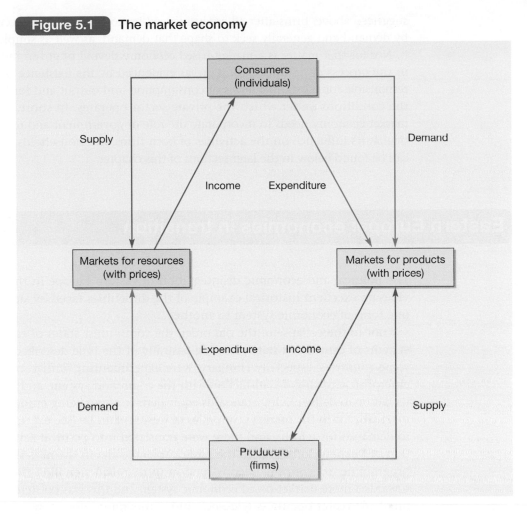

preferences of consumers. If consumer demands change, for whatever reason, this will cause an automatic reallocation of resources, as firms respond to the new market conditions. Equally, competition between producers seeking to gain or retain customers is said to guarantee that resources are used efficiently and to ensure that the most appropriate production methods (i.e. how to produce) are employed in the pursuit of profits.

The distribution of output is also determined by market forces, in this case operating in the markets for productive services. Individuals supplying a resource (e.g. labour) receive an income (i.e. a price) from the firms using that resource and this allows them to purchase goods and services in the markets for products, which in turn provides an income for firms that can be spent on the purchase of further resources (see below). Should the demand for a particular type of productive resource increase – say, as a result of an increase in the demand for the product produced by that resource – the price paid to the provider of the resource will tend to rise and hence, other things being equal, allow more output to be purchased. Concomitantly, it is also likely to result in a shift of resources from uses which are relatively less lucrative to those which are relatively more rewarding.

This matching of supply and demand through prices in markets is described in detail in Chapter 14 and the analysis can also be applied to the market for foreign currencies (see Chapter 16). In practice, of course, no economy operates entirely in the manner suggested above; firms after all are influenced by costs and supply decisions as well as by demand and generally seek to shape that demand, as well as simply responding to it. Nor for that matter is a market-based economy devoid of government involvement in the process of resource allocation, as evidenced by the existence of a public sector responsible for substantial levels of consumption and output and for helping to shape the conditions under which the private sector operates. In short, any study of the market economy needs to incorporate the role of government and to examine, in particular, its influence on the activities of both firms and households. Such an analysis can be found below in the later sections of this chapter.

Eastern Europe: economies in transition

The political and economic disintegration of eastern Europe in the late 1980s provides an excellent historical example of the difficulties faced by states moving from one form of economic system to another.

Prior to the collapse of the old order, the communist states of eastern Europe had systems of centralised state planning basically of the type described above, although some countries, especially Hungary, were experimenting with various forms of free enterprise. Growing dissatisfaction with the command system, and in particular with its failure to deliver living standards equivalent to those being enjoyed at the time by most citizens in the market economies of western Europe (see e.g. Table 5.1), gave rise to demands for reform, and these were translated into political action with the election of Mikhail Gorbachev to the post of Soviet leader in the mid-1980s. Gorbachev's programme of economic reconstruction (*perestroika*) signalled the start of a move towards a more market-based economic system and this was bolstered by his commitment to greater openness (*glasnost*) and democratic reform. By the late 1980s and early 1990s, the old Soviet empire had effectively ceased to exist and the newly independent states, almost without exception, had committed themselves to radical economic change of a kind unthinkable just a few years before.

Table 5.1 Comparative economic indicators, 1988

	Population (million)	GDP ($ billion)	GDP per capita ($)
East Germany	17	156	9360
Czechoslovakia	16	118	7600
Hungary	11	69	6500
Bulgaria	9	51	5630
Poland	37	207	5540
Romania	23	94	4120
European Union	325	4745	14609
West Germany	61	1202	19575

Source: *The Amex Bank Review*, November 1989.

For states anxious to move from an entrenched system of state planning to a market-based economic system, the obstacles can be formidable and can help to slow down the progress of economic (and political) reform. Among the problems faced by eastern European countries in the transitionary phase were:

- The need to create a legal and commercial framework to support the change to a market economy (e.g. company laws, laws on property rights, competition, external trade, the development of an appropriate accounting system).
- The need to establish different forms of free enterprise and to develop financial institutions capable of providing risk and venture capital, at commercial rates of return.
- The need to develop truly competitive markets, free from state control and protection.
- The need to liberalise labour markets and to develop entrepreneurial skills in a workforce traditionally demotivated by the old bureaucratic system.
- The need to allow prices to move to levels determined by market forces, rather than by political decision.
- The need to achieve macroeconomic stability as markets become more open both internally and externally.
- The need to reduce the burden of international debt.
- The need to attract substantial overseas investment to assist in the rebuilding of the collapsed old socialist economies.

Meeting these requirements was not made any easier by economic collapse and the perceived need on the part of some reformers to bring about rapid economic change whatever the consequences. In Russia, in particular, widespread bribery, corruption and criminal activity have helped to undermine an economy struggling with economic and political instability that appears endemic. The recent (2008) problems between Russia and Georgia have also had an effect, with foreign investors withdrawing billions of dollars of foreign investment from Russia because of the risks involved.

Evidence suggests that, given these and other requirements, the process of systemic change is destined to be long and painful for some countries and will be subject to political as well as economic developments, many of which are as yet unpredictable. Central to this process will be the attitude of western countries towards such issues as debt relief, financial assistance, investment and other forms of help, and perhaps understandably the approach thus far has been relatively cautious, particularly given the relative uncertainty that comes from dealing with countries historically perceived to be adversaries. For example, a contemporary analysis by the accountants Ernst & Young in 1992 suggested that the uncertainty was at its greatest in countries such as Russia, Ukraine and Albania and at its least in Hungary, the then Czechoslovakia and Poland, where reforms were often further down the road (see Table 5.2). Hungary's high notional score, for instance, was justified by its relative degree of political and economic stability and its favourable attitude to foreign investment, backed by a legal framework to encourage it. In contrast, in Albania – one of the most rigid of the old communist regimes – political and economic instability, limited business opportunities and a reluctance to change were seen as considerable obstacles to involvement on the part of western companies and governments.

Table 5.2 Eastern Europe: A comparative risk analysis

	Business opportunities	Political risk	Credit rating	Status of economy	Stability of local economy	Business infrastructure	Total
Hungary	2	1	2	3	2	2	12
Czechoslovakia	2	3	2	3	2	2	14
Poland	2	3	3	3	3	2	16
Baltic States	4	3	3	4	3	3	20
Bulgaria	4	3	4	4	3	3	21
Romania	4	4	4	4	4	3	23
Russia and Ukraine	1	4	5	5	4	4	23
Albania	5	4	4	5	5	4	27

Note: Countries are rated on a scale 1 to 5, where low scores are best and high scores worst.
Source: Adapted from the *Daily Telegraph*, 13 May 1992.

With regard to western corporate involvement, in practice this has taken a variety of forms including direct acquisition, joint ventures (which tend to carry tax advantages) and the development of local distribution networks, and much of it has been undertaken by multinational companies seeking to establish market share and to gain low-cost production sites. Coca-Cola, Pepsico, Levi Strauss, Philip Morris, BAT, Mars, Unilever, McDonald's, Procter & Gamble and General Electric have been just some of the organisations that have sought to take advantage of the growing demand for western consumer goods, and Hungary, Poland and the former Czechoslovakia have proved favourable locations for much of the investment. There is no doubt that the case for further investment has been significantly strengthened with the recent process of enlargement within the EU (see Chapter 16) that has involved a number of the old eastern European planned economies. By the same token, political instability in some parts of the old Soviet Empire (see above) acts as a disincentive for foreign investors who can find the risks beginning to outweigh the anticipated benefits.

Politico-economic synthesis

The economic problem of resource allocation, described above, clearly has a political dimension, given its focus on the ownership, control and use of wealth-producing assets within society. This allows links to be made between a country's chosen economic system and its political regime. A useful way of representing possible relationships is illustrated in Figure 5.2. As suggested in Chapter 4, political systems can be characterised as ranging from democratic to authoritarian, depending on the degree of public involvement in decision-making processes. Similarly, economic systems can be seen to range from free market to planned, according to the level of state intervention in the process of resource allocation. This two-dimensional model thus provides for four major combinations of politico-economic systems, ranging from democratic–free-market on the one hand (quadrant 1) to authoritarian–planned on the other (quadrant 3).

Figure 5.2   Politico-economic systems

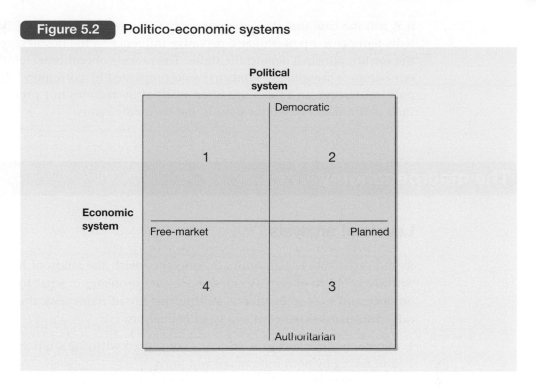

In applying this model to specific cases, it is clear that free-market approaches to resource allocation are predominantly associated with democratic states. Such a link is not surprising. Democracy, after all, includes the notion of individuals being able to express their preferences through the ballot box and having the opportunity to replace one government with another at periodic intervals. In free markets similar processes are at work, with individuals effectively 'voting' for goods and services through the price system and their expressed preferences being reflected in the pattern of resource allocation.

A link between authoritarian regimes and planned economic systems can equally be rationalised, in that government control over the political system is considerably facilitated if it also directs the economy through the ownership and/or control of the means of production, distribution and exchange. In effect, the relative absence of democratic mechanisms, such as free elections and choice between alternative forms of government, is echoed in the economic sphere by the inability of individuals to exercise any real influence over resource allocation. At the extreme, this could involve a government ban on any forms of free enterprise and total government control of the pattern of output and consumption in an economy which is devoid of effective consumer sovereignty.

In practice, of course, the picture is much more complicated than suggested by this simple dichotomy. Some authoritarian states, for instance, have predominantly capitalist economic systems (quadrant 4), while some democratic countries have a substantial degree of government intervention (i.e. moving them towards quadrant 2), either by choice or from necessity (e.g. wartime). Added to this, even in states where the political or economic system appears to be the same, considerable differences can occur at an operational and/or institutional level and this gives each country a degree of uniqueness not adequately portrayed by the model. That said, it is still the case that the basic congruity between democracy and free-market systems represents a powerful and pervasive influence in the business environment of the world's principal democratic states. The process of economic reform – as in eastern Europe – accordingly tends to be accompanied by corresponding pressures for political change and these are often resisted by regimes not prepared to give up their political and economic powers and their élite status.

The macroeconomy

Levels of analysis

As indicated above, economics is concerned with the study of how society deals with the problem of scarcity and the resultant problems of what to produce, how to produce and how to distribute. Within this broad framework the economist typically distinguishes between two types of analysis:

1 **Microeconomic analysis**, which is concerned with the study of economic decision taking by both individuals and firms.
2 **Macroeconomic analysis**, which is concerned with interactions in the economy as a whole (i.e. with economic aggregates).

The microeconomic approach is exemplified by the analysis of markets and prices undertaken in Chapter 14 which shows, for example, how individual consumers in the market for beer might be affected by a price change. This analysis could be extended to an investigation of how the total market might respond to a movement in the price, or how a firm's (or market's) decisions on supply are affected by changes in wage rates or production techniques or some other factor. Note that in these examples, the focus of attention is on decision-taking by individuals and firms in a single industry, while interactions between this industry and the rest of the economy are ignored: in short, this is what economists call a 'partial analysis'.

In reality, of course, all sectors of the economy are interrelated to some degree. A pay award, for example, in the beer industry (or in a single firm) may set a new pay norm that workers in other industries take up and these pay increases may subsequently influence employment, production and consumer demand in the economy as a whole, which could also have repercussions on the demand for beer. Sometimes such repercussions may be relatively minor and so effectively can be ignored. In such situations the basic microeconomic approach remains valid.

In contrast, macroeconomics recognises the interdependent nature of markets and studies the interaction in the economy as a whole, dealing with such questions as the overall level of employment, the rate of inflation, the percentage growth of output in the economy and many other economy-wide aggregates – exemplified, for instance, by the analysis of international trade in Chapter 16 and by the macroeconomic model discussed below. It should be pointed out, however, that while the distinction between the micro and macro approaches remains useful for analytical purposes, in many instances the two become intertwined. UK Chancellor Nigel Lawson's decision (in 1988) to cut the top rate of income tax from 60 per cent to 40 per cent was presented at the time as a means of boosting the economy by providing incentives for entrepreneurs – clearly a macroeconomic proposition. However, to investigate the validity of the Chancellor's view, it is necessary to lean heavily on microeconomic analysis to see how lower taxation might influence, say, an individual's preference for work over leisure. Given that macroeconomic phenomena are the result of aggregating the behaviour of individual firms and consumers, this is obviously a common situation and one which is useful to bear in mind in any study of either the firm or the economy as a whole.

The 'flows' of economic activity

Economic activity can be portrayed as a flow of economic resources into firms (i.e. productive organisations), which are used to produce output for consumption, and a corresponding flow of payments from firms to the providers of those resources, who use them primarily to purchase the goods and services produced. These flows of resources, production, income and expenditure accordingly represent the fundamental activities of an economy at work. Figure 5.3 illustrates the flow of resources and of goods and services in the economy – what economists describe as **real flows**.

In effect, firms use economic resources to produce goods and services, which are consumed by private individuals (private domestic consumption) or government (government consumption) or by overseas purchasers (foreign consumption) or by other firms (capital formation). This consumption gives rise to a flow of expenditures that represents an income for firms, which they use to purchase further resources in order to produce further output for consumption. This flow of income and expenditures is shown in Figure 5.4.

Figure 5.3   'Real flows' in the economy

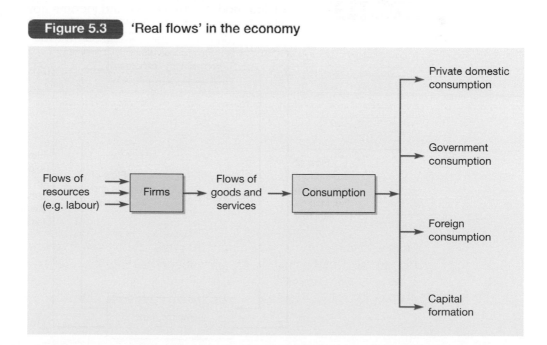

web link

The CFI model is also discussed at
www.bized.ac.uk/learn/economics/macro/notes/income.htm

Figure 5.4 Income flows in the economy

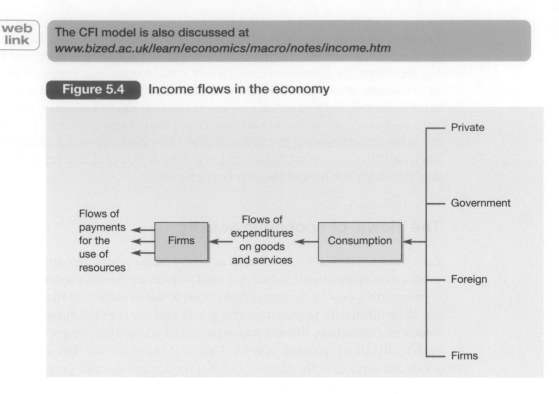

The interrelationship between **income flows** and real flows can be seen by combining the two diagrams into one, which for the sake of simplification assumes only two groups operate in the economy: firms as producers and users of resources, and private individuals as consumers and providers of those resources (see Figure 5.5). Real flows are shown by the arrows moving in an anti-clockwise direction, income flows by the arrows flowing in a clockwise direction.

Figure 5.5 A simplified model of real flows and income flows

Despite a degree of over-simplification, the model of the economy illustrated in Figure 5.5 is a useful analytical tool which highlights some vitally important aspects of economic activity which are of direct relevance to the study of business. The model shows, for example, that:

1 Income flows around the economy, passing from households to firms and back to households and on to firms, and so on, and these income flows have corresponding real flows of resources, goods and services.

2 What constitutes an income to one group (e.g. firms) represents an expenditure to another (e.g. households), indicating that income generation in the economy is related to spending on consumption of goods and services and on resources (e.g. the use of labour).

3 The output of firms must be related to expenditure by households on goods and services, which in turn is related to the income the latter receive from supplying resources.

4 The use of resources (including the number of jobs created in the economy) must also be related to expenditure by households on consumption, given that resources are used to produce output for sale to households.

5 Levels of income, output, expenditure and employment in the economy are, in effect, interrelated.

From the point of view of firms, it is clear from the model that their fortunes are intimately connected with the spending decisions of households and any changes in the level of spending can have repercussions for business activity at the micro as well as the macro level. In the late 1980s, for instance, the British economy went into recession, largely as a result of a reduction in the level of consumption that was brought about by a combination of high interest rates, a growing burden of debt from previous bouts of consumer spending, and a decline in demand from some overseas markets also suffering from recession. While many businesses managed to survive the recession, either by drawing from their reserves or slimming down their operations, large numbers of firms went out of business, as orders fell and costs began to exceed revenue. As a result, output in the economy fell, unemployment grew, investment by firms declined, and house prices fell to a point where some houseowners owed more on their mortgage than the value of their property (known as 'negative equity'). The combined effect of these outcomes was to further depress demand, as individuals became either unwilling or unable to increase spending and as firms continued to shed labour and to hold back on investment. By late 1992, few real signs of growth in the economy could be detected, unemployment stood at almost 3 million, and business confidence remained persistently low.

The gradual recovery of the British economy from mid-1993 – brought about by a return in consumer confidence in the wake of a cut in interest rates – further emphasises the key link between consumption and entrepreneurial activity highlighted in the model. Equally, it shows, as did the discussion on the recession, that a variety of factors can affect spending (e.g. government policy on interest rates) and that spending by households is only one type of consumption in the real economy. In order to gain a clearer view of how the economy works and why changes occur over time, it is necessary to refine the basic model by incorporating a number of other key variables influencing economic activity. These variables – which include savings, investment spending, government spending, taxation and overseas trade – are discussed below.

Changes in economic activity

The level of spending by consumers on goods and services produced by indigenous firms is influenced by a variety of factors. For a start, most households pay tax on income earned, which has the effect of reducing the level of income available for consumption. Added to this, some consumers prefer to save (i.e. not spend) a proportion of their income or to spend it on imported products, both of which mean that the income of domestic firms is less than it would have been had the income been spent with them. Circumstances such as these represent what economists call a **leakage** (or **withdrawal**) from the **circular flow of income** and help to explain why the revenue of businesses can fluctuate over time (see Figure 5.6).

At the same time as such 'leakages' are occurring, additional forms of spending in the economy are helping to boost the potential income of domestic firms. Savings by some consumers are often borrowed by firms to spend on investment in capital equipment or plant or premises (known as investment spending) and this generates income for firms producing capital goods. Similarly, governments use taxation to spend on the provision of public goods and services (public or government expenditure) and overseas buyers purchase products produced by indigenous firms (export spending). Together, these additional forms of spending represent an **injection** of income into the circular flow (see Figure 5.7).

Figure 5.6   The circular flow of income with 'leakages'

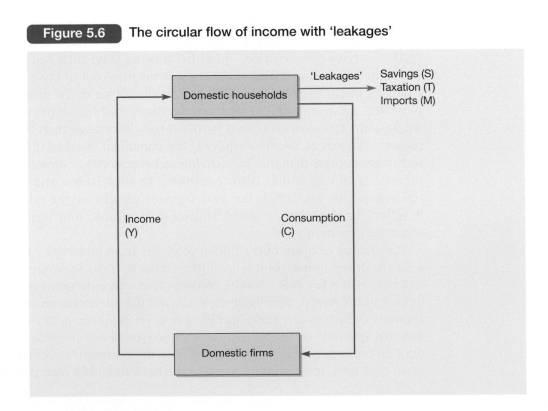

Figure 5.7   The circular flow of income with 'injections' added

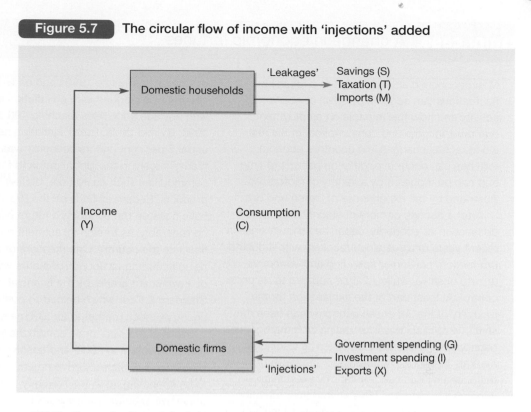

While the revised model of the economy illustrated in Figure 5.7 is still highly simplified (e.g. consumers also borrow savings to spend on consumption or imports; firms also save and buy imports; governments also invest in capital projects), it demonstrates quite clearly that fluctuations in the level of economic activity are the result of changes in a number of variables, many of which are outside the control of firms or governments. Some of these changes are autonomous (i.e. spontaneous), as in the case of an increased demand for imports, while others may be deliberate or overt, as when the government decides to increase its own spending or to reduce taxation in order to stimulate demand. Equally, from time to time an economy may be subject to 'external shocks', such as the onset of recession among its principal trading partners or a significant price rise in a key commodity (e.g. oil price rises in 2007/8), which can have an important effect on internal income flows. Taken together, these and other changes help to explain why demand for goods and services constantly fluctuates and why changes occur not only in an economy's capacity to produce output, but also in its structure and performance over time.

It is important to recognise that where changes in spending do occur, these invariably have consequences for the economy that go beyond the initial 'injection' or 'withdrawal' of income. For example, a decision by government to increase spending on infrastructure would benefit the firms involved in the various projects and some of the additional income they receive would undoubtedly be spent on hiring labour. The additional workers employed would have more income to spend on consumption and this would boost the income for firms producing consumer goods, which in turn may hire more staff, generating further consumption and so on. In short, the initial increase in spending by government will have additional effects on income and spending in the economy, as the extra spending circulates

mini case   A change in economic fortunes

Macroeconomic analysis helps to explain how fluctuations can occur in the level of economic activity and how this impacts on employment, outcome, income and consumption. In the real world, actual changes in a country's economic fortunes can occur over differing periods of time and can be triggered by a variety of factors, as illustrated by the experiences of Japan and Brazil.

After a decade or more of stagnation and deflation in its economy, Japan has shown signs in recent years of a sustained recovery with industrial production, consumer spending and economic growth positive, while inflation appears to be under control. At least part of the explanation for the recovery of the Japanese economy has been the shift in emphasis towards trading with the booming economies in Asia and away from its traditional markets in the US. According to Japanese officials, the economy has become far more stable as Japanese businesses have shifted their attention towards trade with countries such as China, where annual rates of economic growth are on average around 10 per cent.

Brazil, too, has shown that, over time, even apparently intractable economic difficulties can be overcome. In the late 1980s and early 1990s the country was plagued with an inflation problem, with average price rises reaching 490 per cent by 1993. By mid-2008, Brazil's inflation rate was under 5 per cent and its economy was booming, thanks largely to the global demand for commodities such as iron ore, biofuels and food products. Recent oil finds off the Brazilian coast have boosted the economy's future prospects considerably, as foreign investment continues to flow into the country. One measure of the country's rising international economic status was the award of 'investment grade' by the financial rating agency Standard & Poor which helped to push the country's stock market to an all-time high.

While global economic conditions (e.g. the global downturn in 2008) and unsolved economic problems (e.g. Japan's government debt) appear to be impacting upon the recovery process, what these two examples illustrate is that improvements in an economy's performance often take a considerable time. This fact is not always captured well in economists' models of how the macroeconomy operates.

from households to firms and back again. Economists refer to this as the **multiplier effect** to emphasise the reverberative consequences of any increase or decrease in spending by consumers, firms, governments or overseas buyers.

Multiple increases in income and consumption can also give rise to an 'accelerator effect', which is the term used to describe a change in investment spending by firms as a result of a change in consumer spending. In the example above it is possible that the increase in consumption caused by the increase in government spending may persuade some firms to invest in more stock and capital equipment to meet increased consumer demands. Demand for capital goods will therefore rise, and this could cause further increases in the demand for industrial products (e.g. components, machinery) and also for consumer goods, as firms seek to increase their output to meet the changing market conditions. Should consumer spending fall, a reverse accelerator may occur and the same would apply to the multiplier as the reduction in consumption reverberates through the economy and causes further cuts in both consumption and investment. As Peter Donaldson has suggested, everything in the economy affects everything else; the economy is dynamic, interactive and mobile and is far more complex than implied by the model used in the analysis above.[1]

Government and the macroeconomy: objectives

Notwithstanding the complexities of the real economy, the link between business activity and spending is clear to see. This spending, as indicated above, comes from consumers, firms, governments and external sources and collectively can be said to represent total demand in the economy for goods and services. Economists frequently indicate this with the following notation:

Aggregate Monetary Demand = Consumer spending + Investment spending
+ Government spending + Export spending
– Import spending

or
$$AMD = C + I + G + X - M$$

Within this equation, consumer spending (C) is regarded as by far the most important factor in determining the level of total demand.

While economists might disagree about what are the most significant influences on the component elements of AMD, it is widely accepted that governments have a crucial role to play in shaping demand, not only in their own sector but also on the market side of the economy. Government policies on spending and taxation, or on interest rates, clearly have both direct and indirect influences on the behaviour of individuals and firms, which can affect both the demand and supply side of the economy in a variety of ways. Underlying these policies are a number of key objectives which are pursued by government as a prerequisite to a healthy economy and which help to guide the choice of policy options. Understanding the broad choice of policies available to government, and the objectives associated with them, is of prime importance to students of the business environment.

Most governments appear to have a number of key economic objectives, the most important of which are normally the control of inflation, the pursuit of economic growth, a reduction in unemployment, the achievement of an acceptable balance of payments situation, controlling public (i.e. government) borrowing, and a relatively stable exchange rate.

Controlling inflation

Inflation is usually defined as an upward and persistent movement in the general level of prices over a given period of time; it can also be characterised as a fall in the value of money. For governments of all political complexions reducing such movements to a minimum is seen as a primary economic objective (e.g. the current UK government's target for 'underlying inflation' was 2.5 per cent. Under the new Consumer Prices Index the target is now 2 per cent).

Monitoring trends in periodic price movements tends to take a number of forms; in the UK these have included:

1 The use of a **Retail Price Index (RPI)**, which measures how an average family's spending on goods and services is affected by price changes. The RPI has traditionally been the measure used for **headline inflation** in the UK and includes mortgage interest payments.

2 An examination of the **underlying rate of inflation**, which excludes the effects of mortgage payments (known as RPIX in the UK).

3 Measuring **factory gate prices**, to indicate likely future changes in consumer prices.

4 Comparing domestic inflation rates with those of the United Kingdom's chief overseas competitors, as an indication of the international competitiveness of UK firms.

With regard to the latter, the UK now uses a new measure of inflation known as the **Consumer Prices Index (CPI)** to allow for a more direct comparison of the inflation rate in the UK with that of the rest of Europe. The CPI excludes a number of items that have historically been part of the RPIX, especially items relating to housing costs (e.g. mortgage interest payments and council tax).

In addition, changes in **monetary aggregates**, which measure the amount of money (and therefore potential spending power) in circulation in the economy, and movements of exchange rates (especially a depreciating currency – *see* Chapter 16) are also seen as a guide to possible future price increases, as their effects work through the economy.

Explanations as to why prices tend to rise over time vary considerably, but broadly speaking fall into two main categories. First, supply-siders tend to focus on rising production costs – particularly wages, energy and imported materials – as a major reason for inflation, with firms passing on increased costs to the consumer in the form of higher wholesale and/or retail prices. Second, demand-siders, in contrast, tend to emphasise the importance of excessive demand in the economy, brought about, for example, by tax cuts, cheaper borrowing or excessive government spending, which encourages firms to take advantage of the consumer's willingness to spend money by increasing their prices. Where indigenous firms are unable to satisfy all the additional demand, the tendency is for imports to increase. This may not only cause further price rises, particularly if imported goods are more expensive or if exchange rate movements become unfavourable, but also can herald a deteriorating balance of payments situation and difficult trading conditions for domestic businesses.

Government concern with inflation – which crosses both party and state boundaries – reflects the fact that rising price levels can have serious consequences for the economy in general and for businesses in particular, especially if a country's domestic inflation rates are significantly higher than those of its main competitors. In markets where price is an important determinant of demand, rising prices may result in some businesses losing sales, and this can affect turnover and may ultimately affect employment if firms reduce their labour force in order to reduce their costs. Added to this, the uncertainty caused by a difficult trading environment may make some businesses unwilling to invest in new plant and equipment, particularly if interest rates are high and if inflation looks unlikely to fall for some time. Such a response, while understandable, is unlikely to improve a firm's future competitiveness or its ability to exploit any possible increases in demand as market conditions change.

Rising prices may also affect businesses by encouraging employees to seek higher wages in order to maintain or increase their living standards. Where firms agree to such wage increases, the temptation, of course, is to pass this on to the consumer in the form of a price rise, especially if demand looks unlikely to be affected to any great extent. Should this process occur generally in the economy, the result may be a **wages/prices inflationary spiral**, in which wage increases push up prices which push up wage increases which further push up prices and so on. From an international competitive point of view, such an occurrence, if allowed to continue unchecked, could be disastrous for both firms and the economy. Thankfully, such an occurence tends to be relatively uncommon in most economies but, as the problems in Zimbabwe illustrate, hyperinflation can have disastrous consequences for a country's economy and its population (in mid-2008, for example, annual inflation in Zimbabwe was estimated at around 40 million per cent!).

Economic growth

Growth is an objective shared by governments and organisations alike. For governments, the aim is usually to achieve steady and sustained levels of non-inflationary growth, preferably led by exports (i.e. export-led growth). Such growth is normally indicated by annual increases in **real national income** or **gross domestic product** (where 'real' = allowing for inflation, and 'gross domestic product (GDP)' = the economy's annual output of goods and services measured in monetary terms).[2] To compensate for changes in the size of the population, growth rates tend to be expressed in terms of real national income per capita (i.e. real GDP divided by population).

Exactly what constitutes desirable levels of growth is difficult to say, except in very broad terms. If given a choice, governments would basically prefer:

- steady levels of real growth (e.g. 3–4 per cent p.a.), rather than annual increases in output which vary widely over the business cycle;
- growth rates higher than those of one's chief competitors; and
- growth based on investment in technology and on increased export sales, rather than on excessive government spending or current consumption.

It is worth remembering that, when measured on a monthly or quarterly basis, increases in output can occur at a declining rate and GDP growth can become negative. In the United Kingdom, for example, a **recession** is said to exist following two consecutive quarters of negative GDP.

From a business point of view, the fact that increases in output are related to increases in consumption suggests that economic growth is good for business prospects and hence for investment and employment, and by and large this is the case. The rising living standards normally associated with such growth may, however, encourage increased consumption of imported goods and services at the expense of indigenous producers, to a point where some domestic firms are forced out of business and the economy's manufacturing base becomes significantly reduced (often called **deindustrialisation**). Equally, if increased consumption is based largely on excessive state spending, the potential gains for businesses may be offset by the need to increase interest rates to fund that spending (where government borrowing is involved) and by the tendency of government demands for funding to **crowd out** the private sector's search for investment capital. In such cases, the short-term benefits from government-induced consumption may be more than offset by the medium- and long-term problems for the economy that are likely to arise.

Where growth prospects for the economy look good, business confidence tends to increase, and this is often reflected in increased levels of investment and stock holding and ultimately in levels of employment. In Britain, for example, the monthly and quarterly surveys by the Confederation of British Industry (CBI) provide a good indication of how output, investment and stock levels change at different points of the business cycle and these are generally seen as a good indication of future business trends, as interpreted by entrepreneurs. Other indicators – including the state of the housing market and construction generally – help to provide a guide to the current and future state of the economy, including its prospects for growth in the short and medium term.

> **web link** The CBI's website address is *www.cbi.org.uk*

Reducing unemployment

In most democratic states the goal of **full employment** is no longer part of the political agenda; instead government pronouncements on employment tend to focus on job creation and maintenance and on developing the skills appropriate to future demands. The consensus seems to be that in technologically advanced market-based economies some unemployment is inevitable and that the basic aim should be to reduce unemployment to a level which is both politically and socially acceptable.

As with growth and inflation, unemployment levels tend to be measured at regular intervals (e.g. monthly, quarterly, annually) and the figures are often adjusted to take into account seasonal influences (e.g. school-leavers entering the job market). In addition, the statistics usually provide information on trends in long-term unemployment, areas of skill shortage and on international comparisons, as well as sectoral changes within the economy. All of these indicators provide clues to the current state of the economy and to the prospects for businesses in the coming months and years, but need to be used with care. Unemployment, for example, tends to continue rising for a time even when a recession is over; equally, it is not uncommon for government definitions of unemployment to change or for international unemployment data to be based on different criteria.

The broader social and economic consequences of high levels of unemployment are well documented: it is a waste of resources, it puts pressure on the public services and on the Exchequer (e.g. by reducing tax yields and increasing public expenditure on welfare provision), and it is frequently linked with growing social and health problems. Its implication for businesses, however, tends to be less clear-cut. On the one hand, a high level of unemployment implies a pool of labour available for firms seeking workers (though not necessarily with the right skills), generally at wage levels lower than when a shortage of labour occurs. On the other hand, it can also give rise to a fall in overall demand for goods and services which could exacerbate any existing deflationary forces in the economy, causing further unemployment and with it further reductions in demand. Where this occurs, economists tend to describe it as **cyclical unemployment** (i.e. caused by a general deficiency in demand) in order to differentiate it from unemployment caused by a deficiency in demand for the goods produced by a particular industry (**structural unemployment**) or by the introduction of new technology which replaces labour (**technological unemployment**).

A favourable balance of payments

A country's **balance of payments** is essentially the net balance of credits (earnings) and debits (payments) arising from its international trade over a given period of time (see Chapter 16). Where credits exceed debits a balance of payments surplus exists; the opposite is described as a deficit. Understandably governments tend to prefer either equilibrium in the balance of payments or surpluses, rather than deficits. However, it would be fair to say that for some governments facing persistent balance of payments deficits, a sustained reduction in the size of the deficit may be regarded as signifying a 'favourable' balance of payments situation.

Like other economic indicators, the balance of payments statistics come in a variety of forms and at different levels of disaggregation, allowing useful comparisons to be made not only on a country's comparative trading performance, but also on the international competitiveness of particular industries and commodity groups or on the development or decline of specific external markets. Particular emphasis tends to be given to the balance of payments on current account, which measures imports and exports of goods and services and is thus seen as an indicator of the competitiveness of an economy's firms and industries. Sustained current account surpluses tend to suggest favourable trading conditions, which can help to boost growth, increase employment and investment and create a general feeling of confidence amongst the business community. They may also give rise to surpluses which domestic firms can use to finance overseas lending and investment, thus helping to generate higher levels of corporate foreign earnings in future years.

While it does not follow that a sustained current account deficit is inevitably bad for the country concerned, it often implies structural problems in particular sectors of its economy or possibly an exchange rate which favours importers rather than exporters. Many observers believe, for instance, that the progressive decline of Britain's visible trading position after 1983 was an indication of the growing uncompetitiveness of its firms, particularly those producing finished manufactured goods for consumer markets at home and abroad. By the same token, Japan's current account trade surplus of around $120 billion in late 1995 was portrayed as a sign of the cut-throat competition of Japanese firms, particularly those involved in producing cars, electrical and electronic products, and photographic equipment.

Controlling public borrowing

Governments raise large amounts of revenue annually, mainly through taxation, and use this income to spend on a wide variety of public goods and services (see below). Where annual revenue exceeds government spending, a budget surplus occurs and the excess is often used to repay past debt (formerly known in the United Kingdom as the 'public sector debt repayment' or PSDR). The accumulated debt of past and present governments represents a country's **National Debt**. In the UK this stood at over £500 billion in 2007 which was approximately 38 per cent of GDP.

In practice, most governments often face annual budget deficits rather than budget surpluses and hence have a 'public sector borrowing requirement' or PSBR (now known in the UK as **public sector net borrowing** or **PSNB**). While such deficits are not inevitably a problem, in the same way that a small personal over-draft is not necessarily critical for an individual, large scale and persistent deficits are generally seen as a sign of an economy facing current and future difficulties which require urgent government action. The overriding concern over high levels of public borrowing tends to be focused on:

1 Its impact on interest rates, given that higher interest rates tend to be needed to attract funds from private sector uses to public sector uses.
2 The impact of high interest rates on consumption and investment and hence on the prospects of businesses.
3 The danger of the public sector 'crowding out' the private sector's search for funds for investment.
4 The opportunity cost of debt interest, especially in terms of other forms of public spending.
5 The general lack of confidence in the markets about the government's ability to control the economy and the likely effect this might have on inflation, growth and the balance of payments.
6 The need to meet the 'convergence criteria' laid down at Maastricht for entry to the single currency (e.g. central government debt no higher than 3 per cent of GDP).

The consensus seems to be that controlling public borrowing is best tackled by restraining the rate of growth of public spending rather than by increasing revenue through changes in taxation, since the latter could depress demand.

A stable exchange rate

A country's currency has two values: an internal value and an external value. Internally, its value is expressed in terms of the goods and services it can buy and hence it is affected by changes in domestic prices. Externally, its value is expressed as an **exchange rate** which governs how much of another country's currency it can purchase (e.g. £1 = $2 or £1 = €1.20). Since foreign trade normally involves an exchange of currencies, fluctuations in the external value of a currency will influence the price of imports and exports and hence can affect the trading prospects for business, as well as a country's balance of payments and its rate of inflation (see Chapter 16).

On the whole, governments and businesses involved in international trade tend to prefer exchange rates to remain relatively stable, because of the greater degree of certainty this brings to the trading environment; it also tends to make overseas investors more confident that their funds are likely to hold their value. To this extent, schemes which seek to fix exchange rates within predetermined levels (e.g. the ERM), or which encourage the use of a common currency (e.g. the euro), tend to have the support of the business community, which prefers predictability to uncertainty where trading conditions are concerned.

mini case | Digging in for the long term

For firms engaged in international trade, the strength of the currency (i.e. the exchange rate) is an important consideration (see e.g. Chapter 16). As the value of one currency changes against other currencies, this usually alters the price of imported/exported products and this can make them more/less attractive to potential customers. To mitigate the impact of exchange rate changes, some firms engage in a process known as hedging, which basically involves trying to reduce or eliminate exchange rate risks, for example by buying a proportion of a currency forward (i.e. before it is needed) at an agreed price. An alternative strategy is to consider producing the product in different locations (e.g. setting up manufacturing facilities in other countries) which can offset some of the impact of currency fluctuations, as well as providing other potential benefits to a business.

A good example of the latter approach is provided by JCB, the UK-owned private company famous for its yellow construction equipment (e.g. diggers). In the 1990s, the company's business was mainly based in the UK and parts of western Europe, but faced with a limited market and a strengthening pound which made exporting difficult, the firm decided to seek a global presence by investing in manufacturing abroad. Focusing first on the US, JCB built a plant in Georgia in the late 1990s to exploit the US market; this was followed by further plants in Sao Paulo in Brazil and new plants in India near Mumbai. It also acquired a German construction firm in 2005 and opened a further factory near Shanghai in 2006, thereby adding to its global reach.

In addition to the potential currency benefits of operating in different countries, JCB has also gained a number of other advantages, including establishing a global brand name, access to low-cost suppliers and to developing markets, and reducing freight costs and tariff barriers. Globalisation, in short, can offer businesses many 'opportunities', but we must not forget that it can also give rise to substantial 'threats' at the corporate level, not least the danger of low-cost competitors invading one's own markets.

Government and the macroeconomy: policies

Governments throughout Europe and beyond play various key roles in their respective economies. These include the following functions:

- consumer of resources (e.g. employer, landowner);
- supplier of resources (e.g. infrastructure, information);
- consumer of goods and services (e.g. government spending);
- supplier of goods and services (e.g. nationalised industries);
- regulator of business activity (e.g. employment laws, consumer laws);
- regulator of the economy (e.g. fiscal and monetary policies); and
- redistributor of income and wealth (e.g. taxation system).

The extent of these roles, and their impact on the economy in general and on business in particular, varies from country to country as well as over time.

Despite the economic significance of these roles, in most market-based economies democratically elected governments prefer levels and patterns of production and consumption to be determined largely by market forces, with a minimum of government interference. This approach is exemplified by the philosophical stance of the UK and

US governments in the 1980s, that became colloquially known as 'Thatcherism' (UK) and 'Reaganomics' (USA). At the same time, the recognition that market forces alone are unable to guarantee that an economy will automatically achieve the objectives established by governments has meant that state intervention – to curb inflation, encourage growth, reduce unemployment, correct a balance of payments or budgetary problem or restore currency stability – invariably occurs to some degree in all countries. In broad terms, this intervention usually takes three main forms, described as fiscal policy, monetary policy and direct controls. These policy instruments – or 'instrumental variables' – and their effects on the business community are discussed below.

Fiscal policy

As indicated above, each year governments raise and spend huge amounts of money. The UK government's estimates for 2008, for example, suggest that **government spending** will be about £618 billion and is to be allocated in the manner illustrated in Figure 5.8. This spending will be funded mainly from **taxation (direct and indirect)**, and national insurance contributions (see Figure 5.9). The PSNB is estimated at £43 billion.

Figure 5.8 The allocation of UK government spending, 2008 budget

£ billion

Social protection	169
Health	111
Housing and environment	23
Defence	33
Education	82
Public order + safety	33
Industry, agriculture, employment and training	22
Transport	21
Debt interest	31
Other spending	94

Total spending: £618 bn

Source: Adapted from Budget Statement, 2008.

| Figure 5.9 | Sources of government revenue, 2008 budget |

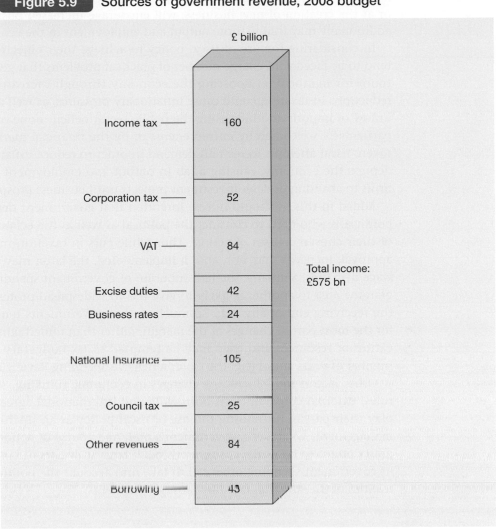

£ billion

Income tax ——— 160

Corporation tax ——— 52

VAT ——— 84

Excise duties ——— 42

Business rates ——— 24

National Insurance ——— 105

Council tax ——— 25

Other revenues ——— 84

Borrowing ——— 43

Total income:
£575 bn

Source: Adapted from Budget Statement, 2008.

Fiscal policy involves the use of changes in government spending and taxation to influence the level and composition of aggregate demand in the economy and, given the amounts involved, this clearly has important implications for business. Elementary circular flow analysis suggests, for instance, that reductions in taxation and/or increases in government spending will inject additional income into the economy and will, via the multiplier effect, increase the demand for goods and services, with favourable consequences for business. Reductions in government spending and/or increases in taxation will have the opposite effect, depressing business prospects and probably discouraging investment and causing a rise in unemployment.

Apart from their overall impact on aggregate demand, fiscal changes can be used to achieve specific objectives, some of which will be of direct or indirect benefit to the business community. Reductions in taxes on company profits and/or increases in tax allowances for investment in capital equipment can be used to encourage business to increase investment spending, hence boosting the income of firms producing industrial products and causing some additional spending on consumption.

Similarly, increased government spending targeted at firms involved in exporting, or at the creation of new business, will encourage increased business activity and additionally may lead to more output and employment in the economy.

In considering the use of fiscal policy to achieve their objectives, governments tend to be faced with a large number of practical problems that generally limit their room for manoeuvre. Boosting the economy through increases in spending or reductions in taxation could cause inflationary pressures, as well as encouraging an inflow of imports and increasing the public sector deficit, none of which would be particularly welcomed by entrepreneurs or by the financial markets. By the same token, fiscal attempts to restrain demand in order to reduce inflation will generally depress the economy, causing a fall in output and employment and encouraging firms to abandon or defer investment projects until business prospects improve.

Added to this, it should not be forgotten that government decision-makers are politicians who need to consider the political as well as the economic implications of their chosen courses of action. Thus while cuts in taxation may receive public approval, increases may not, and, if implemented, the latter may encourage higher wage demands. Similarly, the redistribution of government spending from one programme area to another is likely to give rise to widespread protests from those on the receiving end of any cuts; so much so that governments tend to be restricted for the most part to changes at the margin, rather than undertaking a radical reallocation of resources and they may be tempted to fix budgetary allocations for a number of years ahead (e.g. the Comprehensive Spending Review in the UK).

Other factors too – including changes in economic thinking, self-imposed fiscal rules, external constraints on borrowing and international agreements – can also play their part in restraining the use of fiscal policy as an instrument of demand management, whatever a government's preferred course of action may be. Simple prescriptions to boost the economy through large-scale cuts in taxation or increases in government spending often fail to take into account the political and economic realities of the situation faced by most governments.

Monetary policy

Monetary policy seeks to influence monetary variables such as the money supply or rates of interest in order to regulate the economy. While the supply of money and interest rates (i.e. the cost of borrowing) are interrelated, it is convenient to consider them separately.

As far as changes in **interest rates** are concerned, these clearly have implications for business activity, as circular flow analysis demonstrates. Lower interest rates not only encourage firms to invest as the cost of borrowing falls, but also encourage consumption as disposable incomes rise (predominantly through the mortgage effect) and as the cost of loans and overdrafts decreases. Such increased consumption tends to be an added spur to investment, particularly if inflation rates (and, therefore **'real' interest rates**) are low and this can help to boost the economy in the short term, as well as improving the supply side in the longer term.[3]

Raising interest rates tends to have the opposite effect – causing a fall in consumption as mortgages and other prices rise, and deferring investment because of the additional cost of borrowing and the decline in business confidence as consumer spending falls. If interest rates remain persistently high, the encouragement given to savers and the discouragement given to borrowers and spenders may help to generate a recession, characterised by falling output, income, spending and employment and by increasing business failure.

Changes in the **money stock** (especially credit) affect the capacity of individuals and firms to borrow and, therefore, to spend. Increases in money supply are generally related to increases in spending and this tends to be good for business prospects, particularly if interest rates are falling as the money supply rises. Restrictions on monetary growth normally work in the opposite direction, especially if such restrictions help to generate increases in interest rates which feed through to both consumption and investment, both of which will tend to decline.

As in the case of fiscal policy, government is usually able to manipulate monetary variables in a variety of ways, including taking action in the money markets to influence interest rates and controlling its own spending to influence monetary growth. Once again, however, circumstances tend to dictate how far and in what way government is free to operate. Attempting to boost the economy by allowing the money supply to grow substantially, for instance, threatens to cause inflationary pressures and to increase spending on imports, both of which run counter to government objectives and do little to assist domestic firms. Similarly, policies to boost consumption and investment through lower interest rates, while welcomed generally by industry, offer no guarantee that any additional spending will be on domestically produced goods and services, and also tend to make the financial markets nervous about government commitments to control inflation in the longer term (see below, 'The role of the central bank').

This nervousness among market dealers reflects the fact that in modern market economies a government's policies on interest rates and monetary growth cannot be taken in isolation from those of its major trading partners and this operates as an important constraint on government action. The fact is that a reduction in interest rates to boost output and growth in an economy also tends to be reflected in the exchange rate; this usually falls as foreign exchange dealers move funds into those currencies which yield a better return and which also appear a safer investment if the market believes a government is abandoning its counterinflationary policy. As the UK government found in the early 1990s, persistently high rates of interest in Germany severely restricted its room for manoeuvre on interest rates for fear of the consequences for sterling if relative interest rates got too far out of line.

Direct controls

Fiscal and monetary policies currently represent the chief policy instruments used in modern market economies and hence they have been discussed in some detail. Governments, however, also use a number of other weapons from time to time in their attempts to achieve their macroeconomic objectives. Such weapons, which are designed essentially to achieve a specific objective – such as limiting imports or controlling wage increases – tend to be known as **direct controls**. Examples of such policies include:

- *Incomes policies*, which seek to control inflationary pressures by influencing the rate at which wages and salaries rise.
- *Import controls*, which attempt to improve a country's balance of payments situation, by reducing either the supply of, or the demand for, imported goods and services (see Chapter 16).
- *Regional and urban policies*, which are aimed at alleviating urban and regional problems, particularly differences in income, output, employment, and local and regional decline (see Chapter 13).

A brief discussion of some of these policy instruments is found at various points in the text below. Students wishing to study these in more detail are recommended to consult the books referred to at the end of this chapter.

The role of financial institutions

Interactions in the macroeconomy between governments, businesses and consumers take place within an institutional environment that includes a large number of financial intermediaries. These range from banks and building societies to pension funds, insurance companies, investment trusts and issuing houses, all of which provide a number of services of both direct and indirect benefit to businesses. As part of the financial system within a market-based economy, these institutions fulfil a vital role in channelling funds from those able and willing to lend, to those individuals and organisations wishing to borrow in order to consume or invest. It is appropriate to consider briefly this role of financial intermediation and the supervision exercised over the financial system by the central bank, before concluding the chapter with a review of important international economic institutions.

Elements of the financial system

A financial system tends to have three main elements:

1 *Lenders and borrowers* – these may be individuals, organisations or governments.
2 *Financial institutions*, of various kinds, which act as intermediaries between lenders and borrowers and which manage their own asset portfolios in the interest of their shareholders and/or depositors.
3 *Financial markets*, in which lending and borrowing takes place through the transfer of money and/or other types of asset, including paper assets such as shares and stock.

Financial institutions, as indicated above, comprise a wide variety of organisations, many of which are public companies with shareholders. Markets include the markets for short-term funds of various types (usually termed **money markets**) and those for long-term finance for both the private and public sectors (usually called the **capital market**). **Stock exchanges** normally lie at the centre of the latter, and constitute an important market for existing securities issued by both companies and government.

The vital role played by **financial intermediaries** in the operation of the financial system is illustrated in Figure 5.10 and reflects the various benefits which derive from using an intermediary rather than lending direct to a borrower (e.g. creating a large pool of savings; spreading risk; transferring short-term lending into longer-term borrowing; providing various types of funds transfer services). Lenders on the whole prefer low risk, high returns, flexibility and liquidity, while borrowers prefer to minimise the cost of borrowing and to use the funds in a way that is best suited to their needs. Companies, for example, may borrow to finance stock or work-in-progress or to meet short-term debts and such borrowing may need to be as flexible as possible. Alternatively, they may wish to borrow in order to replace plant and equipment or to buy new premises – borrowing which needs to be over a much longer term and which hopefully will yield a rate of return which makes the use of the funds and the cost of borrowing worthwhile.

The process of channelling funds from lenders to borrowers often gives rise to paper claims, which are generated either by the financial intermediary issuing a claim to the lender (e.g. when a bank borrows by issuing a certificate of deposit) or by the borrower issuing a claim to the financial intermediary (e.g. when government sells stock to a financial institution). These paper claims represent a liability to the issuer and an asset to the holder and can be traded on a secondary market (i.e. a market for existing securities), according to the needs of the individual or organisation holding the paper claim. At any point, financial intermediaries tend to hold a wide range of such assets (claims on borrowers), which they buy or sell ('manage') in order to yield a profit and/or improve their liquidity position. Decisions of this kind, taken on a daily basis, invariably affect the position of investors (e.g. shareholders) and customers (e.g. depositors) and can, under certain circumstances, have serious consequences for the financial intermediary and its stakeholders (e.g. the bad debts faced by western banks in the late 1980s and early 1990s).

Figure 5.10   **The role of financial intermediaries**

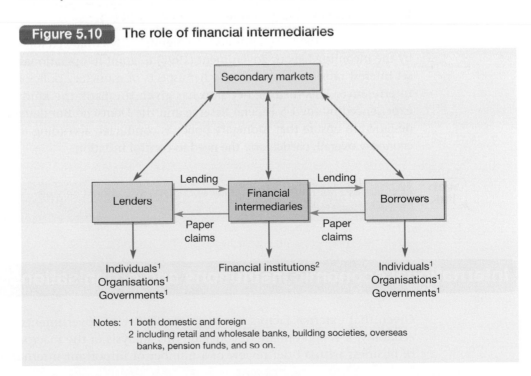

Notes: 1 both domestic and foreign
         2 including retail and wholesale banks, building societies, overseas
         banks, pension funds, and so on.

Given the element of risk, it is perhaps not surprising that some financial institutions tend to be conservative in their attitude towards lending on funds deposited with them, especially in view of their responsibilities to their various stakeholders. UK retail banks, for instance, have a long-standing preference for financing industry's working capital rather than investment spending, and hence the latter has tended to be financed largely by internally generated funds (e.g. retained profits) or by share issues. In comparison, banks in Germany, France, the United States and Japan tend to be more ready to meet industry's medium- and longer-term needs and are often directly involved in regular discussions with their clients concerning corporate strategy, in contrast to the arm's length approach favoured by many of their UK counterparts.[4]

The role of the central bank

A critical element in a country's financial system is its **central** or **state bank**; in the United Kingdom this is the Bank of England. Like most of its overseas counterparts, the Bank of England exercises overall supervision over the banking sector with the aim of maintaining a stable and efficient financial framework as part of its contribution to a healthy economy. Its activities have a significant influence in the financial markets (especially the foreign exchange market, the gilts market and the sterling money market). These activities include the following roles:

- banker to the government;
- banker to the clearing banks;
- manager of the country's foreign reserves;
- manager of the national debt;
- manager of the issue of notes and coins;
- supervisor of the monetary sector; and
- implementer of the government's monetary policy.

In the last case, the Bank's powers were significantly enhanced following the decision by the incoming Labour government (1997) to grant it 'operational independence' to set interest rates and to conduct other aspects of monetary policy free from Treasury interference. This historic decision has given the Bank the kind of independence experienced by the US Federal Reserve and the Deutsche Bundesbank and has been designed to ensure that monetary policy is conducted according to the needs of the economy overall, particularly the need to control inflation.

For further information on the Bank of England you should consult
www.bankofengland.co.uk

International economic institutions and organisations

Given that external factors constrain the ability of governments to regulate their economy, it is appropriate to conclude this analysis of the macroeconomic context of business with a brief review of a number of important international economic institutions and organisations which affect the trading environment. Foremost among these is the European Union, which is examined at length in Chapters 4 and 16. In the discussions below, attention is focused on the International Monetary Fund (IMF), the Organisation for Economic Co-operation and Development (OECD), the European Bank for Reconstruction and Development (EBRD), the World Trade Organisation (WTO) and the World Bank (IBRD).

The International Monetary Fund (IMF)

The IMF is an international organisation currently of 184 member countries. It came into being in 1946 following discussions at Bretton Woods in the USA which sought to agree a world financial order for the post-Second World War period that would avoid the problems associated with the worldwide depression in the inter-war years. In essence, the original role of the institution – which today incorporates most countries in the world – was to provide a pool of foreign currencies from its member states that would be used to smooth out trade imbalances between countries, thereby promoting a structured growth in world trade and encouraging exchange rate stability. In this way, the architects of the Fund believed that the danger of international protectionism would be reduced and that all countries would consequently benefit from the boost given to world trade and the greater stability of the international trading environment.

web link   The IMF's website is *www.imf.org*

While this role as international 'lender of last resort' still exists, the IMF's focus in recent years has tended to switch towards international surveillance and to helping the developing economies with their mounting debt problems and assisting eastern Europe with reconstruction, following the break-up of the Soviet empire.[5] It has also been involved in the past in trying to restore international stability following the global economic turmoil in Asia and elsewhere and some countries would like it to adopt a more enhanced global surveillance role in the wake of the global credit crisis (2008). To some extent its position as an international decision-making body has been diminished by the tendency of the world's leading economic countries to deal with global economic problems outside the IMF's institutional framework. The United States, Japan, Germany, France, Italy, Canada, Britain and Russia now meet regularly as the **Group of Eight (G8)** leading industrial economies to discuss issues of mutual interest (e.g. the environment, eastern Europe). These world economic summits, as they are frequently called, have tended to supersede discussions in the IMF and as a result normally attract greater media attention.

The Organisation for Economic Co-operation and Development (OECD)

The OECD came into being in 1961, but its roots go back to 1948 when the Organisation for European Economic Co-operation (OEEC) was established to co-ordinate the distribution of Marshall Aid to the war-torn economies of western

Europe. Today it comprises 30 members, drawn from the rich industrial countries and including the G7 nations, Australia, New Zealand and most other European states. Collectively, these countries account for less than 20 per cent of the world's population, but produce around two-thirds of its output – hence the tendency of commentators to refer to the OECD as the 'rich man's club'. Currently talks are under way to expand the membership of the Organisation to include other countries such as Chile, Russia and Israel.

 web link   You can access the OECD's website at *www.oecd.org*

In essence the OECD is the main forum in which the governments of the world's leading industrial economies meet to discuss economic matters, particularly questions concerned with promoting stable growth and freer trade and with supporting development in poorer non-member countries. Through its council and committees, and backed by an independent secretariat, the organisation is able to take decisions which set out an agreed view and/or course of action on important social and economic issues of common concern. While it does not have the authority to impose ideas, its influence lies in its capacity for intellectual persuasion, particularly its ability through discussion to promote convergent thinking on international economic problems. To assist in the task, the OECD provides a wide variety of economic data on member countries, using standardised measures for national accounting, unemployment and purchasing-power parities. It is for these data – and especially its economic forecasts and surveys – that the organisation is perhaps best known.

The European Bank for Reconstruction and Development (EBRD)

The aims of the EBRD, which was inaugurated in April 1991, are to facilitate the transformation of the states of central and eastern Europe and beyond from centrally planned to free-market economies and to promote political and economic democracy, respect for human rights and respect for the environment. It is particularly involved with the privatisation process, technical assistance, training and investment in upgrading of the infrastructure and in facilitating economic, legal and financial restructuring. It works in co-operation with its members, private companies and organisations such as the IMF, OECD, the World Bank and the United Nations.

web link   Information on the EBRD can be obtained at *www.ebrd.com*

The World Trade Organisation (WTO)

The World Trade Organisation, which came into being on 1 January 1995, superseded the General Agreement on Tariffs and Trade (the GATT), which dated back to 1947. Like the IMF and the International Bank for Reconstruction and

Development (see below), which were established at the same time, the GATT was part of an attempt to reconstruct the international politico-economic environment in the period after the end of the Second World War. Its replacement by the WTO can be said to mark an attempt to put the question of liberalising world trade higher up the international political agenda.

The WTO can be accessed at *www.wto.org*

With a membership of around 150 states (plus other observers), the WTO is a permanent international organisation charged with the task of liberalising world trade within an agreed legal and institutional framework. In addition it administers and implements a number of multilateral agreements in fields such as agriculture, textiles and services and is responsible for dealing with disputes arising from the Uruguay Round Final Act. It also provides a forum for the debate, negotiation and adjudication of trade problems and in the latter context is said to have a much stronger and quicker trade compliance and enforcement mechanism than existed under the GATT. See also Chapter 16.

The World Bank (IBRD)

Established in 1945, the World Bank (more formally known as the International Bank for Reconstruction and Development or IBRD) is a specialised agency of the United Nations, set up to encourage economic growth in developing countries through the provision of loans and technical assistance. The IBRD currently has over 180 members.

The IBRD can be accessed at *www.worldbank.org* and *http://web.worldbank.org*

The European Investment Bank (EIB)

The European Investment Bank was created in 1958 under the Treaty of Rome and is the financing institution of the European Union. Its main task is to contribute to the integration, balanced development and the economic and social cohesion of EU Member States. Using funds raised on the markets, it finances capital projects which support EU objectives within the European Union and elsewhere. Its interests include environmental schemes, projects relating to transport and energy and support for small and medium-sized enterprises.

For further information on the EIB see *www.eib.org*

Synopsis

Business and economics are inextricably linked. Economics is concerned with the problem of allocating scarce productive resources to alternative uses – a fundamental aspect of business activity. In market-based economies, this problem of resource allocation is largely solved through the operation of free markets, in which price is a vital ingredient. The existence of such markets tends to be associated primarily, though not exclusively, with democratic political regimes.

In all democratic states, government is a key component of the market economy and exercises considerable influence over the level and pattern of business activity – a point illustrated by the use of elementary circular flow analysis. A government's aims for the economy help to shape the policies it uses and these policies have both direct and indirect consequences for business organisations of all kinds.

In examining the economic context in which firms exist, due attention needs to be paid to the influence of a wide range of institutions and organisations, some of which operate at international level. Equally, as markets become more open and business becomes more global, the fortunes of firms in trading economies become increasingly connected and hence subject to fluctuations that go beyond the boundaries of any individual state.

Summary of key points

- Business activity exists in and is affected by the broader macroeconomic environment; it also helps to shape that environment.

- Economics is concerned with how societies allocate scarce economic resources to alternative uses and the 'real costs' of the choices that are made.

- Broadly speaking two main approaches to the problem of resource allocation exist: state planning and the market.

- Most economies in the world are market-based economies which operate through a price mechanism. Within such economies the state also plays a key role in some allocative decisions.

- In market economies economic activity essentially involves 'real flows' and corresponding flows of income and expenditure between producers and consumers.

- Combining these flows into a simple model of the macroeconomy illustrates that income basically flows round the economy in a circular motion.

- Levels of income in the economy are related to levels of output, expenditure and employment.

- Changes in the level of economic activity can be explained by examining changes in one or more of the key economic variables such as consumer spending, saving, government decisions on state spending/taxation and external trade.

- Within the macroeconomy, governments often play a key role in influencing both the levels and patterns of demand in pursuit of their macroeconomic objectives.

- Key government objectives usually include controlling inflation, promoting economic growth, reducing unemployment, and creating a stable macroeconomic environment.

- To pursue these objectives governments use a range of policies, most notably fiscal and monetary policies.

- Government policy decisions take place within a broader economic and financial framework which includes the influence of financial institutions and markets and the requirements which accrue from membership of different supranational and international organisations.

case study   Toyota UK

Toyota's origins can be traced back to the early twentieth century when the inventor of Japan's first automatic loom, Sakidu Toyoda, established a spinning and weaving company. By the 1930s, using funds from selling patent rights to a British machine maker, the company had begun to invest in automotive technology research and soon produced its first prototype passenger vehicle. In August 1937, Kiichiro Toyoda, the son of the original owner, established the Toyota Motor Company, beginning mass production at its Koromo plant in 1938, just before the outbreak of the Second World War.

Despite experiencing considerable difficulties in the post-war period, Toyota recommenced production and began to build up a sales network to market its vehicles. In 1950, the company was split into two parts – production and sales – with the Toyota Motor Company the manufacturing arm of the organisation. Using techniques which have subsequently been emulated by other large companies (e.g. total quality control, just-in-time), Toyota began to increase its output and sales and was beginning to make significant inroads into overseas markets by the mid-1960s. By 1982, when the sales and manufacturing arms of the organisation merged to form the Toyota Motor Corporation, export sales of vehicles had exceeded domestic registrations and Toyota had grown into a large multinational corporation with a range of interests in various parts of the world.

For much of the early post-war period, Toyota focused its attention on the American market and established sales facilities in California in 1957, to be followed by a design base in 1973 and a joint production venture with General Motors in 1984. Less than two years later, the Corporation established its first wholly owned production plant at Georgetown in Kentucky, from which the first of many US-built Toyotas emerged in 1988.

Toyota's development in post-war Europe proceeded along broadly similar lines, with the company establishing local sales and distribution networks, followed by design and production facilities. Initially, production took place under licence (e.g. in Portugal in 1968) or through joint ventures (e.g. with Volkswagen in 1989) and was restricted to commercial vehicles and fork-lift trucks. By the late 1980s, however, the company had signalled its intention of establishing a passenger vehicle manufacturing facility in Europe, as part of its programme of overseas market development. This plant was opened in mid-1992 at Burnaston near Derby and was followed by the opening of an engine plant at Deeside, North Wales, some months later.

Toyota's decision to establish production facilities in Europe is best understood against the political and economic realities of the period. Japan's post-war success in export markets had, by the 1980s, given rise to a huge Japanese balance of payments surplus that was bitterly resented by US and European governments and became the focus of attention in numerous meetings of the G7 countries. As part of this success, the Japanese car industry was under pressure from US and European car manufacturers and their governments to restrain exports, and this ultimately culminated in a system of agreed voluntary restraints (known as VERs) by Japanese car producers, for fear of more draconian measures. Since these restraints did not apply to vehicles produced by Japanese factories overseas ('transplants'), establishing a manufacturing presence outside Japan made sound commercial and political sense. This was particularly true in western Europe, where the EU's Common External Tariff made cars imported from Japan more expensive to consumers and hence relatively less competitive than locally produced vehicles.

The EU's decision to establish a 'single market' within the Union added a further impetus to the decision by Japanese car manufacturers (and others) to seek a European presence. The fact that the United Kingdom was a favoured location for Toyota – and for many other Japanese companies – is not difficult to explain. Apart from providing direct access to the largest single market for motor vehicles in the world, the United Kingdom had a substantial market in its own right and a developed vehicle manufacturing industry with a significant parts and component sector. Added to this, the favourable response given to direct foreign investment by United Kingdom national and local government – including the use of financial and other inducements – made the United Kingdom an attractive proposition and a location of minimal risk for investing multinational corporations.

As far as the choice of Burnaston was concerned, this seems to have been dictated by economic and commercial rather than political factors, although Derbyshire County Council actively lobbied the parent company and offered it a number of inducements to locate in the Midlands. Being centrally placed in Britain and close to the M1, Burnaston offered direct access to all parts of the country and a relatively quick route to the Continent, via the ports and the Channel Tunnel. It also boasted a highly skilled local workforce, a developed infrastructure and a large site with room for further expansion.

There is no doubt that the multi-million Toyota development in Derbyshire has had a considerable impact on the local economy. Apart from the jobs created in building and operating the car plant, further employment has been created directly among local component suppliers and indirectly amongst those involved in providing services and materials and from the extra spending resulting from the growth of jobs. The area has also benefited from the prestige of having attracted a famous company to invest and this has encouraged investment by some other overseas organisations. How far these gains will ultimately be at the expense of the other car-producing areas of Britain still remains to be seen, but economic analysis suggests they may prove significant, particularly as global forces are increasingly shaping the international car industry and making it a highly competitive environment in which to do business.

Case study questions

1 What do you think are the key factors which have made the UK an attractive location for direct foreign investment?

2 To what extent do you think the expansion of the European Union will affect future inward investment decisions?

web link Toyota UK's website is *www.toyotauk.com*

Review and discussion questions

1 To what extent do you agree with the proposition that the market economy is the 'best' form of economic system? Do you have any reservations?

2 Explain how interest rates could be used to boost the economy. Why, then, do governments frequently hesitate to take such steps?

3 Using circular flow analysis, suggest why a large programme of capital expenditure by government (e.g. on new motorways, roads, railways) will benefit businesses. How could such a programme be financed?

4 Which businesses are likely to benefit from a recovery in a country's housing market?

Assignments

1 Imagine you work in the economic development unit of a local authority. Produce a draft report outlining the benefits to the local economy of encouraging direct inward investment. Indicate any disadvantages.

2 You are a trainee journalist on a regional or national newspaper. As part of your first big assignment, you have been asked to provide information on the 'privatisation' of eastern European economies. Using journals and newspapers, provide a scrapbook of information indicating the different ways in which western companies have sought to exploit business opportunities in eastern Europe.

Notes and references

1 Donaldson, P. and Farquhar, J., *Understanding the British Economy*, Penguin, 1988, p. 84.

2 See also the concept of Gross Value Added (GVA) which is an important measure in the estimation of GDP. National Statistics Online has a good explanation of GVA.

3 Real interest rates allow for inflation.

4 See, for example, Neale, A. and Haslam, C., *Economics in a Business Context*, Chapman & Hall, 1991, p. 141.

5 The role of assisting reconstruction in eastern Europe is also undertaken by the European Bank for Reconstruction and Development (EBRD). See text below.

Further reading

Begg, D. and Ward, D., *Economics for Business*, 2nd revised edition, McGraw-Hill, 2006.

Donaldson, P. and Farquhar, J., *Understanding the British Economy*, Penguin, 1991.

Ferguson, K., Essential Economics: *A Guide for Business Students*, Palgrave, 2004.

Griffiths, A. and Wall, S. (eds), *Applied Economics*, 11th edition, Financial Times/Prentice Hall, 2007.

Griffiths, A. and Wall, S., *Economics for Business and Management*, 2nd revised edition, FT/Prentice Hall, 2008.

Macdonald, N. T., *Macroeconomics and Business: An Interactive Approach*, International Thomson Publishing, 1999.

Mulhearn, C., Vane, H.R. and Eden, J., *Economics for Business*, Palgrave, 2001.

Neale, A., Haslam, C. and Johal, S., *Economics in a Business Context*, Thomson Learning, 3rd edition, 2000.

Worthington, I., Britton, C. and Rees, A., *Economics for Business: Blending Theory and Practice*, 2nd edition, Financial Times/Prentice Hall, 2005.

web
link

Web links and further questions are available on the website at:

www.pearsoned.co.uk/worthington

6 The demographic, social and cultural context of business

Ian Worthington

Organisations exist and function within society and consequently are subject to a variety of social influences. These influences, which include demography, social class and culture, can change over time and affect both the demand and supply side of the economy. Marketing organisations recognise and make use of these factors when segmenting markets for consumer goods and services.

Learning outcomes

Having read this chapter you should be able to:

- explain the notions of demography, social class, lifestyles, reference groups, culture and sub-culture
- identify key demographic and social trends that can affect organisations in the private, public and voluntary sectors
- provide examples of how demographic, social and cultural factors can influence both the demand and supply side of the economy
- outline the concept of market segmentation and demonstrate how marketing organisations can use demographic and socio-cultural variables to segment consumer markets

Key terms

ACORN
Ageing population
Birth rate
Cultural diversity
Culture
Death rate
Demographic time-bomb
Demography
Dependent population

Family life cycle
Geo-demographic
  segmentation
Lifestyles
Market segmentation
MOSAIC
Natural population change
Net migration
Primary reference group

Psychographic
  segmentation
Reference group
Secondary reference group
Social class
Social mobility
Sub-culture
VALS

Introduction

As previous chapters have demonstrated, human beings are a critical element of business activity both in their role as producers (e.g. workers, managers, entrepreneurs) and as consumers of outputs provided by the private, public and voluntary sectors. Put simply, business activity ultimately takes place because of and for people, a point well illustrated by the concept of the circular flow of income (CFI) (Chapter 5) and by the systems model introduced in Chapter 1. In order to more fully understand the environment in which business organisations exist and operate, it is important to consider how broader 'social' influences affect business organisations by examining how they can impact upon both the demand and supply side of the economy.

In this chapter we look at three such influences: demography, social aspects and the idea of culture and illustrate how these can affect both the amount and types of goods and services consumed within an economy and different aspects of the production process. In the next chapter, on the resource context, we examine people as a key factor of production and look at a number of areas associated with the concept of the workforce.

As the CFI model clearly shows, both the demand and supply side of the economy are interrelated (e.g. consider the notion of 'derived demand') and the same is often true for demographic, social and cultural influences. For example, in some countries, changing attitudes to female participation in the workforce (a socio-cultural factor) have helped to influence family sizes (a demographic factor) and this in turn has had implications for both the markets for goods and services and for human resources. To simplify the analysis, however, we have chosen to examine the different social influences and their impact on the economy separately but would encourage you to think of the various ways in which the different factors can be interconnected, both in themselves and with other macroenvironmental variables (e.g. the political environment).

The examples provided below are by no means exhaustive and you might like to think of others based on your own interest and/or experience (e.g. public administration students should consider the impact of a changing demographic and socio-cultural environment on the supply of and demand for public sector services such as education, pensions and healthcare). Moreover, the analysis can also be applied across different countries and cultures and ideally should seek to demonstrate the impact of socio-cultural and demographic change on business activity.

The demographic environment of business

Demography is the study of populations both in terms of their overall size and their structural characteristics. From a business point of view the key areas of interest include the age structure of a given population, its gender balance, its geographical distribution and the tendency for both the size and structure of the population to change over time. As noted above, demographic change can have important implications for both the demand and supply side of the economy and hence for organisations of all types.

The size of the population

A country's population normally increases over time and will vary according to such factors as changes in the birth and death rates and in the rate of net migration (see below). For example, the UK population in 1971 was just under 56 million, by 2008 this had risen to 60 million. Estimates suggest that by 2021 the UK will have a population of just under 64 million and that this could peak at almost 67 million by 2050 before it starts to fall back again (see below). In comparison, Russia's current population of around 145 million is projected to fall to about 100 million by 2050 as a result of a declining birth rate and a rising death rate in the wake of the country's economic collapse. If this occurs the world's biggest country will have fewer people than countries such as Uganda and Egypt. It is worth remembering, however, that future population changes are only projections and that these can vary considerably over time as new data become available. For example, in late 2007 the UK's Office for National Statistics provided three projections for the UK population by 2081: 63 million (lowest estimate); 108.7 million (highest estimate); 85 million (most likely estimate). These estimates show considerable variation and indicate how future population changes are relatively unpredictable, which can make forward planning difficult.

Table 6.1 indicates the wide variations that can occur in the size of national populations by examining a range of countries across the globe. Within the EU we can see that major member countries such as France, Germany, Italy and the UK all had populations over 50 million in 2008, while the majority of the new member states had populations below 10 million. These figures are dwarfed, however, by India and China, which had populations of around 1.1 billion and 1.3 billion respectively. Such differences in overall population size have important economic implications in areas such as potential market size, workforce availability, public expenditure, economic growth and international trade.

Table 6.1 Population size in selected countries, 2008

Country	Population (millions)
Germany	82.4
France	64.0
UK	60.9
Italy	58.1
Netherlands	16.6
Greece	10.7
Poland	38.5
Hungary	9.9
Slovakia	5.4
Malta	0.4
USA	303.8
India	1148.0
China	1330.0

Source: Various (including Eurostat).

The age and sex distribution of the population

In addition to examining the overall size of a country's population, demographers are also interested in its structural characteristics, including the balance between males and females and the numbers of people in different age categories. Table 6.2 provides illustrative data for the UK population by age and gender for selected age groups and intervals over the period 1971–2021. As can be seen from the figures in the right-hand column, women outnumber men in the UK population despite the fact that the annual number of male births slightly exceeds that of female births. Moreover, the data clearly point to an **ageing population**, with an increasing percentage of the population in the over 65 group and a decreasing percentage in the under 16 category. Projections suggest that by 2013 the number of over 65s in the UK population will exceed the number who are under 16, a trend which is sometimes described as the **demographic time-bomb** and which has important implications for both the private and public sectors, not least in terms of the overall demand for goods and services including 'public goods' such as education, healthcare, social services, state pensions and social security arrangements.

Table 6.2 Distribution of UK population by age and gender, 1971–2021, at selected intervals

	Under 16 (%)	35–44 (%)	55–64 (%)	Over 65 (%)	All ages (millions)
Males					
1971	27	12	11	10	27.2
2001	21	15	11	14	28.8
2021[1]	18	13	13	18	31.4
Females					
1971	24	11	12	16	28.8
2001	19	15	11	18	30.2
2021[1]	17	12	13	22	32.4

Note: [1] Projections.
Source: Adapted from *Social Trends* (2005).

It is worth noting that the UK's ageing population is a characteristic shared by many other countries, including those in the European Union. Data produced by Eurostat indicate similar trends in both the original EU-15 and in the new accession countries (Table 6.3). In comparison, both India and China have a much smaller percentage of the population in the over 65 category, the figures being 4.8 per cent and 7.4 per cent respectively for 2003.

Table 6.3 Percentage of EU populations aged 65 and over for selected EU countries, 1970–2006

Country	1970	1991	2003	2006
Germany	13	15	17	19
Belgium	13	15	17	17
Spain	9	14	17	17
Finland	9	13	15	16
Denmark	12	16	15	15
Estonia	12	12	16	17
Lithuania	10	11	15	15
Czech Republic	12	13	14	14
Slovakia	9	10	12	12
EU-27 average	12	14	16	17

Source: Adapted from Eurostat and ONS.

Other structural characteristics

Populations can also be examined in a number of other ways including their ethnicity and geographical distribution. For instance, in the 2001 population census in the UK, around 8 per cent of people surveyed described themselves as belonging to a minority ethnic group, with the largest grouping being Indian, accounting for almost 2 per cent of the total population and nearly 23 per cent of those in the ethnic minority category. The census data show that, in general, minority ethnic groups in the UK have a younger age structure than those in the 'White Group' and tend to be highly concentrated in large urban centres, particularly London. For the UK population as a whole, the majority of people live in England, with significant concentrations in regions such as the south-east, the Midlands, the north-west and the north-east, a fact which has important economic, political and social ramifications. Moreover, inter-regional movements of population, together with other factors such as international migration and differential birth and death rates, can result in significant local and regional variations in population over time with a knock-on effect for both the public and private sectors (for example, demand for housing and school places).

Population change

As the previous analysis indicates, populations can change in either size and/or structure, with important consequences for economic activity both within and between countries. The size and structure of a country's population depend on a number of variables, the most important of which are the birth rate, the death rate and the net migration rate.

The birth rate

Birth rates tend to be expressed as the number of live births per thousand of the population in a given year. In many countries this figure has been falling steadily over a long period of time for a number of reasons. These include:

- A trend towards smaller families as people become better off and health improves and death rates fall.
- The increased availability of contraception.
- The trend towards later marriages and later childbearing for social and/or economic reasons.
- Declining fertility rates.
- Changing attitudes towards women and work.

In some countries governments have offered financial and other incentives to married couples to try to reduce the birth rate (e.g. China) as a means of controlling population growth. In other countries incentives have been offered to try to reverse the actual or potential decline in the birth rate because of its economic consequences (e.g. France, Singapore). Declining birth rates are, of course, an important contributor to an ageing population; they can also have other consequences. For instance, a recent increase in the birth rate in the UK has led to a call by the Optimum Population Trust for British couples to restrict themselves to 2 children in order to reduce the impact of population growth on the natural environment.

The death rate

Like birth rates, **death rates** are usually measured per thousand of the population in a given year. For developed economies such as the UK this figure has tended to fall over time before reaching a plateau. Among the main contributors to this trend have been:

● Rising living standards, including better housing, sanitation and nutrition.
● Developments in medical technology and practice.
● Better education.
● Improved working conditions.

The difference between the birth rate and the death rate represents the **natural change** in the population (i.e. increase or decrease).

Net migration

Apart from the movement of population within a country (internal migration), people may move from one country to another for a variety of reasons. The balance between those leaving (emigrants) and those entering (immigrants) a country over a given period of time represents the rate of **net migration**. Along with changes in the birth and/or death rate, this can be a significant factor in population change and can have important consequences for the economy (e.g. the gain or loss of certain skills) and for the political system. In the UK, recent estimates (2007) suggest that around 70 per cent of the country's future population growth might come both directly and indirectly from migration, much of which is related to EU enlargement.

Influences on the rate of net migration include:

● Legal barriers (e.g. immigration laws).
● Economic migrancy.
● The numbers fleeing persecution.
● Government policy.
● Political developments.

Demographic change and business

Changes in the size and/or structure of a country's population can have important consequences for enterprises in the public, private and voluntary sectors both in the short and long term. Given increased globalisation and international trade, the impact of demographic change has an international as well as a national dimension for a growing number of trading organisations.

The following examples provide illustrations of how a changing demography can influence both the level and pattern of demand within an economy and in turn help to explain why changes can occur in a country's economic and industrial structure (see Chapter 12) and why some countries engage in international trade (see Chapter 16). Demographic change can also have important effects on the supply side of the economy.

You should try to think of other examples.

- As populations grow in size the demand for many types of goods and services also tends to grow (e.g. energy, consumer durables, food). A growing population also provides a larger workforce, other things being equal.
- An 'ageing population' increases the demand for a range of public, private and voluntary sector goods and services (e.g. healthcare, pensions, specialist holidays, sheltered housing). It also creates an increasingly **dependent population**.
- A declining birth rate influences the demand for education, children's products, childcare, certain TV programmes, comics, toys, etc. It can also reduce the numbers of young people available to enter the workforce to replace those who retire.
- Changes in the ethnic make-up of the population can affect the demand for particular food products, clothing and media services and can place increased demands on public authorities (e.g. documents printed in different languages). Some researchers also argue that a more diverse workforce can improve an organisation's performance.
- The regional redistribution of the population will affect the consumption of a range of goods and services including housing, education, healthcare, transport, energy and many day-to-day products. It can also affect prices (e.g. in the housing market) and the make-up of the local labour market.

On a more general level, it is also worth noting that demographic change can impact on a country's social as well as its economic structure and that this can result in increased (or reduced) demands on a range of organisations, particularly those in the public sector. For example, the growing imbalance being experienced in many countries between an increasing and dependent elderly population and a diminishing population of working age touches on many areas of public policy, from healthcare and social provision on the one hand to pensions and fiscal policy on the other. Governmental responses to the consequences of demographic change can have both direct and indirect consequences for a wide variety of organisations across the economy.

The social context

Since organisations exist and operate in society, they are subject to a variety of societal influences that operate at both a general and specific level. In this section we consider some of the key factors within an organisation's social environment, starting with the concept of social class. The notion that organisations also have responsibilities to society is examined in Chapter 9.

Social class

Throughout history, all societies have normally exhibited a certain degree of social and economic inequality that has given rise to the tendency to classify individuals into different social categories. For example, in India the 'caste system' has been an important source of social differentiation and one which has exerted a key influence over the life and opportunities available to members of the different castes. In other countries, including the United Kingdom, the categorisation of individuals has often been based around notions of **social class**, the idea of grouping people together who share a similar social status which is related to certain common features such as educational background, income and occupation. Whereas in some types of social system, movement between groups is either very difficult or impossible (e.g. the caste system), in others **social mobility** is frequently observed, with some individuals able to move relatively quickly between the different social strata (e.g. upper class, middle class, working class) as their personal circumstances change.

In practice, the process of allocating individuals to a particular class category has generally been based on socio-economic criteria such as income, wealth and occupational status. Advertisers and market researchers – including the Institute of Practitioners in Advertising – have tended to favour a scheme known as 'ABC1' (see Table 6.4) which uses an individual's occupation as a basis for allocation, the assumption being that a person's job is closely linked to key aspects of her/his attitudes and behaviour, including their choice of car, clothes, home furnishings, holidays, reading material and so on. There is even evidence to suggest that class might be influential in an individual's choice of retail outlets (e.g. different UK supermarket chains appear to attract customers from different socio-economic groups).[1]

Table 6.4 The ABC1 system of social grading

Social grading	Social status	Occupation
A	Upper middle class	Higher managerial, administrative and professional
B	Middle class	Intermediate managerial, administrative and professional
C1	Lower middle class	Supervisory or clerical, junior managerial, administrative and professional
C2	Skilled working class	Skilled manual workers
D	Working class	Semi and unskilled manual workers
E	Lowest subsistence level	State pensioners or widows, casual workers, lowest grade workers

Similar systems of classification have also been/are used for official purposes (e.g. the UK 10-year census of population). In the 1990s in the UK, government statistics used what was called the Registrar General's Social Scale – subsequently renamed 'Social Class based on Occupation' – to group the UK population into seven different categories according to their occupation (e.g. Group I was professional; Group II was managerial and technical; Group V was unskilled occupations). This system has now been replaced by NS-SEC (the National Statistics Socio-Economic Classifications) which again focuses on occupation as the key criterion for class allocation. NS-SEC is shown in Table 6.5. The figures in the right-hand column represent the socio-economic classification of the UK population of working age in the summer of 2003.[2]

Table 6.5 National Statistics Socio-Economic Classifications (NS-SEC)

Category	Occupation	Estimated % of working population in 2003
1	Higher managerial and professional occupations	10.8
1.1	Employers and managers in larger organisations (e.g. company directors, senior managers, senior civil servants, senior police and armed forces officers)	
1.2	Higher professionals such as doctors, lawyers, teachers, social workers, clergy	
2	Lower managerial/professional occupations including nurses, midwives, journalists, actors, musicians, prison officers, etc.	22.2
3	Intermediate occupations, for example clerks, secretaries, driving instructors	10.3
4	Small employers and own-account workers such as publicans, farmers, taxi drivers, window cleaners, painters and decorators	7.7
5	Lower supervisory, craft and related occupations including plumbers, printers, train drivers and butchers	9.4
6	Semi-routine occupations, for example shop assistants, hairdressers, bus drivers, cooks	13.3
7	Routine occupations such as labourers, couriers, waiters, refuse collectors	9.0
8	People who have never had paid work or are long-term unemployed	16.5

Source: Office of National Statistics.

While it would be unwise to assume that a factor such as a person's social class will invariably affect their choice of goods and services, empirical evidence reveals some interesting variations in the levels of expenditure on particular products among different groups in the UK population, a fact not lost on marketing organisations which often use socio-economic criteria as one way to segment a market (see below). According to data produced in the annual survey of Social Trends in the UK (see Table 6.6), total expenditure was highest among the managerial and professional group and was almost double that of people in the never worked/unemployed category. Within this overall pattern of expenditure some interesting data emerges, particularly with regards to priorities, as indicated by expenditure on different items by the different social groupings. For instance, expenditure on housing, fuel and power was highest among the never worked/long-term unemployed group while spending on health was highest among the managerial group. Note that some of the high levels of spending among the former group, in areas such as education and communication, are probably largely to do with the fact that this category also contains students.

Table 6.6 Household expenditure (£/week) by socio-economic classification of household, 2006

	Managerial and professional occupations	Intermediate occupations	Routine and manual occupations	Never worked and long-term unemployed[1]
Transport	100.81	70.18	52.49	41.76
Recreation and culture	82.65	67.35	54.46	31.95
Food and non-alcoholic drink	56.70	49.49	45.99	38.05
Housing, fuel and power	56.04	51.83	50.03	63.51
Restaurant and hotels	59.44	41.48	35.51	28.65
Clothing and footwear	35.25	25.45	22.44	25.98
Alcohol and tobacco	12.86	12.69	13.11	8.79
Communication	14.81	14.69	12.13	11.72
Education	15.84	5.24	2.58	15.85
Health	7.32	4.31	4.52	1.37
All household expenditure	676.37	513.81	418.01	323.11

Note: [1]This category includes students.
Source: Adapted from *Expenditure and Food Survey*, ONS.

Lifestyles

Another factor that can clearly affect people's attitudes and behaviour is the **lifestyle** that they choose to adopt. Lifestyles are basically concerned with the way in which people live and how they spend their money, decisions which are not necessarily always linked to their socio-economic position. Two individuals with the same occupation – and nominally in the same social class – may have entirely different lifestyles, a point well illustrated by examining two university lecturers. My own lifestyle is highly sophisticated, environmentally sensitive, artistic and cosmopolitan; that of a colleague – who happens to teach marketing – is narrow, parochial, philistine and consumption-driven. Then, what would one expect?!

Joking apart, lifestyle analysis provides another way of seeking to categorise and explain human behaviour, based on factors such as an individual's interests, activities and opinions as well as on their demographic characteristics. In essence, the proposition is that by examining distinctive patterns of consumer response, a marketing organisation can build up a clearer picture of an individual's habits, preferences and behaviour and by doing so can design more effective and appealing products, marketing programmes and/or communications that can be aimed at specific lifestyle groups.

While we should be cautious of over-generalising, the evidence suggests that in many countries the way in which people spend their time and money has changed considerably in recent decades as a result of changes in demography, working patterns, technology, income and a range of other factors. Once again we can illustrate this by looking at longitudinal data collected through the annual survey of social trends in the UK. These data show, for example, that:

● Cinema attendance in 2004 was the second highest figure in 30 years.
● In 2002/3 around 45 per cent of homes in the UK could access the Internet; this was four times the number in 1998/9. In 2007 84 per cent of households had Internet access with a broadband connection.

- UK residents took over 41 million holidays abroad in 2003, six times the number in 1971.
- Household spending on communications (including mobile phones) increased more than ninefold in real terms between 1971 and 2006.
- Between 1974 and 2005/6, household purchases of fruit in the UK increased by 77 per cent (measured in grams/person per week). Fruit juice purchases, for example, rose tenfold per week during this period.
- In 1993 80 per cent of men and 73 per cent of women held at least one plastic card (e.g. credit/debit/store card); by 2003 this had risen to 91 per cent and 90 per cent respectively.
- The number of licensed cars on Britain's roads more than doubled in the period 1971–2006.
- The number of households with regular use of two cars increased fourfold over the same period.
- In 1996/7 16 per cent of households had a mobile phone; by 2006 the figure was 80 per cent.
- About 60 per cent of homes had a CD player in 1996/7; by 2006 this had topped 80 per cent. During the same period sales of home computers grew from under 30 per cent to 67 per cent.
- Since 1974 UK consumers have halved their consumption of red meat and sales of butter, margarine and cooking fats have also fallen.
- During the period 1997–2003 the amount of household waste collected for recycling more than doubled while the amount of land dedicated to organic food production grew more than sevenfold. By 2006/7 recycling rates had reached 31 per cent.

If we take changing expenditure patterns in the UK as an indication of changes in lifestyles then there has been a discernible shift in emphasis from essential products such as food, housing, water and fuel to the less essential items such as communications, foreign travel, recreation and culture (see Table 6.7). For example, after allowing for inflation, UK household expenditure on food and drink rose by only 52 per cent between 1971 and 2006 whereas spending on communication rose by over nine times. Interestingly spending on alcohol and tobacco actually fell over the same period while spending on healthcare doubled, suggesting a shift in public concern towards a healthier lifestyle (see Mini case: Fit for purpose?).

Table 6.7 Volume of household expenditure on selected items, 1971–2006, expressed as index numbers (base year 1971)

Category of spending	1971	1991	2003	2006
Food and non-alcoholic drink	100	117	141	152
Alcohol and tobacco	100	92	91	89
Housing, water, fuel	100	138	156	160
Health	100	182	205	212
Communication	100	306	846	956
Recreation and leisure	100	283	610	783
Household expenditure abroad	100	298	712	763

Source: Adapted from ONS.

In light of the discussion on inflation in Chapter 5, it is worth noting that such changes in spending patterns over time are reflected in changes in the official 'basket of goods and services' used to calculate the Retail Prices Index in the UK. The 1980s saw CDs, CD players and condoms added to the basket, with computers, camcorders and mobile phone charges added in the next decade. By 2004/5 dishwater tablets had replaced dishwasher powder, wooden garden furniture sets had replaced plastic sets and leather sofas had replaced ordinary ones. More bizarrely, hamsters and popcorn bought in cinemas had been added to the index while baguettes, corned beef and writing paper were dropped (see e.g. the *Guardian*, 22 March 2005, p. 20). By 2007/8, the RPI contained fruit smoothies, USB sticks, peppers, muffins and small oranges and had discarded microwaves, TV repairs, washable carpets and 35 mm camera films. What does this tell us about the changing lifestyles and spending habits of UK citizens; are people in the UK getting healthier?

mini case · Fit for purpose?

One of the important social trends in recent years has been the move towards healthier lifestyles, a development which has been spurred on by concerns over the increased incidence of obesity, diabetes, heart disease and cancer – problems often associated with rising levels of affluence. Along with this trend have come numerous business opportunities including the growth in the number of fitness clubs, health farms and activity holidays and a general rise in the sale of products such as vitamin supplements, fruit juices, blood pressure monitors and books promoting healthier diets. Grocery retailers too have not been slow to exploit the new situation, offering a range of chilled, ready made 'healthier option' meals, often endorsed by a well-known personality (e.g. the UK grocery retailing chain Sainsbury's has used Jamie Oliver, the TV chef, to promote its products; Oliver has also been involved in a well-publicised campaign to improve the nutritional value of school meals in the UK).

As with any change of this kind there tend to be losers as well as winners. For example, according to research by Mintel, sales of the UK's favourite snack, the potato crisp, are in decline as consumers switch to products generally held to be healthier such as dried fruit, cereal bars and nuts. A particular concern for many consumers has been the high fat and high salt content of products such as crisps and this has driven some companies to produce low salt and/or low fat brands and to change the types of fat being used in the product in an effort to boost sales (e.g. the UK-based Walker's Snack Products has a variety cooked in olive oil). Interestingly enough, the apparent trend towards healthier eating in the UK stands in contrast to the experiences in some other European countries, particularly those bordering the Mediterranean (e.g. Italy, Greece, Spain and Portugal). Reports suggest that there has been something of a retreat from the 'Mediterranean diet' of fruit and vegetables and a move towards foods with high fat, sugar and salt content as a growing number of consumers in these countries are influenced by sedentary lifestyles, supermarket shopping and fast-food restaurants.

Many of the trends referred to above are, of course, mirrored in consumer aspirations and behaviour in other countries, particularly in respect of issues such as healthier lifestyles, increased foreign travel, greater access to communications technology and more environmentally friendly products (though not necessarily rodent purchases!). As the following examples illustrate, changes in consumer lifestyles can represent both an opportunity and a threat to trading organisations and can have important implications for businesses and countries alike.

- Coca-Cola has seen a decline in profits as consumers have switched to bottled water, fruit juice and other non-fizzy drinks as part of a healthier diet.
- GlaxoSmithkline has targeted the Italian market with its non-smoking products in the wake of the ban by the Italian government on smoking in public places.
- Beer consumption in Germany has dropped dramatically as young Germans reject a product that they evidently regard as 'uncool' and less healthy than some alternatives.
- Some French wine companies have introduced wine in cartons with a straw to attract the 'eat on the go' young consumer.
- Smoking restrictions in countries such as the UK, Germany, Italy and France have had an impact in various ways (e.g. increase in home drinking; rise in sales of patio heaters; reduced use of slot machines in public houses).
- Sales of Guinness to Africa (especially Nigeria) have grown substantially.
- China has overtaken the USA in sales of televisions and mobile phones and Chinese consumers are increasingly buying a wide range of western consumer goods from luxury confectionery and designer clothes to expensive cars and foreign beers).
- With a rapidly expanding economy and growing liberalisation in many areas of private life, the sex industry in China is booming (see e.g. the *Guardian,* 25 June 2005, p. 20). The country now provides 70 per cent of the world's sex toys and there is a growing (sic) domestic market.
- Sales of organic food are growing significantly across Europe and beyond. The global market for organic food in 2005 was worth about £15 billion, with Europe responsible for just under half.
- With the immense popularity of the iPod and iTunes (its online record store), Apple has become one of the world's fastest-growing brands.
- Other brands in the technology/lifestyle field that are increasing in value include BlackBerry, Google, Amazon, Yahoo and eBay.
- Social networking sites (e.g. Facebook; MySpace) have become very popular particularly in the UK where it is estimated that 25 per cent of adults use such sites around 23 times every month.

Other social influences

While it is important to consider the influence of broad social factors such as class and lifestyles, it is also worth remembering that consumers are individuals and that they are subject to influences that operate at a personal level. Such influences include the wide variety of individuals and groups with whom we come into contact during our lifetime and who may influence our attitudes, values, opinions and/or behaviour. Primary among these are our interactions within the family, with friends or work colleagues and through our involvement with sports and social clubs, religious organisations, trade unions and so on. Such groups are sometimes referred to as **reference groups**.

Groups that have a regular or direct (i.e. face-to-face) influence on us are known as **primary reference groups** while those whose influence tends to be more indirect and formal are known as **secondary reference groups**. The former, in particular, can be very influential in shaping our attitudes and behaviour including our decisions on consumption.

The importance of reference groups, especially family and friends, is recognised by both economists and marketers. Economists, for example, use the notion of 'households' (see Chapter 5) to indicate that the consumption of goods and services often takes place within a collective family framework, as in the case of groceries, holidays, vehicles and many other everyday products. Marketers use concepts such as the **family life cycle** to show changing patterns of consumption as the individual moves from being a child in a family to being a parent with different needs and responsibilities.

While it is difficult to be precise about when and how far an individual's demand is shaped by the family and other reference groups, it is not difficult to think of particular examples when this is likely to be the case. For many services such as builders, restaurants, hotels, hairdressers and car repairs, consumers often rely on the advice of a trusted friend or colleague and many firms can gain new business through such word-of-mouth recommendations. Equally, through membership and/or support of a particular group or club, individuals may be tempted to purchase particular goods and/or services (e.g. football kit, trainers, a CD, tickets), especially those with a desirable 'brand name' and endorsed by a well-known personality (e.g. sportsperson, musician, singer, film star). In such cases, the demand for the product is often less price sensitive (see Chapter 14) since it is a 'must have' product.

The cultural environment

Culture

The term **culture** generally refers to a complex set of values, norms, beliefs, attitudes, customs, systems and artefacts which are handed down from generation to generation through the process of socialisation and which influence how individuals see the world and how they behave in it. Defined in this way, culture can be seen to have at least three important features:

- it comprises both material (e.g. human artefacts such as buildings, literature, art, music) and abstract elements (e.g. rituals, symbols, values);
- it is socially learned and transmitted over time; and
- it influences human behaviour.

As a concept, 'culture' is often applied in a variety of circumstances at both the macro and micro level: terms such as 'western culture', 'Asian culture', 'European culture', 'New York City culture', 'youth culture', 'pop culture', 'entrepreneurial culture' and 'research culture' are just some of the examples of its usage in the modern world. What they have in common is that they imply certain shared aspects of human belief, understanding and behaviour that link individuals together into some form of definable group and/or range of activities.

In a business context, it can be easy to underestimate the degree to which a person's perceptions, attitudes and behaviour can be shaped by cultural influences, some of which may be relatively enduring (e.g. certain 'core' values and beliefs) while others may be more open to change (i.e. secondary beliefs and values). In the United States, for example, American citizens believe in the right of individuals to bear arms and this is enshrined in the US Constitution. The buying and selling of handguns and rifles is thus acceptable within American society, despite the fact that they are frequently used in violent crimes including robbery and murder. In other countries, trade in such weapons tends to be seen as highly questionable by most people and is usually heavily regulated by the government to certain types of weapons for use in acceptable pursuits such as hunting or rifle shooting. Cultural differences such as this can, of course, apply not only to the kinds of goods and services that are consumed (e.g. eating horsemeat in France is acceptable but not in the UK) but also to other aspects of both the production and consumption process and this can have important implications for an organisation's behaviour.

Examples include:

- Who decides what is bought, how it is bought or where it is bought (e.g. in some cultures women have predominantly been the purchasers of household products).
- What colours are acceptable (e.g. the colour associated with bereavement varies across cultures).
- How far harmonisation of products and marketing activities is feasible (e.g. the EUs perennial debates over what constitutes an acceptable definition of certain products such as sausages, Feta cheese, chocolate).
- What factors can enhance the prospect of a sale (e.g. bribes are acceptable in some cultures).
- How business is conducted (e.g. the length of negotiations, the meaning of a handshake).
- The method of communicating with the target audience (e.g. in the UK a single shared language allows organisations to use national media).
- How customer enquiries/complaints are dealt with (e.g. UK businesses using call centres in India often give their operators British names and train them to talk about everyday British preoccupations such as the weather and sport).

In effect, culture not only influences an individual's response to products and the nature of the buying and selling process, but it also exercises a significant influence on the structure of consumption within a given society. For companies which can gain acceptability on a global scale, despite cultural differences between countries, the potential benefits are huge (e.g. global brands such as Coca-Cola, McDonald's, Nike).

While the so-called 'Americanisation' of consumption is not to everyone's taste, other forms of cultural exportation are often more acceptable and can prove highly lucrative for the country concerned. In the UK, for example, overseas earnings from culture and arts-related tourism make a significant contribution to the country's 'invisible earnings' (see Chapter 16) and many other countries benefit in similar ways.

mini case   National cultures

Recognising and responding to cultural differences between countries can have an important impact on how successful organisations are in international trade. But is it possible to generalise about a country's culture?

One academic who has made a significant contribution in this area is Professor Geert Hofstede, who has developed a theory of culture which allows comparisons to be made between the main cultural characteristics in different countries. Hofstede's research is based on data collected from IBM employees across the world while he was working at the company as a psychologist. On the basis of his research Hofstede identified four cultural dimensions; later he added a fifth. These dimensions can be used to compare value systems at different levels, from the family through to the state.

The five cultural dimensions are as follows:

1 *Power distance* – this is concerned with the degree to which the members of a society accept an unequal or hierarchical power structure. In societies where the power distance is large there is a perception that inequality exists and subordinates tend to be more dependent on their superiors. This can result in an autocratic or paternalistic style of management or governance (e.g. in some African countries) which can evoke either positive or negative reactions. Where the power distance is small, individuals tend to see themselves more as equals and management/governance styles tend to be more consultative and less hierarchical (e.g. in northern European countries).

2 *Uncertainty avoidance* – this focuses on how members of society cope with uncertainty in their lives. Where levels of anxiety are generally high, this results in high uncertainty avoidance and people in these cultures are deemed to be more expressive and emotional (e.g. Latin American countries) than in low uncertainty avoidance countries (e.g. many Asian countries).

3 *Individualism* – refers to the extent to which individuals in society see themselves as independent and autonomous human beings or as part of a collectivity. High individualist countries tend to be countries such as the United States, the UK, Canada and Australia; low individualism is said to be prevalent in Asian and Latin American countries.

4 *Masculinity* – is concerned with how far a society is predisposed to aggressive and materialistic behaviour and is linked to gender role. Hofstede associates masculinity with toughness, assertiveness and materialism and with a predisposition to conflict and competition. Femininity, in contrast, is characterised as caring, sensitive and concerned with the quality of life; the result is a more accommodating style based on negotiation and compromise. Hofstede's analysis suggests the more masculine countries include Austria and Japan, while Scandinavian countries tend to be the most feminine.

5 *Long-term orientation* – relates to the degree to which a society embraces a long-term view and respect for tradition. In societies with a short-term orientation people tend to stress the 'here and now', typified by western countries. Eastern cultures, by comparison, are generally held to have a longer-term orientation that emphasises concern for the future and for tradition as well as the present.

One of the benefits of Hofstede's research is that it reminds us that cultural differences can and do occur between states and, as a result, there is no 'one-size-fits-all' style of management or governance that would be suitable across all countries. For companies which are multinational organisations, management styles and approaches in the country of origin may not necessarily be suitable in other parts of the organisation for cultural reasons. Vive la différence!

Sub-culture

A society is rarely, if ever, culturally homogeneous. Within every culture **sub-cultures** usually exist, comprising groups of individuals with shared value systems based on common experiences, origins and/or situations. These identifiable sub-groups may be distinguished by nationality, race, ethnicity, religion, age, class, geographical location or some other factor and their attitudes, behaviour, customs, language and artefacts often reflect sub-cultural differences. At times such differences can be relatively easily accommodated and ultimately may become institutionalised through the legal and/or political process (e.g. the Scottish and Welsh Assemblies – see Chapter 4). At other times sub-cultural differences can be the source of a considerable degree of conflict between various sub-groups, resulting in serious divisions within a society and even in war and genocide.

The UK provides a good example of the notion of **cultural diversity** and can be used to illustrate how this can influence the demand for goods and services. In addition to nationality groups such as the Irish, Scots and Welsh, the country has provided a home for successive generations of immigrants from around the globe and this has created a rich mix of ethnic and other sub-groups, often concentrated in particular parts of the country and having their own language, traditions and lifestyles. In Leicester, for example, where a significant proportion of the population is of Asian origin, there is a substantial Asian business community, part of which has developed to cater specifically for the local ethnic population (e.g. halal butchers, saree shops), as well as attracting custom from the wider community (e.g. Indian restaurants). Many Asian businesses in Leicester are small, family owned enterprises, employing members of the extended family in keeping with cultural traditions. Aspects such as the organisation and financing of the business, its network of relationships and the working conditions for staff are also frequently influenced by cultural values, traditions and norms, although changes in these areas are becoming more apparent, especially among second and third generation Asian-owned enterprises.

Application: market segmentation

Marketers have long recognised the importance of demographic, social and cultural factors in shaping people's demand for goods and services. This is exemplified by the concept of **market segmentation**.

In essence, market segmentation refers to the practice of dividing a market into distinct groups of buyers who share the same or similar attitudes and patterns of behaviour and who might require separate products or marketing to meet their particular needs. By segmenting a market into its broad component parts, businesses should be able to focus their marketing efforts more effectively and efficiently, for example by developing product offerings and marketing programmes which meet the requirements of the different market segments.

Markets can be segmented in a variety of ways and this tends to differ between consumer markets and those which involve business to business transactions. Table 6.8 below outlines some of the major variables used in segmenting consumer markets. As the table indicates, demographic, social and cultural factors provide a basis for identifying distinct market segments within the markets for consumer goods and services. In practice, of course, marketers may use either one (e.g. demography) or a combination (e.g. age, location and social class) of different variables to segment a market they are seeking to target.

Table 6.8 Methods of segmenting consumer markets

Type of segmentation	Key segmentation variables	Examples
Demographic	Age, gender, religion, ethnic group, family size, family life cycle stage	Children's products, ethnic foods, 18–30 holidays, retirement homes, cars
Socio-economic	Social class, income, occupation	Luxury products, convenience services, discount goods
Geographic	Country, region, urban/suburban/ rural, town/city, climate	Country clothing, air conditioning, regional specialities
Geo-demographic	House type and location	Conservatories, lawn mowers
Psychographic	Lifestyles, values, personality	Health/healthier products, cosmetics, cigarettes
Mediagraphic	Media habits (e.g. papers read)	Specialist magazines, eco-friendly holidays
Behavioural	Behavioural characteristics including time/occasion of purchase, loyalty, user status, benefits sought, attitude to product, etc.	Mother's day products, disposable cameras, toothpaste

A good example of combining the different variables is provided by the notion of **geo-demographic segmentation** which focuses on the relationship between an individual's geographical location and her/his demographic characteristics, given that close links frequently exist between a person's place and type of residence and factors such as income, family size and attitudes. One well-known scheme of this type is **ACORN** (A Classification Of Residential Neighbourhoods) which uses 40 variables from population census data to differentiate residential areas. Another is **MOSAIC**, developed by Experian, which draws on a variety of data sources (e.g. census data, financial data, property characteristics, demographic information) and uses a range of sophisticated analytical techniques to produce household profiles at full postcode level. Under the MOSAIC scheme, UK households are currently divided into 11 groups with names such as 'Symbols of Success', 'Suburban Comfort' and 'Grey Perspectives' and these are then further sub-divided into 61 types, again with interesting and evocative names including 'Golden Empty Nesters', 'Sprawling Subtopia' and 'Childfree Serenity'. For a fuller description of MOSAIC and Experian's other products (e.g. commercial MOSAIC) and methodology you should access the company's website at *http://www.experian.co.uk* and follow the links.

With regard to factors such as social class and lifestyles, these tend to be grouped under the notion of **psychographic segmentation**, an approach which has attracted considerable attention in recent years given the reciprocal link between lifestyles and consumption indicated above. Lifestyle segments can be developed either as 'off-the-shelf' products by marketing agencies/management consultancies or can be customised for/by individual companies, although the latter often tend to be both complex and expensive to design. One established and popular example of the former is **VALS** (Values And Lifestyles) developed by SRI International. Under this model, individuals are allocated to different categories on the basis of a combination of demographic and lifestyle factors such as age, education, income and levels of self-confidence and then these categories are grouped into a number of broader segments which reflect a category's predominant orientations. Thus, under VALS 2, the three broad groups identified were (1) people who were *principle-orientated* (i.e. guided by their views of how the world should be); (2) people who were *status-orientated* (i.e. guided by the opinions and actions of others); (3) people who were *action-orientated* (i.e. guided by the desire for social and physical activity, variety in life and risk taking). Again you can gain further information on this scheme by visiting the SRI website at **www.sric_bi.com**.

Synopsis

All organisations are an integral part of the society in which they exist and carry out their activities and as a result they are affected by a range of influences emanating from the demographic, social and cultural environment. These influences can change over time and help to shape both the demand and supply side of business activity. Businesses and other organisations need to be aware of and respond to the process of societal change and to the opportunities and threats that such change can engender.

Summary of key points

- Organisations exist and operate within society and are subject to a variety of demographic and socio-cultural influences.

- Demography is concerned with population variables, including population size, structure and distribution.

- Changes in demography are primarily related to changes in birth and/or death and/or net migration rates.

- Demographic change can affect both the demand and supply side of the economy.

- The social context of business includes factors such as social class, lifestyles and reference group influences. The consumption of goods and services in an economy can be linked to such factors.

- The cultural environment of business comprises those institutions and other forces which help to shape society's basic attitudes, values, perceptions, preferences and behaviour.

- Societies usually also contain sub-cultures which can influence a person's beliefs, attitudes and actions.

- Like demography and social factors, cultural influences can change over time and can affect organisations. Businesses need to be sensitive to such change.

- The importance of demographic, social and cultural factors in business can be illustrated by the concept of market segmentation.

case study | The effects of an ageing population

There is no doubt that the world's population is ageing. In 2000 there were 69 million people in the world over the age of 80 years and this is the fastest growing segment of the population (see Table 6.9). By 2050 it is estimated that this figure will have risen to 379 million, which represents 4 per cent of the world's population. In 2000 many countries already had higher percentages of over 80s including Sweden (5.1 per cent), Norway and Britain (both 4 per cent). In Japan (the fastest ageing country in the 1990s) it is predicted that by 2015 over 25 per cent of the population will be over 65 years of age.

Table 6.9 shows that in all parts of the world the fastest growing segments are the older ones; for the more developed countries reductions in the size of the 0 to 59 age groups are predicted. The predictions are made on the assumption that present trends in life expectancy and fertility rates will continue.

Why is the world population ageing?

There are two main causes – increased life expectancy and lower fertility rates. Figure 6.1 shows the fertility rates and Figure 6.2 shows the life expectancy for the same groups of the world's population between 1950 and 2050.

Fertility rates have fallen dramatically in all parts of the world since 1950 and this trend is expected to continue into the future although some countries may buck the trend in certain years (e.g. fertility rates in the UK increased in the period 2001–7). Conversely life expectancy has risen in all parts of the world and is also expected to continue to do so. Putting these two trends together means that the average age of the world population is increasing. (The factors behind these changes have already been discussed in this chapter.) There are of course wide differences between countries but the general picture is one of convergence.

What are the implications of the ageing population for business?

Production

Demand patterns vary a great deal with age and if the grey population is increasing in size businesses will have to respond to the changing demands. If the American experience is repeated in the rest of the world the grey population will spend more on education and leisure services. Many retirees take the opportunity to return to education to pursue their interests.

Table 6.9 Projected growth rates between 2000 and 2050, percentages

	0–14	15–59	60+	80+
World	0.15	0.79	2.35	3.40
More developed countries	−0.34	−0.42	1.07	2.23
Less developed countries	0.21	1.01	2.87	4.22
Least developed countries	1.26	2.38	3.37	4.07

Sources: *World Population Prospects*, United Nations, 2000.

Table 6.10 gives an example of how the level of weekly expenditure on selected products can vary by age. It can be seen that the older age groups spent less on beer and cider, cigarettes and visiting the cinema or theatre but more on holidays in the UK and medical insurance than the younger age groups.

As businesses respond to these changes there will be a shift of resources towards the service sector and

this will bring about further change in industrial structure (see Chapter 12).

Marketing

Demographic change has long been recognised as an important part of the marketing environment and one that needs continual monitoring. This is especially the case in the USA where the trends now evident in

Figure 6.1   Projected fertility rates between 1950 and 2050

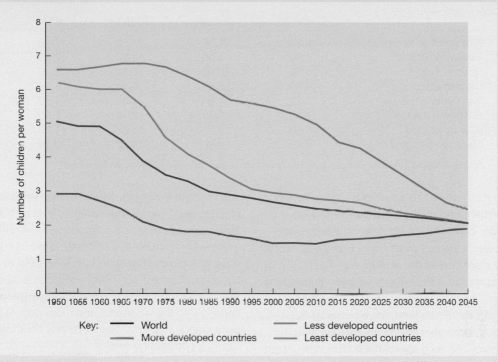

Source: United Nations, 2000.

Figure 6.2   Projected life expectancy between 1950 and 2050

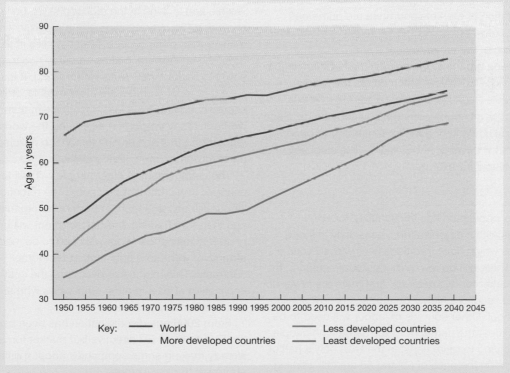

Source: United Nations, 2000.

Table 6.10 Expenditure on selected products by age of head of household, UK, 2002, £ per week

	Under 30	30 to 49	50 to 64	65+
Eating out at restaurant	9.30	11.60	11.50	11.40
Take away meals	4.90	4.80	2.90	2.20
Beer and cider	9.90	10.60	10.80	5.10
Cigarettes	5.60	6.80	6.10	4.80
Visit cinema/theatre	1.30	1.50	1.30	1.20
Holiday in the UK	1.50	2.30	2.70	5.80
Holiday abroad	5.50	12.50	14.50	11.20
Medical insurance	0.40	0.80	1.70	3.20

Source: Adapted from *www.statistics.gov.uk/CC1/SearchRes.asp?tem=household+expenditure+age.*

Europe started earlier and where the older population is large, affluent and with a great deal of market power. Older consumers have been dubbed 'woofs' by marketeers – well off older folk – and are accepted as an important part of the market.

Those currently in their 40s have been dubbed the 'third agers'. As they reach the 50–75 year age group they will have more free time, have better health, more money and higher expectations than their predecessors. The third agers in the USA have much higher demand than their predecessors for education and leisure services – they make heavy use of sports centres, cinemas and evening classes.

Demography is also important to marketers in the segmentation of markets and there are numerous examples of where age is the segregating factor. In recognition of the different needs and wants of the different age groups in the holiday market there is the 18–30 holiday company which caters for young people while Saga Holidays cater for the over 50s. Interestingly, given the comments already made, Saga Holidays is now offering the kind of holidays often associated with younger travellers – like elephant riding in Nepal for example.

HRM

A greying population has implications for HR strategies within organisations, especially in those industries which have traditionally employed young people. There will be fewer young people entering the labour market for two reasons: first there are fewer of them and second a higher percentage is now staying on at school. Other sources of labour will need to be found to meet the demand. At the same time people are continuing to retire early; in the USA only a half of men between the ages of 60 and 65 are still working

and in some European countries the percentage is much lower. Policies implemented in the 1980s and 1990s by organisations downsizing have created a 'retire early' culture among many, and some pension rules which penalise individuals who wish to work beyond retirement age have worked to exacerbate this. The combination of fewer younger people coming into the workforce and more people leaving early means that employers in many countries are facing a contracting market.

One possibility is the increased participation of older people in the labour force. This means that ageist HRM practices will have to change. Employers often view older workers as more expensive, less flexible and lacking in the required skills, but statistics show that the over-40s age group receives less training than other groups. Many studies in this area have shown that age makes no difference to the ability to acquire new skills with training. It is often the case that older workers are more reliable, are more experienced and have less absenteeism than younger workers. Many employers all around the world are recognising this and are implementing policies which positively encourage older workers.

The employment of older people will call for changes in recruitment practices. The retention of labour will become more important for organisations and therefore training and development will take on greater significance. Work will need to be made more attractive, with more part-time or temporary contracts. This might also overcome the cost implication of having older employees who are higher up incremental pay scales.

From 2006 age discrimination has been banned in the EU under an EU directive but market forces are already making some companies adopt a different approach to older workers.

Financial

There are financial implications of an ageing population. The Potential Support Ratio (PSR) shows the number of persons aged 15 to 64 years per one person of 65 years and over. It gives an indication of the dependency burden of an ageing population on the working population. This fell from 12:1 to 9:1 between 1950 and 2002 and is forecast to fall further to 4:1 by the year 2050 (see Table 6.11).

Again Table 6.11 shows a similar pattern all over the world – there will be an increasing financial burden on people of working age as a result of ageing populations. Within the overall figures there are marked differences. In Japan for instance, the ratio is forecast to fall from 4:1 in 2002 to 1:1 in 2050. In the USA, where immigration is generally higher (and therefore ageing is less pronounced), the ratio is forecast to fall from 5:1 to 3:1.

Table 6.11 Projected Potential Support Ratio, 2002 and 2050

	2002	2050
World	9:1	4:1
More developed countries	5:1	2:1
Less developed countries	12:1	5:1
Least developed countries	17:1	10:1

Source: United Nations, 2002.

This means that a higher proportion of the population will depend upon a smaller proportion of the population for support – in terms of resources for health care and the payment of pensions. Many countries are looking at their pension provisions to try to reduce the cost of dependency. In the UK for example there has been a shift in the burden of pension provision from the state to individuals and many companies have ended their 'final salary' pension schemes. Nevertheless, it is still estimated that to meet the demand for pensions of the ageing population by 2030 the UK needs a 5 per cent annual growth rate in GDP. This is much higher than growth rates have been. In the past in the UK, state pensions have been paid out of current taxation but this is likely to change so that state pensions will be funded from investments. Changes in the retirement age also help to reduce the cost of dependency.

In addition to the cost of pensions, an increase in the average age of a population has implications for health care and the cost of health care. Although this case study makes the point that the greying population is fitter and healthier than ever before, there are of course implications for the demand for health care. For example, the percentage of 65-year-olds in the UK with Altzheimer's disease is 5 per cent, and this rises to 20 per cent in the over-80s. Therefore there is a need for greater provision for health care, whether this is done by the state or by individuals.

As well as these major changes the ageing populations will mean changes in:

- popular culture, which for some time has been dominated by youth;
- crime rates – as most crime is carried out by younger people, crime rates should fall;
- family relationships – with falling birth rates and longer life expectancy the 'beanpole' family structure will become the norm.

It is clear from this discussion that the ageing population being experienced by much of the world has big implications for business in many diverse areas.

Case study questions

1 Think of some examples of goods and services for which demand will rise as a consequence of an ageing population. How should marketers address this new buyer segment?

2 What types of policy can organisations use to:
   (a) encourage the older worker to stay in employment for longer?
   (b) recruit older workers into the workplace?

Review and discussion questions

1 What is meant by an 'ageing' population? Examine some of the key ways in which an ageing population can affect the supply side of the economy.

2 In a country of your own choice, identify some of the major social trends over the last decade. How are these trends reflected in changing patterns of consumption?

3 What is meant by the term 'culture'? To what extent do you agree with the proposition that globalisation could destroy local cultural diversity?

4 Why do marketers segment markets? Give examples of particular markets where demographic segmentation might be appropriate.

Assignments

1 Assume you work in the HR department of a large retail organisation that is seeking to replace staff who are about to retire. Because of demographic and other trends you anticipate problems in recruiting school leavers in sufficient numbers. Produce a report outlining the problem to senior executives and suggest possible solutions. Provide justifications for your recommendations.

2 Choose three countries from different continents. Produce data to show the age distribution of the population in each of the countries in a given year. Account for any differences in the age profile of the three countries and suggest ways in which these differences might affect their respective economies in both the short and the long term.

Notes and references

1 See e.g. Worthington, I., Britton, C. and Rees, A., *Economics for Business: Blending Theory and Practice*, 2nd edition, Financial Times/Prentice Hall, 2005, pp. 86–9.

2 The figure for long-term unemployment includes students and others who are not officially in paid employment (e.g. housewives).

Further reading

Hofstede, G., *Culture's Consequences: Comparing Values, Behaviors, Institutions and Organizations Across Nations*, 2nd edition, Sage, 2003.

Hofstede, G., *Cultures and Organizations: Software of the Mind*, 2nd edition, McGraw-Hill, 2004.

Kotler, P., Wong, V., Saunders, J. and Armstrong, G., *Principles of Marketing*, 4th European edition, Financial Times/Prentice Hall, 2005, Chapter 10.

Masterson, R. and Pickton, D., *Marketing: An Introduction*, McGraw-Hill, 2004, Chapter 4.

Morrison, J., *The International Business Environment*, Palgrave, 2002, Chapters 5 and 6.

Office of National Statistics, *Social Trends 38*, Palgrave Macmillan, 2008. Available free online.

Worthington, I., 'The Social and Economic Context', in Rose, A. and Lawton, A., *Public Services Management*, Financial Times/Prentice Hall, 1999, pp. 26–43.

Web links and further questions are available on the website at:

www.pearsoned.co.uk/worthington

7 The resource context: people, technology and natural resources

Chris Britton

Businesses carry out a variety of activities, but their main activity is to produce goods and services to be sold on the market. In the production process inputs are turned into outputs. Key inputs into the production process are people, technology and natural resources.

Learning outcomes

Having read this chapter you should be able to:

● illustrate the importance of people, technology and natural resources to business

● explain what determines the quality of labour in the economy

● demonstrate the effect of technological change on business

● outline the main issues affecting natural resources

Key terms

Capital	Minimum wage	Resources
Computer-aided design (CAD)	Natural resources	Social capital
	Negademand	Stock
Derived demand	Net investment	Technological change
Educated workforce	Non-renewable resources	Technological
Factor of production	NVQs	unemployment
Fixed capital	Occupational immobility	Technology
Geographical immobility	Occupational structure	Trade union
Gross investment	Participation rate	Wage rate
Immobility of labour	People	Wages
Information technology	Process innovation	Workforce
Infrastructure	Product innovation	Working capital
Innovation	Renewable resources	Working week
Investment	Replacement investment	
Land	Research and development	

Introduction

The main aim of business is to produce goods and services that people want. This production cannot take place without people, technology and natural resources. In economics these three are called the factors of production and are categorised under the headings of labour, capital and land. This chapter will consider each of these in turn. Resources can be renewable or non-renewable. **Renewable resources** would include labour, water, fishing stocks, soil, air and solar power even though many of these might not be renewable for a long period of time. **Non-renewable resources** would be most minerals including oil, iron ore and coal, agricultural land, forests and electricity (in so far as most electricity is derived from minerals).

People

As indicated in Chapter 6, **people** are important in the economy as both producers and consumers of goods and services. For most products that are produced people are the most important input into the production process. Therefore the quantity and quality of the people available in an economy will have a considerable impact upon the economy's ability to produce.

The quantity of people available for work depends upon a variety of factors:

● the size of the total population;
● the age structure of the population;
● the working population;
● the length of the working week; and
● the wage level.

As well as the quantity of labour, productivity will be affected by its quality. This in turn depends upon:

● education and training;
● working conditions;
● welfare services (e.g. national insurance schemes which cover sickness pay, the NHS which maintains the health of workers; also many firms provide their own welfare services like private pension plans, and so on);
● motivation; and
● the quality of the other factors of production.

Some of the quantitative factors have already been discussed in the previous chapter. In this section we concentrate on the idea of the 'workforce' and associated issues, before considering the question of labour quality.

The workforce

The **workforce** is the number of people who are eligible and available to work and offer themselves up as such. The size of the workforce will be determined by the age at which people can enter employment, which in the United Kingdom is 16 years, and the age at which they leave employment. In the United Kingdom the retirement age for men is 65 years and for women will be 65 by 2020. Those included in the definition of the workforce are:

- those working in paid employment, even if they are over retirement age;
- part-time workers;
- the claimant unemployed;
- members of the armed forces; and
- the self-employed.

The workforce in 2008 was 31.7 million, which is about 51 per cent of the total population. The importance of the workforce is twofold: it produces the goods and services needed in the economy; and through the payment of taxes it supports the dependent population (i.e. the very old and the very young).

An important determinant of the size of the workforce is the **participation rate** (i.e. the proportion of the population who actually work).

Table 7.1 shows that the participation rate for women in the UK was 74.2 per cent in the summer of 2008; somewhat lower than the male figure of 83.8 per cent. The figures have, however, been converging over the years. Activity rates were higher for married than unmarried women.

Table 7.1 Economic activity by gender (% men 16–64 and women 16–59), June 2008

	Men	Women
Economically active	83.8	74.2
In employment	80.0	72.5
Unemployed	3.8	1.7
Economically inactive	16.2	25.8

Source: Adapted from various tables, www.statistics.gov.uk.

The trend has been for increased participation rates for women over time as families have become smaller and because of the changing role of women in society as a whole, labour-saving devices in the home, and government legislation to promote equal pay and treatment. Also important in this process are the changes in industrial structure which have led to more part-time service jobs (*see* Chapter 12).

The participation rates for both married and unmarried women have moved in a cyclical way, both dipping during the recession of the early 1980s. The general trend, however, is quite different. The participation rate of unmarried women fell between 1973 and 1998 (74 per cent to 66 per cent of the 16–59/64 age group). The participation rate for married women increased dramatically over the same period, from 55 per cent in 1973 to 74 per cent in 1998.

Table 7.2 gives some comparisons with other EU countries. The United Kingdom has the second-highest activity rates for men and women after Denmark. There are marked differences in the activity rates for women across the EU, but in every country they were lower than the male activity rate.

web link

For more information on albour markets see *www.dti.gov.uk*, *http://europa.eu.int/comn/eurostat* and *www.oecd.org*

Table 7.2 Economic activity rates* by sex for selected EU countries (%), 2006

	Males	*Females*	*All*
UK	77.3	65.8	71.5
France	68.5	57.7	63.0
Germany	72.8	62.2	67.5
Belgium	67.9	54.0	61.0
Italy	70.5	46.3	58.4
Denmark	81.2	73.4	77.4
EU-27 average	71.6	57.2	64.4

Note: *As a percentage of the working-age population.
Source: Adapted from Table 4.7, *Social Trends*, 2007, ONS, UK.

The length of the working week

The average length of time for which people work is also a significant determinant of the quantity of labour that is available in an economy. Generally, the shorter the **working week**, the less labour there is available. There has been, over the last hundred years, a gradual reduction in the length of the working week; 40 hours is now roughly the norm, with a gradual increase in the number of holidays that people take. More recently this trend has been reversed: the average working week in the UK was 43 hours in 2007. Table 7.3 shows the length of the average working week in selected EU countries.

Table 7.3 Average hours worked per week* for selected EU countries, 2007

	All
UK	43.0
France	41.0
Germany	41.7
Belgium	41.2
Italy	41.1
Denmark	40.4
Netherlands	40.9
EU 15 average	41.8
EU 25 average	41.8

Note: * Full-time employees.
Source: Eurostat, 2008.

Both men and women in the UK work a longer week than men and women in all other EU countries.

Wages

It is clear that **wages** will affect how much people are willing to work and therefore the overall supply of labour in the economy. The analysis here will use the basic tools of demand and supply described in Chapter 14. It is advisable to review that chapter before proceeding. The market for labour can be likened to the market for any other commodity, in that there will be a demand for and a supply of labour. The demand for labour will come from the firm which wishes to produce goods and services that can be sold in the market. The demand for labour is a '**derived demand**' as its demand is derived from the demand that exists for what it produces. The demand curve can be assumed to be a normal downward-sloping demand curve which indicates that – everything else being equal – as the wage rate goes up the demand for labour goes down.[1] The supply of labour comes from people. It is equally likely that the total supply curve has the normal upward slope, indicating that as the wage rate increases the supply of labour increases. It is argued that as the wage rate increases past a certain level people would prefer to substitute leisure for wages. The individual supply curve will therefore bend backwards at that wage rate. The total supply curve, however, will be upward sloping, indicating that those not working will be encouraged to offer their services and that those already working might be encouraged to work overtime.

Assuming for the time being that the labour market is a totally free market, the **wage rate** and the amount of labour being used will be determined by the forces of demand and supply, as in Figure 7.1. The equilibrium wage rate is £W and the equilibrium quantity of labour is L. If there is a change in the level of demand or supply, there will be a corresponding change in the wages and quantity of labour.

Trade unions and wages

In the UK there are four different types of **trade union**:

1 *Craft unions*. They represent one particular craft or skill, like the Boilermakers Union, which was formed in 1834 and was the longest-lived craft union in the TUC when it merged with the GMB in 1982. These were the earliest type of union.
2 *Industrial unions*. They have members doing different jobs but in the same industry. Industrial unions are more common in other countries but some UK unions come close to this type; for example, the National Union of Miners.

Figure 7.1 The market for labour

3 *General unions.* They contain members doing different jobs in different industries, like the Transport and General Workers Union.

4 *White collar unions.* They represent the non-manual workers like teachers, social workers, and so forth. An example is UNISON.

 web link | For information on trade unions in the UK see *www.tuc.org.uk*

One of the main aims for all types of union has been to counteract, and protect their members from, the power of the employer. As far as wages are concerned, this has been achieved through collective bargaining. Over the years a situation has been reached where hardly any wage contracts are negotiated individually. Rather, they are collectively negotiated by trade unions and employers. Although there does seem to be a trend away from collective bargaining, coinciding with the anti-trade union legislation of the 1980s and decline in the membership and power of the trade unions, the majority of wage increases are still negotiated by trade unions.

It is argued that the activities of trade unions through collective bargaining have served to increase the wage rate above its equilibrium level and thus cause unemployment. Figure 7.2 demonstrates this effect. Assume that the market clearing wage rate is £W and the quantity of labour being used is L. Assume now that a trade union enters the market that has the power to enforce a wage increase to £W_1. At this wage rate the market does not clear, the demand for labour is L_1 while the supply of labour is L_2. There is therefore excess supply of labour, or unemployment. In this way trade unions are blamed for keeping wages at too high a level so that the market cannot clear.

Figure 7.2 can be used to illustrate the argument of those who oppose the setting of a minimum wage (see Mini case: The minimum wage). Although this argument seems plausible enough, it is not quite as simple as it seems. There are other market imperfections which prevent the market from operating as smoothly as suggested and which contribute towards creating unemployment. There are some industries

Figure 7.2 The effect of trade unions on the labour market which have only one or two employers who can exercise a great deal of power over the market. The arguments over the **minimum wage** are also more complicated and centre on much wider economic and social issues. There are additional factors which may prevent people moving easily and smoothly between jobs. For example, people may not easily be able to change jobs if they are geographically or occupationally immobile.

mini case | The minimum wage

The UK government introduced a minimum wage in April 1999. By October 2008 the minimum wage was £5.75 per hour for workers over the age of 22 years, and £4.77 per hour for workers between the ages of 18 and 21 years. It is estimated to affect over 1 million people

What are the arguments for and against a minimum wage?

1 It will create unemployment – this can be illustrated using Figure 7.2. The market clearing wage rate is £0W per hour. If a minimum wage is set above this level (£0W$_1$) there will be excess supply of labour or unemployment. The minimum wage is a rigidity introduced into the market which is preventing the market from clearing.
   But Figure 7.2 tells us little about the effect of a particular minimum wage. For some occupations a minimum wage of £5.75 per hour will be well below the market clearing rate of £0W and therefore will have no impact on the market at all. It will only affect the low paid occupations. The actual effect of a minimum wage will depend upon the shapes of the demand and supply curves shown in Figure 7.2 – there may be other factors like the elasticity of demand which will influence the impact of the minimum wage. If the very low paid receive an increase in their wages, they will have greater spending power and so the demand for goods and services will rise. As the demand for labour is a derived demand, there will be a corresponding increase in the demand for labour – thus using up the excess supply of labour. A study in 2003[2] found that the introduction of the minimum wage had had no significant adverse effects on the level of employment.

2 It will increase costs to the employers who will pass these increased costs on to the consumer in the form of higher prices. It was estimated that a minimum wage of £3.60 (when it was first introduced) would add around 0.75 per cent to the national wage bill, and about 1 per cent to the annual rate of inflation.
   But there is no evidence that this happened. Employers are faced with a choice – instead of increasing prices to consumers they could accept lower profits or attempt to increase productivity in line with wage increases. In fact a minimum wage might reduce costs of recruiting and training if it reduces labour turnover.

3 A minimum wage might encourage employers to cut back spending on training.
   But one way of increasing the productivity of workers so that the minimum wage does not have inflationary consequences is to train workers, so the minimum wage might actually increase the provision of training.

There is no evidence that the introduction of the minimum wage in the UK had any of the negative effects claimed by dissenters. Twenty of the EU-27 members have minimum wages in operation which vary widely. In January 2008 Romania had the lowest hourly rate (€0.66) while Luxembourg had the highest (€9.06); the UK was the third highest with a minimum hourly wage rate of €7.85. The corresponding federal minimum wage in the US was €3.90, but there are wide differences between US states as some offer higher rates than this. These figures do not measure purchasing power, however, as they do not take into account the cost of living in each country.

Immobility of labour

People are **geographically immobile** for a variety of reasons:

- The cost of moving. It is an expensive business to move to another part of the country, particularly to areas where housing costs are high, like London.
- There may be shortages of housing in certain areas, or it may be difficult or even impossible to sell a house in other areas.
- There will be many social ties in the form of family and friends that people may be reluctant to leave.
- For people with children, schooling will be important. For example, parents are reluctant to relocate when their children are working for GCSE or A-level examinations.

People are also **immobile occupationally** for the following reasons:

- Some jobs require some natural ability that an individual might not possess (e.g. entertainers, footballers, and so on).
- Training is required by many occupations (e.g. doctors, engineers). Without this training an individual could not do the job and the length of training might be a deterrent.
- To enter some occupations (like starting up your own business), a certain amount of capital is required. In some cases the amount of capital needed will be very high (dry cleaning, for example, where the machines are expensive to purchase), and for many this might prove to be a barrier to mobility.

In order to help people to be more mobile so that the labour market works more smoothly, the government over the years has evolved a variety of policies. Job centres and the like attempt to overcome the lack of knowledge of jobs that are available. Training schemes are offered so that people can retrain, and relocation allowances can be paid to alleviate the cost of moving.

These are some of the factors that determine the number of people who are available in an economy for producing goods and services. However, it is not just the quantity of labour but also its quality that is important. The quality of the workforce is determined by many factors already mentioned, but most importantly by the level of education and training of the workforce.

The level of education and training of the workforce

An **educated workforce** is necessary for an advanced industrial nation, in terms of both general qualifications and specific job-related training. The UK does not fare well in either of these areas compared with other countries. There has been a dramatic improvement over the last 30 years in the qualifications gained by school leavers in the UK but it is still the case that in 2005 2.7 per cent of school leavers left without any qualifications and 16.9 per cent of school leavers attained GCSE grade D–G as their highest qualification.[3]

In the UK, a stated aim of the government is to increase the proportion of young people staying on at school after the statutory minimum leaving age. And although the staying on rate has improved since the 1970s it still remains low internationally.

In 2004 only 73 per cent of 17-year-olds in the UK were still in full-time education compared with 90 per cent in France, Germany and Finland. One such policy is the payment of Educational Maintenance Allowances (EMAs) to young people as an incentive to stay on in full-time education after the age of 16. It is too soon to judge the success of this policy but there is evidence from other countries that similar schemes have been successful in reducing the drop-out rate. The UK government also has in place policies aimed towards vocational courses for the over-16s. Table 7.4 gives some examples of these.

Table 7.4 Examples of vocational courses for over-16s

Year	Scheme	Description
1983	Youth Training Scheme	Provided work-related training for 16- and 17-year-olds, both on and off the job. Largely introduced to fill the gap left by the demise of the traditional apprenticeships.
1985	Certificate of Pre-vocational Educatiol	Full-time vocational courses for over-16s containing an element of work experience.
1992	National Vocational Qualifications (NVQs), General National Vocational Qualifications (GNVQs)	A comprehensive system of vocational qualifications at four levels of achievement.
1998	Work-based Training for Young People	This replaced the Youth Training Scheme with the aim of ensuring that young people have access to post-compulsory education or training.
2004	National Qualifications Framework	This brings together general and vocational qualifications into one framework.

National Vocational Qualifications (**NVQs**) are qualifications that cover a specific skill like plumbing or carpentry while General National Vocational Qualifications (GNVQs) are more general and indicate a broad knowledge of an area like the built environment. NVQ level 2 equates to GNVQ intermediate level and is equivalent to five GCSE grades A* to C. NVQ level 3 equates to GNVQ advanced level and is equivalent to two GCE A-levels, and level 4 equates to a degree or higher vocational qualification.

In 2004 these were all brought together as a National Qualifications Framework, part of which is shown in Table 7.5.

Table 7.5 National Qualifications Framework, up to level 3

Level	General	Vocational	Occupational
3 Advanced	A level	BTEC national award	NVQ level 3
2 Intermediate	GCSE (grade A*–C)	BTEC first diploma	NVQ level 2
1 Foundation	GCSE (grade D–G)	BTEC introductory certificate	NVQ level 1

Source: Qualifications and Curriculum Authority, *www.qca.org.uk*, 2005.

The UK government has used a variety of policies in an attempt to increase educational attainment and training. These include:

- the National Literacy and Numeracy Strategy, launched in 1998, which provides for a dedicated literacy hour and one mathematics lesson every day for primary school children;
- the use of Education Action Zones in areas of educational disadvantage;
- the introduction of the Education Maintenance Allowance, which offers financial incentives to young people from low-income homes to remain in education;
- an increased number of Modern Advanced Apprenticeships;
- e2e (entry to employment), which is an entry to a level 1 programme that uses work-based learning;
- in 2001 43 Learning and Skills Councils were set up with responsibility for all post-16 education up to university level;
- in 2002 Sector Skills Councils were set up;
- several new National Skills Academies have been established in recent years.

As well as school and higher education, job-related training is important in improving the quality of the workforce. Training at work can be of two types: on-the-job training and off-the-job training. There has been the development of a competence-based approach to training, which partly stems from the introduction of NVQs. The system is designed to be easily understood and to provide workers with the skills that are needed by industry. It is designed to unify what is a very diverse system of qualifications existing in the United Kingdom at present. Recent developments include:

- In 2006 the Train to Gain scheme channelled funding of adult skills in order to subsidise training in the workplace.
- The Commission for Employment and Skills was set up in 2008 to bring industry into the heart of decision making.

These two initiatives were proposed by the Leitch Report (2006) which looked at training and skills in the UK.

The government sponsors training programmes in the UK for adults, aimed at long-term unemployed or disadvantaged adults. Successful completion of these programmes has increased over time, and the proportion still unemployed after the scheme fell from 53 per cent in 1990–1 to 48 per cent in 1999/2000.

The government also sponsors training for young people. This includes Apprenticeships and Advanced Apprenticeships. These schemes are designed for the 16–25-year age group and aim to provide training leading to recognised vocational qualifications – Apprenticeships at NVQ level 2 and Advanced Apprenticeships at NVQ level 3.

The Investors in People initiative has had an impact on training as it is based on four principles:

- top-level commitment to develop all employees;
- regular reviews of training and development of all employees;
- action to train and develop employees throughout their employment; and
- evaluation of the outcome of training as a basis for continuous improvement.

By October 2005, over 30 000, UK organisations had achieved recognition under the standard, representing 38 per cent of the UK workforce.

The number of women receiving job-related training has increased over the last twenty years relative to men, and there has been a gradual increase for both sexes over the time period. There are significant differences between industries, with, for example, the service sector having a much higher level of training than agriculture, forestry and fishing, and between occupations.

Training is an important issue not just for school leavers and the unemployed but for all employees. The *National Employers' Skills Survey*, carried out in the UK in 2007 found that 21 per cent of vacancies were skill shortage vacancies. It was encouraging that 48 per cent of establishments had a training plan and 67 per cent provided training.

For information on training schemes see
www.dfes.gov.uk
www.warwick.ac.uk/ier (Institute for Employment Research)
www.nfer.ac.uk (National Foundation for Employment Research)
www.lsc.gov.uk
www.ssda.org.uk

Occupational structure of the population

There will be changes in the **occupational structure** of the population over time. These will be caused by changes in industrial structure and technological change. There has been an increase in the number of non-manufacturing jobs at the same time as a fall in the number of manufacturing jobs. There are more women in the workforce now because there has been an increase in demand for the types of goods that have been produced by women. There has also been an increase in the availability and quality of labour-saving devices in the home, which has released women into the workforce. There has been a decrease in the average family size so that if women leave the workforce to look after their children they now do so for a shorter period of time. There has also been a change in attitude towards women working.

Figure 7.3 shows the structure of occupations in the UK by gender. There is a higher percentage of men than women in the professional/managerial occupations and there are more men working in skilled trades than women. Women are clearly concentrated in clerical/selling-type occupations.

There was a fundamental change in the nature of working life throughout the 1980s and on into the 1990s, and this has to do with the notion of 'flexibility'. There has been an increase in the incidence of part-time working, for both men and women, and an increased use of temporary contract and flexible working patterns. In 2007, 6.3 million people worked part time in the UK; this represents about a fifth of the workforce. Approximately 3.8 million people were self-employed.

| Figure 7.3 | Occupational structure of UK workforce by gender, 2008 |

Source: Adapted from www.statistics.gov.uk/cci/nugget–print.asp?ID=1654.

Technology

Technology is defined as 'the sum of knowledge of the means and methods of producing goods and services' (*Penguin Dictionary of Economics*). It is increasingly science based, encompassing things like chemistry, physics and electronics, and refers to the organisation of production as well as the actual techniques of production itself. **Technological change** leads to the introduction of new products, changes in the methods and organisation of production, changes in the quality of resources and products, new ways of distributing the product and new ways of storing and disseminating information. Technology has a very big impact upon the world of business in all of these areas and has an important effect on the level and type of investment that takes place in an economy and therefore the rate of economic growth.

Technological change

There have been massive changes in technology in the past ten years. This section will consider a few of these and assess their impact upon business and the economy.

Information technology

Developments in **information technology** have had the effect of transforming existing business activities as well as creating entirely new ones, involving the collection, handling, analysis and transmission of information. There has been a massive increase in the demand for information, and, on the supply side, continued advances in the miniaturisation of components. These will continue even when the

capabilities of the silicon chip have been exhausted, with the development of superconductors and optronics. There are also the advances in the computing area such as
the development of new languages and artificial intelligence.

Advances in information technology have many impacts upon business. They
are creating new products and making old products more profitable to produce
through things like **computer-aided design (CAD)**. The effects they are having on
the different functions carried out by businesses can easily be seen:

● *Administration*. The administration of businesses has been revolutionised by the
introduction of information technology. Most businesses have computer systems, records have been computerised and filing has become unnecessary.
● *Communication*. This has been eased by the introduction of fax machines and e-
mail. Video conferencing has contributed to the change in working practices by
making it possible for people to work anywhere. Telecommunications companies, such as BT, are working on desktop video conferencing systems, where the
video camera is attached to the desktop PC.
● *Production*. The use of CAD will shorten the design and planning phase of the
product and shorten the life cycle of the product. Japan applied this very early
on in the field of consumer electronics and many of the products are withdrawn
from sale and redesigned within a very short period of time.
● *Storage and distribution*. The computerisation of stock control has had implications for the storage requirements of firms. It has made implementation of the
just-in-time method of stock control possible. This is easily seen in the case of
supermarkets where the use of bar-codes on products makes it possible to carry
out a stock check of a whole supermarket in a matter of hours. The shelves can
then be loaded up as the stock check continues. Similarly, the use of bar-codes
with Electronic Point of Sale (EPOS) makes stock control simpler.
● *Electronic Funds Transfer at Point of Sale (EFTPOS)*. This system has also had a revo-
lutionary effect in the area of retailing. Most shops now accept credit cards or
Switch cards where funds are immediately transferred from bank accounts to the
supermarkets.
● *The Internet*. The potential for the Internet is enormous, although it is still, relatively speaking, in its infancy. In 2008 there were an estimated 1.5 billion people
wired to the Internet. The highest percentage population penetration was in the
US (73.6 per cent), the lowest in Africa (5.3 per cent). In October of that year
work started on laying 9300 miles of cable under the Indian Ocean which will
connect East Africa to the Internet. This is intended to be operational by the
middle of 2009 and opens up Africa for the possible siting of call centres given
the prevalence of European languages spoken there.

One aspect of business where information technology has become particularly
important is in providing opportunities for firms to interact immediately with their
customers and suppliers, whoever and wherever they might be. Concepts such as e-
commerce, e-business and e-markets are now part of the business lexicon and are
now an important area of study for undergraduate and postgraduate students alike.
If you would like further information on this rapidly developing feature of the contemporary business environment, we have provided an additional chapter on
e-business which is available via the Companion Website to this text.

Other technological developments

- *New materials*. There are two main developments in this area: the development of materials in the high-tech industries like technical ceramics and the upgrading of materials used in lower-range products like coated sheet metal.
- *Biotechnology*. This is expected to have wide-ranging effects on many fields. The development of new products like computers that can imitate the activity of the brain can shorten the development process for certain products by speeding up existing processes.
- *Energy*. The kind of developments that can take place in this field are the use of superconductors to transport electricity and research which might make solar energy a viable source of energy.

These are the new emerging industries which are creating new products and making old products more profitable to produce. It has been estimated that the output of these emerging industries is 20 per cent for consumption within the industries themselves, 20 per cent for final consumption and 60 per cent for consumption in the traditional industries.

Technology and investment

The second input into the production process after people is **capital**. In economics, capital has a special meaning; it refers to all man-made resources which are used in production. Capital is usually divided into **working capital** and **fixed capital**. Working capital consists of the stocks of raw materials and components used in producing things. Fixed capital consists of buildings, plant and machinery. The main difference between the two is that fixed capital gives a flow of services over a long period of time, while working capital needs to be replaced on a regular basis. Because of its nature, working capital is much more mobile than fixed capital (i.e. it can be used for other purposes much more easily). Capital is a '**stock**' of goods used in the production process, a stock which is continually being used and therefore needing to be replaced. This stock provides a flow of services for the production process.

Capital includes a wide diversity of items, including factory premises, machinery, raw materials in stock, transport vehicles and partly finished goods. As well as these, there is what is often called '**social capital**', which refers to capital that is owned by the community such as schools and hospitals. There is also spending on the **infrastructure**, which is important to all businesses rather than being linked to one particular business. The main components of this are transport, energy, water and information. The transportation system is obviously very important to a developed economy. Road, rail, air and water are used to transport goods, services and raw materials. The capital stock in transport and communications in the UK was £311.1 billion in 2006. The same is true for energy and water; both are used by industry in great quantities, and a good infrastructure in these is essential. The information distribution system is also part of the infrastructure and would include telephone systems and the post.

Table 7.6 shows the capital stock of the United Kingdom in 1998 and 2006 by industry. The level of capital stock increased over the period by 22 per cent, but there are marked differences between industries, ranging from a growth of 92 per cent in real estate, renting and business activities to a fall of minus 30 per cent in mining and quarrying.

Table 7.6 Gross capital stock in 1998 and 2006 by industry at 2003 replacement costs in UK (£ billion)

Industry	1998	2006	% change
Agriculture, forestry and fishing	45.0	41.0	−8.9
Mining and quarrying	132.5	115.3	−30.0
Manufacturing	367.0	356.2	−2.9
Electricity, gas and water supply	160.4	175.3	+9.3
Construction	23.6	38.3	+62.3
Distribution	157.8	229.2	+45.2
Hotels and restaurants	47.4	68.4	+44.3
Transport and communications	198.1	311.1	+57.0
Financial intermediation	91.8	120.8	+31.6
Dwellings	1586.2	1812.5	+14.3
Real estate, renting and business activities	163.4	313.7	+92.0
Public administration	291.2	337.2	+15.8
Education	109.7	138.3	+26.1
Health and social welfare	73.5	99.2	+35.0
Other services	115.0	173.5	+50.9
Total	**3549.5**	**4329.8**	**+22.0**

Source: Adapted from Table 2.2.2., *Capital Stocks, Capital Consumption and Non-Financial Balance Sheets*, ONS, UK, 2007.

The increase in the stock of capital over time is called **investment**. Investment will serve to increase the productive potential of the firm and the economy. Investment usually refers to the purchase of new assets, as the purchase of second-hand assets merely represents a change in ownership and therefore does not represent a change in productive potential. Investment is important for the firm as it is a mechanism for growth; it is an integral part of the innovation process and can have disastrous results for a firm if an investment goes wrong. Generally, the higher the level of investment in a country, the higher will be the level of economic growth.[4]

Total or **gross investment** can be broken down into replacement investment, which is investment to replace obsolete or worn-out machines, and new investment, which is any investment over and above this. This includes investment by firms, individuals (in dwellings mainly) and governments (see Figure 7.4). As might be expected, the level of investment is affected by the state of the economy. There was a fall in the level of investment in the early 1980s and again in the early 1990s, both of these as a result of the recession in the economy (see Figure 7.5). The level of investment in 2006 represented 23 per cent of GDP.

There is an important relationship between investment and technological change which runs in both directions. Investment can form the basis for improvements in technology while improved technology which brings about new ways of producing goods will lead to greater investment. For private firms the main determinants of the level of investment will be the rate of technological change and the scope for extra profit as a result of these changes.

Figure 7.4 Categories of investment in the UK, 2006

Source: Adapted from Table 16.20, *Annual Abstract of Statistics*, ONS, UK, 2007.

Innovation and technology

There are two types of innovation that can occur as a result of technological change: **product Innovation** and **process innovation**. Product innovation is the development of new products, like the microprocessor, which will have far-reaching effects on business. New products impact upon the industrial structure of a country, as new industries grow and old industries disappear. This in turn will lead to changes in the occupational structure of the workforce, as we have seen. It has even had the effect of reducing the benefits large firms derive from economies of scale in cases where the technological change can be exploited by small firms as well as it can by large firms. Another example of product innovation which has affected the level of competition in the market is the development of quartz watches, which allowed Japan to enter

Figure 7.5 Gross fixed investment in UK manufacturing industry (2003 prices), 1979–2006

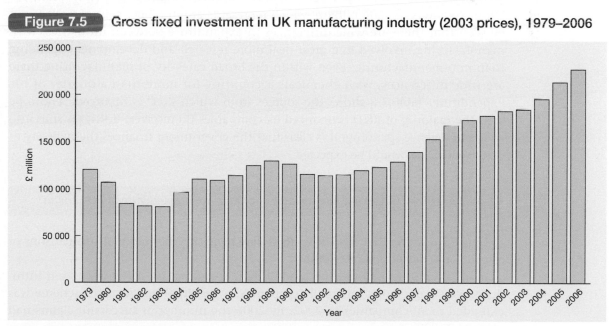

Source: Adapted from *www.statistics.gov.uk*.

the market and compete with Switzerland. Process innovation, on the other hand, refers to changes that take place in the production process, like the introduction of assembly-line production in the manufacture of cars. The two types of innovation are related, as the above examples show. The microprocessor (product innovation), which is a new product, has led to massive changes in the way that production and offices operate (process innovation).

Not all innovation is technological in nature; for example, changes in fashion in clothing are not technological. Innovative activity is important for all industry whether manufacturing or non-manufacturing. In some industries (e.g. pharmaceuticals, computers), innovation is essential if firms wish to remain competitive. A CBI survey of 408 companies in the UK found that the innovation activities of 84 per cent of the sample had been adversely affected by the economic slowdown post-September 11.[5]

For further information on research by the CBI see
www.cbi.org.uk (Confederation of British Industry)

Research and development

Most, but not all, technological changes have occurred through the process of **research and development** (R&D). 'Research' can be theoretical or applied, and 'development' refers to the using of the research in the production process. Most research and development carried out by private companies is directed towards applied research and development. It is designed to develop new products and production processes which will render production more profitable. It is also aimed at improving existing products and processes. Most basic theoretical research carried out in the United Kingdom is financed from public sources and is undertaken in places like the universities.

Table 7.7 shows that the level of research and development expenditure in the UK in 2006 was £14 306 million, which represents around 2 per cent of GDP. It can be seen that there are wide differences in expenditure between industries, with manufacturing involved in a great deal more research and development spending than non-manufacturing. Even within the broad category of manufacturing there are wide differences, with chemicals accounting for more than a quarter of the expenditure. Table 7.8 shows the sources from which R&D is financed. As can be seen the majority of R&D is financed by companies themselves. If R&D is split into civil and defence spending, it is clear that the government finances the majority of defence R&D, as would be expected.

For information on R&D see *www.oecd.org* or *http://europa.eu.int/comm.eurostat*

Figure 7.6 shows that the UK tends to fare badly in international comparisons of research and development spending.

In an attempt to increase the level of R&D spending, the UK government introduced R&D tax credits for small companies in the 2000 budget. This scheme was extended to all companies in 2002. By 2006 the number of successful claims had reached 22 000.

Table 7.7 Spending on R&D (£ million) in 2006 (2006 prices)

Product group	£ million	% of total
All product groups	14 306	100
All products of manufacturing industry	10 796	77
Chemical industries	4 624	33
Mechanical engineering	874	6
Electrical machinery	1 216	9
Aerospace	1 836	13
Transport	913	7
Other manufactured products	1 333	9
Non-manufactured products	3 322	24

Source: Adapted from Table 20.4, *Annual Abstract of Statistics*, ONS, UK, 2007.

Table 7.8 Sources of funds for R&D within industry in the UK for selected years

	1985	1989	1990	1993	1996	1999	2000	2001	2002	2003	2004	2005	2006
Total (£ million)	5 122	7 650	8 082	9 069	9 362	10 231	10 417	11 164	11 865	12 163	12 668	13 310	14 306
Government funds (%)	23	17	17	12	10	10	9	9	7	9	10	8	8
Overseas funds (%)	11	13	15	15	22	23	21	24	27	24	23	27	27
Mainly own funds (%)	66	69	68	72	69	67	70	67	66	67	66	65	65

Source: Adapted from *Annual Abstract of Statistics*, various years, ONS, UK.

Figure 7.6 R&D spending as a percentage of GDP, all sectors, selected countries, 2005 unless otherwise indicated

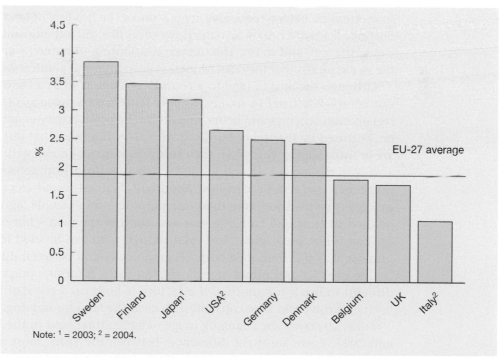

Note: [1] = 2003; [2] = 2004.

Source: Chapter 5, *Eurostat Yearbook*, 2007.

Limits to technological change

Technological change has many effects on the economy and the environment and if uncontrolled can lead to problems, like high levels of unemployment or the exhaustion of natural resources. One area of concern is energy. The world's stock of energy is finite and we are still heavily dependent upon fuel which was formed millions of years ago. The development of nuclear power again represents a finite source of energy, and also carries with it other problems like the disposal of nuclear waste and the possibility of accidents. For these and other reasons the scale of technological change needs to be controlled.

It is also the case that technological change can lead to high levels of unemployment in industries that are in decline. This type of unemployment often takes on a regional bias as the older traditional industries tend to be located in particular parts of the country. **Technological unemployment** is in some respects inevitable as in a changing world it would be expected that new industries would emerge and old industries die. The problem can be tackled by the government and industry through retraining, but what is also needed is a new and more flexible view of work where less time is spent working and more on leisure. Technological change can also give rise to the opposite problem of skill shortage in new industries, where particular skills are required. Technological change has not led to the massive increase in unemployment predicted by many in the 1970s and 1980s.

Natural resources

In economics, **natural resources** are put under the heading of **land** as a factor of production. It would include all natural resources like the soil, minerals, oil, forests, fish, water, the sun, and so on. The uneven distribution of natural resources throughout the world means that they can be used as economic and political weapons.

Although the area of land in a country is fixed, land as a factor of production is not completely fixed in supply as more land can be made available through land reclamation schemes and better irrigation. The productivity of agricultural land can be increased by the use of fertilisers. It is true, however, that our natural resources are in finite supply. And often their true extent is not known with certainty.

It is in the area of natural resources that the distinction between renewable and non-renewable resources is most important. Natural resources can be either. Land can often be used for more than one purpose – for example, agricultural land can be used to grow one crop one year and another the next – but oil, once it is used up, cannot be used again. And even though land can be used for more than one purpose it is still immobile both geographically and between different uses. Land can be used for agriculture or industry, but using it for one purpose makes it more difficult to use it for another. If a factory is built on a piece of land, it would be both expensive and time consuming to clear the land for farming.

Table 7.9 shows the changing usage of agricultural land in the UK between 1971 and 2007. There are slight differences between the years, most notably the inclusion of 'set aside' land in the 1993, 1997, 2000, 2003 and 2007 columns. This was part of EU Common Agricultural Policy where farmers were paid not to use land in an attempt to reduce the overproduction of agricultural goods.

Table 7.9 The use of agricultural land in 1971, 1993, 1997, 2000, 2003 and 2007 in the UK (thousand hectares)

	1971	1993	1997	2000	2003	2007
Crops	4838	4519	4990	4709	4478	4350
Bare fallow	74	47	29	33	29	165
Grasses	7240	6770	6687	6767	6884	7141
Rough grazing*	6678	5840	5878	5803	5565	5552
Set aside	–	677	306	572	689	440
Woodland and other land on agricultural holdings	285	678	763	789	792	954
Total	19 115	18 531	18 653	18 579	18 438	18 602

Note: * Includes sole-right rough grazing and common rough grazing.
Source: Adapted from Table 21.3, *Annual Abstract of Statistics*, ONS, UK, 2008.

Protection of the environment

Increased knowledge of the effects of depletion of natural resources has led to increased environmental awareness among the population. There has been an increased interest in conservation and recycling and the search for alternative forms of energy. A survey by the Department of the Environment found that 90 per cent of the adult population in the UK were either 'fairly concerned' or 'very concerned' about the environment. The issues which caused concern included traffic congestion, global warming, air and water pollution and depletion of the ozone layer. This change in public opinion has already had a major impact on the way in which business operates and is likely to have even bigger effects.

Governments in the UK and elsewhere have a variety of targets for environmental protection relating to issues such as greenhouse gas emissions, biodiversity, renewable energy, recycling, packaging and so on. Some of these targets are set through negotiations with other countries at both international (e.g. Kyoto Protocol) and supranational (e.g. EU) levels and hence are influenced by political, economic, social and technological considerations and by a variety of state and non-state actors (see Chapter 4). Given the growing importance of environmental issues in business, a separate chapter on ethics and the natural environment has been added below (see Chapter 9).

Pressure groups concerned with the environment include *www.foe.co.uk* (Friends of the Earth) and *www.greenpeace.org*

mini case   Oil prices

The Organisation of Petroleum Exporting Countries (OPEC) was formed in 1960 as a cartel of the major producers and exporters of crude petroleum. It did not have much impact upon the market until the 1970s when it enforced massive increases in the price of oil. It did this through cutting back on the supply of oil, as shown in Figure 7.7. The demand curve (DD) for oil is drawn as highly inelastic in shape. The supply curve for oil prior to 1973 is shown as SS, and the equilibrium price of oil was $2.50 per barrel. In 1973 OPEC exercised its market power by restricting the output of oil to Q_2. As a result of this the price of oil rose to $12.00 per barrel.

In 2008 it is difficult to believe that the price of oil was ever $2.50 per barrel. Up to 2003 the price of oil remained below $25 per barrel but volatility in the market and rapid price rises after 9/11 and the invasion of Iraq saw a peak of $140 per barrel in June 2008. Why have prices been so volatile and why have they risen so rapidly? There are two main reasons:

Figure 7.7   The operation of OPEC in the market for oil

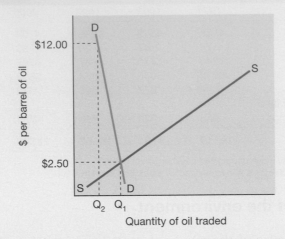

1 Supply factors

No one knows the true extent of oil reserves in the world but they are finite; in the UK, for example, North Sea oil production has halved since 1999. In addition, OPEC does not want to see the price of oil fall to too low a level and will manipulate supply to achieve this. The power of OPEC to raise price in such a way depends upon its ability to restrict the supply of oil to Q_2. There are two provisos to this:

- Inherent in the operation of cartels is the incentive to cheat since if one country exceeds its quota its profitability will be increased at the expense of other countries. Such cheating was commonplace in OPEC from the late 1970s onwards. In addition to this, OPEC does not control as much of the world supply of oil as it did – it accounts for only 40 per cent of world oil production (down from 70 per cent in 1973). Both of these mean that OPEC has less power to restrict supply.
- OPEC does not want the price of oil to be too high as it encourages the search for alternative sources of energy. In the 1970s higher prices encouraged energy saving and the search for alternative sources and forms of energy.

OPEC has stated that it would like to see the price of oil remain around $100 per barrel.

2 Demand factors

The demand for oil is high and rising, especially in the developing countries. It is estimated that Russia, India and China consume 20.7 million barrels of oil per day – taking up the reduction in demand from the US where oil consumption fell in the first half of 2008. In addition, speculation on the future price of oil has also had a big impact upon demand. When growth rates slow down investors tend to move into commodities like oil. Predictions that the price of oil could reach $200 per barrel have not helped. Speculation has two effects – it makes the price more volatile, but also means that price responds to factors which are based on perceptions rather than real forces. For example, the seemingly unrelated testing of rockets in North Korea had an impact on oil prices.

The weakening of the US$ has impacted upon the price of oil as oil is traded in dollars – it takes more dollars to buy the same amount of oil. The strengthening of the US$ and the acceptance of a rescue package for the US financial markets in October 2008 led to a fall in the price of oil to $93 dollars per barrel, but it is difficult to predict what will happen in the future. In the short term at least the anticipated worldwide recession in the wake of the global financial crisis is likely to result in a reduction in oil prices and seems destined to trigger a response from OPEC in the form of a reduction in supply in order to stop oil prices falling.

One important resource in business whose exploitation and use has a significant impact on the natural environment is energy. The UK is not well endowed with high-grade minerals; the main natural resource is energy. There is a good deposit of coal and the discovery of North Sea oil and gas has made the UK self-sufficient in energy supplies. The usage of energy has doubled since 1970 but as Table 7.10 shows there has been a change in the relative importance of the different sources of energy.

Table 7.10 Primary usage of energy in the UK (heat supplied basis); percentage of total

	1950	1970	2000	2001	2002	2003	2004	2005	2006
Solid fuel	78.6	30.7	6.8	7.2	6.9	6.8	6.5	5.9	5.9
Gas	5.9	10.7	37.6	38.2	40.0	39.6	40.4	40.8	40.7
Oil	12.2	47.2	47.9	46.1	46.5	44.7	43.8	42.9	42.7
Electricity	3.3	11.4	7.0	7.6	7.6	7.8	7.8	8.8	9.0
Renewable energy	-	-	0.9	0.9	1.0	1.2	1.3	1.7	1.8

Source: Adapted from Table 22.4, *Annual Abstract of Statistics*, ONS, 2008.

Coal has lost its place to oil and gas as the most important sources of energy. The increase in the usage of both oil and gas is due to the discovery of North Sea oil and gas in the UK. The biggest single user of energy in the UK is transport (33 per cent of energy produced), followed by the domestic sector (28 per cent) and industry (20 per cent). A small but growing source of energy in the UK is renewables, with the government's target by 2020 being 15 per cent.

There is great variation in the fuels used for the generation of electricity across Europe as Table 7.11 shows.

Table 7.11 Fuel used for electricity generation, selected EU countries (%), 2004

	Nuclear	Coal and lignite	Oil	Gas	Renewable energy	Other
France	78.3	4.5	1.0	3.7	11.5	0.9
Belgium	55.4	10.7	2.0	27.9	2.3	1.8
Sweden	51.1	0.7	1.3	1.0	45.4	0.5
Spain	22.7	28.3	8.5	20.2	18.0	2.3
Germany	27.5	48.3	1.7	11.6	9.6	1.3
UK	20.2	33.3	1.2	39.9	3.7	1.6
Netherlands	3.8	23.3	2.8	63.3	6.6	0.2
EU-15	32.3	25.4	4.7	21.4	14.8	1.5
EU-25	31.0	29.5	4.5	19.9	13.7	1.4

Source: Adapted from Figure 3, *Electricity Production by Fuel*, European Environment Agency, 2008.

There has been a dramatic rise in the amount of electricity generated by nuclear power and several EU countries use it as their primary generator of electricity. While its use produces lower emissions of greenhouse gases, there is an increased risk of accidental leakage of radioactivity as well as the problem of the disposal of radioactive waste. Electricity generation from oil and gas has tended to fall and an EU Directive now requires 20 per cent of electricity (for the EU-15 countries) to come from renewable sources by 2020. There is clearly a growing demand for alternative sources of energy.

The alternatives of hydro, wind and solar energy sources will also grow in importance. In the UK the government has tried to promote the search for renewable energy sources through projects like the Non-Fossil Fuel Obligation which requires regional electricity boards to obtain a certain percentage of their electricity from clean sources. It also funds experimental work in the search for new sources of energy.

As well as recycling and searching for new sources of energy there is the concept of 'negademand' where the use of less produces negative demand for those commodities. This concept can be applied to energy and water saving, driving, shopping, etc.

> **web link**
>
> For information on the natural environment in the UK see *www.environment-agency.gov.uk* or *www.the-environment-council.org.uk* or *www.business-in-the-environment.org.uk*
>
> In the EU see *www.eea.eu.int* (The European Environment Agency) or *www.europa.eu.int/comm/environment/index*
>
> In the world see *www.oecd.org*

Synopsis

This chapter looked at the three main inputs into the production process: people, technology and natural resources. It considered each in turn and examined their importance to business and the main factors which determine both the quality and the quantity of these factors of production.

People are important in two ways: they are the producers of goods and services, and also the consumers of goods and services. The quantity of human resources available in an economy depends upon things like total population size, participation rates, length of working week and wages. The quality depends upon such things as the level of health care, education and training. There have been significant changes in the labour market over recent years.

One of the main features of the last 50 years has been the massive changes in technology that have had an enormous impact upon business, resulting in new products and markets and new methods of production and distribution.

As far as natural resources are concerned, the traditional view was that they were fixed in supply and therefore did not receive much consideration. However, with increased environmental awareness there is growing concern that this is not the case and that many of our natural resources are non-renewable and therefore need to be conserved.

Each of the three inputs into the production process has been considered separately but they are interlinked and difficult to separate in reality. It has already been said that the productivity of people will be affected by the technology at their disposal, and this is also true of natural resources. All of the three inputs are 'stocks', from which streams of resources flow to firms. These flows are crucial to business, as without them production could not take place. Both the quantities and qualities of our stocks of these resources are important, as too is the replacement of the stocks that are being used.

Summary of key points

- Three main resources are used in the production of goods and services – labour, capital and land.

- The quantity of labour available depends upon population size, regulations in the labour market, the length of the working week and wage levels.

- The level of education and training determines the quality of available labour.

- The quantity and quality of capital depends on the level and type of investment taking place, the extent of research and development and the level of innovation.

- The quantity and quality of land is an important element in the production process and will depend on many things, including environmental controls.

case study   Resource prices

As we saw in Chapter 1, resources such as labour, technology and raw materials constitute inputs into the production process that are utilised by organisations to produce outputs. Apart from concerns over the quality, quantity and availability of the different factors of production, businesses are also interested in the issue of input prices since these represent costs to the organisation which ultimately have to be met from revenues if the business is to survive. As in any other market, the prices of economic resources can change over time for a variety of reasons, most, if not all, of which are outside the direct control of business organisations. Such fluctuations in input prices can be illustrated by the following examples:

- Rising labour costs – e.g. rises in wages or salaries and other labour-related costs (such as pension contributions or healthcare schemes) that are not offset by increases in productivity or changes in working practices. Labour costs could rise for a variety of reasons including skills shortages, demographic pressures, the introduction of a national minimum wage or workers seeking to maintain their living standards in an inflationary period.
- Rising raw material costs – e.g. caused by increases in the demand for certain raw materials and/or shortages (or bottlenecks) in supply. It can

also be the result of the need to switch to more expensive raw material sources because of customer pressure, environmental considerations or lack of availability.

- Rising energy costs – e.g. caused by demand and/or supply problems as in the oil market in recent years, with growth in India and China helping to push up demand and coinciding with supply difficulties linked to events such as the war in Iraq, hurricanes in the Gulf of Mexico or decisions by OPEC.
- Increases in the cost of purchasing new technology/capital equipment – e.g. caused by the need to compete with rivals or to meet more stringent government regulations in areas such as health and safety or the environment.

As the above examples illustrate, rising input prices can be the result of factors operating at both the micro and macro level and these can range from events which are linked to natural causes to developments of a political, social and/or economic kind. While many of these influences in the business environment are uncontrollable, there are steps business organisations can (and do) often take to address the issue of rising input prices that may threaten their competitiveness. Examples include the following:

▶

- Seeking cheaper sources of labour (e.g. Dyson moved its production of vacuum cleaners to the Far East).
- Abandoning salary-linked pension schemes or other fringe benefits (e.g. company cars, healthcare provisions, paid holidays).
- Outsourcing certain activities (e.g. using call centres to handle customer complaints, or outsourcing services such as security, catering, cleaning, payroll, etc.).
- Switching raw materials or energy suppliers (e.g. to take advantage of discounts by entering into longer agreements to purchase).
- Energy-saving measures (e.g. through better insulation, more regular servicing of equipment, product and/or process redesign).
- Productivity gains (e.g. introducing incentive schemes).

In addition to measures such as these, some organisations seek cost savings through divestment of parts of the business or alternatively through merger or takeover activity. In the former case the aim tends to be to focus on the organisation's core products/services and to shed unprofitable and/or costly activities; in the latter the objective is usually to take advantage of economies of scale, particularly those associated with purchasing, marketing, administration and financing the business.

Case study questions

1 If a company is considering switching production to a country where wage costs are lower, what other factors will it need to take into account before doing so?

2 Will increased environmental standards imposed by government on businesses inevitably result in higher business costs?

Review and discussion questions

1 Why are industries such as electricity 'natural monopolies'? What other examples are there of natural monopolies?

2 Think of one technological advance that has recently been made. What have been the effects of that change on the economy, business and the consumer?

3 In what ways can the general and specific skills of the British workforce be improved?

4 What impact will a much stronger Organisation of Petroleum Exporting Countries (OPEC) have on the market for energy?

5 What impact will increased use of the Internet, both for customer information and purchasing, have on call centres?

Assignments

1 You work in the economic development unit of your local council. The unit is compiling a bid to central government in order to win some resources to improve the basic infrastructure in the locality. Your job is to identify the economic problems that exist in your local town and explain why an increase in resources would overcome the problems. Write a briefing paper to the management committee of the unit on your results.

2 You are a member of your local Chartered Institute of Personnel and Development branch and have been asked to give a talk on 'Flexibility in Working Practices' to a group of trainee managers from a variety of functional and industrial backgrounds. They are particularly interested in three questions:

● What is meant by flexibility?
● Why is flexibility needed?
● What are the implications of greater flexibility?

(Sources for this would include the second edition of this text and *People Management*, CIPD.)

Notes and references

1 For further reading on this area see Begg, D., Fischer, S. and Dornbusch, R., *Economics*, McGraw-Hill, 2005.

2 See paper entitled 'The impact of the introduction of the minimum wage in UK', by Mark Stewart (*www.warwick.ac.uk/res2003/abstracts*).

3 See Table 6.5, *Annual Abstract of Statistics*, ONS, UK.

4 The relationship between investment and the rate of growth is difficult to prove, but there does seem to be high correlation between the level of investment in a country and its associated level of economic growth. It should be remembered, however, that high correlation does not prove that one thing causes another.

5 *Economic Downturn Hits Vital Innovation*, CBI survey, May 2002.

Further reading

Donaldson, P., *Understanding the British Economy*, Penguin, 1991.

Simon, J.L., *The Economics of Population Growth*, Princeton University Press, 1997.

Welford, R. and Starkey, R., *The Earthscan Reader in Business and Sustainable Development*, Earthscan, 2001.

Willaert, D., *World Atlas of Ageing*, WHO, Geneva, 1998.

Worthington, I., Britton, C. and Rees, A., *Economics for Business: Blending Theory and Practice*, Financial Times/Prentice Hall, 2nd edition, 2005.

web link

Web links and further questions are available on the website at:
www.pearsoned.co.uk/worthington

8 The legal environment

Diane Belfitt and Martin Morgan-Taylor

Businesses, like individuals, exist and carry on their activities within a framework of law which derives from custom and practice, from the judicial decisions of the courts and from statutes enacted by governments. This legal environment not only constrains and regulates a firm's operations, but also provides an enabling mechanism through which it is able to pursue its objectives, particularly the achievement of profits through entrepreneurial activity. Like the political and economic environment with which it is intertwined, the legal environment of business is a key influence on the business organisation and an important area of study for students of business. This can be demonstrated by an examination of a number of the fundamental areas in which the law impinges on the operations of an enterprise.

Learning outcomes

Having read this chapter you should be able to:

● understand the idea of 'law' and the sources from which laws are derived

● outline the court system, including the role of the European Court of Justice

● discuss the basic features of the laws of contract and agency

● analyse the reason for statutory intervention to protect the consumer and some of the principal pieces of legislation in this field

Key terms

Acceptance	Customs	Principal
Agent	Delegated legislation	Private law
Capacity	Intention to create legal	Public law
Case law	relations	Statute law
Codes of practice	Judicial precedent	Tort
Consideration	Legislation	Trust
Criminal law	Offer	

Introduction

It is almost universally accepted that for a society to exist and function in an ordered way a set of rules is required to regulate human behaviour. Irrespective of whether these rules are laid down in custom or practice or in statute, they constitute a means of regulating and controlling the activities of individuals and groups, and of enforcing minimum standards of conduct – even though they may be ignored or flouted on occasions. This framework of rules and the institutions through which they are formulated and enforced represent what is normally understood as the 'law', which invariably evolves over time in response to changing social, economic and political circumstances (e.g. the influence of pressure groups). As one of the constraining (and enabling) influences on business organisations, this legal environment is an important area of study for students of business, hence the tendency for courses in business-related subjects to have specialist modules or units on different aspects of business law (e.g. contract, agency, property and so on).

The aim of this chapter is not to examine business law in detail or to provide a definitive insight into particular areas of the law as it relates to business organisations. Rather it is to raise the reader's awareness of the legal context within which businesses function and to comment briefly on those aspects of law which regularly impinge on a firm's operations. Students wishing to examine business law in more detail should consult the many specialist texts which have been written in this field, some of which are listed at the end of this chapter.

Classification of law

Laws relating to both individuals and organisations can be classified in a number of ways: international and national, public and private, criminal and civil. In practice there are no hard and fast rules to classification and some categories may overlap (e.g. where a person's behaviour is deemed to infringe different areas of law). Nevertheless, distinguishing laws in these terms serves as an aid to explanation and commentary, as well as helping to explain differences in liabilities and in legal remedies in England and Wales (e.g. a child under the age of 10 cannot be held criminally liable).

Public and private law

Put simply, **public law** is the law which concerns the state, whether in international agreements or disputes or in the relationship between the state and the individual. Thus public law consists of international treaties and conventions, constitutional law, administrative law and criminal law. In contrast, **private law** is law governing the relationships between individuals and comprises laws in respect of contract, tort, property, trusts and the family.

Criminal law

Criminal laws relate to a legal wrong (criminal offence) – a breach of a public duty, punishable by the state on behalf of society. Decisions on whether or not to bring a prosecution in a particular instance are taken by the Crown Prosecution Service (in England and Wales) and the matter may or may not involve trial by jury, according to the seriousness of the alleged offence and the plea of the defendant(s). In some cases, the consent of both magistrates and defendants is required for a case to remain in the magistrates' court although this may change in the very near future. Moreover, while the criminal process may also arise from a private prosecution, such prosecutions are rare and, in these cases, the Attorney-General (the government's senior law officer) has the right to intervene if he or she sees fit.

Tort

A **tort** is a civil wrong other than a breach of contract or a breach of trust and is a duty fixed by law on all persons (e.g. road users have a duty in law not to act negligently). The law of tort, therefore, is concerned with those situations where the conduct of one party threatens or causes harm to the interests of another party and the aim of the law is to compensate for this harm. The most common torts are negligence, nuisance, defamation and trespass.

Trusts

A **trust** is generally defined as an 'equitable obligation imposing on one or more persons a duty of dealing with property, over which they have control, for the benefit of other persons who may enforce the obligation'. This property may be in the form of money or stocks and shares or in other types of asset, particularly land, where trusts have become a very common way of permitting persons who are forbidden to own legal estates in land to enjoy the equitable benefits of ownership. Partnerships, for example, cannot hold property as legal owners, so often several partners will act as trustees for all the partners (as a partnership has no separate corporate identity it cannot own property – see Chapter 10). Similarly, minors may not hold legal estates, so their interests must be protected by a trust, administered by an individual or an institution.

---

mini case   Banking on advice

Banks have duties as well as rights when dealing with the day-to-day affairs of their customers. Failure to discharge these duties, in some circumstances, may be deemed negligent behaviour.

In September 1995 the High Court ruled that Lloyds Bank had been negligent in lending money to two of its customers for use on a speculative property deal which had failed to come off because of a collapse in the property market in the late 1980s. In essence the customers had claimed that the bank owed them a duty of care in advising them on the merits of a loan to invest in property speculation and that it had been in breach of its duty when agreeing to proceed with the loan. In effect the claimants were arguing that they had been badly advised and that this had resulted in a loss which was not only suffered but also reasonably foreseeable.

In finding for the claimants – who were suing Lloyds under the tort of negligence – the judge ruled that the bank manager was in breach of his duty of care in advising them to proceed and that the couple had relied on his advice, including claims made in the bank's promotional literature. While a ruling of this kind sent shock waves through the financial community, it is, as yet, uncertain whether it set a legal precedent. Certainly, this is likely to prove a far more significant question to Lloyds (and other financial institutions) than the £77 000 compensation awarded to the claimants by the High Court.

Sources of law

Laws invariably derive from a number of sources including custom, judicial precedent, legislation and international and supranational bodies (e.g. the EU). All of these so-called legal sources of the law can be illustrated by reference to English law, which applies in England and Wales. Where laws made by Parliament are to apply only to Scotland or Northern Ireland the legislation will state this. Similarly, any Act which is to apply to all four home countries will contain a statement to this effect.

Custom

Early societies developed particular forms of behaviour (or **customs**) which came to be accepted as social norms to be followed by the members of the community to which they applied. In England many of these customary rules ultimately became incorporated into a body of legal principles known as the common law. Today customs would be regarded as usage recognised by law, whether by judicial precedent (**case law**) or through statutory intervention and hence they are largely of historical interest. Occasionally, however, they are recognised by the courts as being of local significance and may be enforced accordingly as exceptions to the general law (e.g. concerning land usage).

Judicial precedent

Much of English law is derived from **judicial precedent** (previous decisions of the courts). The present system of binding precedent, however, is of fairly recent origin, dating from the latter part of the nineteenth century, when advances in recording legal judgments and a reorganisation of the court structure facilitated its general acceptance.

In essence, judicial precedent is based on the rule that the previous decisions of a higher court must be followed by the lower courts – hence the significance of the court structure. In any judgment will be found a number of reasons, arguments, explanations and cases cited and these must all be considered carefully by judges to determine whether there are material differences in the case before the court and the earlier decision. To reach a decision, the court must find what is termed the *ratio decidendi* of the previous case. Put very simply, the *ratio* of a case are the essential steps in the legal reasoning which led the court to make that particular decision. Anything which cannot be regarded as a *rationes* is termed *obiter dicta* or 'things said by the way'. The whole of a dissenting judgment in a case is regarded as *obiter*. *Obiter dicta* are not binding but may be regarded as persuasive arguments if the facts of the case permit.

Clearly there are times when, perhaps because of the position of a court in the hierarchy, decisions are not to be regarded as binding precedent. However, if the judgment has been delivered by a jurisdiction which has a common law system (e.g. Canada, Australia) or, most importantly, by the Judicial Committee of the Privy Council, then those decisions will be regarded as being of persuasive precedent, and may be used to help the court reach its own decision.

Legislation

A substantial proportion of current law – including laws governing the operations of business organisations – derives from **legislation** or **statute**, enacted by the Queen (or King) in Parliament. As Chapter 4 indicated, the initiative in this sphere lies effectively with the government of the day which can virtually guarantee a bill will become law, if it has a working majority in the House of Commons.

Apart from a limited number of bills proposed by backbench MPs (private members' bills), the vast majority of legislation emanates from government and takes the form of Acts of Parliament or delegated legislation. Acts of Parliament are those bills which have formally been enacted by Parliament and have received the Royal Assent and, except where overridden by EU law, they represent the supreme law of the land. In addition to creating new laws (e.g. to protect the consumer), statutes may also be used to change or repeal existing laws. In some instances they may be designed to draw together all existing law (a consolidating Act) or to codify it or to grant authority to individuals or institutions to make regulations for specific purposes (an enabling Act). Under the Consumer Credit Act 1974, for instance, the Secretary of State for Trade and Industry is permitted to make regulations governing the form and content of credit agreements under delegated authority from Parliament.

As its name suggests, **delegated legislation** is law made by a body or person to which Parliament has given limited powers of law-making – as illustrated by the example above. More often than not, authority will be delegated to a Minister of the Crown, but it may also be conferred on local authorities or other public undertakings, either through the use of a statutory instrument or by some other means of delegation. Since Parliament remains sovereign, such legislation is required to receive parliamentary approval and scrutiny, but time tends to prevent anything other than a cursory glance at a limited proportion of the legislation of this kind. It does, however, remain subject to judicial control, in so far as the body granted authority may be challenged in the courts for exceeding its powers (*ultra vires*).

In addition to these two principal forms of domestic legislation, developments in the law also emanate from Britain's membership of the European Union. Under the Union's main treaties – or those parts to which the British government has agreed –

Union legislation becomes part of the law and takes precedence over domestic legislation, although the latter may sometimes be required to implement it. Accordingly, law which is inconsistent with Union law is repealed by implication and British citizens, like their counterparts elsewhere in the EU, become subject to the relevant Union laws (unless an 'opt-out' has been negotiated).[1]

Whereas the provisions of the main treaties represent primary legislation, the regulations, directives and decisions emanating from the Union's institutions are secondary (or subordinate) legislation, made under the authority conferred by the Treaty of Rome (1957) and by subsequent Acts (e.g. the Maastricht Treaty 1992, the Amsterdam Treaty 1997, the Nice Treaty 2001 and the Lisbon Treaty 2007). As Chapter 4 indicated, regulations are of general application throughout the Member States and confer individual rights and duties which must be recognised by the national courts. Their purpose is to achieve uniformity throughout the EU, as in the requirement for heavy goods vehicles to fit tachographs to control drivers' hours.

Directives, by contrast, are not directly applicable; they are addressed to member states and not individuals, although a directive may create rights enforceable by an individual citizen, as they become directly applicable if a member state fails to implement its provisions within the prescribed time limits. The aim of EU directives is to seek harmonisation or approximation between national laws rather than to achieve uniformity; hence the method of implementation is left to the discretion of the individual state, usually within a given time limit (e.g. the Companies Act of 1981 implemented the Union's fourth directive on company accounts by allowing small and medium-sized companies to reduce the amount of information provided to the Registrar of Companies).

Decisions, too, are binding, but only on the member state, organisation or individual to whom they are addressed and not on the population generally. In practice, EU decisions become effective from the date stated in the decision, which is generally the date of notification, and they are enforceable in national courts if they impose financial obligations.

The legal system: the courts

A country's legal system can be said to have two main functions: to provide an enabling mechanism within which individuals and organisations can exist and operate (e.g. companies are constituted by law) and to provide a means of resolving conflicts and of dealing with those who infringe the accepted standards of behaviour. These functions are carried out by a variety of institutions, including the government and the courts, and a detailed analysis of the legal system within a state would require consideration of the interrelationship between politics and law. Since the political system has been examined in Chapter 4, the focus here is on the courts as a central element of a country's legal system, with responsibility for interpreting the law and administering justice in democratic societies. It is worth remembering, however, that political and governmental activity take place within a framework of law and that framework is itself a product of the political process at a variety of spatial levels.

The English legal system

Under the English legal system, a useful distinction can be made between courts on the basis of their status. The superior courts are the House of Lords, the Court of Appeal and the High Court. Law reports generally emanate from the higher courts – these cases involve a major point of law of general public interest (e.g. *R v R*, 1991). Inferior courts, in contrast, have limited jurisdiction and are subject to the supervisory jurisdiction of the High Court. The current hierarchy of courts is illustrated in Figure 8.1. For domestic purposes (i.e. not concerning EU legislation), the highest court is the House of Lords, which is the final court of appeal for both civil and criminal cases. Decisions reached by the Law Lords are binding on all other courts, though not necessarily on their Lordships themselves.

Like the House of Lords, the Court of Appeal has only appellate jurisdiction. In the case of the Civil Division of the court, its decisions bind all inferior courts and it is bound by its own previous decisions and by those of the House of Lords. The Criminal Division similarly is bound by the decisions of the Law Lords, but not by the Court of Appeal's Civil Division, nor is it bound by its own previous decisions where these were against a defendant, as exemplified in a number of celebrated cases in recent years.

The High Court is divided into three separate divisions: Chancery, Queen's Bench and Family, and has virtually unlimited original jurisdiction in civil matters, many of which are of direct relevance to business organisations. The Family court deals with such things as adoption, wardship and contested divorce cases, while the Chancery court deals with cases concerning trusts, property and taxation. Claims in

Figure 8.1 The hierarchy of courts

contract and tort are the responsibility of the Queen's Bench division, which has two specialist courts to deal with commercial matters and with ships and aircraft. It also exercises the criminal jurisdiction of the High Court – the latter being entirely appellate in instances referred to it by the magistrates' courts or the Crown Court.

In criminal cases the Crown Court has exclusive original jurisdiction to try all indictable offences and can hear appeals against summary conviction or sentence from magistrates' courts. Broadly speaking, the latter largely deal with less serious offences (especially motoring offences), where trial by judge and jury is not permitted – an issue still under discussion following the publication of the Runciman Report (1993). Whereas magistrates' courts have both criminal and civil jurisdiction – with the emphasis towards the former – the jurisdiction of the county courts is entirely civil and derived solely from statute. Amongst the issues they deal with are conflicts between landlords and tenants and disputes involving small claims (e.g. concerning consumer matters) where a system of arbitration provides for a relatively inexpensive and quick method of resolving problems.

In disputes with a supranational dimension – involving EU member states, institutions, organisations, companies or individuals – ultimate jurisdiction rests with the European Court of Justice. Under Article 220 (ex 164) of the Treaty of Rome, the court is required to ensure that in the application and interpretation of the Treaty the law is observed. As indicated elsewhere, in carrying out this function, the court has adopted a relatively flexible approach in order to take account of changing circumstances (see Chapter 4). Few would dispute that its judgments have had, and will continue to have, a considerable influence on the development of EU law.

mini case Jean-Marc Bosman – a case of foul play?

An example of how EU law affects individuals and organisations in member states is provided by the case of Jean-Marc Bosman, a Belgian football player who successfully challenged the transfer fee system operated by Europe's football authorities in the mid-1990s.

Bosman, who had been under contract to the Belgian club Liège, had sought a transfer to a French team when his contract expired but had his ambitions thwarted when Liège demanded a very high transfer fee. In the judgment of the European Court of Justice, clubs could no longer demand a fee for players out of contract if the player was headed for another EU member state. According to the judges, the system allowing for a fee to be imposed violated the right enshrined in the Treaty of Rome that European citizens could go from one EU country to another in pursuit of work. They also held that the rule limiting the number of foreign players a club could field in European matches violated the principle of the free movement of workers.

As a final comment, it is perhaps worth stating that while conflict remains an enduring feature of daily life, many disputes are settled without recourse to the courts, often through direct negotiation between the parties concerned (e.g. Richard Branson's attempts to reach a negotiated settlement with British Airways over its alleged 'dirty tricks' campaign). Moreover, even where negotiations fail or where one party declines to negotiate, a dispute will not necessarily result in court action, but may be dealt with in other ways. Disputes over employment contracts, for example, tend to be dealt with by a specialist tribunal, set up by statute to exercise specific functions of a quasi-legal nature. Similarly, complaints concerning maladministration by public (and increasingly private) bodies are generally dealt with by a system of 'ombudsmen', covering areas as diverse as social security benefits and local authority services. Financial services such as banking and insurance are covered by the Financial Services Ombudsman.

Business organisations and the law

Business organisations have been described as transformers of inputs into output in the sense that they acquire and use resources to produce goods or services for consumption. As Table 8.1 illustrates, all aspects of this transformation process are influenced by the law.

It is important to emphasise from the outset that the law not only constrains business activity (e.g. by establishing minimum standards of health and safety at work which are enforceable by law), but also assists it (e.g. by providing a means by which a business unit can have an independent existence from its members), and in doing so helps an enterprise to achieve its commercial and other objectives. In short, the legal environment within which businesses operate is an enabling as well as a regulatory environment and one which provides a considerable degree of certainty and stability to the conduct of business both within and between democratic states.

Given the extensive influence of the law on business organisations, it is clearly impossible to examine all aspects of the legal context within which firms function. Accordingly, in the analysis below attention is focused primarily on contract law, agency, and some of the more important statutes enacted to protect the interests of the consumer, since these are areas fundamental to business operations. Laws relating to the establishment of an enterprise and to the operation of markets are discussed in Chapters 10 and 17 respectively.

Table 8.1 Law and the business organisation

Business activity	Examples of legal influences
Establishing the organisation	Company laws, partnerships, business names
Acquiring resources	Planning laws, property laws, contract, agency
Business operations	Employment laws, health and safety laws, contract, agency
Selling output for consumption	Consumer laws, contract, agency

Contract law: the essentials

All businesses enter into contracts, whether with suppliers or employees or financiers or customers, and these contracts will be important – and possibly crucial – to the firm's operations. Such contracts are essentially agreements (oral or written) between two or more persons which are legally enforceable, provided they comprise a number of essential elements. These elements are: offer, acceptance, consideration, intention to create legal relations and capacity.

Offer

An **offer** is a declaration by the offeror that they intend to be legally bound by the terms stated in the offer if it is accepted by the offeree (e.g. to supply component parts at a particular price within a specified time period). This declaration may be made orally or in writing or by conduct between the parties and must be clear and unambiguous. Furthermore it should not be confused with an 'invitation to treat', which is essentially an invitation to make an offer, as is generally the case with advertisements, auctions and goods on display. Tenders are offers; a request for tenders is merely an invitation for offers to be made.

Termination of an offer can happen in several ways. Clearly an offer is ended when it is accepted but, that apart, an offer may be revoked at any time up to acceptance. It is of no consequence, legally, that an offer may be kept open for a certain time. It is only when some consideration is paid for 'buying the option' that the time factor is important and this 'buying the option' would generally be a separate contract in any case. If an offer is for a certain length of time, then later acceptance is ineffective, and even where there is no specified time limit, the courts will imply a reasonable time. Thus, in *Ramsgate Victoria Hotel v Montefiore* (1866), shares in the hotel were offered for sale. After several months the offer was 'accepted' but the court held that too much time had passed, bearing in mind that the purpose of the shares offer was to raise money.

Another way for an offer to come to an end is by the failure of a condition. Although a genuine offer is always held to be firm and certain, sometimes it may be conditional and not absolute. Thus, should A wish to buy a model car from B, B may agree but impose conditions on the deal, such as stating that A must collect at a specific time on a certain day at a particular place and must pay in cash. This is known as a 'condition precedent' and failure to complete the conditions will nullify the agreement. There is another type of condition, called a 'condition subsequent' where there is a perfectly good contract which runs until something happens. For instance, a garage may have a good contract with an oil company to buy petrol at £x per 1000 litres until the price of oil at Rotterdam reaches \$$x$ per barrel. It is only when oil reaches the stipulated price that the contract ends.

Acceptance

Just as an offer must be firm and certain, the **acceptance** of an offer by the person(s) to whom it was made must be unequivocal and must not contain any alterations or additions. Accordingly, any attempt to alter the terms of an offer is regarded as a counter-offer and thus a rejection of the original offer, leaving the original offeror free to accept or decline as he or she chooses.

While acceptance of an offer normally occurs either in writing or verbally, it may also be implied by conduct. In the case of *Brogden v Metropolitan Railways Co.* (1877) Mr Brogden had supplied the company for many years without formalities. It was then decided to regularise the position and a draft agreement was sent to him. He inserted a new term, marked the draft 'approved' and returned it to the company where it was placed in a drawer and forgotten about, although both parties traded with each other on the terms of the draft for more than two years. Following a dispute, Mr Brogden claimed there was no contract. The House of Lords decided differently, saying that a contract had been created by conduct.

Inferring the acceptance of an offer by conduct is quite different from assuming that silence on the part of the offeree constitutes acceptance; silence cannot be construed as an acceptance. Equally, while the offeror may prescribe the method of acceptance (although this is regarded as permissive rather than directory), the offeree may not prescribe a method by which he or she will make acceptance. For instance, an offer may be made by fax, thus implying that a fast response is required; therefore a reply accepting the offer which is sent by second-class mail may well be treated as nugatory.

There are some rules about acceptance which are important. Postal acceptance, for example, is a good method of communication and one which is universally used by businesses, but to be valid for contractual purposes a communication must be properly addressed and stamped and then placed into the hands of the duly authorised person (i.e. the post box or over the counter). An acceptance sent to a home address may be nullified if there has been no indication that this is acceptable. Similarly, acceptance of the offer must be effectively received by the offeror where modern, instantaneous methods of communication are used. Thus if a telephone call is muffled by extraneous sound, then the acceptance must be repeated so that the offeror hears it clearly.

Consideration

Together, offer and acceptance constitute the basis of an 'agreement' or meeting of minds, provided the parties are clear as to what they are agreeing about (i.e. a *consensus ad idem* exists). However, English courts will rarely enforce a 'naked promise'. As a result, a promise must have 'consideration'. **Consideration** has been defined as some right, interest, profit or benefit accruing to one party or some forbearance, detriment, loss or responsibility given, suffered or undertaken by the other. In commercial contracts, the consideration normally takes the form of a cash payment in return for the goods or services provided (i.e. the 'price' in a contract of sale). It does not need to be the full market value, but it must be something tangible. In contracts involving barter, however, which are sometimes used in international trade, goods are often exchanged for other goods or for some other form of non-pecuniary consideration (e.g. information or advice).

Intention to create legal relations

Not every agreement is intended to create a legally binding relationship. For example, most domestic agreements – such as the division of household chores – would not constitute a contract recognised in law. In commercial agreements, however, it is generally accepted that both parties intend to make a legally binding contract and therefore it is unnecessary to include terms to this effect. Should such a presumption be challenged, the burden of proof rests with the person who disputes the presumption.

Capacity

A contract may be valid, voidable or void and one of the factors which determines this is the contractual capacity of the respective parties to the agreement. Normally speaking, an adult may make a contract with another adult which, if entered into freely and without any defects, and which is not contrary to public policy, is binding upon them both (i.e. valid). However, the law provides protection for certain categories of persons deemed not to have full contractual capacity (e.g. minors, drunks and the mentally disordered); hence the practice by firms of excluding people under the age of 18 from offers of goods to be supplied on credit.

Concentrating on minors – those below voting age – the law prescribes that they can only be bound by contracts for 'necessaries' (e.g. food, clothing, lodging) and contracts of employment that are advantageous or beneficial, as in the case of a job which contains an element of training or education. In most other instances, contracts with minors are void or voidable and as such will be either unenforceable or capable of being repudiated by the minor.

In the case of business, legal capacity depends on the firm's legal status. Unincorporated bodies (e.g. sole traders, partnerships) do not have a distinct legal personality and hence the party to the agreement is liable for their part of the bargain. Limited companies, by contrast, have a separate legal identity from their members and hence contractual capacity rests with the company, within the limits laid down in the objects clause of its Memorandum of Association (see Chapter 10).

Other factors

To be enforceable at law a contract must be legal (i.e. not forbidden by law or contrary to public policy). Similarly, the agreement must have been reached voluntarily and result in a genuine meeting of minds. Consequently, contracts involving mistakes of fact, misrepresentation of the facts, or undue influence or duress may be void or voidable, depending on the circumstances. In insurance contracts, for instance, the insured is required to disclose all material facts to the insurer (e.g. health record, driving record), otherwise a policy may be invalidated. In this context a 'material fact' is one which would affect the mind of a prudent insurer, even though the materiality may not be appreciated by the insured.

Agency

As business activity has become more specialised and complex, firms have increasingly turned to outside individuals to carry out specialist functions such as freight forwarding, overseas representation, insurance broking and commercial letting. These individuals (known as **agents**) are authorised by the individual or organisation hiring them (known as the **principal**) to act on their behalf, thus creating an agency relationship. As in other areas of commercial activity, special rules of law have evolved to regulate the behaviour of the parties involved in such a relationship.

In essence, the function of an agent is to act on behalf of a principal so as to effect a contract between the principal and a third party. The agent may be a 'servant' of the principal (i.e. under their control as in the case of a sales representative) or an 'independent contractor' (i.e. their own master as in the case of an estate agent) and will be operating with the consent of the principal whether by contract or implication. Having established a contractual relationship between the principal and the third party, the agent generally leaves the picture and usually has no rights and duties under the contract thus made.

With regard to an agent's specific obligations under an agency agreement, these are normally expressly stated under the terms of the agreement, although some may also be implied. Traditionally the common law of agency prescribes, however, that agents:

- *Obey the lawful instruction of the principal*, otherwise they may be in breach of contract.
- *Exercise due care and skill*, in order to produce a deal which is to the principal's best advantage.
- *Act personally*, rather than delegate, unless expressly or implicitly authorised to do so.
- *Act in good faith*, thus avoiding conflicts of interest or undisclosed profits and bribes.
- *Keep proper accounts*, which separate the principal's funds from those which belong personally to the agent.

Moreover, in so far as an agent is acting under the principal's authority, the principal is bound to the third party only by acts which are within the agent's authority to make. Consequently *ultra vires* acts only affect the principal if he or she adopts them by ratification and the agent may be liable for the breach of the implied warranty of authority to the third party.

In addition to these common law duties owed by the principal, the Commercial Agents (Council Directive) Regulations 1993 apply when an agent falls within the definition of a commercial agent (Reg. 2(1)). They apply to transactions involving the sale or purchase of goods and they bestow certain rights and obligations upon both the principal and agent. It is clear that these duties overlap to some extent with the common law duties. Regulation 3 provides the agent's duties to their principal:

- a commercial agent must look after the interests of her/his principal and act dutifully and in good faith;
- make proper efforts to negotiate and, where appropriate, conclude the transactions;
- communicate to their principal all the necessary information available to them;
- comply with reasonable instructions given by the principal.

Regulation 4 specifies the duties of the principal:

- to act dutifully and in good faith;
- to provide the commercial agent with the necessary documentation relating to the goods in question;
- to obtain necessary information for the agent. This is a higher standard, perhaps requiring searching for data, than under the common law, where all the principal needs to do is to disclose information in their possession;
- to notify the agent within a reasonable period of time if the usual volume of trade is likely to be significantly reduced;
- to inform the agent within a reasonable period of time of the principal's acceptance, refusal, or non-acceptance of a commercial transaction arranged by the agent.

Law and the consumer

Neo-classical economic theory tends to suggest that laws to protect the consumer are unnecessary. However, modern economists (in particular behavioural economists) have shown that the traditional assumption of working markets is not necessarily reliable, so regulation is sometimes required. If individuals are behaving rationally when consuming goods and services, they would arrange their consumption to maximise their satisfaction (or 'utility'), in the words of an economist. Products which because of poor quality or some other factor reduced a consumer's utility would be rejected in favour of those which proved a better alternative and this would act as an incentive to producers (and retailers) to provide the best products. In effect, market forces would ensure that the interest of the consumer was safeguarded as suppliers in a competitive market arranged their production to meet the needs and wants of rational consumers.

The 'ideal' view of how markets work is not always borne out in practice. Apart from the fact that consumers do not always act rationally, they often do not have access to information which might influence their choice of products; in some cases they may not even have a choice of products (e.g. where a monopoly exists) although this situation can change over time (e.g. through privatisation of state monopolies). Also, given the respective resources of producers and consumers, the balance of power in the trading relationship tends to favour producers who can influence consumer choices using a range of persuasive techniques, including advertising.

Taken together, these and other factors call into question the assumption that the consumer is 'sovereign' and hence the extent to which individuals have inherent protection in the marketplace from powerful (and, in some cases, unscrupulous) suppliers. It is in this context that the law is seen to be an important counterbalance in a contractual relationship where the consumer is, or may be, at a disadvantage, and this can be said to provide the basis of legal intervention in this area.

Existing laws to protect consumers are both civil and criminal and the relevant rights, duties and liabilities have been created or imposed by common law (especially contract and tort) or by statute. Significantly, as the examples below illustrate, a large element of current consumer law has resulted from statutory intervention, much of it in the last 30 years. Indeed, a sizeable quality of consumer protection law comes from the EU by way of directives. These laws – covering areas as diverse as trade descriptions, the sale of goods and services, and consumer credit and product liability – indicate a growing willingness on the part of governments to respond to the complaints of consumers and their representative organisations and to use legislation to regulate the relationship between business organisations and their customers. Europe is keen to encourage consumers to take advantage of cross-border EU markets by harmonising consumer protection. To this end Europe has been adopting consumer protection directives, the most significant recent one being the Unfair Commercial Practices Directive, which has caused a lot of the pre-existing domestic law to be replaced.

The Consumer Affairs Directorate in the Department of Business, Enterprise and Regulatory Reform is a useful source of reference on consumer law – see *www.berr.gov.uk/consumers/index/html*

Trade Descriptions Act 1968 and the Consumer Protection from Unfair Trading Regulations 2008

Until recently the main aim of the Trade Descriptions Act was to protect consumers from traders who misdescribe goods or give a false description of services in the process of trade. Under the Act – which imposed an obligation on local authorities to enforce its provisions (via Trading Standards Officers) – a trader could be convicted of a criminal offence in three main areas:

1 Making a false trade description of goods.
2 Making a false statement of price.
3 Making a false trade description of services.

The penalty for such offences could be a fine on summary conviction and/or imprisonment following conviction on indictment.

However, these provisions have largely been replaced by criminal sanctions as described in The Consumer Protection from Unfair Trading Regulations (2008). These extend criminal liability beyond simply misleading practices to include, in part, aggressive practices such as coercion and harassment. The OFT (see Chapter 17), local authorities and the enforcement bodies also have powers to seek 'stop now' orders against such practices.

The Consumer Credit Act 1974

The Consumer Credit Act, which became fully operational in May 1985, controls transactions between the credit industry and private individuals (including sole traders and business partnerships) up to a limit of £15 000. Under the legislation consumer credit agreement is defined as a personal credit providing the debtor with credit up to the accepted limit. This credit may be in the form of a cash loan or some other type of financial accommodation (e.g. through the use of a credit card). The Act also covers hire purchase agreements (i.e. a contract of hire which gives the hirer the option to purchase the goods), conditional sale agreements for the sale of goods or land, and credit sale agreements, where the property passes to the buyer when the sale is effected.

The main aim of this consumer protection measure is to safeguard the public from trading malpractices where some form of credit is involved. To this end the Act provides, among other things, for a system of licensing controlled by the Office of Fair Trading (see Chapter 15) which must be satisfied that the person seeking a licence is a fit person and the name under which he or she intends to be licensed is neither misleading nor undesirable. Providing credit or acting as a credit broker without a licence is a criminal offence, as is supplying a minor with any document inviting them to borrow money or obtain goods on credit. (Note that the Consumer Credit Bill has been re-introduced in 2005 and so the above rules may change.)

A further protection for the consumer comes from the requirements that the debtor be made fully aware of the nature and cost of the agreement and his or her rights and liabilities under it. The Act stipulates that prior to the contract being made the debtor must be supplied with certain information, including the full price of the credit agreement (i.e. the cost of the credit plus the capital sum), the annual rate of the total charge for credit expressed as a percentage (i.e. the annual percentage rate), and the amounts of payments due and to whom they are payable. In addition, the debtor must be informed of all the other terms of the agreement and of their right to cancel if this is applicable. In the case of the latter, this applies to credit agreements drawn up off business premises, and is designed to protect individuals from high-pressure doorstep sellers who offer credit as an incentive to purchase.

Sale of Goods Act 1979

Under both the Sale of Goods Act 1979 (as amended), the Unfair Contract Terms Act 1977 and the Unfair Terms in Consumer Contracts Regulations 1999 consumers are essentially seen as individuals who purchase goods or services for their own personal use from other individuals or organisations selling them in the course of business. A computer sold, for example, to a student is a consumer sale, while the same machine sold to a secretarial agency is not, since it has been acquired for business purposes. This legal definition of a consumer is important in the context of laws designed specifically to provide consumer protection, as in the case of the Sale of Goods Act which governs those agreements whereby a seller agrees to transfer ownership in goods to a consumer in return for a monetary consideration, known as the 'price'. Where such an agreement or contract is deemed to exist the legislation provides consumers with rights in respect of items which are faulty or which do not correspond with the description given to them, by identifying a number of implied conditions to the sale. In the case of contracts for the supply of services (e.g. repair work) or which involve the supply of goods and services (e.g. supplying units and fitting them in a bathroom or kitchen), almost identical rights are provided under the Supply of Goods and Services Act 1982 (as amended).

The three main implied conditions of the 1979 Act are relatively well known. Under section 13, goods which are sold by description must match the description given to them and it is of no significance that the goods are selected by the purchaser. This description may be on the article itself or on the packaging or provided in some other way, and will include the price and possibly other information (e.g. washing instructions) which the consumer believes to be true. A shirt described as 100 per cent cotton, for instance, must be just that, otherwise it fails to match the description given to it and the consumer is entitled to choose either a refund or an exchange.

The second condition relates to the quality of the goods provided. Under section 14(2) of the Act goods had to be of 'merchantable quality', except where any defects are drawn specifically to the attention of the purchaser before the contract is made or where the buyer has examined the goods before contracting and the examination ought to have revealed such defects. As 'merchantable quality' was a matter of some controversy the phrase was amended to 'satisfactory quality' and this is defined in section 1 of the Sale of Goods and Services Act 1994, but the general expectation is that a product should be fit for the purpose or purposes for which it is normally bought, bearing in mind questions of age, price and any other relevant factors (e.g. brand name). A new top-of-the-range car should have no significant defects on purchase, whereas a high-mileage used car sold for a few hundred pounds could not reasonably evoke such expectations in the mind of the consumer. Thus, while the implied condition of 'satisfactory' applies to sale goods and used goods as well as to full-price purchases of new goods, it needs to be judged in light of the contract description and all the circumstances of a particular case, including the consumer's expectations.

The third implied condition derives from section 14(3) of the legislation, namely that goods are fit for a particular purpose (i.e. capable of performing the tasks indicated by the seller). Section 14(3) comes into its own when a use or range of uses is made known to the seller. Accordingly, if the seller, on request from the purchaser, confirms that goods are suitable for a particular purpose and this proves not to be the case, this would represent a breach of section 14(3). Equally, if the product is unsuitable for its normal purposes, then section 14(2) would also be breached and the consumer would be entitled to a refund of the price.

It is worth noting that 'satisfactory' and 'fitness for a purpose' are closely related and that a breach of one will often include a breach of the other. By the same token, failure in a claim for a breach of section 14(2) is likely to mean that a claim for a breach of section 14(3) will also fail. Moreover, if, on request, a seller disclaims any knowledge of a product's suitability for a particular purpose and the consumer is willing to take a chance, any subsequent unsuitability cannot be regarded as a breach of section 14(3). The same applies if the buyer's reliance on the skill or judgement of the seller is deemed 'unreasonable'. The quality and fitness obligations are only owed when goods are sold in the course of a business, whilst section 13 applies to all sales.

The remedies available for breach of these implied terms was rejection, or damages if the short-term right to reject the goods had been lost, such as by the lapse of an unreasonable period of time (which will depend upon the circumstances of each case). The only exception to this has traditionally been that of durability, that is, where the goods have failed before goods of that type could reasonably be expected to fail. Durability has always been treated as a damages only breach, so as to avoid overcompensating the buyer.

However, the Sale and Supply of Goods to Consumers Regulations 2002 has granted the consumer/buyer new remedies. The Regulations come from the European Consumer Guarantees Directive (1999/44/EC) and seek to continue the move towards harmonising the cross-border sale of consumer goods. The DTI, keen not to reduce the pre-existing levels of consumer protection, added the new remedies to those already existing. The result is that the consumer still retains the short-term right to reject the goods for nonconformity. The period of time to exercise this option is quite short, normally a number of weeks at most. However, if this remedy is lost due to lapse of time, the consumer now has four new paired remedies: repair or replace, price reduction or rescission. It must be noted that the damages awarded for rescission, the last remedy, will include a sum knocked off for 'beneficial use', reflecting the amount of use the consumer managed to get out of the goods. Until these Regulations the consumer had no right to require a repair or a replacement, and could only sue for damages.

Moreover, the Regulations now remove the problem of goods damaged in transit. Under the old law, the risk passed to the consumer/buyer once the goods had been handed over to a third-party carrier, the result being that the purchaser would find both the carrier and the seller blaming one another for the loss. Ultimately, the consumer would go uncompensated unless they decided to sue both parties. The Regulations now require that goods must actually be received by the consumer/buyer in conformity with the contract, so risk passes later. Lastly, the manufacturer must bear the return cost for any defective goods under a manufacturer's guarantee.

These new remedies only apply to consumers/buyers of goods sold in the course of a business. Section 15A of the Sale of Goods Act applies to business-to-business sales where there is only a slight breach of an implied condition of description or quality. The provision seeks to prevent a business buyer from rejecting goods due to a technical breach, and imposes an award of damages only. As damages are based on loss, damages for a technical breach will probably be very low. As a result, businesses which find that they can get the goods cheaper elsewhere will no longer be encouraged to seek to reject goods for minor breaches. This also recognises that rejections of goods is not the norm in business; normally a recalculation of the price takes place. Having theoretical rights is one thing, but in business one may need to trade with the other party again.

As a final comment, under the Sale and Supply of Goods and Services Act 1982, section 3, there is an implied condition that a supplier acting in the course of business must carry out the service with reasonable care and skill and within a reasonable time, where a specific deadline is not stated in the contract. Reasonable care and skill tends to be seen as that which might be expected of an ordinary competent person performing the particular task, though this will, of course, depend on the particular circumstances of the case and the nature of the trade or profession. As in the case of the Sale of Goods Act, any attempt to deprive the consumer of any of the implied conditions represents a breach both of the Unfair Contract Terms Act 1977 and the Unfair Terms in Consumer Contracts Regulations 1999.

Exclusion or limitation clauses in consumer contracts are subject to the Unfair Contract Terms Act 1977 and the Unfair Terms in Consumer Contracts Regulations 1999, which currently operate as a dual regime, giving the consumer the choice of actions. Under the former any clause seeking to exclude or limit liability for personal injury/death or the statutory implied terms against a consumer is void while all other clauses are subject to the test of reasonableness. Under the latter regulations a term that has not been individually negotiated will be unfair if it is contrary to good faith by causing a significant imbalance between the parties. The situation is a little different in business deals although personal injury/death still cannot be excluded. Thus, where a reference is made on a product or its container or in a related document to a consumer's rights under sections 13 to 15 of the Sale of Goods Act, there must be a clear and accessible notice informing consumers that their statutory rights are not affected when returning an item deemed unsatisfactory. It is an offence under the Fair Trading Act 1974 to display notices stating 'no refunds' or 'no refunds on sale goods'. The aim is to ensure that buyers are made fully aware of their legal rights and are not taken advantage of by unscrupulous traders who seek to deny them the protection afforded by the law.

The Consumer Protection Act 1987

The Consumer Protection Act 1987 came into force in March 1988 as a result of the government's obligation to implement EC Directive 85/374 which concerned product liability. In essence the Act provides for a remedy in damages for any consumer who suffers personal injury or damage to property as a result of a defective product by imposing a 'strict' liability on the producers of defective goods (including substances, growing crops, ships, aircraft and vehicles). Naturally, the onus is on the complainant to prove that any loss was caused by the claimed defect and a claim can be made where damage to property, personal injury or death has occurred. In the case of the latter, for example, a relative or friend could pursue an action and, if American experience is anything to go by, could be awarded very substantial damages if liability can be proven. As far as property is concerned, damage must be to private rather than commercial goods and property and must exceed £275 for claims to be considered.

While the Act is, *inter alia*, intended to place liability on the producers of defective goods, this liability also extends to anyone putting a name or distinguishing mark on a product which holds that person out as being the producer (e.g. supermarkets' own-brand labels). Similarly, importers of products from outside the EU are also liable for any defects in imported goods, as may be firms involved in supplying components or parts of the process of manufacture of a product. To prevent a firm escaping its liability as a supplier claiming it is unable to identify its own suppliers, the legislation provides a remedy: any supplier unable or unwilling to identify the importing firm or previous supplier becomes liable itself for damages under the Act.

Firms seeking to avoid liability for any claim have a number of defences under section 4 of the Act. Specifically these are:

● That the defendant did not supply the product in question.
● That the product was not manufactured or supplied in the course of business.
● That the defect did not exist at the time the product was distributed.
● That where a product has a number of components, the defect is a defect of the finished product or due to compliance with any instructions issued by the manufacturer of the finished product.
● That the defect is attributable to the requirement to comply with existing laws.
● That the state of scientific and technical knowledge at the time the product was supplied was not sufficiently advanced for the defect to be recognised.

Of these, the last – the so-called development risks or 'state of the art' defence – is the most contentious, given that it applies largely to products such as new drugs and new technology where the implications of their usage may not be apparent for some years. As recent cases have shown, manufacturers faced with damages from claimants who appear to have suffered from the use of certain products often decide to settle out of court without accepting liability for their actions.

 web link   The annual Report of the Office of Fair Trading (OFT) contains useful commentary on consumer protection issues, including codes of practice and the powers of the OFT. See *www.oft.gov.uk*

Codes of practice

Alongside the protection provided by the law, consumers may be afforded a further measure of security when the organisation they are dealing with belongs to a trade association which is operating under a **code of practice** (e.g. the Association of British Travel Agents). In essence, codes of practice represent an attempt by trade associations to impose a measure of self-discipline on the behaviour of their members by establishing the standards of service customers should expect to receive and by encouraging acceptable business practices. In addition, such codes of conduct invariably identify how customer complaints should be handled and many offer low-cost or no-cost arbitration schemes to help settle disputes outside the more formal legal process.

While codes of practice do not in themselves have the force of law, they are normally seen as a useful mechanism for regulating the relationship between business organisations and their customers and accordingly they have the support of the Office of Fair Trading, which often advises trade associations on their content. Businesses, too, usually find them useful, particularly if through the establishment of a system of self-regulation they are able to avoid the introduction of restrictions imposed by the law.

Synopsis

All business activities, from the establishment of the organisation through to the sale of the product to the customer, are influenced by the law. This legal environment within which businesses exist and operate evolves over time and is a key influence on firms of all sizes and in all sectors, as illustrated by an examination of some of the main laws governing the relationship between a business and its customers. The majority of consumer laws are of relatively recent origin and derive from the attempts by successive governments to provide individuals with a measure of protection against a minority of firms which behave in ways deemed to be unacceptable. Concomitantly, they also provide reputable organisations with a framework within which to carry out their business and, as such, act as an incentive to entrepreneurial activity in market-based economies.

Summary of key points

- The legal rules within which businesses exist and operate are an important part of the external environment of business organisations.

- Laws affecting businesses derive from a variety of sources including custom, the decisions of the courts and legislation.

- Laws are sometimes made at international and supranational level (including Europe).

- Contract, agency and consumer protection are three key areas governing the day-to-day work of businesses.

- Offer, acceptance, consideration, intention to create legal relations and capacity are central elements of contract law.

- Agency relationships are a common feature of business practice.

- The relationship between businesses and their customers is governed by a variety of laws, many of which derive from statute.

- In addition to the protection provided to consumers by the law, many organisations also operate under agreed codes of conduct.

case study — The sale of goods on the Internet

The sale of consumer goods on the Internet (particularly those between European member states) raises a number of legal issues. First, there is the issue of trust, without which the consumer will not buy; they will need assurance that the seller is genuine, and that they will get the goods that they believe they have ordered. Second, there is the issue of consumer rights with respect to the goods in question: what rights exist and do they vary across Europe? Last, the issue of enforcement: what happens should anything go wrong?

Information and trust

Europe recognises the problems of doing business across the Internet or telephone and it has attempted to address the main stumbling blocks via Directives which are incorporated into member states' own laws. The Consumer Protection (Distance Selling) Regulations 2000 attempts to address the issues of trust in cross-border consumer sales, which may take place over the Internet (or telephone). In short, the consumer needs to know quite a bit of information, which they may otherwise have easy access to if they were buying face to face. Regulation 7 requires *inter alia* for the seller to identify themselves and an address must be provided if the goods are to be paid for in advance. Moreover, a full description of the goods and the final price (inclusive of any taxes) must also be provided. The seller must also inform the buyer of the right of cancellation available under Regulations 10–12, where the buyer has a right to cancel the contract for seven days starting on the day after the consumer receives the goods or services. Failure to inform the consumer of this right automatically extends the period to three months. The cost of returning goods is to be borne by the buyer, and the seller is entitled to deduct the costs directly

flowing from recovery as a restocking fee. All of this places a considerable obligation on the seller; however, such data should stem many misunderstandings and so greatly assist consumer faith and confidence in non-face-to-face sales.

Another concern for the consumer is fraud. The consumer who has paid by credit card will be protected by section 83 of the Consumer Credit Act 1974, under which a consumer/purchaser is not liable for the debt incurred, if it has been run up by a third party not acting as the agent of the buyer. The Distance Selling Regulations extend this to debit cards, and remove the ability of the card issuer to charge the consumer for the first £50 of loss (Regulation 21). Moreover, section 75 of the Consumer Credit Act 1974 also gives the consumer/buyer a like claim against the credit card company for any misrepresentation or breach of contract by the seller. This is extremely important in a distance selling transaction, where the seller may disappear.

What quality and what rights?

The next issue relates to the quality that may be expected from goods bought over the Internet. Clearly, if goods have been bought from abroad, the levels of quality required in other jurisdictions may vary. It is for this reason that Europe has attempted to standardise the issue of quality and consumer rights, with the Consumer Guarantees Directive (1999/44/EC), thus continuing the push to encourage cross-border consumer purchases. The implementing Sale and Supply of Goods to Consumer Regulations 2002 came into force in 2003, which not only lays down minimum quality standards, but also provides a series of consumer remedies which will be common across Europe. The Regulations further amend the Sale of Goods Act 1979. The former DTI (now BERR), whose job it was to incorporate the Directive into domestic law (by way of delegated legislation), ensured that the pre-existing consumer rights were maintained, so as not to reduce the overall level of protection available to consumers. The Directive requires goods to be of 'normal' quality, or fit for any purpose made known by the seller. This has been taken to be the same as our pre-existing 'reasonable quality' and 'fitness for purpose' obligations owed under sections 14(2) and 14(3) of the Sale of Goods Act 1979. Moreover, the pre-existing remedy of the short-term right to reject is also retained. This right provides the buyer a short period of time to discover whether the goods are in conformity with the contract. In practice, it is usually a matter of weeks at most. After that time has elapsed, the consumer now has four new remedies that did not exist before, which are provided in two pairs. These are repair or replacement, or price reduction or rescission. The pre-existing law only gave the consumer a right to damages, which would rarely be exercised in practice. (However, the Small Claims Court would ensure a speedy and cheap means of redress for almost all claims brought.) Now there is a right to a repair or a replacement, so that the consumer is not left with an impractical action for damages over defective goods. The seller must also bear the cost of return of the goods for repair. So such costs must now be factored into any business sales plan. If neither of these remedies is suitable or actioned within a 'reasonable period of time' then the consumer may rely on the second pair of remedies. Price reduction permits the consumer to claim back a segment of the purchase price if the goods are still useable. It is effectively a discount for defective goods. Rescission permits the consumer to reject the goods, but does not get a full refund, as they would under the short-term right to reject. Here money is knocked off for 'beneficial use'. This is akin to the pre-existing treatment for breaches of durability, where goods have not lasted as long as goods of that type ought reasonably be expected to last. The level of compensation would take account of the use that the consumer has (if any) been able to put the goods to and a deduction made off the return of the purchase price. However, the issue that must be addressed is the length of time that goods may be expected to last. A supplier may state the length of the guarantee period, so a £500 television set guaranteed for one year would have a life expectancy of one year. On the other hand, a consumer may expect a television set to last ten years. Clearly, if the set went wrong after six months, the consumer would only get £250 back if the retailer's figure was used, but would receive £475 if their own figure was used. It remains to be seen how this provision will work in practice.

One problem with distance sales has been that of liability for goods which arrive damaged. The pre-existing domestic law stated that risk would pass to the buyer once the goods were handed over to a third-party carrier. This had the major problem in practice of who would actually be liable for the damage. Carriers would blame the supplier and vice versa. The consumer would be able to sue for the loss, if they were able to determine which party was responsible. In practice, consumers usually went uncompensated and such a worry has put many consumers off buying goods over the Internet. The Sale and Supply of Goods to Consumer Regulations also modify the transfer of risk, so that now the risk remains with the seller until actual delivery. This will clearly lead to a slight increase in the supply of goods to consumers, with the goods usually now being sent by insured delivery. However, this will avoid the problem of who is actually liable and should help to boost confidence.

Enforcement

Enforcement for domestic sales is relatively straightforward. Small-scale consumer claims can be dealt with expeditiously and cheaply under the Small Claims Court. Here claims under £5000 for contract-based claims are brought in a special court intended to keep costs down by keeping the lawyers' out of the court room, as a victorious party cannot claim for their lawyers' expenses. The judge will conduct the case in a more 'informal' manner, and will seek to discover the legal issues by questioning both parties, so no formal knowledge of the law is required. The total cost of such a case, even if it is lost, is the cost of issuing the proceedings (approximately 10 per cent of the value claimed) and the other side's 'reasonable expenses'. Expenses must be kept down, and a judge will not award value which has been deliberately run up, such as first-class rail travel and stays in five star hotels. Residents of Northampton have hosted a trial of an online claims procedure, so that claims may now be made via the Internet. (*www.courtservice.gov.uk* outlines the procedure for MCOL, or Money Claims Online.) Cases will normally be held in the defendant's court, unless the complainant is a consumer and the defendant a business.

▶

Enforcement is the weak point in the European legislation, for there is, as yet, no European-wide Small Claims Court dealing with transnational European transactions. The consumer is thus forced to contemplate expensive civil action abroad in a foreign language, perhaps where no such small claims system exists – a pointless measure for all but the most expensive of consumer purchases. The only redress lies in EEJ-Net, the European Extra-Judicial Network, which puts the complainant in touch with any applicable professional or trade body in the supplier's home member state. It does require the existence of such a body, which is unlikely if the transaction is for electrical goods, which is one of the most popular types of Internet purchase. Therefore, until Europe provides a Euro Small Claims Court, the consumer cross-border buyer may have many rights, but no effective means of enforcement. Until then it would appear that section 75 of the Consumer Credit Act 1974, which gives the buyer the same remedies against their credit card company as against the seller, is the only effective means of redress.

Case study questions

1 Consider the checklist of data which a distance seller must provide to a consumer purchaser. Is this putting too heavy a burden on sellers?

2 Is a consumer distance buyer any better off after the European legislation?

3 Are there any remaining issues that must be tackled to increase European cross-border consumer trade?

Review and discussion questions

1 Why are laws to protect the consumer felt to be necessary? What other means do consumers have of protecting their interest in the marketplace?

2 To what extent does the supranational structure of European Union law infringe the principle of the supremacy of Parliament?

3 Do you think that tobacco companies should be made retrospectively liable for the safety of their product? Justify your answer.

4 Examine the case for and against increased government control over business practices.

Assignments

1 You are a trading standards officer in a local authority trading standards department. You have been asked to talk to a group of school sixth-form students on the Sale of Goods Act 1979. Prepare suitable PowerPoint slides outlining the following:

   (a) The main provisions of the 1979 Act.
   (b) The customer's rights in the event of a breach of the implied conditions.
   (c) The sources of help and advice available to an individual with a consumer problem.

2 Imagine you work for a Citizens' Advice Bureau. A large part of your work involves offering advice to individuals with consumer problems. Design a simple leaflet indicating some of the principal pieces of legislation in the field of consumer protection and their main provisions. Your leaflet should also give guidance as to further specialist sources of help and advice.

Notes and references

1 'Opt-outs' may sometimes be negotiated, however. Britain initially opted out of the Social Chapter of the Maastricht Treaty, which includes a provision for a 48-hour maximum working week. Within the Union an attempt was made to treat this issue as a health and safety measure which could then be applicable to British firms by majority (not unanimous) vote of the member states. After the 1997 election, the new Labour government decided to 'opt in' to the Social Chapter. The 48-hour working restrictions are now causing concern in a number of areas, notably transport, deep sea fishing and the health service.

Further reading

Atiyah, P., *The Sale of Goods*, 11th edition, Longman, 2005.

Bradgate, R., *Commercial Law*, 4th edition, OUP, 2005.

Card, R. and James, J., *Law for Accountancy Students*, 7th edition, Butterworths, 2002.

Davies, F. R., *Davies on Contract – Concise Course Texts*, 9th edition, Thompson, 2004.

Web links and further questions are available on the website at:
www.pearsoned.co.uk/worthington

9 The ethical and ecological environment

Ian Worthington and Dean Patton

There is a growing body of opinion that businesses have a duty to fulfil objectives that stretch beyond the simple well-being of the organisation to the promotion of greater corporate social responsibility, particularly with regard to the natural environment. This chapter looks at the reasons which lie behind this perspective and speculates on how businesses can be encouraged to accommodate environmental policies into their strategic management techniques.

Learning outcomes

Having read this chapter you should be able to:

● demonstrate the involvement that business has with other elements of society

● identify a corporation's primary and secondary stakeholders and their respective interests

● define the meaning of corporate social responsibility and determine the actions business needs to undertake in order to be considered socially responsible

● analyse the benefits that are available to business from following a strategy of corporate social responsibility

Key terms

Business culture
Business ethics
Competitive advantage
Corporate social responsibility (CSR)
Eco-label
Eco-Management and Audit Scheme (EMAS)

Environmental management systems (EMS)
Genetically modified (GM) foods
Learning curve effect
Life-cycle analysis
Market niche

Polluter pays principle
Resource-based view
Self-regulation
Stakeholders
Sustainable development
Top-down approaches

Introduction

In May 1999 the largest ever survey of global public opinion took place into the changing expectations of businesses in the twenty-first century. Twenty-five thousand people in 23 countries on 6 continents were interviewed about their perceptions of the roles and responsibilities of business organisations in the social and environmental as well as the economic spheres. This worldwide survey – known as the Millennium Poll on Corporate Social Responsibility (**CSR**) – confirmed what many business researchers and corporate leaders had come to recognise over the course of the previous decade or so. Namely, that a firm's social and environmental performance was no less important to the general public (and, therefore, customers) than its traditional roles of making profits, paying taxes and complying with the law. While there were differences in the strengths of opinions expressed in the different countries surveyed, the overall message of the poll was clear: consumers believe that business organisations should behave in a socially and environmentally responsible way and should be held accountable for their actions across a range of areas from protecting the health and safety of their employees, through avoiding unethical business practices, to protecting the natural environment.

In the analysis below, the focus is on ethical and ecological issues in business which have become an increasingly important aspect of the macroenvironmental context within which firms exist and operate. This development can be illustrated in a number of ways. For example, many larger organisations now publish annual social and environmental reports which are designed to highlight improvements in the firm's performance on a range of indicators (e.g. employee training; charitable donations; reduction in carbon omissions) to a variety of stakeholder groups including customers, shareholders, creditors, employees, suppliers, NGOs and government (see below). To achieve these claimed improvements, a growing number of firms in recent years have appointed senior executives and managers with responsibility for directing, monitoring and auditing the social and environmental performance of the business and for communicating this both internally and externally to the various interested parties. In the lexicon of business, concepts such as corporate social responsibility, social responsiveness, corporate social performance, corporate citizenship and corporate sustainability have become relatively commonplace, as have notions such as supply chain ethics, green marketing and triple bottom line accounting. Parallel developments have also taken place in the academic world as a growing number of business and management programmes now incorporate the study of business ethics, CSR and sustainable development into the curriculum, supported by a burgeoning literature in these fields and an expanding group of international journals on the ethical and environmental aspects of business (e.g. the *Journal of Business Ethics*; *Journal of Environmental Management*; *Business Strategy and the Environment*).

To provide an insight into how businesses can be affected by ethical and ecological pressures, the chapter begins with a general discussion of the notions of business ethics and corporate social responsibility before moving on to a more detailed examination of the very topical issue of environmental management in business. For students wishing to investigate these issues in more detail, we have recommended some useful sources in the 'Further reading' section at the end of the chapter. You could also consult the websites of leading multinational corporations and bodies such as business representative organisations (e.g. Confederation of British Industry; Institute of

Directors; Chambers of Commerce), environmental NGOs (e.g. Greenpeace; Friends of the Earth; Forum for the Future), advocacy groups (e.g. Business in the Community) and the various international groups/agencies whose work includes consideration of ethical and environmental issues in business (e.g. UN, World Bank).

Ethics and business

As we saw in the previous chapter, business organisations exist and function within a framework of law emanating from various sources including government. In many areas of life laws essentially direct what individuals and/or organisations can or cannot do and set minimum standards of behaviour based on underlying ethical principles. Not all ethical aspects of business, however, are covered by government legislation or the common law, as in the case of selling weapons to overseas governments or paying low wages to workers producing a product in other countries. By the same token, not all laws governing individual or organisational behaviour raise what would be regarded as important ethical issues.

As Crane and Matten (2004) suggest, **business ethics** is basically concerned with those issues in business that are not covered by law or where there is no definite consensus on what is 'right' or 'wrong' behaviour. Accordingly they define business ethics as 'the study of business situations, activities and decisions where issues of right and wrong are addressed', stressing quite rightly that in terms of organisational behaviour right and wrong should be seen in a moral sense, not from a financial or strategic point of view. It might make financial sense, for instance, for an organisation to exploit cheap labour or flush its waste products into a river at no cost to the business, and it might not be illegal, but is it ethical? As the Millenium Poll and other surveys have illustrated, a firm's stance on ethical issues in business are an important aspect of its external environment and one that applies to enterprises of all kinds and in all sectors of the economy.

While it is beyond the scope of this chapter to discuss all the potential ethical dilemmas faced by modern business organisations, it is worth noting that these have tended to intensify and broaden as business activity has become more globalised and as technological transformation has given rise to the globalisation of communications and the 24-hour instant news culture. Multinational corporations in particular are facing much closer scrutiny by different groups of stakeholders that are increasingly willing to pressurise larger businesses to behave in a more ethically and ecologically sustainable way. Allegations that some high-profile western companies are (sometimes unwittingly) exploiting child labour in the developing world or are involved in ethically questionable commercial practices (e.g. bribery; price fixing) or in environmentally damaging activities (e.g. illegal logging; oil exploration in unspoiled natural environments) inevitably attract media attention and can result in significant damage to a firm's reputation and, potentially, its bottom line. By the same token, firms recognised for having a good ethical stance may find favour with the different stakeholder interests and this could bring organisational benefits of various kinds, including increased sales, access to new customers/markets, improvements in labour recruitment and retention, lower insurance premiums and less scrutiny by governments and/or NGOs.

Whether 'good ethics' and 'good business' are always complementary has been the subject of considerable debate in both practitioner and academic circles and is one which is far from resolved.[1] That said, what is clear is that the question of ethics in business and the related concept of corporate social responsibility are no longer peripheral issues and have been rapidly moving up the corporate agenda in most large business organisations in recent years. If firms are to avoid the potential risks posed by a poor ethical performance (e.g. Enron) and/or exploit the anticipated opportunities offered by a positive ethical stance (e.g. the Co-operative Bank), they need to put in place appropriate mechanisms for managing the ethical issues they face (e.g. values statements; codes of ethics; accredited auditing and reporting systems). They also need to think more broadly about society's expectations or corporate behaviour and of their obligations and responsibilities beyond those to the immediate owners of the business. This notion of a firm's social responsibilities is the issue to which we now turn.

Corporate social responsibility (CSR)

As indicated above, the idea of CSR essentially means that business organisations have responsibilities that go beyond mere profit making and encompass voluntary activities and actions that affect people, their communities and the natural environment. The question of whether, and how far, a firm should engage in such activities if they might adversely affect profitability remains a contested arena. A central theme in this debate has been the issue of the central purpose of the business organisation and the knowledge, abilities and responsibilities of those that run profit-seeking enterprises. Under the neo-classical view of the firm, private sector businesses exist to make profits for the owners (e.g. shareholders) and the responsibility of the firm's managers is to act in a way which enhances the position of the providers of capital, for example by maximising profits and/or shareholder value. Writing in *The New York Times* in 1970, the economist Milton Friedman basically echoed this perspective when he argued that the social responsibility of a business was to increase its profits so long as it obeyed the law and operated ethically.[2] In Friedman's opinion a firm's directors were not only ill-equipped to make decisions on social and environmental matters but, as agents for the firm's owners (the principals), they also had a fiduciary responsibility to the shareholders, not to some broader conception of the social good. Under this interpretation, allocating some of the firm's resources to the pursuit of socially responsible objectives could effectively be construed as unethical since it involves spending money that belongs to other individuals.

This conventional view of the role of business in society has been challenged on a number of grounds and, to many observers of the business scene, now seems very outdated, narrow and arguably naïve. As Chapter 1 has indicated, businesses exist within and draw their resources from the broader society and therefore could be said to have a moral obligation to take account of their social and environmental performance. Added to this, shareholders are only one of the groups with which the firm interacts and consequently there are other stakeholder interests to whom a business has responsibilities and obligations when carrying out its activities (see e.g.

Chapter 10). Such **stakeholders** are both internal (e.g. employees) and external (e.g. customers) to the organisation and under the stakeholder view of the firm (see e.g. Freeman, 1984) businesses have a social responsibility to take into account the interests of all parties affected by their actions and decisions, not just the owners of the business. In contrast to the neo-classical view of the firm, the stakeholder approach stresses the necessity for managers to try to operate the business to the benefit of all stakeholder groups and to seek to gain an effective balance between the different interested parties. Using some of the firm's profits to achieve such an outcome is not necessarily detrimental to the firm's owners and indeed may ultimately help to enhance shareholder value, particularly over the longer term.

More recent discussions of why businesses should take account of their social and environmental responsibilities have tended to focus on the strategic benefits of CSR; in essence how acting 'responsibly' can leverage advantage for the business on both the demand and the supply side (see e.g. McWilliams *et al.*, 2006). Writers such as Porter and Kramer (2002), for example, have argued that a firm can gain a **competitive advantage** by investing in CSR, particularly if its actions in this area become an intrinsic part of its business and corporate differentiation strategies. One important element in this debate has been the application of a **resource-based view (RBV)** of the firm in which social and environmental responsibility are portrayed as an organisational resource/capability that can lead to sustained competitive advantage.[3] Under this perspective, engaging in CSR has the potential to enhance a firm's reputation with key stakeholder groups and this could give it an advantage over its rivals that is both valuable and potentially difficult to imitate. One arena where this might be particularly important is with regard to an organisation's environmental performance, given the growing international concerns over the impact of business activity on the natural environment. This is an issue to which we now turn in more detail.

Environmental management: an issue of corporate responsibility

Organisations accepting responsibility for the impacts they have on air, land and water is just one of the issues to be addressed within the debate on business attitudes towards corporate responsibility. It is, however, the one area where governments, communities and business have worked most closely to improve their understanding of the issues and resolve the identified problems; in particular, to reconcile the perceived need for economic growth with the demand for greater environmental protection and reduced levels of ecological degradation.

Historically, economic development and growth through business activity have been portrayed as beneficial to the well-being of a society and as an important influence on the quality of life of its citizens. Accordingly, organisational practices and processes designed to increase production and consumption have generally been encouraged and welcomed, even though their detrimental effects on the natural environment have been recognised for some time.[4]

While growth invariably remains an objective of governments, its environmental impact has become part of the political agenda at both national and international level, where particular concern has been expressed about the extent of ecological degradation, the rate at which limited resources are being depleted, the frequency and scale of accidents caused as a result of business practice and the global threat of climate change with its attendant problems. Pessimists have argued that in the pursuit of growth many countries may have already surpassed levels of usage of essential resources and sustainable levels of pollution, and have blighted future generations for the sake of present consumption. The more optimistic view is that individual and collective action can give rise to sustainable development which allows for present requirements to be met without compromising the ability of successive generations to meet their own needs. The concept of scarcity and choice is not new, but the way in which human needs are to be met while seeking not to compromise the future is the practical challenge that will face society and therefore all business organisations.

It is the philosophy of **sustainable development** that many argue is the only way forward for the world economy. The problem of environmental degradation is closely related to the issue of economic growth, and both industry and society need to balance environmental protection with economic development. The difficulties in finding an appropriate balance lie not just in the need to reconcile a range of conflicting interests but also in the relative lack of information on the relationship between economic development and its long-term impact on the natural environment.

The seriousness of the situation and its potentially disastrous consequences suggest that an environmental revolution is needed which may require a dramatic change in the behaviour of society and industry as both consumers and producers. Much attention has, of course, been focused on political initiatives which are testimony to the widely accepted view that environmental policy needs to be formalised and co-ordinated at international level if it is to be effective in tackling the salient issues. **Top-down approaches**, however, can only be part of the overall solution and much depends on the actions of firms and individuals in the marketplace and on their willingness to accept responsibility for their own behaviour and its consequences. In short, concern for the environment needs to be expressed through the actions of a myriad of actors, and for a revolution in environmental responsibility to be successful it must permeate all levels of society, including members of the business community.

Business response to environmental concerns

Corporately responsible actions and/or expenditures have a trade-off cost: the alternatives that the money, resources, time and effort could have been used for if they had not been devoted to more socially oriented goals. As indicated previously, this is generally known as the 'opportunity cost', the notion that in a world of finite resources, whatever a business chooses to do, it does at the expense of something else, the opportunity forgone. As a result, the timing of returns is a critical factor in the decision-making process. The returns to investment in greater environmental responsibility are, however, likely to be of a long-term nature, a situation which may offer little comfort to firms, particularly small businesses that are fighting for survival and need short-term returns. Thus while businesses, in general, may want to provide a more environmentally responsible policy – particularly if their stakeholders are forcing them to look to the wider concerns of business practice and process – the implementation of such a policy may only occur if it is deemed to be in the best interests of the business: that is, where the resources are used in an optimum way to provide sufficient reward for the hierarchy of stakeholders.

Business culture at present is still largely driven by short-term profit and the stakeholders that generally hold the most influence are the providers of financial capital, the shareholders or owners of the business. In order to develop greater environmental awareness in business it is necessary to review the way objectives are prioritised to take account of the viewpoints of indirect stakeholders, thus ensuring that the issue of sustainable development is brought on to the corporate agenda. The willingness and/or ability of a firm to be corporately responsible for its own sake has little, if any, precedent in current business practice; organisational policy is far more dependent upon the business environment in which the organisation works. All business activity, by definition, involves some environmental damage and the best a business can achieve is to clear up its own mess while searching hard for ways to reduce its impact on the environment.

It is, therefore, impossible to expect the type of business environment not to influence the level of corporate responsibility, and the degree of change, the intensity of competition and the scale of complexity will all be factors in the creation of policy, whether this be to increase market share or to reduce the levels of air emissions.

If firms are to provide a greater level of corporate responsibility, does society have to resort to the use of laws and government regulation, or will business perceive the change in societal expectations and decide voluntarily to act more responsibly towards the general environment? The answer probably lies somewhere between the two, but there is obviously a close association between the level of legislative impact upon a firm and the degree of perceived impact the organisation would expect to have upon the environment that may lead to the implementation of environmental management systems. Sethi puts forward a threefold typology:[5]

1 *Social obligation*. A situation where the organisation uses legal and economic criteria to control corporate behaviour. The strategy is, therefore, reactive and dependent upon change instigated by the market or through legislation. The organisation exhibits an exploitative strategy, giving in to environmental concerns only when it can obtain direct benefit. The principal stakeholder in this type of organisation is the shareholder and the pursuit of profit the primary objective.

2 *Social responsibility*. This type of organisation tries to go beyond the requirements prescribed by law and instead seeks to conform to the current values and norms of society. The organisation will, therefore, accept responsibility for solving current environmental problems and will attempt to maintain current standards of both the social and physical environment. In order to achieve this the organisation must be accountable to a range of stakeholders and this assumes that profit, although the dominant motive, is not the only one.

3 *Social responsiveness*. This organisation exhibits a proactive strategy, actively seeking future social change. The policies of the organisation are followed with a fervent zeal, the business seeks to lead the field in terms of promoting a corporately responsible attitude. It accepts public evaluation of its policies and procedures and is prepared to impinge upon profit to maintain the high profile it has established through its corporately responsible actions.

As Seth's typology indicates, business responses to CSR can vary and some firms will tend to take a reactive and/or defensive approach in which their response to environmental concerns tends to be minimal and compliance driven. In contrast, other businesses may actually follow a socially responsible approach as a result of the possible advantages it might afford the organisation. In general the hypothesis can be supported that a better society produces a better environment for business. Further, environmental proactivity often makes sound investment sense, leading to increases in market share, a lowering of costs through energy and material savings and finally an improvement in the 'corporate image'. Provision for responsible behaviour is therefore financially good for the business. A further possible impetus for implementing environmental management systems could come from political rather than economic sources. In simple terms, organisations that instigate their own environmental policies and/or regulations tend to face a reduced threat from external regulatory bodies and this improves company image while reducing possible checks upon corporate practices and processes.

The Body Shop's website address is *www.thebodyshop.com*

In essence, the conclusions reached highlight the fact that organisations will not necessarily pursue a proactive role in the development of environmentally responsible policies. The initial short-run costs are prohibitive when the payback is generally assumed to be over the long term. What might be required is a re-education of those involved in the decision-making process so that they understand the benefit of a longer-term view and can identify policies that offer a sustainable competitive advantage over time. This is true for all strategy and is therefore applicable to the implementation of environmental policies.

mini case | Environmental performance in the small firms sector

Numerically, small firms dominate the global economy. In the UK, for example, approximately 97 per cent of firms have fewer than 50 employees. These firms account for 50 per cent of the total working population and around one-third of the country's GDP. The economic importance of the sector has grown since 1979 and as a consequence the environmental impact of the sector has also become more significant.

The small-firm sector has not, however, kept pace with the general environmental awareness of business. Small firms have continually underperformed in the use of environmental audits, knowledge of environmental legislation and the publication of environmental reports.

A number of reasons have been put forward for the perceived failure of small firms to become environmentally aware. These include:

1 *Cost*. Small firms have limited resources and in general do not perceive an economic gain from implementing environmental policies.

2   *Lack of expertise.* Small firms simply do not have the human or physical resources for developing improved environmental practices. In addition they are very sceptical of inviting expensive outside consultants to investigate their existing practices.

3   *Ignorance of legislation.* The plethora of small firms limits the ability of any agency to monitor the whole sector. As a consequence many small firms rely upon the fact that 'what they do not know cannot hurt them'. Small firms are notoriously 'ignorant' about their environmental responsibilities and rely to some extent upon the problems of scale that monitoring agencies face.

4   *Scale advantages.* Small firms cannot spread the cost of any environmental initiatives over a large product range. Nor can they benefit significantly from the improved public relations often generated by environmental good practice.

These factors may have led to a market imperfection in the development of environmental responsibility within business. As a result, new and imaginative initiatives are needed to create greater interest within the small-firm sector and to improve its environmental practices.

Methods of encouraging environmental concern within business

The quality of the existing environment and improvements in it would be regarded by economists as a form of public good. This is a good for which the principle of exclusion does not apply; it can be jointly consumed by many individuals simultaneously, at no additional cost and with no reduction in the quality or quantity of the public good consumed by any citizen.

The fact that the principle of exclusion does not apply creates the 'free-rider' problem because some groups will believe that others will take on the burden of paying for the public good, in this case the extra cost incurred to improve the quality of the environment. Historically, the government has taken charge of public goods (e.g. the fire and police services or the provision of street lighting) in order to ensure that they are provided and not left to the vagaries of the market. Recent events suggest, however, that state intervention in the future cannot be taken for granted, particularly in areas where market solutions appear possible.

Government intervention

Direct action by government within the business sector has not led to improved environmental responsibility. Nationalised industries have not been the bastions of the ecological environment and in some instances in the United Kingdom (e.g. the 'tall stacks' policy) have appeared to disregard the environmental degradation that they created. Indirect action through regulation or legislation may be more effective, but this is not in keeping with the general policy of *laissez-faire* which operated in the United Kingdom under the Conservative government throughout the 1980s and in the 1990s and has been largely followed by the Labour government post-1997.

Furthermore, there are a number of dangers associated with a reliance solely upon a regulatory system as a means of control. Laws tend to be reactive and there may be significant differences between the letter and the spirit of the law. Industry may hold a monopoly of expertise, making government regulation ineffective. Finally, transnational issues (e.g. leaks from nuclear power stations, global warming, acid rain) are far too multifarious and intricate to resolve through regulation. This is not to say that the legal system is always ineffectual, but simply that it is not a precise means of control, often providing the unscrupulous with scope to act as they please.

Indeed, regulation has become an increasingly complex tool to control business practice.[6] The globalisation of business means that organisations are having to deal with different legislative controls and requirements in different countries. In some instances, company policies change from country to country to meet the lowest standards possible. The tragedy at Bhopal, in India, illustrated how the multinational organisation Union Carbide was willing to accept lower standards of safety in a Third World plant than would have been deemed appropriate for a domestic plant in the United States. It pursued a policy of satisfying the law or regulatory frameworks of the individual host country. Similar arguments can be made for the many shipping organisations registering under flags of convenience which allow cost reductions.

Alternatively, to sell in all markets may require working to the highest common denominator. Not all countries operate the same environmental standards and, although the EU has attempted to standardise some legislation there are still differences in what environmental requirements organisations must fulfil in different countries. Conforming to the stringent requirements of certain markets may improve the competitive position of firms in other markets.

Proposed or possible regulation may also persuade organisations to consider the impact of their activities, particularly if in future more stringent legislation looks likely as governments accept the principle of the **polluter paying** for any environmental damage caused. To judge by American experience, it is possible that retrospective action may be taken, with companies being penalised for decisions taken years previously.[7]

For some organisations legal compliance is an end in itself, for others regulations form a minimum standard of behaviour. The culture of the organisation, within obvious cost constraints, will determine the level of behaviour above the law. For the organisation that sees its responsibilities over and above the law, there may be some additional benefits. Those organisations that develop environmentally sensitive processes and systems first will have greater experience than those slower to react, who may find themselves overtaken by the quickening rate of new legislation. It may also be the case that those firms that undertake environmental initiatives first are able to develop a competitive advantage over other businesses in the same sector because they are able to take advantage of benefits associated with experience and **learning curve effects**. There is, however, a danger that organisations view the use of environmental management tools as a one-off measure. Like any business plan, such a process must be regularly reviewed in order to take account of our increasing knowledge of this subject and the changing needs of the organisation.

To summarise, legislation and regulation do have an important role to play in improving the environmental performance of business overall; this is most evident when governments have the relevant information concerning business practice and process. Frequently, however, business possesses the necessary information and the government has to incur a significant resource cost to acquire the relevant knowledge; suggesting that other tools of control are necessary to instil within business the required corporate responsibility. A strong argument can be made for providing greater information concerning products to the consumer, thereby offering the opportunity to individuals to make more informed decisions about which products to consume. Such a policy would reduce the level of government involvement and help to educate individuals as to the part they play in creating environmental hazards and damage.

Market mechanisms

The increased level of environmental awareness among the population – owing to the easier availability of information – has already led to more informed choices being made by various stakeholder groups that interact with business.[8] Customers, suppliers, employees and investors are all more aware of their responsibilities to the environment, and there are various ways in which their considered decisions can influence the overall objectives of business and ensure that the organisation is corporately responsible for its actions. Increasingly, discerning consumers offer a powerful inducement to firms and despite the lack of perfect information some product switching is already occurring. Firms seeking to maintain current market share, or looking for new opportunities, must be aware of these changes. There has been a number of eco-labelling schemes that have been developed which have assisted consumers in identifying products which are thought to have the least impact upon the environment in their particular class.

An EU **eco-label** was launched in 1993, but take-up has been slow across EU members and only around 200 products have been successfully introduced and certified under the scheme. In the UK the former Department of the Environment, Transport and the Regions (DETR) decided in 1998 no longer to continue with the scheme and called upon the EU member states to push for an 'integrated product policy'.

Well-labelled eco-friendly products are far more prevalent in Europe, where there is a much broader view of nature rather than a focus upon particular issues, such as animal rights or certified forestry schemes. This has led to better-regulated and publicised initiatives on encouraging and labelling eco-friendly products. For example, nine national eco-labels are currently operated in seven EU member states (the Netherlands and Spain each have two) and eco-label schemes in Europe are generally well respected, with certification controlled by independent bodies.

The forerunner of these various labels was established in Germany in 1978 and was colloquially known as the 'Blue Angel'. The label has been adopted by more than 4300 products and 90 product groups, and it is claimed that the majority of households look out for the Blue Angel when choosing environmentally friendly products. Other labels include, in the Netherlands, Stichting Milieukeur; in France, NF Environnement; in Finland, Norway and Sweden, the Nordic White Swan. Most importantly, businesses that wish to apply for these labels will have to provide proof of environmental performance from their suppliers to qualify. In this way products will be evaluated using **life-cycle analysis**, a cradle-to-grave assessment of a product's impact upon the environment.

Further emphasis upon the environment has been created with the introduction of a number of **environmental management systems (EMS)** standards. The UK developed the first EMS (British Standard 7750) but this has subsequently been replaced by ISO 14001 to allow the introduction of a common international EMS standard. There is, however, a European Union EMS standard known as the **Eco-Management and Audit Scheme (EMAS)** which is generally regarded as the most demanding EMS standard. EMS standards have followed the same basic approach as the quality standards and it is hoped that these EMS standards will be able to enjoy the same level of success as the quality standards (BS 5750/ISO 9001). This theme is highlighted by the actions of the Body Shop which demanded that Peter Lane, the organisation chosen to distribute its stock, had satisfactorily to pass an environmental audit before being given the contract. The point is further supported by the actions of B&Q, a UK chain of hardware stores, which has audited not only its own products but those of its suppliers. These audits were the precursor of implemented environmental policies, including the delisting of a large peat supplier who refused to desist from sourcing from Sites of Special Scientific Interest. It seems safe to argue that business will in future face greater pressures to meet new demands from the more discerning customer, be they individuals or other businesses.

It is interesting to note that premiums paid to insurance companies have increased in line with losses incurred for environmental damage caused by normal business activity. In the same way that householders who can demonstrate increased security measures in their homes are rewarded with lower premiums, companies which demonstrate evidence of environmental safeguards may also reap such rewards. More critically, failure to demonstrate extensive environmental management systems may lead to a refusal to offer insurance cover. Moreover, lending institutions may not wish to be associated with poorly safeguarded organisations. In the United States, a further development in legislation means that lending institutions may be held liable for environmental damage caused by plant held as collateral for loans. As a result there has been a significant tightening in the flow of funds to polluting industries such as scrap merchants, businesses dealing with hazardous waste, pulp and paper mills and petrol filling stations. Similar trends are evident in the United Kingdom, where banks have become increasingly careful about loans made to small businesses that have any conceivable environmental risk potential. Therefore, finance that is already limited is being further reduced not because of the viability of the business but because of the environmental liability hanging over them. Thus, while the United Kingdom is yet to see this type of legislation, banks and other lending institutions are already very aware of their environmental responsibilities and this is increasingly encapsulated in their lending policies.

External pressure

There has been a considerable amount of pressure from external groups upon business; these have ranged from *ad hoc* groups formed in local communities to large transnational organisations like Greenpeace. The size and scale of the groups may differ but their objectives are similar: to use whatever power they have at their disposal to influence the decision-making process, and there have been a number of notable successes. For many groups, however, this does not go far enough and accordingly the calls for increased democratisation of the decision-making process to include wider stakeholder groups are becoming more frequent and vociferous.

Effective democratisation assumes greater stakeholder access, with attendant changes in structure and culture; the depth of access and the magnitude of change depends upon the degree to which democratisation is embraced. Participatory democracy may be the most effective form, if yet a largely untested philosophy; however, the success of such an approach will require not only involvement in the decision-making processes, but also access to information and expert knowledge which provide the basis for effective power and influence. Significantly, this approach has still to be culturally accepted by the majority of businesses in the United Kingdom.

Finally, there are the dangers of companies burying their heads in the sand in the hope that the 'new environmentalism' is the latest management fad. The costs, however, of a late response and the possible threat of legal action as well as punitive fines could be critical for those that are slow to develop environmentally sensitive policies. Organisations must realise that the stakes are high and that the costs of getting it wrong (e.g. a serious incident causing environmental damage) are significant in terms of company image, fines, lost production, lost sales, insurance premiums and customer loyalty.

Self-regulation

As noted previously, industry is frequently the holder of the information and expertise required for the effective and efficient implementation of regulation. To regulate, the government has to acquire that information and this can be an expensive process. However, if industry were to **self-regulate** and adopt environmental controls without waiting for the government, then this process of information gathering could be avoided. There are obvious drawbacks to this type of approach. Mintzberg has pointed out that often the implementation of self-regulation is a response by business to attempt to offset on-coming regulation. This has two very positive outcomes for the business sector. First, it offers credibility with society that as a sector it has the interests of the environment in mind when conducting business. Second, it provides a convenient smokescreen for practices which may be regarded as dubious by an external body. It is, therefore, inherent in the idea of self-regulation that the organisation can be trusted to fulfil the environmental requirements of the rest of society.

Growing public awareness of environmental issues and the subsequent regulation of business activities have demonstrated that society is not prepared to allow business to be conducted without restriction or without consideration of its impact upon the environment. The assumption that organisations will abide by the rules and norms of their society has been seen to be misplaced. If society is to trust managers of businesses, it must ask by whose social norms they are controlling their organisations. The growing trend for annual environmental reports is a positive step in this direction; many FTSE 100 companies now publish a separate 'green' report which recognises the impact that business has on the environment. The Body Shop has gone one stage further with the publication of a 'values' report, a wide-ranging, independently verified audit of the company's track record on the issues of the environment, animal protection and human relationships within the business. Most reports, however, provide little in the way of substantive statements and disclosures of what remains very sensitive information and, not being covered by any regulation or standard, they tend to lack consistency. Governments are, therefore, likely to be forced to continue to monitor self-regulatory systems and to retain the power to enforce environmental objectives.

---

mini case | **Carbon footprinting**

Walkers Snackfoods (UK) is a subsidiary of Pepsico (US) and produces a range of snack products including Walkers Crisps, Doritos, Wotsits and Quavers. In 2005, the company agreed to participate in a pilot study with the Carbon Trust (a government-sponsored body) aimed at helping businesses to cut their carbon emissions across the supply chain, thereby reducing the carbon footprints of their products. Working with the Trust, and with the different organisations involved in its supply chain, Walkers collected data on carbon emissions at each stage of the life cycle of one of its leading products, from the raw materials stage (i.e. potato production, vegetable oil manufacture etc.) to the ultimate disposal of the package after consumption. These data provided the company with an insight into the

carbon impact of its activities on the environment and pointed to areas in which that impact could be reduced to the advantage of both the company and the natural environment (e.g. by saving on energy usage). On certain packets of Walkers Crisps consumers will now find a logo identifying the carbon footprint associated with the product throughout its life cycle (i.e. grams of CO_2 emitted per packet). How far this will influence consumers in their choice of brands remains to be seen, but it is noteworthy that a number of other leading brand names (e.g. Tesco) have indicated their intention of carbon footprinting their products in the future.

Note: Several other companies have been involved in similar initiatives with the Carbon Trust, including Boots, Cadbury Schweppes, and Marks & Spencer.

web link

For further details see the Carbon Trust website at *www.carbontrust.co.uk*

The benefits to business from the implementation of environmental policies

The previous section has indicated that industry is being driven to develop more environmentally friendly policies; the implication is that organisations would revert to previous policies if the forces driving environmentalism were negated. This assumption, however, fails to take account of the benefits that the implementation of corporately responsible policies has brought some organisations. The drive for greater corporate responsibility has emanated from North America where companies are increasingly expected to draw up their own plans for meeting environmental obligations, putting a premium on having accurate knowledge about their own performance. Business strategists within North America have suggested that in the coming years environmentalism will be at the cutting edge of social reform and therefore one of the most important areas that business must consider. The commitment of industry, however, lags behind the rhetoric and this is particularly true within business in the UK. In order to improve environmental performance there needs to be an increase in information and training, not simply about the environmental consequences, but also concerning the benefits that are being obtained by organisations that are adopting greater corporate responsibility.

Efficiency of factor inputs

Business strategists as well as organisations have already generated a considerable amount of pro-environmental jargon; PPP (Pollution Prevention Pays), WOW (Wipe Out Waste) and WRAP (Waste Reduction Always Pays) are some of the better-known acronyms. The obvious message is that more efficient use of materials and energy will reduce cost, provide a positive effect on the company's accounts and improve the bottom line. In essence, the argument is that by reducing pollution and resource utilisation firms can become more 'eco-efficient' and this can save money as well as protecting the environment. The message that businesses are beginning to receive is that too much attention has been extended to labour and capital costs at the expense of material and energy costs and the new environmental management systems are highlighting this issue.

Improved market image

The image that organisations portray to the rest of society is increasingly important, owing to the development of rapid information flows. Creating this image can be expensive and resources may be wasted as a result of a careless action or remark. A good example of this would be the aggressive marketing campaign used by Monsanto to introduce **genetically modified (GM) foods** into the European market. This campaign had not taken account of the specific market conditions in Europe and the acute concerns of the consumer towards food products. As a result the campaign backfired. In a similar vein a chance remark by a BP representative concerning the oil spillage from the tanker *Braer* in the Shetlands (see case study) was used in an advertising campaign by Greenpeace to illustrate the lack of responsibility shown by large corporations. BP spent an undisclosed sum promoting and implementing a green strategy in order to project the image of an organisation that cares. It can be assumed that the Greenpeace advertisement will have at the very least reduced the effectiveness of this campaign.

Given the current climate of public opinion, organisations which are seen to be improving their levels of corporate responsibility and are able to communicate this to the consumer are likely to improve their market share and to develop customer loyalty (e.g. Varta's development of technology which reduced the heavy metal content of its consumer batteries). The image that a company portrays could also affect the quality of human resources available. Increasingly employees are taking into account an organisation's record on corporate responsibility when deciding upon future employment. The claims of companies must, however, be supported by actions that can be readily communicated and understood by the consumer. Initiatives such as the eco-label and ISO 14001/EMAS will assist in providing clear statements of intent that provide better information for a more informed purchase.

Providing new market niches

The clear message from the market is that there is a growing number of consumers who are prepared to be more discerning about the type of goods they buy, thereby taking into account the impact their purchases have upon the environment. As a result, a number of **market niches** has developed and this has proved attractive to business, given that consumers are prepared to pay extra for a product that is less harmful to the environment. In many cases this means that margins can be increased, a factor which is sometimes contrary to market trends.

In addition to this, there are other market opportunities that result from the need to take action to improve the degree of environmental responsibility. Levels of environmental expenditure are increasing, and this extra expenditure must be generating revenue for those organisations providing the right type of product or service. There are significant market opportunities available, for example, in pollution reduction, energy saving and waste control technologies, and if it is assumed that the push towards more sustainable development will continue, then there will be further opportunities for firms in the field of product and process design.

Proactive legislative compliance

The legislative framework within which businesses operate involves a growing number of regulatory bodies. As indicated in various chapters, legislation from the UK government is supported and often surpassed by EU directives, and organisations seeking to operate successfully in the Single Market must demonstrate compliance if they wish to compete. Regulations which were once confined to product and process now often extend to the way in which decisions are made within organisations and it seems more likely that the Cadbury Report on corporate governance has started a process of increased democratisation of the decision-making process which businesses will have difficulty in preventing. Past organisational performance on environmental issues has not instilled confidence and trust, and it is unlikely that mere rhetoric will calm the calls for more accountability. In future it seems more likely that the demand will be for a socially responsive organisation that accepts full public evaluation of its activities and makes itself accountable to all interested parties; in short, an organisation which is proactive in developing greater corporate responsibility and which is committed in practice as well as in principle to the concept of sustainable development.

Corporate responsibility without intervention?

Many businesses at present appear to be taking up the challenge of corporate responsibility if only out of the slow realisation that it is in their own interest – that is, to avoid regulation, to increase market share and/or to reduce costs. In its purest form, corporate responsibility could be supported for its own sake as representing a noble way for corporations to behave and such a stance can be closely associated with a business attitude of social responsiveness. Since this approach can conflict with a key objective of business – namely, profit maximisation – the question is whether the two are mutually exclusive or if a way can be found to combine profitability and corporate responsibility. Many observers believe that a business environment which is allowed to operate without government intervention seems unlikely to engender corporately responsible organisations. By the same token, legislation on its own cannot be expected to oversee all aspects of business, including the impact that firms have on the natural environment.

Arguably what is required is that a tone is set, through both legislation and societal norms and values, that provides clear signals to businesses; it will then be up to organisations to interpret these signals and to transmit them into policies which provide for the wants of society and at the same time satisfy the requirements of legislation. In this way corporate responsibility will tend to be seen as essential to competitive advantage and will become an integral part of the strategic management process. In short, the pursuit of a philosophy of sustainable development can be instilled into business practice without the excessive use of intervention that so often impinges upon the entrepreneurial flair of organisations. Businesses, however, need to play their part.

Synopsis

The ethical and ecological context of business operations and decisions has become increasingly important as individuals, groups and governments show a greater inclination to look beyond the commercial impact of the business community. Concepts such as business ethics, corporate social responsibility and environmental management have become mainstream issues in the world of business and firms face growing pressures to consider and improve upon their social and environmental performance. While the relative costs and benefits of a proactive response remain open to dispute, many observers believe that 'doing good' can pay, not least by reducing organisational 'threats' and enhancing business 'opportunities'.

Summary of key points

- Business ethics is concerned with issues of 'right' and 'wrong' behaviour in a business context.

- Corporate social responsibility (CSR) is the idea that organisations should be held accountable for the effects of their actions on people, their communities and the environment.

- CSR has become an important consideration for modern businesses, alongside traditional concerns with profitability and growth.

- Being socially responsible as a business does not preclude being profitable.

- Increasingly, business organisations have to take account of the views of their stakeholders on questions of social responsibility.

- One area where this has become particularly significant is with regard to the impact of business operations and decisions on the natural environment.

- Different businesses respond in different ways, ranging from reactive stances through to more proactive environmental approaches which go beyond compliance with regulatory demands.

- The key 'drivers' of corporate environmental responsiveness include government intervention, market forces, external pressures and self-regulation by organisations.

- Firms which implement environmental policies can find they benefit from improved resource efficiency, enhanced market image, new market opportunities, increased competitive advantage and anticipatory reaction.

case study

The *Braer* oil tanker disaster

Introduction

The *Braer* was built by Oshima Shipbuilding in Nagasaki in 1975; it was a single-engined vessel, 241.5 m long, with a dead weight of 89 730 tons. It was registered with the Norwegian classification society Det Norske Veritas (DNV) in 1985 and according to that particular institution had an exceptional record. The ship was required to undergo rigorous surveys every five years and an annual inspection; the last periodic survey was carried out in July 1989 while the last annual inspection occurred in May 1992. Records show that neither of these inspections found anything that could improve seaworthiness and DNV regarded the *Braer* as a very good ship. The vessel itself had not previously been involved in a shipping casualty and Skuld Protection and Indemnity, the insurers of the ship, stated that in their opinion it was a sound ship managed by a sound and responsible company.

The emergency began at about 5.30 a.m. on 5 January 1993 when the tanker, carrying 85 000 tons of light crude oil from Norway to Quebec was passing through the 22-mile gap between Shetland and Fair Isle. The storm force seas had somehow managed to drive seawater into the fuel tank and by 6 a.m. the *Braer* was

without power and drifting sideways towards Shetland. The first tug was dispatched from Lerwick harbour, 30 miles from the incident, at approximately 7.30 a.m., a crucial delay of at least 90 minutes from the time the engines failed. Despite the efforts of the salvage crews, the tanker hit the rocks at 11.30 a.m.; by 3 p.m. there were already reports of large oil slicks, with their subsequent effects on wildlife in the area.

Consequences of the oil spillage

The environmental impact of the wrecked *Braer* oil tanker near Sumburgh Head in Shetland was described by the World Wide Fund for Nature as 'potentially catastrophic'. The site of the disaster is a region of high cliffs and sheltered coves teeming with wildlife all year round. At the time Sumburgh Head was due to be designated a special protection area under the European Community birds directive. The oil coating the rocks settled on plants and fish in the intertidal zone and moved through the food chain, poisoning the feeding sea birds and threatening both the otter and seal population which had a stronghold in the area. A spokesperson for the Wildfowl and Wetlands Trust stated that they were particularly worried about the spillage, in light of a previous incident in 1979 when the ▶

Esso Bernicia spilled 1174 tonnes of fuel oil at Sullem Voe. This spillage had been fatal for all the ducks in the immediate area and the general population declined by 25 to 30 per cent.

While many Shetlanders were dismayed by the threat to the birds and sea life caused by the pollution, their main concern was the economic threat to the fishing and fish farming industries. In spite of oil wealth, Shetland still earned much of its living from fish. Almost a third of the islands' 10 000-strong labour force worked in the fish industry, including fishermen, fish processors and salmon farmers. A spokesperson for the Shetlands Fishermen Association stated that 'the Shetlands were more dependent on fish than any other part of the EC'. Without fishing, the future of the community appeared doubtful. The Shetland salmon industry alone was worth approximately £35 million of the £80 million turnover of the islands' fishing industry. Although the ship's cargo was largely harmless to fish because the oil floats upon the surface, the chemical dispersants employed against oil slicks produce an oily emulsion that can kill fish as it sinks to the sea bed. The combination of dispersant and oil was known to be more toxic than oil alone.

Historical precedent

The *Braer* disaster was yet another example of oil tankers which have come to grief on the seas. In 1967 the *Torrey Canyon* disaster released 30 000 tons of oil in a 35-mile-long slick off Cornwall. It was the first and remains the largest oil disaster in the United Kingdom. At the time one senior government official claimed that it had created 'an oil pollution problem of unparalleled magnitude'. There has been a regular stream of similar occurrences since this date, including:

1970   *Pacific Glory*, 3500 tons of oil
1978   *Eleni V*, 5000 tons of oil
        Amoco Cadiz, 223 000 tons of oil
1979   *Atlantic Empress* and *Aegean Captain*,
        1.2 million barrels of oil
1987   *Exxon Valdez*, 240 000 barrels of oil
1990   *American Trader*, 7600 barrels of oil
1992   *Aegean Sea*, 24 million gallons of oil

From July 1993, under anti-pollution rules negotiated by the International Maritime Organisation (IMO), all new tankers had to be constructed with a double-skinned hull. Since 1995 existing vessels also have to meet more stringent standards. In practice, this has

sometimes meant sending many older ships to the scrapyard because they are not worth the cost of rebuilding to meet these standards. However, as a spokesperson for the IMO indicated at the time, ships built in the 1970s were regarded as technically out of date but needed to be retained to meet the demand for oil. With 136 governments involved during that period and a world tanker fleet of 2900 ships, it was accepted that change could not happen overnight.

The issues of corporate responsibility

The ship's course

Environmental experts initially found it difficult to understand why the captain of the *Braer* had followed a course that took it so close to the Shetland coastline. The waters around the Shetland Isles are classified as 'an area to be avoided' and this was confirmed by the IMO. Furthermore, International Collision Regulations say a ten-mile protection zone is necessary to avoid the risk of oil pollution and severe damage to the environment and the economy of Shetland. The regulations stipulated that all shipping of more than 5000 gross tons should avoid the area. The main reason offered for the presence of the *Braer* in the area was the extreme bad weather, which may have led the captain to put the safety of the crew before any risk to the environment. Weather forecasts can, however, be brought into the equation, since the vast majority of crews usually relied on three-day forecasts rather than the longer ten-day forecasts that were available. In effect the dependence on the shorter prediction means that the crew was committed to a route as soon as a vessel left port. Paul Roberts, a representative of Oceanroutes, which advised the shipping industry on weather conditions along prime trading routes, stated that oil tankers did not have standard routes: 'From Norway it is fairly natural for tankers to go around the top of Britain. If conditions are horrendous we might recommend the Channel, but extra miles means extra days means lots of bucks.'

Safety standards and flags of convenience

There has been a gradual increase over the years in the number of owners cutting costs by registering ships under overseas 'flags of convenience'. At times of worldwide recession, some owners burdened by ageing fleets have adopted the lower safety standards of countries such as Cyprus, Panama and Liberia, whose flag was carried by the *Braer*. The

Merchant Navy Officers' union, NUMAST, said it had warned the government about the dangers of allowing so-called coffin ships to carry dangerous goods around Britain's coast. More than 60 per cent of foreign ships checked in British ports in 1991 were found to have defects. The union's then general secretary, John Newman, said a disaster was inevitable given the increasing amounts of hazardous cargoes being carried by vessels with 'safety records up to 100 times worse than British vessels'.

The structure of the ship's hull

US legislation, in response to the *Exxon Valdez* disaster, had concentrated on the gradual introduction of double-hulled tankers and the phasing out of the older oil carriers with a single-skinned hull. This stance was subsequently incorporated into new international law which required all new tankers to be constructed using the double-hull technique. This belated response hides a number of issues. First, the legislation does not indicate what should happen to the vessels built before 1993 but which were still very much in use. Second, it has been cogently argued by Joe Nichols, technical manager at the International Tanker Owners' Pollution Federation, that the double hull would not necessarily have prevented either the *Braer* or the *Exxon Valdez* disaster. Moreover the double-hull design itself can cause problems through the build-up of gases and new so-called mid deck designs may yet prove superior. Legislation, in other words, may not be sufficiently flexible to accommodate all the necessary safety requirements.

The level and quality of training offered to the crew

The concentration upon the technical and safety requirements of the tanker could have meant that an important issue had been overlooked. Approximately 80 per cent of oil spills are caused by human error, which indicates an urgent need to harmonise training procedures throughout the seafaring world. Although tanker crew members must have internationally recognised certificates of training, it is notoriously difficult to obtain uniformity within the awarding bodies. Possibly of more concern is the incidence of such certificates being purchased from markets in the Far East. According to a director of the International Shipping Federation 'there are indications that the overall world training standards have diminished'.

The depressed costs of chartering vessels

Training problems may be a symptom of the very low charter rates for oil tankers caused by over-capacity in the industry. A company which during that period invested in an up-to-date tanker with the necessary pollution control measures needed to make approximately $60 000 a day on charter rates, compared to the $15 000 a day offered by the hard-bargaining oil companies. In effect charterers were not prepared to pay for quality shipping and could be said to have indirectly sponsored the continuation of substandard shipping.

The delayed request for assistance

Comparison has been made between the *Braer* and the *Amoco Cadiz* (1978) disasters, given the critical delay by the *Braer*'s captain in acknowledging the fact that the tanker was in extreme danger and in need of salvage under Lloyd's 'open form'. The *Braer*'s captain may have felt in no imminent danger as the ship was lying roughly midway between the islands when the power failed, and he may have assumed that the tanker had a good chance of making it through the channel to relative safety. With the benefit of hindsight, it is difficult to understand how someone in such a position could make a rational decision based upon some form of cost-benefit analysis, given that the intangible costs of ecological and environmental damage and the secondary effects of lost income and quality of life would at the time be unquantifiable.

Conclusion

The *Braer*, built in 1975, was owned by B & H Ship Management of New York. The pollution protection held by the company was in keeping with that of other businesses with interests in shipping: B & H had contributed to a 'protection and indemnity' club under the management of Skuld in Oslo. These clubs are groups of like-minded shipowners which were formed at the turn of the twentieth century to provide for areas not covered by conventional policies. The cover they offer is compulsory for ships carrying 2000 tonnes or more of crude oil to or from UK ports. If this was not enough, the state-supported International Oil Pollution Compensation Fund, administered by the IMO, came into force, providing a ceiling of £662 per tonne of ship. In the case of the *Braer* this would be £54.63 million. Both schemes come under UK law. In effect, shipowners become liable for damage caused by the spillage itself, for the clean-up costs, and any damage caused by the clean-up measures. Skuld provided a standard $500 million-worth of coverage which in this case was never going to be enough once the full scale of the disaster was known, and this has led to renewed calls for raising minimum levels of compensation paid on oil spills. These calls have been consistently thwarted by tanker owners who face rising premiums and other costs. It is widely accepted that the compensation levels are set too low now and that delays in paying out compensation are far too long.

Case study questions

1 In the *Braer* case who are the stakeholders, what are their interests and how might they influence future decisions to avoid further environmental incidents such as the tanker disaster?

2 What part do you think that environmental organisations can play in reducing the likelihood of future environmental disasters of this kind?

Review and discussion questions

1 To what extent are governments responsible for establishing the parameters by which organisations conduct business? Should a business be free to decide its own level of corporate responsibility?

2 Consider the case for greater democracy in the decision process of firms. To what extent is it feasible for businesses to implement the recommendations of the Cadbury Report?

3 Writers have argued that the only objective of business is to make profit, within the boundaries established by government. Do you agree?

Assignments

1 As a group, select an environmental issue (e.g. business or natural feature) and write a report to the leader of a local pressure group which details an environmental impact assessment of the issue. The report should make clear reference to:
(a) a cost-benefit analysis, carried out by the group, of the salient factors;
(b) any legislation/regulation that concerns the case; and
(c) the provision of a stakeholder map that illustrates who the stakeholders are, their importance to the case and their ability to affect future decisions.

2 As a newly appointed trainee manager you have been asked to look afresh at the business, with particular reference to the implementation of an environmental management system. Your immediate superior has asked you to write a report. Accordingly, you are required to:
(a) consult the available literature and identify what you consider to be the necessary processes and procedures that would comprise an environmental management system;
(b) indicate the areas within the organisation that need to be addressed; and
(c) explain how such a policy should be implemented within the organisation.

Notes and references

1 For a discussion see, for example, Vogel, D. (2005).

2 Friedman, M., 'The social responsibility of business is to increase its profits', *New York Times Magazine*, 13 September 1970, pp. 7–13.

3 See e.g. Hart, S., 'A natural resource-based view of the firm', *Academy of Management Review*, 20, pp. 986–1014, 1995.

4 For a fuller discussion of the issues involved see Worthington, I., Britton, C. and Rees, A., *Business Economics: Blending Theory and Practice*, 2nd edition, Financial Times/Prentice Hall, 2005, Chapter 14.

5 Sethi, S. P., 'Dimensions of corporate social performance: an analytical framework', *California Management Review*, Spring 1975.

6 The complexity associated with implementing environmental policy is illustrated by the setting up of the Environment Agency in the UK. This is a 'quango' which has taken over the functions of the National Rivers Authority, Her Majesty's Inspectorate of Pollution and the local authority waste regulators, and has the task of regulating the water, air and land environment in an integrated way.

7 Simon, B., 'Sharks in the water', *Financial Times*, 27 November 1991.

8 Peattie, K., *Green Marketing*, Pitman Publishing, 1992.

Further reading

Bansal, P. and Roth, K., 'Why companies go green: a model of ecological responsiveness', *Academy of Management Journal*, 43 (4), 2000, pp. 717–36.

Cairncross, F., *Green Inc: A Guide to Business and the Environment*, Earthscan Publications, 1995.

Cannon, T., *Corporate Responsibility: A Textbook on Business Ethics, Governance, Environment*, Pitman, 1994

Crane, A. and Matten, D., *Business Ethics*, Oxford University Press, 2004. A second edition was published in 2006.

Esty, D. C. and Winston, A. S., *Green to Gold: How Smart Companies Use Environmental Strategy to Innovate, Create Valve and Build Competitive Advantage*, Yale University Press, 2006

Frederick, W. C., Post, J. E. and Davis, K., Business and Society: *Corporate Strategy, Public Policy, Ethics*, 8th edition, McGraw-Hill, 1996.

Freeman, R. E., *Strategic Management: A Stakeholder Perspective*, Prentice Hall, 1984.

Kolk, A., *Economics of Environmental Management*, Financial Times/Prentice Hall, 2000.

McWilliams, A., Siegel, D.S. and Wright, P.M., 'Corporate Social Responsibility: Strategic Implications', *Journal of Management Studies*, 43(1), 2006, pp. 1–18.

Mercado, S., Welford, R. and Prescott, K., *European Business*, 4th edition, Financial Times/ Prentice Hall, 2001, Chapter 11.

Pearce, D. and Barbier, E., *Blueprint for a Sustainable Economy*, Earthscan Publications, 2000.

Pearce, D. W. and Turner, R. K., *Economics of Natural Resources and the Environment*, Harvester Wheatsheaf, 1990.

Porter, M. E. and Kramer, M. R., 'The Competitive Advantage of Corporate Philanthropy', *Harvard Business Review*, 80(12), 2002, pp. 56–69.

Roberts, P., *Environmentally Sustainable Business: A Local and Regional Perspective*, Paul Chapman Publishing, 1995.

Vogel, D., *The Market for Virtue: The Potential and Limits of Corporate Social Responsibility*, Brookings Institution, 2005.

Welford, R., *Corporate Environmental Management: Systems and Strategies*, Earthscan Publications, 1996.

Welford, R. and Gouldson, A., *Environmental Management and Business Strategy*, Pitman Publishing, 1993.

Welford, R. and Starkey, R. (eds), *Business and the Environment*, Earthscan Publications, 1996.

Worthington, I., Britton, C. and Rees, A., *Economics for Business: Blending Theory and Practice*, 2nd edition, Financial Times/Prentice Hall, 2005, Chapter 14.

Web links and further questions are available on the website at:

www.pearsoned.co.uk/worthington

Migration

In an increasingly globalised world, companies often look to international migration of labour to fill jobs as they can no longer rely on their own domestic labour markets to do this. The international migration of labour is important – although it has no overall effect on the world population it has significant effects for individual countries. In 2006 the migrant population was 192 million, which represented 2.9 per cent of the world population (as opposed to 2.1 per cent in 1960).[1] In 2006 the USA accounted for 20 per cent of the total; the Russian Federation was second with

7 per cent. The table below shows net migration for selected European countries between 2000 and 2005. It indicates that there was a net inflow for Europe as a whole but a net outflow from eastern Europe, the highest outflow being in the Ukraine. The table shows the most important countries in each area for migration – Spain for southern Europe and Germany for western Europe. In northern Europe, the UK was the biggest in terms of numbers while Ireland was the biggest in terms of the migration rate.

International migration for selected European areas/countries, 2000 to 2005

Area	Net migration (000)	Migration rate per 1000 population
Europe	1083	1.5
Eastern Europe	−105	−0.3
of which Ukraine	−140	−2.9
Northern Europe	232	2.4
of which UK	137	2.3
Ireland	39	9.8
Southern Europe	600	4.1
of which Spain	405	10
Western Europe	356	2
of which Germany	220	2.7

Source: Adapted from annexe to *International Migration 2006*, UN

Although not shown in the table above, there were differences between the developed and the developing world in this time period. The net migration rate was +2.2 for the developed countries and −0.6 for developing countries.

There are push factors and pull factors which give rise to labour migration: push factors include poverty in the home country, natural disasters and political fear; pull factors include the possibility of employment, better standards of living and better education. Migration can be permanent or temporary. In 2006 there were 4 million permanent migrants into the OECD countries and 2.5 million temporary migrants. Permanent migration is dominated by family migration where families join previous labour

migrants. The rate of migration has been slowing and is expected to fall further with the slowdown in the OECD countries. In addition, many countries have also started to tighten their immigration policies in response to the slowdown and the subsequent rises in unemployment.

The debate over labour migration is often heated and not based in fact, but the costs and benefits of migration need to be considered in both the sending countries and the receiving countries. It is often argued that immigrants take jobs away from people in the host country but this is not sustained by research. An IOM report[2] found that in western Europe immigrants are often not in direct competition with the home population and take jobs at both ends of the spectrum. At the low-skill, high-risk and low-paid end, where it is difficult to fill vacancies from the home labour force, and at the high-skill, high-paid end, where home-grown skills may not be available, research in the US showed that the average income of immigrants is around 20 per cent lower than that of the home workforce. In the US it was estimated that GDP grew by $8 billion in 1997 purely because of immigration. Another argument often used, but again not borne out by research, is that immigration represents a drain on welfare, health and education spending in the host country. A Home Office report found that in the UK between 1999 and 2000 immigrants contributed £2.1 billion more in taxes than they received in benefits.[3]

The migration of skilled labour is an obvious benefit to the host country but for the sending country it represents a 'brain drain' – education, skills and knowledge are lost. This is not all negative, however, as migrants often return home, bringing with them newly acquired skills and knowledge – a 'brain gain'. The OECD estimates that between 20 and 50 per cent of migrants return to their home countries within five years. There has been a big increase in the number of foreign students which has risen by 50 per cent from 2000 to 2005 in the OECD countries. The countries that have benefited most are the US, the UK, Australia and France. This brings in short-term benefits in the form of extra income for fees but this type of migration is often temporary as the students return home at the end of their studies.

One benefit of migration to the country of origin is what is called remittances – migrants sending money home to their families – estimated to be $100 billion in 2004 but thought to be possibly twice this figure when informal channels are taken into account. These flows rival development aid from developed to developing countries. The biggest recipient in 2004 was India and the second biggest was Mexico. Diaspora associations (groups of émigrés from one country which link together in the host country) can also contribute to development and help relations between the host country and the country of origin. They are also instrumental in circular migration where émigrés return home.

International migration is important to business. Research carried out in 2007 in UK businesses[4] found that nearly 40 per cent of HR managers reported skill shortages, with engineering being the worst. Between 20 per cent (companies with 100 to 249 employees) and 50 per cent (companies with over 250 employees) of UK businesses said that they were looking overseas to fill skill shortages. Over a third of the HR managers felt that membership of the EU and the associated free movement of labour was instrumental in meeting the skills gap. Of course much has changed since mid-2007 and the global economic slowdown has led to increased unemployment and a corresponding fall in vacancies in the labour market. It has also led to increased public hostility to migration and many countries have started to tighten their immigration policies.

Notes

1   UN, *International Migration Report*, 2008.
2   *World Migration Report*, IOM, 2005.
3   UK Home Office, 2002.
4   'Is the UK up to it?' *Vedior*, June 2007.

Part Three

FIRMS

10 Legal structures

Ian Worthington

Market-based economies comprise a rich diversity of business organisations, ranging from the very simple enterprise owned and operated by one person, to the huge multinational corporation with production and distribution facilities spread across the globe. Whatever the nature of these organisations or their scale of operation, their existence is invariably subject to legal definition and this will have consequences for the functioning of the organisation. Viewing the business as a legal structure provides an insight into some of the important influences on business operations in both the private and public sectors.

Learning outcomes

Having read this chapter you should be able to:

● discuss the legal structure of UK business organisations in both the private and public sectors

● compare UK business organisations with those in other parts of Europe

● illustrate the implications of a firm's legal structure for its operations

● explain franchising, licensing and joint ventures

Key terms

Articles of Association
'Black economy'
Company
Company directors
Consortium
Consumer societies
Executive directors
Franchising
Gearing
Golden share

Joint venture
Licensing
Managing director
Memorandum of
    Association
Nationalised industry
Non-executive directors
Partnership
Private limited company
Public corporation

Public limited company
    (PLC)
Public sector
    organisations
Shareholders
Sole trader
Stakeholders
Unlimited personal liability
Workers' co-operatives

Introduction

Business organisations can be classified in a variety of ways, including:

- size (e.g. small, medium, large);
- type of industry (e.g. primary, secondary, tertiary);
- sector (e.g. private sector, public sector); and
- legal status (e.g. sole trader, partnership, and so on).

These classifications help to distinguish one type of organisation from another and to focus attention on the implications of such differences for an individual enterprise. In the discussion below, business organisations are examined as legal structures and the consequences of variations in legal status are discussed in some detail. Subsequent chapters in this section investigate alternative structural perspectives in order to highlight how these too have an important bearing on the environment in which businesses operate.

Private sector organisations in the UK

The sole trader

Many individuals aspire to owning and running their own business – being their own boss, making their own decisions. For those who decide to turn their dream into a reality, becoming a sole trader (or sole proprietor) offers the simplest and easiest method of trading.

As the name suggests, a **sole trader** is a business owned by one individual who is self-employed and who may, in some cases, employ other people on either a full-time or a part-time basis. Normally using personal funds to start the business, the sole trader decides on the type of goods or services to be produced, where the business is to be located, what capital is required, what staff (if any) to employ, what the target market should be and a host of other aspects concerned with the establishment and running of the enterprise. Where the business proves a success, all profits accrue to the owner and it is common for sole traders to reinvest a considerable proportion of these in the business and/or use them to reduce past borrowings. Should losses occur, these too are the responsibility of the sole trader, who has **unlimited personal liability** for the debts of the business.

Despite this substantial disadvantage, sole proprietorship tends to be the most popular form of business organisation numerically. In the United Kingdom, for example, it is estimated that about 80 per cent of all businesses are sole traders and in some sectors – notably personal services, retailing, building – they tend to be the dominant form of business enterprise. Part of the reason for this numerical dominance is the relative ease with which an individual can establish a business of this type. Apart from minor restrictions concerning the use of a business name – if the name of the proprietor is not used – few other legal formalities are required to set up the enterprise, other than the need to register for Value Added Tax if turnover exceeds a certain sum (e.g. £67 000 in 2008) and/or to fulfil any special requirements laid down by the local authority prior to trading (e.g. some businesses require licences). Once established, of course, the sole trader, like other forms of business, will be subject to a variety of legal requirements (e.g. contract law, consumer law, employment law) – though not the requirement to file information about the business in a public place. For some, this ability to keep the affairs of the enterprise away from public scrutiny provides a further incentive to establishing this form of business organisation – some of which may operate wholly or partly in the **black economy** (i.e. beyond the gaze of the tax authorities).

A further impetus towards sole ownership comes from the ability of the individual to exercise a considerable degree of control over her/his own destiny. Business decisions – including the day-to-day operations of the enterprise as well as long-term plans – are in the hands of the owner and many individuals evidently relish the risks and potential rewards associated with entrepreneurial activity, preferring these to the relative safety of employment in another organisation. For others less fortunate, the 'push' of unemployment rather than the 'pull' of the marketplace tends to be more of a deciding factor and one which clearly accounts for some of the growth in the number of small businesses in the United Kingdom in the later part of the twentieth century.

Ambitions and commitment alone, however, are not necessarily sufficient to guarantee the survival and success of the enterprise and the high mortality rate among businesses of this kind, particularly during a recession, is well known and well documented. Part of the problem may stem from developments largely outside the control of the enterprise – including bad debts, increased competition, higher interest rates, falling demand – and factors such as these affect businesses of all types and all sizes, not just sole traders. Other difficulties, such as lack of funds for expansion, poor marketing, lack of research of the marketplace and insufficient management skills are to some extent self-induced and emanate, at least in part, from the decision to become a sole proprietor rather than some other form of business organisation. Where such constraints exist, the sole trader may be tempted to look to others to share the burdens and the risks by establishing a partnership or co-operative or limited company or by seeking a different approach to the business venture, such as through franchising. These alternative forms of business organisation are discussed in detail below.

The partnership

The Partnership Act 1890 defines a **partnership** as 'the relation which subsists between persons carrying on a business in common with a view to profit'. Like the sole trader, this form of business organisation does not have its own distinct legal personality and hence the owners – the partners – have unlimited personal liability both jointly and severally. This means that in the case of debts or bankruptcy of the partnership, each partner is liable in full for the whole debt and each in turn may be sued or their assets seized until the debt is satisfied. Alternatively, all the partners may be joined into the action to recover debts, unless by dint of the Limited Partnership Act 1907, a partner (or partners) has limited liability. Since it tends to be much easier to achieve the same ends by establishing a limited company, limited partnerships are not common, nor can all partners in a partnership have limited liability. Hence in the discussion below, attention is focused on the partnership as an unincorporated association, operating in a market where its liability is effectively unlimited.

In essence, a partnership comes into being when two or more people establish a business which they own, finance and run jointly for personal gain, irrespective of the degree of formality involved in the relationship. Such a business can range from a husband and wife running a local shop as joint owners, to a very large firm of accountants or solicitors, with in excess of a hundred partners in offices in various locations. Under the law, most partnerships are limited to 20 or less, but some types of business, particularly in the professions, may have a dispensation from this rule (Companies Act 1985, s 716). This same Act requires businesses which are not exempt from the rule and which have more than 20 partners to register as a company.

While it is not necessary for a partnership to have a formal written agreement, most partnerships tend to be formally enacted in a Deed of Partnership or Articles, since this makes it much easier to reduce uncertainty and to ascertain intentions when there is a written document to consult. Where this is not done, the Partnership Act 1890 lays down a minimum code which governs the relationship between partners and which provides, amongst other things, for all partners to share equally in the capital and profits of the business and to contribute equally towards its losses.

In practice, of course, where a Deed or Articles exist, these will invariably reflect differences in the relative status and contribution of individual partners. Senior partners, for example, will often have contributed more financially to the partnership and not unnaturally will expect to receive a higher proportion of the profits. Other arrangements – including membership, action on dissolution of the partnership, management responsibilities and rights, and the basis for allocating salaries – will be outlined in the partnership agreement and as such will provide the legal framework within which the enterprise exists and its co-owners operate.

Unlike the sole trader, where management responsibilities devolve on a single individual, partnerships permit the sharing of responsibilities and tasks and it is common in a partnership for individuals to specialise to some degree in particular aspects of the organisation's work – as in the case of a legal or medical or veterinary practice. Added to this, the fact that more than one person is involved in the ownership of the business tends to increase the amount of finance available to the organisation, thus permitting expansion to take place without the owners losing control of the enterprise. These two factors alone tend to make a partnership an attractive proposition for some would-be entrepreneurs, while for others the rules of their professional body – which often prohibits its members from forming a company – effectively provide for the establishment of this type of organisation.

On the downside, the sharing of decisions and responsibilities may represent a problem, particularly where partners are unable to agree over the direction the partnership should take or the amount to be reinvested in the business, unless such matters are clearly specified in a formal agreement. A more intractable problem is the existence of unlimited personal liability – a factor which may inhibit some individuals from considering this form of organisation, particularly given that the actions of any one partner are invariably binding on the other members of the business. To overcome this problem, many individuals, especially in manufacturing and trading, look to the limited company as the type of organisation which can combine the benefits of joint ownership and limited personal liability – a situation not necessarily always borne out in practice. It is to this type of business organisation that the discussion now turns.

Limited companies

In law a **company** is a corporate association having a legal identity in its own right (i.e. it is distinct from the people who own it, unlike in the case of a sole trader or partnership). This means that all property and other assets owned by the company belong to the company and not to its members (owners). By the same token, the personal assets of its members (the **shareholders**) do not normally belong to the business. In the event of insolvency, therefore, an individual's liability is limited to the amount invested in the business, including any amount remaining unpaid on the shares for which they have subscribed.[1] One exception to this would be where a company's owners have given a personal guarantee to cover any loans they have obtained from a bank or other institution – a requirement for many small, private limited companies. Another occurs where a company is limited by guarantee rather than by shares, with its members' liability being limited to the amount they have undertaken to contribute to the assets in the event of the company being wound up. Companies of this type are normally non-profit-making organisations – such as professional, research or trade associations – and are much less common than companies limited by shares. Hence in the discussion below, attention is focused on the latter as the dominant form of business organisation in the corporate sector of business.[2]

Companies are essentially business organisations consisting of two or more individuals who have agreed to embark on a business venture and who have decided to seek corporate status rather than to form a partnership.[3] Such status could derive from an Act of Parliament or a Royal Charter, but is almost always nowadays achieved through 'registration', the terms of which are laid down in the various Companies Acts. Under legislation, enacted in 1985, 1989 and 2006 individuals seeking to form a company are required to file numerous documents, including a **Memorandum of Association** and **Articles of Association**, with the Registrar of Companies. If satisfied, the Registrar will issue a Certificate of Incorporation, bringing the company into existence as a legal entity. As an alternative, the participants could buy a ready-formed company 'off the shelf', by approaching a company registration agent who specialises in company formations. In the United Kingdom, advertisements for ready-made companies appear regularly in magazines such as *Exchange and Mart* and *Dalton's Weekly*.

web link

Companies' House can be accessed at *www.companieshouse.gov.uk*

Information on how companies are created, run and wound up is contained in the 2006 Companies Act which essentially consolidates all previous legislation and case law into one Act of Parliament. As this Act shows, under British law a distinction is made between public and private companies. **Public limited companies** (PLCs) – not to be confused with public corporations, which in the UK are state-owned businesses (see below) – are those limited companies which satisfy the conditions for being a 'PLC'. These conditions require the company to have:

- a minimum of two shareholders;
- at least two directors;
- a minimum (at present) of £50 000 of authorised and allotted share capital;
- the right to offer its shares (and debentures) for sale to the general public;
- a certificate from the Registrar of Companies verifying that the share capital requirements have been met; and
- a memorandum which states it to be a public company.

A company which meets these conditions must include the title 'public limited company' or 'PLC' in its name and is required to make full accounts available for public inspection. Any company unable or unwilling to meet these conditions is therefore, in the eyes of the law, a 'private limited company', normally signified by the term 'Limited' or 'Ltd'.

Like the public limited company, the **private limited company** must have a minimum of two shareholders, but its shares cannot be offered to the public at large, although it can offer them to individuals through its business contacts. This restriction on the sale of shares, and hence on their ability to raise considerable sums of money on the open market, normally ensures that most private companies are either small or medium sized, and are often family businesses operating in a relatively restricted market; there are, however, some notable exceptions to this general rule (e.g. Virgin). In contrast, public companies – many of which began life as private companies prior to 'going public' – often have many thousands, even millions, of owners (shareholders) and normally operate on a national or international scale, producing products as diverse as computers, petro-chemicals, cars and banking services. Despite being outnumbered by their private counterparts, public companies dwarf private companies in terms of their capital and other assets, and their collective influence on output, investment, employment and consumption in the economy is immense.

Both public and private companies act through their **directors**. These are individuals chosen by a company's shareholders to manage its affairs and to make the important decisions concerning the direction the company should take (e.g. investment, market development, mergers and so on). The appointment and powers of directors are outlined in the Articles of Association (the 'internal rules' of the organisation) and so long as the directors do not exceed their powers, the shareholders do not normally have the right to intervene in the day-to-day management of the company. Where a director exceeds his or her authority or fails to indicate clearly that they are acting as an agent for the company, they become personally liable for any contracts they make. Equally, directors become personally liable if they continue to trade when the company is insolvent and they may be dismissed by a court if it considers that an individual is unfit to be a director in view of their past record (Company Directors Disqualification Act 1985).

The 2006 Act sets out in detail the duties of company directors, including the duty to promote the success of the organisation, to exercise reasonable care, skill and diligence and to give appropriate consideration to issues that go beyond the balance sheet. For example, directors of UK companies now have a duty to consider the impacts of their business operations on the environment and the community generally and quoted public companies must report on issues of social and environmental responsibility as part of an expanded review of the business (see Chapter 9).

In practice it is usual for a board of directors to have both a chairperson and a managing director, although some companies choose to appoint one person to both roles. The chairperson, who is elected by the other members of the board, is usually chosen because of their knowledge and experience of the business and their skill both internally in chairing board meetings and externally in representing the best interest of the organisation. As the public face of the company, the chairperson has an important role to play in establishing and maintaining a good public image and hence many large public companies like to appoint well-known public figures to this important position (e.g. ex-Cabinet ministers). In this case knowledge of the business is less important than the other attributes the individual might possess, most notably public visibility and familiarity, together with a network of contacts in government and in the business world.

The **managing director**, or chief executive, fulfils a pivotal role in the organisation, by forming the link between the board and the management team of senior executives. Central to this role is the need not only to interpret board decisions but to ensure that they are put into effect by establishing an appropriate structure of delegated responsibility and effective systems of reporting and control. This close contact with the day-to-day operations of the company places the appointed individual in a position of considerable authority and he/she will invariably be able to make important decisions without reference to the full board. This authority is enhanced where the managing director is also the person chairing the board of directors and/or is responsible for recommending individuals to serve as executive directors (i.e. those with functional responsibilities such as production, marketing, finance).

Like the managing director, most, if not all, **executive directors** will be full-time executives of the company, responsible for running a division or functional area within the framework laid down at board level. In contrast, other directors will have a non-executive role and are usually part-time appointees, chosen for a variety of reasons, including their knowledge, skills, contacts, influence, independence or previous experience. Sometimes, a company might be required to appoint such a director at the wishes of a third party, such as a merchant bank which has agreed to fund a large capital injection and wishes to have representation on the board. In this case, the individual tends to act in an advisory capacity – particularly on matters of finance – and helps to provide the financing institution with a means of ensuring that any board decisions are in its interests.

In Britain the role of company directors and senior executives in recent years has come under a certain amount of public scrutiny and has culminated in a number of enquiries into issues of power and pay. In the Cadbury Report (1992), a committee, with Sir Adrian Cadbury as chairperson, called for a non-statutory code of practice which it wanted applied to all listed public companies. Under this code the committee recommended:

- a clear division of responsibilities at the head of a company to ensure that no individual had unfettered powers of decision;
- a greater role for non-executive directors;
- regular board meetings;
- restrictions on the contracts of executive directors;
- full disclosure of directors' total enrolments;
- an audit committee dominated by non-executives.

The committee's stress on the important role of non-executive directors was a theme taken up in the Greenbury Report (1995) which investigated the controversial topic of executive salaries in the wake of a number of highly publicised pay rises for senior company directors. Greenbury's recommendations included:

- full disclosure of directors' pay packages, including pensions;
- shareholder approval for any long-term bonus scheme;
- remuneration committees consisting entirely of non-executive directors;
- greater detail in the annual report on directors' pay, pensions and perks;
- an end to payments for failure.

Greenbury was followed by a further investigation into corporate governance by a committee under the chairmanship of ICI chairman Ronald Hampel. The Hampel Report (1998) advocated company self-regulation and called for greater shareholder responsibility by companies and increased standards of disclosure of information; it supported Cadbury's recommendation that the role of chairperson and chief executive should normally be separated. A year later, the Turnbull Report (1999) considered the issue of corporate governance and information disclosure from the perspective of risk management, arguing that companies need to take steps to manage and disclose corporate risks formally.

As far as the issue of non-executive directors was concerned, this was investigated further by the Higgs Committee which was set up in 2002 and which reported the following year. In essence the Higgs Report set down a code of non-binding corporate guidelines regarding the role of non-executive directors on company boards. Like the Cadbury Report, Higgs recommended that the role of chairperson and chief executive should be kept separate and that the former should be independent, though not necessarily non-executive. As for non-executive directors, Higgs recommended that at least half the board should be independent and that non-executives should play key roles in areas such as strategy, performance, risk and the appointment and remuneration of executive directors. The latter issue, in particular, has been an area of considerable controversy in the UK in recent years and seems destined to remain so for some time.

mini case   Companies under pressure

Public companies have to satisfy the conflicting demands of a range of stakeholder groups (see below), not least their shareholders who expect the organisation to operate in their interest. On the whole, individual shareholders are usually relatively quiescent, leaving the strategic and day-to-day decisions to the organisation's directors and senior executives. As an increasing number of public companies have found, however, many shareholders are becoming more actively involved in corporate decisions which they believe affect their investments and have been willing to voice their feelings at shareholders' meetings and to the media. This is particularly true of large corporate investors.

In the 5th edition of this book we reported on the rise of shareholder militancy at Daimler-Benz, with shareholders expressing dissatisfaction over the company's poor performance and its effect on shareholder value. This is only one issue that has been exercising company shareholders in recent years, however. At the large UK retail chain Marks & Spencer, for example, investors are unhappy at the decision to combine the position of executive chairman annd chief executive in contravention of City corporate governance rules; at Exxon Mobil shareholder concerns have focused on the company's environmental record, particularly with regard to its impact on climate change. At other companies, executives' pay and rewards have been the central issues that have provoked shareholder anger.

From a company's point of view, challenges such as these are not especially welcome and the board of directors may be forced to spend time and resources to justify its actions to the protestors. Apart from the negative publicity that shareholder revolts can evoke, large corporations are particularly concerned when the protests come from very large corporate investors such as pension funds, since their reactions can affect not only the current but also the future position of the organisation.

Co-operatives

Consumer co-operative societies

Consumer societies are basically 'self-help' organisations which have their roots in the anti-capitalist sentiment which arose in mid-nineteenth-century Britain and which gave rise to a consumer co-operative movement dedicated to the provision of cheap, unadulterated food for its members and a share in its profits. Today this movement boasts a multibillion-pound turnover, a membership numbered in millions and an empire which includes thousands of food stores (including the Alldays convenience chain purchased in 2002), numerous factories and farms, dairies, travel agencies, opticians, funeral parlours, a bank and an insurance company, and property and development business. Taken together, these activities ensure that the Co-operative Group remains a powerful force in British retailing into the early twenty first century. Indeed, it is the world's largest consumer co-operative employing around 85 000 people (in 2007) following the merger of the Co-operative Group and United Co-operatives. Survey evidence indicates that in retailing it is the UK's most trusted and ethical brand name.

 web link The Co-operative Group's website address is *www.co-operative.coop*

Although the co-operative societies, like companies, are registered and incorporated bodies – in this case under the Industrial and Provident Societies Act – they are quite distinct trading organisations. These societies belong to their members (i.e. invariably customers who have purchased a share in the society) who elect Area Committees to oversee trading areas. These committees have annual elections and meetings for all members and these in turn appoint members on to regional boards and elect individual member directors to the Group Board. The Group Board also includes directors of corporate members who are representatives of other societies. Individual stores may also have member forums. Any profits from the Group's activities are supposed to benefit the members. Originally this took the form of a cash dividend paid to members in relation to their purchases, but this was subsequently replaced either by trading stamps or by investment in areas felt to benefit the consumer (e.g. lower prices, higher-quality products, modern shops, and so on) and/or the local community (e.g. charitable donations, sponsorship). The twice-yearly cash dividend was, however, reintroduced in 2006, a move which saw a significant increase in the membership of the organisation.

The societies differ in other ways from standard companies. For a start, shares are not quoted on the Stock Exchange and members are restricted in the number of shares they can purchase and in the method of disposal. Not having access to cheap sources of capital on the stock market, co-operatives rely heavily on retained surpluses and on loan finance, and the latter places a heavy burden on the societies when interest rates are high. The movement's democratic principles also impinge on its operations and this has often been a bone of contention as members have complained about their increasing remoteness from decision-making centres. Some societies have responded by encouraging the development of locally elected committees to act in an advisory or consultative capacity to the society's board of directors and it looks likely that others will be forced to consider similar means of increasing member participation, which still remains very limited.

> **web link**
>
> The Co-operative Commission has put forward numerous proposals for changes which are designed to improve the performance of societies. See *www.co-opcommission.org.uk*

The movement's historical links with the British Labour Party are also worth noting and a number of parliamentary candidates are normally sponsored at general elections. These links, however, have tended to become slightly looser in recent years, although the movement still contributes to Labour Party funds and continues to lobby politicians at both national and local level. It is also active in seeking to influence public opinion and, in this, claims to be responding to customer demands for greater social and corporate responsibility. Among its initiatives are the establishment of a customer's charter (by the Co-operative Bank) and the decision to review both its investments and the individuals and organisations it does business with, to ascertain that they are acceptable from an ethical point of view.

Workers' co-operatives

In Britain, **workers' co-operatives** are found in a wide range of industries, including manufacturing, building and construction, engineering, catering and retailing. They are particularly prevalent in printing, clothing and wholefoods, and some have been in existence for over a century. The majority, however, are of fairly recent origin, having been part of the growth in the number of small firms which occurred in the 1980s.

As the name suggests, a workers' co-operative is a business in which the ownership and control of the assets are in the hands of the people working in it, having agreed to establish the enterprise and to share the risk for mutual benefit. Rather than form a standard partnership, the individuals involved normally register the business as a friendly society under the Industrial and Provident Societies Acts 1965–78, or seek incorporation as a private limited company under the Companies Act 1985. In the case of the former, seven members are required to form a co-operative, while the latter only requires two. In practice, a minimum of three or four members tends to be the norm and some co-operatives may have several hundred participants, frequently people who have been made redundant by their employers and who are keen to keep the business going.

The central principles of the movement – democracy, open membership, social responsibility, mutual co-operation and trust – help to differentiate the co-operative from other forms of business organisation and govern both the formation and operation of this type of enterprise. Every employee may be a member of the organisation and every member owns one share in the business, with every share carrying an equal voting right. Any surpluses are shared by democratic agreement and this is normally done on an equitable basis, reflecting, for example, the amount of time and effort an individual puts into the business. Other decisions, too, are taken jointly by the members and the emphasis tends to be on the quality of goods or services provided and on creating a favourable working environment, rather than on the pursuit of profits – although the latter cannot be ignored if the organisation is to survive. In short, the co-operative tends to focus on people and on the relationship between them, stressing the co-operative and communal traditions associated with its origins, rather than the more conflictual and competitive aspects inherent in other forms of industrial organisation.

Despite these apparent attractions, workers' co-operatives have never been as popular in Britain as in other parts of the world (e.g. France, Italy, Israel), although a substantial increase occurred in the number of co-operatives in the 1980s, largely as a result of growing unemployment, overt support across the political spectrum and the establishment of a system to encourage and promote the co-operative ideal (e.g. Co-operative Development Agencies).[4] More recently, however, their fortunes have tended to decline, as employee shareholding and profit schemes (ESOPs) have grown in popularity. It seems unlikely that workers' co-operatives will ever form the basis of a strong third sector in the British economy, between the profit-oriented firms in the private sector and the nationalised and municipal undertakings in the public sector.

Public sector business organisations in the UK

Public sector organisations come in a variety of forms. These include:

- central government departments (e.g. Department of Innovation, Universities and Skills);
- local authorities (e.g. Lancashire County Council);
- regional bodies (e.g. Regional Development Agencies);
- non-departmental public bodies or quangos (e.g. the Arts Council);
- central government trading organisations (e.g. The Stationery Office); and
- public corporations and nationalised industries (e.g. the BBC).

Some of these were discussed in Chapter 4, which examined the political environment, and numerous other references to the influence of government on business activity can be found throughout the book. In the discussion below, attention is focused on those public sector organisations which most closely approximate businesses in the private sector, namely, public corporations and municipal enterprises. An examination of the transfer of many of these public sector bodies to the private sector – usually termed 'privatisation' – is contained in Chapter 17.

Public corporations

Private sector business organisations are owned by private individuals and groups who have chosen to invest in some form of business enterprise, usually with a view to personal gain. In contrast, in the public sector the state owns assets in various forms, which it uses to provide a range of goods and services felt to be of benefit to its citizens, even if this provision involves the state in a loss. Many of these services are provided directly through government departments (e.g. social security benefits) or through bodies operating under delegated authority from central government (e.g. local authorities, health authorities). Others are the responsibility of state-owned industrial and commercial undertakings, specially created for a variety of reasons and often taking the form of a **public corporation**. These state corporations are an important part of the public sector of the economy and have contributed significantly to national output, employment and investment. Their numbers, however, have declined substantially following the wide-scale privatisation of state industries which occurred in the 1980s and this process has continued through the 1990s and beyond with the sale of corporations such as British Coal, British Rail and British Energy (see Chapter 17).

Public corporations are statutory bodies, incorporated (predominantly) by special Act of Parliament and, like companies, they have a separate legal identity from the individuals who own them and run them. Under the statute setting up the corporation, reference is made to the powers, duties and responsibilities of the organisation and to its relationship with the government department which oversees its operations. In the past these operations have ranged from providing a variety of national and international postal services (the Post Office), to the provision of entertainment (the BBC), an energy source (British Coal) and a national rail network (British Rail). Where such provision involves the organisation in a considerable degree of direct contact with its customers, from whom it derives most of its revenue, the corporation tends to be called a **nationalised industry**. In reality, of course, the public corporation is the legal form through which the industry is both owned and run and every corporation is to some degree unique in structure as well as in functions.

As organisations largely financed as well as owned by the state, public corporations are required to be publicly accountable and hence they invariably operate under the purview of a 'sponsoring' government department, the head of which (the Secretary of State) appoints a board of management to run the organisation. This board tends to exercise a considerable degree of autonomy in day-to-day decisions and operates largely free from political interference on most matters of a routine nature. The organisation's strategic objectives, however, and important questions concerning reorganisation or investment, would have to be agreed with the sponsoring department, as would the corporation's performance targets and its external financing limits.

The link between the corporation and its supervising ministry provides the means through which Parliament can oversee the work of the organisation and permits ordinary Members of Parliament to seek information and explanation through question time, through debates and through the select committee system. Additionally, under the Competition Act 1980, nationalised industries can be subject to investigation by the Competition Commission (see Chapter 17), and this too presents opportunities for further parliamentary discussion and debate, as well as for government action.

A further opportunity for public scrutiny comes from the establishment of industry-specific Consumers' or Consultative Councils, which consider complaints from customers and advise both the board and the department concerned of public attitudes to the organisation's performance and to other aspects of its operations (e.g. pricing). In a number of cases, including British Rail before privatisation, pressure on government from consumers and from other sources has resulted in the establishment of a 'Customers' Charter', under which the organisation agrees to provide a predetermined level of service or to give information and/or compensation where standards are not achieved. Developments of this kind are already spreading to other parts of the public sector and in future may be used as a means by which governments decide on the allocation of funds to public bodies, as well as providing a vehicle for monitoring organisational achievement.

It is interesting to note that mechanisms for public accountability and state regulation have been retained to some degree even where public utilities have been privatised (i.e. turned into public limited companies). Industries such as gas, electricity, water and telecommunications are watched over by newly created regulatory bodies which are designed to protect the interests of consumers, particularly with regard to pricing and the standard of service provided. Ofgas, for example, which used to regulate British Gas, monitored gas supply charges to ensure that they reasonably reflected input costs and these charges could be altered by the regulator if they were seen to be excessive. Similarly, in the case of non-gas services, such as maintenance, the legislation privatising the industry only allowed prices to be raised to a prescribed maximum, to ensure that the organisation was not able to take full advantage of its monopoly power. The regulator of the gas market is now Ofgem – see Chapter 17.

An additional source of government influence has come through its ownership of a **golden share** in a privatised state industry which effectively gives the government a veto in certain vital areas of decision making. This notional shareholding – which is written into the privatisation legislation – tends to last for a number of years and can be used to protect a newly privatised business from a hostile takeover, particularly by foreign companies or individuals. Ultimately, however, the expectation is that this veto power will be relinquished and the organisation concerned will become subject to the full effects of the market – a point exemplified by the government's decision to allow Ford to take over Jaguar in 1990, having originally blocked a number of previous takeover bids (see also Chapter 4 Mini case: The demise of the VW law).

The existence of a golden share should not be equated with the decision by government to retain (or purchase) a significant proportion of issued shares in a privatised (or already private) business organisation, whether as an investment and/or future source of revenue, or as a means of exerting influence in a particular industry or sector. Nor should it be confused with government schemes to attract private funds into existing state enterprises, by allowing them to achieve notional company status in order to overcome Treasury restrictions on borrowing imposed on public bodies. In the latter case, which often involves a limited share issue, government still retains full control of the organisation by owning all (or the vast majority) of the shares – as in the case of Consignia (formerly known as the Post Office). In March 2001 Consignia was incorporated as a government-owned public company. This change in legal status allowed the company more freedom to borrow and invest in the business, to make acquisitions and to enter into joint ventures and to expand internationally. The name Consignia was subsequently dropped in favour of the brand name Royal Mail.

Municipal enterprises

UK local authorities have a long history of involvement in business activity. In part this is a function of their role as central providers of public services (e.g. education, housing, roads, social services) and of their increasing involvement in supporting local economic development initiatives (see Chapter 13). But their activities have also traditionally involved the provision of a range of marketable goods and services, not required by law but provided voluntarily by a local authority and often in direct competition with the private sector (e.g. theatres, leisure services, museums). Usually such provision has taken place under the aegis of a local authority department which appoints staff who are answerable to the council and to its committees through the department's chief officer and its elected head. Increasingly, though, local authorities are turning to other organisational arrangements – including the establishment of companies and trusts – in order to separate some of these activities from the rest of their responsibilities and to create a means through which private investment in the enterprise can occur.

One example of such a development can be seen in the case of local authority controlled airports which are normally the responsibility of a number of local authorities who run them through a joint board, representing the interests of the participating district councils (e.g. Manchester International Airport). Since the Airports Act 1986, local authorities with airports have been required to create a limited company in which their joint assets are vested and which appoints a board of directors to run the enterprise. Like other limited companies, the organisation can, if appropriate, seek private capital and must publish annual accounts, including a profit and loss statement. It can also be privatised relatively easily if the local authorities involved decide to relinquish ownership (e.g. East Midlands Airport is part of the Manchester Airports Group).

Such developments, which have parallels in other parts of the public sector, can be seen to have had at least four benefits:

1 They have provided a degree of autonomy from local authority control that is seen to be beneficial in a competitive trading environment.
2 They have given access to market funds by the establishment of a legal structure that is not fully subject to central government restrictions on local authority borrowing.
3 They helped local authority organisations to compete more effectively under the now defunct system of compulsory competitive tendering (CCT), by removing or reducing charges for departmental overheads that are applied under the normal arrangements.
4 They have provided a vehicle for further private investment and for ultimate privatisation of the service.

Given these benefits and the current fashion for privatisation, there is little doubt that they will become an increasing feature of municipal enterprise in the foreseeable future. That said, local authorities are restricted in their degree of ownership of companies following the passage of the 1990 Local Government and Housing Act.

Business organisations in mainland Europe

Sole traders, partnerships, co-operatives and limited companies are to be found throughout Europe and beyond, and in many cases their legal structure is similar to that of their British counterparts. Where differences occur, these are often a reflection of historical and cultural factors which find expression in custom and practice as well as in law. Examples of some of these differences are contained in the discussion below, which focuses on France, Germany, Denmark and Portugal.

France

Numerically, the French economy is dominated by very small businesses (i.e. fewer than ten employees), the majority of which are sole traders. As in Britain, these are owner-managed-and-operated enterprises, with a husband and wife often assuming joint responsibility for the business. Formal requirements in this type of organisation tend to be few, although individuals as well as companies engaging in a commercial business are required to register before trading officially begins. Since this process is relatively simple and there are no minimum capital requirements nor significant reporting obligations, sole traderships tend to be preferred by the vast majority of individuals seeking to start a business and they are particularly prevalent in the service sector. They carry, however, unlimited personal liability for the owner, whose personal assets are at risk in the event of business failure.

Most of the remaining French business organisations are limited companies, many of which are Petites et Moyennes Entreprises (PMEs) – small and medium enterprises – employing between 10 and 500 employees. These companies come in a variety of legal forms, but two in particular predominate: the Société à Responsabilité Limitée (SARL) and the Société Anonyme (SA). A new company form, the Société Anonyme Simplifée was created by statute in 1994 and combines the legal status of a corporation with the flexibility of a partnership.

The SARL tends to be the form preferred by smaller companies, whose owners wish to retain close control of the organisation; hence many of them are family businesses – an important feature of the private sector in France. This type of enterprise can be established (currently) with a minimum capital of €7500, cannot issue shares to the general public, has restrictions on the transfer of shares and is run by individuals appointed by the shareholders – usually the shareholders themselves and/or relatives. In practice, these various restrictions help to ensure that the owner-managers remain dominant in the organisation and the appointed head of the company will invariably be the most important decision maker. Concomitantly, they help to provide the organisation with a defence against hostile takeover, particularly by overseas companies looking for a French subsidiary in order to avoid the special rules which apply to branches and agencies (e.g. a foreign parent company has unlimited liability for the debts of its branch or agency, since these do not have a separate legal identity).

The SA is the legal form normally chosen by larger companies seeking access to substantial amounts of capital. In the case of a privately owned company, the minimum capital requirement is currently €37 000; if publicly owned the minimum is €225 000 million. Where capital assets are substantial, this tends to ensure that financial institutions are large shareholders in SAs and many of them have interests in a wide range of enterprises which they often manage through a holding company (see below). One advantage of this arrangement is that it provides the financial institution with a means of managing its investments and of exerting influence over companies in which it has a large minority stake. Another is that it provides a means of defending French companies from hostile takeovers and hence small and medium enterprises often seek backing from holding companies to help fend off foreign predators.

As in Britain, the legal basis of the SA provides for a clear distinction between the roles of the owners (the shareholders) and the salaried employees, and it is the former who appoint the company's board of directors. In smaller companies, the chairperson and managing director is often the same person and many smaller French companies continue to have extremely strong central control, often by the head of the owning family. In larger companies, the two roles are normally separated, with the managing director assuming responsibility for the day-to-day operations of the enterprise and forming the link between the board and the company's senior executives and managers, some of whom may have considerable delegated authority.

It is worth noting that in companies with more than 50 employees, there is a legal requirement to have elected work councils, and workers' delegates have the right to attend board meetings as observers and to be consulted on matters affecting working conditions. In companies with more than ten employees, workers have the right to elect representatives to look after their interests and regular meetings have to take place between management and workers, over and above the obligation of employers to negotiate annually on pay and conditions. Despite these arrangements and the legal right for unions to organise on a company's premises, trade union membership – outside state-run companies – remains low and hence union influence tends to be limited. Recent steps to encourage local agreements on pay and conditions seem destined to reduce this influence even further – a situation which has parallels in Britain.

Germany

All major forms of business organisation are to be found in Germany, but it is the limited company which is of particular interest. Some of these are of relatively recent origin, having formerly been East German state-owned enterprises which have undergone privatisation following the reunification of the country.

In numerical terms it is the private limited company (*Gesellschaft mit beschränkter Haftung* – GmbH) which predominates and which is the form chosen by most foreign companies seeking to establish an enterprise in Germany. As in Britain, this type of organisation has to be registered with the authorities and its founding members must prepare Articles of Association for signature by a public notary. The Articles include information on the purpose of the business, the amount of capital subscribed, the members' subscriptions and obligations and the company's name and registered address. Once the registration process is complete – usually a matter of a few days – the personal liability of the members becomes limited to the amount invested in the business. Currently, the minimum amount of subscribed share capital required for registration is €10 000, half of which must be paid up by the company itself.

Large numbers of GmbHs are owned and run by German families, with the banks often playing an influential role as guarantors of part of the initial capital and as primary sources of loan finance. As in France, this pattern of ownership makes hostile takeovers less likely, as well as ensuring that the management of the enterprise remains in the hands of the owners. Significantly, the management of a proposed GmbH is subject to quality control, being required to prove that they are qualified for the task prior to trading. This requirement stands in stark contrast to arrangements in Britain, where no such guarantees are needed, other than those implicit in a bank's decisions to help finance a proposed venture on the basis of a business plan.

The procedures for establishing other types of business organisation are similar to those of the GmbH, although in the case of the public limited company (*Aktiengesellschaft* – AG), the current minimum amount of capital required at start-up is €50 000 in negotiable share certificates. Unlike British companies, the AG usually consists of two boards of directors, one of which (the supervisory board) decides on longer-term strategy, while the other (the managing board) concentrates on more immediate policy issues, often of an operational kind. Normally half the members of the supervisory board (*Aufsichtrat*) are elected by shareholders, while the other half are employees elected by the workforce, and it is the responsibility of the board to protect the interests of employees as well as shareholders.

Such worker representation at senior levels is an important element of the German system of business organisation and even in smaller enterprises workers have the right to establish works councils and to be consulted on social and personnel issues and on strategic decisions. Equally, all employees have a constitutional right to belong to a trade union – most of which are organised by industry rather than by craft or occupation, as is largely the case in the United Kingdom. Consequently, German companies typically negotiate with only one union, usually in an atmosphere which stresses consensus and an identity of social and economic interests, rather than conflict and confrontation.

Corporate finance is another area in which German experience differs from that in the United Kingdom, although the situation has changed to some degree in recent years. Historically, in Britain a substantial amount of company finance has been raised through the stock market and this is also the case in the United States and Japan. In Germany (and for that matter in France, Italy and Spain), the banks and a number of other special credit institutions play a dominant role, with bank loans far outstripping joint-stock financing as a source of long-term capital. Traditionally, German banks have been willing to take a longer-term view of their investment, even at the expense of short-term profits and dividends, and this has benefited German companies seeking to expand their operations. In return, the banks have tended to exert a considerable amount of influence in the boardrooms of many German companies, usually by providing a substantial number of members of a company's supervisory board, including the chairperson.

Denmark

Denmark, like France, is a country whose economy is dominated by small businesses, many of which are sole traders. As in other countries, there are very few regulations governing the establishment of this type of enterprise, other than the need to register for VAT if turnover exceeds a predetermined limit and to meet taxation and social security requirements. In keeping with practice throughout Europe and beyond, sole traders have unlimited personal liability and this imposes a considerable burden on the organisation's owner and family, who often run the business jointly. The same conditions also apply in the case of Danish partnerships – whether formal or informal – with the joint owners having full and unlimited liability for all debts accruing to the organisation.

Limited companies in Denmark also reflect practice elsewhere, being required to register under the Companies Act and having a legal existence separate from the owners and employees. Three main types of limited liability company can be distinguished:

1 The *Anpartselskaber* (ApS), which is a private joint-stock company, often run by a family and owned and controlled by a handful of individuals, one of whom may simultaneously occupy the roles of main owner, chairperson and managing director. Many of these companies began life as sole traders, but for reasons of taxation and liability have registered as an ApS.

2 The *Aktieselskaber* (A/S), which is a quoted or (more regularly) unquoted public limited company, subject essentially to the same regulations as the ApS, but having a much larger minimum capital requirement on registration. A large number of A/S companies are still small businesses, run by family members who wish to retain control of the enterprise as an increase in assets occurs.

3 The AMBA is a special kind of limited company – in essence a tax-free co-operative with its own regulations. Many of these companies have grown over the years through merger and acquisition and some of them belong to larger Danish companies and employ a substantial number of workers. They tend to be concentrated in farm-related products, but can also be found in the service sector, especially wholesaling and retailing.

Portugal

A brief look at Portuguese business organisations reveals a range of legal structures which includes sole traders, joint ventures, complementary groups, unlimited companies, limited partnerships and public and private limited companies. In the case of the latter, capital requirements tend to be an important distinguishing feature with the Public Limited Company or Corporation (*Sociedade Anonima* – SA) having a much larger minimum capital requirement than the private company (*Sociedade Por Quotas or Limitada* – LDA) as in other countries.

The public sector in mainland Europe

Given the number of countries involved, it is impossible to survey the whole of the public sector in the rest of Europe. Students with an interest in this area are encouraged to read further and to consult the various specialist sources of information covering the countries they wish to investigate. A number of general points, however, are worthy of note:

1 Public sector business organisations can be found in all countries and invariably exist because of the decision by the state to establish a particular organisation under state ownership and control, or to nationalise an existing private business (or industry).

2 In some countries (e.g. France, Greece, Portugal) the state has traditionally played an important role in business and still controls some key sectors of the economy.

3 State involvement in business often includes significant shareholdings in a number of large enterprises, not only by the national government but also by regional and/or local government (e.g. in Germany).

4 State intervention often occurs in organisations or industries which can be deemed 'problematic' (e.g. in Greece).

5 Privatisation of state-owned enterprises has occurred throughout Europe and in other parts of the world. In the former East Germany, for example, most of the state-owned companies have been transferred to private ownership, by turning them initially into trusts which became the vehicle for privatisation and/or joint ventures. Similarly in Portugal, the wholesale nationalisation of the economy after the 1974 Revolution has been reversed and the government is committed to a phased programme of privatisation, involving employees and small investors as well as large national and international organisations (see also Chapter 17 for a further discussion).

This latter point serves to re-emphasise that the business environment is subject to change over time and the fashions of today may tomorrow become things of the past. This fluctuating environment is as applicable to the public sector as it is to the private sector of the economy.

Legal structure: some implications

For businesses in the private sector, the choice of legal structure has important implications. Among the factors which the aspiring entrepreneur has to take into account when deciding what form of business enterprise to establish are:

- the degree of personal liability;
- the willingness to share decision-making powers and risks;
- the costs of establishing the business;
- the legal requirements concerning the provision of public information;
- the taxation position;
- commercial needs, including access to capital; and
- business continuity.

For some, retaining personal control will be the main requirement, even at the risk of facing unlimited personal liability and reducing the opportunities for expansion. For others, the desire to limit personal liability and to provide increased capital for growth will dictate that the owner seeks corporate status, even if this necessitates sharing decision-making powers and may ultimately result in a loss of ownership and/or control of the enterprise.

This link between an organisation's legal structure and its subsequent operations can be illustrated by examining three important facets of organisational life: the organisation's objectives, its sources of finance and its stakeholders. As the analysis below illustrates, in each of these areas, significant differences occur between alternative forms of business organisation, both *within* the private sector and *between* the state and non-state sectors of the economy. In some cases, these differences can be attributed directly to the restraints (or opportunities) faced by an organisation as a result of its legal status, suggesting that the legal basis of the enterprise conditions its operations. In other cases operational considerations tend to dictate the organisation's legal form, indicating that these are as much a cause of its legal status as a result of it – a point well illustrated by the workers' co-operative and the public corporation.

Organisational objectives

All business organisations pursue a range of objectives and these may vary to some degree over time. New private sector businesses, for example, are likely to be concerned initially with survival and with establishing a position in the marketplace, with profitability and growth seen as less important in the short term. In contrast, most well-established businesses will tend to regard profits and growth as key objectives and may see them as a means towards further ends, including market domination, maximising sales revenue and/or minimising operating costs.

Organisational objectives are also conditioned by the firm's legal structure. In sole traders, partnerships and some limited companies, control of the enterprise rests in the hands of the entrepreneur(s) and hence organisational goals will tend to coincide with the personal goals of the owner(s), whatever the point in the organisation's life cycle. In public companies, however – where ownership tends to be separated from control – the goals of the owners (shareholders) may not always correspond with those of the directors and senior managers who run the organisation, particularly when the latter are pursuing personal goals to enhance their own organisational position, status and/or rewards.

It is worth noting that the possibility of goal conflict also occurs where an individual company becomes a subsidiary of another organisation, whether by agreement or as a result of a takeover battle. This parent–subsidiary relationship may take the form of a holding company which is specially created to purchase a majority (sometimes all) of the shares in other companies, some of which may operate as holding companies themselves. Thus, while the individual subsidiaries may retain their legal and commercial identities and may operate as individual units, they will tend to be controlled by a central organisation which may exercise a considerable degree of influence over the objectives to be pursued by each of its subsidiaries. It is not inconceivable, for example, that some parts of the group may be required to make a loss on paper, particularly when there are tax advantages to be gained by the group as a whole from doing so.

Workers' co-operatives and public corporations provide further evidence of the relationship between an organisation's legal status and its primary objectives. In the case of the former, the establishment of the enterprise invariably reflects a desire on the part of its members to create an organisation which emphasises social goals (e.g. democracy, co-operation, job creation, mutual trust) rather than the pursuit of profits – hence the choice of the 'co-operative' form. Similarly in the case of the public corporation, a decision by government to establish an entity which operates in the interests of the public at large (or 'national interest') favours the creation of a state-owned-and-controlled organisation, with goals laid down by politicians and generally couched in social and financial terms (e.g. return on assets, reinvestment, job creation) rather than in terms of profit maximisation.

This apparent dichotomy between the profit motive of the private sector and the broader socio-economic goals of public bodies has, however, become less clear-cut over the last decade, as an increasing number of state-owned organisations have been 'prepared' for privatisation and successive governments have sought to bring private money into public projects by creating public/private partnerships. Equally, in other parts of the public sector – including the health service and local government – increasing stress is being laid on 'best value' and on operating within budgets – concepts which are familiar to businesses in the private sector. While it is not inconceivable that a change in government could reverse this trend, current evidence suggests that a shift in cultural attitudes has occurred and public bodies can no longer rely on unconditional government support for their activities. If this is the case, further convergence is likely to occur between state and privately owned bodies, with the former moving towards the latter rather than vice versa.

Finance

Business organisations finance their activities in a variety of ways and from a range of sources. Methods include reinvesting profits, borrowing, trade credit and issuing shares and debentures. Sources include the banks and other financial institutions, individual investors and governments, as well as contributions from the organisation's original owners.

In the context of this chapter it is appropriate to make a number of observations about the topic as it relates generally to the business environment:

1 All organisations tend to fund their activities from both internal (e.g. owner's capital, reinvested profits) and external sources (e.g. bank borrowing, sale of shares).
2 Financing may be short term, medium term or longer term, and the methods and sources of funding chosen will reflect the time period concerned (e.g. bank borrowing on overdraft tends to be short term and generally needed for immediate use).
3 Funds raised from external sources inevitably involve the organisation in certain obligations (e.g. repayment of loans with interest, personal guarantees, paying dividends) and these will act as a constraint on the organisation at some future date.
4 The relationship between owner's capital and borrowed funds – usually described as an organisation's **gearing** – can influence a firm's activities and prospects in a variety of ways (e.g. high-geared firms with a large element of borrowed funds will be adversely affected if interest rates are high).
5 Generally speaking, as organisations become larger many more external sources and methods of funding become available and utilising these can have implications for the structure, ownership and conduct of the organisation.

This latter point is perhaps best illustrated by comparing sole traders and partnerships with limited companies. In the case of the former, as unincorporated entities neither the sole trader nor the partnership can issue shares (or debentures) and hence their access to large amounts of external capital is restricted by law. Companies have no such restrictions – other than those which help to differentiate a private company from a public one – and consequently they are able to raise larger amounts by inviting individuals (and organisations) to subscribe for shares. Where a company is publicly quoted on the stock market, the amounts raised in this way can be very large indeed and the resultant organisation may have millions of owners who change on a regular basis as shares are traded on the second-hand market.

Organisations which decide to acquire corporate status in order to raise funds for expansion (or for some other purposes) become owned by their shareholders, who may be the original owners or may be individual and institutional investors holding equity predominantly as an investment and with little, if any, long-term commitment to the organisation they own. As indicated above, in the latter case, a separation tends to occur between the roles of owner (shareholder) and controller (director) and this can lead to the possibility of conflicting aims and objectives or differences in opinion over priorities within the enterprise – a problem discussed in more detail below under 'Stakeholders'.

A further illustration of the relationship between an organisation's legal structure and its ability to raise finance is provided by the public corporation. In this case, as a public body accountable to Parliament and the public via government, the public corporation is normally required to operate within a financial context largely controlled by government and this will be conditioned by the government's overall fiscal policy, including its attitude to the size of the Public Sector Borrowing Requirement (PSBR). One aspect of this context in Britain has been the establishment of external financing limits (EFLs) for each nationalised industry, arrived at by negotiation between government and the board running the public corporation, and used as a means of restraining monetary growth and hence the size of the PSBR. Unfortunately this has also tended to prevent the more financially sound corporations, such as British Telecom before privatisation, from borrowing externally on a scale necessary to develop their business – a restriction which tends to disappear when the corporation becomes a fully fledged public company, either through privatisation or by some other means.

Stakeholders

All organisations have **stakeholders**; these are individuals and/or groups who are affected by or affect the performance of the organisation in which they have an interest. Typically they would include employees, managers, creditors, suppliers, shareholders (if appropriate) and society at large. As Table 10.1 illustrates, an organisation's stakeholders have a variety of interests which range from the pursuit of private gain to the more nebulous idea of achieving public benefit. Sometimes these interests will clash as, for example, when managers seek to improve the organisation's cash flow by refusing to pay suppliers' bills on time. On other occasions, the interests of different stakeholders may coincide, as when managers plan for growth in the organisation and in doing so provide greater job security for employees and enhanced dividends for investors.

Table 10.1 Organisational stakeholders and their interests

Types of stakeholder	Possible principal interests
Employees	Wage levels; working conditions; job security; personal development
Managers	Job security; status; personal power; organisational profitability; growth of the organisation
Shareholders	Market value of the investment; dividends; security of investment; liquidity of investment
Creditors	Security of loan; interest on loan; liquidity of investment
Suppliers	Security of contract; regular payment; growth of organisation; market development
Society	Safe products; environmental sensitivity; equal opportunities; avoidance of discrimination

The legal structure of an organisation has an impact not only on the type of stakeholders involved but also to a large degree on how their interests are represented. In sole traders, partnerships and smaller private companies, the coincidence of ownership and control limits the number of potential clashes of interest, given that objectives are set by and decisions taken by the firm's owner-manager(s). In larger companies, and, in particular, public limited companies, the division between ownership and control means that the controllers have the responsibility of representing the interests of the organisation's shareholders and creditors and, as suggested above, their priorities and goals may not always correspond.

A similar situation occurs in public sector organisations, where the interest of taxpayers (or ratepayers) is represented both by government and by those individuals chosen by government to run the organisation. In this case, it is worth recalling that the broader strategic objectives of the enterprise and the big decisions concerning policy, finance and investment tend to be taken by politicians, operating with advice from their officials (e.g. civil servants, local government officers) and within the context of the government's overall economic and social policies. The organisation's board of management and its senior executives and managers are mainly responsible for the day-to-day operations of the business, although the board and the person chairing it would normally play a key role in shaping overall objectives and decisions, through regular discussions with government and its officials.

One important way in which public sector organisations differ from their private sector counterparts is in the sanctions available to particular groups of stakeholders who feel that the organisation is not representing their best interests. Shareholders in a company, for example, could withdraw financial support for a firm whose directors consistently disregard their interests or take decisions which threaten the security and/or value of their investment, and the possibility of such a reaction normally guarantees that the board pays due attention to the needs of this important group of stakeholders. The taxpayer and ratepayer have no equivalent sanction and in the short term must rely heavily on government and its agencies or, if possible, their power as consumers to represent their interest *vis-à-vis* the organisation. Longer term, of course, the public has the sanction of the ballot box, although it seems highly unlikely that the performance of state enterprises would be a key factor in determining the outcome of general or local elections.

The relative absence of market sanctions facing state-owned organisations has meant that the public has had to rely on a range of formal institutions (e.g. parliamentary scrutiny committees, consumer consultative bodies, the audit authorities) and on the media to protect its interest in areas such as funding, pricing and quality of service provided. As these organisations are returned to the private sector, the expectation is that the sanctions imposed by the free market will once again operate and shareholders in privatised utilities will be protected like any other group of shareholders in a privately owned enterprise. To what extent this will occur in practice, of course, is open to question, while the newly privatised public corporations face little, if any, competition. Government, it seems, prefers to hedge its bets on this question, at least in the short term – hence the establishment of regulators with powers of investigation into performance and some degree of control over pricing.

mini case   Big Mac gets bigger and more selective

Growth through franchising has become a preferred option for many organisations, typified by McDonald's, which is the world's biggest fast food chain. Established in 1955 when Raymond Croc opened his first burger restaurant, McDonald's was estimated to have had in excess of 20 000 outlets spread across the globe by the end of 1996. Contrary to popular predictions, the organisation continued to expand at a significant rate and benefited from the opening of new markets in eastern Europe and the Far East. In the mid-1990s, for example, it was estimated that at its current rate of growth, a new McDonald's was opening somewhere in the world every three hours.

When considering applicants for a coveted McDonald's franchise the company has always been concerned to ensure that its reputation for quality and service is maintained. Potential franchisees have to demonstrate not only a successful track record in a previous occupation, but also that they have the necessary financial resources and a willingness to commit themselves to the organisation. Individuals making the grade have traditionally been offered two kinds of franchise scheme. The conventional franchise involves a 20-year agreement between the franchisee and the company under which the latter buys and develops the site which the former takes over and operates for an agreed price, as well as paying McDonald's a royalty fee based on a pre-agreed percentage of turnover. Under the other option – the business facilities lease – the individual leases the restaurant normally for a three-year period, prior to being offered the opportunity to convert to a conventional franchise if funds permit.

Like any business, McDonald's fortunes have fluctuated over time. In late October 2002 McDonald's announced its intention of sharply cutting back on its expansion plans and redirecting its efforts towards supporting its existing chain of restaurants (see the *Guardian*, 23 October 2002). By 2005, McDonald's claimed to have over 30 000 local restaurants serving nearly 50 million people each day in more than 119 countries. Adverse publicity, following the documentary *Super Size Me* appears to have led to a consumer backlash in recent years and the company has closed some stores, while opening new ones. McDonald's strategy is to undertake a programme of worldwide restructuring coupled with more careful targetting of the market. This includes getting the 'right restaurants' in the 'right places' and responding to local requirements (e.g. Kosher outlets in some Israeli branches of McDonald's).

web link   The website for McDonald's is *www.mcdonalds.com*

Franchising, licensing and joint ventures

To complete this review of the legal structure of business organisations, it is useful to consider three developments which have a legal aspect: franchising, licensing and joint ventures. All three may be seen as a means of carrying out a business venture in a way that reduces some of the risks normally faced by the entrepreneur.

Franchising

Franchising, which has grown significantly in recent years, is an arrangement where one party (the franchiser) sells the right to another party (the franchisee) to market its product or service. In terms of their legal status the parties involved could be any of the forms described above, but in practice it is usually the case that the franchiser is a company while the franchisee tends to be a sole trader or partnership. Both parties in law have a separate legal identity, but the nature of the contract between them makes their relationship interdependent and this has important implications for the operation of the franchise.

Franchise arrangements come in a variety of forms. Probably the best known is the 'business format franchise' (or 'trade name franchise') under which the franchiser agrees to allow the franchisee to sell the product or service with the help of a franchise package which contains all the elements needed to set up and run a business at a profit. These would typically include the brand name, any associated supplies, promotional material and other forms of support and assistance. In return the franchisee usually pays an initial sum or fee for the use of the service and its various elements, remits royalties based on sales and/or profits, agrees to make a contribution for consultancy, training and promotion, and undertakes to maintain standards. Wimpy, Kentucky Fried Chicken, Burger King, Prontaprint and Dynarod are examples of this type of franchise.

Other forms include manufacturer/retailer franchises (e.g. car dealers), manufacturer/wholesaler franchises (e.g. Coca-Cola, Pepsi) and wholesaler/retailer franchises (e.g. Spar and Mace) and it is estimated by the industry's trade body   the British Franchise Association – that in retailing alone franchising accounts for over 20 per cent of sales in the United Kingdom. One indication of its growing significance is the spread of franchising into further and higher education, with universities and other colleges of higher education franchising some of their courses to local further education colleges, which in turn may franchise some of their courses to schools and/or sixth-form colleges. Another indicator is the decision by many clearing banks and firms of accountants to establish franchise sections to help and advise individuals who want to open a franchise or who have already done so and are seeking further guidance.

The British Franchise Association's main website is *www.thebfa.org*

Undoubtedly the mutual benefits to be derived from a franchise arrangement help to explain its popularity as a way of doing business in both domestic and external markets and it has proved an attractive vehicle for some companies seeking rapid overseas expansion, without undertaking substantial direct investments – although this is sometimes necessary to support the operation (e.g. McDonald's had to invest in a plant to make hamburger buns in the United Kingdom). Equally, many would-be entrepreneurs find the security of a franchise more attractive than other methods of starting a business, especially as there is some evidence to suggest that franchises have better survival rates than the more conventional forms of independent enterprise (e.g. sole traders).

Current indications are that this popularity is likely to continue into the foreseeable future, although it is more likely that greater selectivity of potential franchisees will occur as the franchise industry becomes more mature and attempts to gain an increased degree of public respectability. Franchisees, too, are likely to become more particular about the businesses they agree to deal with, as they endeavour to join the enterprise culture. It is, after all, the franchisee who has to bear the financial risk of the business in return for a share in the profits; the franchiser has a reputation to think about.

Licensing

Licensing is another form of non-equity agreement under which a firm in one country (the licensor) authorises a firm in another country (the licensee) to use its intellectual property (e.g. patents, copyrights, trade names, know-how) in return for certain considerations, usually royalty payments. Licences may be granted to individuals, independent companies, subsidiaries of a multinational company or to government agencies and the rights granted may be exclusive or non-exclusive.

Companies invariably enter into licensing agreements to gain certain advantages. These might include:

● Reducing competition by sharing technology.
● Seeking overseas profits without direct foreign investment.
● Protecting an asset from potential 'pirates'.
● Avoiding restrictions on foreign investment or imports imposed by other countries.
● Recouping some research and development costs.
● Gaining a share of an overseas market.

Needless to say, most organisations granting licences tend to be based in the advanced industrial economies and are frequently multinationals which regard their trade marks and technologies as an integral part of their asset base. One problem of transferring the use of such assets to another firm is that the owner loses a degree of control over the asset, including the quality of production, and this may affect the product's image and sales elsewhere. Another is the possibility of the licensee dominating the market after the agreement ends, even to the extent of excluding the licensor from the marketplace by aggressive competition or the development of an alternative product.

Joint ventures

The term **joint venture** tends to be used in two ways: to describe a contractual agreement involving two or more parties, or to describe a jointly owned and independently incorporated business venture involving more than one organisation. It is the latter usage which is mainly applied here.

Joint ventures – which are popular with international companies – can take a variety of legal forms and almost every conceivable type of partnership may exist, ranging from two companies joining together in the same domestic market (e.g. Sainsbury's and British Home Stores set up the Savacentre chain), to joint private/public sector ventures between participants from different countries. Sometimes numerous organisations may be involved and these may be based in one country or in several. Where this occurs the term **consortium** is often used, as in the case of TransManche Link (TML), the international joint venture which built the Channel Tunnel.

As with licensing and franchising, joint ventures have increased in popularity in the last 25–30 years and have been one of the ways in which international companies have sought to develop an overseas market, particularly in the face of import restrictions, or heavy research and development costs. Multinational car companies have been active in this field – as evidenced by past links between General Motors and Toyota, Ford and Mazda – and these arrangements look likely to continue as markets become more global. For western companies wishing to exploit the gradual privatisation of the former planned economies of eastern Europe, joint ventures with indigenous producers are likely to prove a safer bet than direct inward investment, particularly given the degree of economic and political uncertainty. They are also likely to prove more politically acceptable in states seeking to establish their own economic independence and identity after almost 50 years of regional domination.

Synopsis

Market-based economies throughout Europe and beyond have a range of business organisations with broadly similar legal structures. These legal structures help to determine not only the ownership and control of the enterprise, but also other aspects of its operations, including its objectives, its access to finance and its external relationships and obligations. Viewing businesses as legal entities provides a useful insight into a number of the external influences which impinge upon their daily existence and highlights some of the consequences faced by organisations which transfer from public (i.e. state) to private ownership. It also sheds light on other important developments in entrepreneurial activity, including franchising, licensing and joint ventures.

Summary of key points

- Business organisations have a legal structure.

- The three commonest forms of business in the private sector are sole traders, partnerships and limited companies.

- Whereas the owners of the first two types of business organisation face unlimited personal liability, in companies the legal separation of the firm from its owners affords the latter limited personal liability.

- Companies are normally run by directors who are appointed to represent the interest of the owners (the shareholders). In public companies this separation of ownership and control is a key distinguishing feature.

- Other forms of business organisation exist in the public sector (e.g. the public corporation) and the 'third sector' (e.g. the co-operative).

- Government-owned businesses are increasingly adopting private sector forms of organisation to provide for greater flexibility and freedom of action.

- The legal status of the organisation has implications for the objectives of the enterprise, how it is financed and for its stakeholder relationships.

---

case study   The entrepreneurial spirit

Business studies textbooks teach us that new businesses invariably come into existence to satisfy the needs and ambitions of their owners. Once established, it is assumed that an enterprise will begin to grow and that the owner(s) will sanction this and take steps to bring it about. As the two case studies below illustrate, these assumptions may be correct or not, according to specific circumstances. Arguing from the particular to the general needs to be approached with caution in business, as in any other field of study.

T & S Stores PLC

Like many medium- to large-sized businesses, T & S Stores started from relatively modest origins and was the brainchild of one individual, Kevin Threlfall, a Wolverhampton entrepreneur.

A barrow boy by background, Threlfall received his early business training working from the age of 12 on his parents' pitch in West Midlands markets.

Despatched to public school, Threlfall soon found this market background was treated contemptuously by his fellow pupils and this made him determined to prove his worth in the business world. On leaving school he began providing pet-foods in bulk, before selling out his business and founding the Lo Cost food chain in 1972. This was subsequently bought for £1.5 million by Oriel Foods, later owned by the Argyll Group.

Threlfall's T & S Stores grew from the Wolverhampton market stalls and quickly expanded into retail outlets, with their emphasis on discount tobacco and convenience shopping. Using day-glo starbursts offering low-priced cigarettes, Threlfall cleverly attracted customers into his stores where they were tempted by the use of colourful confectionery gondolas and other techniques into impulse purchases of products carrying high margins. By keeping costs to a minimum, Threlfall was able to turn his company into a highly profitable enterprise with a stock market capitalisation of almost £140 million by 1991 and a chain of almost 600 stores.

In 1989, T & S acquired the Dillons and Preedy chains from Next for £54 million and subsequently purchased 22 stores from Johnson News Group for £4.25 million in February 1991, thus helping to increase the organisation's interest in convenience stores, which Threlfall believed would be the company's main area of future growth. Trading from outlets larger than most of the T & S shops and offering an extended range of grocery and frozen-food lines, Threlfall's One Stop convenience stores generally achieved higher gross margins than the core tobacco shops and helped to contribute to the company's strong net cash position in the early 1990s. Despite these developments, Threlfall maintained close contacts with what was happening on the ground and attempted to maintain a degree of individual customer attention in a field of retailing which is rapidly changing.

Threlfall's entrepreneurial skills, coupled with the gains from introducing National Lottery and other facilities in many of the group's outlets, continued to strengthen the organisation's financial and trading position. With hundreds of stores and increasing turnover and pre-tax profits, T & S attracted outside investment from reputable fund managers who expressed confidence in the management's strategy of refocusing the business towards the growing convenience store market. Turnover by 2001 was recorded at £933 million; in 1995 it had been £445 million.

T & S was subsequently acquired by Tesco in January 2003 and now trades under the One Stop brand, with some stores being converted to the Tesco Express format. An Office of Fair Trading investigation into the acquisition concluded that the purchase of T&S by Tesco did not lead to any significant lessening of competition.

Dave Noble (Windsurfing)

Unlike Kevin Threlfall, Dave Noble came from a non-business background and had no ambitions as a child to seek a career in industry or commerce. Following A-levels at the local grammar school in Woking, Noble went to Aberystwyth University where he obtained a degree in philosophy, before continuing his studies at postgraduate level. After a brief spell doing research, he left university and worked on building sites, subsequently returning to study for a postgraduate certificate of education, a move which was to take him into teaching in Loughborough.

With the start of a family, Noble gave up his full-time teaching post to look after the children, continuing as a supply teacher as and when circumstances allowed. As a keen windsurfer, with an established reputation in the sport, he decided to use some of his time at home to make his own boards, buying the necessary fittings from suppliers to the trade. As requests from friends for similar equipment began to grow, Noble found himself dealing with suppliers on a larger scale and spending an increasing amount of his time making and equipping windsurfing boards. Before he had fully realised what was happening, Noble found himself in business as a sole trader, operating in the leisure industry, a growing sector in the UK economy.

With an initial injection of his own capital, supported by a weekly income from the government's Enterprise Allowance Scheme, Noble established his own venture in late 1986/early 1987, operating from home in Shepshed in Leicestershire. Despite only limited expenditure on advertising, the business began to grow quickly, allowing the venture to become totally self-financing. Before long, it became obvious that new premises would be needed and so in 1989 the Noble family (now five in total) moved to a Georgian house in the village of Wymeswold on the Leicestershire/Nottinghamshire border. Apart from providing adequate space for a growing family, the new house had numerous outbuildings suitable for making and selling equipment and for storing supplies and material. It was also sufficiently close to Shepshed to allow Noble to keep his existing customer and supplier bases which were fundamental to the success of the business.

Noble's initial enthusiasm at working from his village home – in a manner reminiscent of a traditional cottage industry – was soon to be dampened following complaints from neighbours who objected to the traffic from customers seeking boards and other equipment. Consequently, the business was forced to relocate to the nearby Wymeswold Airfield Industrial Estate, where Noble acquired two units from which to operate. Like other units on the estate, Noble's premises were relatively basic, but provided sufficient space for production, storage and sales and had more than adequate parking for customers and suppliers. Being in a rural location, with no houses in the immediate vicinity, complaints concerning disturbance ceased to be a problem for the business.

Despite the successive moves, Noble's business continued to grow, even in the recession years in the early 1990s. Part of this growth was manifestly attributable to the increased demand for leisure products, and the decision to add mountain bikes and ski equipment to the range of items on offer was clearly beneficial, although by no means part of a deliberate strategy of diversification. The most significant factor in the firm's success, however, and one which resulted in the need to hire additional staff to meet the increased demand, appears to have been Noble's deliberate policy of keeping customers and suppliers happy. By paying all his bills on time, Noble was able to strike good bargains with suppliers and to pass savings on to the customer in the form of highly competitive prices which other traders could not meet. In addition, Noble and his staff did their best to meet their customers' needs individually, even if it meant working extra hours and incurring some additional expense.

By the mid-1990s Dave Noble (Windsurfing) had become a formidable operator in the marketplace, with a dominant share of the market in the East Midlands and a loyal and extensive customer base. As the firm continued to prosper, Noble eventually planned to sell his business to the staff and to go into semi-retirement. He has, however, maintained an interest in the leisure industry, importing snowboards which he sells to the trade via mail order. He has recently taken back control of parts of the main business as the anticipated sale did not materialise and this is now being run by two of his sons.

Case study questions

1 What characteristics have Threlfall and Noble in common which might help to explain their success as entrepreneurs?

2 Can you identify any changes in the external environment of either of the businesses in the case study which proved beneficial to their development?

web link You can find information on this and other companies at *www.hoovers.com*

Review and discussion questions

1 Numerically, the sole proprietorship is the most popular form of business organisation throughout Europe. How would you account for this?

2 To what extent is corporate status an asset to a business organisation? Does it have any disadvantages?

3 Examine the implications of privatising a public sector business organisation.

4 Discuss how the legal status of a business affects its objectives, its methods of finance and its stakeholders.

5 How would you explain the rise in the popularity of franchising in recent years?

Assignments

1 You have recently been made redundant and decide to set up your own small business, possibly with a friend. Assuming that you have £25 000 to invest in your new venture, draft a business plan which is to be presented to your bank manager in the hope of gaining financial support. Your plan should include a clear rationale for the legal form you wish your business to take, your chosen product(s) or service(s), evidence of market research, an indication of anticipated competition and supporting financial information.

2 You work in a local authority business advice centre. One of your clients wishes to start a business in some aspect of catering. Advise your client on the advantages and disadvantages of the various legal forms the proposed enterprise could take.

Notes and references

1 Liability may be extended where a company continues trading after insolvency.

2 It is also possible to have unlimited companies.

3 Under regulations issued in 1992 it is possible to have single member private companies with limited liability status, but these are the exception rather than the general rule.

4 A similar growth occurred in the number of 'community businesses' in Scotland during this period. Though not strictly 'co-operatives', they are also part of the so-called third sector of business.

Further reading

Campbell, D. J. and Craig, T., *Organizations and the Business Environment*, Butterworth-Heinemann, 2005.

Morrison, J., *The International Business Environment*, 2nd edition, Macmillan, 2006.

Palmer, A. J. and Hartley, R., *The Business Environment*, 5th edition, McGraw-Hill, 2005.

Worthington, I., Britton, C. and Rees, A., *Economics for Business: Blending Theory and Practice*, 2nd edition, Financial Times/Prentice Hall, 2005.

Web links and further questions are available on the website at:

www.pearsoned.co.uk/worthington

11 Size structure of firms

Chris Britton

Businesses range in size from the single proprietor at one extreme to the large multinational at the other which employs thousands of people over several countries. The structure of these businesses will be very different and the problems they face will vary as a result of the differences in size. The size structure of business will depend on many factors which range from choice (the sole proprietor may choose to remain small) to external factors which are beyond the control of the firm.

Learning outcomes

Having read this chapter you should be able to:

- outline the size structure of UK industry
- provide reasons for why organisations grow in size
- demonstrate the way in which organisations grow and the methods of finance
- explain the limitations to growth
- survey the level of merger activity in the United Kingdom and the European Union
- demonstrate the role and importance of the small-firm sector
- discuss the idea of networking between firms

Key terms

Capital market	External growth	Networking
Concentration	Flexible firm	Profit
Conglomerate merger	Gearing	Small firm
Debentures	Horizontal merger	Stock Exchange
Diseconomies of scale	Industrial concentration	Subcontracting
Diversification	Internal growth	Takeover
Dividends	Joint venture	Vertical integration
Enterprise	Merger	Virtual organisation
Equity	Money market	
Establishment	Multinational corporation	

Introduction

There has been an increase in the level of industrial concentration in the United Kingdom over the last one hundred years. In 1909 the largest hundred companies produced 16 per cent of manufacturing output; by 1990 this had risen to around 30 per cent. Such an increase in the size of business organisations gives rise to worries about the concentration of power in the hands of a few producers and abuses of this power. If the companies are multinationals, they may be beyond the control even of national governments. More recently the trend towards greater concentration has been reversed, and there seems to be a movement towards employment in smaller units. This chapter will look at the size structure of British industry and the reasons for such a structure, with some international comparisons. It will consider the role of small and large firms in the economy. It will also examine the reasons for growth, the ways in which organisations grow, the financing of growth and the limits to growth. It will also consider the relatively more recent trend towards co-operation in production, rather than competition, through activities like joint ventures and networking.

The size structure of UK industry

When looking at the size of firms it is important to define the terms used in official data. The firm, or '**enterprise**', is the organisation as a whole, and it might be comprised of several units or '**establishments**'. Small firms like the corner shop will mostly be enterprises with only one establishment. Large firms like Sainsbury's will have many establishments as they have branches in most towns.

There are many different ways to measure the size of firms. Common measures used are turnover, the value of output, the capital employed or the level of employment. Such measurement is beset by problems, not least the difficulty of defining the small firm, as will be seen later in this chapter. The three measures mentioned above might give conflicting pictures, as an industry which is becoming increasingly mechanised will probably have rising levels of average capital employed and output but falling average levels of employment. Table 11.1 shows the 'top ten' companies in the United Kingdom using two of these measures and it illustrates the point that different measures of the size of a firm will give different rankings.

Some of these names will be familiar to the reader while others are less so. Compass Group plc, for example, is a food service organisation which provides catering and support services to its clients.

The most common measure of size used is the level of employment. Table 11.2 shows the size structure of units in all industries by the number of employees in the United Kingdom in 2006. The table shows that smaller firms predominate in terms of numbers, with 98.4 per cent of firms employing fewer than 100 employees. In terms of employment, however, these firms account for only 34.0 per cent of the total level of employment in manufacturing. At the other end of the scale establishments with over 500 employees account for only 0.3 per cent of the total number but 54.6 per cent of total employment. The pattern of size structure varies across industries and over time. In the last 20 to 30 years there seems to have been an increase in the importance of small firms and a decline in the importance of large firms in their contribution to employment. In 1980 establishments with fewer than 200 employees accounted for 31.9 per cent of total employment and establishments with more than 500 employees accounted for 49.8 per cent. The comparable figures from Table 11.2 are 38.7 per cent and 54.6 per cent. Even the short period of time from 1991 to 2000 saw a shift in the importance of small firms. There was an increase of 188 968 in the number of units employing fewer than 20 people, while there was a decrease of 13 332 in the number of units employing more than 20 employees. A similar pattern emerges with employment, with an increase in employment of 313 800 in the smaller units and a decrease in employment of 882 800 in the larger units.

Many of the large companies listed in Table 11.1 operate in more than one country and are therefore multinationals. **Multinational corporations** strictly defined are enterprises operating in a number of countries and having production or service facilities outside the country of their origin.[1] Multinationals pose particular problems for governments and economies because of their size. They are considered later in this chapter.

Table 11.1 The ten largest companies in the UK, 2007

Ranking by turnover	Ranking by employment
1 Tesco plc	1 Compass Group plc
2 Vodafone Group plc	2 Group 4 Securicor plc
3 BP International plc	3 Tesco plc
4 Tesco Stores plc	4 HSBC Holdings plc
5 Aviva plc	5 Unilever plc
6 Unilever plc	6 Royal Mail Holdings plc
7 WPP 2005 Ltd	7 Royal Mail Group plc
8 BT Group plc	8 Sainsbury's Supermarkets Ltd
9 British Telecommunications plc	9 Tesco Stores Ltd
10 J. Sainsbury plc	10 The Royal Bank of Scotland Group plc

Source: *Key British Enterprises*, 2007.

Table 11.2 Size structure of UK industry by employment, 2006

Employment size group	Number of units	% of total	Employment (000s)	% of total
1–9	1 064 170	83.0	3 906	15.2
10–19	118 120	9.2	1 638	6.4
20–49	60 575	4.7	1 874	7.3
50–99	18 925	1.5	1 316	5.1
100–199	9 120	0.7	1 217	4.7
200–499	5 510	0.4	1 691	6.6
500 and over	4 415	0.3	14 065	54.6

Source: Adapted from Table 1, *http://stats.berr.gov.uk/ed/sme/smestats2006.xls* 'UK whole economy'! A1

Organisational growth

The reasons for organisational growth

Firms grow in size for many reasons; growth could be an explicit objective of management or could be necessary for the successful operation of the firm:

- Growth could be a managerial objective if it brings benefits to management such as greater security and higher remuneration.
- It could be that the market in which the business operates is expanding and growth is necessary to maintain market share. This is especially the case as markets become more international.
- Growth enables the organisation to reap the benefits of economies of scale (see Chapter 15).
- Growth enables firms to diversify into other markets, which means that risk can be spread further.
- Industries which are capital intensive will of necessity be comprised of large firms.
- In the area of product development it is possible that the necessary research and development could only be carried out by large companies.
- Growth could be pursued as a defensive strategy, as a reaction to the activities of competitors.

Table 11.3 provides an illustration of how the stated objectives of EU firms for engaging in merger activity can change over time and gives some indication of the reasons for growth. Much of this shift can be explained by changing market conditions which resulted from the creation of the Single European Market in 1992. The relaxation of trade restrictions in the run-up to 1992 encouraged much greater competition, and hence expansion and strengthening of market position have assumed much greater importance since 1985, together accounting for nearly 75 per cent of mergers. It was expected that the increased competition would force companies to concentrate more upon their core activities and as a result diversification as a motive for merger fell from 17.6 per cent in 1985 to 2.1 per cent of cases in 1992.

Table 11.3 Main motives for mergers in Europe, 1985–1992

Motive	% of times mentioned			
	1985–86	1989–90	1990–91	1991–92
Expansion	17.1	26.9	27.7	32.4
Diversification	17.6	3.0	2.8	2.1
Strengthening market position	10.6	45.3	48.2	44.4
Rationalisation and synergies	46.5	17.7	13.3	16.2
Research and development	2.4	0.6	0	0
Other	5.9	6.4	8.0	5.0

Source: *European Economy*, no. 57, 1994. Reproduced by permission of the Office for Official Publications of the European Communities.

The OECD[2] recognises that there are efficiencies involved in growth and it classifies these into 'static' and 'dynamic' efficiencies. Static efficiencies are one-off improvements such as economies of scale in production. Dynamic efficiencies are those that enable improvements in cost, quality, service or new product development on an ongoing basis. In considering the benefits of a takeover or merger, for example, it may be that the dynamic efficiencies will eventually overtake the initially bigger static efficiencies. Examples of dynamic efficiencies include:

- Economies of scale and scope in R&D.
- Better risk-spreading especially for R&D.
- Increased financial resources for R&D.
- Better intellectual property rights protection.

In industrial economics firm size is seen as a function of growth. It is suggested that although there is no limit on the size of a firm there are limits on the rate of expansion. Growth rates are seen to depend on different things by different theorists, including the availability of finance, the level of consumer demand and the limitations of management. These theories, however, are primarily concerned with large firms and their development. Small firms are seen as potentially large firms that failed to grow for some reason or other. One interesting theory of growth is the stages model, where the firm is seen as passing through various stages in its development from small sole proprietor/partnership through the decision to expand into a large organisation. This again is a 'grow or fail' theory which does not apply well to industries which are dominated by successful small firms, as will be seen later in the chapter.

mini case   Mars and Wrigley

In May 2008 Mars surprised the market by taking over Wrigley in a $23 billion deal. The takeover was a friendly one and was negotiated in less than three weeks. Unusually, both companies are private family-owned businesses which possibly meant that there were compatibilities which made the takeover more feasible and meant that the decision-making timescale could be short. What will the takeover mean for both companies?

For Mars, it enables diversification into a new market – chewing gum has a much healthier image than other confectionary and the dental benefits of chewing gum are well documented. The gum market has a higher growth rate than other forms of confectionary – 20 per cent in 2007. Wrigley has a big presence in Asia and China in particular, where growth in the confectionary market is particularly high, and Mars will be able to tap into these distribution networks. The new company will take the market leader's position away from Cadbury's Trident brand with 14 per cent of the world market against 10 per cent (Cadbury).

For Wrigley, the premium offered over its share price was generous (28 per cent) and the takeover will bring access to more extensive distribution networks. Wrigley will be a standalone subsidiary which means that managers at Wrigley are allowed to keep their jobs and to remain in the location of their HQ. Bill Wrigley, the company's executive chairman, said that 'this combined entity will have the resources and critical mass to explore new geographies and categories that might have been beyond our reach in the past'.

The takeover will have implications for other companies in the market – Cadbury for example. Commentators cannot agree whether the Mars–Wrigley takeover has made Cadbury a more likely takeover target or predator, as it will retain the number 1 position outside the USA. Nestlé and Kraft have been identified as possible companies for either possibility. There is also speculation of an alliance with Hershey's, which holds 43 per cent of the US chocolate markets, a company that Cadbury has held talks with in the past.

Methods of growth

Firms grow in size internally as part of normal business operation or externally through takeover and merger.

Internal growth

Growth is a natural process for many firms that start small, capture a segment of the market and then continue to expand either by producing more of the same goods or by extending their product lines. The advantage of **internal growth** over external growth is that the company grows within the existing structure of management; there are none of the problems of bringing together two different management systems. There might also be economies of scale from building a bigger plant that might not be available when companies merge and plant size does not change. Set against these, internal growth has certain disadvantages and this is why most of the growth in the size of organisations has occurred through external growth.

External growth

Growth by acquisition is called **external growth** and occurs through **takeover** or **merger.** A merger is the voluntary coming together of two companies with the agreement of the management of both companies, the result of which is the creation of a new legal identity. A takeover is where one company makes an offer to the shareholders of another. If the management of the threatened company resist it is called a hostile takeover, but if the price offered to shareholders is high enough they will accept. Takeover bids can be and have been successfully fought off by the management of the second firm. A holding company is a new company that is formed to acquire assets in other companies. The acquired companies retain their independent identities but are directed by the holding company.

External growth can be seen to have a number of advantages:

1 It is fast, so that productive capacity can be increased very quickly.
2 The acquiring firm has access to an established management team and system.
3 If the shares of the acquiring company have sufficiently high values relative to the acquired firm, there might be no need for additional cash to be raised.
4 The purchase of existing assets could be cheaper than building new productive capacity.

But set against these is the fact that the process might not be an easy one; it is a difficult job to merge two companies smoothly and successfully and there are likely to be many teething problems. Research by Coopers & Lybrand (now PriceWaterhouse Coopers) found that top executives regarded half of the takeovers in which they had been involved as failures. The main reasons for failure were lack of planning and managerial problems.

Although the definitions of merger and takeover are clear enough, it is often difficult to tell them apart in practice and they are usually put together in official publications under the heading of acquisitions. In order to understand fully the motivation for mergers and takeovers it is important to recognise that there are different types of mergers.

Horizontal mergers

A **horizontal merger** is where a combination between firms at the same stage in a production process takes place; for example, between two car manufacturers or between two brewers. The vast majority of mergers that take place are of this type and many of our largest companies have been formed through horizontal merger. Examples include mergers between banks and building societies. The motives for this type of merger are:

- *To benefit from economies of scale.* Horizontal mergers allow the merged firms a greater level of specialisation and the benefits of other economies of scale (see Chapter 15).
- *Greater market share.* When firms come together there will be a reduction in competition in the market and the resulting firm will have a much larger share of the market.
- *Rationalisation of output.* If the level of demand for a good is shrinking, merger between the producers could be necessary in order to rationalise output.
- *Reaction to competitors.* In markets where mergers are taking place, companies may feel that they have to do the same in order to maintain their market position.

The takeover of the American company Anheuser–Busch (which makes Budweiser) by Belgian company InBev (which makes Stella Artois) in 2008 is an example of a horizontal takeover (see International business in action: 'A lot of bottle').

Vertical mergers

A vertical merger involves firms at different stages of the same production process. It is vertical since it runs along the production process from extraction of raw materials to distribution. An example would be a merger between a car manufacturer and a metal-pressing company. **Vertical integration** can take place 'backwards' towards the beginning of the production process or 'forwards' towards the end of it and it can occur for several reasons:

1 In the case of backwards integration, to control the supplies of raw materials with respect to their quantity and quality. This brings greater security to the acquiring firm.
2 To restrict supplies of the raw materials to competitors.
3 In the case of forwards integration, to control the quality of the outlets for the finished product. Manufacturers finance the majority of advertising and they might well feel that a forwards merger would enable them to ensure that the good was being sold in the most appropriate setting.
4 In both cases, economies of scale are possible if different parts of the production process are brought together.
5 Again, vertical mergers can be carried out as a reaction to the activities of competitors.

An example of a vertical takeover is the proposed aquisition of Continental (a German tyre producer) by Ashaeffler (a maker of car parts, especially ball bearings) in 2008.

Conglomerate mergers

These mergers are neither vertical nor horizontal but involve a merger between firms involved in producing different goods. The bid made during 2008 by advertising giant WPP for the market research group TNS would be an example of a conglomerate merger, although the markets are highly complementary. The main motivation for this type of merger is diversification. It reduces the risk involved in producing for only one market and allows the firm to spread risk further. It can also provide the firm with another option if the original market declines in size.

As far as the economy is concerned, the main gains of mergers are in increased efficiency resulting from economies of scale and also the increased scope for research and development. A common view is that merger and takeover activity serves the purpose of rationalising business. The weak businesses go and the strong survive. Even when a takeover is carried out for the purpose of asset stripping this will be the case.

Growth by merger and takeover

Growth through merger and takeover first appeared in the USA over a hundred years ago and merger activity tends to come in waves (see the discussion later in this chapter). Five periods of heightened merger activity have been identified in the USA:

- The period 1880 to 1905 – this coincided with the proliferation of the joint stock company and the international establishment of stock exchanges. This period was characterised by mergers of a horizontal nature.
- The 1920s – at this time the mergers were largely vertical in nature, as manufacturers took control of both suppliers and distributors.
- The 1960s – mergers in this period were mainly about diversification and the establishment of conglomerates.
- The post-1980 period – this wave of activity took place in a period of recession and was largely about cost-cutting and rationalisation.
- The late 1990s – as companies in mature industries attempted to become global operators. The pace of this surge of activity slowed for a period after September 11th 2001, but by 2004 the boom in activity had restarted.
- Early 2000s – from 2004 to 2007 the boom continued until the credit crunch in the USA caused a sharp fall in merger activity, including a 36 per cent decline in the first half of 2008.

The first two periods of heightened merger activity in the USA had little effect in Europe; however, there were waves of activity in Europe which coincided with the last two. The first wave of merger activity in Europe came in the 1960s after obstacles to trade were removed by the establishment of the EEC in 1957. The second wave of mergers came in the 1980s in the run-up to the establishment of the Single European Market in 1992. As yet there is little evidence of an increase in merger activity as a result of EMU in Europe.

The most recent surge of activity in the USA did not reach the EU until 2005 – the value of mergers and acquisitions in Europe in the first quarter of 2005 was three times higher than the same period in 2004 and there are several pending large deals. The motivation for this activity seems to be the synergies achieved through mergers with similar companies – it seems that national companies are trying to become European companies.

The recent fall in merger activity seen in the USA has been echoed in Europe (e.g. 35.4 per cent decline in activity in the first half of 2008) which is suffering from the same economic malaise. The only part of the world not affected as yet is Asia where the value of deals rise by 27.4 per cent in the same time period.

Finance for growth

Internal sources

As part of its operation the firm will generate income in the form of **profit**. Part of this profit will be distributed in the form of **dividends** to shareholders, the rest can be used for reinvestment and to finance growth. Although this is seen as a relatively easy and cheap source of finance, it does carry an opportunity cost and therefore should be judged on its rate of return like any other source of finance. Table 11.4 shows that internal funds were the largest single source of finance for industry during the 1990s. It also shows that the totals available and the pattern of sources vary a great deal from year to year. (This data is no longer compiled by the Office for National Statistics.)

Table 11.4 Sources of funds for industry, 1990, 1994 and 1997 (£ million)

Source	1990	1994	1997
Internal funds	33 838	61 406	56 363
Banks and other short-term borrowing	19 911	−4 841	6 630
Loans and mortgages	9 120	4 557	4 384
Ordinary shares	1 880	8 495	19 616
Debentures and preference shares	6 367	1 008	10 640
Other capital issues	7 485	5 067	10 526
Other overseas investment	11 233	−1 400	25 938
Other	1 444	3 766	953
Total	91 278	78 056	135 050

Source: *Financial Statistics*, January 1993, 1996 and 1999. Crown copyright 1999. Reproduced by permission of the Controller of HMSO and of the Office for National Statistics, UK.

External sources

As the size and availability of retained earnings will be limited, most firms will also have to seek other sources of finance for expansion. There are many external sources of finance and a typical firm's capital structure will comprise a combination of these. The sources are as follows.

Banks

Banks provide short- and medium-term finance to companies in the form of loans or overdrafts. The relative cost of these depends upon how the firm wishes to use the funds. Loans carry a lower rate of interest but the interest is paid on the whole amount, while the interest on overdrafts is only paid on the amount drawn. British banks have been criticised by many for failing to provide longer-term finance for business, as banks do in other countries.

Capital market

The **capital market** is the place where stocks and shares are traded and is therefore a key provider of long-term finance to firms. The main institution in the capital market is the **Stock Exchange**. The capital market is made up of two parts: the primary part which involves the buying and selling of new stocks and shares; and the secondary part which involves the buying and selling of existing stocks and shares. It is therefore the primary part of the market that is the source of finance for firms. The secondary part of the market is, however, also important in this process as individuals and organisations are more likely to buy stocks and shares with the knowledge that there is a ready market on which they can be traded at a later date.

The main institutions that buy stocks and shares are the insurance companies, pension funds, investment trusts, unit trusts and other large financial institutions such as building societies.

A new issue of shares takes place when an existing company needs extra finance or when a company becomes a public limited company.

Types of stocks and shares

1 *Preference shares*. These are shares in a company which carry a fixed dividend. Holders have preference over other shareholders in the payment of dividends and on the liquidation of the firm. Preference shares usually carry no voting rights, and so holders have little influence over how the company is run.
2 *Ordinary shares*. Ordinary shares are called the '**equity**' of the company. They do not usually carry a fixed dividend; the company declares a dividend, depending upon its performance in that year. This means that in good years ordinary shareholders could receive high dividends, while in bad years possibly none at all. Ordinary shares are therefore more risky than preference shares, and in recognition of this they usually carry voting rights, so that holders can exercise some influence over how the company is run.
3 *Debentures*. **Debentures** or loan stock are bonds which are given in exchange for a loan to the company. The company agrees to repay the borrowed amount at some date in the future and to make annual payments of interest in the meantime. Interest on debentures is paid before payment of any dividends and the interest is allowable against tax. A debenture holder is a creditor of the company, a shareholder is an owner of the company.

New issue of shares

A company will go to an issuing house or merchant bank which will advise it on the type and number of shares to issue, the price at which they should be offered and other matters. They will often carry out the issue of shares on behalf of the firm. A new issue of shares is not a big source of finance for growth as it is fairly expensive; retained earnings are more convenient and cheaper. Also the amount of information that is required from companies which issue shares to the general public can act as a disincentive.

It is worth noting that in the UK the Stock Market has two main equity markets: the main market and the Alternative Investment Market (AIM). The main market deals in the shares of the large and well-established companies. The Alternative Investment Market provides an opportunity for growing smaller companies to raise capital and have their shares traded in a market without the considerable expense of a full market listing.

Money market

The **money markets** provide short-term finance for companies, often for as brief a period as overnight.

Government and other institutions

The government is a source of finance for firms. Through its regional policy it gives tax allowances, loans, grants and training allowances to firms in certain parts of the country (see Chapter 13). It has many schemes for helping business, particularly small businesses. This will be covered more fully later in this chapter.

Other sources

Other sources include trade credit and hire purchase (i.e. receiving assets now and paying later). This is only a small source of finance for companies. As Table 11.4 shows, industry draws a fairly high proportion of its funding from overseas. This includes finance from many different sources, including individuals, governments, financial institutions overseas and companies.

Firms will typically go for a mixture of different types of finance. The exact combination will depend upon many factors, including their relative costs, their availability and the desired capital structure of the firm. A firm's desired capital structure will largely depend upon the type of market in which it operates. The different types of finance are classified under the two headings of debt and equity. Debt refers to all types of capital on which payments have to be made each year regardless of how the firm has performed; this would include loans and preference shares. Equity refers to ordinary shares where the payment of a dividend depends upon the performance of the firm. As a source of finance, debt is generally cheaper but it is also more risky since in bad years the firm will have to meet the interest payments. The ratio of debt to equity is called the **gearing** of the company. Debt is not well suited to firms in industries where profits fluctuate and such firms will have lower gearing than those in more stable markets.

Limits to growth

Several factors tend to act as a limit to organisational growth:

- To finance growth, excessive borrowing might have taken place and the firm may have trouble meeting debt repayments; therefore there is increased risk of bankruptcy.
- A serious constraint to growth might be the abilities of management. As organisations grow in size they may experience **diseconomies of scale**, which are mainly to do with managerial problems, like communication and control.
- If the size of the market for the product is stagnant or declining it may be both unnecessary and impossible for the firm to grow.
- Government policies, too, can have an important impact on growth. Every government has policies on competition which seek to limit anti-competitive practices and which normally regulate merger activity (see Chapter 17).

Merger activity in the United Kingdom

There are two common ways of measuring the level of merger activity – by the number of transactions or by the total value of the transactions. Figure 11.1 shows the level of merger activity in the UK according to the number of companies acquired in the UK by UK companies. It can be seen that there was a sharp rise in

Figure 11.1 UK merger activity by number, 1983–2007

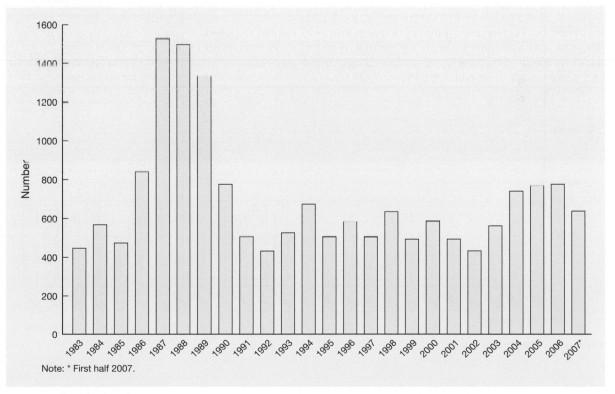

Note: * First half 2007.

Source: *www.statistics.gov.uk*.

merger activity in the mid-1980s and a downturn in 1989. The cyclical pattern continues into the 1990s but the amplitude is reduced. This cyclical pattern is repeated in other countries and in the EU as a whole and it implies that the level of mergers is in some way related to the state of the economy. The rise in the mid-1980s was due partly to an improvement in the state of the economy and partly to the liberalisation of the financial markets, which made finance for takeover bids more freely available. The fall in 1989 was due partly to the recession and partly to the problems that some companies subsequently experienced by overstretching themselves in the mid-1980s. The subsequent rise in the level of merger activity was due to the restructuring which took place in many diverse industries in the 1990s like the financial services sector and the public utilities.[3]

Figure 11.2 shows the level of merger activity in the UK according to the value of the transactions, and the same cyclical path can be discerned although the peaks and troughs do not exactly coincide with the number of transactions. The use of the value of the transactions as a measure of merger activity is problematic in that it will be distorted by any very high-value deals that take place, as in 1995–7 and 2000 when the number of transactions fell but their value rose. The first half of 2007 showed record activity but by the end of the year markets had slowed because of the impact of the global financial crisis (see International business in action: 'The global financial crisis').

Figure 11.2   UK merger activity by value, 1983–2007

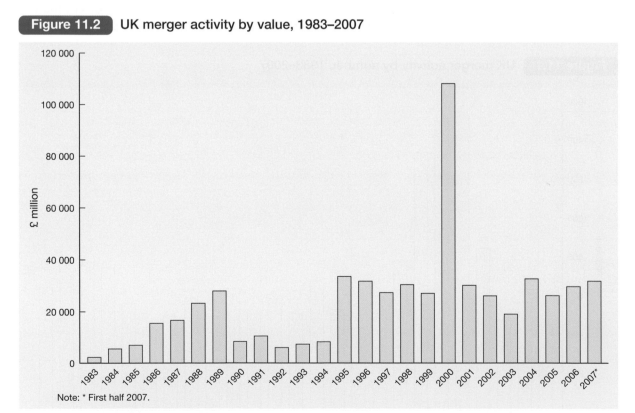

Note: * First half 2007.

Source: *www.statistics.gov.uk.*

Global merger activity

The same pattern seen in the UK data is also evident in the EU and the world as a whole (see Table 11.5). There was a decline in merger and acquisitions in the early 2000s followed by a surge in activity in 2004. During the 1990s the boom in merger activity was dominated by the telecommunications sector, while in the 2004/5 recovery the activity was taking place mainly in the financial services sector.

Table 11.5 Cross-border mergers and acquisitions to and from OECD countries, 1999–2007 ($ billion)

Year	Outwards	Inwards
1999	801	775
2000	1166	1136
2001	606	585
2002	376	410
2003	321	338
2004	422	444
2005	673	635
2006	847	818
2007	1028	1033

Source: Adapted from Table 2.3, *International Investment Perspectives*, OECD, 2007.

The high volume of merger and acquisition activity in the first half of 2007 meant that it was a record year even though the pace slowed in the second half of the year as the credit crunch took hold – worldwide mergers and acquisitions totalled $4.5 trillion, a 24 per cent increase over 2006. The global financial crisis has had an impact on the level of merger and acquisition activity – the value of global mergers and acquisitions was $729.9 billion in the first quarter of 2008 (down by 24.2 per cent on the previous year) and the lowest level since the third quarter of 2006. In quarter 2 the level of activity was down by 36 per cent.[4] It is difficult to predict what will happen in the second half of 2008, but the consensus among commentators is that the level of activity will be 25 per cent lower than in 2007.

Small firms

There are serious problems in the analysis of the small-firm sector, including the lack of data over a long period of time and the problem of defining exactly what is a **small firm**. The Bolton Report,[5] published in 1971, was the report of a committee set up to look into the role of small firms in the UK economy. It used various definitions for statistical purposes, depending upon the industry being considered, on the grounds that what is small in one industry might be large in another. Table 11.6 shows the size distribution of firms based on their turnover for a selection of industries for 2007.

Table 11.6 Size of companies by turnover across different industries, 2007 (%)

Industry	Turnover size ('000)		
	up to £250	£250–£500	over £500
Agriculture, forestry and fishing	86	9	5
Mining and quarrying and public utilities	40	10	50
Manufacturing	53	14	33
Construction	70	13	17
Wholesaling	48	14	38
Retailing	63	19	18
Financial services	49	11	40
Business services	76	10	15

Source: Adapted from Table B2.2, *UK Business Activity by Size and Location*, National Statistics, 2007.

It is clear from Table 11.6 that the definition of 'big' will vary with the industry. In the Bolton Report the definition used for small firms in manufacturing was 'less than 200 employees', while in construction it was 'less than 25 employees'. In some industries turnover limits were chosen while in others a mixture of employment and turnover was used. Although this is confusing and makes comparison between industries and countries difficult, it was accepted that there could not be a single definition which would apply to all sectors. The EU in 1994 recommended to its members that they use 'less than 250 employees' as the definition of a small to medium-sized enterprise (SME), in order to facilitate the easy comparison of data across member states. A further refinement of the definition used by Eurostat based on numbers employed is shown in Table 11.7.

Table 11.7 Classification of firms by employment size

Number of employees	Type of firm
0–9	micro businesses
10–99	small enterprises
100–499	medium-sized enterprises
500+	large enterprises

Applying this definition to Table 11.2, it can be seen that 83 per cent of manufacturing firms in the UK are micro businesses, 15.4 per cent are small, 1.1 per cent are medium sized and 0.3 per cent are large. Although there are some national differences (the southern-most countries have relatively more micro businesses than the northern countries) the pattern of size structure is similar in the EU as a whole – 92 per cent of all enterprises are micro businesses, 7.4 per cent are small, 0.5 per cent are medium sized and 0.1 per cent are large.[6]

It is important to note that the definition of SME used within the EU changed in 2005. For grant-aid purposes an SME must have no more than 25 per cent of its capital owned by a larger enterprise and must meet specific criteria with regard to numbers of employees, turnover or balance sheet totals. A 'micro firm' is one with 0–9 employees, a maximum annual turnover of 2 million euros or a maximum balance sheet total also of 2 million euros. The equivalent figures for a 'small firm' are

10–49 employees, 10 million euros turnover or 10 million euros balance sheet total; for a 'medium-sized firm' 50–249 employees, 50 million euros turnover or 43 million euros balance sheet total. Using these definitions it is estimated that 99 per cent of all enterprises in the EU (prior to enlargement) were SMEs and that they provided around 65 million jobs.

No matter how small firms are defined, they will suffer from similar problems, which are very different from those faced by larger companies.

Trends in the small-firm sector

The percentage share of small establishments in total manufacturing employment in the UK was in decline for the 1930s up to the early 1970s, when its importance increased dramatically.[7] In recent years the percentage has stayed around 40 per cent. Table 11.2 showed that for UK industry small firms are very important in terms of the number of businesses, accounting for 99 per cent of total firms. Even though they were less important in terms of employment, they still accounted for 39 per cent of total employment. Figure 11.3 shows the share of employment of small firms by sector; as can be seen, there is a great deal of variation between sectors.

Reasons for the growth in the small-firm sector

There has clearly been a resurgence in the importance of the small-firm sector which appears to have been more pronounced in the United Kingdom than in other countries. Why? Some causal factors are as follows:

Figure 11.3 Share of small firms in employment by sector, 2007

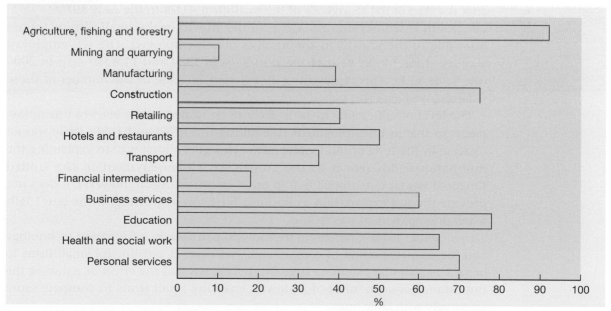

Source: Adapted from Figure 3, UKN 08/92, BERR, 2008.

1 *The changing pattern of industry.* In Chapter 12 it is shown that there has been a change in the industrial structure of the United Kingdom away from manufacturing and towards services. Since many services are dominated by small firms, there will be a corresponding change in average firm size. However, this does not provide the full explanation as there has been a growth in the share of small firms even in the manufacturing sector. And it does not explain the international differences since there have been similar changes in industrial structure in other countries too.

2 *Changes in consumer spending habits.* A move from mass-produced goods to more specialised products puts small firms at an advantage as they can react more quickly to changes in demand and shorter product life cycles.

3 *Flexible specialisation and the growth of subcontracting.* A debate which started in the late 1980s centres round the idea of the **flexible firm**.[8] As a result of the recession of the early 1980s there was a drive by firms to reduce their costs in order to remain competitive. One way of reducing overhead costs was to move to a flexible firm structure whereby the firm's activities are divided into core and peripheral activities. The core activities, which are central to the activities of the firm, would be kept 'in-house' and carried out by full-time permanent workers. The peripheral activities would be carried out by temporary workers or would be subcontracted. The firm has then reduced its overheads and can react to peaks in demand by increasing the amount of temporary labour it uses or increasing the amount of **subcontracting**. This might also have had the effect of increasing the relative importance of the small-firm sector.

4 *Reorganisation and job reduction.* There has been an increase in the phenomenon of downsizing by organisations in an attempt to reduce costs. Ninety per cent of large companies have reorganised and cut jobs since 1985.

5 *Government policy.* After the Bolton Report there was a much greater interest in the role of the small firm in the regeneration of the economy and in the provision of jobs. But most of the initiatives designed to help the small firm came after the start of the resurgence of the small-firm sector in the early 1970s.

6 *The growth in self-employment.* A part of the growth in the small-firm sector has been due to the growth in the number of self-employed. The self-employed accounted for 9.8 per cent of the workforce in 1984 and 11.8 per cent in 2006 (see Table 11.8). This represents a 20 per cent increase in the number of those self-employed over this period.

   The level of self-employment is likely to be related to the level of unemployment, so that as unemployment rose during the 1970s and 1980s there was an increase in the level of self-employment. This goes a long way to explaining the international differences as the growth in self-employment in the United Kingdom has far outstripped that in other countries. Again, however, it does not provide the full explanation as business births were growing in the late 1960s when unemployment was falling.

7 *Technological change.* Changes in technology, particularly information technology and the miniaturisation of components, has made it possible for small firms to benefit to a similar extent to large firms. This has had the effect of reducing the importance of economies of scale and enabling small firms to compete more effectively with large ones.

Table 11.8 Percentage of workforce self-employed, 1984–2006 (UK)

Year	% self-employed
1984	9.8
1985	10.0
1986	10.0
1987	10.9
1988	11.3
1989	12.1
1990	12.3
1991	11.9
1992	11.3
1993	11.2
1994	11.7
1995	11.6
1996	11.6
1997	11.5
1998	10.9
1999	10.8
2000	10.6
2001	11.3
2002	11.2
2003	11.6
2004	11.7
2005	11.6
2006	11.8

Source: Adapted from *Annual Abstract of Statistics* (various), ONS, UK.

8 *Competitive forces.* As far as the international differences are concerned, the Bolton Report found that industry in the United Kingdom was biased towards large size in comparison with other countries. So what may have happened as a result of competitive forces is that the balance of industry in the United Kingdom has moved towards the norm of other countries.

The role of the small-firm sector

The growing importance of the small-firm sector implies that small firms do have a valuable role in the economy apart from being a mere provider of employment. The areas in which the small firm has advantages over large firms are those where there are:

1 *Clearly defined small markets.* It is not worthwhile for large firms to enter such markets since there are no economies of scale and no scope for mass production.
2 *Specialist, quality, non-standardised products.* Again it would not be worth a large firm entering such a market as the benefits of large-scale production cannot be reaped.
3 *Geographically localised markets.* For example, the small corner shop.
4 *Development of new ideas.* It is often argued that the small firm is the 'seedbed' of ideas and that, because of greater motivation and commitment on the part of the owner of the small firm, it is very conducive to invention and innovation.

Aid to the small-firm sector

The thinking on small firms has changed over time. Initially they were viewed favourably, but after the Second World War the dominant thinking was that large-scale production could take advantage of large economies of scale and that costs would be lower and production more efficient. It was not until more recently that the interest in the small-firm sector has increased again. The main reasons for the renewed interest are seen in the results of empirical studies which have shown that the role of the small firm is greater than previously thought in areas such as innovation, the balance of payments and employment.

The main argument for giving support to the small-firm sector is that it has a valuable role to play in the economy. In the 1980s and 1990s, for example, small firms were seen as a mechanism for reducing the very high levels of unemployment. Between 1983 and 1993 the small-firm sector created 2.5 million jobs. The basic premise for support is that small firms are at a disadvantage with respect to large businesses in areas such as raising capital, research and development and risk bearing. The 2007 EU Observatory Survey of SMEs in Europe found that there were three main problems facing small firms:

- The burden of regulation – reported as acting as a constraint by 36 per cent of SMEs within Europe. It is estimated that large firms spend €1 per employee on regulatory compliance compared to €10 for SMEs. All EU governments had introduced measures to reduce this burden and the Commission has a commitment to reduce the administrative demands on small businesses by 25 per cent.
- Access to finance – including cash flow problems resulting from late or non-payment of bills. In the UK all public limited companies are required by law to state in their annual reports the average length of time it takes to pay their bills. The Federation of Small Business in the UK publishes a 'name and shame' list of slow payers.
- Access to new markets – between 1996 and 2004 it has been estimated that 60 per cent of the UK's productivity growth came from exporting firms. Only 8 per cent of European SMEs report turnover from exports.

Government policy

Within the UK national policy for small firms has increasingly become a vital component of governmental attempts to create a competitive economy capable of achieving sustainable economic growth. To this end policy initiatives in recent years have become more focused and have tended to adopt a multi-agency approach, aimed at improving the environment in which small businesses emerge and grow, and at fostering enterprise and innovation. Key developments over the last decade or so have included:

- *Business Link* – a national network of 'one-stop shops' to provide information and support to small firms.
- *Direct Access Government* – a 'one-stop shop' on the Internet that provides businesses with access to regulatory guidance and forms.
- *The Enterprise Zone* – another Internet-based initiative to help firms with finding

information on issues such as finance, exporting, technology, innovation and management.

● *The Teaching Company Scheme (TCS)* – the government's premier technology transfer mechanisms for linking UK higher education establishments and businesses.

● *The SMART Awards* – designed to promote technological development and innovation.

There have also been a number of legislative and fiscal changes aimed at reducing the burdens on small businesses (e.g. levels of corporation tax). Some of the more recent developments have included the launch of the University for Industry (UfI), the Enterprise Fund, the University Challenge Fund, the Small Business Service (SBS) and the EU SME Initiative. The latter – introduced in December 1997 – was designed to assist SMEs in rural areas or areas of industrial decline to become more competitive in overseas markets. There have also been attempts to reduce the flow and improve the quality of regulation affecting smaller businesses and an action plan to make the UK the number one location for starting and growing a business.

As the mini case 'the small-firm sector' illustrates, the UK government's 2008 Enterprise Strategy provides a framework of five key 'enablers' aimed at developing an enhanced enterprise culture in the UK. Among the measures proposed under the strategy are a net reduction in the regulatory burden on small firms (of 25 per cent by 2010); changes to the insolvency rules; cross-border mentoring and work placements in SMEs; a women's enterprise campaign; a global entrepreneurship week; a National Enterprise Academy; improvements in the Business Link and business support services; changes to the Small Firms Loans Guarantee Scheme; expansion of the Enterprise Capital Fund; a refocused Small Business Research Initiative; changes to public procurement processes to help SMEs gain access to public contracts. Further information on government small-firm policy is available via the Department of Business Enterprise and Regulatory Reform website (*www.berr.gov.uk*).

mini case   The small-firm sector

Over the years the UK government, like most others, has introduced policies designed to aid the small-firm sector. The latest initiative launched in March 2008 is the Enterprise Strategy, designed to make the UK the most enterprising economy in the world and the best place to start and grow a business. The Strategy aims to boost enterprise skills and to increase knowledge, to help both new and existing business to grow and to ease the burden of regulations, especially on small firms. Five key enablers are identified:

● building an enterprise culture – to provide everyone with the understanding of enterprise so that ideas can be turned into wealth;

● knowledge and skills – encouraging enterprise throughout education, starting in primary schools and continuing through universities to become embedded in the workplace;

● access to finance – to ensure that entrepreneurs and small businesses have both the knowledge and the opportunity to access finance to advance their enterprise;

● regulatory framework – legislation will be kept to a minimum and regulatory burdens reduced;

● business innovation – ensuring that UK business can capitalise on global trends through help in developing innovative products and processes.

Although not specifically aimed at the SME sector, policies proposed under each of the five enablers should have a positive effect on small businesses as two of the five enablers are identified as particular problems for small firms – access to finance and the burden of regulation.

Networking between firms

A more recent trend in industry which is well documented is towards co-operation rather than competition.[9] This co-operation can take many forms: for example, subcontracting, networking (both formal and informal) and joint ventures. Such co-operation can be (and is) used by large as well as small and medium-sized enterprises. For large companies it is a way to grow and diversify without risk. For smaller firms it allows them to stay small but at the same time to benefit from some of the advantages of large-scale production like specialisation.

Subcontracting

There has been an increase in the amount of subcontracting, where firms do not carry out the whole of the production process themselves but subcontract some of their activities to other firms. This represents a rejection of vertical integration and it is related to the notion of the flexible firm mentioned earlier. Subcontracting goes some way to explaining the phenomenal growth rate in 'business services' that occurred in the 1980s. It is increasingly common for businesses to subcontract specialist work in areas such as human resource management to outside consultancies. 'Partnering' between companies and consultancies is becoming more common where the consultancy is retained on a semi-permanent basis to give advice on a whole range of human resource matters from recruitment to planning for succession. This will obviously boost the small-firm sector. There has also been an increase in 'partnership sourcing' as large firms are developing long-term relationships between themselves and their suppliers. This phenomenon brings benefits to the large firms in the form of reducing stock levels and associated costs and facilitating just-in-time production methods. It also brings benefits to small firms, many of which are the suppliers, in the form of greater security.

Networking

Networking refers to the relationships that exist between organisations and the people within those organisations. These relationships can be of different types, both formal and informal, and there is increasing recognition of the importance of these relationships, especially to small firms (e.g. they may be based on the exchange of goods and services, like the relationship between a firm and its supplier or client). Subcontracting is an example of this kind of network but there are other links not based on exchange, like the relationship between a firm and the bank manager or other advisers. There are also informal links between the entrepreneur and family and friends, and between entrepreneurs in different organisations. There might also be co-operative links between firms. This can be seen in the market for executive recruitment where there has been a growth in the links between consultancies, particularly for international work. The creation of the Single European Market and the increased internationalisation of business left the smaller consultancies in a weak position relative to the large international recruitment firms like Korn Ferry International, which have branches in most European countries. The smaller consultancies have reacted by forming networks. There are basically two types of network:

1 Where firms are members of a network but where the network has a different name from the individual firms and the firms operate under their own name (i.e. the network has an identity of its own). The members are independent firms that co-operate in carrying out their business. There are 16 such groups in Europe including EMA Partners International and AMROP Heuer Group.

2 Where firms are part of a network of independent firms but where the network does not have a separate identity and the firms operate under their own names. There are ten such groups in Europe.

web link   For information on companies mentioned see *www.kornferry.com*, *www.ema-partners.com* and *www.amrop.com*

The firm is seen as existing within a spider's web of relationships, as Figure 11.4 shows. It is possible for two firms to be linked in a variety of ways; in one market they may be competitors, in the next co-operators, customers in another and suppliers in another.

Networking has taken on greater significance because of changes that are taking place in the economy, which include the reversal of the trend towards higher industrial concentration, the adoption of Japanese methods of production, the decline of 'mass markets' and technological change that requires greater specialisation than previously. All of these changes favour the formation of networks.

The role of strategic alliances between firms has been recognised, especially in the small firm sector where expansion through other means is often impossible and in the process of internationalisation.[10]

Figure 11.4   A typical network

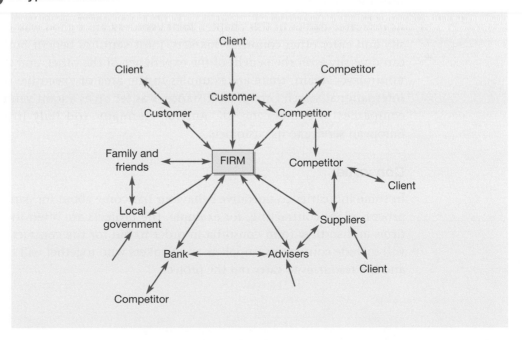

The virtual organisation

The **virtual organisation** is a network-based structure built on partnerships where a small core operating company outsources most of its processes. It is a network of small companies which specialise in various aspects of production. The organisation can be very big in trading terms but very small in the numbers of permanent staff. The process is typically mediated by information technology.

The main benefit of the virtual structure is that it helps organisations to deal with uncertainty. When virtual organisations are managed properly they can simultaneously increase efficiency, flexibility and responsiveness to changes in market conditions. The organisation is reaping the benefits of specialisation without having to develop those specialisms itself. Therefore overhead costs are minimised, as too are training costs and support costs. Information technology assumes many of the co-ordinating and managing roles that managers and committees carry out in large organisations. Information technology enables communication and the sharing of information across geographical boundaries. It is often the case, however, that the creation of a virtual organisation is driven solely by cost considerations rather than strategic considerations, in which case the benefits might not be realised. There will be a loss of control over outsourced activities and it may actually cost more to manage such activities. The organisation can become locked into contracts and specific relationships so that flexibility is reduced. There may be a lack of commitment of key resources (i.e. contractors) to the company and the loss of a contractor will be very serious.

There is some evidence that the incidence of virtual organisations is on the increase, facilitated by developments in information technology. It is a matter of 'wait and see' if this will become the dominant organisational structure in the future.

Joint ventures

As indicated earlier in this chapter, **joint ventures** are a good way for firms to diversify and enter other countries' markets. Joint ventures benefit both parties as each can diversify with the benefit of the experience of the other, and the level of risk is minimised. Again, there are examples in the area of executive recruitment. The International Search Group, for instance, was set up as a joint venture between five companies in France, the UK, Austria, Germany and Italy in order to offer a European service to its customers.

Consortia

In some industries co-operative behaviour has come about for particular reasons. In process plant contracting, for example, the projects are often too large for single firms and so they form consortia in order to bid for the contract. The consortium will include contractors, suppliers and bankers who together will have the expertise and the resources to carry out the project.

Multinationals

At the opposite end of the scale from the very small business are companies which have the capability to produce goods or services in more than one country but where control usually resides in a central location. **Multinationals** are often well-known household names, as the examples below illustrate:

● UK multinationals – BP, Glaxosmithkline.
● European multinationals – Nestlé, Volkswagen.
● USA multinationals – General Motors, IBM.

These multinationals are huge organisations and their market values often exceed the GNP of many of the countries in which they operate. They are estimated to account for a quarter of the world's output.

The growth in the multinationals is due to relaxation of exchange controls making it easier to move money between countries, and the improvements in communication which make it possible to run a worldwide business from one country. See Chapter 3 for a full discussion of the operation of multinational enterprises.

 web link

For information on the companies mentioned on this page see: *www.bp.com, www.gsk.com, www.nestle.com, www.vw.com, www.gm.com* and *www.ibm.com*

Synopsis

This chapter has looked at the size structure of industry in the United Kingdom and Europe as a whole. It examined the motives for and the methods of growth, as well as the sources of finance for such growth. The role of the small firm was considered, as too was the role of the multinational. Although many industries are dominated by huge companies, the trend seems to be moving away from growth towards a process of disintegration for a variety of reasons. As a result of this trend there has been an upsurge in the small-firm sector, and an increase in the level of co-operative behaviour between firms.

Summary of key points

● The size structure of firms varies greatly within industries, within a country and between countries.

● Firms can grow internally through organic growth or externally through merger and takeover.

● There are many motivations for growth, including increased market share, the reaping of economies of scale, the diversification of risk.

- Growth can be financed internally through reinvested profits or externally through banks, the capital market and the money market.

- There are limits to organisational growth, such as diseconomies of scale.

- The level of merger activity in the UK and in Europe follows a cyclical pattern and is related to economic conditions.

- The small-firm sector is an important source of output and employment, and this importance has increased over time.

- Many factors have influenced the growth of the small-firm sector, including the changing pattern of industries, changes in demand, technological change, the trend towards increased subcontracting and government policy.

- At the other end of the size spectrum, multinational corporations have a massive impact on world output and employment through their activities.

case study   Grocery retailing in the UK

The grocery retailing market in the UK is dominated by four major players. Table 11.9 shows the market shares of the major firms in 2007. As the table illustrates, out of the four, Tesco is the clear market leader.

Table 11.9 Market share for grocery retailing in the UK, 2007

Retailer	Market share %
Tesco	27
Asda	14.5
Sainsbury	14
Morrisons	10
Somerfield	4
Co-op Group	4
M & S	4
Waitrose	3.5
Iceland	2
Lidl	2
Aldi	1.8
Netto	1
Others	12.2

The grocery retailing market is one dominated by large firms; the market is an oligopoly (see Chapter 15) as four major players account for over 65 per cent of the market and their behaviour exhibits some of the characteristics of an oligopoly, as will be seen later on in this case study. Another group of retailers of interest in Table 11.9 comprises Iceland, Lidl, Aldi and Netto – these are the discounters. They offer a much reduced range of products (around 2000 instead of the 30,000 offered by the big supermarkets) at a discounted price. In the UK they hold a small part of the market but in other European countries they play a much more important role – in Germany, for example, the discounters account for 40 per cent of the market. The 'Others' category in Table 11.9 includes all the small local and corner shop grocery retailers.

Tesco has diversified into many different areas including electricals, clothing, finance, insurance and telecommunications. It has 2000 stores and is still growing at a high rate. It is estimated that in 2008, Tesco accounts for £1 in every £7 spent by the British public. Tesco is also the third biggest employer in the UK and has recently become the biggest non-food retailer in the UK. It is the fourth biggest retailer in the world behind Wal-Mart (which owns Asda), Carrefour and Home Depot. It has diversified internationally and now has more floor space outside the UK than in the UK. It has a presence in local markets through its Tesco Expresses and the One Stops.

Has Tesco become too big?

By 2008 the British public's love affair with Tesco appeared to be reaching an end, with claims from many different quarters that Tesco had become too big. The criticisms have become increasingly loud and vociferous:

- For many years, Tesco has been accused of predatory behaviour with respect to planning rules and regulations. It has been very active in lobbying local councillors and politicians and has been accused of forcing the small corner shops out of business.
- In the USA Barak Obama has criticised Tesco for its relationship with trade unions.
- In the UK Tesco has come under fire for not meeting RSPCA standards of care for the chickens sold in its stores.
- It has been accused of importing food from Zimbabwe and exploiting workers in India.

There is even an organisation of pressure groups with an interest in the activities of Tesco called the Tescopoly Alliance which serves as a rallying point for anti-Tesco feeling.

In addition to this negative publicity, the three Fs (rising food prices, rising fuel prices and the world financial crisis) has led to changes in consumer behaviour as households try to cut back on their spending. There is evidence that consumers are moving away from the big four supermarkets towards the discount stores like Aldi, Iceland and Lidl. The market share of Aldi rose to 2.9 per cent in 2008. The discounters work by offering only around 2000 products at much lower prices than the big four supermarkets. Tesco has responded by dramatically cutting the prices of 3000 basic foodstuffs. As the market is an oligopoly, economic theory suggests that the other large players will do the same and there is evidence that this is happening as both Sainsbury and Asda have reduced the price of basic food items. Commentators are predicting that this is the start of a full-scale price war – only time will tell.

Although its sheer size provides Tesco some immunity from these factors, the general view of Tesco is of a giant that does not listen to either its critics or its customers. All of this is not good news for Tesco. The situation is reminiscent of the early 1990s in the UK, when the then market leader – Sainsbury – appeared to become arrogant and not interested in listening to its customers. Its near demise left the market clear for Tesco to expand.

Case study questions

1 Why do small corner supermarkets manage to survive in the grocery retail market?

2 Has there been a price war between the big four supermarkets in the UK?

Review and discussion questions

1 What impact is the global financial crisis ('credit crunch') likely to have on merger and acquisition behaviour?

2 Can you see any dangers in the creation of super utilities (large, diversified organisations which supply a range of utilities – gas, electricity and water)?

3 What advantages does networking bring to small firms and the economy as a whole?

4 How has the balance between large and small firms in manufacturing changed in the last ten years? Do you expect these trends to continue?

Assignments

1 You are an information officer at your local business advice centre and you have been given the job of designing and writing a leaflet aimed at the proprietors of small firms, outlining the government aid that is available to small businesses. Your brief is to keep the leaflet short and readable but with maximum information. (Information on government aid will be available at your local library or business advice centre.)

2 As part of 'Business Week' you have been asked to give a short talk to local sixth-formers doing Business Studies A-level on the size structure of UK industry. Prepare your talk by choosing two industries, describing and giving reasons for the typical size structure of the firms in those industries.

Notes and references

1 *Penguin Dictionary of Economics.*

2 See OECD, *Dynamic Efficiencies in Merger Analysis*, May 2008.

3 *See* case study in Chapter 8 of the 2nd edition of this book.

4 Thomson merger news available at www.thomsonmergernews.com

5 *The Bolton Committee Report*, HMSO, 1971.

6 *Panorama of EU Industry*, 1994, European Commission.

7 See Figures 9.4 in the 5th edition of this book.

8 Atkinson, J., 'Flexibility, uncertainty and manpower management', Report no. 89, Institute of Manpower Studies, 1984.

9 Pyke, F., 'Co-operative practices among small and medium-sized establishments', *Work, Employment and Society*, 2 (3), September 1988.

10 See case study at the end of Chapter 13 of the 2nd edition of this book.

Further reading

Griffiths, A. and Wall, S., *Applied Economics*, 11th edition, Financial Times/Prentice Hall, 2005.

Stanworth, J. and Gray, C., *Bolton 20 Years On: The Small Firm in the 1990s*, Chapman, 1991.

Web links and further questions are available on the website at:
www.pearsoned.co.uk/worthington

12 Industrial structure

Chris Britton

Within any economy, there will be a whole range of industries that produce a variety of products for a variety of users. The particular combination of industries within a country is called the industrial structure of that country. There will be international differences in industrial structures, because of differences in the many factors that affect the determination of industrial structure.

Learning outcomes

Having read this chapter you should be able to:

● explain the concept of industrial structure and illustrate how it is measured

● outline the industrial structure of the United Kingdom and the European Union as a whole

● analyse the reasons for particular industrial structures and the factors which influence industrial structure

● illustrate how and why the industrial structure of the United Kingdom and the European Union has changed over time

Key terms

Crowding out
Deindustrialisation
Entrepreneurship
Industrial structure
Life cycle model

Manufacturing sector
Primary sector
Productivity
Secondary sector
Skill shortages

Standard Industrial
   Classification (SIC)
Tertiary sector

Introduction

A country can produce many different and diverse types of goods and services ranging from the production of cars to the delivery of legal services to farming. The mix of these and the combination of industries that exist to produce them is called the **industrial structure** of a country. There are likely to be large differences in industrial structure between countries for many reasons. This chapter will look at the industrial structure of the European Union as a trading bloc and the United Kingdom in particular. There is a need for the industrial structure of a country to be measured in some way so that changes over time can be identified and international comparisons made. This chapter will look at the definitions of industries, the problems with such definitions and the official classification of industry used by the government in the United Kingdom. It will also identify the changes in industrial structure and the causes of these changes.

The structure of industry

The process of production

In Chapter 7 the three factors of production – labour, land and capital – were considered. Textbooks often add a fourth factor of production to this list, called 'entrepreneurship'. **Entrepreneurship** is the process of bringing together the other factors in order to produce goods and services. A firm produces goods and services because they are demanded and because a profit can be earned by selling them. Figure 12.1 shows a much simplified profit and loss account for a car manufacturer.

The items on the expenditure side represent the payments to the factors of production. Wages are payments to labour, raw materials and an element of overheads would be the payments to capital, and the payment for land would be included in overheads. The payment to the entrepreneur is in the form of profit.

Figure 12.1 A simplified profit and loss account

Revenues	£m	Expenditures	£m
Sales of cars	30.0	Raw materials	7.5
		Wages and salaries	10.0
		Overheads (rent, rates lighting, etc.)	2.5
			20.0
		Profit	10.0
	30.0		30.0

What has happened in this process is that the factors of production have been combined to make finished cars and in the process value has been added to the initial value of the raw materials.

The car manufacturer can be thought of as being in the centre of a process of production which links together raw materials at one end with the consumers at the other end. The raw materials are extracted and processed and then the finished goods are sold. In economic terminology, the extraction of raw materials is called *primary production*, the manufacture of cars is called *secondary production* and the distribution of the finished cars is called *tertiary production* (see Figure 12.2). Although this simple path from primary production through to tertiary production is the case for many industries, it is likely to be much more complicated in practice.

The discussion at present is confined to a single firm, but it can be moved to the *industry level*. The industries that deal with natural resources like farming and mining comprise the **primary sector**. Industries which process these natural resources comprise the **secondary sector**, which will include manufacturing, construction and energy suppliers. The service industries make up the **tertiary sector**. There are great difficulties involved in such a classification of industry, as will be seen later, but consideration will now be given to the official classification of industry in the United Kingdom.

The Standard Industrial Classification

The **Standard Industrial Classification (SIC)** of economic activity is the official classification of industries in the United Kingdom into different sectors. It was introduced in 1948 and has been updated and changed on occasions to take account of the development of new products and industries for producing those products. It was changed in 1980, mainly in order to bring the United Kingdom classification in line with the activity classification used by the Statistical Office of the European Communities (Eurostat), which is called Nomenclature générale des activités économiques dans les Communautés européennes (NACE).

> Data on industrial structure in the UK is available from *www.statistics.gov.uk*
> For the EU from *http://europa.eu.int/comm/eurostat*

Figure 12.2   A simplified production process

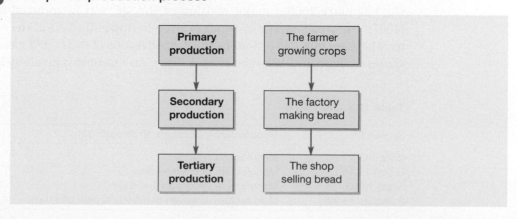

The 1980 SIC is shown in Table 12.1. The 1980 classification had ten *divisions* (denoted by a single digit). Each of these is divided into *classes* (two digits), which in turn are divided into *groups* (three digits) and *activity headings* (four digits). In total there are ten divisions, 60 classes, 222 groups and 334 activity headings.

Table 12.1 SIC (80)

Division	Industry
0	Agriculture, forestry and fishing
1	Energy and water supply industries
2	Extraction of minerals and ores other than fuels; manufacture of metals, mineral products and chemicals
3	Metal goods, engineering and vehicle industries
4	Other manufacturing industries
5	Construction
6	Distribution, hotels and catering; repairs
7	Transport and communication
8	Banking, finance, insurance, business services and leasing
9	Other services

The term 'production industries' refers to divisions 1 to 4 of the above classification; the term 'manufacturing industries' refers to divisions 2 to 4. The SIC does not comply exactly with the broad classification of industry used in the last section. The primary sector of the economy is found in division 0 and parts of divisions 1 and 2; the secondary sector in parts of divisions 1 and 2 and all of divisions 3 to 5. The tertiary sector would be divisions 6 to 9.

The SIC is changed periodically to reflect changes taking place in industry, most notably in 1990, 2003 and 2008 (see below). In 1990 the EC approved a new statistical classification of economic activities in the EU (NACE Rev. 1). This means that the United Kingdom had to introduce a new SIC in 1992. The standardisation of industrial classification across Europe makes interstate comparisons easier. The SIC (92) which replaced SIC (80) was based on NACE Rev. 1. It had 17 sections instead of the ten divisions of SIC (80); each of these sections was denoted by a letter from A to Q. The sections were divided into subsections which were denoted by the addition of another letter. The subsections were then broken down into two-digit divisions and again into groups (three digits), into classes (four digits) and into subclasses (five digits).

In January 2003 the EU made a minor revision of NACE Rev 1, which was known as NACE Rev 1.1. As a result, the UK government had to introduce a new SIC (2003).[1] On 1 January 2008 a major revision of the SIC was introduced in the UK – SIC (2007), the broad outline of which is given in Appendix 12.1 at the end of this chapter. There are now 21 sections (A to U), 88 divisions (2 digit), 272 groups (3 digit), 615 classes (4 digit) and 191 subclasses (5 digit). An example is given in Table 12.2. Some

Table 12.2 SIC (2007)

Section C	Manufacturing (Divisions 10 through 33)
Division 13	Manufacture of textiles
Group 13.1	Manufacture of other textiles
Class 13.93	Manufacture of carpets and rugs
Subclass 13.93/1	Manufacture of woven or tufted carpets and rugs

sections are subdivided more than others, Section A (Agriculture, Forestry and Fishing), for example, only has 3 divisions while Section C (manufacturing) has 24. The level of detail depends upon the diversity of production included within the section.

The new SIC brings the UK in line with the European Union (NACE rev 2) and the United Nation's International Standard Industrial Classification of all economic activities (ISIC rev 4). The main differences between SIC (2007) and SIC (2003) are in the number of sections and the distribution of industries between the sections. For example, Section K in SIC (2003) is now distributed across 3 sections (L, M and N). There is a much more detailed breakdown of the service sector which illustrates the increased importance of this sector in the economy.

Problems in classifying industries

The classification of industry is problematic. Firms could be grouped together according to similarities in what they produce but some firms produce a range of goods for quite different markets. Firms could be grouped together according to what they 'do', so that if their production processes are similar they could be considered as part of the same industry. The service industries are particularly problematic as they have traditionally been defined by the function they perform, but developments in technology have led to these functions overlapping and therefore becoming more difficult to distinguish: for example, publishing and printing. All of this leads to industries that are seemingly very diverse being grouped together in the SIC. Although the SIC does not succeed in overcoming all of these problems, it does provide an accepted classification of industry which can be used for many purposes. The information collected provides a basis for comparing the structure of industry within a country over time and between countries.

Measuring industrial structure

The structure of industry in a country is not static, and it changes over time for a variety of reasons. For example:

● The development of new products means that new industries come into existence (e.g. the inventions and innovations in the field of electronic games).
● New patterns of demand mean that some industries will be declining while others become increasingly important.
● Changes in society will be reflected in industrial structure. For example, according to the Census in 1851, 22 per cent of the workforce in the United Kingdom was engaged in agriculture, forestry and fishing while in 2007 the figure was 1.4 per cent. This obviously reflects the movement away from an agriculturally based society to an industrial society.

Industrial structure is usually measured by the level of employment or output of the various sectors of the economy, and changes in industrial structure over time can be observed by looking at the changes in the employment and output levels in different industries. These will usually (but not always) paint the same picture; a sector in decline will have falling employment and output.

Industrial structure in the EU

Figure 12.3 shows the industrial structure of the EU as a whole measured by employment in 1979, 2004 (EU-15) and 2005 (EU-27). This figure illustrates two things: first, that there has been a change in industrial structure during this time period; and second that there is a difference between the EU-15 countries and some of the newer members of the EU. During the period there has been a steady fall in the level of employment in agriculture and manufacturing and a rise in employment in the service sector. In 2004, 5 per cent of the working population of the EU-15 was employed in agriculture, 25 per cent in industry and 70 per cent in the service sector. This trend away from employment in the primary and secondary sectors towards the service sector is evident in other advanced industrial economies. Table 12.3 shows that while there are some differences in industrial structure between countries, the tertiary sector in all cases is predominant in employment terms (except India and China).

Table 12.3 Percentage employed in different sectors of selected countries, 2007

	Agriculture	Industry	Services
UK	1.4	22.3	76.4
Germany	2.3	30.0	67.7
Slovenia	2.5	38.3	55.9
France	3.4	22.9	73.8
EU-27	4.4	27.1	67.1
Ireland	6.0	27.0	67.0
Portugal	10.0	30.0	60.0
Poland	16.1	29.0	54.9
Romania	29.5	23.2	47.1
Japan	1.4	26.5	72.0
USA	1.4	19.8	78.9
China	43.0	25.0	32.0
India	60.0	12.0	28.0

Source: *www.cia.gov*.

Within the EU, the UK has a smaller agricultural sector in terms of employment than other EU countries (and the EU average) and also has the biggest service sector. Table 12.3 also shows that the newer members of the EU have had an impact on the average, many of which have big agricultural sectors: the two biggest are shown in the table – Poland and Romania. There are exceptions to this pattern as Portugal has a big agricultural sector and Slovenia has a structure much more in line with EU-15 members. Four other countries are shown for comparison, including the fast-developing economies of China and India, which have very different patterns of industrial structure.

Industrial structure can also be gauged by looking at output figures. Here the same pattern is evident – the importance of the primary and secondary sectors of the main industrial countries has declined in importance – reasons for this will be considered later in this chapter. Table 12.4 shows the contribution of the output of the three sectors to GDP for the same countries as in the previous table.

Figure 12.3 Percentage shares in employment in the three main sectors of the EU, 1979, 2004 (EU-15) and 2005 (EU-27)

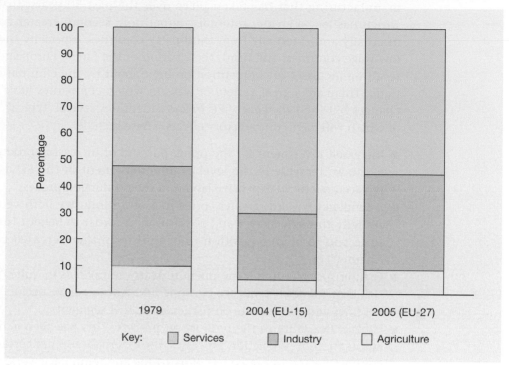

Source: Adapted from Table 2, *Eurostat Yearbook*, 2008.

Table 12.4 Contribution towards GDP for different sectors of selected countries, 2007 (%)

	Agriculture	Industry	Services
UK	0.9	23.4	75.7
Germany	0.8	29.0	70.1
Slovenia	2.0	34.4	63.5
France	2.2	21.0	76.7
EU – 27	2.0	27.1	70.7
Ireland	5.0	46.0	49.0
Portugal	8.1	25.4	66.5
Poland	4.1	31.6	64.4
Romania	7.9	35.6	56.5
Japan	1.4	26.5	72.0
USA	0.9	20.5	78.5
China	11.3	48.6	40.1
India	17.6	29.4	52.9

Source: *www.cia.gov*.

Using output to assess industrial structure makes China and India look more similar to the others. In the EU there are three main reasons for the restructuring of manufacturing that has taken place over the past 30 years: first, deregulation, which has led to greater internal competition; second, greater competition both internally and externally from third-party countries, especially the less developed, low-wage countries; and third, the creation of the Single European Market and the resulting increases in competition brought about by the elimination of barriers to trade. There are a great variety of ways in which companies have reacted to these changes but the *Panorama of EU Industry* identifies several 'typical' responses, some of which will have contradictory effects. These include:

● Increased investment for the prime purpose of increasing productivity. This has led to an increase in the level of unemployment in the EU as machinery has replaced relatively expensive labour in the production process.
● A tendency towards greater concentration in industry both vertically and horizontally through merger and acquisition, in order to benefit from economies of scale and to be in a position to benefit from the increased competition (see Chapter 11).
● Greater specialisation in production. Many companies in quite diverse industries (window frames, chemicals, clothing and textiles) have decided to reduce product lines and concentrate on particular market segments.
● Greater flexibility in the production process. This has been achieved by greater automation in production processes, the externalisation of certain activities, subcontracting and increased use of part-time and temporary workers.

Industrial structure in the UK

The United Kingdom does not fare well in international comparisons, as the trend is the same as in the EU but the decline in the **manufacturing sector** has been more pronounced in the United Kingdom and the jobs lost in manufacturing have not been offset by jobs created in the service sector. It is also true that while there has been a relative decline in the output of manufacturing in all countries, it is only in the case of the United Kingdom that there has been an absolute decline.

Figure 12.4 shows a graph of employment in manufacturing in four countries over the period 1974 to 2005. It is clear from this graph that the decline in employment in manufacturing has been much greater in the United Kingdom than the others. The United Kingdom started from a much higher base in 1974 and in 2004 had the lowest level of employment in manufacturing except for Japan, which had been experiencing a sharp economic slump.

Table 12.5 gives an indication of the change in industrial structure in Great Britain between 1978 and 2008. It is important to realise that when different years are compared the figures will be affected by the state of the economy in each of those years, but nevertheless the comparison will give an indication of changes in the relative importance of the three sectors of the economy. The change in the Standard Industrial Classification that occurred during this period would have had a minimal effect on the figures and has been corrected as far as possible.

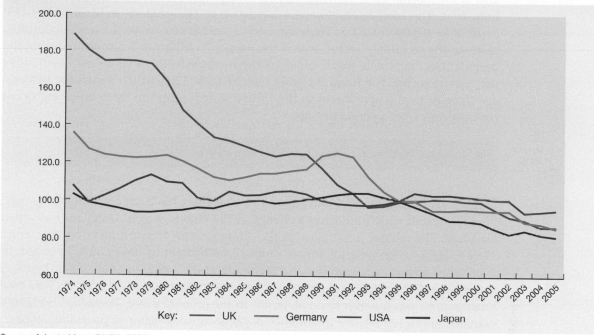

Figure 12.4 Index of employment in manufacturing industry in selected countries (1995 = 100)

Key: —— UK   —— Germany   —— USA   —— Japan

Source: Adapted from OECD, 2008.

Table 12.5 Total numbers in employment mid-June 1978, 2004 and 2008 (UK)

Section	1978 (000s)	2004 (000s)	2008 (000s)
A/B/C	650	569	483
Total primary	**650**	**569**	**483**
D	7 130	4 420	3 153
E	684	283	190
F	1 871	1 839	2 214
Total secondary	**9 685**	**6 542**	**5 557**
G	5 333	6 387	7 106
H			
I	1 704	1 579	1 860
J	2 795	4 659	6 633
K			
L	5 598	6 615	8 023
M			
N			
O–Q	1 097	1 581	2 017
Total tertiary	**16 527**	**20 821**	**25 639**
Total employment	**26 862**	**278 932**	**31 679**

Source: www.statistics.gov.uk.

There has been an increase in the level of total employment during this period and a substantial change in the pattern of employment between the different industries. The level of employment has fallen in the primary sector from 650 000 in 1978 to 483 000 in 2008. There has been a similar change in the level of employment in the secondary sector, which fell from 9.7 million to 5.5 million during the period. These falls were partly offset by the increase in the level of employment in the tertiary sector. The trend is clearly seen in Table 12.6, which shows the percentage share of total employment in the United Kingdom in the three broad sectors of the economy over a period of time.

 web link For data on employment/output by sector see *www.oecd.org*

It is clear from Table 12.6 and Figure 12.5 that there has been a shift in the pattern of employment which indicates a change in the structure of industry in the United Kingdom. The relative importance of the primary sector has declined over the period 1969 to 2008, accounting for 3.6 per cent of employment in 1969 and 1.5 per cent in 2008. The increase experienced at the beginning of the 1980s was due to North Sea oil and the most recent decline was due to the decline of the coal industry. This fall is a continuation of a much longer trend of decline in the primary sector. There has also been a dramatic fall in the relative importance of the secondary sector in providing employment, which fell from 46.8 per cent to 17.5 per cent of employment during the period. Again this table shows that the relative importance of the service sector has increased.

Before consideration is given to the reasons for these changes, the other key indicator of changes in industrial structure will be considered – the level of output.

Figure 12.5 Percentage share of total employment of the secondary and tertiary sectors of the UK economy

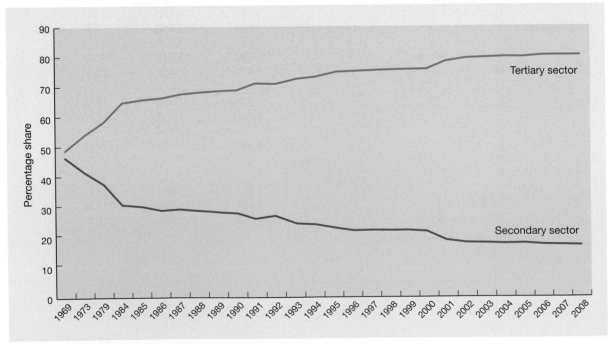

Source: *www.statistics.gov.uk.*

Table 12.6 Percentage share of total employment of primary, secondary and tertiary sectors (UK), 1969–2008

Year	Sector		
	Primary	Secondary	Tertiary
1969	3.6	46.8	49.3
1973	3.5	42.1	54.3
1979	3.1	38.2	58.7
1984	3.8	31.1	65.1
1985	3.6	30.5	65.8
1986	3.3	29.9	66.3
1987	3.0	29.5	67.6
1988	2.7	29.0	68.3
1989	2.4	28.5	68.9
1990	2.5	28.1	69.1
1991	2.4	26.4	71.2
1992	1.6	27.4	71.0
1993	2.1	25.0	72.9
1994	1.9	24.6	73.5
1995	1.7	23.6	74.9
1996	1.8	22.6	75.6
1997	1.7	22.4	75.9
1998	1.7	22.3	76.0
1999	1.6	22.5	76.0
2000	1.7	22.1	76.2
2001	1.5	19.5	79.0
2002	1.4	18.6	80.0
2003	1.4	18.5	80.1
2004	1.4	18.3	80.3
2005	1.4	18.2	80.3
2006	1.4	17.9	80.7
2007	1.4	17.8	80.8
2008	1.5	17.5	80.9

Source: Adapted from *www.statistics.gov.uk*.

These figures show a similar pattern to those on employment. There has been a fall in the relative importance of the secondary sector and an increase in the importance of the tertiary sector. There was an increase in the importance of the oil and natural gas industries in the late 1970s and early 1980s because of the production of North Sea oil and gas; this trend, however, has now been reversed. The broad classification used in Table 12.7 hides the fact that there are differences within the sectors, where some industries grow while others decline in importance.

Table 12.7 Output by industry 1987–2004 (% of total GDP)

Industry	1987	1989	1991	1993	1995	1997	1999	2001	2003	2004
Agriculture, forestry and fishing	1.9	1.8	1.7	1.9	1.9	1.5	1.2	1.0	1.0	1.0
Energy and water supply	6.2	4.7	4.8	4.7	3.8	2.3	2.0	1.8	1.7	1.7
Manufacturing	23.9	23.0	20.7	19.8	20.1	21.2	19.3	17.4	15.0	14.4
Construction	6.1	7.1	6.1	5.0	5.1	5.3	5.4	5.9	6.2	6.3
Services	61.9	63.4	66.7	68.6	69.1	69.7	73.7	73.5	75.8	76.3

Source: Adapted from Table 12.5, *Regional Trends* 40, 2008, ONS, UK.

The changes in relative sizes of the different sectors of the economy in the United Kingdom are the same as in other countries. It is only in the United Kingdom that there have been periods of absolute decline in the output of manufacturing industries, as Figure 12.6 shows. This decline in manufacturing is regarded by many as relatively unimportant; it is seen as a natural process of change which started with the Industrial Revolution and the movement from the land. To some extent this natural growth argument is supported by Tables 12.3 and 12.4. Spain, which is the least developed of those in the table, has the highest level of employment in the agricultural sector.

This change in industrial structure is a trend which is evident in other countries. It might also be the case that some of the growth in the service sector is illusory. For example, if firms are externalising services that they once carried out themselves, there is actually not an increase in the amount of work done but a change in where it is done. It is not surprising that employment levels in manufacturing should fall, given the expansion of services and increases in productivity. What is more disturbing is that the absolute value of output in manufacturing has fallen and while similar patterns can be observed in other countries, the United Kingdom does not fare very well in international comparisons.

Causes of changes in industrial structure

There are several explanations put forward for the changes that take place in industrial structure. Broadly speaking these can be classified into demand and supply factors.

Figure 12.6 Output of manufacturing industry in the UK, 1979–2007 (2003 = 100)

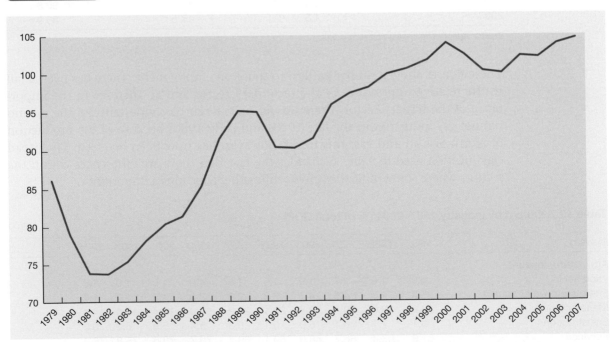

Source: *www.statistics.gov.uk.*

mini case   The life cycle model

A common way of looking at a product and the organisation that produces it is through the use of the 'life cycle model', where the position of the product in its life cycle will have implications for such things as the marketing of that product. The life cycle model can be applied equally to a market, an industry or even an industrial sector, where the position in its life cycle will have implications for industrial structure, market structure (see Chapter 15) and for the strategic choices which will confront the organisation in that industry.

The four phases in a life cycle – development, growth, maturity and decline – are shown in Figure 12.7.

The first phase is the development, birth or entry phase of the life cycle when the industry is in its infancy and growth is still very low. The growth phase is where there is rapid growth in sales and profitability. Firms are likely to have larger market shares and there will be lower costs due to economies of scale and the experience effects. The maturity phase, where growth has stabilised, is

the most common state of the majority of industries and it could last a very long time.

The decline phase is where the growth rate starts to fall for many possible reasons, for example technological change which has made the industry obsolete or changing patterns of demand by consumers, to mention two. There is likely to be cost cutting and the market can be 'niched', possibly looking to overseas markets.

Various points can be made about this life cycle. First, a product or an industry may not go through all of these stages; for example, an industry may not make it past the development stage for a variety of reasons, as in the case of the disc cameras which never found popularity with the public. Second, the length of each of the stages of the life cycle is not uniform and is likely to vary a great deal between industries – this can be seen by applying the model to the agricultural sector, where the growth phase lasted for several hundreds of years. Third, it is possible to miss the decline phase altogether, through diversification

Figure 12.7   A life cycle

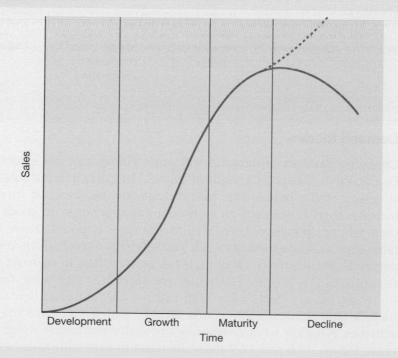

and innovation, in which case the growth path runs along the dotted line in the figure and the organisation has embarked upon another life cycle. The implications of the stage in the life cycle for various factors are summarised in Table 12.8.

It is important to note that the behaviour of organisations will affect the shape of the life cycle of the product and the industry. Porter[2] looks at the strategic possibilities which confront a firm at various stages in its life, depending upon its position in the market – a leader or a follower. One important factor is that a product might be at a different stage in its life cycle at different geographical locations, so an industry which is saturated in the West might be able to extend its life by expanding into other countries.

Table 12.8 Implications of the different stages of the life cycle

Stage	Development	Growth	Maturity	Decline
Market growth	Low	Very rapid	Slowing or constant	Negative
Degree of competition	Low because there are few firms in the industry	Increasing as new firms enter	High Market stabilising	Declining Tendency towards oligopoly or monopoly
Marketing activities	Market research Promotion of new product	Promotion Increasing market share	Maintaining or increasing market share Product differentiation	Depends on strategy
R&D expenditure	High on new products and processes	Mainly on processes	Fairly low	Depends on strategy
Costs	High	Slower rate of increase (economies of scale)	Cost cutting	Depends on strategy
Profits	Low or zero	Growing fairly rapidly	Margin of profit squeezed by competition	Falling

Demand factors

Changing patterns of demand will cause changes in the structure of industry. Demand will change as a result of changes in tastes and fashions, changes in the structure of the population, and changes in the levels of income. As income increases there is normally an increase in total spending on goods and services but there will be differences between different types of goods. There will be relatively large increases in expenditure on goods which have high income elasticities of demand[3] and relatively small increases or even falls in demand for other goods. Goods with low income elasticities are necessities like food, fuel, clothing and footwear. Luxury items have high income elasticities of demand; these would include things like durable goods, alcohol and services like tourism and leisure activities. Naturally what constitutes a necessity and luxury would change over the years. Figures 12.8 and 12.9 show the trend in expenditure on selected goods and services over a period of time in the United Kingdom.

Figure 12.8 Expenditure on selected goods in the UK, 1983–2006

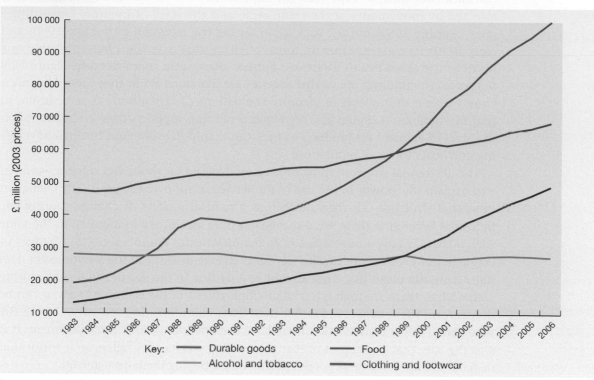

Key:
— Durable goods
— Alcohol and tobacco
— Food
— Clothing and footwear

Source: www.statistics.gov.uk.

Figure 12.9 Expenditure on services in the UK, 1983–2006

Source: www.statistics.gov.uk.

Figure 12.8 shows that the expenditure on food and clothing has remained fairly constant over time, as expected. The expenditure on durable goods is much more affected by movements in the trade cycle and the level of income. Expenditure grew over the 1980s but fell back again during the recession of the late 1980s and early 1990s. The expenditure on tobacco fell steadily over the 1980s, probably as a result of increased health awareness but has risen again more recently. Figure 12.9 reinforces the findings above that services are like durables in that their demand is closely linked to the level of income. The pattern of expenditure is very similar to that for durables. It should also be remembered that suppliers have an impact upon the level of demand for products as they can manipulate demand through advertising and other forms of promotion.

The differential effects of rising income on demand for goods and services would in part explain the growth in the size of the service sector over the years. The change in industrial structure can then be seen as a natural process of change. During the Industrial Revolution there was a movement from agriculture to industry, in the same way as there is now a movement from manufacturing towards services. Changes in demand, however, cannot explain all of this change. Growth in the service sector does not necessarily mean that there should be a decline in the size of the manufacturing sector when there are high levels of unemployment in the economy. Labour can be drawn from the unemployed rather than from manufacturing industry. During the time period under consideration there have been periods of high unemployment. It is also the case that the import of manufactured goods has not fallen, so it is not that demand has fallen for those goods but that we are buying them from abroad.

Supply factors

Changes in industrial structure can also be triggered by changes in supply conditions. The oil crisis of the 1970s is a good example of this. As a result of the massive increase in oil prices, there was a concerted campaign to reduce the consumption of oil and a search for other forms of energy. Technological change gives rise to new products and/or new processes of production. Different industries will vary in the scope for technological change and for increases in productivity (this is considered more fully later in this chapter).

Demand and supply forces are interlinked so it is often difficult to separate their effects as new products will generate new demands or could be developed to meet new demands.

Added to these internal factors is the fact that the United Kingdom is part of an international economy and competition from abroad will have an impact on the structure of industry through both demand and supply factors.

Deindustrialisation

The decline in the importance of manufacturing has been termed '**deindustrialisation**' by many economists. The following causes are put forward for deindustrialisation.

'Crowding out'

The argument here is that the growth in the size of the public sector has been at the expense of the private sector. The resources that could have been used to expand the private sector have instead been used in the public sector, so that the public sector has '**crowded out**' the private sector. This was a popular argument used in the 1980s to call for reductions in public spending. With higher levels of unemployment the argument loses its validity because it is not just a matter of using resources in the private or public sector – they are lying idle. As a result the 'crowding out' argument is less popular now. It is also argued that the higher rates of interest which might accompany higher spending on the public sector discourage private spending. Again, there is little concrete evidence that lower investment results from higher rates of interest. It could be that investment falls because of lower returns on that investment, and the returns on capital employed have been lower in the United Kingdom than in other countries.

Productivity

In terms of **productivity** the UK has not performed as well as other countries, as the mini case study shows. Low productivity has implications for international competitiveness. It can be offset by lower wages in order to stop costs from rising which might be passed on in the form of higher prices. Although the UK wages are relatively low compared with those of many of its competitors, they are not low enough to offset the low productivity levels completely. Alternatively the exchange rate could fall so that prices remain competitive internationally. Although this happened after the UK left the ERM, for long periods during the 1970s, 1980s and 1990s the UK exchange rate was high, and hence its international competitiveness was adversely affected.

---

mini case   Productivity

There are a number of ways of measuring productivity. The productivity of labour can be measured by output per person employed or by output per hour worked. Neither of these are perfect measures because they will both be affected by the amount of capital employed and the productivity of this capital, but as there are great problems involved in measuring the productivity of capital this problem will be ignored for the time being. Table 12.9 shows output per person employed in selected countries in 2006.

These figures show that the UK has not performed well compared with the other countries listed (with the exception of Germany). It is the case that in both the USA and the UK workers work longer hours; it is therefore better to look at output per hour worked (see Table 12.10).

Taking the number of hours worked into account changes the position of both the USA and the UK; France now has the highest productivity levels and UK has the lowest. It appears that there is still a 'productivity gap'

Table 12.9 Output per person employed, selected countries, 2006 (EU-27 = 100)

USA	140.3	EU-27	100
France	125.3	Euro Area	110.3
Germany	106.4		
UK	110.3		

Source: Adapted from Table 1.3, *Europe in Figures*, Eurostat, 2008.

between the UK and other countries. Why is this the case? Writers in this area[4] identify three main periods of history: the Golden Age (between 1950 and 1974) was a period of fast productivity growth in the western world when the EU countries started to catch up with productivity levels in the USA; the slowdown period (1974–1995) when productivity grew very slowly; and the rebound (1995 to now) where productivity has been growing very quickly, especially in the USA and in industries linked to ICT. During the slowdown period, productivity in the UK grew faster than other EU countries because of the deregulation of labour markets which took place during that time. This growth, however, was not enough to close the productivity gap.

Two main reasons put forward for the UK's poor performance are:

- *The quality of the inputs used.* There are two main inputs into the production process – labour and capital. Improving the quantity and quality of both of these will have an impact on productivity levels. As discussed in the text of this chapter, the UK fares badly on both of these counts.
- *How these inputs are used.* This is measured by 'total factor productivity', which measures the efficiency of both labour and capital. Recent figures are not available for total factor productivity but figures for 1999 showed that UK did rather better on this measure of productivity.[5]

Table 12.10 Comparative output per hour worked, selected countries, 2006 (EU-15 = 100)

USA	116.7	EU-15	100
France	119.7	EuroArea	102.3
Germany	110.0		
UK	89.8		

Source: Adapted from Table 1.3, *Europe in Figures*, Eurostat, 2008.

International competition

Because of competition from both the developed world and the developing world, where wage rates are lower than the UK rates, the United Kingdom has lost markets. At home much demand for goods and services is met by imports. Internationally the United Kingdom has lost markets too, as the level of its exports has fallen. There is evidence of this from the UK balance of payments. For example, in the mid-1980s the United Kingdom started to import more manufactured goods than it exported for the first time since the Industrial Revolution, and there was a widening deficit on the balance of payments in manufactured goods. High exchange rates have not helped the situation and have contributed to the decline. It is argued that the United Kingdom competes badly in both price and quality.

Specialisation

The United Kingdom tends to specialise in sectors which do not have great export potential; its percentage shares in sectors like electrical equipment, computers and transport equipment are less than the EU averages. The energy sector is of great importance to the United Kingdom economy.

Research and development

In the United Kingdom the proportion of spending on research and development has not changed very much over the last 20 years. This is not the case for other countries. It is also true that in the United Kingdom a much greater percentage of R&D is financed by government rather than private industry (see Chapter 7).

The educational system

The educational system in the United Kingdom is said to be biased towards the arts and pure sciences rather than applied scientific, engineering and business-type subjects. In the United Kingdom, 30 per cent of engineers have a professional qualification, while in Germany the figure is 70 per cent. Five per cent of UK retail workers have received training similar to an apprenticeship; in Germany the corresponding figure is 75 per cent. As far as international trade is concerned the United Kingdom also lags behind other European countries in its language training.

Level and type of investment

The level of investment in the United Kingdom is low. This means that the stock of capital may be too low and that it will be relatively 'old' (see Chapter 7).

Non-price factors

Non-price factors include quality, design and after-sales service. The United Kingdom is late compared to other countries to take up total quality management. These techniques were started in the West but then taken up and honed by the Japanese and are now being used worldwide. Quality management schemes can only be successful if other conditions are right, like a well-trained and qualified and highly motivated workforce.

Skills shortages in manufacturing

Even in times of high unemployment, there are still **skill shortages**. In the UK just over one fifth of employers reported a shortage of skills in their workforce in 2004 and 20 per cent of vacancies were hard to fill because of skill shortages.[6] Shortages exist within sectors as diverse as construction and childcare.

The financial system

It is often argued that the UK banks are less supportive of business than banks in other countries. In the United Kingdom, banks tend to offer only short-term to medium-term finance for industry; the only long-term finance would be in the form of mortgages. In other countries banks are large providers of long-term finance to industry through the purchase of stocks and shares.

Lack of qualified managers

It is argued that manufacturing has not recruited the best-qualified candidates for management, although management training can overcome this to some extent.

North Sea oil

The existence of North Sea oil has had a mixed effect on the United Kingdom. On the one hand it has led to an inflow of cash which has helped the balance of payments, but it has also served to keep the exchange rate of the pound higher than it would have been in its absence. A higher exchange rate has the effect of making United Kingdom goods more expensive abroad and foreign goods cheaper in the United Kingdom. Thus there is a corresponding deterioration in the balance of payments. The high exchange rate makes the United Kingdom less competitive in international markets, and as the biggest part of what we export is industrial goods, this sector will be most affected.

Government policy

During the 1980s the United Kingdom government repeated the argument that the decline in manufacturing was not important. It was seen as the working of the market mechanism, and would be replaced by services. The government therefore took a relaxed view of the decline. In the early 1980s the adherence to a strict monetarist policy of high interest rates and cut-backs in government expenditure all contributed to the decline in manufacturing.

Synopsis

Industrial structure refers to the relative sizes of the different industries in the economy. Firms are grouped together into industries and industries are grouped together into sectors in some way, although this is often difficult to do. The government has an official Standard Industrial Classification which has been changed to bring it in line with the EU classification.

The size of industries and sectors of the economy is measured by looking at the level of employment or the level of output. In the United Kingdom the primary sector is small and declining, although there was an increase in its importance in the 1980s due to the discovery and extraction of North Sea oil and gas. The secondary sector has also been declining in importance, in terms of both employment and output. The biggest sector of the economy at present is the tertiary sector. This pattern is similar to what is happening in other industrialised countries, although the detail varies slightly between countries. The industrial structure of a country and the way it changes depend upon many factors, most of which have been considered in this chapter.

Summary of key points

● Each country has a particular mix of primary, secondary and tertiary sectors which make up its industrial structure.

● Over the last 100 years there has been a shift in industrial structure in all countries, firstly from agriculture to manufacturing and then from manufacturing to services.

- This shift has taken place both in terms of employment and output.

- Changes in demand are one of the major causes of changes in industrial structure, as evidenced by the case study.

- Supply factors like technological change are also important in the process of change.

- The decline in manufacturing has been termed deindustrialisation and this process has been particularly pronounced in the UK.

- Reasons put forward for this include 'crowding-out', productivity, investment, research and development, the educational system and the high value of the pound.

Appendix 12.1 The Standard Industrial Classification (SIC), 2007

Division	Industry
Section A	Agriculture, forestry and fishing
Section B	Mining and quarrying
Section C	Manufacturing
Section D	Electricity, gas, steam and air conditioning supply
Section E	Water supply, waste management and remediation activities
Section F	Construction
Section G	Wholesale and retail trade; repair of motor vehicles and motor-cycles
Section H	Transportation and storage
Section I	Accommodation and food service activities
Section J	Information and communication
Section K	Financial and insurance activities
Section L	Real estate
Section M	Professional, scientific and technical activities
Section N	Administrative support service activities
Section O	Public administration and defence; compulsory social security
Section P	Education
Section Q	Human health and social work activities

Section R	Arts, entertainment and recreation
Section S	Other service activities
Section T	Activities of households as employers
Section U	Activities of extra-territorial organisations and bodies

case study   Spending on leisure services

The growth of the service sector has been partly due to changes in the spending patterns of consumers. Many services have high income elasticities of demand and as income has increased over time so has spending on services. Figure 12.9 illustrates this point and the cyclical pattern in spending is further evidence of the link between spending on services and income. This case study will look at spending on leisure services in general and then go on to look at theme parks in particular to investigate factors which influence industrial structure.

The relationship between income and spending can also be illustrated with cross-sectional data, where households are broken into deciles, or tenths, according to their income levels. The first income decile represents the lowest tenth of income earners and the highest decile indicates the highest tenth of income earners. Figure 12.10 shows that spending on food falls steadily as a percentage of their total spending as income increases. Figure 12.11 shows that the percentage spent on all services and leisure services within that rises as income rises.

Theme parks in the UK

The USA is the market leader in theme parks. On average every American visits a theme park once a year, in the UK the figure is once every three years while in Europe the average is once every five years. The European market is therefore seen as having great growth potential. Theme parks make an important contribution to the level of employment, GDP and the balance of payments through tourism, but there is little official information available.

Demand factors

Within the sector there are differences. The popularity of zoos for example has declined over the last 20 years – many have closed or diversified. Windsor Safari Park was rescued from receivership by Legoland in the 1990s. Such diversification can be seen as a way of avoiding the decline phase of the life cycle (see mini case). Having said that, the UK market is exhibiting some signs of being a saturated market – the total number of visitors to theme parks in 2003, for example, was 13.5 million, which represents a growth of only 3 per cent from 1999. Total revenue rose by 20 per cent during that time period, mainly due to higher admission charges and increased in-park spending.

Factors which influence demand are:

● *Economic conditions.* Economic recession has two contradictory effects on spending on theme parks: on the one hand it may increase spending since it makes foreign holidays less attractive and on the other it may reduce expenditure because of lower income. The latter certainly seems to be true for in-park spending, which accounts for around 46 per cent of such spending.
● *The weather* has a major impact on attendance at theme parks, and explains why although demand has grown over the last 10 years this growth has been cyclical. The weather in the UK has become increasingly unpredictable and this was the main reason for a fall in admissions in 2007.
● *Location.* The catchment area of a theme park is thought to be within a radius of 150–200 kilometres. Many theme parks have tried to overcome this problem by extending the use of the parks beyond the 'day trip' by offering accommodation on site. The growth in the short

Figure 12.10 Percentage of spending on food and non-alcoholic drinks in UK, 2006

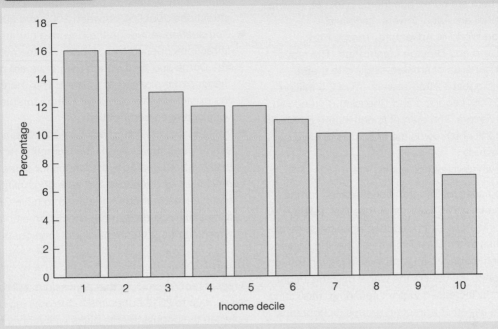

Source: Adapted from Table A7, *Family Spending*, ONS, 2007

Figure 12.11 Percentage of spending on services by income decile in the UK, 2006

Source: Adapted from Table A7, *Family Spending*, ONS, 2007.

break holiday has helped, and some parks offer a discount on a two-day ticket.

● *Demographic change.* The ageing of populations has led to a gradual change of emphasis in theme parks away from the high profile 'white knuckle' rides towards a more family atmosphere.

● *The high value of the pound* has put off foreign visitors from visiting the UK and at the same time made foreign travel relatively cheaper for UK travellers.

● *September 11 2001* had a very big impact on the numbers of foreign tourists visiting the UK and so too did the Iraq War in 2003.

Supply factors

In the UK there are numerous theme parks of varying size. The big 6 are Alton Towers, Legoland, Chessington World of Adventure, Thorpe Park, Flamingo Land and Drayton Manor Park. The rest of the market consists of smaller, single-site theme parks. The biggest – Alton Towers – had 2.5 million visitors in 2006; Legoland and Chessington received 1.4 million visitors. The market is dominated by Merlin Entertainment which owns the first 4 of the big 6 as well as Tussauds.

Factors which influence supply are:

● *Extended season.* The traditional season for the theme parks is the summer and school holidays. Many parks have extended their opening periods – sometimes to include Christmas. Opening hours have been extended into the evening, even though the entrance fee covers the whole day, this might well lead to increased in-park spending. Marketing has been aimed at attracting groups (school trips or corporate customers) in the weekdays during term time.

● *Diversification.* Theme parks have started to offer special events out of season, like fireworks displays, classical music concerts and Halloween parties to boost attendance. Given demographic changes, the parks have started to offer other attractions as well as the white knuckle rides to appeal to the whole family – like puppet shows or magic shows. Some are even offering children's birthday parties.

● *Cost considerations.* Theme parks employ a high number of temporary and part-time employees and so any legislation which affects the employment of these types of workers will impact upon costs. Tickets are now available on the Internet – this cuts administrative costs and gives the theme park more control over its own marketing. The rising cost of energy has also had a significant impact, with electricity used to power rides and other attractions doubling between 2003 and 2006.

● *Competition.* Although there were a number of attractions opened to coincide with the millennium (the Dome and the London Eye) there are no new theme parks planned at present. This means that the existing theme parks will not be threatened with increased competition.

● *The growing burden of red tape/bureaucracy.* Two examples of these are (1) the Gambling Act (2005) which introduced age restrictions for some gaming machines and reduced the type of gaming machines permitted (2) the need to have CRB (Criminal Records Bureau) checks on employees which carries both financial and time costs.

The future

A recent report[7] predicts that admissions will rise by 7 per cent up to 2012 but points to the opening of a gap between the popular theme parks with money to upgrade attractions and the smaller, less well off parks that will not be able to do this. The American Adventure, for instance, closed in 2007.

This case study has shown that the major impetus for the growth of this sector has come through the demand factors, most of the items considered as supply factors have merely been reactions to the demand characteristics. It therefore shows how important demand is in the determination of and changes to industrial structure.

Case study questions

1 Assuming that virtual reality machines become really popular, what are the implications for the recreation park providers?

2 How might theme parks avoid the decline phase of their life cycle?

 web link

See *www.balppa.org* (British Association of Leisure Parks, Piers and Attractions); *www.alva.org.uk* (Association of Leading Visitor Attractions); *www.alton-towers.co.uk*; *www.lego.com*

Review and discussion questions

1 Select industries in various stages of their life cycles. How closely do the observed characteristics of these industries correspond with the expected characteristics summarised in Table 12.7?

2 On what basis could you judge whether manufacturing was more important to an economy than services?

3 What would be the effect on the industrial structure of a country of the discovery of large supplies of oil?

4 What is the difference between an industry and a market?

5 What policies can governments introduce to increase productivity?

Assignments

1 You are the research assistant for an MP who is to participate in a debate on the importance of the manufacturing sector to the economy. You have been asked to produce a list of the arguments that are likely to be used by both sides in the debate: that is, reasons why the decline does matter and the set of counter-arguments. Provide a suitable list.

2 You work for an organisation which provides European intelligence to local businesses and the media. Your line manager has to give a presentation at an international conference on the likely effects that enlargement of the EU will have on industrial structure and has asked you to research the topic. You are required to:

● collect the necessary information on the industrial structures of the potential new entrants;
● assess the impact that the accession of these countries would have on the industrial structure of the EU;
● assess the likely impact of membership on the industrial structures of the countries themselves.

Notes and references

1 See Chapter 10 of the 5th edition for further details on SIC (2003).

2 Porter, M., *Competitive Advantage: Creating and Sustaining Superior Performance*, The Free Press, New York, 1985.

3 See Chapter 14.

4 See *http://cep.lse.ac.uk* (Centre for Economic Performance) for articles on productivity.

5 See mini case study on productivity in Chapter 9 of the 4th edition of this text for figures on total factor productivity.

6 See *www.lsc.gov.uk* (Learning and Skills Council) for information on skills shortages.

7 See Mintel Report, *Theme Parks – UK*, January 2008.

Further reading

Cook, G., *Economics and Business Studies Update: A Student Guide*, Hidcote Press, 2008.

Donaldson, P., *Understanding the British Economy*, Penguin, 1991.

Jones, T. T. and Cockerill, T. A. J., *Structure and Performance of Industries*, Philip Allan, 1984.

Worthington, I., Britton, C. and Rees, A., *Business Economics: Blending Theory and Practice*, 2nd edition, Financial Times/Prentice Hall, 2005.

web link

Web links and further questions are available on the website at:
www.pearsoned.co.uk/worthington

13 Government and business

Ian Worthington

In any society multiple interactions exist between government and business and these occur at a variety of spatial levels and in a wide range of contexts. One such interaction stems from the government's attempts to alleviate the problems of regional and/or local economic decay and decline and these tend to be the focus of governmental policies at local, regional, national and even supranational level. While such measures are formulated and administered by governmental agencies, business organisations in market economies often exercise considerable influence on government decisions. This influence can be enhanced if the views of the business community are expressed through powerful and persuasive representative organisations.

Learning outcomes

Having read this chapter you should be able to:

● explain the rationale for government involvement in the economy

● demonstrate the nature and scope of United Kingdom government regional policy

● identify government policy initiatives at sub-regional level, including the role of local government in economic development

● characterise the role of business as an influence on government

Key terms

Assisted Area
Business angels
Business Link
Chambers of Commerce
City Action Teams
City Challenge
City Grant
Community initiatives
Confederation of British Industry
English Partnerships
Enterprise grants
Enterprise zones

European Structural Funds
Externalities
Industrial policies
Inner City Task Forces
Local Enterprise Agencies
Market failure
Merit goods
Negotiated environment
Public goods
Region
Regional chambers
Regional Development Agencies

Regional government offices
Regional Selective Assistance
Single Regeneration Budget
Trade associations
Urban Development Corporations
Urban Regeneration companies

Introduction

All democratic market-based economies accept the need for government involvement in the day-to-day workings of the economy. The critical question, therefore, is not whether a role for government should exist, but *what* that role should be and *where* the boundaries should be drawn between private and public (i.e. collective) action. Governments of a 'socialist' persuasion normally favour a substantial role for the state as both producer and regulator, whereas non-socialist administrations tend to prefer limited state influence that is directed towards improving the operation of the free market. Either way, the actions of the state in the economy can be influential at both the macro and the micro level and this has important implications for the conduct of business in the non-state sector.

In examining the role of government in the macroeconomy, Chapter 5 emphasised how changes in fiscal and monetary policy could be used to influence aggregate levels of income, output and employment in the economy and how attempts to regulate the overall level of economic activity were related to a government's macroeconomic policy objectives. By way of contrast, in this and a number of subsequent chapters (especially Chapter 17) the focus is on the ways in which government actions impinge upon the operations of firms and markets and the rationale underlying the decisions by the state to intervene at the micro level. Such interventions may take place at the request of the business community or despite its opposition, but it is rare for them to occur without business expressing an opinion which it expects government to take into consideration. This role of business as an important influence on government policy is examined in the concluding section of this chapter.

Government and business: an overview

In considering reasons for government intervention in the economy, economists have traditionally pointed to the problem of **market failure**. This is the notion that if left entirely to their own devices, markets can operate in a way which is not always economically or socially desirable. To this extent interventionist policies can be portrayed as an attempt by governments of all political complexions to deal with the problems inherent in the operation of free markets.

The key areas of 'market failure' are well known. Primary concerns include:

1 The unwillingness of markets to produce goods and services which are either unprofitable or which it is not practical to provide through private means (i.e. **public good** such as defence, social services and so on).
2 The likely under-provision of certain goods and services felt to be of general benefit to the community (i.e. **merit goods** such as education, libraries and so on).
3 The failure to take into account the external costs and benefits of production or consumption (i.e. **externalities** such as pollution, congestion and so on).
4 The danger of monopoly power if businesses can be freely bought and sold.
5 The under-utilisation of economic resources (e.g. unemployment resulting from demand deficiency, new technology or structural or frictional problems).

6 The tendency for output to be determined and distributed on the ability to pay rather than on the basis of need or equity.

Government responses to these problems have normally taken a number of forms, including public ownership, legislation and administrative or fiscal regulation, and examples of all these approaches can be found to a greater or lesser extent in all countries. In recent years, however, under the influence of economists of the 'new right', governments have begun to take steps to disengage the state from some of its activities (e.g. public ownership) and have increasingly turned to market solutions to problems emanating primarily from the operation of the market system itself (e.g. schemes to charge for the use of roads which are heavily congested).

While all forms of government intervention in the economy invariably have direct or indirect consequences for businesses, it is possible to distinguish certain policies which are designed specifically to influence the industrial and commercial environment – sometimes described as 'industrial policies'. In the United Kingdom and elsewhere, these have typically included:

- attempts at direct industrial intervention (e.g. the establishment of the National Enterprise Board);
- privatisation policies;
- policies relating to competition and monopoly control; and
- policies designed to influence industrial location and to encourage economic regeneration at different spatial levels.

Though it cannot be claimed that such measures amount to a single and coherent policy for business, nevertheless they indicate that successive governments accept they have an important role to play in shaping the environment in which private businesses function. Competition and privatisation policy – discussed in detail in Chapter 17 – tend to focus on the operation of markets and on the benefits which derive from private provision under a competitive market structure. Government spatial policies – the subject-matter of this chapter – are mainly concerned with addressing the problems of regional disparities in income, employment and output, and the associated problem of localised economic decline as businesses fail or decide to relocate their premises.

Regional policy

Regions

A **region** is a geographical area which possesses certain characteristics (e.g. political, economic, physical) which give it a measure of unity that allows boundaries to be drawn round it, thus differentiating it from surrounding areas. In the United Kingdom the standard planning regions have traditionally been the North, North West, Yorkshire/Humberside, East Midlands, West Midlands, South West, East Anglia, South East, Wales, Scotland and Northern Ireland, with each of these further divided into sub-regions based on administrative counties and on designated metropolitan areas. These planning regions and sub-regions historically have formed the units of classification for a wide range of official government statistics (see Chapter 18).

With the establishment of the **regional government offices** and the setting up of the **Regional Development Agencies (RDAs)** the regional map of the UK has become influenced by these structures. Moreover, outside London, **regional chambers** have been established in each of the eight current English regions (the North West, North East, Yorkshire and the Humber, West Midlands, East Midlands, East of England, South East, South West) to represent the various regional interests in relation to the work of the region's RDA. The membership of the regional chambers – mostly called 'Assemblies' – includes representatives of the local authorities, employer and employee groups, the small business sector, the health service, educational establishments, rural and environmental groups and other regional stakeholders. At the time of writing there are no directly elected regional assemblies in England (excluding London) of the kind found in many other European states, although the government has sanctioned the use of referendums on the issue of regional government. One such referendum, in the North East in 2004, produced a vote against a directly elected assembly.

For information on regional chambers, regional assemblies and regional development generally, you should consult the websites of the Department for Business Enterprise and Regulatory Reform at *www.berr.gov.uk* and the Department for Communities and Local Government at *www.communities.gov.uk*

The basis of regional policy

Many countries have a recognisable regional policy of one kind or another. Such policies are generally designed to identify and demarcate those geographical areas which are experiencing substantial economic and/or social problems and which are felt to require government assistance. Using a range of socio-economic indicators – such as unemployment levels, population density, economic activity rates, income – governments tend to distinguish those regions which depart significantly from the national average and designate these regions **assisted areas**. These areas then become the focus of government assistance and tend to be given priority in the provision of financial aid for capital projects and for measures designed to increase employment and growth. Such aid generally comes in a variety of forms and may include assistance from international and supranational sources, as in the case of EU regional policy (see below).

UK regional policy

The origins of UK regional policy can be traced back to the 1930s when the government first began to provide help to a number of depressed areas in the form of low-interest loans, subsidised rents and the establishment of government trading estates. By the closing decades of the twentieth century the system had evolved into one in which the government designated three types of assisted area that became eligible for regional aid. These were:

1 Development areas (DAs);
2 Intermediate areas (IAs);

3 Northern Ireland – which received special regional help owing to the problems it was experiencing in attracting investment in industrial and commercial projects.

The areas qualifying for government regional assistance under this scheme underwent some revision in 1993. Subsequently, following new European Commission rules on regional aid in March 1998, all EU member states were required to further revise their Assisted Areas maps by 1 January 2000 in preparation for the enlargement of the EU. The UK's initial response – which was submitted to the Commission in July 1999 – was rejected and the proposed regional aid map had to be adjusted following consultation with the various interested parties. The revised proposals for a new Assisted Areas map for the UK were published on 10 April 2000.

web link Information on the new Assisted Areas arrangements is available via the Europa website

Under this scheme regional aid was available in those areas covered by existing EU law (e.g. Amsterdam Treaty Articles 87[3]a and 87[3]c). These areas, designated Tiers 1 and 2, remained in force until the end of 2006, subject to adjustments to reflect any significant socio-economic changes which occured during the period. Where any additions were made to the agreed regional aid map, these had to be offset by exclusions in other areas to maintain the overall population ceiling.

The UK government also designated a new Tier 3 which extended outside Tiers 1 and 2 and where the emphasis was on aid to small and medium-sized enterprises in the form of enterprise grants. This decision was designed to complement other measures to encourage smaller businesses, including the establishment of the Small Business Service (SBS) and the creation of the Enterprise Fund (see Chapter 11).

Within the designated areas **Regional Selective Assistance (RSA)** has traditionally been the main form of discretionary grant aid. This was administered by the Regional Development Agencies and designed to secure employment opportunities and increase regional competitiveness and prosperity. In order to qualify, businesses had to be investing in fixed capital items, with minimum fixed costs over £500 000, and had to demonstrate that a project met a number of predetermined criteria, including creating/safeguarding jobs and contributing positive benefits to both the regional and the national economy. Grants were available to firms of all sizes in Tier 1 and Tier 2 Assisted Areas, with the regional aid guidelines allowing higher maximum grant levels in areas designated Tier 1 (e.g. Cornwall).

In Tier 2 and 3 areas **Enterprise Grants** were also available to SMEs investing in fixed capital items. The maximum fixed costs had to be no more than £500 000 and the grant ceiling was 15 per cent of those costs, up to a maximum grant of £75 000. The grant was specifically, though not exclusively, targeted at high growth businesses seeking to maximise value added projects with demonstrable quality outputs and aimed to support projects in these areas that would not otherwise have gone ahead without grant aid.

In April 2004, Regional Selective Assistance and Regional Enterprise Grants in England were replaced by Selective Finance for Investment in England (SFIE). SFIE is discretionary and normally takes the form of a grant (or occasionally a loan), with a minimum threshold of £10 000. The aim of the scheme is to support new investment projects that lead to long-term improvements in productivity, skills and employment in the assisted areas. Support under the scheme – which is administered by the RDAs – was made available to business of all sizes located in (or planning to locate in) an assisted area and which could meet certain criteria (e.g. employment benefits). Assistance was also available to SMEs investing in Tier 3 areas and further support was provided through agencies such as English Partnerships, the RDAs and the Learning and Skills Council as well as through the Regional Venture Capital Funds and the long-standing Small Firms Loan Guarantee Scheme.

Following a revision in the European Commission's guidelines on regional aid, a new Assisted Areas map for the UK came into effect for the period 2007–2013. Under the new scheme, 4 per cent of the UK's population remain eligible for regional aid up to agreed levels under Article 87(3)(a) and a further 19.3 per cent under Article 87(3)(c), with the whole of Northern Ireland a designated Assisted Area. As in the previous period, the main form of discretionary grant aid in England is Selective Finance for Investment in England (SFIE). For Wales and Scotland, the equivalent schemes are via Regional Selective Assistance.

The Regional Government Offices are a useful source of information on what grants are available for businesses in particular regions of the UK. Try typing Regional Government Offices into Google and follow the links.

Regional aid within the European Union

In addition to any funding provided by the national government, businesses in the member states of the European Union can also benefit from grant aid under agreed European programmes that have been designed to tackle national and regional disparities within the EU. The majority of this aid is provided from **European Structural Funds** which are used to assist those areas that compare unfavourably with the EU's average levels of prosperity. The EU's four structural instruments have traditionally been:

1 The European Regional Development Fund (ERDF).
2 The European Social Fund (ESF).
3 The European Agricultural Guidance and Guarantee Fund (EAGGF).
4 The Financial Instrument for Fisheries Guidance (FIFG).

For the period 2000–2006 it has been estimated that around €195 billion was spent by these four sources of funding, with a further €18 billion provided through the Cohesion Fund (see Table 13.1). There was also an additional allocation for new Member States from 2004.

Under the new Structural Fund Regulations which came into effect on 1 January 2000, the EU identified three priorities or 'objectives' for grant aid. These were:

● Objective 1 – promoting the development and structural adjustment of regions whose development is lagging behind.
● Objective 2 – supporting the economic and social conversion of industrial, rural, urban and fisheries areas facing structural difficulties.
● Objective 3 – supporting the adaptation and modernisation of policies, systems of education, training and employment.

In the period 2000–2006 it has been estimated that Objective 1 areas covered around 22 per cent of the EU population and probably commanded around 70 per cent of the designated funding, with 11.5 per cent going to Objective 2 Areas and

12.3 per cent to support Objective 3 in areas not accorded Objective 1 status. The main aims and focus of funding in the three areas is shown in Table 13.2.

Alongside the three key objectives, the EU also designated a number of **community initiatives** which focus on finding common solutions to specific problems and which accounted for around 5 per cent of spending from the Structural Funds over the same period. Interreg III, for example, focused on cross-border, transnational and international co-operation and was funded under the ERDF. Urban II sought to promote sustainable development in the troubled urban districts of the EU through the design and implementation of innovative models of development for economic and social regeneration, again funded under the ERDF. Leader+ promoted rural development through local initiatives using funds from the EAGGF.

Smaller amounts of funding were also provided under schemes to promote innovative actions and for the adjustment of fisheries structures outside the Objective regions, with the former designed to encourage the testing of new ideas and practices that might not be funded under the traditional programmes of the Structural Funds.

With the enlargement of the EU in May 2004, the issue of further reform of EU regional policy has obviously become increasingly important and a variety of schemes were put forward by member states, culminating in new arrangements for the period 2007–2013. Under the new scheme, the EU has budgeted for €308 billion of expenditure under the Structural and Cohesion Funds which are designed to pursue its 3 main objectives of Cohesion and Regional Policy; Convergence, Regional Competitiveness and Employment; European Territorial Co-operation. The UK is expected to receive around €9.4 billion (at 2004 prices) from the Structural Funds (i.e. ERDF; ESF; Cohesion Fund) during this period.

Table 13.1 European Structural Funds, 2000–2006

Fund	Main focus
European Regional Development Fund	Designed to redress the main regional imbalances within the EU through the development and structural adjustment of regions whose development is lagging behind. Funding supports investment in sites and facilities for business, infrastructure, local economic development initiatives, environmental protection and improvement, tourism and cultural projects, etc.
European Social Fund	Aimed primarily at improving employment opportunities and reducing social exclusion by promoting employability and equal opportunities and by investing in human resources, particularly through education and training initiatives.
European Agricultural Guidance and Guarantee Fund	Designed to support rural development and encourage rural restructuring and diversification in order to promote economic prosperity and social inclusion, while protecting and maintaining the environment and rural heritage.
Financial Instrument for Fisheries Guidance	Aims to contribute to achieving a sustainable balance between fishery resources and their exploitation. Funds projects to modernise the structure of the fisheries sector and related industries and to encourage diversification of the workforce and the industry into other sectors.

Information on European Structural Funds can be found on the websites of the Regional Government Offices. The EU's own website also contains substantial amounts of information on funding and on policy.
See *http://europa.eu.int/comm/regional_policy*

Table 13.2 Objective areas and funding

Main funding instruments	EU Objective areas	Main aims of funding	Main focus of funding	Eligible areas within EU
ERDF/ESF/ EAGGF/FIFG	Objective 1	To support development in the less prosperous regions of the EU so as to narrow the gap between development levels in the various regions.	Funding for take-off of economic activities by supporting projects concerning infrastructure, human resources, and aid for production sectors.	Regions where GDP per head is at or below 75 per cent of EU average (e.g. Saxony, Western Greece, Galicia, Sicily, Algarve, West Wales and the Valleys, Merseyside, South Yorkshire, Cornwall and the Isles of Scilly).
ERDF/ESF	Objective 2	To revitalise areas facing structural difficulties whether industrial, rural, urban, or dependent on fishery.	Funding for economic and social conversion.	Eligible areas must meet specified criteria related to structural decline. Covers 18 per cent of EU population.
ESF	Objective 3	To support national efforts to modernise policies and systems of education, training and employment.	Funding aimed at combating unemployment and developing human resources.	All areas have Objective 3 status outside Objective 1 regions.

mini case　Attracting foreign inward investment

Though not the only factor explaining the destination of direct inward investment, government grant aid and other forms of assistance are clearly important in determining where multinational enterprises decide to locate new factories and offices. In 1994, for example, the South Korean electronics company, Samsung, announced a £450 million investment in a new complex on Teesside which was expected to bring up to 3000 jobs to the area by the turn of the century. As an incentive to the company, the British government offered nearly £60 million in regional selective assistance and further contributions were promised by the local county council, the TEC and English Partnerships, the government-backed development agency. Sadly for the North East, Samsung subsequently cancelled its planned investment in the wake of the global economic crisis.

Other announcements of further multi-billion pound investments in Britain by huge Korean conglomerates (*chaebol*) seem to confirm the importance of regional incentives in locational decisions. Not that the Far East has been the only source of such inward investment. In August 1995, the German industrial giant Siemens indicated its intention to build a £1.1 billion semi-conductor factory on Tyneside near the site of the Swan Hunter shipyard. All the indications were that this decision was heavily influenced by the personal intervention of the then Prime Minister, John Major, and his deputy, Michael Heseltine, in a deal which included a substantial package of state aid. As in the Samsung case, Siemens qualified for contributions from the DTI in the form of regional selective assistance, together with funding from local authorities and other agencies, and help from English Partnerships to develop the site.

While for both Tyneside and Britain, Siemens' decision was something of a triumph, economic events – particularly the collapse of prices of semi-conductors – undermined Siemens' overseas investment plans. In 1998 the company announced the closure of its plant on Tyneside.

UK urban policy

The urban 'problem'

The progressive decline and decay of urban areas – with its associated unemployment amongst the low paid, unskilled and ethnic members of the population – first came to prominence in the 1960s and gave rise to an Urban Programme aimed predominantly at funding capital projects and education schemes in deprived inner-city locations. Implicit in this programme was the view that the urban 'problem' was largely one of physical decline coupled with failings on the part of individuals which could be corrected by selected government intervention, designed to improve the prospects and environment faced by local citizens. This largely 'pathological' perspective was ultimately exposed by both academic research and community projects undertaken in the 1970s, with the result that government came to see the problem as one of economic and social change, and its impact on the local environment. This 'structuralist' view suggested that policy should be directed towards economic development through partnership between the centre, the localities and the private sector, with the emphasis on schemes to overcome structural weaknesses. Riots in several large UK cities in the 1980s served to emphasise that the problem was particularly acute in those inner-city core areas that had suffered a significant loss of industry and population over a number of years.

The focus of policy implementation: 1970s–2000

Whereas regional policy is managed centrally through a single government department, urban policy has traditionally operated through a variety of agencies including local authorities, voluntary organisations, quangos and a number of independent bodies set up by central government. The relative importance of these agencies in implementing government policy has changed significantly over time.

The initial focus of policy implementation under the Urban Programme was the local authorities which acted as a channel for central government funds into projects designed to regenerate economic activity (e.g. by providing premises), to improve the physical environment (e.g. by clearing land or renovating buildings) and to meet social needs (e.g. by providing community facilities for deprived groups). This role was further enhanced by the Inner Urban Areas Act 1978 which conferred wide powers on certain designated local authorities to assist industry wherever a need was felt to exist and where government help was seen to be appropriate. Central to the government's strategy was its attempt to regenerate inner-city areas through capital investment and through environmental improvement, some of which was to be funded from the private sector. To encourage private sector investment, local authorities in the designated areas were allowed to declare industrial and commercial improvement areas and to give financial assistance to companies which located in such areas.

With the election of the Conservative government in 1979, a number of new initiatives were introduced which indicated a move towards an even more spatially selective policy for urban areas. These initiatives – which included Enterprise Zones, Urban Development Corporations, freeports and City Action Teams (see below) – frequently by-passed local authorities or reduced their powers over the allocation of resources and/or land use, and were seen by many commentators as a vote of no confidence in local government's ability to stimulate urban regeneration. At the heart of the new approach lay an attempt by central government to turn inner-city areas into investment opportunities for the private sector by clearing dereliction and improving infrastructure. The basic idea, as the *Financial Times* (30 October 1990) pointed out, was to reduce downside risk to a level where private investors would see enough potential to develop in cities rather than take softer profits elsewhere.

In March 1988 the government launched its 'Action for Cities' initiative which covered a range of programmes administered by different government departments that were designed to promote industrial and commercial investment and hence create employment in the inner-city areas. Programmes under this initiative were co-ordinated by a special unit located at the Department of the Environment and local co-ordination occurred through City Action Teams. After 1994, in an attempt to achieve greater co-ordination in policy and to introduce competition for resources, the government began to amalgamate a wide range of inner-city programmes under the **Single Regeneration Budget (SRB)**, with the funds initially being administered by the newly integrated regional government offices which brought together the existing regional offices of a number of major government departments (e.g. Environment, Trade and Industry, Transport, Employment). It also established a new development agency (**English Partnerships**) that was to draw its public funding from the SRB. From April 1999 English Partnerships' regional functions and the SRB Challenge Fund became the responsibility of the newly established **Regional Development Agencies**. The latter have been set up to take the lead in delivering more effective and integrated regeneration programmes which promote sustainable economic, social and physical regeneration within the regions. They are seen as a key actor in developing and delivering partnership-based regeneration strategies at sub-national level.

Selected urban policy instruments

The Urban Programme

Historically the Urban Programme, which was designed to help combat the economic, social and environmental problems of urban areas, was the main mechanism for allocating funds to those inner-city areas facing the greatest need. Of the 57 designated local authority areas which fell into this category, 9 were 'partnership authorities', where the government formed a close partnership with local authority agencies to tackle the problem of urban decay (e.g. Hackney, Liverpool, Manchester, Salford). The remaining 48 'programme authorities' (including Barnsley, Bolton, Sandwell, Wrekin) had no such partnership, but were eligible for government assistance for projects which contributed to the economic development of the inner area. In both cases, requests for funds had to be submitted from or via the local authorities which assessed the application and paid the grant for projects receiving official approval.

With the advent of the Single Regeneration Budget, the Urban Programme was gradually phased out and all cities, towns and rural areas were brought within the remit of government regeneration policy. Since the new regime was designed to be competitive, towns and cities within an area were effectively required to compete for funding against each other.

Urban Development Corporations (UDCs)

Urban Development Corporations were independent development agencies, established by central government to oversee inner-city development within designated areas. The first two such areas were London Docklands and Merseyside which gained UDCs in 1980. Subsequently, UDCs were established in Trafford Park (Manchester), the Black Country (Birmingham and surrounding districts), Teesside, Tyne and Wear, Cardiff Bay, Central Manchester, Leeds, Sheffield and Bristol. These ten agencies – whose powers of development within their designated areas superseded those of the local authorities in their area – ceased operations in 1998.

Using funds mainly provided by central government and employing around 500 permanent staff in total, the UDCs had the following objectives:

1 To bring land and buildings into effective use.
2 To encourage the development of industry and commerce.
3 To ensure housing and other social facilities are available in order to encourage people to live and work in the designated area.

To achieve these aims, corporations were given wide powers to acquire, reclaim, assemble, develop, sell or lease land and to provide the necessary infrastructure. In addition they had powers to build houses for rent or sale and to renovate and reuse existing buildings. In short, they were the development control authorities for their areas.

A fundamental aspect of the UDC's role as an agency for urban regeneration was its ability to act as a catalyst for encouraging private sector investment. Using public money to bring about environmental improvement and infrastructural development, corporations sought to attract private investors by removing some of the abnormal costs of development such as land clearance and servicing. This 'pump-priming' role cost the taxpayer over £500 million in the early 1990s, with the lion's share of the funds going to the London Docklands Development Corporation (LDDC), whose fortunes were considerably affected by the collapse in property prices in the late 1980s and early 1990s.

Enterprise Zones (EZs)

Like UDCs, **Enterprise Zones** were first established in the early 1980s, with the first batch of 11 EZs being designated in 1981 with a planned lifespan of 10 years. By the late 1980s the number of EZs had risen to 27, though the number has fluctuated over time as some of the original EZs (e.g. Corby) were wound up and new ones announced in the wake of the closure of a large number of pits in the United Kingdom coal industry.

In essence, Enterprise Zones were small areas of territory within a locality where the government was seeking to encourage industrial and commercial activity by the removal of certain tax burdens and other impediments to enterprise (e.g. bureaucratic procedures). Among the principal benefits for firms located or locating in an EZ were:

● Exemption from rates on industrial and commercial property.
● Allowances of 100 per cent for corporation and income tax purposes on all capital expenditure related to industrial and commercial development.
● A greatly simplified planning regime.

In addition, businesses normally faced fewer requests from public bodies for statistical information and were often exempt from other administrative procedures.

Whether EZs were successful in attracting enterprise and in creating significant numbers of jobs in inner-urban areas is open to dispute. Some evidence exists to suggest that the net job-creation effect has been relatively small and that many of the 'new' jobs are simply relocations by local businesses moving to take advantage of the benefits offered to firms within an EZ. However, according to an evaluation of EZs in the later 1990s it is estimated that the experiment helped to create over 50 000 net new jobs at a cost in the region of £1700 per year, per job.

City Action Teams (CATs)

City Action Teams were designed to bring together government departments, local authorities, local community groups, voluntary organisations and businesses working in inner-city areas. In addition to providing information and advice to any business working in or moving to an inner-city area, a CAT could help with funding for schemes which safeguarded or created jobs, improved the environment, provided training places or encouraged enterprise and the growth of business. It also funded feasibility studies and assisted with consultancy fees for local projects. With the recent change in emphasis of government regeneration policy, funding for CATs has steadily fallen and was a mere £1 million by 1995/6. Like UDCs, City Action Teams have been phased out.

City Challenge

City Challenge was designed to concentrate resources on key areas in the 1990s. Under the initiative, local authorities in partnership with the private sector, local organisations and the local community were asked to draw up detailed plans for solving the problems of their area and special government funds were allocated to acceptable projects. The first eleven partnerships completed their five-year programmes to bring self-sustaining economic regeneration in deprived areas by March 1997. Nineteen Round 2 partnerships finished their programmes the following year.

City Grant

City Grant is the descendant of the Urban Development Grant – an idea copied from the United States after the Toxteth and Brixton riots in the early 1980s. The aim of the grant is to support private sector capital projects which benefit local areas (e.g. bringing derelict land and buildings into use) by bridging any adverse gap between the estimated costs of a project and its expected market value, thus allowing a developer to make a reasonable profit on the venture. Large-scale projects that give rise to new jobs or housing and which improve the environment have been the focus of the grant aid, and priority generally has been given to schemes within City Challenge areas before those from the 57 local authorities that are part of the old Urban Programme. In recent years, City Grant has been administered by English Partnerships (*www.englishpartnerships.co.uk*).

Inner-City Task Forces

Task Forces were composed of small teams of civil servants from various government departments and people on secondment from the private sector who worked directly with local authorities and local businesses to stimulate economic development in inner-city areas. Their role was to co-ordinate and monitor the whole range of government initiatives within the designated area. The Task Force programme ceased on 31 March 1998.

More recent developments in urban policy

With the change of government in 1997, urban policy in the UK has taken on a more targeted and focused approach, with funding increasingly being directed towards a range of economic, social and environmental initiatives. Key developments have included:

- *The New Deal for Communities programme* – designed to combat social exclusion through focused and intensive neighbourhood renewal projects in the most deprived neighbourhoods. This scheme is scheduled to end in 2011.
- *SRB Challenge Round 5 and 6* – which included a more regional focus and an increased emphasis on partnership capacity building. The majority of new resources were concentrated in the most deprived areas.
- *Housing estate regeneration* – through Housing Action Trusts and Estate Action.
- *Coalfields initiatives* – especially the Coalfields Regeneration Trust and the Enterprise Fund.
- Initiatives to tackle problems such as education, drugs, health and crime.

In 1998 the government established an Urban Task Force chaired by Lord Rogers to examine the causes of urban decline and to recommend solutions to bring people back into towns and cities. In its report in June 1999 the Task Force made 105 recommendations, including the establishment of **Urban Regeneration Companies**

(URCs) to lead and co-ordinate redevelopment and new investment in declining areas. This suggestion was subsequently endorsed in a White Paper on Urban Renaissance published in 2000 which also underlined the need to create local strategic partnerships in order to develop a co-ordinated approach to strategy formulation and implementation.

To emphasise the increased importance being attached to tackling urban issues and problems the government established a Cabinet Committee on Urban Affairs and an Urban Policy Unit within the DETR. It also announced a review of the work of English Partnerships, the discontinuation of the national rounds of the SRB (after Round 6) and an Urban Summit to discuss the whole area of urban regeneration policy. This meeting, which took place in late 2002, examined the idea of developing 'sustainable communities', a concept which was subequently taken up in a White Paper published in February 2003 (*Our Towns and Cities: The Future*). In essence, the idea was to revitalise the UK's towns and cities through local schemes of urban regeneration which would involve a range of stakeholders including the private sector. As the government recognised, to achieve this aim would require substantial co-ordination of existing and future government programmes and a high degree of co-operation both within and between different tiers of government. In keeping with this philosophy, the government set up a review of sub-national economic development and regeneration which reported in July 2007. To achieve its aims of strengthening economic performance at regional, city and local level, the government announced its intention to enhance the role of local government in promoting economic development and neighbourhood renewal (see below) and its wish to further devolve power and resources to the regional and local level. It also announced a number of other reforms at sub-national level, including changes to the role of the Learning and Skills Council and a streamlining of the regional tier outside London.

Local government and business in the UK

The basis of local economic development

As a major service provider, consumer, employer and landowner, local government has always played an important role in the economy and its influence on business activity at local level remains considerable. Large local authorities annually spend hundreds of millions of pounds, employ tens of thousands of workers and support many thousands of additional jobs through the placement of contracts with local businesses. Further employment is also created through the 'multiplier effect', as local authority employees spend their income in the local economy and local citizens consume local authority services such as transport and leisure.

Not content with local economic conditions, many local authorities have actively intervened in the local economy by establishing economic development programmes which are designed to alleviate the familiar problems of unemployment, industrial decline and environmental decay. These programmes – often co-ordinated through an economic development unit within the local authority – normally comprise a range of initiatives designed to create or safeguard local jobs by supporting local businesses and encouraging enterprise in a variety of ways (see below). While the origins of such initiatives can be traced back to the nineteenth century, the majority of measures have been introduced in the last 25 to 30 years and represent a move from a reactive to a proactive role by local authorities in local economic development.

The basis for such local authority intervention is partly legal and partly political. Under the law, local authorities in the United Kingdom can only engage in activities for which they have statutory authority, whether granted by public statute (i.e. applying to all authorities) or by private Act (i.e. applying to a specific authority). These statutes not only impose specific duties on local authorities to provide certain services (e.g. education, special housing, care in the community), but also may grant both general and permissive powers which allow local government to engage in different forms of development activity such as the purchase and sale of land and other assets, the granting of financial assistance to industry, and the provision of promotional and advisory services. It is worth noting that the 1989 Local Government and Housing Act introduced, for the first time, a clear statutory basis for local authorities' economic development activities. Under subsequent legislation (i.e. The Local Government Act 2000) local authorities in England and Wales now have a duty to prepare 'community strategies' which improve the economic, social and environmental well-being of their area and its inhabitants and contribute to the achievement of sustainable development in the UK.

A number of more recent changes serve to underline local authority involvement in local economic development. For example, the introduction of the Local Area Business Growth Incentive (LABGI) scheme in 2005 permits local authorities to receive a proportion of increases in local business rate revenues to spend on their own priorities, including schemes to promote local business growth. In addition, the government has made it easier for local authorities to borrow to support investment through the introduction of the Prudential Borrowing Regime (in 2004) and has given statutory authority for local government to form partnerships with the local business community to set up Business Improvement Districts (BIDs) aimed at enhancing local areas. Added to this the recent sub-national review of economic development and regeneration (see above) highlights the government's intention to consider creating a focused statutory economic duty on upper tier authorities to carry out an assessment of the economic challenges and circumstances within their local economy and to perform the LABGI scheme to give a clearer incentive to local authorities to promote economic growth.

Funds for local economic development come from local, national and supranational sources, though not all authorities qualify for all three. By far the largest contribution has come normally from locally generated income, which includes the council tax, local authority reserves and revenue derived from charging for local authority services. Central funding includes the government's block grant to support local authority services, income from other centrally funded programmes (e.g. environment) and from the various initiatives which are part of the government's regional and urban policy. In the case of the latter, these have traditionally been available to authorities within the assisted areas and/or the Urban Programme areas, though some funds have been channelled through other agencies (e.g. the Scottish and Welsh Development Agencies).

Supranational support from the European Union has come mainly from the ERDF and has been used in the assisted and Urban Programme areas to fund infrastructural projects (e.g. Tyne and Wear Metro, Liverpool Ring Road). In addition, further funding may also be available under certain circumstances from the European Social Fund (e.g. for training), the European Coal and Steel Community (e.g. for support for declining steel and coal areas), the European Investment Bank (e.g. low-interest loans for infrastructural investment) and a number of other sources. More often than not, these funds have been directed at those areas identified by the national government as areas of greatest need – hence the decision by the United Kingdom government in the 1980s to extend the number of authorities covered by its Urban Programme, thus qualifying those added to the list for EU financial aid (see discussion above). As with other funds from non-local sources, EU funding has increasingly required the provision of match funding and the establishment of cross-community partnerships before funds can be accessed for economic development purposes.

Types of intervention

Local authority aid to industry and commerce takes a wide variety of forms, but three areas in particular are worth noting: help with land and buildings; financial assistance; and the provision of information, advice and other support services. These were three of the major priorities identified by local authorities in a survey carried out in the late 1980s by the chartered accountants Deloitte, Haskins & Sells.[1]

As far as land and buildings are concerned, local councils as planning authorities, landowners and site developers clearly have an important role to play in industrial development, and despite some attempts by central government to reduce their influence, their involvement in the local property market has remained significant over time. Among the key activities undertaken by local government in this area have been:

1 The identification of land available for industrial use (e.g. local authority registers of vacant land and land use), including services connected with attracting inward investment.
2 The provision of local-authority-owned land for industrial and commercial development.
3 The supply of on-site infrastructure (e.g. roads, drainage).
4 Land reclamation and site assembly.
5 Environmental improvement (including derelict land).
6 Advice and help to private sector developers.

In addition, local authorities have often been involved in the provision and/or conversion of premises for business use (including starter units, workshops and small factories) and have encouraged the development of a number of science parks, usually working in conjunction with private companies and institutions of higher education.

Financial assistance has also been important in encouraging business activity, with local authorities sometimes providing grants to firms seeking to move to new premises or to expand and/or convert existing buildings, particularly if additional jobs are likely to be created. Funds – mainly in the form of grants or loans – have also been made available to firms wishing to purchase new equipment or to establish certain types of enterprise (e.g. co-operatives) or to meet some of the costs of creating jobs for the unemployed or to cover rental charges. Added to this, some councils established Enterprise Boards, which were essentially trading companies concerned with the provision of long-term development capital for investment in local businesses and property. Using funds from local sources, the boards invested in local companies – usually by taking an equity stake – and managed their portfolio of investments through a specially created company which was independent of the local authority. Through such investments the boards sought to attract additional funds from financial institutions such as pension funds, thus creating a financial leverage which was designed to multiply the impact of the support from the public sector.[2]

To complement these direct forms of intervention, all local authorities have sought to encourage local economic development through their promotional and advisory activities which are aimed at both existing and would-be entrepreneurs. Many councils, for example, produce publicity material, booklets, leaflets, information packs and other types of promotional literature, extolling the advantages of their area for tourism or for industrial and commercial use; this can be one of the factors encouraging investment, including direct inward investment by multinational companies, particularly if it is supported by financial and/or other incentives offered by the local authority (e.g. the Toyota development at Burnaston near Derby) or under regional or urban assistance programmes (e.g. the Nissan plant near Sunderland).

Similarly, as active providers of information to businesses on matters such as vacant premises and sites, local labour market conditions, housing availability and sources of finance, local councils deliberately promote their respective areas and many make use of trade fairs or trade delegations to ensure that the 'message' is not restricted to a domestic audience but also reaches potential overseas investors. For the most part, these activities tend to be co-ordinated through the economic development unit or some other agency operating under the purview of an authority's chief executive officer. Significantly, however, an increasing number of authorities have established specialist marketing departments in an effort to 'sell' their area to organisations and individuals who are likely to contribute to the regeneration of the local economy through investment in capital assets and through job creation.

Partnership with the private sector

While local authorities acting alone can be an important agency for local economic development, their support for local businesses often occurs through some form of partnership with the private sector and, increasingly, with a range of other agencies (e.g. local authorities have been asked by central government to set up 'strategic partnerships' to tackle cross-sector issues within the local community). Such partnerships – including the establishment of Local Enterprise Agencies – are increasingly seen as a vital element in effective economic regeneration in the SME sector at both local and regional level.

Local Enterprise Agencies (known as Enterprise Trusts in Scotland) date back to the early 1970s, but their main period of growth began a decade later, with the number of agencies reaching around 300 by the end of the 1980s. Using funds provided by industry and commerce and by central and local government, LEAs act essentially as business development organisations assisting both new and existing enterprises. Their core activity is to provide information and business counselling (often referred to as 'signposting') which points individuals wishing to start a business to sources of help or assists those already running a business with specific problems. In addition most LEAs provide a number of other services, including business training, workspace, help with the preparation of business plans, provision of *ad hoc* services (e.g. solicitors), advice on marketing, taxation, personnel matters and help in locating premises. In recent years LEAs have worked increasingly in partnership with other support organisations, particularly through the **Business Link** network and the Learning and Skills Council. There is also a National Federation of Enterprise Agencies (NFEA) which represents LEA views in government circles.

Unlike Enterprise Boards which were essentially interventionist bodies established by Labour local authorities, Enterprise Agencies are independent organisations which are either private sector initiatives or more regularly a partnership between the public and private sectors, operating through a board which is private sector led. Increasingly, LEAs have tended to work together to provide a more effective service to small businesses, as exemplified by the formation of the Local Investment Networking Company (LINC) in 1987. LINC – which was run jointly by a number of LEAs located throughout the United Kingdom and sponsored by several large companies including BP and Lloyds Bank – was established to help small businesses seeking funding and additional managerial input to find suitable investors. The aim of the organisation was to help both small start-up and growing firms whose financial requirements tended to fall into an 'equity gap' (below £250 000) which was often difficult to bridge through conventional sources. It did this by bringing together private investors willing to invest in new or expanding small businesses and companies looking for such investment and/or additional management skills to aid their development. LINC was replaced in 1999 by the National Business Angels Network – a network of informal investors (**business angels**) willing to invest time and money in supporting cash-starved entrepreneurs.

Further encouragement to the creation of public and private sector partnerships comes from organisations such as Business in the Community (BITC), which also operates as an umbrella organisation for local enterprise agencies. BITC's main role is to encourage the involvement of the business community in a wide range of issues affecting local areas and, in particular, in economic development at local, sub-regional and regional levels. The assumption is not only that the business sector has a responsibility to the local community but also that it has the skills, experience, expertise, contacts and other resources which help to increase the chances of such economic development initiatives being successful.

Within the area of economic development and enterprise, BITC has been particularly active in encouraging community-based partnerships between businesses, government, local groups and individuals aimed at regenerating urban and rural communities, and in this it often works alongside national organisations such as the Action Resource Centre and the Civic Trust. In addition, through a range of initiatives on community enterprise, customised training, business support, innovation and partnership sourcing, the organisation has sought to develop closer links between firms and their local communities in the belief that such community involvement is a natural part of successful business practice, as well as a key influence on the quality and quantity of business activity at local level.

Business as an influence on government

Both individually and collectively, business organisations in a market economy are an important influence on government decision making; they are an essential part of what has been termed the **negotiated environment** in which individuals and groups bargain with one another and with governments over the form of regulation of the environment that a government may be seeking to impose.[3]

At an individual level, it tends to be large companies – and in particular multinational corporations – that are in the strongest position to influence government thinking, by dint of their economic and political power, and many of them have direct contacts with government ministers and officials for a variety of reasons (e.g. large defence contractors supply equipment to the Ministry of Defence). In addition, many large businesses use professional lobbyists, or create their own specialist units, whose role is to liaise directly with government agencies and to represent the interest of the organisation at national and/or supranational level (e.g. in Brussels), using the kind of techniques described in Chapter 4. While such activities do not ensure that governments will abandon or amend their proposals or will pursue policies favourable to a particular company's position, they normally guarantee that the views of the organisation are considered alongside those of the other vested interests. Added weight tends to be given to these views when they are supported by all the leading firms in an industry (e.g. the tobacco lobby's fight against a complete ban on tobacco advertising).

The voice of business is also heard in political circles through various voluntary representative organisations such as Chambers of Commerce, employers' associations, trade associations and the Confederation of British Industry (CBI). **Chambers of Commerce**, for example, largely represent the views and interests of small businesses at local level, but also have a national organisation that lobbies in Whitehall and Brussels. In contrast, **trade associations** – which are sometimes combined with employers' associations – are usually organised on an industry basis (e.g. the Society of Motor Manufacturers and Traders) and handle consultations with appropriate government agencies, as well as providing information and advice to members about legislation and administration pertinent to the industry concerned.

---

mini case   Oiling the wheels?

Lobbying government is a legitimate activity in democratic countries; in some cases pressure groups may help to push a government towards a particular policy decision, in others they may cause it to abandon a course of action it had originally intended to take. Either way, governments usually deny that lobbying has any effect on their decisions.

The UK Labour government's proposals to impose a tax on the use of superstore car parks provides an interesting example of lobbying activity. According to a report in the *Observer* (26 July 1998) the supermarket chain Tesco received prior notice of the government's plans for a car park tax. The information on government thinking appears to have been provided by a firm of lobbyists which had close links with the Labour leadership when in opposition. The firm told undercover reporters from the newspaper that advance knowledge of the proposal

▶

had been useful in planning Tesco's campaign against the tax.

The evidence seems to suggest that as late as May 1998 the government still intended to go ahead with the charge for car parking and that it was to be included in a forthcoming Department of Transport White Paper. Following a meeting in late May between Tesco and the minister responsible for transport affairs, the plan was shelved and an alternative arrangement involving corporate support for subsidised community transport was subsequently announced in the delayed White Paper. Both the government and Tesco deny that any deal was done over the car park tax, although the company admits that lobbying did take place and that it had made a £12 million donation to the Millennium Dome project earlier that year. As the *Observer* points out, there is of course no suggestion that the Dome donation and the outcome of the car park tax issue were in any way related.

The Confederation of British Industry (CBI)

The largest employers' association overall, representing thousands of companies employing millions of workers, is the **CBI**, whose members are drawn from businesses of all types and sizes and from all sectors, but especially manufacturing. Through its director-general and councils – and supported by a network of regional offices and a permanent staff which has representation in Brussels – the organisation promotes the interests of the business community in discussions with governments and with national and international organisations, as well as seeking to shape public opinion. Part of its influence stems from its regular contacts with politicians, the media and leading academics and from the encouragement it gives to businesses to take a proactive approach to government legislation and policy. Additionally, through its authoritative publications – including the Industrial Trends Surveys and reports – the CBI has become an important part of the debate on government economic policy generally, as well as a central influence on legislation affecting the interests of its members.

A good example of its more proactive approach in recent years was its attempt to shape government thinking on environmental policy in the 1990s and to harmonise the work of both government and businesses in this area by promoting its own 'Action Plan'. To this end the CBI established a group of staff dedicated especially to work on environmental issues of interest to business and set up a policy unit and a management unit to provide information, contacts and advice to the various parties involved. The policy unit's role was to monitor developments in legislation, liaise with government departments and enforcement agencies (e.g. the former National Rivers Authority), lobby government and other organisations, provide information and advice, and help to formulate CBI policy on vital environmental issues. The management unit produced promotional literature for businesses, organised conferences and seminars on specific topics, conducted surveys and provided advice on financial and other assistance available to its members to help them develop good environmental management practices within their organisation.

In a report published in late 1998, entitled 'Worth the Risk – Improving Environmental Legislation', the CBI launched an attack on what it called an overprescriptive approach to environmental laws. It called upon government to listen to industry and to concentrate pollution control on the biggest risk areas. According to the chairman of the CBI's environmental protection panel, the existing approach to legislation did not take account of the cost of regulation and its impact on the competitiveness of industry. By using a risk-based approach, the CBI argued that the government could achieve a better system of regulation without compromising business competitiveness.

In the last few years the CBI's views and position on environmental issues – and a host of matters from transport to taxation – have become more widely articulated through its comprehensive website (*www.cbi.org.uk*) and through its information and research services (see e.g. *www.cbi.org.uk/policymatrix.htm*). The easily accessible policy briefs on topics of interest and concern to the CBI are a useful resource for students of business, as are its 'policy briefs', which summarise the CBI's policy positions on key business topics.

While it is impossible to say with any degree of certainty how influential industry is in shaping government policy in this or other areas, there is little doubt that the views of leading industrialists and their representative bodies and associations have received increased attention, particularly under past Conservative administrations. Regular pronouncements by senior government ministers frequently refer to the fact that a particular policy or piece of legislation has been framed 'with industry in mind' and there are clear signs that the Labour government under Tony Blair had sympathies in the same direction. It is not without just cause that the CBI claims that it has 'unparalleled access to decision-makers in Whitehall, Westminster and Brussels' and that it is often consulted informally before new proposals are published for full public debate. Nor is it particularly surprising that a former head of the CBI (Sir Digby Jones) has been given a role in government by the incoming Prime Minister, Gordon Brown.

Synopsis

State involvement in business activity takes many forms and can be seen as an attempt by government to tackle the problems caused by the operation of the free market. One such problem – regional imbalance – is normally the focus of a government's regional policy that seeks to correct economic disparities through spatially selective forms of assistance. Similarly, the adverse consequences associated with urbanisation and localised economic decay and decline have generally given rise to a range of government initiatives, often in partnership with the private sector, and involving different forms of state intervention at local, national and supranational level.

Local government, too, has been active in this sphere and has used a variety of means to encourage local economic development and to support the local business community, both as agent for central government and as sponsor in its own right. Many of its activities have involved direct collaboration with businesses and with the voluntary organisations which represent them, and the private sector has remained a key influence on government policy at all spatial levels. Given the increasing emphasis on free market activity, the voice of business is destined to remain a key input into the process of economic decision making in Britain and elsewhere for the foreseeable future.

Summary of key points

- Government involvement in the workings of market-based economies is often rationalised on the grounds of 'market failure'.

- Market failure is the notion that if left entirely to their own devices markets do not always deliver economically or socially desirable outcomes.

- Different forms of government intervention occur, some of which are designed specifically to influence the industrial and commercial environment and can be loosely called 'industrial policies'.

- Regional policy seeks to reduce disparities in the economic and social performance of different areas of a country, predominantly through different systems of grant aid for business and for other projects.

- Funds for such projects may be available from local, national, international and/or supranational agencies.

- Urban policy is targeted at problems in urban areas including unemployment, social exclusion, physical decline and environmental degradation.

- Over the years governments have experimented with a range of policies and schemes to regenerate urban locations.

- Local authorities are normally involved in the implementation of the various centrally devised schemes and also support local businesses through their own programmes of local economic development as well as through their various roles in the local community.

- Increasingly many of the current schemes require the establishment of multi-sector partnerships involving government, business and other agencies.

- Business involvement in the development of local communities can bring certain commercial benefits.

- Businesses can also gain influence in the policy sphere through their actions and through their representative organisations.

case study   Government and business – friend or foe?

As we have seen, governments intervene in the day-to-day working of the economy in a variety of ways in the hope of improving the environment in which industrial and commercial activity takes place. How far they are successful in achieving this goal is open to question. Businesses, for example, frequently complain of over-interference by governments and of the burdens imposed upon them by government legislation and regulation. Ministers, in contrast, tend to stress how they have helped to create an environment conducive to entrepreneurial activity through the different policy initiatives and through a supportive legal and fiscal regime. Who is right?

While there is no simple answer to this question, it is instructive to examine the different surveys which are regularly undertaken of business attitudes and conditions in different countries. One such survey by the European Commission – and reported by Andrew Osborn in the *Guardian* on 20 November 2001 – claimed that whereas countries such as Finland, Luxembourg, Portugal and the Netherlands tended to be regarded as business-friendly, the United Kingdom was perceived as the most difficult and complicated country to do business with in the whole of Europe. Foreign firms evidently claimed that the UK was harder to trade with than other countries owing to its bureaucratic procedures and its tendency to rigidly enforce business regulations. EU officials singled out Britain's complex tax formalities, employment regulations and product conformity rules as particular problems for foreign companies – criticisms which echo those of the CBI and other representative bodies who have been complaining of the cost of over-regulation to UK firms over a considerable number of years.

The news, however, is not all bad. The Competitive Alternatives study (2002) by KPMG of costs in various cities in the G7 countries, Austria and the Netherlands indicated that Britain is the second cheapest place in which to do business in the nine industrial countries (see *www.competitivealternatives.com*). The survey, which looked at a range of business costs – especially labour costs and taxation – placed the UK second behind Canada world-wide and in first place within Europe. The country's strong showing largely reflected its competitive labour costs, with manufacturing costs estimated to be 12.5 per cent lower than in Germany and 20 per cent lower than many other countries in continental Europe. Since firms frequently use this survey to identify the best places to locate their business, the data on relative costs are likely to provide the UK with a competitive advantage in the battle for foreign inward investment (see Mini case, above).

Case study questions

1 How would you account for the difference in perspective between firms who often complain of government over-interference in business matters and ministers who claim that they have the interests of business at heart when taking decisions?

2 To what extent do you think that relative costs are the critical factor in determining inward investment decisions?

Review and discussion questions

1 Why should a government committed to the free market intervene in the working of the economy?

2 Explain the connection between 'market failure' and the need for some form of government regional policy.

3 Why are some local authorities more interventionist than others?

4 Why have cross-sector partnerships to tackle social and economic problems become so fashionable in recent years?

Assignments

1   You are employed in the publicity and promotion unit of a local authority. Part of your work involves promoting the area as a suitable location for industrial and commercial activity. Your task is to produce a leaflet – for distribution to potential clients – indicating the advantages of locating within the area and the forms of assistance available.

2   You are the chairperson of the local Chamber of Commerce. The local authority has written to you concerning its plans to pedestrianise the town (or city) centre and asking for the reaction of local businesses. Your task is to produce a short report, for the next meeting of the Chamber, outlining the benefits and disadvantages to the local business community of such a scheme and indicating how the Chamber of Commerce could make its views known in political circles.

Notes and references

1   Deloitte, Haskins & Sells, *Local Authority Assistance to Growing Businesses*, London, 1989.
2   Many Enterprise Boards were set up by Metropolitan County Councils. Their activities have generally continued, despite the abolition of these councils.
3   See Thomas, R. E., *The Government of Business*, 3rd edition, Philip Allan, 1987.

Further reading

Adams, J., Robinson, P. and Vigor, A., *A New Regional Policy for the UK*, IPPR, 2003.

Griffiths, A. and Wall, S. (eds), *Applied Economics: An Introductory Course*, 10th edition, Financial Times/Prentice Hall, 2004, esp. ch. 11.

Ho, S. Y., *Evaluating British Urban Policy: Ideology, Conflict and Compromise*, Ashgate, 2003.

Hornby, W., Gammie, R. and Wall, S., *Business Economics*, 2nd edition, Financial Times/Prentice Hall, 2001.

Imrie, R. and Raco, M. (eds), *Urban Renaissance? New Labour Community and Urban Policy*, Policy Press, 2003.

McKeown, P., 'Regional Policy', in Atkinson, B., Livesey, F. and Milward, B., *Applied Economics*, Macmillan, 1998.

Mulhearn, C., Vane, H. R. and Eden, J., *Economics for Business*, Palgrave, 2001, Chapter 7.

Williams, R. H., *European Spatial Policy and Planning*, Paul Chapman Publishing, 1996.

Worthington, I., Britton, C. and Rees, A., *Economics for Business: Blending Theory and Practice*, 2nd edition, Financial Times/Prentice Hall, 2005, Chapter 11.

Web links and further questions are available on the website at:
www.pearsoned.co.uk/worthington

A lot of bottle

Many organisations have ambitions to grow and to increase their market share, turnover and profitability. For very large businesses operating on an international scale, merger or acquisition is a popular way of achieving such objectives and can result in the creation of a huge company with a truly global reach. In the discussion below, we focus on one major example, InBev's acquisition of Anheuser-Busch in 2008.

Prior to the takeover deal, the Belgium-based InBev was one of the world's leading brewers of beer with around 13 per cent of the world market. While the roots of the business go back to the fourteenth century, InBev itself came into being in 2004 following a merger between Belgium's Interbrew and the Brazilian brewer AmBev. With key global brands such as Skol, Brahma Chop, Stella Artois, Becks, Leffe, Staropramen and Hoegaarden, the company had a portfolio of products that could appeal to different markets across the globe. Annual group sales in 2006/7 were around 40 billion pints and its turnover was estimated to be around 14 billion euros.

InBev's main rival at the time was the London-based SABMiller, a merger of South African breweries and Miller, which created a business with key brands such as Snow and Miller Lite that helped to give the company a similar market share and annual sales to those of InBev. The latter's other main competitors were Anheuser-Busch and Heineken, each with a market share of just under 9 per cent and key brands such as Bud.Light (AB), Budweiser (AB) and Heineken. Like InBev and SABMiller, these two companies were also businesses that had grown from previous mergers/acquisitions as the world's leading brewers sought to dominate the growing global market, especially in the developing countries in the Far East and South America.

While there was some opposition by the Anheuser-Busch board to the InBev takeover, the deal went through in the second half of 2008 and has led to the creation of a huge global company named Anheuser-Busch InBev. The takeover brings into being a brewing colossus that is expected to sell around 65 billion pints of beer a year, about a fifth of the total world market. Apart from the obvious opportunities to make significant cost savings and economies of scale from combining the two businesses, the new company brings together some of the major global brands that are sold to beer drinkers throughout the world. It also brings into being an organisation that seems destined to become one of the world's top consumer goods companies, alongside such famous names as PepsiCo and Procter & Gamble.

As markets become increasingly globalised, we should expect to see more mega-deals of this kind, as multinational companies battle for an advantage in a highly competitive, international business environment. Cross-national mergers/acquisitions of the kind discussed here make obvious economic and commercial sense and provide the participants with numerous potential benefits, some of which were discussed in Chapter 11. Whether they ultimately benefit the consumer, however, is a matter of opinion. Certainly in a market such as this, there are many who feel that the increasing concentration of production in fewer and fewer hands might mean that one of the consequences of globalisation could be the gradual demise of local brands of beer and the homogenisation of a product that no longer reflects its local origins. In short, globalisation may not necessarily always be good news, it's all a matter of taste.

Part Four

MARKETS

14

The market system

Chris Britton

As part of their normal production activity, businesses are involved in buying (inputs – like labour and raw materials) and selling (outputs – the finished product). Buying and selling take place in markets and although there are many different types of market the basic analysis remains the same.

Learning outcomes

Having read this chapter you should be able to:

● explain the working of the market system

● apply the theory to the real world

● demonstrate the importance of key concepts like elasticity to business

● discuss the wider economic effects of changes in market forces

Key terms

Buyers' market	Equilibrium quantity	Market system
Complements	Excess demand	Normal goods
Cross-price elasticity	Excess supply	Price ceiling
Demand	Factor market	Price controls
Demand curve	Free market	Price elasticity
Effective demand	Income elasticity	Price floor
Effective supply	Inelasticity	Product market
Elasticity	Inferior goods	Sellers' market
Elasticity of demand	'Law of demand'	Substitutes
Elasticity of supply	'Law of supply'	Supply
Equilibrium price	Market	Supply curve

Introduction

As indicated in Chapter 5, the market system is an economy in which all of the basic economic choices are made through the market. The **market** is a place where buyers and sellers of a product are brought together. The nature and location of the market depends on the product. For example, within your local town there is likely to be a vegetable market where you would go to buy vegetables. Here, buyers and sellers meet face to face in the same location, but this is not always the case. The market for used cars might be the local newspaper classified section; the sale of stocks and shares passes through a broker so that the buyer never meets the seller. There are many different types of market, involving different buyers and sellers. Firms sell the goods and services they produce to households on the **product markets**, while in the **factor markets** firms are buying resources such as labour and raw materials. The discussion in this chapter will concentrate on the product markets but much of the analysis could also be applied to the factor markets.

A **free market** system is one in which the basic economic choices are made through the market, without any intervention by the government. In reality, markets are not completely free; governments intervene in markets for many reasons and in many different ways (see Chapter 17), but in this chapter such intervention will be ignored.

The market mechanism

In every market there will be a buyer and a seller, and somehow they have to be brought together so that a sale can take place. The market mechanism is the way in which this takes place in a market economy. In the product market, the buyer is the household and the seller is the firm. In economic language the household **demands** the good or service and the firm **supplies** the good or service. Each of these will be considered separately first and then brought together.

Demand

The quantity demanded refers to the quantity of a good or service that households are willing and able to purchase at a particular price. This definition shows that it is **effective demand** that is important; although many people would like to own a Rolls-Royce they could not afford it and so their demand is not effective on the market. The demand for a good or service depends on a number of factors, the most important of which are:

- the price of the good;
- the prices of other goods;
- disposable income; and
- tastes.

Table 14.1 The demand for 'Real Brew' draught beer

Price (£ per pint)	Quantity demanded (000s of pints/week)
0.90	83
1.00	70
1.10	58
1.20	48
1.30	40
1.40	35
1.50	32

To begin with, the relationship between quantity demanded and price will be looked at, assuming that the other factors above remain the same. This assumption will be relaxed in the subsequent analysis.

Table 14.1 shows what happens to the quantity demanded of beer as the price per pint goes up. Note that demand is measured over some period of time. The information is then presented in a graphical form in Figure 14.1; the line joining the various combinations of price and quantity demanded is called a **demand curve**. The demand curve shows that if all of the other factors which influence demand are constant then as price goes up, quantity demanded goes down. This is commonly referred to as **the law of demand**. What happens when price rises is that some individuals will cut down their consumption of beer and others may switch to other types of beer. There are some goods where this relationship might not hold:[1] for example, in the stock market where a rise in share prices might lead to the expectation of further price rises and therefore an increase in demand on the part of those wishing to make a capital gain. However, these exceptions are rare and it is therefore safe to assume that the law of demand holds.

If the price of beer changes, there is a movement along the demand curve. For example, if the price of beer goes up from 90p a pint to £1.00 a pint, the quantity demanded goes down from 83 000 pints per week to 70 000 pints per week. In drawing the demand curve the assumption was made that other factors affecting demand are constant. If this assumption is relaxed, what happens to the demand curve?

Figure 14.1 A demand curve for 'Real Brew' draught beer

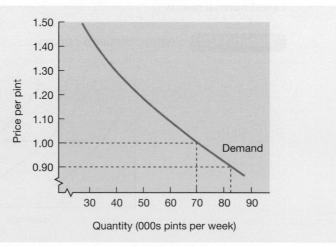

Price of other goods

The quantity of beer consumed will be affected by the prices of other goods. These other goods are likely to be **substitutes** or **complements**. A substitute for beer may be lager, and if the price of lager goes down, some individuals may switch from beer to lager; thus the demand for beer goes down. What happens to the demand curve is that at all price levels, the demand for beer is now lower. Thus the demand curve shifts to the left, indicating that at £1.00 per pint only 60 000 pints of beer are demanded per week. If the price of a substitute goes up, there will be an increase in the demand for beer. The demand curve moves to the right. These movements are shown in Figure 14.2. The closer the goods are as substitutes and the greater the change in the price of the substitute, the greater will be the shift in the demand curve.

A complementary good is one which tends to be consumed with another good. For beer, it is possible that individuals eat crisps or smoke cigarettes at the same time as drinking beer. The relationship is the opposite of that for substitutes. If the price of a complement goes up, individuals might be less likely to drink beer, and demand will fall. The demand curve moves to the left. If the price of a complement goes down, the demand for beer will rise. Again the closer the goods are as complements, and the greater the price change of that complement, the greater will be the shift in the demand curve.

Disposable income

Changes in disposable income will clearly affect demand. If the economy moves into recession, then retail sales and the housing market might suffer. As incomes increase once the economy recovers, then such sectors will pick up again. Higher incomes will lead to increased consumption of most goods. If your income is boosted, how will this affect your consumption? You might buy more textbooks, and probably spend more money on leisure activities and clothes. Most students might also drink an extra pint of beer per week. Thus an increase in disposable income will lead to an increase in demand for these goods, indicated by a rightward shift in the demand curve. As incomes fall the demand for these goods will fall, indicated by a leftward shift in the demand curve. These types of goods are called **normal goods**.

Figure 14.2   Shifting demand curves

There are goods, however, that experience a fall in demand as a result of income increases. These goods are called **inferior goods**. A good example is hard toilet paper; as individuals become richer, they are likely to substitute more expensive soft toilet paper, and thus the demand for hard toilet paper will fall.

Tastes

Taste includes attitudes and preferences of consumers, and will be affected by such things as fashion, and advertising campaigns by producers or by governments. For example, a successful advertising campaign by the government pointing out the effects of smoking would cause tastes to change and demand for cigarettes to fall.

The demand curve, then, is downward sloping, indicating that as the price of the good rises the quantity demanded by households falls, shown by a *movement along the demand curve*. Changes in the other determining factors lead to *movements of the demand curve*.

Supply

The other side of the market is the supply side. In the market for goods and services it is the firm that is the supplier. The quantity supplied of a good is defined as the quantity that firms are willing and able to supply to the market at a particular price. Again notice the wording of the definition is such that it only includes **effective supply** and, as with demand, it is measured over a specific time period.

The quantity supplied to the market depends on a number of factors, the most important of which are:

● the price of the good;
● the prices of other goods;
● the prices of the resources used to produce the good;
● technology;
● expectations; and
● number of suppliers.

In the same way as for demand, all factors other than price will be assumed to be constant and the relationship between quantity supplied and price will be considered first.

Table 14.2 provides some information on price and quantity supplied of beer. The same information is represented graphically in Figure 14.3; the line joining the points together is called the **supply curve**. The upwards-sloping curve illustrates **the law of supply**. This states that, as the price of a good rises, the quantity that firms are willing to supply also rises. This is because if costs are constant as we have assumed, then higher prices must mean higher profits to the firm.

Note that there is no supply at a price below 90p per pint; this is the minimum price required by the producer to produce the beer. If the price per pint changes there is a movement along the supply curve in the same way as for demand. If any of the other factors listed above change there will be a movement of the supply curve.

Table 14.2 The supply of 'Real Brew' draught beer

Price (£ per pint)	Quantity supplied (000s of units/week)
0.90	0
1.00	35
1.10	43
1.20	48
1.30	55
1.40	60
1.50	68

Other prices

The supply of one good can be influenced by the price of another. For example, if the brewery in which Real Brew beer is brewed is also producing lager, then an increase in the price of lager (with the price of beer remaining the same) will encourage the firm to produce less beer and more lager, as lager is now more profitable to produce. The supply curve for beer would shift to the left, indicating that at every possible price, less is now supplied than before. If the price of lager fell, the supply of beer would increase. This is shown by a rightward shift of the supply curve. The size of the shift would depend upon the degree to which the goods could be substituted for each other in production, and the size of the price change. These shifts are illustrated in Figure 14.4.

Goods can also be complements in their production process; for example, beef and leather hides. An increase in the price of beef would increase not only the supply of beef but also the supply of hides. There would be a corresponding shift in the supply curve for hides.

Figure 14.3   The supply of 'Real Brew' draught beer

Figure 14.4   Shifting supply curves

The prices of the resources used in the production of the good

If any of the costs of production (wages, rent, rate of interest, and so on) increased, then the profitability of that good at each price would fall and there would be a tendency for supply to be reduced. The supply curve would move to the left. If costs of production fell there would be an increase in supply and a rightward movement of the supply curve. The extent of the shift depends upon the size of the price change, the significance of that factor in production, and the degree to which the factor could be substituted for another factor.

Technology

As illustrated in Chapter 7, technical development in all aspects of production has led to great improvements in output per worker. Such improvements generally result in either more being produced with the same resources, or the same being produced with fewer. In most cases it would also lead to a substitution of one factor of production for another. For example, car production becomes less labour intensive as robotic techniques take over. Even such a product as traditional British beer has benefited from significant technical improvements in production. The effect of such advances would result in increased supply at each price level and hence a movement of the supply curve to the right.

Business expectations

Expectations play a crucial role in the decision making of firms. Good expectations of the future would encourage firms to invest in new plant and machinery, which would increase their productive potential. Chancellors of the Exchequer are occasionally accused of trying to 'talk the economy up': that is, they may paint a rosy picture of the current and future state of the economy in the hope that this will enhance business expectations, and help pull the economy out of recession. If business does become increasingly confident, or perhaps more inclined to take risks, then this would shift the supply curve to the right. The reverse would shift it to the left.

The number of suppliers

As the number of suppliers in a market increases the supply will rise; the supply curve shifts to the right. If suppliers leave the market, supply will fall and the supply curve moves to the left.

Price determination

The market is the place where buyers and sellers meet and where demand and supply are brought together. The information on demand and supply is combined in Table 14.3 and presented graphically in Figure 14.5.

Table 14.3 The supply and demand for 'Real Brew' draught beer

Price (£ per pint)	Quantity demanded (000s/wk)	Quantity supplied (000s/wk)
0.90	83	0
1.00	70	35
1.10	58	43
1.20	48	48
1.30	40	55
1.40	35	60
1.50	32	68

The equilibrium price

At a price of £1.20, the quantity demanded is the same as the quantity supplied at 48 000 pints per week. At this price the amount that consumers wish to buy is the

Figure 14.5 The market for 'Real Brew' draught beer

same as the amount that producers wish to sell. This price is called the **equilibrium price** and the quantity being bought and sold is called the **equilibrium quantity**. The point of equilibrium can be seen on the diagram at the point where the demand and supply curves cross.

At price levels above £1.20 the quantity that producers wish to supply is greater than the quantity consumers wish to buy. There is **excess supply** and the market is a 'buyers' market'. At prices less than £1.20 consumers wish to buy more than producers wish to supply. There is **excess demand** and the market is a **sellers' market**.

In competitive markets, situations of excess demand or supply should not exist for long as forces are put into motion to move the market towards equilibrium. For example, if the price level is £1.30 per pint, there is excess supply and producers will be forced to reduce the price in order to sell their beer. Consumers may be aware that they are in a **buyers' market** and offer lower prices, which firms might accept. For one or both of these reasons, there will be a tendency for prices to be pushed back towards the equilibrium price. The opposite occurs at prices below equilibrium and price is pushed upwards towards equilibrium.

Shifts in demand and supply

So long as the demand and supply curves in any market remain stationary, the equilibrium price should be maintained. However, there are numerous factors that could shift either or both of these curves. If this were to happen, then the old equilibrium would be destroyed and the market should work to a new equilibrium. How does this happen?

In Figure 14.6 the original equilibrium price for Real Brew draught beer is P_1. Assume that the demand curve moves from D_1 to D_2. This increase in demand could be due to a variety of factors already mentioned. For example, the price of a rival drink may have increased; disposable income could have risen; or sales may have benefited from a successful advertising campaign. In any event, at the old equilibrium price there now exists an excess of demand over supply of Q_1Q_3. It is likely that price will be bid upwards in order to ration the shortage in supply. As

Figure 14.6   A shift in the demand curve

price rises, demand is choked off and supply exhausted. Eventually, there is a movement to a new equilibrium of P_2. At this new price both supply and demand at Q_2 are higher than they were at the previous equilibrium. If, alternatively, the demand curve had shifted to the left, then the process would have been reversed and the new equilibrium would have been at a level of demand and supply less than Q_1, with a price below P_1. Illustrate this process diagrammatically for yourself.

In Figure 14.7 there is a shift in the supply curve from S_1 to S_2. Refer back in this chapter to envisage specific reasons for such a shift. At the original equilibrium price of P_1 there would now be an excess supply over demand of Q_1Q_3. Price would therefore fall in a free market. As it does, demand will be encouraged and supply diminished. Eventually there will be a new equilibrium at P_2 with a higher quantity demanded and supplied than at the previous equilibrium. If the supply curve had instead shifted to the left, then market forces would have resulted in a lower quantity supplied and demanded than before. Once again, illustrate this diagrammatically for yourself.

The analysis so far has been relatively straightforward; it has been assumed that either the demand or the supply curve moves alone. However, it is likely that in any given time period both curves could move in any direction and perhaps even more than once.

Given the many factors that may shift both the demand and the supply curves, it is easy to imagine that markets can be in a constant state of flux. Just as the market is moving towards a new equilibrium, some other factor may change, necessitating an adjustment in an opposite direction. Given that such adjustment is not immediate, and that market conditions are constantly changing, it may be the case that equilibrium is never actually attained. It is even possible that the very process of market adjustment can be destabilising.[2] The constant movement of price implied by the analysis may also be detrimental to business. The firm might prefer to keep price constant in the face of minor changes in demand and supply.

Figure 14.7   A shift in the supply curve

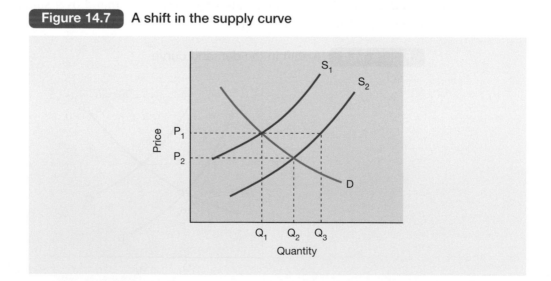

mini case   The price of gold

Gold as a commodity has always had a particular historical economic importance and its price is very volatile. Over 84 per cent of the gold mined each year goes into the production of jewellery, but it is the role of gold as a store of wealth that gives it such volatility. Until the 1970s the US, the UK and many other countries pegged their currencies to the value of gold – 'the gold standard'. As a result, central banks kept stocks of gold, as well as other currencies, which gives gold increased importance as a commodity.

The price of gold has been increasing since 2001 to hit $1000 per ounce in March 2008. By June the price had fallen to $880 per ounce. Explanations for these movements in gold prices can be found in the theory of demand and supply.

Supply factors

First, as a natural resource, the supply of gold is inelastic; it is mined in over 60 countries but the amount mined is small and getting smaller each year. This means that the supply curve will be inelastic (see below) – SS in Figure 14.8. Any changes in demand will have a bigger impact upon price than if the supply curve was elastic. Draw a more elastic supply curve in Figure 14.8 and see what impact that has on price.

Once the gold standard had been rejected by countries, their central banks started to sell off some of their stocks of gold; this led to increases in market supply and therefore falls in the price of gold. You should be able to draw this on a demand and supply diagram.

Demand factors

The increase in the price of gold that took place between 2001 and 2008 has mainly been down to demand factors:

- there has been higher demand for gold from oil-producing countries such as Russia and Qatar, which do not wish to hold the surpluses they have accumulated in dollars (from exporting oil), which by 2008 was a weakened currency;

- an increasingly wealthy Chinese population has been buying gold as a store of wealth;
- western pension funds have also been very active in the closed exchanges where they can buy 'shares' in gold bars.

The effect of increasing demand is shown in Figure 14.8. Increases in demand from D_1 to D_2 to D_3 cause price to increase fairly sharply.

Figure 14.8   The market for gold

At the time of writing, the price of gold had already fallen from its peak of $1000 per ounce and the main reason for this was the stabilising of the US$. It is clear that the forces of demand and supply are very evident in the market for gold and the supply characteristics make its price more susceptible to changes in demand. This may change in the future as deep-sea mining equipment should go into action in 2010, and if gold is found in significant quantities, the supply of gold will become more elastic. Shocks to the global financial system (e.g. the global financial crisis in 2007/8) also affect the price of gold as investors look for 'safe havens' for their money. Historically, gold has been seen as one such safe haven.

Price controls

Governments occasionally take the view that a particular equilibrium price is politically, socially or economically unacceptable. In such circumstances, one course of action is the imposition of **price controls**. This involves the institutional setting of prices at either above or below the true market equilibrium. For example, if it was felt that the equilibrium price of a good was too high, then the government might try to impose a lower price on the market. This would now be the maximum acceptable price or **price ceiling**. Price may not rise above this ceiling. Alternatively, the equilibrium price could be seen as too low. In this case, a higher price, or **price floor** is imposed, below which price should not fall.

Figure 14.9 illustrates the market for a basic foodstuff. Imagine that it is wartime and the disruption has shifted the supply curve to the left. This could be largely due to a movement of resources away from the production of this good and towards munitions. The free market price at P_1 is seen to be unacceptably high relative to the pre-war price, and the decision is made to impose a price ceiling of P_2. It is hoped that such a ceiling will alleviate the problems of consumers who could not afford the free market price. The problem now is that at the price ceiling only Q_3 units will be supplied, whereas demand is for Q_2. The volume of output Q_3Q_2 therefore represents an excess of demand over supply. Many customers are frustrated in their desire to purchase that good. To help bring order to the situation, a system of rationing might be introduced. This could allocate the limited output between the many customers in a more orderly fashion than 'first come, first served'. For example, one unit could be allocated per person and priority could be given to the old and the sick. This does not solve the problem of excess demand. It is commonly found in such situations that illegal trading starts to emerge at a price above the ceiling. To obtain the good many would be willing to pay a higher price. This is commonly referred to as black market trading.

Figure 14.10 illustrates the market for a specific type of labour. The downward-sloping demand curve indicates that, at lower wages, employers will wish to take on additional workers. The supply curve shows how more people will offer themselves for work as wage rates increase. At the intersection of the curves, the market

Figure 14.9   Imposition of a price ceiling

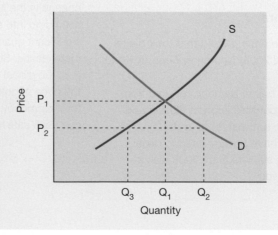

Figure 14.10   Imposition of a price floor

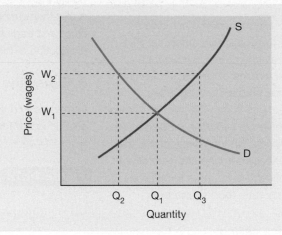

is in equilibrium. Imagine that this equilibrium wage is seen to be too low, and the authorities seek to impose a minimum wage of W_2. Employers are not permitted to pay any less than this amount. It is hoped that the policy will improve the welfare of workers by raising their living standards to some acceptable level.

At this minimum wage, employment becomes more attractive, and Q_3 persons seek employment. On the other hand, employers only wish to take on Q_2 workers. There is now a situation of excess supply. Only Q_2 find work, the remainder Q_2Q_3 are unsuccessful. The policy has actually reduced the level of employment from Q_1 to Q_2. In such a situation, there will be a temptation to flout the legislation. For example, unscrupulous employers observing the ranks of unemployed would realise that many would willingly work at less than the minimum wage.

The above examples illustrate the problems that arise once price is imposed away from its equilibrium. Further examples of such price controls would include the guaranteed minimum prices to farmers within the Common Agricultural Policy (CAP) of the European Union (see case study at the end of Chapter 12 of the previous edition of this book), and various post-war attempts to control the cost of rented accommodation at a price affordable to the low paid. The former has been associated with overproduction and the need to control the mountains of excess supply, while the latter tended to result in landlords taking their properties off the rental market in order to seek more profitable returns. The success of such policies requires careful control and monitoring. In many circumstances, it might be better to consider alternative ways of achieving the policy goals.

mini case   What can be done about rising food prices?

Rising world food prices (see case study at the end of the chapter) have implications for the whole world, but especially for poorer countries where incomes are low and the demand for food is high; 2008 has seen food riots in countries from Mexico to Pakistan to Burkina Faso. Even consumers in the USA have seen the rationing of rice in supermarkets. What can governments do? Demand and supply diagrams can be used to analyse some of the possibilities.

1 Price controls

One possibility is the introduction of a maximum price ceiling below the equilibrium price – at P in Figure 14.11.This has been done in India for a number of years on a range of goods and several Far Eastern countries on petrol. In 2008 the Chinese government has frozen the price of certain essential goods. There are two main problems with the use of price ceilings. First, as described in the text, there is now excess demand at the enforced price level and no incentive for more to be produced so this may lead to greater food shortages.

Figure 14.11   Price ceiling

   Second, this type of price control is expensive and cannot be maintained in the long run. For example, it is estimated that the cost of the price ceiling on petrol in Malaysia is 10 per cent of government spending.

2 Rationing

In the face of food shortages, one possibility is that rationing will take place so that individuals will only be allowed a certain quantity of the product in question. This would be more equitable than a first-come, first-served basis for distribution or black market trading where the rich have more market power than the poor. The problem with food markets is that they are not free markets; there are trading blocs and trading rules which prevent an equitable distribution of food worldwide.

3 Subsidies

Farmers could be paid subsidies to increase their production of foodstuffs. These are shown in Figure 14.12.

Figure 14.12   Payment of subsidies

   The payment of a subsidy to a producer is like the opposite of a tax – it means that the costs of production are lower so that supply can be increased. The supply curve moves from S to S_1 and price falls. This overcomes the first problem with price controls – the lack of incentive to increase production. The use of demand and supply diagrams show how problems with the market mechanism can be addressed in theory. The problem is that we live in the real world and the solutions to the food crisis are more likely to be political rather than economic. For example, will the west turn away from the use of biofuels? Will trade policies be changed so that the worldwide distribution of food can be more equitable?

Elasticity of demand

It has been shown that as long as other factors affecting demand remain constant, a decrease in price would be expected to increase the quantity demanded by consumers. This knowledge is obviously of importance to business, in that it implies that sales will expand as the good becomes more price competitive. It does not, however, say anything about the degree to which sales might increase. As prices change, will demand change by a large or a small amount? At the end of the day, will the extra sales bring in more or less total revenue? In short, a measure is needed of the responsiveness of demand to price changes. In the same way the responsiveness of quantity demanded to other factors like income or other prices can also be measured. It is also important to be aware of the responsiveness of supply to changes in prices. All of these are measured by the concept of **elasticity**.

Price elasticity of demand

Figure 14.13 illustrates two different-shaped demand curves and shows the effect of a price increase from 40p to 60p in each case. On the left-hand diagram, the increase in price causes demand to fall from 25 to 20 units. Total revenue received by the producer (i.e. price multiplied by the number of units sold) changes from £10.00 (40p × 25 units) to £12.00 (60p × 20 units). As illustrated, the area A represents the gain in revenue as a result of the price change, while B shows the loss of revenue. In this case there is a clear net gain. The reason for this is that the significance of the price rise is greater than the fall in demand. Compare this with the right-hand diagram. The same price rise now causes total revenue to fall from £20.00 (40p × 50 units) to £6.00 (60p × 10 units). The loss of revenue, area B^1, is clearly greater than the gain in revenue, area A^1. There is a net loss of revenue. This is a situation where the decrease in demand is of greater significance than the increase in price.

The traditional way of measuring the responsiveness of demand to a change in price is via the concept of **price elasticity**, the formula being:

$$\text{Price elasticity of demand (Ep)} = \frac{\text{Percentage change in quantity demanded}}{\text{Percentage change in price}}$$

$$\text{Ep} = \frac{\% \text{ change QD}}{\% \text{ change P}}$$

The significance of this formula lies in whether the value of price elasticity is greater or less than 1. If it is greater, then the percentage change in quantity demanded is greater than the percentage change in price. Demand is referred to as being relatively **elastic**, or responsive to price changes. If, on the other hand, the percentage change in quantity demanded is less than the percentage change in price, then price elasticity will be less than 1. Demand is now referred to as being relatively **inelastic**, and demand is not very responsive to price changes.

The higher or lower the value of price elasticity, the greater or lesser the responsiveness of demand to the price change. Table 14.4 demonstrates the connection between price elasticity and total revenue. It will be observed that if price elasticity is greater than 1, then there is a negative relationship between price changes and total revenue. For example, an increase in price results in a decrease in total revenue. Whereas, if elasticity is less than 1, then there is a positive relationship.

Table 14.4 Elasticity and total revenue

Elasticity	Price change	Change in total revenue
Elastic	Upward	Downward
	Downward	Upward
Inelastic	Upward	Upward
	Downward	Downward

Calculating elasticity

From the information portrayed in Figure 14.13, in the left-hand diagram price rose from 40p to 60p and demand fell from 25 to 20 units; thus:

$$Ep = \frac{\% \text{ change QD}}{\% \text{ change P}} = \frac{5/25 \times 100}{20/40 \times 100} = \frac{20\%}{50\%} = 0.4$$

This shows that demand is inelastic. One problem with this measurement is that if you measured elasticity when price fell from 60p to 40p the answer would be different:

$$Ep = \frac{\% \text{ change in QD}}{\% \text{ change in P}} = \frac{5/20 \times 100}{20/60 \times 100} = \frac{25\%}{33.3\%} = 0.75$$

The reason for this variation is that the percentage change in each case is being measured from a different base. When price rises from 20p to 40p, this is a 50 per cent rise. Yet when it falls from 60p to 40p this is only a 33.3 per cent fall. The value of elasticity therefore varies. To avoid this ambiguity, elasticity is measured as the percentage change from the average value of price and quantity before and after the change, that is:

$$\% \text{ change} = \frac{\text{Change in value} \times 100}{\text{Average value}}$$

Figure 14.13 Responsiveness of demand to a price change

The value of elasticity for the price increase and decrease must now be identical:

$$Ep = \frac{\% \text{ change QD}}{\% \text{ change P}} = \frac{5/22.5 \times 100}{20/50 \times 100} = \frac{22.2\%}{40\%} = 0.55$$

The determinants of elasticity

There are a number of factors which determine how responsive quantity demanded is to price changes. First, the nature of the good and how it is viewed by consumers. A good which is a necessity will have a low value of elasticity, as an increase in price will not have a very big impact on the quantity consumed. Goods like cigarettes will have inelastic demand because they are habit forming. The tastes of consumers will be important: whether they view a television, for example, as a necessity or a luxury will determine the value of elasticity. Another factor is whether substitutes are available for the good or not. If there is no substitute for a particular good and the household wishes to continue to consume it, an increase in price will have little effect on the level of demand. Other factors include the importance of the good in the household's total expenditure. The smaller the proportion of the household's budget which is spent on a particular good, the smaller will be the effect on demand of any change in price.

Income elasticity of demand

Income elasticity of demand is a measure of the responsiveness of quantity demanded to changes in income. It can be negative in the case of inferior goods, where an increase in income leads to a fall in the demand for a good, or positive in the case of a normal good, where an increase in income leads to an increase in demand. There is also a difference between luxuries and necessities. Luxuries will have positive income elasticities with values over 1. This means that an increase in income will cause an increase in demand for that good and that a 1 per cent increase in income will cause a more than 1 per cent increase in demand. A necessity on the other hand will also have a positive income elasticity but its value will lie somewhere between 0 and 1, showing that an increase in income of 1 per cent causes an increase in demand by less than 1 per cent.

Income elasticity is calculated in a similar way to price elasticity except that it is income which is changing rather than the price of the good:

$$\text{Income elasticity} = \frac{\% \text{ change in quantity demanded}}{\% \text{ change in income}}$$

The effect of changes in income on the overall level of expenditure depends upon the type of the good being considered, as Table 14.5 shows.

Table 14.5 Income elasticity and total expenditure

Type of good	Income elasticity	Change in total expenditure brought about by an increase in income of 1%
Inferior	Negative	Downward
Normal	Positive	Upward
Luxury	Positive and above 1	Upward by more than 1%
Necessity	Positive between 0 and 1	Upward by less than 1%

Cross-price elasticity of demand

Cross-price elasticity of demand is a measure of how the demand for one good is affected by changes in the prices of other goods. It is calculated with the formula:

$$\frac{\text{Cross-price}}{\text{elasticity}} = \frac{\text{\% change in quantity demanded of good X}}{\text{\% change in the price of good Y}}$$

Like income elasticity it can be positive or negative depending this time upon the nature of the relationship between the goods. If the goods are substitutes for one another, as the price of Y goes up, the quantity demanded of X will also rise, as consumers substitute the relatively cheaper good (e.g. margarine for butter). Therefore cross-price elasticity will be positive. If the goods are complements, as the price of Y rises the demand for X will fall and cross-price elasticity will be a negative value. The size will depend upon how closely the goods are related, either as substitutes or complements.

Elasticity of supply

The concept of elasticity can be applied to supply as well as demand, and is a measurement of how responsive quantity supplied is to changes in the price of a good. Figure 14.14 illustrates two differently shaped supply curves and the effect of the same price change in each case.

Elasticity of supply is measured with the following formula:

$$\text{Elasticity of supply} = \frac{\text{\% change in quantity supplied}}{\text{\% change in price}}$$

The higher the numerical value, the more responsive is supply to changes in price.

The main determinants of the elasticity of supply for a good are the nature of the production process and the time-scale in question. It may well be easier to increase the supply of manufactured goods than agricultural goods, given the nature of the production processes involved. Even agricultural goods can be increased in supply, given time to replant stock, so supply is more responsive to price changes in the longer time period.

Figure 14.14 Responsiveness of supply to a price change

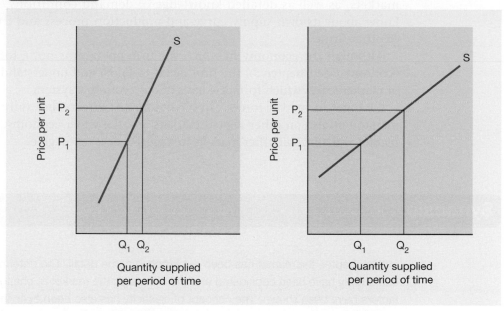

The importance of the market to business

All firms operate in markets, whether they are localised, national or international. Although firms might be able to influence the market conditions that face them, they need a knowledge of their own markets and how markets fit together in the market economy. Firms often have a range of products and they need to be aware of the differing conditions in each of their markets. They need a knowledge of the shape and position of the demand curve they face, including knowledge of the following aspects:

- The nature of the good they produce.
- The way in which it is viewed by consumers.
- The factors which affect the demand for their good.
- Any changes likely in the future which will affect the market.
- Any likely government intervention in the market.

Only through this information can the firm hope to retain markets, expand existing markets and move into new ones.

An understanding is also needed of the concept of elasticity of demand. Knowing how the demand for its product responds to changes in its price will help the firm in its pricing policy. Measures of income elasticity help the firm in forecasting the effects of changes in income on the demand for its products. Economic growth will affect markets with high income elasticities much more than markets with low income elasticities. This knowledge will also help the firm in developing its marketing strategy. For example, goods with low income elasticities could be marketed as 'economical', thus hopefully increasing the market share.

If the firm wishes to be successful in existing markets and to expand into new markets, as well as detailed knowledge of demand conditions, it also needs to know about its own supply curve and production process and the supply curves of other firms.

Although the economy in which the firm operates is not a totally free market economy (see Chapter 5), the firm needs to know and understand the importance of market forces which form the basis of our economic system.

Changes in market forces can have dramatic effects, not only on the affected market but also on other related markets and the wider economy. Changes in one market will affect all other markets to a greater or lesser degree.

Synopsis

In this chapter, the market has been examined in some detail. The determinants of demand and supply have been considered and the effects on the market of changes in any of these factors have been shown. The concept of elasticity has also been examined and calculated and the importance of all these issues to business has been demonstrated.

Summary of key points

- In a free market both the quantity being traded and the price of a product are determined by the forces of demand and supply.

- The demand for a good or service depends upon a number of factors, including price, the price of other goods, the income of consumers, tastes and so on.

- The supply of a good or service also depends upon a range of influences, including price, the costs of production, technology and the number of suppliers.

- Changes in demand and supply cause changes in the price of the product and the quantity being traded.

- Where demand and supply are equal, the market is said to be in equilibrium.

- Where this occurs, equilibrium price and quantity result.

- Intervention in the market mechanism can take the form of minimum or maximum prices, taxation or subsidy.

- Elasticity is a measure of the responsiveness of demand or supply to various factors, including price, income and the price of other goods.

- It is important for businesses to be aware of the demand and supply characteristics of the good or service they are producing.

case study   The international food crisis

2008 saw rapidly increasing food prices worldwide. The price of wheat rose 130 per cent in the year up to March 2008 and has risen threefold since 2000. The price of wheat jumped by 25 per cent in one day in February 2008. The cost of 1 tonne of Thai rice rose by 30 per cent in April 2008. The price rises are not confined to cereals; dairy and meat prices are also rising as feed costs of cattle rise. These price rises have important implications for many people – especially the poor, who are being priced out of the market. Demand and supply diagrams can be used to analyse the reasons for the price rises. They can also be used to consider the remedies. Reasons put forward are as follows.

1 Growing demand for food

It is estimated that the world's richest 20 per cent consumes 16 times more food than the world's poorest 20 per cent. The growing affluence of countries like India and China has led to a massive increase in the demand for foodstuffs. Added to this is the growth in the world population, estimated to rise from 6.6 billion in 2008 to 9.2 billion in 2050. These factors push the demand for food upwards.

The supply of foodstuffs is fairly inelastic (as it takes time to increase supply) so the supply curve in Figure 14.15 is shown as very steep (S). Increases in demand (D_1, D_2, D_3 etc.) push price upwards, the inelastic nature of supply makes this happen quicker.

2 Global warming

Many countries are experiencing adverse weather conditions which have contributed to a fall in the supply of many agricultural products. In Canada (the second largest wheat exporter in the world) drought is expected to reduce the harvest by a quarter in 2008. Australia (third largest producer) has been experiencing a drought for the last 5 years which has led to a fall in annual production of 25 million tonnes of grain in 2000 to 9.8 million in 2006.

Figure 14.16 demonstrates this effect. With demand constant, the falls in supply lead to increases in price. Of course, given the above discussion, demand is not constant and so the effects are intensified.

3 Palm oil and biofuel

The demand for palm oil is rising for two main reasons: because consumers are demanding more non hydrogenated oil in foodstuffs; and, second, because palm oil can be used in biofuel and the demand for that is increasing. It is impossible for farmers to increase the production of palm oil as drought and flooding in the countries that produce palm oil have reduced the crop and it takes eight years for a palm oil tree to mature before supply can be increased. Whether supply should be increased at all is in dispute as the use of land for the production of palm oil reduces the amount of food that can be

Figure 14.15   Increased demand for food

Figure 14.16   The effect of global warming

grown and Greenpeace argue that the carbon dioxide released by the deforestation that has taken place to plant palm oil trees is more than the savings in CO_2 from the use of biofuels. Land used for biofuel production is not being used for food production. It is estimated that the USA now devotes a third of its output of maize to car fuel. Figure 14.16 shows the impact of this on food prices.

All of these factors and more are impacting on the price of food at the same time, so the combined effect is even bigger and, at the time of writing, there is no indication of these problems abating. In the normal operation of the market mechanism, increasing prices indicate to the producers that resources should be switched to produce more in order to meet the excess demand. Given the factors

mentioned above, this is not likely to happen. This means that action needs to be taken by governments or supra-national organisations. Possible remedies can also be analysed using demand and supply diagrams, and this has been done in the second mini case study in this chapter.

Case study questions

1 What has happened in the market for food since the writing of this case study? Use demand and supply diagrams to analyse this.

2 A solution used by some grain exporters has been to restrict the export of grain in order to feed their own populations. How could you show this using a demand and supply diagram?

 web link Information is available from *www.wfp.org* and *www.fao.org*

Review and discussion questions

1 Show the effects on the market for houses of the following:
   (a) a fall in income levels;
   (b) a rise in the rate of interest;
   (c) the lack of a 'feel good factor' in the economy.

2 Considering the market for CDs, show the effects of the following changes using demand and supply diagrams:
   (a) an increase in the number of people owning CD players;
   (b) a fall in the cost of producing CDs; and
   (c) a movement away from releasing music on LP and towards releasing music on CD.

3 Have the changes you predicted in your answers to questions 1 and 2 actually happened in the real world? If not, why not?

Assignments

1 You are a journalist on a local newspaper and have been asked to write an article on the current state of the housing market in your locality. You should identify factors which influence house prices in general and more specifically in your region. The following information from the Nationwide house price index may help (*www.nationwide.co.uk/hpi*).

Region	Average house prices, quarter 1, 2008	% change since quarter 4, 2007
East Anglia	£179 868	–2
East Midlands	£153 066	–1.3
London	£296 772	–2.3
North	£132 439	–0.6
North West	£154 124	–3.1
South East	£211 119	–1.6
South West	£196 711	–3.1
Scotland	£149 834	–0.9
Wales	£151 499	–2.2
West Midlands	£160 715	–2.5
Yorkshire and Humberside	£151 764	–1.9
UK	£179 363	–2.5

2 You work in the marketing department of a company that produces light bulbs. The company is considering increasing the price of its light bulbs by 20 per cent. At present a 100 watt light bulb costs 80p. The only information that is available is a study carried out in the previous year on the sensitivity of sales to price, the results of which are shown opposite:

Price	Sales (million)
80p	5800
100p	4000

Write a report for your manager on the likely effects of the proposed price increase, explaining the concept of elasticity of demand and the factors which are likely to affect it for this product.

Notes and references

1 In such cases the demand curve would be upward sloping, indicating that as price rises demand rises. Other examples include 'snob goods', which are consumed because of their price.

2 In the markets described in this chapter there is an automatic tendency for the market to move back towards equilibrium once it is disturbed. However, it is possible for the demand and supply curves to be so shaped that once the market is disturbed it tends to move away from equilibrium rather than towards it. This is called the cobweb model. The interested reader should look at R. Lipsey, *An Introduction to Positive Economics*, Weidenfeld & Nicolson, 1989.

Further reading

Begg, D., Fischer, S. and Dornbusch, R., *Economics*, 7th edition, McGraw-Hill, 2003.

Griffiths, A. and Wall, S., *Applied Economics: An Introductory Course*, 10th edition, Financial Times Prentice Hall, 2004.

Lipsey, R. and Chrystal, A., *Economics*, 10th edition, Oxford University Press, 2004.

Worthington, I., Britton, C., and Rees, A., *Economics for Business: Blending Theory and Practice*, 2nd edition, Financial Times/Prentice Hall, 2005.

Web links and further questions are available on the website at:

www.pearsoned.co.uk/worthington

15 Market structure

Chris Britton

All businesses operate in a market which will be peculiar to that industry. Each market will have its own particular characteristics which depend upon many factors, and although it is not possible to have a model which describes every market, there are some economic models which provide some guidance to the kind of characteristics and behaviour that will be found in individual markets.

Learning outcomes

Having read this chapter you should be able to:

- explain the market structures of perfect competition, monopoly, oligopoly and monopolistic competition and indicate their implications for the behaviour of firms

- demonstrate the applicability of these predictions to the real world

- apply Porter's five-forces model to an analysis of the structure of industries

- understand the measurement of competition by concentration ratios

- survey differences in industrial concentration between industries, countries and over time

- indicate what determines market structure and what determines the behaviour of firms

Key terms

Abnormal profits
Average costs of production
Barriers to entry
Barriers to exit
Cartel
Collusion
Concentration ratio
Contestable market
Differentiation
Economies of scale
Five-forces model
Homogeneous products
Interdependence

Market structure
Minimum efficient scale of production (MES)
Monopolistic competition
Monopoly
Monopsony
Natural monopoly
Non-price competition
Normal profits
Oligopoly
Perfect competition
Perfect knowledge
Perfect mobility

Price competition
Price discrimination
Price leadership
Price maker
Price taker
Price war
Sticky prices
Structure–conduct–performance model (S–C–P)
Transaction cost economics

Introduction

In economics the behaviour and the performance of firms in an industry are thought to depend upon some basic structural characteristics. This view is exemplified by the **structure–conduct–performance model**, where structure determines conduct, which in turn determines performance. The basic elements included under these headings are given in Table 15.1.

The structure–conduct–performance model provides a good framework for classifying and analysing an industry. A simple example of the process can be seen in the soap powder industry. Here the market is dominated by two large producers, Unilever and Procter & Gamble. This apparent lack of competition gives rise to certain behavioural characteristics like the massive amount of advertising, the existence of many brand names and fairly uniform prices. This process will be considered in more detail later in the chapter, but the example serves to indicate the relationship between the structure of the market and the behaviour and ultimately the performance of firms in an industry.

> **For more information on these companies see *www.unilever.com* and *www.procterandgamble.com***

'**Market structure**' refers to the amount of competition that exists in a market between producers. The degree of competition can be thought of as lying along a continuum with very competitive markets at one end and markets in which no competition exists at all at the other end. This chapter looks at the two extremes (perfect competition and monopoly), and the market structures which exist between. The theory predicts the effects of market structure on behaviour and performance in those markets. However, as with the working of the market mechanism, the real world is often different from the theory and therefore this chapter will look at real markets and the relevance of the theory to the real world. The structure–conduct–performance model is open to criticism[1] since it says little about what determines structure in the first place. It also tends to view the firm as passive in the face of market structure, accepting the implications for conduct and performance, rather than actively trying to change and mould market structure. Michael Porter's 'five-forces model'[2] will be used to broaden out the analysis.

Table 15.1 Structure–conduct–performance model

Structural factors
- Amount of actual competition: (a) seller concentration; and (b) buyer concentration.
- Existence of potential competition.
- Cost conditions.
- Demand conditions.
- Existence of barriers to entry.

Conduct factors
- Pricing policy.
- Amount of advertising.
- Merger behaviour.
- Product differentiation.

Performance factors
- Profitability.
- Technological innovation.

Market structure is important not only because of the implications it has for conduct and performance but also because it has an impact upon the strategic possibilities which face the organisation, its ability to act strategically and the likely effects of such strategic behaviour (*see* Chapter 18).

In addition, this chapter will examine how the level of competition is measured in a market, how the level of competition varies between industries and countries, and how and why this has changed over time.

Market structures – in theory and practice

As mentioned above, market structures can be thought of as lying along a continuum with perfect competition at one end and monopoly at the other (*see* Figure 15.1). Both of these market structures are unrealistic representations of the real world, but are useful as benchmarks in assessing the degree of competition in a market. Between these two extremes lie other market structures, which are more realistic. Two will be described, oligopoly and monopolistic competition.

Perfect competition

This is the most competitive market structure. A number of conditions need to be fulfilled before **perfect competition** is said to exist. These conditions are as follows:

1 There are so many buyers and sellers in the market that no *one* of them can influence price through its activities.
2 The good being sold in the market is **homogeneous** (i.e. all units of the good are identical).
3 **Perfect knowledge** exists in the market. This means that producers have perfect knowledge of prices and costs of other producers and that consumers know the prices charged by all firms.
4 There exists **perfect mobility** of both the factors of production and consumers. This means that people, machines and land can be used for any purpose, and that consumers are free to purchase the good from any of the producers.
5 There are no **barriers to entry or exit** in the industry. There is nothing to prevent a new firm setting up production in the industry.

Figure 15.1   Market structures

Naturally, this is a highly theoretical model and these conditions are unlikely to be all met in reality, but if they did, and the theory is followed through, the conclusion is that there will only be one price in the market for the good being sold. For example, if one firm is charging a higher price for the good than other firms, everyone in the market will know (because of perfect knowledge), and because the good is homogeneous and because of perfect mobility on the part of consumers, consumers will simply purchase the good from another firm. The firm that was charging a higher price will be forced to reduce the price of the good in order to sell it, or face mounting stocks of the good. There is therefore only one price for the good and this will be determined by *market* demand and supply – that is, total demand and total supply, no one consumer or producer having enough market power to influence the price. Accordingly, the firm is said to be a **price taker**.

Price determination in perfect competition

Firms need to cover costs of production and to earn a certain level of profits in order to stay in business. This minimum level of profits is called **normal profit**, and profits over and above this level are called **abnormal profits**. If the firm is trying to maximise its profits it will decide what level of output to produce by setting the cost of producing the last unit of the good equal to the revenue gained from selling the last unit: in economic terminology, where marginal cost equals marginal revenue. Included in cost would be elements of wages, rent, rates, interest, raw materials *and* normal profits. If these costs are not being covered the firm will be making a loss.

As there is only one price in perfect competition, the revenue derived from selling the last unit must be equal to its price. Therefore, the price of the good depends on the level of marginal cost.

In the short run, individual firms can earn abnormal profits, but these are not sustainable in the longer term. If one firm is earning abnormal profits, given the assumption of perfect knowledge, everyone will know and, since freedom of entry exists, other firms will enter the market in order to earn abnormal profits. This means that there is an increase in market supply and price will fall back to a level where abnormal profits have been competed away. Similarly when losses are being made, freedom of exit means that supply will be reduced and price will rise again until normal profits have been regained.

The implications of perfect competition for market behaviour and performance are summarised in Table 15.2. Perfect competition involves very restrictive assumptions,

Table 15.2 Implications of perfect competition for conduct and performance of firms in an industry

Extent of market power	The firm has no market power at all.
Price	There will only be one price for the good. The firm will be a '**price taker**'.
Advertising	There will be no advertising, as all units of the good are the same and everyone knows this.
Profitability	There can be no abnormal profits, except possibly in the very short run if a producer reduces price and captures a larger share of the market.

which will rarely be fulfilled in the real world. The usefulness of the model lies in its role as an *ideal market* in which competition is at a maximum, rather than in its applicability to the real world.

An example of perfect competition?

The nearest example to perfect competition is probably the fruit and vegetable market in the centre of a large town. The goods will be fairly homogeneous, with perhaps slight variation in the quality. Knowledge will be almost perfect with respect to prices charged, as consumers could quickly walk around the market and ascertain the price of tomatoes, for example. Mobility of consumers is also high because the sellers are located in the same place. Thus the conditions for perfect competition nearly hold. The prediction is that there will be only one price for a particular good. Again this prediction is nearly fulfilled; the price of tomatoes tends to be rather similar across such a market, and when one trader reduces the price towards the end of the day, others tend to follow suit. Another market which is said to be close to perfect competition is the stock exchange, although with the increasing use of computers this is less likely to be true in the future.

Monopoly

Monopoly lies at the opposite end of the spectrum to competition. In its purest form a monopolistic market is one in which there is no competition at all; there is a single producer supplying the whole market. The monopolist has considerable market power and can determine price or quantity sold, but not both because he or she cannot control demand. The power of the monopolist depends on the availability of substitutes, and on the existence and height of barriers to entry. If there are no close substitutes for the good being produced, or if there are high barriers to entry, the power of the monopolist will be high and abnormal profits can be earned in the long run.

A monopolist could also be a group of producers acting together to control supply to the market: for example, a **cartel** such as OPEC (Organisation of Petroleum Exporting Countries).

For information on OPEC see *www.opec.org*

In monopolistic markets the producer might be able to charge different prices for the same good: for example, on an aeroplane it is quite likely that there will be passengers sitting in the same class of seat having paid very different prices, depending upon where and when the tickets were bought. Essentially they are paying different prices for the same service, and the producer is said to be exercising **price discrimination**. Why is this possible? There are certain conditions that must hold for this type of price discrimination to occur. First, the market must be monopolistic and the producer must be able to control supply. Second, there must be groups of consumers with different demand conditions. For example, the demand for train travel by the commuter who works in London will be more inelastic than the demand of a student going to London for the day, who could use alternative forms of transport or even not go. This means that the willingness to pay among consumers will vary. The final condition necessary is that it must be possible to separate these groups in some way. For example, telephone companies are able to separate markets by time so that it is cheaper to phone after a certain time; British Rail used to separate groups by age for certain of its railcards.

The monopolist will maximise its profits by charging different prices in different markets. Price discrimination is often thought of as a bad thing as the monopolist is exploiting the consumer by charging different prices for the same good. But there are some advantages, in that it makes for better use of resources if cheap airline tickets are offered to fill an aeroplane which would otherwise have flown half-full. It can also lead to a more equitable solution in that higher-income users pay a higher price than lower-income users. The main problems with the notion of price discrimination is not that it is always a bad thing, but that it is the monopolist who has the power to decide who is charged what price.

Again the effects of monopoly on the behaviour and performance of the firm can be predicted (*see* Table 15.3). Like perfect competition, this is a highly theoretical model and is mainly used as a comparison with perfect competition to show the effects of the lack of competition.

Table 15.3 Implications of monopoly for conduct and performance of firms in an industry

Extent of market power	The firm has absolute market power.
Price	There will only be one price for the good, except in the case of price discrimination. The firm is a '**price maker**'.
Advertising	There will be no need for advertising, as there is only one firm producing the good.
Profitability	Abnormal profits can exist in the long run as there is no competition which might erode them away.

A comparison of perfect competition and monopoly

● It would be expected that price would be higher under monopoly than under perfect competition because of the absence of competition in the monopolistic market. It is argued, for example, that the large telephone companies (including BT) are overcharging the consumer. The benefits of the considerable technological advances that have been made in this area have not been passed on fully to the consumer. This can only be sustained by virtue of the monopolistic power of the companies. *But*, to counter this it could be argued that a monopolist is in a better position to reap the benefits of economies of scale, therefore it is possible that price might be lower.

● There might be less choice under monopoly since firms do not have to continually update their products in order to stay in business. *But*, it is also possible to think of examples where monopolies provide greater choice (e.g. in the case of radio stations), where under perfect competition all radio stations would cater for the biggest market, which would be for pop music. A monopolist, however, would be able to cover all tastes with a variety of stations.

● There is less incentive to innovate under monopoly, since the monopolist is subject to less competition. *But*, equally, a monopolist might have more incentive to innovate as it can reap the benefits in terms of higher profits. It may also have more resources to devote to innovation.

As can be seen there is not a clear set of arguments that imply that perfect competition is better than monopoly, and, as will be seen in Chapter 17, this is taken into account in UK competition policy.

An example of monopoly?

Although it is easy to think of examples of industries where the dominant firm has a great deal of monopoly power, there is no such thing as a pure monopoly, as substitutes exist for most goods. For example, British Rail used to have monopoly power in the market for rail travel, but there are many alternative forms of travel. This point highlights the difficulties of defining markets and industries discussed in Chapter 10. The nearest examples of monopolies are the old public utilities, like gas, electricity, water and so on, many of which have been privatised.

The government, in determining whether monopoly power exists in a market, has a working definition of what constitutes a monopoly. It is when 25 per cent of the market is accounted for by one firm or firms acting together. This would form grounds for investigation by the Competition Commission. The process of UK competition policy is discussed in Chapter 17 in more detail. The sources of monopoly power are the existence of barriers to entry and exit and the availability of substitutes (these will be discussed later in this chapter).

For information on the the operation of the Competition Commission see
www.competition-commission.org.uk

Oligopoly

In both perfect competition and monopoly firms make independent decisions. In the case of monopoly there are no other firms in the industry to consider; in the case of perfect competition the firm has no power to affect the market at all. So for different reasons they act as though they have no rivals. This is not true in the case of oligopoly. **Oligopoly** is where a small number of producers supply a market in which the product is differentiated in some way. The characteristics of oligopoly are:

● A great deal of **interdependence** between the firms; each firm has to consider the likely actions of other firms when making its decisions.
● A lack of **price competition** in the market; firms are reluctant to increase their prices in case their competitors do not and they might lose market share. Firms are also reluctant to reduce their prices, in case other firms do the same and a price war results which reduces prices but leaves market share unchanged and so everyone is left worse off.[3]
● The lack of price competition means that different forms of **non-price competition** take place, such as branding or advertising. Oligopolists will sell their products not by reducing the price but through heavy advertising, brand names or special offers. The Premier points scheme was a good example of such non-price competition. The purchase of petrol from certain outlets gave the customer

points which were accumulated on their Premier points card and then redeemed for money-off vouchers to be spent at Argos. Table 15.4 shows the implications of oligopoly for conduct and performance of firms in an industry.

The way in which price is determined in an oligopolistic market is through either **price leadership** or some sort of **collusion**. Price leadership is where one firm takes the lead in setting prices and the others follow suit. The price leader is not necessarily the firm with the lowest cost, as it depends upon the power of the firm. So price could be set at a higher level than in a competitive market. Collusion is an explicit or implicit agreement between firms on price, which serves to reduce the amount of competition between firms. Collusion is illegal in most countries as it is seen as a form of restrictive practice, but this does not mean that collusion does not take place. A cartel is a form of collusion where firms come together to exercise joint market power. Cartels are now illegal in most countries, but the most famous of all is OPEC which has had a dramatic effect on the oil industry over the last 30 years. Collusive agreements, as well as possibly being harmful to the consumer, tend to be unstable as there is great temptation on the part of individual firms/countries to cheat. What is clear in the case of oligopoly is that once price is set there is a reluctance to change it. Therefore price competition is replaced by non-price competition of the sort mentioned above.

Table 15.4 Implications of oligopoly for conduct and performance of firms in an industry

Extent of market power	A great deal of market power.
Price	A stable price level. Prices set by price leadership or collusion.
Advertising	Much advertising and branding. Non-price competition is common.
Profitability	Abnormal profits can exist, their extent depends on the strength of competitors.

The most often quoted examples of oligopoly are the market for tobacco and the market for soap powder. Both of these markets are dominated by a very small number of producers and both exhibit the predicted characteristics. There is little price competition and price is fairly uniform in both markets. There is a high degree of non-price competition in both markets – high advertising, strong brand names and images, and the use of special offers or gifts at times in order to sell the goods.

Compared with monopoly and perfect competition, oligopoly is a much more realistic market structure, with many markets exhibiting the characteristics stated above. Table 15.5 gives a few examples.

Table 15.5 The top firms' share of the market in the UK (percentages)

Industry	Percentages
Cigarettes[a]	91*
Brewing[b]	89**
Sugar and artificial sweeteners[c]	79*
Ice cream[c]	68*
Jeans[c]	13*

Note: * Top three firms in the industry; ** Top five firms.
Source: [a] Keynote Report; 2007; [b] Keynote Report, 2008; [c] Mintel Report, 2008.

It is interesting to note that the market shares of the top firms in all of these industries have decreased since the publication of the last edition of this text. For three of these products, this has mainly been down to an increase in the market's share of own-brand products. For sugar there has been an increase of 20 per cent in the market's share of own brands between 2002 and 2006 and the corresponding figures are 22 per cent for jeans and 3 per cent for ice creams. More will be said about this later in the chapter.

For information and reports on specific industries see *www.mintel.co.uk* and *www.keynote.co.uk*

Monopolistic competition

A market structure of monopolistic competition exists when all of the conditions for perfect competition are met except for the existence of a homogeneous good, so that each firm has a monopoly over its own good but there is a great deal of competition in the market from other suppliers producing very similar products. In **monopolistic competition** the good is slightly **differentiated** in some way, either by advertising and branding or by local production. There does not have to be a technical difference between the two goods, which could be identical in composition, but there must be an 'economic difference' – that is, a difference in the way the goods are perceived by consumers. There is also some degree of consumer loyalty, so that if one firm reduces price, consumers might not necessarily move to that firm if they believe that the difference between the brands justifies the higher price. Abnormal profits can exist in the short run but cannot persist since new firms are free to enter the industry and compete away abnormal profit (*see* Table 15.6).

Table 15.6 Implications of monopolistic competition for conduct and performance of firms in an industry

Extent of market power	The firm has little market power.
Price	There will be small differences in price.
Advertising	There will be heavy advertising and branding.
Profitability	Small abnormal profits can exist in the short run but will be competed away in the longer run.

An example of monopolistic competition?

There are many examples of this type of industry: for example, the paint industry where ICI is the only producer of Dulux but there are many other types of paint on the market.

How accurate is the theory?

The implications of the theory of market structures for the behaviour and performance of firms are summarised in Table 15.7.

Table 15.7 Implications of theory for behaviour of firms

	Market power	*Price*	*Advertising*	*Profitability*
Perfect competition	None	One price	None	Only normal profits
Monopoly	Absolute	Price discrimination possible	None	Abnormal profits
Oligopoly	High	One price	High	Abnormal profits
Monopolistic competition	Little	Small differences in price	High	Only normal profits in long run

As argued above, both perfect competition and pure monopoly tend to be based on assumptions that are somewhat unrealistic and should be regarded as 'ideal types' of market structure, in the sense that they establish the boundaries within which true markets exist and operate, and against which they can be analysed. In contrast, oligopoly and monopolistic competition are much nearer to the types of market structure which can be found in the real world, and economic theory does appear to explain and predict behaviour in these markets to a certain extent. In oligopolistic markets, for example, price tends to be **sticky** and much of the competition between firms occurs in non-price ways, particularly branding, advertising and sales promotion (*see* Table 15.8). Occasionally, however, **price wars** do occur – as in the petrol market in the 1980s and more recently between the four biggest supermarkets.

Table 15.8 shows the top advertisers in the United Kingdom ranked for 2006; their ranks in 1994 are also given. The names in the list are familiar and largely expected from the predictions: for example, Procter & Gamble is one of the two companies which together with Unilever account for around 90 per cent of the market for washing powder. A less familiar name is Reckitt Benckiser which subsequently acquired Boots in 2007.

Table 15.8 Top advertisers in the UK, 2006

Rank			
2006	*1994*	*Advertiser*	*Total adspend (£000)*
1	1	Procter & Gamble	181 023
2	3	Unilever	177 167
3	–	Central Office of Information Communication	140 758
4	36	L'Oréal Golden	120 121
5	48	British Sky Broadcasting	118 306
6	–	DFS Furniture	107 286
7	2	British Telecom	92 241
8	–	Orange	88 982
9	32	Reckitt Benckiser	83 790
10	19	Tesco	76 101

Source: Adapted from *Advertising Statistics Yearbook*, 1995 and 2007, Advertising Association, WARC.

For information on advertising see *www.adassoc.org.uk*

It is much more difficult to judge how accurate the behavioural implications are. Lack of data is one problem, as is the fact that only one structural characteristic has been considered here – the level of competition between producers. The other structural factors listed in Table 15.1 will also have an effect, like the level of demand, the degree of competition between the buyers and the degree of potential competition. Profitability, price and advertising, for instance, will be affected by the level of demand in the market.

Porter's five-forces model

Porter's model[4] says that the structure of an industry and the ability of firms in that industry to act strategically depend upon the relative strengths of five forces: current competition, potential competition, the threat of substitute products, the power of buyers and the power of suppliers. Each of these five forces will be examined in turn. The case study at the end of this chapter uses this model to analyse the airline industry.

Current competition

Current competition has already been considered under the heading of market structure but the important point to remember is that by acting strategically firms can change the structure of the industry. Firms in a highly competitive market might be unhappy with the lack of power they have over various factors like pricing and may through their strategic actions try to change the situation. If they are successful there will be a change in the level of current competition and therefore in market structure.

Potential competition (or threat of new entry)

It has been shown that market structure or current competition affects the behaviour of firms in an industry. However, looking at the number of firms in an industry does not provide the whole picture. It is possible that firms in an oligopolistic market might act in a way consistent with perfect competition because of the threat of potential competition. This threat can affect the behaviour of firms even if it does not happen. The degree of potential competition depends upon the existence and height of barriers to entry and exit.

Barriers to entry

Barriers to entry are any barriers which prevent or inhibit the entry of firms into the industry. There are several sources of barriers to entry.

Some industries are what are called **natural monopolies** in that the production process is such that competition would be wasteful. The old public utilities are good examples of these, as it would be very wasteful for there to be two national grid systems in the electricity industry.

Some production processes are subject to **economies of scale**. As firms grow in size, or as the scale of production increases, certain economies occur which serve to reduce the **average cost of production**. The scale of production can be increased in many ways, for example by increasing the capacity of the existing plant, by increasing the number of plants or by increasing the product range. Figure 15.2 shows how the average *cost* of production changes as the *scale* of production changes.

The downward-sloping part of the curve shows falling average cost or economies of scale. The upward-sloping part shows rising average cost or diseconomies of scale. Economies of scale reduce average cost and therefore benefit the producer and also the consumer if they are passed on in lower prices.

The sources of economies of scale are usually classified under three headings: technical; marketing; and financial.

Technical economies come from increased specialisation and indivisibilities. The larger the scale of production the more the production process can be broken down into its component parts and the greater the gain from specialisation. There are certain indivisibilities involved in production, which only large firms can benefit from. For example, a small firm cannot have half a production line as that is meaningless, but might not be big enough to use a whole production line. Another type of indivisibility is involved in the notion of fixed costs. Fixed costs like the cost of rates or the fees of an accountant, for example, remain the same irrespective of the level of production. Therefore the greater the level of production, the lower will be the average cost of items as it is being spread over a larger output.

Marketing economies come from spreading marketing costs over a larger output, so that average costs will be lower. The company can also take advantage of bulk buying, and will probably have a specialised department devoted to marketing.

Financial economies come from the fact that larger companies find it easier and often cheaper to borrow capital.

Added to these is *risk diversification* which is possible with larger companies as they may well have interests in other industries. All of these economies of scale give rise to falling average cost and therefore explain the downward-sloping part of the cost curve in Figure 15.2. Economies of scale are a very effective barrier to entry. If the incumbent firm in an industry has lower average cost as a result of economies of scale, it will be hard for a newcomer to compete effectively at a smaller scale of production. Gas, electricity and water are examples of this. The production processes of these goods are subject to economies of scale and it is therefore

Figure 15.2   A firm's average cost curve

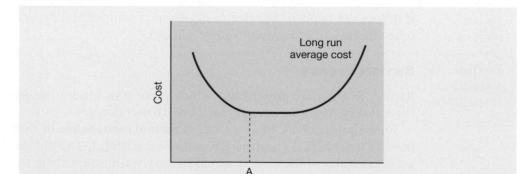

difficult for others to come into the market in competition with established firms. This is why such industries are called 'natural monopolies'.

Barriers to entry can be legal ones, as in the case of patents and franchises which serve to restrict competition and prevent new firms from entering an industry. Advertising and branding can also be barriers, in that industries where brand names are well established are difficult to enter without massive expenditure on advertising. Some industries require a high initial capital investment to enter, for example, dry cleaning, where the machinery is very expensive. Switching costs can also be regarded as a barrier to entry. If the consumer has to bear a cost in switching from one good to another that might be enough to deter the consumer from doing so and therefore serve as a barrier to entry. The recent practice of the building societies and banks of offering low fixed-rate mortgages with penalties for early withdrawal can be seen as an example of the introduction of switching costs into the market.

A **contestable market**[5] is one in which there are no barriers to entry or exit. This means that all firms (even potential entrants) have access to the same technology and there are therefore no cost barriers to entry. It also means that there are no sunk or unrecoverable costs which would prevent a firm leaving the industry. It follows that it is possible to ensure that firms behave in a competitive way, even if the market structure they operate in is imperfectly competitive, by ensuring that the market is contestable. What is regulating market behaviour then is not *actual* competition but *potential* competition.

mini case   Open Skies and Contestability

The 'Open Skies' agreement between the USA and the EU signed in 2007 and introduced in 2008 is a policy designed to make markets more contestable. It eases restrictions on air travel between the US and the EU so that any airline can fly to US destinations and not necessarily from its home nation, as was previously the case. British Airways can now fly from Paris to New York, whereas it could only fly from London Heathrow to New York. Similarly any US airline can do the same for European destinations.

This policy is not designed to break up existing companies or to introduce more competition into the market directly. It makes the market more contestable – it opens the market up for the possibility of competition. The agreement has led to structural changes in the market (see the case study at the end of this chapter for more details of the air industry). For example, as a direct result of this deal:

- British Airways has launched a new airline called OpenSkies which flies between Paris and New York.

- Virgin Atlantic has increased the number of flights from London to New York.
- Continental and Delta have started flying from London Heathrow to New York.

Theory predicts that more competition will lead to lower prices. Unfortunately this agreement has come into force at a time of rapidly rising oil prices so this is unlikely to happen – Virgin Atlantic has said that prices cannot be any lower. It is also argued by EU airlines that the agreement is unbalanced. US airlines can fly between EU destinations (from Paris to London for example) but EU airlines cannot do the same within the USA. In addition to this, US carriers are allowed to buy up their EU rivals but foreign ownership of US airlines is not allowed. The agreement is being introduced in stages and US markets should be completely open to competition by 2010; whether this happens or not will have to be seen.

Barriers to exit

Exit barriers are those which prevent or deter exit from an industry; they are mainly related to the cost of leaving the industry. The cost of exit depends upon how industry-specific the assets of the firm are. If we take physical assets as an example, a printing press is highly specific to the printing industry and could not be used for anything other than printing. There will be a second-hand market for printing presses but it would probably have to be sold at a loss, therefore incurring a high cost. A van, however, would be different, as it is still a physical asset but one that would not be specific to a particular industry, therefore the loss involved in selling would be less. Generally speaking, the more industry-specific an asset is the lower will be the second-hand value and the higher the cost of exit. An intangible asset like knowledge of the market or expenditure on research and development cannot be resold and must be left in the market, and therefore is a sunk cost – a non-recoverable cost.

Barriers to entry and exit can be 'innocent' or can be deliberately erected. Economies of scale can be regarded as innocent barriers to entry since they are inherent in the production process. Advertising and branding can be thought of as deliberately erected barriers to entry since they increase the expense of any firm entering the market. Similarly, the introduction of penalty clauses on mortgages is a deliberately erected barrier since it incurs switching costs for the consumer.

Where innocent barriers to entry or exit are low, potential competition will be high and firms within such a market are faced with the choice of accepting the situation or deliberately erecting some barriers. This is an example of strategic behaviour on the part of firms; whether it is attempted or not depends on the likelihood of success and the relative costs and benefits. It is another area where game theory is used to formulate strategic possibilities.[6]

The threat of substitute products

The threat from substitute products largely depends upon the nature of the good being traded in the market and the extent of product differentiation. It has a clear impact upon market structure, because if there are no substitutes for a good the producer of that good will face little competition and have a great deal of market power. However, as was seen earlier, even industries which appear to be pure monopolies like the former British Rail face competition from substitutes since there are other ways to travel. Much of the expenditure by firms to differentiate their products is designed to reduce the threat from substitute products.

The power of buyers

So far this chapter has concentrated on the competition between producers in a market, but the amount of competition between buyers will also have an impact on an industry. Markets will range from those where there are many buyers, as in the case of retailing, through markets where there are a small number of buyers, as in the case of car and parts manufacturers, to markets where there is only one buyer.

This latter type of market is called a **monopsony**, and it is the buyer who has a great deal of market power rather than the seller. An example of this is the coal industry, where the majority of output goes to the electricity producers. Increasingly in retailing the giant retailers are exerting a great deal of power over the manufacturers. TOYS 'R' US, the world's largest toy retailer, is involved very early on by manufacturers in the design process for new toys and as a result gets many exclusives that are not available in other toy shops.

The level of buyer power could be measured in the same way as seller power (*see* later in this chapter), but no data are collected centrally on the level of buyer concentration. It is clear, however, that there are many markets in which powerful buyers can and do exert a great deal of control over suppliers, and this power is an important source of marketing economies of scale. It is possible to put together the level of competition between producers and consumers in order to predict behaviour. For example, a market which consists of a single buyer and a single seller will have quite different characteristics from a market which has many buyers and sellers. The existence of strong buyers might have beneficial effects on the market as they could offset the power of strong producers or it could lead to higher seller concentration as sellers come together to counteract the power of the buyer.

In markets where there are strong sellers and weak buyers the producers' power can be offset by, for example, consumer advice centres or watch-dog bodies, as in the case of the former public utilities.

A distinction can be made between existing and potential customers. Existing customers are particularly significant to firms in industries where repeat orders are important or where goods are supplied on a regular basis, as in grocery retailing. It is no surprise that the large grocery retailers are using loyalty cards to increase the loyalty of existing customers. The power of existing customers is much lower where the firm supplies goods on a one-off basis, although the firm cannot disregard existing customers as this will affect its reputation and the ability to attract potential customers. Potential customers might be new to the market or can be buying from an existing competitor at present.

Power of suppliers

The power of suppliers over the firm is likely to be extremely important in certain markets, depending upon the nature of the product being supplied. For example: Is the product highly specialised? Is the same or similar product available from elsewhere? How important is the product in the production process? The importance of good and reliable supplies has assumed greater significance since firms have started to adopt just-in-time production methods. Reducing stock levels to reduce costs can only be effective if firms can depend upon their suppliers; hence there has been the development of partnership sourcing as firms develop long-term relationships with their suppliers.

Another important factor here is whether or not the firm itself can produce the components it needs in the production process. If it can the power of suppliers is greatly reduced. The decision as to whether to produce or to buy from a supplier is the subject of a relatively new area of economics called **transaction cost economics**.[7]

Measuring the degree of actual competition in the market

In industrial economics the level of competition in a market is measured by concentration ratios. These measure the percentage of value added, total output or employment that is produced by a stated number of the largest firms in the industry. The common numbers are three or five. The five-firm concentration ratio measures the percentage of employment or output accounted for by the five largest firms in the industry.

Table 15.9 shows the five-firm concentration ratios for a selection of industries in 2004 as measured by output.

Table 15.9 Five-firm concentration ratios for selected industries in the UK, 2004

Industry	Output (%)
Sugar and sugar by-products	99
Tobacco	99
Iron and steel	61
Pharmaceutical products	57
Rubber products	45
Leather goods	30
Footwear	25
Legal service	9
Other business services	5

Source: Adapted from Appendix 1, 'Concentration ratios for businesses by industry in 2004', Sanjiv Mahajan, *Economic Trends*, ONS, October 2006.

Although Table 15.9 shows only a small selection of industries, it does show that there is a wide variation in the degree of concentration across industries. Only two services industries are listed because there is a general lack of data on the service sector. Generally services are less concentrated than manufacturing industries because of the nature of the production process and the fact there is less scope for economies of scale. The differences between the market shares of sugar and tobacco in Tables 15.5 and 15.9 are due to the fact that the large producers also produce the own-brand labels.

While it is relatively easy to compare the level of concentration in particular industries over time it is more difficult to make any conclusion about the 'average' level of concentration (*see* Mini case: Concentration in this chapter). Table 15.10 gives an illustration of the percentage share of total employment and sales of the largest 100 private firms in the United Kingdom between 1979 and 1992. Although these are not concentration ratios as such, the data do provide an indication of how concentration has changed over time in aggregate. The change in the Standard Industrial Classification during this period has only a small impact on the figures. Note how the level of 'average' concentration decreased slightly during the first part of the period, reversing the trend of the first half of this century where industrial concentration increased. The reason for the decrease is largely the process of privatisation and the growth in the small-firm sector during the 1970s and 1980s.

Table 15.10 100 largest private enterprise groups

Year	Percentage share of total Employment	Sales
SIC(68)		
1979	12	18
SIC(80)		
1980	13	15
1981	13	16
1982	12	15
1983	12	16
1984	15	19
1985	9.5	14
1986	9.7	15.4
1987	10.8	17.1
1988	9.4	17.6
1989	12.1	21.6
1990	14.6	23.6
1991	14.9	21.2
1992	16.9	24.9

Source: *Census of Production*, various. Crown copyright. Reproduced by permission of the Controller of HMSO and of the Office for National Statistics, UK.

In the later part of the period concentration started to rise again, mainly due to the industrial restructuring taking place and the increased level of merger activity identified in Chapter 11. As the UK government ceased publication of these figures in 1992 it is difficult to assess what has happened to concentration more recently.

Making comparisons between different countries tends to be difficult because of this problem of 'averaging' concentration and because of national differences in the way in which data are collected and reported. Moreover official EU publications on industry have changed the way in which they report data, so comparisons over time are problematical. Available evidence suggests, however, that in the 1960s concentration increased in Europe and stabilised by the 1970s before declining in the last quarter of the twentieth century, as in the United Kingdom.

One of the main arguments for the creation and expansion of the Single European Market was that the bigger market would allow greater economies of scale through the growth in the size of firms. Chapter 11 has already identified an increase in merger activity in the EU in the late 1980s in the run-up to 1992 and Table 15.11 shows the change in the five-firm concentration ratios according to value added in selected sectors in the EU between 1986 and 1991.

Most sectors experienced an increase in concentration levels, although there are differences between the sectors. Aerospace is one sector where concentration increased by 20 per cent, mainly due to the growth of British Aerospace and Rolls-Royce. The level of concentration in the EU has risen as a result of increased merger activity and a competition policy which is torn between promoting competition by preventing market domination and the need to establish European competitiveness by encouraging it.

Despite the difficulties in comparing concentration ratios, the general view of industrial economists is that concentration is greater in the United Kingdom than in other member states.

Table 15.11 Five-firm concentration ratios on a value-added basis (%) for selected sectors in the EU

Sector	1986	1991	% change
Tobacco	58.39	59.16	0.76
Chemicals	42.25	41.48	−0.77
Rubber and plastic products	14.78	21.71	6.93
Iron and steel	47.21	82.31	35.10
Aerospace	51.24	71.97	20.72
Computers	34.08	33.17	−0.91
Drink	39.73	43.24	3.50
Food	16.92	20.37	3.45
Printing and publishing	19.20	19.34	0.14

Source: Commission of the European Communities, *European Economy*, no. 57, 1994. Reproduced by permission of the Office for Official Publications of the European Communities.

mini case Concentration

Although it is difficult to talk about the 'average' level of concentration in a country, the government in the UK produced data on the percentage share of the largest 100 enterprises in employment and output up to 1992 (*see* Table 15.10). These data show that concentration increased in the first half of this century but has stabilised and even fallen at times. A report in 2002[8] found that the concentration of industry in the EU had reduced both geographically and industrially in the last quarter of the twentieth century. Between 1970 and 2000 there was less geographical concentration of industry in France, Germany and the UK (63 per cent in 1970 and 58 per cent in 2000). Using the Gini coefficient to measure concentration[9] there had been a small fall in concentration in manufacturing as a whole and also in the majority of industries. The most concentrated industries were motor vehicles, motorcycles, aircraft, electrical apparatus, chemicals, petroleum and coal products. It is also true that the relative importance of the small firm to both output and employment has increased over recent years at the expense of larger organisations. What are the reasons for these changes?

The main benefits to result from increased size and concentration are the economies of scale discussed in the text. The techniques of mass production which produced standardised goods at low cost rely upon the economies of specialisation and division of labour. Although there are many industries which are still dominated by very large organisations, the recent trends in firm size and concentration indicate that smaller firms are increasingly able to compete with large firms. In unsegmented markets where the product is standardised the techniques of mass production are still appropriate, but increasingly there is a movement to a more flexible approach to manufacturing. This has been called the 'Japanisation' of industry.

● Changes in consumer demand have led to a demand for a bigger range of products so that markets are increasingly segmented and there is greater product differentiation. Under such conditions the benefits of economies of large-scale production have little significance, and large-scale organisations are less responsive to changes in demand than small firms. The use of 'flexible manufacturing systems' gives much greater flexibility in production and enables firms to produce a wider range of products at lower cost than traditional methods of production.

● Developments in information technology like Computer Aided Design (CAD) and Computer Aided Manufacturing (CAM) have exacerbated this trend since they serve to reduce the minimum efficient scale of production and make economies of scale possible at lower levels of output. Thus small firms can benefit from economies of scale in the same way as large firms. CAD and CAM make possible the manufacture of different products so that the product mix can be altered quickly.

● Economies of scope exist where a firm can produce two or more products at a lower per unit cost than if it produced each product separately. They result where related activities use similar labour and equipment and where producing related goods is a way of using up excess capacity. The economies stem from the spreading of fixed costs over larger output. Since economies of scope are not due to increased scale of production they can be realised by large and small firms alike. One small firm industry which has benefited from economies of scope is executive recruitment consultancy, where firms increasingly offer a range of related services like training audits and succession planning.

● Techniques like just-in-time production are more accessible to small firms since they eradicate the need for keeping large inventories and the associated costs of storage.

Reasons for high concentration

Many industries in the United Kingdom are highly concentrated and it is believed that the United Kingdom has higher concentration ratios than other large industrial countries. Why are there different market structures between industries?

Referring back to Figure 15.2, the point at which the curve becomes horizontal (A in diagram) is called the **minimum efficient scale of production** or **MES**. It is the point at which all economies of scale have been reaped by the firm, and the point at which firms that wish to maximise their efficiency must operate.

The higher the MES relative to the total output of the industry, the fewer will be the number of firms operating in an industry and therefore the higher will be the level of concentration. For example, if the MES in an industry is half of the industry output, the industry could only support two firms, as smaller firms could not achieve low enough costs to compete with the large firms.

As the scale of production continues to increase, average costs eventually start to rise. This is due to diseconomies of scale, which are mostly attributed to managerial inefficiencies. These are the difficulties faced by management in controlling, co-ordinating and communicating in a large organisation.

Firms in every industry will face differing average cost curves and therefore market structures will be different. In services, for example, because of the nature of the product, the scope for economies of scale is small and, accordingly, the MES is small relative to the size of the total market and the industries tend to be unconcentrated. The level of concentration in manufacturing tends to be much higher because of the nature of the production process and the scope for economies of scale.

The size of the MES is not the only explanation of why there are different market structures. If it was, one might expect that the same industry would have similar levels of concentration in different countries, but this is not the case, as indicated above. The strength of the five forces will differ greatly between industries and will therefore give many different structures. Obviously government policy can influence the type of market structure, and this will differ between countries. It is also true that the significance of barriers to entry varies between countries. Empirical results from West Germany and the United Kingdom show that in both countries barriers to entry are high, but that in the United Kingdom advertising is the most important barrier, while in West Germany it is economies of scale.

Synopsis

In this chapter, four different market structures were considered that embraced the whole spectrum of competition: perfect competition; monopoly; oligopoly; and monopolistic competition. Each of these market structures gives predictions about the behaviour of firms in those markets. Generally the more realistic of these market structures predict well what happens in the real world. This analysis was then incorporated into Porter's five-forces model which includes further factors largely ignored by traditional economic theory. Nevertheless, these factors are particularly important in certain industries, like the power of the giant retailers as buyers and the importance of potential customers to industries where the level of repeat business is high.

The amount of competition in a market is measured using concentration ratios and evidence on concentration was examined both within the United Kingdom and between countries as far as that was possible.

Summary of key points

- There are four different market structures identified by business economists. These are (arranged with most competitive first): perfect competition, monopolistic competition, oligopoly and monopoly.

- Perfect competition is a market structure which is very competitive and where the producers are 'price takers'.

- Pure monopoly is a market structure with a single producer that is a 'price maker'.

- Monopolistic competition is a market structure where there is a great deal of competition but where the product is slightly differentiated, so producers have a little market power.

- Oligopoly is a market structure where there is a small number of large producers, interdependent in their decision making. This is a common market structure.

- The determinants of market structure include the existence and height of barriers to entry and exit and the existence of economies of scale.

- Knowledge of market structure gives some indication of likely behaviour of firms with respect to factors like pricing and advertising.

A Porter's five-force analysis of the airline industry

Like many other industries in 2008, the airline industry is under threat from a variety of sources. Increasing oil prices, the credit crunch and environmental concerns are just three of the issues which are having a dramatic effect on the industry. How will these affect the industry? This case study uses Porter's five-forces model to analyse this.

Current competition

There are hundreds of airlines in the world. Some are very big like British Airways and American Airways and some are smaller like the low-cost airlines Ryanair and easyJet. The rising price of oil is having a dramatic effect on market structure. In the year up to September 2008, 26 airlines had gone out of business. Rising fuel prices impact more on the smaller airlines as they typically operate older aircraft which are less fuel efficient. More casualties are expected by the end of 2008, especially among the 70 smaller airlines operating in Europe.

The credit crunch is also having an effect: IATA estimates that in 2008 global passenger capacity grew faster than the demand for seats. Even national flag carriers are having problems; at the time of writing it is not clear whether the attempts to save Alitalia will be successful. Problems faced by holiday companies also impact on the airline industry. The collapse of XL Leisure Group in 2008 left 85 000 holidaymakers stranded and a further 200 000 without a holiday. One way in which airlines try to protect themselves and provide 'seamless travel' to their customers is through the formation of strategic alliances. There are three main alliances.

The Open Skies agreement has opened the door to possible strategic alliances between airlines and one was under consideration at the end of 2008 – between American Airlines, British Airways and Iberia. This has been heralded as the advent of the global mega-alliance.

Power of buyers

There are two main reasons for air travel – leisure and business. It is estimated that business travel accounts for around 15 per cent of air travel and leisure 85 per cent. Over the last 50 years the demand for air travel has increased greatly. Demographic factors, including

Table 15.12 Major airline alliances, 2008

Oneworld Alliance	Aer Lingus, American Airlines, British Airways, Cathay Pacific, Finnair, Iberia, Japan Airlines, LAN, Malév, Royal Jordanian, Qantas
Star Alliance	Air Canada, Air China, Air New Zealand, ANA, Asian Airlines, Austrian Airlines, BMI, LOT Polish Airlines, Lufthansa, Scandinavian Airlines, Shanghai Airlines, Singapore Airlines, South African Airlines, Spanair, TAP Portugal, Thai Airways International, United Airlines, US Airways
Sky Team	Aeroflot, Aeromexico, Air France, Alitalia, China Southern, Continental Airlines, CSA Czech Airlines, Delta Airlines, KLM, Korean Air, Northwest Airlines

increased life expectancy and better health, have meant that all ages travel more than before. The average growth rate in air travel over the last 20 years is around 5 per cent per annum [10]. Both travel for leisure and travel for business are cyclical and will depend upon economic growth and this demand is highly susceptible to external forces. There was a sharp drop in air travel after 11 September 2001, for example (see Chapter 1), and the effects of the credit crunch will be felt on the volume of air travel. It is generally believed that the demand for leisure travel is price elastic: as prices go down travel increases sharply (and vice versa). It is also generally believed that business travel is price inelastic, that business travellers are less concerned about what they pay as someone else picks up the bill (this is questionable given the extent to which the low-cost, no-frills airlines have expanded in the business market).

The annual growth rate in the numbers of passengers carried has fallen from 12 per cent in 2004 to 5 per cent in 2007. Table 15.13 shows the breakdown of air travel by area and predicted growth rates up to 2011, and it can be seen that these are variable. There has been faster growth in the developing countries, especially China.

▶

Table 15.13 Air traffic by area

Area	Percentage of global air traffic in 2007	Growth rate forecast 2007–2011
Europe	40	+5.0
Asia/Pacific	28	+5.9
North America	17	+4.2
Middle East	7	+6.8
Latin America	4	+4.4
Africa	3	+5.6

Source: Adapted from IATA, 2008.

Another issue which might impact on the level of demand for air travel is the environmental impact of flying. The International Civil Aviation Organisation has a carbon emission calculator on its website. The UK government has announced that it will introduce a new tax which will replace the current air-passenger duty in 2009. The new tax will be much higher than the current tax and it is argued that it represents a more realistic assessment of the environmental costs of air travel.

Power of suppliers

There are two main organisations which dominate the supply of aircraft to airlines – Boeing Company (US based) and Airbus SAS (European based). Both companies have full order books but are experiencing delays in production. Airbus has delayed deliveries of its A380 because of wiring problems and Boeing is experiencing ongoing industrial action by employees. Another supplier of importance is the oil industry – oil represents a third of the operating costs of the airlines. Because of rises in the oil price, the price of jet fuel rose by 80 per cent between 2007 and 2008.

Threat of new entry

The threat of new entry is low because the airline business carries very high fixed costs – there are the costs of purchasing and maintaining the aeroplanes and the cost of landing at airports. All of these are fixed costs which do not change if an aircraft is half-empty. Airspace was deregulated in the 1970s in the USA and in the 1990s in Europe, such that any qualified airline can fly anywhere in the EU without government agreement.

This increased the level of competition and allowed the smaller low-cost airlines to establish themselves. The Open Skies agreement has also reduced barriers to entry for competition by existing airlines if not by new companies. In order to fly, airlines have to pay airport charges and these are very high especially in the bigger airports (this is why the low-cost airlines often operate to and from smaller, less well known airports) and this may be prohibitive. The problems with Terminal 5 at Heathrow in 2008 led to delays in the transfer of BA flights to the new terminal and a backlog of airlines waiting to take up BA's empty slots.

Threat of substitutes

For international travel there is really no substantial competition to air travel; sea travel accounted for only 10 per cent of international trips in 2007. Domestically, the airlines are in competition with all other sorts of travel and there is evidence from the UK that between 2003 and 2007, the fastest growing mode of transport for domestic destinations was railways (up from 6.2 per cent to 7.1 per cent). This growth took place at the expense of road travel rather than air travel, which remained static. Europe has been opened up as a destination for railway travel with the opening of the Channel Tunnel.

The low-cost airlines are cheaper than other methods of travel and of course much faster. The fact that in Europe countries are joined and the rail network is more developed may in part explain why the low-cost airlines do not yet have much of the market (5 per cent) compared with the UK (20 per cent) and the USA (22 per cent).

The Future

The airline industry is experiencing a period of rapid structural change for a number of reasons, which have been considered above. It is argued by many commentators that this restructuring is necessary and that the industry that emerges will be much stronger.

Case study questions

1 Why is there unlikely to be a price war between the low-cost providers in the airline industry?

2 What might be the effect on the industry of the proposed strategic alliance between British Airways, American Airlines and Iberia mentioned in the text?

web link For further details see e.g. *www.iata.org*; *www.icao.org*; *www.oneworld.com*; *www.staralliance.com*; *www.skyteam.com*

Review and discussion questions

1 Use Porter's five-forces model to analyse two industries of your choice. Try to choose industries which have contrasting market structures.

2 What economies of scale are likely to exist in retailing?

3 Think of examples of a market which is very competitive and a market which is not very competitive. Does the behaviour of the firms in these markets comply with the predictions in Table 15.7?

4 Why are goods like washing powders and coffee advertised more heavily than goods like matches or bread?

Assignments

1 You are working in the strategic planning department of a large recorded music producer and have been asked to write a briefing document for a board meeting on the structure of the industry. Use either the S–C–P model or Porter's five-forces model as a framework for this briefing. (Sources of information: Competition Commission reports, the previous editions of this book, media and local libraries, Mintel and Keynote.)

2 You are working in the local consumer advice centre which each week produces an information sheet giving the prices of a typical 'basket of goods' in local shops. Choose ten branded items (like Nescafé, for example) to constitute your basket of goods and survey three types of retail outlet: a small corner shop, a mini-market on a local main road and a large supermarket. Design an information sheet and present the information you have gathered in the form of a table. Include a list of bullet points which might explain any differences in price.

Notes and references

1 See Hay, D. A. and Morris, D. J., *Industrial Economics: Theory and Evidence*, Oxford University Press 1979, for a summary of the criticisms which are beyond the scope of this book.

2 Porter, M., *Competitive Strategy: Techniques for Analyzing Industries and Competitors*, The Free Press, New York, 1980.

3 For a full discussion of this, see Begg, D., Fischer, S. and Dornbusch, R., *Economics*, 7th edition, McGraw-Hill, 2003.

4 Porter, M., *Competitive Strategy: Techniques for Analyzing Industries and Competitors*, The Free Press, New York, 1980.

5 Baumol, W. J., Panzar, J. C. and Willig, R. D., *Contestable Markets and the Theory of Industry Structure*, Harcourt Brace Jovanovich, 1988.

6   In this context students should note the use of game theory to model and predict the behaviour of firms in oligopolistic markets. For a simple introduction to this area, see Griffiths, A. and Wall, S., *Applied Economics: An Introductory Course*, 9th edition, Financial Times/Prentice Hall, 2001.

7   Williamson, O. E., 'The Economics of Organisation: The Transaction Cost Approach', *American Journal of Sociology*, 87 (3), 1981, pp. 548–77.

8   'Location and Concentration of Industries' *European Economy Special Report* no. 2, 2002.

9   Worthington, I., Britton, C. and Rees, A., *Economics for Business; Blending Theory and Practice*, 2nd edition, Financial Times/Prentice Hall, 2005.

10 Keynote Report on Airlines, 2008.

Further reading

Begg, D., Fischer, S. and Dornbusch, R., *Economics*, 8th edition, McGraw-Hill, 2005.

Griffiths, A. and Wall, S., *Applied Economics: An Introductory Course*, 10th edition, Financial Times/Prentice Hall, 2004.

Jones, T. T. and Cockerill, T. A. J., *Structure and Performance of Industries*, Philip Allan, 1984.

Worthington, I., Britton, C. and Rees, A., *Economics for Business: Blending Theory and Practice*, 2nd edition, Financial Times/Prentice Hall, 2005.

web
link

Web links and further questions are available on the website at:
www.pearsoned.co.uk/worthington

16 International markets and trade

Chris Britton

The importance of international markets will vary between firms and industries but most businesses do not operate solely within national boundaries. Businesses which operate in the export market will obviously need an understanding of international markets but even the sole proprietor producing for a small local market may well use imported raw materials in the production process and so will be affected by changes that take place internationally.

Learning outcomes

Having read this chapter you should be able to:

- explain why international trade takes place
- examine the international organisations which serve to promote free trade
- outline the balance of payments position in the United Kingdom
- describe the working of the foreign exchange markets

Key terms

Balance of payments
Balance of trade
Capital account
Common agricultural policy (CAP)
Common external tariff (CET)
Common market
Current account
Current balance
Customs union
Deficit
Devaluation

European Economic Area (EEA)
European Monetary System
Exchange control
Exchange rate
Exchange Rate Mechanism (ERM)
Financial account
Fixed exchange rate
Floating exchange rate
Foreign direct investment
Free trade
Import control

Import penetration
Invisible trade
J-curve effect
Multinational enterprises
Qualitative control
Quota
Single market
Specialisation
Speculation
Subsidy
Surplus
Tariff
Visible trade

Introduction

International markets are important to most firms; even if they do not produce for the export market they may well be dependent upon raw materials which are imported and they will almost definitely be affected by movements in the exchange rate. Britain, like all other advanced industrial countries, is highly dependent upon international markets and that dependence has grown over the years. What makes international trade different from trade within a country is that the trade is taking place across national borders. Thus a system for international payments is needed. It is essential for students of business to have an understanding of international markets, exchange rates and the balance of payments.

International trade – why it takes place

Trade between countries takes place because resources are unevenly distributed through the world and the mobility of the factors of production is limited, consequently some countries are better at producing certain goods than others. Some countries could not actually produce a particular good: for example, Britain cannot produce minerals that are not indigenous or fruit that can only be grown in tropical weather conditions. If there is a demand for these goods in Britain, there are a number of possibilities: either the British could do without these goods; or an attempt could be made to grow them (in the case of the fruit) despite the climatic conditions; or Britain could buy the goods from other countries that can produce them. In other words it can trade for them.

It is easy to see that if country A can produce video cameras more cheaply than country B and B can produce wheat more cheaply than A, **specialisation** should occur and A should produce video cameras and B should produce wheat and they should trade with one another. Complete specialisation is, however, unlikely, for strategic reasons. It is also true that even if country A can produce both goods more cheaply than country B there is scope for benefits from trade. As this may not be so easy to imagine, Table 16.1 gives a numerical example. Country A can produce 100 video cameras or 100 units of wheat using 100 workers. Country B can produce 20 video cameras or 40 units of wheat with the same number of workers. Country A can therefore produce both goods at lower cost than country B. To show that even in this situation trade will benefit the world, assume that both countries produce both goods and that they each devote half of their workforce to each good.

Table 16.1 Production of video cameras and wheat

	Number of units that 100 workers can produce	
	Video cameras	Wheat
Country A	100	100
Country B	20	40

The total output of video cameras is 60 units and of wheat is 70 units. Country A is 5 times more efficient at producing video cameras than country B, but only 2.5 times more efficient than B in producing wheat (see Table 16.2). It would therefore benefit both countries if production was rearranged. If B specialised completely in wheat and A produced 35 units of wheat and 65 video cameras, world output would be as indicated in Table 16.3.

Table 16.2 Production of video cameras and wheat

	Video cameras	Wheat
Country A	50	50
Country B	10	20
	—	—
	60	70

Table 16.3 Production of video cameras and wheat

	Video cameras	Wheat
Country A	65	35
Country B	0	40
	—	—
	65	75

In short, world output has been increased and everyone is better off provided that trade takes place. This simplified example illustrates the basic argument for **free trade**. Free trade brings the advantages of higher world output and higher standards of living. Countries will produce the goods in which they have a cost advantage and trade with other countries for other goods. So countries can buy goods at lower prices than they could be produced for at home. Where economies of scale are present, the savings as a result of specialisation can be immense.

Theoretically, free trade brings most benefit; however, there are often restrictions to such trade and it is unlikely that complete specialisation will take place. Most countries would regard being totally dependent on another country for a particular good as a risky proposition.

Restrictions to international trade

There are a number of things that governments do to restrict international trade. These restrictions include:

- **Quotas** A physical limitation on the import of certain goods into a country, sometimes by mutual agreement (e.g. voluntary export restraints).
- **Tariffs** A tax placed on imported goods.
- **Exchange controls** A limit to the amount of a currency that can be bought, which will limit the import of goods.
- **Subsidies** Payments made to domestic producers to reduce their costs and therefore make them more competitive on world markets.

● **Qualitative controls** Controls on the quality of goods rather than on quantity or price.

All of these serve to restrict international trade, and therefore reduce specialisation on a world level. They invite retaliation and could lead to inefficiencies. **Import controls** have a wide effect on industry. The 200 per cent tariffs that the Americans threatened to impose on French cheeses and wines at the end of 1992 if the GATT talks were not successful, would have impacted on many other industries like the bottle-making industry or the insurance industry. But there are powerful arguments used in support of import controls. For example, they can be used to protect industries, whether these industries are 'infant' industries or strategic industries. In the 1999 debate within the EU on bananas, it was argued by the African, Caribbean and Pacific countries which receive preferential treatment in the EU for their bananas that the relaxation of these preferential terms might lead to the complete devastation of their economies. Import controls can also be used to improve the balance of payments position in the case where a deficit exists.

The United Kingdom is a member of a number of international organisations that serve to promote free trade and control the restrictions to free trade, like the World Trade Organisation (see Chapter 5 and the Mini case below).

mini case The World Trade talks

The 'Doha round' of trade talks was aimed at reducing world trade barriers with the specific aim of helping the developing countries. The talks started in 2001 and were due to end in 2004 but collapsed in 2003 as poorer countries refused to continue until concessions had been promised by the richer countries. Talks restarted in 2004 but stalled again in 2006 and then restarted in July 2008. This time the talks only lasted nine days before they collapsed. There are 149 countries involved in the WTO talks, which makes agreement difficult to achieve. However, there are calls for negotiations to start again as the issues are important. The World Bank estimates that the abolition of agricultural subsidies would increase global trade by $300 billion per year by 2015. Agricultural tariffs and subsidies have disastrous effects on developing countries which are highly dependent on agriculture – in Africa, for example, 70 per cent of the population is involved in agricultural production.

The WTO wants the EU to open up its markets more readily to foreign producers. For example, the EU produces sugar at three times the world price but keeps imports of sugar out of the EU with high tariffs. The EU has offered to cut tariffs on some goods (in exchange for concessions) but wants to maintain them on 'sensitive' food products. The WTO also wants the USA to reduce the subsidies it pays to its farmers. The US has offered to reduce agricultural subsidies by up to 50 per cent, again in return for concessions. Both the EU and US want increased access to non-agricultural markets in newly developing countries like India and Brazil. These countries are reluctant to do this as the reduction of trade barriers may lead to an influx of cheap manufactured goods from China.

Complete failure of the Doha talks could see the end of multilateral trade agreements and an increased reliance on bilateral trade agreements negotiated between countries. This is problematic for businesses where bilateral agreements overlap, causing difficult regulatory requirements. The real losers in this will be the developing nations; anti-poverty groups argue very strongly that increased trade is better for these countries than increased aid. If developing countries do not become self-sufficient in trade they will continue to need aid in the future.

web link

For information on the work of the World Trade Organisation see *www.wto.org*

The European Union (EU)

The EU was established in 1958 by the Treaty of Rome. The six original members, France, West Germany, Italy, Holland, Belgium and Luxembourg, were joined in 1972 by the United Kingdom, Ireland and Denmark. Greece joined in 1981, followed by Spain and Portugal in 1986 and Austria, Finland and Sweden on 1 January 1995. In 2004 ten further countries joined the EU, mainly from eastern Europe: Czech Republic, Cyprus, Estonia, Hungary, Latvia, Lithuania, Malta, Poland, Slovakia and Slovenia. In January 2007 Romania and Bulgaria were admitted. These countries, along with the former East Germany, currently constitute the 27 member states of the Union, a number which is likely to grow further by the end of the decade. Other countries which are waiting to join are Croatia and Turkey.

As a result of the enlargement of the EU, a new constitution was put forward which included changes in voting rights, the size of the EU commission and maintaining national sovereignty. The new constitution had to be ratified by all member states of the EU. The new constitution was shelved in 2005 after 'no' votes in referenda held in France and the Netherlands. In 2007 a new reform treaty was agreed by EU leaders – the Lisbon Treaty – again needing to be ratified by all 27 members of the EU. Many members ratified it through their parliaments but in Ireland, the only country to hold a public vote, the vote was against ratification of the treaty. This has caused turmoil within the EU. Some have argued that the treaty is dead (Poland has decided not to put the treaty forward for ratification because of the Irish 'no' vote) while some argue that the treaty should never have been put to a public vote at all so that the 'no' vote can be ignored. The President of the EU has vowed to solve this problem by the end of 2008 so that the treaty can be put in place in 2009.

> **web link**
> For information on the European commission see *http://europa.eu.int/comm/index_en.htm*
> For European statistics see *http://europa.eu.int/comm/eurostat*

The primary aim of the Treaty of Rome was to create a '**common market**' in which member states were encouraged to trade freely and to bring their economies closer together, ultimately culminating in the creation of a '**single market**' within the Union. To bring this about, a protected free trade area or '**customs union**' was established, which involved the removal of tariff barriers between member states and the institution of a **common external tariff (CET)** on goods from outside the Union. Institutional structures (see Chapter 4) and Union policies – most notably the **common agricultural policy (CAP)** – also contributed to this end and to the creation of a trading bloc of immense proportions. Within this bloc, member states were expected to gain numerous advantages, including increased trade and investment, huge economies of scale and improvements in productivity and cost reductions. To support the goal of increased trade and co-operation between community members, a **European monetary system** was established in 1979 in which a majority of member states undertook to fix their exchange rates within agreed limits (see below).

A significant step towards the creation of a single market – capable of competing effectively with the United States and Japan – was taken in 1986 when the then 12 community members signed the Single European Act. This Act established 31 December 1992 as the target date for the creation of a Single European market: an area (comprising the 12 EU countries) without internal frontiers, in which the free movement of goods, services, people and capital was to be ensured within the provisions contained in the Treaty. Among the measures for making the single market a reality were agreements on the following issues:

- the removal or reduction in obstacles to cross-border travel and trade (e.g. customs checks);
- the harmonisation or approximation of technical and safety standards on a large number of products;
- closer approximation of excise duties and other fiscal barriers (e.g. VAT);
- the removal of legal obstacles to trade (e.g. discriminatory purchasing policies);
- the mutual recognition of qualifications.

Further steps in the development of the EU came with the decision to establish a **European Economic Area (EEA)** – which permits members of the European Free Trade Area (EFTA) to benefit from many of the single market measures – and, in particular, from the Treaty on European Union, agreed by the 12 member states in December 1991 at Maastricht. Apart from the institutional changes mentioned in Chapter 4, the Maastricht Treaty contained provisions for:

- increased economic and monetary union between member states;
- a single currency;
- a social charter to protect workers' rights;
- a common foreign and security policy;
- community citizenship.

These various measures were scheduled to be introduced over a number of years, although in some cases – most notably the United Kingdom – specially negotiated 'opt-out' clauses meant that some provisions were not implemented simultaneously by all member states (e.g. the single currency; the social charter).

European monetary union was finally achieved on 1 January 1999 with the creation of the Eurozone. Eleven members of the EU were included – the UK, Denmark and Sweden chose not to participate, while Greece failed the convergence criteria for membership but has since joined in 2001. In 2007, Slovenia joined the Eurozone and in 2008 Malta and Cyprus joined, taking the total up to 15 (EU-15). The Eurozone is effectively a single economic zone since it operates with a single currency – the euro (see the text later in this chapter) and members have given up sovereignty over monetary policy, which is now determined by the European Central Bank. National sovereignty over fiscal policy has been retained, so there can be some differences in tax rates and government spending, but this is to operate in a framework of 'harmonisation'. The creation of the Eurozone enables increased specialisation across the whole of Europe and bigger economies of scale. It embraces more than 300 million people and is responsible for one-fifth of the world's output and as such comes a close second to the USA as an economic superpower.

The UK has chosen not to join the Eurozone and the single currency until a referendum has been held. In 1997 the Chancellor of the Exchequer set out five economic tests of whether the UK should join or not. These were:

1 Are business cycles and economic structures of the UK and the Eurozone compatible and *sustainable*?
2 If problems emerge, is there sufficient flexibility to deal with them?
3 Would joining EMU encourage long-term investment in the UK?
4 What impact would it have on the competitive position of the UK's financial services industry?
5 Will joining EMU promote higher growth, stability and employment?

By 2008, the debate over membership of the euro in the UK has receded from the political agenda (at least for the time being) in view of the more pressing problems encountered by the EU during the year over the new constitution and the global financial crisis.

The balance of payments

The **balance of payments** is a record of a country's international trade with other countries over a period of time, usually a year. It records the flows of money rather than goods, so that an import will be recorded as a negative amount since the money is flowing out of the country to pay for the good, and an export is recorded as a positive amount. Money flows into and out of a country for two basic reasons: first, in exchange for goods and services (current transactions), and second, for investment purposes (capital transactions). In the UK these two flows are recorded separately in the UK balance of payments accounts which are produced by the government. Since 1992, when customs posts were abolished, balance of payment figures have been collected through Intrastat and are based on VAT returns.

For information on the balance of payments in the UK see *www.statistics.gov.uk*
For information on international trade see *www.oecd.org* and *www.wto.org*

Current transactions

In the UK the **current account** records the flows of money received and paid out in exchange for goods and services. It is subdivided into **visible trade** (the import and export of goods) and **invisible trade** (the import and export of services). Invisible trade includes:

1 Services like banking, insurance, tourism.
2 Interest, profits and dividends.
3 Transfers, which include grants to developing countries, payments to international bodies like the EU and private transfers such as gifts.

The balance of these flows on visible trade is called the **balance of trade** and the balance on the current account overall is called the **current balance**. It is to one of these balances that journalists and politicians are usually referring when they talk about the balance of payments. Table 16.4 shows the balance of payments for the United Kingdom in 2007. It can be seen that the balance of trade was –£89 515 million, the invisible balance was +£29 840 million and the current balance was –£59 675 million. More will be said later about the history of the balance of payments in the United Kingdom.

Table 16.4 UK balance of payments, 2007 (£m)

Visible balance		–89 515
Invisible trade		
Services	38 331	
Current income	5 302	
Current transfers	–13 793	
Invisible trade balance		29 840
Current account balance		–59 675
Capital account balance		2 528
Financial account		
Direct investment	–20 903	
Equity capital		
Reinvested earnings		
Other capital transactions		
Portfolio investment	79 925	
Equity securities		
Debt securities		
Financial derivatives	–17 871	
Other investments	18 361	
Reserve assets	–1 191	
Net transactions on financial account		58 321
Balancing item		–1 174

Source: Adapted from *www.statistics.gov.uk/statbase/tsdataset/asp?vlink=209&more=Y.*

Capital transactions

As well as these current transactions there are flows of money for investment purposes. These include funds from both the public and private sectors and long-term and short-term monetary movements.

Long-term capital transactions include:

● Overseas investment in the United Kingdom (e.g. purchase of shares, acquisition of real assets, purchase of government securities by non-residents).
● UK private investment overseas, where UK residents buy shares, acquire real assets, and so on, in overseas countries. The capital account does not include interest, dividends or profits but only flows of money for investment purposes. A capital transaction can give rise to a current flow in the future. If a non-resident bought shares in a UK company the initial amount would appear on the capital account. The resulting flow of dividends paid in the future would be recorded as a flow on the invisible account.
● Official long-term capital (i.e. loans from the UK government to other governments).

Short-term transactions include:

- Trade credit – as goods are often not paid for as they are received the physical export and import of goods is not matched with an inflow or outflow of money. In order that the balance of payments balances, these amounts would be included here as trade credit.
- Foreign currency borrowing and lending abroad by UK banks.
- Exchange reserves held by other countries and other organisations in sterling.
- Other external banking and money market liabilities in sterling.

These capital transactions are recorded in the UK balance of payments as changes from the previous year; they are not a record of all the transactions that have taken place over time. If money is flowing into the United Kingdom for investment purposes there is an increase in the UK liabilities and these are shown as positive amounts on the balance of payments. If money is flowing out of the country there is an increase in the UK assets and these are shown as negative amounts in the balance of payments.

Until 1986, capital flows to/from the private sector and capital flows to/from the public sector were shown in two separate accounts. In 1986 the format of the balance of payments was changed to show all capital transactions in one account under the heading of 'UK transactions in external assets and liabilities'. In 1998 the format of the balance of payments was changed once more to bring it into line with the standards published in the fifth edition of the *IMF Balance of Payments Manual*. The UK balance of payments now comprises three sections:

- the current account, as before;
- the **capital account**, which records capital transfers and transfers of non-financial assets into and out of the UK. As Table 16.4 shows, the balance on this account was £2528 million in 2007;
- the **financial account**, which gives the balance of trade in financial assets. This section of the balance of payments is itself subdivided between direct investment, portfolio investment, other investments and reserve assets. The balance on the financial account for 2007 was +£58 321 million.

Speculative flows of currencies would appear in the financial account of the balance of payments. Portfolio investment is the purchasing of shares in companies while direct investment is the setting up of subsidiaries. Reserve assets shows the change in official reserves – an increase in official reserves is shown as a negative amount and a decrease is shown as a positive amount.

The balance of payments overall should balance as negative flows will be balanced by positive flows. As this is often hard to understand two examples will be given.

Example 1

If a UK resident buys foreign goods there will be a negative entry in the current account equal to the value of those goods. That individual has to pay for those goods in foreign currency and could do this by using money from a foreign currency bank account if he or she has one, or by borrowing the foreign currency from a bank in that country. Either way there is an increase in the amount of liabilities and the same amount would be shown as a positive amount in the capital account.

Example 2

If a foreign investor purchased shares in a UK company, there would be a positive amount recorded in the capital account. The investor might pay for these shares by using sterling from a sterling bank account and so there would be an equal negative amount shown in the capital account.

The balance of payments should therefore always balance but invariably fails to do so, owing to errors and omissions in the recording process, and so a balancing item is included to ensure that it does. As can be seen from Tables 16.4 and 16.5, the balancing item can be very large, and this calls into question the accuracy of the figures.

Table 16.5 UK balance of payments, 1994–2007 (£m)

	1994	1996	1998	2000	2001	2002	2003	2004	2005	2006	2007
Visible balance	−11126	−13722	−21813	−32976	−40648	−46675	−47665	−57944	−68789	−77555	−89515
Invisible balance	4358	6721	17841	8882	18257	29060	28926	32262	32804	26830	29840
Current account	−6768	−7001	−3972	−24094	−22391	−17615	−18739	−25682	−30985	−50725	−59675
Capital account	33	1260	516	1527	1206	868	1296	2073	1491	853	2528
Financial account	2126	3961	2219	24944	23816	10272	15961	27028	33954	44800	58321
Balancing item	4609	1780	1237	−2377	−2631	6475	1482	−3419	−4460	5072	−1174
Drawings on (+) or additions to (−) official reserves	−1045	510	164	−3915	3085	459	1559	−193	−656	426	−1191

Source: Adapted from *www.statistics.gov.uk/statbase/tsdataset.asp?vlink=209&more=Y.*

Equilibrium in the balance of payments

If the balance of payments always balances how can there be a deficit on the balance of payments? The answer is that the media and politicians are referring to the current balance or the balance of trade rather than the overall balance of payments position. A balance of payments surplus on the current account is where the value of exports exceeds the value of imports. A deficit is where the value of imports exceeds the value of exports. As explained above, if there is a surplus on the current account, this will be matched by an outflow in the capital account, for example a reduction in the size of sterling bank balances, or an increase in official reserves. The opposite is true for a deficit. This implies that there cannot be a balance of payments problem; however, persistent surpluses or deficits on the current account are considered to be problematic. A persistent deficit has to be financed in some way, either through borrowing, to increase the external liabilities, or by selling more of its assets. A deficit will also lead to pressure on the exchange rate, as will be shown later. A continued surplus is also a problem, since one country's surplus must mean that other countries are experiencing a deficit, and they will be faced with the problem of financing the deficit. Political pressure will be brought to bear, and there is the possibility of the introduction of tariffs or other import controls in order to reduce a deficit.

Methods of correcting balance of payments deficits

Since **surpluses** are not regarded as being such a problem as **deficits**, this section will concentrate on action needed to overcome a deficit, although the actions would be reversed for a surplus. When there is a current account deficit, the outflow of funds is greater than the inflow of funds from international trade. The authorities need to increase exports and/or reduce imports. Thus:

1 A fall in the exchange rate will have the double effect of making exports cheaper abroad and imports dearer at home, thus encouraging exports and discouraging imports. This will be explained fully later.
2 To increase exports British companies that produce for the export market could be subsidised. This would have the effect of reducing the price of UK goods abroad, making them more competitive.
3 Import controls could be imposed to restrict the level of imports coming in to the country.
4 A rise in the rate of interest would make Britain more attractive to investors and therefore increase capital flows into Britain and help offset the current account deficit.

The history of the balance of payments in the United Kingdom

Table 16.5 gives a summary of the balance of payments in the United Kingdom between 1994 and 2007. The table shows that the current account was in deficit for the whole period. The weaknesses on the current account pre-date this and are somewhat hidden in the overall figures. The current account deficits started in 1987, the visible balance has been in deficit since 1983 (and still is) and within this the non-oil balance has been in deficit since 1982. This did not show in the overall current account figures until 1987 because of the offsetting effect of invisibles and oil. The United Kingdom's underlying weaknesses on the current account come from several sources:

1 Exports have risen but imports have risen faster. In the United Kingdom there is a high propensity to import goods.
2 The collapse of oil prices during the 1990s reduced the value of the United Kingdom's oil exports.
3 The recession of the early 1980s left the UK manufacturing base in an extremely weak position. This meant that it was difficult to produce enough goods for export or even to meet domestic demand, so the balance of payments was hit from both directions. The changes in the structure of industry in the United Kingdom described in Chapter 12 have implications for the balance of payments, as services are less exportable than goods.
4 The consumer booms that occurred in the late 1980s and in the late 1990s led to increases in the level of imports.

5 The impact of oil has been twofold. First, as the United Kingdom is now an oil-exporting country it brings in revenue which helps to improve the balance of payments. Second, it has tended to keep the exchange rate higher than it would have been, as will be shown in the next section, which makes UK goods less competitive in world markets and will therefore lead to a worsening of the balance of payments.

6 The high value of the pound in the late 1990s hit the UK's export market.

7 The most recent deterioration is due to a fall in the level of non-European exports, especially to Asia and Russia.

Figure 16.1 shows the breakdown of the current account between visibles and invisibles and it is clear that good performance on invisibles has partly offset poor performance in visibles.

Figure 16.1 **Components of the current account, UK, 1991–2007**

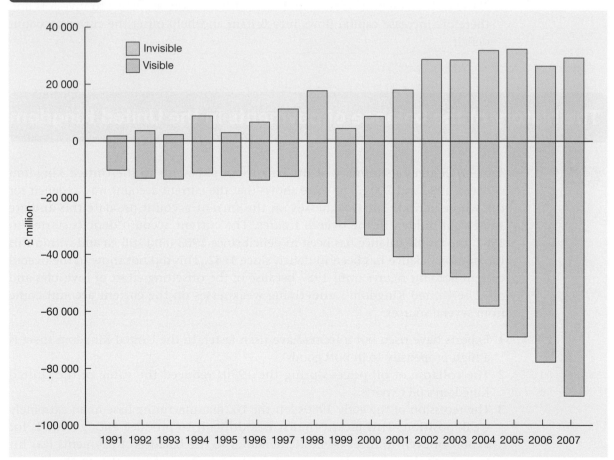

Source: Adapted from *www.statistics.gov.uk/statbase/tsdataset.asp?vlink=209&more=Y.*

mini case The current account of the balance of payments

Figures on the balance of payments are produced every month by the government in the UK and are often seized upon by commentators as indications of either an improvement in the UK's economic performance or a deterioration, depending upon the details of the figures. There are a number of reasons why their observation is incorrect. First, balance of payments figures are notoriously unreliable, and are often revised by very large amounts. In June 1996, for example, the estimated deficit on the balance of payments for 1995 was revised from £6.7 billion to £2.9 billion because of the discovery of large investment flows. Second – and this applies to all short-term economic indicators – there are very short-term changes in economic variables which are not translated into long-term trends. So the balance of payments can vary quite dramatically each month due to short-term factors which are evened out over the course of the year. In addition, the balance of payments, like other indicators, often does not behave as expected.

Figure 16.2 shows the UK current balance for the period 1970 to 2007. Two points can immediately be made about the behaviour of the balance of payments. First, the data move in a cyclical way and are therefore affected by the trade cycle. Second, the balance of payments generally improves in times of recession (e.g. the early 1980s and early 1990s) and worsens in times of boom. The reasons for this are twofold – in a recession the level of imports falls as income falls and the level of exports is unlikely to fall unless other countries are experiencing the same level of economic downturn. The balance of payments therefore improves. Usually the balance of payments improves enough in a recession to push it into surplus, although this did not happen in the early 1990s when the UK's current account remained in the red.

The unpredictability of the balance of payments is very evident in the figures for the 1990s. In 1994 the balance of payments improved, despite the recovery in economic conditions which would have

Figure 16.2 UK current balance, 1970–2007 (£ million)

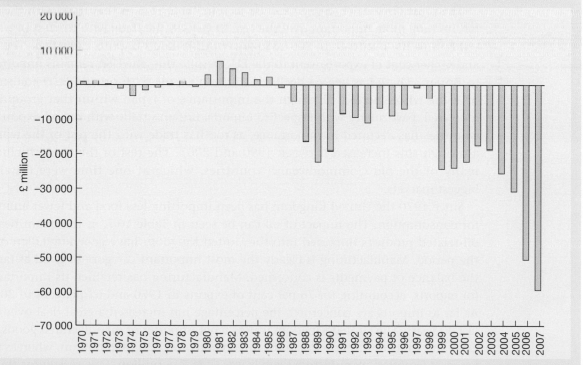

Source: Adapted from *www.statistics.gov.uk/statbase/tsdataset.asp?vlink=209&more=Y.*

been expected to worsen the balance of payments. This improvement continued in the late 1990s despite economic conditions which implied the opposite. The balance of payments should have suffered as a result of the high value of the pound and the economic turmoil in Asia and Russia. One possible explanation for the apparently contrary behaviour of the balance of payments is the J-curve effect (see Figure 16.7). It could be that the improvement in the balance of payments in the mid-1990s was caused by the fall in the value of the pound after the UK left the ERM, even though that happened in 1992, because of the time lags involved. Similarly, the effects of the high value of the pound were not evident until 1999 onwards.

The deficit on the balance of payments in the UK in the last quarter of 2001 was the worst ever, mainly due to the global economic downturn after September 11. The two main contributors were the collapse in investment income abroad and the increase in direct payments to the EU. Commentators were surprised at the speed with which the balance of payments had been affected, although the UK was not as badly affected as other countries. The balance of payments did recover in 2002–2003 but the deficit deepened in 2004–2007. There are two main reasons for the high deficits seen in this period: UK banks are paying higher interest to foreign banks and UK consumers are borrowing heavily to buy imported products.

The multitude of factors which impact upon the balance of payments and the difficulties involved in accurate data collection make the balance of payments figures unreliable and very difficult to predict. The use of one month's figures by commentators to prove either that recovery is under way or that a recession is imminent is unsound.

Patterns of trade

Over time, patterns of trade change, for many reasons, Table 16.6 shows UK patterns of trade by destination/source and Table 16.7 shows UK trade by type of good. From these tables it is possible to look at how the country's patterns of trade have changed.

The most obvious change, as can be seen in Table 16.6, is that trade with the EU has become more important over the last 30 years while trade with the rest of western Europe has declined. In 2007 55 per cent of Britain's imports came from the EU and 60 per cent of exports went to the EU. Despite this, the USA remains important to Britain. There has been a decline in Britain's trade with other OECD countries over the whole period, although the importance of Japan within that group has increased, particularly with respect to imports. Britain's trade with the oil-exporting countries has declined in importance, as too has trade with the rest of the world, although this increased between 1990 and 2007. The rest of the world includes many of the old Commonwealth countries, which at one time were Britain's biggest markets.

Since 1970 the United Kingdom has been importing less food and fewer animals for consumption. The impact of oil can be seen in Table 16.7, as the quantities of oil-related products imported into the United Kingdom have generally fallen over the period. Manufacturing is clearly the most important category of good as far as the balance of payments is concerned. Manufacturing has retained its importance for exports, accounting for 76 per cent of exports in 1970 and 62 per cent in 2007. As far as imports are concerned, the percentage has increased a great deal over the last 30 years. The United Kingdom is now a net importer of manufactured goods. In 2007 the value of imported manufactured goods was £203 836 million, whereas the value of exported manufactured goods was £138 716 million. One reason for this is

Table 16.6 UK's imports and exports of goods by destination/source (%)

	1970		1980		1990		2003		2007	
	Exports	Imports	Exports	Imports	Exports	Imports	Exports	Imports	Exports	Imports
European Union	32	32	46	44	53	52	59	58	60	55
Other W. Europe	13	12	12	12	9	13	4	6	4	8
United States	12	11	10	12	13	11	18	12	15	8
Other OECD countries, of	11	10	6	7	5	7	4	6	6	7
which Japan	2	2	1	4	2	6	2	3	2	3
Oil-exporting countries	6	11	10	9	6	2	4	2	4	2
Rest of the world	18	14	12	11	10	10	12	18	13	21

Source: Adapted from Tables 19.5, 19.6, *Annual Abstract of Statistics*, various, ONS, UK.

Table 16.7 Pattern of trade by type of good (%)

	1970		1990		2003		2007	
	Exports	Imports	Exports	Imports	Exports	Imports	Exports	Imports
Food and animals	3	20	4	8	3	7	4	7
Beverages and tobacco	3	2	3	1	2	2	2	2
Crude materials except fuels	3	12	2	5	2	2	2	3
Minerals, fuels	3	14	8	7	9	5	11	10
Chemicals and related products	9	6	13	9	17	11	18	11
Manufactured goods	24	20	15	17	12	13	13	13
Machinery	40	19	41	30	42	40	37	30
Miscellaneous manufacturing	9	7	13	15	12	16	12	16
Total manufacturing	76	46	69	70	67	72	62	67
Others	3	2	2	!	!	!	!	!

Source: Adapted from Tables 19.1, 19.3, *Annual Abstract of Statistics*, various, ONS, UK.

the increased import penetration in the United Kingdom. Table 16.8 shows import penetration in UK manufacturing for 1970, 1980, 1990, 1994, 1996, 2003 and 2005 from which it can be seen that the penetration has increased over this time period.

Table 16.8 Import penetration[a] in manufacturing in UK (%)

1970	1980	1990	1994	1996	2003	2005
16.6	26.2	36.7	50[b]	56	60	62

Notes: [a]Measured as $\dfrac{\text{import value}}{\text{home demand}} \times 100$

[b]New SIC definition.

Source: *Annual Abstract of Statistics*, 1972, 1982, 1992, 1996, 1999, 2005, 2008.
Crown copyright. Reproduced by permission of the Controller of HMSO and of the Office for National Statistics, UK.

In 2007, the percentage of Britain's trade with the rest of the world stood at a similar level to that in 1970 but the percentages were reversed, with the country exporting less to the rest of the world and importing more. For 2007, China accounted for 6 per cent of the rest of the world total imports.

Exchange rates

The **exchange rate** of a currency is the price of that currency in terms of other currencies. If each country has its own currency and international trade is to take place an exchange of currencies needs to occur. When a UK resident buys goods from France, these must be paid for in euros. The individual will probably purchase euros from a bank in exchange for sterling in order to carry out the transaction. There must therefore be an exchange rate between sterling and euros. Likewise there will be exchange rates between sterling and all other currencies.

Basically, there are two types of exchange rate: the **floating exchange rate**; and the **fixed exchange rate**. There are also hybrid exchange rate systems which combine the characteristics of the two main types.

The floating exchange rate

A floating exchange rate is one that is determined within a free market, where there is no government intervention, and the exchange rate is free to fluctuate according to market conditions. The exchange rate is determined by the demand for and the supply of the currency in question.

As far as sterling is concerned, the demand for the currency comes from exports – that is, overseas residents buying pounds either to buy British goods and services or for investment purposes. The supply of pounds comes from imports – that is, UK residents who are buying foreign currencies to purchase goods and services or for investment purposes and who are therefore at the same time supplying pounds to the market.

The market for sterling can then be drawn using simple demand and supply diagrams. In Figure 16.3, the price axis shows the price of £1 in terms of US dollars and the quantity axis shows the quantity of pounds being bought and sold. The equilibrium exchange rate is determined by the intersection of demand and supply at £1 = $2. As this is a totally free market, if any of the conditions in the market change the exchange rate will also change.

Figure 16.3 The determination of the exchange rate of £ for $

The demand for and supply of sterling, and therefore the exchange rate, is affected by:

1 Changes in the balance of payments.
2 Changes in investment flows.
3 Speculation in the foreign exchange markets.

Changes in the balance of payments

Figure 16.4 shows the effect on the exchange rate of changes in the balance of payments. The original demand curve is DD and the original supply curve is SS. At the equilibrium exchange rate of £1 = $2 the demand for pounds is equal to the supply of pounds. In other words, if the demand for pounds comes from exports and the supply of pounds comes from imports, imports and exports are equal and the balance of payments is in equilibrium. Now it is assumed that a balance of payments deficit appears, caused by the level of imports rising while the level of exports stays the same. If exports remain the same there will be no change in the demand curve for pounds. As imports rise there will be a rise in the supply of pounds to the market; the supply curve moves to the right to S^1S^1. At the old exchange rate of £1 = $2, there is now excess supply of pounds, and as this is a free market there will be downward pressure on the value of the pound until equilibrium is re-established at the new lower exchange rate of £1 = $1. At this exchange rate the demand for pounds is again equal to the increased supply of pounds and the balance between imports and exports is re-established.

How does this happen? When the value of the pound falls two things happen: the price of imports rises and the price of exports falls. Thus the level of imports falls and the level of exports rises and the deficit is eradicated. A simple numerical example illustrates this point:

At old exchange rate £1 = $2:

An American car which costs $20000 in USA costs £10000 in UK.
A British car which costs £10000 in UK costs $20000 in USA.

Figure 16.4   The effect of changes in the balance of payments on the exchange rate

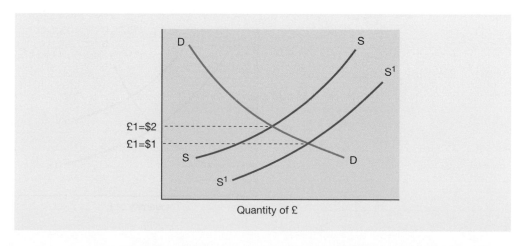

If the exchange rate falls to £1 = $1:

The American car still costs $20000 in USA but now costs £20000 in UK.
The British car still costs £10000 in UK but now costs $10000 in USA.

Therefore a depreciation in the exchange rate has made imports dearer (the American car) and exports cheaper (the British car). Thus a fall in the value of the pound helps to re-establish equilibrium in the balance of payments.

In the case of a surplus on the balance of payments, the exchange rate will rise, making exports more expensive and imports cheaper and thereby re-establishing equilibrium in the balance of payments. You should test your understanding of the working of the foreign exchange markets by working through what happens if a surplus develops.

A fall in the value of the pound in a free market is called a 'depreciation' in the value of the pound, a rise in its value is called an 'appreciation'.

Changes in investment flows

In Figure 16.5, the original equilibrium exchange rate is £1 = $2. If there is an increase in the level of investment in the UK from overseas, there will be an increase in the demand for pounds. The demand curve moves to the right (to D^1D^1), and the exchange rate rises to £1 = $2.5.

The effect of speculation

If the exchange rate of sterling is expected to rise, **speculators** will buy sterling in order to make a capital gain by selling the currency later at a higher exchange rate. There will be an increase in the demand for pounds and the exchange rate will rise. If the exchange rate is expected to fall, speculators will sell sterling in order to avoid a capital loss, there will be an increase in the supply of sterling and therefore a fall in the exchange rate. Illustrate these changes yourself using demand and supply diagrams.

Figure 16.5   The effect of changes in the investment flows on the exchange rate

The important thing about speculation is that it tends to be self-fulfilling. If enough people believe that the exchange rate is going to rise and act accordingly, the exchange rate will rise.

The main advantage of the floating exchange rate is the automatic mechanism it provides to overcome a balance of payments deficit or surplus. Theoretically, if a deficit develops, the exchange rate will fall and the balance of payments is brought back into equilibrium. The opposite occurs in the case of a surplus. Of course in reality it does not work as smoothly or as quickly as the theory suggests. A depreciation is supposed to work as demonstrated in Figure 16.6.

There are, however, a number of problems which may occur to prevent this self-correcting mechanism working properly. First, if in the United Kingdom the goods which are imported are necessities that cannot be produced at home, then even if their price goes up as a result of a depreciation, they will continue to be demanded. Thus, not only will the balance of payments deficit not be automatically rectified, another economic problem will result, that of inflation. The United Kingdom will continue to buy the imported goods at the new higher price. A second problem occurs on the other side of the equation. It is assumed above that, as the price of exports falls, more exports are sold. This presupposes that in the United Kingdom the capacity is there to meet this increased demand, but this may not be the case, especially if the economy is fully employed already or if the export-producing industries are not in a healthy enough state to produce more.

These problems give rise to what is called the '**J-curve effect**'. A fall in the exchange rate may well lead to a deterioration in the balance of payments in the short term, until domestic production can be increased to meet the extra demand for exports and as substitutes for imported goods. Once this can be done there will be an improvement in the balance of payments, hence the J-curve effect pictured in

Figure 16.6   The effect of depreciation

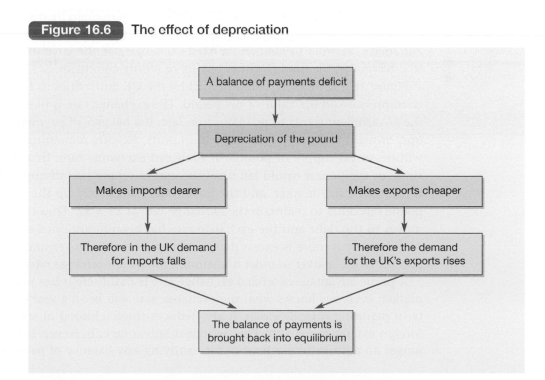

Figure 16.7. The effect of a fall in the exchange rate is limited and the curve levels off after a certain time period. The depreciation in the value of the pound seen when Britain left the ERM did not have an immediate effect on the balance of payments and many argued that this was due to the J-curve effect.

One big disadvantage of the floating exchange rate is that it introduces uncertainty into the market, and for firms that operate internationally, this is another variable which needs to be considered when planning. Moreover, since the possibility of speculation exists with the floating exchange rate, this can be destabilising and unsettling to markets, something which businesses do not welcome.

Figure 16.7 J-curve

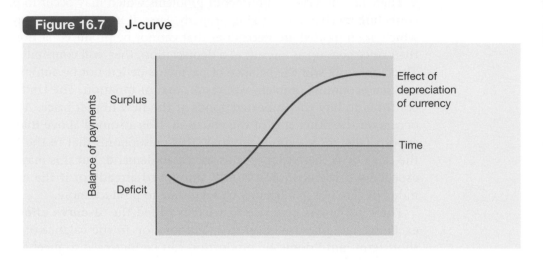

The fixed exchange rate

The fixed exchange rate is one that is fixed and maintained by the government. An exchange rate can be fixed in terms of other currencies, gold or a basket of other currencies. In order to maintain a fixed exchange rate the government has actively to intervene in the market, either buying or selling currencies.

Figure 16.8 shows the action needed by the UK authorities in the case of downward pressure on the value of the pound. The exchange rate is fixed at £1 = $2, and the government wants to maintain that rate. If a balance of payments deficit develops, brought about by an increase in imports, exports remaining the same, there will be excess supply of pounds at the fixed exchange rate. In a free market the value of the pound would fall until the excess supply had disappeared. However, this is not a free market, and the government must buy up the excess supply of pounds in order to maintain the exchange rate at £1 = $2. Thus the demand curve moves to the right and the exchange rate has been maintained at the same level. Alternatively if there is excess demand for pounds, the government has to supply pounds to the market in order to maintain the fixed exchange rate.

A prime advantage of a fixed exchange rate is that there is less uncertainty in the market; everyone knows what the exchange rate will be in a year's time, and long-term planning is made easier. It also reduces the likelihood of speculation in the foreign exchange markets. One serious disadvantage, however, is that there is no longer an automatic mechanism for rectifying any balance of payments problems

Figure 16.8   The effect of changes in the balance of payments on a fixed exchange rate

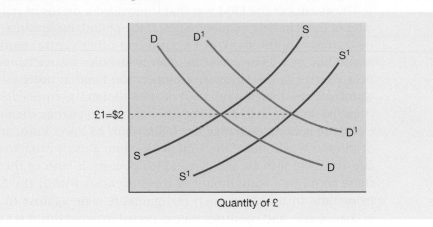

Quantity of £

as there is in the case of the floating exchange rate and this means that government intervention is necessary not just to support the exchange rate, but also to overcome any balance of payments problems. Added to this, a fixed exchange rate is not sustainable in the case of persistent deficits or surpluses. In the event of a surplus, the government must supply pounds to the market and if the surplus persists then eventually the government will exhaust its reserves and might well have to revalue the pound (i.e. increase the exchange rate of the pound). In the case of a persistent deficit, the size of the government's reserves will be increasing over time and the government may have to **devalue** the pound to correct the problem.

There are, then, advantages and disadvantages to both types of exchange rate and there have been hybrid exchange rate systems which serve to combine the advantages of both systems. In such an exchange rate system the exchange rate is basically fixed but is allowed to fluctuate by a small amount either side of the central value. The **Exchange Rate Mechanism (ERM)** of the European Union was an example of this. When the United Kingdom entered the ERM the exchange rate was fixed against other member currencies but allowed to vary by 6 per cent either side of the central value before action was needed.

Over the years the United Kingdom has had a variety of different types of exchange rate. Before the First World War and for some time between the wars, the exchange rate was fixed in terms of gold – the gold standard. From the Second World War until 1972, the United Kingdom was part of the Bretton Woods system of fixed exchange rates, where the pound was fixed in terms of dollars. Then from 1972 to 1990, there was a floating exchange rate. In 1990, however, Britain joined the Exchange Rate Mechanism of the European Union, which was again a fixed exchange rate. In September 1992, the pound left the ERM and was allowed to float once more.

The Exchange Rate Mechanism

In October 1990, the United Kingdom joined the ERM, which was a system of fixed exchange rates. The currencies within the ERM were fixed against the European currency unit (ECU) and were therefore fixed against one another. Exchange rates were allowed to fluctuate by a small percentage around their par values. The ECU was a weighted basket of EU currencies, designed to act as a unit of account and eventually as an international currency.

The essence of the ERM was that it provided a means of stabilising the exchange rates of participating member states. If the pound, for instance, strayed too far from its central rate the Bank of England and other central banks of ERM members would buy or sell currencies in order to stabilise the exchange rate. Each member held reserves in the European Co-operation Fund in order to settle debts between countries, and these funds could be used to stabilise currencies. Another thing that could be done to help an ailing currency was to change the domestic rate of interest. If the pound's exchange rate fell towards its lower limit, an increase in the rate of interest would make the United Kingdom a more attractive place for investors and therefore increase the demand for pounds. If both of these approaches failed, there could be a realignment of the currencies within the ERM. This happened from time to time, but such realignments were against the spirit of the fixed exchange rate, and countries were expected to avoid this if possible.

Britain's reasons for entering the ERM in 1990 were as follows:

- To enjoy the benefits of fixed exchange rates and, in particular, less uncertainty and reduced speculation.
- As part of the government's anti-inflationary stance, since the discipline of the ERM would force the United Kingdom's rate of inflation towards the lower European average.
- As part of Britain's commitment to Europe, the Maastricht Treaty and the Delors plan called for economic and monetary union between the countries of the EU.

Figure 16.9 shows the fluctuations in sterling's exchange rate after joining the ERM. The exchange rate of the pound was much more stable while the UK was a member

Figure 16.9 **Exchange rate of sterling with the Deutschmark**

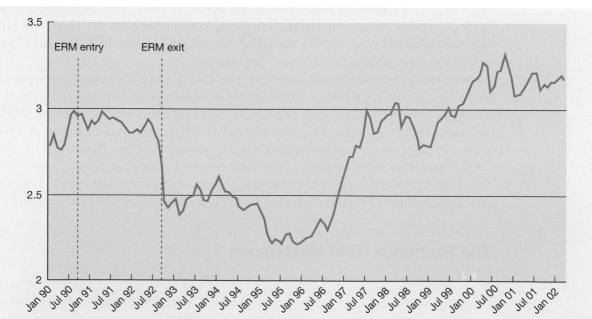

Source: Adapted from *www.statistics.gov.uk/statbase/tsdataset.asp?vlink=210&more=Y.*

of the ERM, but sterling ran into problems in mid-1992, mainly as a result of speculation against the pound. The Bank of England intervened in the market but was unable to stop the fall in the value of the currency. An increase in interest rates was announced but then withdrawn very quickly because of political pressures and the effect such a move would have on UK industry in the midst of recession. In the end the pound was suspended from the ERM and allowed to float, and subsequently fell in value sharply.

web link   For information on exchange rates see *www.bankofengland.co.uk*

The single European currency

On 1 January 1999 the single European currency – the euro – was introduced. In order to qualify for membership of the single currency, EU members had to fulfil strict convergence criteria with respect to inflation rates, budget deficits and the rates of interest.[1] In the end all countries qualified except Greece, where there were problems with high inflation rates. The UK, Denmark and Sweden decided not to join the single currency while Greece, Slovenia, Malta and Cyprus have since joined. Each of the currencies of these 15 members is fixed to the euro at a specified rate, but each is a sub-unit of the euro rather than a separate currency.

Even though the UK has not joined the single currency, many businesses in the UK have already adapted to its existence. Many large companies use the euro for accounting purposes – Marks & Spencer stores are fully equipped to accept the euro. Even without entry, preparation is necessary for practical reasons, since many large companies have started to invoice and pay bills in euros – computer systems will have to be adapted to allow for this. There will also be a cost involved in the UK as banks are charging fairly high commission for converting euros, particularly for small users. Preparation is also a strategic issue for business. First, EMU will result in greater competition, as price differences will be more obvious to consumers. The cost of converting currencies serves to increase the costs of UK businesses and make them less competitive. Second, EMU will probably result in more mergers and acquisitions across Europe and this will have dramatic effects on the structures of industries.

In the UK the debate over the single European currency continues, although as previously noted this issue has been pushed into the background by other problems. The pro single currency camp claims that the UK will be further marginalised in Europe if it does not join in the single currency. It also argues that there are great benefits to membership – a reduction in transaction costs like the cost of currency exchange, a reduction in the uncertainty caused by changing exchange rates, lower interest rates and the continuance of London as a financial centre in currencies. The anti camp argues just as vociferously that all of this would be at the expense of the loss of sovereignty – the UK would be unable to change its exchange rate in order to boost the competitiveness of UK goods. The performance of the euro since its birth has been variable. Figure 16.10 shows the value of the euro against sterling since January 1999 when €1 was worth 70p. In June 2008 one euro was worth 79p in the UK.

Figure 16.10 Exchange rate of the euro with sterling

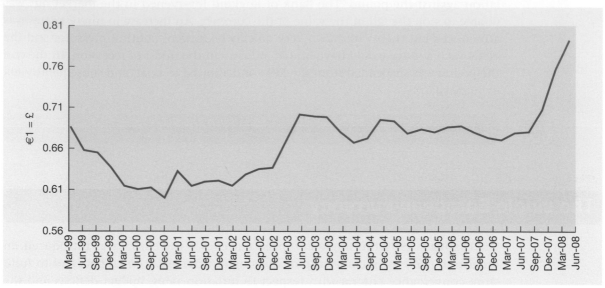

Source: Adapted from *www.bankofengland.co.uk*.

There are a number of problems brewing in Europe. First, there are the problems associated with the lack of agreement on the new constitution which have already been discussed. Second, it seems that the imposition of a single interest rate across Europe has caused problems as some countries are growing and could bear a higher rate of interest while others are in recession and therefore could not. Third, member countries have to act to reduce the size of their budget deficit if it exceeds 3 per cent of GDP. Again this might be acceptable in a booming economy but not in an economy heading for recession. At the end of 2008 there is not much evidence of economic convergence and there is a strong anti-euro feeling in parts of the EU.

Exchange rates and business

Reference has already been made to the fact that changes in exchange rates can affect businesses in several ways. These would include:

- making it easier or harder to export (as prices change);
- making it easier or harder for foreign competitors to penetrate the domestic market (again through the price effect);
- causing uncertainty in both trading and investment terms;
- adding to or reducing the cost of imported raw materials and component parts.

In addition, if a falling exchange rate causes inflationary pressures within the economy, this could add to a firm's production costs (e.g. through higher wage bills) and could encourage the government to introduce counter-inflationary policies which might subsequently depress demand in the home market.

For businesses regularly involved in currency dealing and/or multinational activities, changing currency values can also bring other gains or losses. Shell and Allied Lyons, for example, lost over £100 million each on currency gambles in the early 1990s by entering into deals when the exchange rate between currencies was not fixed in advance. In contrast, Unilever's record profits for the financial year 1992/93 included substantial overseas earnings, some of which were the direct result of a weaker pound, which in turn meant that remitted profits increased when converted back into sterling. Clearly the introduction of a single European currency will impact upon such gains or losses.

Synopsis

This chapter has looked at the international marketplace and, in particular, the benefits that derive from international trade. Consideration has also been given to some of the restrictions that exist to free trade and the organisations that are active in promoting it. Patterns of trade in the United Kingdom have been examined, as well as a recent history of the balance of payments position. Exchange rates were covered, including an analysis of how businesses are affected by changes in the value of currencies.

Summary of key points

- International trade takes place because it increases the output of the whole world.

- Despite this there are restrictions to international trade which include tariffs and quotas, but there are international organisations which seek to limit these and promote free trade.

- The balance of payments is a record of one country's trade with other countries.

- A balance of payments deficit is a situation where imports are greater than exports, a balance of payments surplus is the opposite, where exports are greater than imports.

- The exchange rate is the price of one currency in terms of another.

- A floating exchange rate is determined by the free market, a fixed exchange rate is determined by the government or some other authority.

- The euro is a single currency introduced into circulation in January 2002 by the members of the Eurozone.

case study · Enlargement of the European Union

The European Union has gone through five enlargements, increasing its initial membership of 6 countries in 1957 to 27 members in 2008. The reasons for the establishment of the EU are well documented in this chapter and they provide the rationale for the enlargement of the EU. EU-27 covers an area of 4 million km^2 and a population of 493 million people. In population size it is the third largest after China and India. Its trade with the rest of the world accounts for 20 per cent of global trade and trade between members accounts for two-thirds of all EU trade. Figure 16.11 shows current membership of the EU and candidates for membership.

Figure 16.11 A map of Europe

The benefits arising from the enlargement of the EU include:

1 *Political stability* – expansion of the EU gives European leaders the chance to bring political stability to Europe and end the divisions which twice last century ended in war. Membership of the EU should help to entrench the new-found democracies of the former communist countries in eastern Europe. In addition, the size of the EU makes possible a concerted and joint response to the severe financial problems currently facing the world.

2 *Economic benefits* – the fifth enlargement of the EU increased the size of the population of the EU by about 30 per cent. This enhanced the EU position as a major trading bloc in the world. At the time of the last two enlargements, the new members had growing economies which extended the market size for existing members and the potential growth of the EU.

EU candidates

In 2008 there were three candidate countries – Turkey, Croatia and the Former Yugoslav Republic of Macedonia. The first two of these are in accession negotiations to join the EU while the last has not yet reached that stage. Other Balkan countries – Albania, Bosnia and Herzegovina, Montenegro, Serbia and Kosovo – are potential candidates countries. Table 16.9 gives some basic information on the three candidates.

The accession of these countries will expand the population of the EU by a further 16 per cent. The GDPs are all significantly lower than the EU-27 average but this was also true for the two newest members of the EU – Bulgaria and Romania. This should not then be an impediment to accession but there are other factors which need to be taken into account. There is the impact on the EU budget as the accession of poorer countries with large agricultural sectors has implications for both regional aid and the Common Agricultural Policy budget which together account for around 80 per cent of the EU's budget. The feeling among existing members (particularly the older members) is not as positive as it was at the time of the last two accessions, largely because of the effects of the credit crunch and the perceived loss of jobs to the poorer members of the EU. In addition to this there is the problem of relations with Russia (especially important to the Baltic states) and in the case of the Former Yugoslav Republic of Macedonia, Greek objection to the country's name. Most commentators expect further expansion to happen more slowly in the future, not least because EU treaties need to be amended to accommodate additional members.

Case study questions

1 What are the main economic benefits to *existing* members of enlarging the EU?

2 What are the main economic benefits to the *applicants* of joining the EU?

Table 16.9 Population and GDP per capita for EU candidate countries

Country	Population size (million)	GDP per capita as a % of EU-27 average
Turkey	72.5	29
Croatia	4.4	27
Former Yugoslav Republic of Macedonia	2	50

Source: Eurostat, 2008.

Review and discussion questions

1 For a business considering expansion into Europe, what methods of expansion are available?

2 Using demand and supply diagrams, show the effect on the market for foreign exchange of the following:
   (a) a decreased level of imports;
   (b) a fall in the rate of interest; and
   (c) the development of a balance of payments surplus.

3 What is the likely effect on a system of fixed exchange rates of continued speculation in one of the member currencies?

4 Explain why businesses generally prefer fixed rather than floating rates of exchange.

5 How might the US government help its ailing steel industry without resorting to trade sanctions?

Assignments

1 You work in a local chamber of commerce and have been asked to make a presentation to its members on the arguments for and against UK membership of the single European currency. The audience is likely to be mixed in its attitude to the single European currency. Prepare the presentation, anticipating and answering any possible questions the audience might have.

2 You work for a trade union in the hosiery industry which strongly supports the use of import restrictions to protect its workers from competition from countries where wage rates are much lower. You have been asked to take part in a debate on the issue by the local Conservative MP, who is a champion of the free market. Present a set of arguments that will counter any points that your opponent is likely to make.

Notes and references

1   See the 2nd edition of this book, Chapter 13.

Further reading

Ellis, J. and Williams, D., *International Business Strategy*, Pitman Publishing, 1995.

Griffiths, A. and Wall, S., *Applied Economics,* 10th edition, Financial Times/Prentice Hall, 2004.

Worthington, I., Britton, C. and Rees, A., *Business Economics: Blending Theory and Practice*, 2nd edition, Financial Times/Prentice Hall, 2005.

Web links and further questions are available on the website at:

www.pearsoned.co.uk/worthington

17 Governments and markets

Ian Worthington

The central role played by government in the operation of the economy and its markets has been a recurrent theme of this book. Paradoxically, many of the government's interventionist policies have been designed to remove existing barriers to the operations of free markets and to promote greater competition and choice. In some cases, the government's strategy has been to disengage the state from some of its involvement in the economy – as in the case of 'privatisation'. In other cases, policy changes and legislation have been deemed the appropriate course of action – as in the government's approach to competition policy and to the operation of the labour market.

Learning outcomes

Having read this chapter you should be able to:

● outline the rationale underlying the government's approach to markets

● analyse and evaluate UK privatisation policy and give examples of privatisation in other countries

● explain the changing nature of UK competition policy, including the legislative and institutional framework within which it operates

● identify government initiatives in the labour market and, in particular, its approach to employment and trade union power

Key terms

Competition Act 1998
Competition Commission
Competition policy
Director General of Fair Trading
Economic efficiency

Keynesianism
Labour market
Labour market flexibility
Learning and Skills Council
Monetarism

New Deal
Office of Fair Trading
Privatisation
Third way
Training and Enterprise Councils

Introduction

A belief in the virtue of competition and in the need to develop competitive markets remains a central tenet of government economic policy in capitalist states. At the heart of this belief lies the widely accepted view that competition provides the best means of improving **economic efficiency** and of encouraging wealth creation. Proponents of this view argue that competition:

- ensures an efficient allocation of resources between competing uses, through the operation of the price system;
- puts pressure on firms to perform as efficiently as possible;
- provides a mechanism for flexible adjustment to change, whether in consumption or in the conditions of supply;
- protects consumers from potential exploitation by producers, by offering alternative sources of purchase.

It follows that an absence or lack of competition in either the factor or product markets is seen as detrimental to the well-being of the economy as a whole and that governments have a responsibility for ensuring wherever possible that markets operate freely, with a minimum of state interference.

Much of the philosophical basis for this perspective can be traced to the **monetarists** who tended to dominate official thinking in Britain and elsewhere for much of the last two decades of the twentieth century. Broadly speaking, monetarists argue that levels of output and employment in the economy are supply-determined, in contrast to the **Keynesian** view which emphasises the importance of demand in shaping economic activity. Accordingly, supply-side policies seek to improve the output responsiveness of the economy, by focusing on the workings of markets and in particular on removing the obstacles which prevent markets from functioning efficiently.

The influence of the supply-side approach to economic management can be seen in a number of key areas, and in particular, in the UK government's policy of privatisation and in the reforms in the labour market in the 1980s. Concerns over competition and potential abuses of market power also figure prominently in governmental approaches to monopolies and mergers. These three aspects of government intervention in markets – privatisation, competition policy and labour market reforms – are considered separately below and illustrate how state involvement can be a key influence in the environment of individual business organisations on both the input and output side.

Privatisation policy

On privatisation

In its broadest sense, **privatisation** involves the transfer of assets or different forms of economic activity from the public sector to the private sector. In the United Kingdom such transfers occurred throughout the 1980s and 1990s under different

Conservative administrations. Although the current Labour government has continued the process to some degree (e.g. with the partial privatisation of the National Air Traffic Services), the heyday of huge state sell-offs in Britain has probably passed. In government circles the talk is now of public/private partnerships as a mechanism for increasing private sector investment in the public services – part of what has become known as the **third way** in British politics.

In practice, the term privatisation has been applied to a range of activities that involve a measure of state disengagement from economic activity. Typically these have included:

- The sale of government-owned assets, especially nationalised industries (e.g. British Telecom, British Gas) or industries in which the government had a substantial shareholding (e.g. BP).
- The contracting out of services normally provided by the public sector (e.g. school meals, hospital cleaning).
- The deregulation or liberalisation of activities over which the state had previously placed some restriction (e.g. the deregulation of bus routes or postal services).
- The injection of private capital into areas traditionally financed by the public sector, including various Private Financing Initiatives aimed at large public sector projects such as building schools, hospitals and roads.
- The sale of local authority-owned property to private citizens or organisations (e.g. council houses, school playing fields).
- The privatisation of government agencies (e.g. Her Majesty's Inspectors for Education).

Of these, the sale of state assets – especially the public corporations and nationalised industries – has been the main plank of UK privatisation policy and the one which has captured the most public and media attention. For this reason, in the discussion below attention is focused on this aspect of the privatisation programme.

The scope of government asset sales in the period 1979–96 is indicated in Table 17.1. In the first phase, between 1979 and 1983, these tended to generate relatively small sums of money compared with what was realised in later years and generally involved the sale of government shares in companies such as British Aerospace, Britoil, BP, ICL and Ferranti. Between 1983 and 1988, the government disposed of a

Table 17.1 Major asset sales, 1979–1996

Amersham International	British Telecom	National Grid
Associated British Ports	Britoil	Railtrack
British Aerospace	Cable & Wireless	Rolls-Royce
British Airports Authority	Electricity industry	Rover Group
British Airways	Enterprise Oil	Royal Ordnance
British Coal	Fairey Aviation	Sealink (British Rail)
British Energy	Ferranti	Short Brothers
British Gas	Forestry Commission	Unipart (Rover)
British Petroleum	Istel (Rover)	Water authorities
British Rail Hotels	Jaguar (British Leyland)	Wytch Farm onshore oil (British Gas)
British Steel	National Bus Company	
British Sugar Corporation	National Enterprise Board Holding	

number of its largest industrial and commercial undertakings, including British Telecom, British Gas and British Airways, along with Rolls-Royce and Jaguar. These were followed by the sale of British Steel, the Rover Group, the National Bus Company and, more significantly, by the regional water authorities and the electricity industry in the late 1980s and early 1990s.[1] In the most recent phase, major sales have included British Coal, Railtrack, the flotation of the National Grid, the privatisation of the nuclear industry and the selling off of the National Air Traffic Services (NATS). It is worth noting that Railtrack, having gone through a period of administration, has subsequently been turned into a not-for-profit organisation called Network Rail.

In disposing of national assets governments have used a number of different methods, including selling shares to a single buyer, usually another company (e.g. the sale of Rover), selling shares to the company's management and workers (e.g. the management buyout of the National Freight Corporation), and selling shares on the open market for purchase by individuals and institutions (e.g. the stock market flotation of British Telecom). In some cases the process took place in several stages, as a proportion of shares was released on to the market over several years (e.g. BP); in other cases a one-off sale occurred, with investors invited to subscribe for the whole of the equity (e.g. British Steel). As Figure 17.1 indicates, proceeds from privatisation sales between 1979 and 1991 exceeded £34 billion, with the majority of the revenue being raised in the mid- to late 1980s. Estimates for the period 1991–4 suggest that privatisation yielded a further £25–£30 billion for the Exchequer. Over the whole period of privatisation it is thought that total revenues

Figure 17.1   Proceeds from privatisation

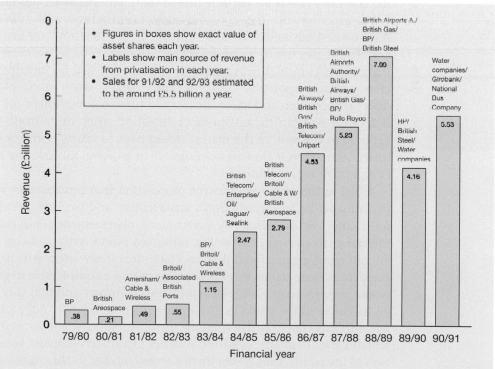

Source: Cook, G. C., *Privatisation in the 1980s and 1990s*, Hidcote Press, 1992.

from the sale of state-owned industries amounted to around £100 billion (at 2000 prices). This is equivalent to approximately 2 per cent of total government expenditure (or revenues) for that period. Interestingly, these amounts now seem rather modest when set against the significant sums invested by the UK Treasury in supporting Northern Rock during the 2008 credit crisis. As part of this support, the bank has been 'nationalised' in order to protect the taxpayers' interest.

Postscript

The global financial crisis (see 'International business in action', below) has resulted in a number of governments taking steps to protect their financial institutions. In some cases this has meant the nationalisation or part-nationalisation of those institutions. While this suggests a reversal of the privatisation process, in reality this should be seen as a particular response aimed at addressing a specific problem. It is not a general trend.

Rationale

The roots of privatisation policy lie in the attempt by the Conservative government, then under the leadership of Margaret Thatcher (1979–90), to tackle the perceived deficiencies in the supply side of the UK economy. Central to the government's philosophy was the belief that the free market was a superior method of allocating economic resources and that large-scale state involvement in business activity hampered economic progress. 'Rolling back the frontiers of the state' – by reducing the size of the public sector – was consequently seen as a key component in improving the country's economic performance at both national and international level.

The government's case for privatisation centred round the claim that the sale of state-owned businesses would improve their efficiency and general performance, and would give rise to increased competition that would broaden consumer choice. Under state control, it was argued that businesses had no incentive to strive for efficiency or to respond to consumer preferences, since many of them lacked any direct competition and all of them could turn to government for financial support, if revenue was insufficient to meet operating costs. In contrast, firms which were exposed to the 'test' of the market would have to satisfy both the consumer and the financial markets if they were to survive or to avoid takeover by more efficient and competitive organisations.[2]

Allied to this argument was the proposition that privatisation would improve the performance of an organisation's management and workers. Freed from the need to meet objectives laid down by government, management could concentrate on commercial goals such as profitability, improved productivity and cost reduction, and on encouraging greater flexibility and technical innovation within the organisation. Implicit in these claims was the acceptance that a considerable degree of restructuring would need to occur within each privatised company and that this was likely to act as an incentive to the workforce to improve its performance. Additional encouragement was also expected to derive from the use of employee share-ownership schemes, under which current employees within a newly privatised company were offered a proportion of the equity, thus giving them a vested interest in the organisation's fortunes.

The sale of shares to employees and to the public generally was also presented as a benefit of privatisation in that it helped to encourage wider share ownership and to create a 'share-owning democracy', with increased sympathies towards capitalist modes of production (and possibly the Conservative party). Concomitantly, the sale of state assets also served to reduce the size of the public sector borrowing requirement (PSBR) – since revenue from sales was counted as negative public expenditure – and this helped to reduce the government's debt burden and to take some of the pressure off interest rates, as well as releasing funds for use by the private sector.

Criticisms of privatisation

Opponents of privatisation have likened the process to 'selling the family silver' – disposing of important national assets for short-term financial gains. Under privatisation, these assets, once owned by the general public, have passed into the hands of those individuals and organisations able and willing to buy shares including overseas buyers who could ultimately gain control of important parts of British industry, unless prevented from doing so by government action (e.g. through a 'golden share'). To add to this criticism, some observers claimed that valuable assets, bought over many years by public funds, were sold off too cheaply to private investors who have reaped the benefit at the expense of the general public. Only industries which were not attractive to the stock market have tended to remain in public ownership and this has meant that the taxpayer has had to pay the bill to support their continued existence.

Further criticisms have included the loss of future government revenue from the sale of profitable state-owned businesses and the problem of ensuring that commercial goals are not allowed to displace completely the broader economic goals once pursued by nationalised industries (e.g. the possible closure of unprofitable rural telephone boxes or railway lines under privatisation). In essence, the fear has been that once freed from government regulation, privatised companies will tend to replace the loss-making 'public service' element of their former activities with products or services that offer the greatest levels of profit. While this will benefit some consumers, the cost is likely to be borne by other buyers who have limited market power and, in some cases, no alternative product to turn to.

This problem of lack of choice has been particularly acute where the privatisation of a state monopoly has given rise to a private monopoly, as initially was the case with many of the privatised utilities. Despite the establishment of 'regulators' to oversee the operations of some of the newly privatised concerns (see Table 17.2) and to act as a kind of proxy for true competition, some opponents still feel that the interest of consumers is not fully protected under the current arrangements. They also feel that exploitation through higher prices or other abuses of market power remains possible. Evidence from investigations by the former Monopolies and Mergers Commission (see below) and from the regulatory authorities suggests that this view is not without foundation. This evidence has also conveniently been used by the Treasury in recent years as a justification for levying windfall taxes on the profits of the privatised utilities as a means of boosting Exchequer revenues.

Table 17.2 Key regulatory bodies for selected privatised utilities

Name	Date established	Main activities
Office of Tele-communications (OFTEL)	1984	Regulated BT – especially line rentals, inland calls, overseas calls; provided conditions for new entrants and regulated the equipment market. Its duties have now passed to OFCOM (see below).
Office of Water Services (OFWAT)	1989	Regulates domestic and non-domestic supply by water and sewerage companies. Regulates price increases to customers.
Office of Gas and Electricity Markets (OFGEM)	2000	Regulates the gas and electricity industries in England, Scotland and Wales with the aim of enhancing customer choice and value by promoting competition and controlling monopolies. Replaced OFGAS and OFFER.
Office of Communications (OFCOM)	2003	Regulates the UK communications industries with responsibilities for television, radio, telecommunications and wireless communications services.

web link

Regulatory body websites include *www.ofcom.gov.uk*, *www.ofwat.gov.uk*, *www.ofgem.gov.uk*

Privatisation overseas

Before offering an assessment of privatisation in the United Kingdom, it is worth noting that most other states have embarked on similar experiments in economic liberalisation, irrespective of their size, ideology or level of economic development. At the end of the 1980s it was estimated that worldwide sales of state assets to the private sector exceeded $25 billion or about £14 000 million and this figure has continued to grow with the ongoing privatisation process in eastern Europe and elsewhere. For example, according to *The Economist* (23 November 1996), in the period 1985–95 the combined revenues from privatisation in France, Germany, Italy, the Netherlands and Spain alone were in excess of $70 billion, with France having the lion's share of $34 billion. For the same period the United Kingdom's receipts were estimated at $85 billion, making it the most significant privatisation programme within the OECD.

The following examples of overseas privatisation give some idea of the wide range of state assets from different sectors of the economy that have been sold by governments of different political complexions over the last two to three decades.

- In Portugal major privatisations between 1989 and 1997 included banks, insurance companies, public utilities and businesses producing cement, oil, paper products, tobacco and beer.
- In the Netherlands privatisations have included the national airline (KLM) and the water, gas and electricity utilities.
- In Brazil part of the country's rail network has been sold off; in Jamaica privatisation has included the National Commercial Bank and the Caribbean Cement Company.

- In France privatisations range from chemicals and oil to insurance, banking, public utilities, vehicles and parts of the motorway network.
- In India the government has divested a significant proportion of public sector enterprises with sales including businesses involved with steel, zinc and petrochemicals.
- In China the government has proceeded cautiously with privatisation, starting with the sale of the smaller state-owned enterprises to private owners and more recently the partial privatisation of some larger listed companies.

Arguably the most dramatic and exciting experiments in privatisation have taken place in eastern Europe, particularly among the transition economies which have moved from a planned economic system towards private enterprise. In the newly unified Germany, for instance, the federal government decided to appoint a special privatisation agency (Treuhand) to oversee and assist in the large-scale privatisation of former East German state industries and firms, and other governments (including those in Hungary, the Czech Republic and Poland) have embarked on similar programmes of rolling privatisation and have undertaken legal and institutional changes to speed up the process. While progress has varied in the different states and has generally been influenced by questions of economic and political stability (e.g. in the Russian Federation), the large-scale sell-off of public assets by the former communist states will undoubtedly continue into the foreseeable future. Current evidence suggests that the transition in these countries is proving a significantly more painful experience than that encountered in states already possessing a market-based economic system (see e.g. the article by Nick Potts in the Further reading section at the end of the chapter).

mini case   Government to the rescue

While privatisation has gripped the imaginations of governments of all persuasions for the last two to three decades, there often comes a time in economic history when circumstances dictate that a particular economic orthodoxy has to be temporarily (if not permanently) abandoned. Arguably one of the best examples of this was the decision by the US government to take the two American mortgage giants Fanny Mae and Freddie Mac into temporary public ownership.

The two companies concerned account for about 50 per cent of all US home loans and play an active role in buying up mortgages from lenders, parcelling them up and then selling them on to financial institutions across the globe. With the onset of the credit crisis in 2007/8, Fanny Mae and Freddie Mac were faced with multi-billion-dollar losses as homeowners defaulted and house prices tumbled.

While the two US institutions were far from being the only businesses facing severe financial problems, their importance to the US housing market meant that their precarious position threatened not just the property market in America, but also the wider global financial system (see 'International business in action: The global financial crisis').

In an effort to reassure the financial markets, the US decided that the two government-sponsored enterprises should become government-owned businesses on a temporary basis, what in the US is known as 'conservatorship'. For the foreseeable future, Fanny Mae and Freddy Mac are to be run by the Federal Housing Finance Agency and underwritten by public money. This is similar to the arrangement in the UK, where Northern Rock Building Society – another victim of the credit crisis – has been temporarily nationalised by the UK government.

Assessment[3]

Measured against some of the UK government's stated objectives, privatisation appears to have been successful, and has involved a transfer of ownership of over 7 per cent of GDP from the public to the private sector. Apart from the fact that many other national governments have sought to emulate Britain's approach to asset sales, the privatisation programme has been cited as an important component of the improvement in the supply side of the economy after 1979. It has also been a critical element in promoting the free market approach which has come to dominate governmental thinking in Britain and elsewhere for over two decades. All of this has evidently been achieved with the support of the British public (although some opinion polls have indicated a decline in the popularity of privatisation). In 1979, for instance, only 7 per cent of adults owned shares in public companies. By the early 1990s this figure had risen to 25 per cent, or 11 million shareholders, many of whom had bought shares for the first time in the 1980s with the sale of the big public utilities.

This significant growth in the number of ordinary shareholders can be explained in a number of ways. For a start, most stock market flotations were accompanied by extensive and costly advertising campaigns which helped to raise public awareness and to attract investors (e.g. British Gas's 'Tell Sid' campaign). Added to this, investors in public utilities were often offered special incentives to buy shares in businesses they dealt with on a regular basis (e.g. cheaper telephone bills) or in which some of them worked and therefore had a vested interest. Perhaps most importantly, and with the benefit of hindsight, some privatisation stock appears to have been sold at substantially lower prices than the market would bear and this guaranteed quick profits for people who bought and then sold immediately as prices rose. In the circumstances it is not surprising that many flotations were hugely oversubscribed – a fact which led to criticism that some privatisation stock had been considerably undervalued.

Many shareholders who invested for longer-term capital gains also benefited from underpricing of share issues and in some cases received free additional shares and other benefits (including annual dividends) by holding on to their investment. An analysis by Gary Cook of the share performance of privatised companies shows that some of the earlier privatisations have produced spectacular long-term gains, though some privatised company shares performed less well.[4] Cable & Wireless shares, for example, were issued at an average price of 56p in the early 1980s and were trading at 588p by August 1991. Similarly, BT's initial issue price of 130p in 1984/5 had risen to 391p by the same date, a threefold increase despite the stock market crash in 1987.

Whatever the reason for the growth in share ownership, it is clear that privatisation, along with the sale of council houses, helped the Conservative government of the day to claim that it encouraged the growth of a 'property-owning democracy' in which an increasing number of citizens held a stake in the success of the economy and therefore in the performance of the private sector. That said, it is still the case that the majority of shares in public companies are held by individuals in better-paid professional and managerial occupations and that overall the percentage of *all* UK shares owned by individuals has fallen dramatically over the last 30 years. In contrast, the holdings of institutional investors (such as insurance companies and pension funds) have risen rapidly – a fact which not only gives them significant influence over the future of many public companies, but which also suggests that the claim of wider share ownership has to be treated with a degree of caution.[5]

Notwithstanding this latter point, the government's relative success in selling state assets also helped it initially to achieve another one of its objectives – that of reducing the size of the PSBR. From the early 1980s onwards, public expenditure as a percentage of GDP fell substantially – partly as a result of the revenues from the privatisation programme – and by the latter part of the decade the government had a budget surplus (or public sector debt repayment) as revenue exceeded spending. Once again, however, this apparent benefit needs to be seen in context. For a start, much of the improvement in public finances during this period was a result of the government's restraint on public spending, rather than the effects of privatisation, though the receipts clearly helped the government to balance its books. Added to this, by the early 1990s, as the recession took hold, public spending rapidly began to outstrip the amounts raised in revenue, causing a dramatic growth in the size of government borrowing, despite a decade of privatisation receipts. Understandably, some critics have asked whether the sale of valuable state assets was in vain and distracted the incumbent government from addressing some of the underlying structural weaknesses in the British economy.

With regard to privatisation as a spur to greater organisational efficiency and performance, this is an area in which assessment is particularly problematical. Part of the difficulty arises from the fact that direct comparisons between state and privatised companies are often impossible, since some goods and services have not normally been provided by both the public and private sectors simultaneously (e.g. railways). In addition, even where such provision occurs (e.g. the health service), the public sector usually has to pursue a number of non-commercial objectives laid down by politicians and this makes direct comparisons somewhat unfair, particularly if profitability alone is taken as a measure of performance.

One way of approaching some of these problems is to attempt a comparison between the performance of an organisation before privatisation and its performance after it has become part of the private sector – using measures such as relative profitability, productivity or levels of service. Yet, once again, significant methodological difficulties exist which call into question the validity of many of the conclusions. Industries such as British Gas and British Telecom, for instance, have always been profitable and profits have tended to grow since privatisation; but this could as easily reflect the benefits of monopoly price rises as improvements in efficiency resulting from a change in ownership. Conversely, the decline in the fortunes of the once publicly owned steel industry could be interpreted as a decline in efficiency and/or performance under privatisation, when in fact a combination of overcapacity in the world steel industry and the impact of the recession have clearly been the main culprits.

Comparisons of productivity can also be misleading and usually fail to take into account the substantial 'economic' costs of privatisation (e.g. large-scale redundancies). Many state industries were substantially restructured prior to flotation in order to attract investors, and the resulting job losses – invariably at the taxpayer's expense – helped many newly privatised businesses to claim substantial productivity gains in their first few years of trading. Perhaps ironically, the greatest improvements in productivity in the period 1984–91 often occurred within industries nationalised at the time – such as British Coal and British Rail – whose massive redundancy programmes helped them to outpace the productivity gains of manufacturing industry by anything up to three times, according to Treasury figures. In such circumstances, it would be easy – though probably unreasonable – to conclude that while being privatised was good for productivity, it was not as good as not being privatised!

Further complications arise when one compares the performance of privatised companies which have remained monopolies with the performance of those which have consistently operated under competitive market conditions. Writing in the heyday of privatisation (the *Guardian*, 3 March 1993), Victor Keegan argued that the fortunes of companies such as British Steel, Rolls-Royce and Rover had been seriously affected by the sort of violent cyclical disturbances which had previously driven them into the public sector and that this had significantly influenced their attractiveness to private investors. In comparison, businesses which had faced little effective competition in some areas of the market (e.g. Cable & Wireless, British Airways) and those facing none (e.g. the water companies, British Gas) had invariably performed well for their shareholders; though the price of this success had frequently been paid by customers (in the form of inflated charges) and workers (in the form of redundancy).

Keegan's conclusion, that it is competition rather than ownership which acts as a spur to increased efficiency, is one that is widely held and underlies some of the recent attempts by government and by the regulatory bodies to identify ways of reducing the monopoly power of the privatised public utilities. The proposition is that under a more competitive market structure the commercial pressures of the marketplace force management to seek ways of improving organisational efficiency and performance, for fear of the consequences if they fail to meet the needs of the consumer and the investor. If left to their own devices, the large utilities are unlikely to put themselves to such 'tests' voluntarily, and this approach would presumably find favour with shareholders who have a vested interest in maximising revenue. Paradoxically, in order to improve the position of the consumer, government may be forced to intervene more aggressively and imaginatively in the marketplace, in order to promote greater competition among producers and increased choice for the consumer. Such intervention could easily be justified under current competition policy.

Competition policy

Whereas privatisation has focused on the balance between public and private provision within the overall economy, UK government **competition policy** has largely been concerned with regulating market behaviour and in particular with controlling potential abuses of market power by firms acting singly or in concert in specific markets. To achieve these aims, successive British governments have relied mainly on legislation, as well as on a measure of self-regulation and persuasion, and have generally taken a more liberal view of market structures than that taken in the United States, where monopolies have been deemed illegal for over a century. This legislative framework to regulate market activity, and the institutional arrangements established to support it, are considered immediately below.

web link

There are lots of useful websites relating to UK competition policy. A good starting point is the Office of Fair Trading (OFT) which is at *www.oft.gov.uk*
You could also try the Competition Commission at *www.competition-commission.org.uk* and the Deparment of Business, Enterprise and Regulatory Reform at *www.berr.gov.uk*

The evolving legislative framework

Official attempts to control market behaviour through statutory means date back to the late 1940s with the passage of the Monopolies and Restrictive Practices Act 1948. This Act, which established the Monopolies Commission (later the Monopolies and Mergers Commission), empowered it to investigate industries in which any single firm (a unitary monopoly), or a group of firms acting together, could restrict competition by controlling at least one-third of the market. Following such an investigation, the Commission would publish a report which was either factual or advisory and it was then the responsibility of the relevant government department to decide what course of action, if any, to take to remove practices regarded as contrary to the public interest. In the event, the majority of the Commission's recommendations tended to be ignored, though it did have some success in highlighting the extent of monopoly power in the United Kingdom in the early post-war period.

In 1956 investigations into unitary monopolies were separated from those into restrictive practices operated by a group of firms, with the enactment of the Restrictive Trade Practices Act. This Act, which outlawed the widespread custom of manufacturers jointly enforcing the retail prices at which their products could be sold, also required firms to register any form of restrictive agreement that they were operating (e.g. concerning prices, sales, production) with the Registrar of Restrictive Practices. It was the latter's responsibility to bring such agreements before the Restrictive Practices Court and they were automatically deemed 'against the public interest', unless they could be justified in one of a number of ways (e.g. benefiting consumers, employment, exports). Further extensions to the Act in 1968 (to cover 'information agreements') and in 1973 (to cover services) were ultimately consolidated in the Restrictive Trade Practices Act 1976. This new Act vested the responsibility for bringing restrictive practices before the court in the recently established Director General of Fair Trading (see below).

A further extension of legislative control came with the passage of the Monopolies and Mergers Act 1965. The Act allowed the Monopolies Commission to investigate actual or proposed mergers or acquisitions which looked likely to enhance monopoly power and which involved, at that time, the takeover of assets in excess of £5 million. The aim of this Act was to provide a means of regulating activities which threatened to be contrary to the public interest, by permitting government to decide which mergers and acquisitions should be prohibited and which should be allowed to proceed and, if necessary, under what terms. Additional steps in this direction were taken with the passage of the Fair Trading Act 1973 and the Competition Act 1980, the main provisions of which are summarised below:

1 A scale monopoly exists where at least 25 per cent of a market is controlled by a single buyer or seller; this can be applied to sales at local as well as national level and can include monopolies resulting from nationalisation.

2 Investigations can occur when two related companies (e.g. a parent and a subsidiary) control 25 per cent of a market or when separate companies operate to restrict competition even without a formal agreement (e.g. tacit collusion).

3 Mergers involving gross worldwide assets of over £70 million or a market share of over 25 per cent can be investigated.

4 Responsibility for overseeing consumer affairs, and competition policy generally, lies with the Director General of Fair Trading (DGFT), operating from the Office of Fair Trading (OFT). The DGFT has the power to make monopoly references to the renamed Monopolies and Mergers Commission (MMC) and to advise the relevant government minister on whether merger proposals should be investigated by the MMC.

In the latter context, it is worth noting that while there was no legal obligation on companies to inform the OFT of their merger plans, the Companies Act 1989 introduced a formal procedure enabling them to pre-notify the DGFT of merger proposals, in the expectation that such pre-notification would enhance the prospects for rapid clearance in cases which were deemed straightforward.

While the question of market share still remains an important influence on official attitudes to proposed mergers or takeovers, there is no doubt that in recent years increasing attention has focused on anti-competitive practices and under the Competition Act 1980 such practices by individuals or firms – as opposed to whole markets – could be referred to the MMC for investigation. In addition the Act allowed the Commission to scrutinise the work of certain public sector agencies and to consider the efficiency and costs of the service they provided and any possible abuses of monopoly power, and similar references could also be made in the case of public utilities which had been privatised (e.g. under the Telecommunication Act 1984, the Gas Act 1986, the Water Industry Act 1991).

Additional statutory control has also come in the form of EU legislation governing activities which have cross-border implications. Article 81 (formerly Article 85) of the Treaty of Rome prohibits agreements between enterprises which result in a restriction or distortion in competition within the Union (e.g. price fixing, market sharing). Article 82 (formerly Article 86) prohibits a dominant firm, or group of firms, from using their market power to exploit consumers, while further Articles prohibit the provision of government subsidies if they distort, or threaten to distort, competition between industries or individual firms.

Moreover, under Regulation 4064/89 which came into force in September 1990, concentrations or mergers which have a 'Community dimension' have become the subject of exclusive jurisdiction by the European Commission. Broadly speaking, this means that mergers involving firms with a combined worldwide turnover of more than €5 billion became subject to Commission control, provided that the EU turnover of each of at least two companies involved exceeded €250 million and the companies concerned did not have more than two-thirds of their EU turnover within one and the same member state. Mergers which do not qualify under the regulation remain, of course, subject to national competition law.

Since previous editions of this book were published the UK government has acted to bring UK competition policy into line with EU law. Under the **Competition Act 1998** – which came into force on 1 March 2000 – two basic prohibitions have been introduced:

1 A prohibition on anti-competitive agreements, based closely on Article 85 of the Treaty of Rome (now Article 81).

2 A prohibition of abuse of dominant position in a market, based on Article 86 (now Article 82).

These prohibitions, which replace a number of other pieces of legislation (e.g. the Restrictive Trade Practices Act 1976; the Resale Prices Act 1976; the majority of the Competition Act 1980), were designed to be enforced primarily by the DGFT, together with the utility regulators, who would have concurrent powers in their own sphere of operations. Companies breaching either or both of the prohibitions would be liable to fines and may be required to pay compensation to third parties affected by their anti-competitive behaviour.

mini case   Accusations of price fixing

Governments in market-based economies normally argue that markets work best when there is competition between businesses and that this benefits consumers in a variety of ways, including increased choice and more competitive prices. For a market to work effectively and in the interests of consumers, firms involved in the supply side of the market (e.g. producers and retailers) need to work independently and should not collude or share information with their rivals in any way that could distort competition. Cartels, price fixing and other anti-competitive practices are usually outlawed by governments, but this does not guarantee that such practices do not exist in some markets.

To illustrate the 'problem' of anti-competitive behaviour, we can examine a number of recent cases in the UK where there have been allegations of 'price fixing' by suppliers/retailers:

- Major supermarkets were accused of price fixing of dairy products and were fined over £100 million after admitting they acted together on the pricing of milk, butter and cheese.
- British Airways and Virgin Atlantic admitted colluding to fix fuel surcharges for passengers on the transatlantic route and large fines were imposed.

- In 2008, the Office of Fair Trading accused the tobacco groups Imperial and Gallagher of collaborating with some major retailers (including major supermarkets) on the prices of cigarettes and rolling tobacco.
- OFT is also investigating over a hundred British construction companies that are alleged to have fixed bids when tendering for major contracts such as schools, hospitals and private sector developments.

A central feature of all these cases is the claim that the alleged collaboration between the companies involved worked to the disadvantage of consumers (whether individuals, other businesses or public sector bodies such as local authorities). In short, price fixing – whatever form it takes – tends to make products/services more expensive than they would be under truly competitive market conditions. Under UK law, firms that are found to engage in such practices can be fined up to 10 per cent of their UK turnover, although this rarely happens, particularly as some of the accused tend to admit a degree of liability in exchange for a reduced fine.

With the passage of the Enterprise Act in 2002, further significant changes have been introduced, including the addition of strong deterrents for individuals involved in breaches of competition law, the modernisation of the monopoly and merger rules, and the restructuring and extension of the powers of the competition authorities (see below). Whereas the Fair Trading Act emphasised the notion of the 'public interest' in examining anti-competitive practices, the new legislation applies the test of a 'substantial lessening of competition' when the competition authorities are called upon to assess an existing or planned merger. To be deemed a 'relevant merger situation', one of two thresholds has to be met: the value of UK turnover of the enterprise acquired/to be acquired exceeds £70 million (the turnover test); or the share of goods/services in the UK or a large part of the UK that is/will be held by the merged enterprise is at least 25 per cent (the share of supply test).

In a further development in 2004, the European Commission adopted a regulation which gives the national competition authorities and courts additional responsibilities for the application of Articles 81 and 82 (see above). In essence the Office of Fair Trading and the sectoral regulators now have the power to enforce EC competition rules and, as a consequence, the Competition Act 1998 has been amended to bring it in line with the new European system.

The institutional framework

The formulation and implementation of UK competition policy has traditionally involved a variety of agencies, including the former Department of Trade and Industry, the **Office of Fair Trading**, the Monopolies and Mergers Commission and the Mergers Panel. Of these, the MMC (now the Competition Commission) and the OFT deserve special attention.

From its foundation in 1948 until its replacement in 1999, the Monopolies and Mergers Commission remained a statutory body, independent of government both in the conduct of its inquiries and in its conclusions which were published in report form. Funded by the DTI, the Commission had a full-time chairperson, and around 35 other part-time members, three of whom were deputy chairpeople and all of whom were appointed by the Secretary of State for Trade and Industry. Such appointments normally lasted for three years at the outset and included individuals drawn from business, the professions, the trade unions and the universities. To support the work of the appointed members, the Commission had a staff of about 80 officials, two-thirds of whom it employed directly, with the remainder being on loan from government departments (especially the DTI) and increasingly from the private sector.

It is important to note that the Commission had no legal power to initiate its own investigations, instead, references – requests for it to carry out particular inquiries – came either from the Secretary of State for Trade and Industry or the Director General of Fair Trading, or from the appropriate regulator in the case of privatised industries and the broadcasting media. Where a possible merger reference was concerned, the initial evaluation of a proposal was made by a panel of civil servants (the Mergers Panel) who considered whether the merger should be referred to the MMC for further consideration. The decision then rested with the Secretary of State, who took advice from the Director General of Fair Trading before deciding whether the proposal should be investigated or should be allowed to proceed.

Under the legislation, references to the Commission could be made on a number of grounds. As indicated above, these included not only monopoly and merger references but also references concerned with the performance of public sector bodies and privatised industries and with anti-competitive practices by individual firms (i.e. competition references). In addition, the Commission was empowered to consider general references (involving practices in industry), restrictive labour practices and references under the Broadcasting Act 1990, as well as questions of proposed newspaper mergers, where special provisions apply.

On receipt of a reference, the Commission's chairperson appointed a small group of members to carry out the relevant inquiry and to report on whether the company (or companies) concerned was operating – or could be expected to operate – against the public interest. Supported by a team of officials, and in some cases including members appointed to specialist panels (e.g. newspaper, telecommunications, water and electricity), the investigating group gathered a wide range of written and oral evidence from both the party (parties) concerned and from others likely to have an interest in the outcome of the inquiry. In reaching its conclusions, which tended to take several months or more, the group had to take into account the 'public interest', as defined under section 84 of the Fair Trading Act 1973, which stressed the importance of competition, the protection of consumer interests and the need to consider issues related to employment, trade and the overall industrial structure. While in most references, issues relating to competition were the primary concern, the Commission was able to take wider public interest issues into account and could rule in favour of a proposal on these grounds, even if the measure appeared anti-competitive.

The culmination of the Commission's inquiry was its report which, in most cases, was submitted to the Secretary of State for consideration and was normally laid before Parliament, where it often formed the basis of a debate or parliamentary questions. In the case of monopoly references judged to be against the public interest, the Secretary of State – with the advice of the DGFT – decided on an appropriate course of action, which could involve an order to prevent or remedy the particular adverse effects identified by the Commission. In the case of merger references, a similar procedure occurred in the event of an adverse judgement by the Commission. The Secretary of State, however, was not bound to accept the Commission's recommendations, nor was he or she able to overrule the conclusion that a merger does not operate, or may be expected not to operate, against the public interest.

It is important to note that at all stages of this multi-stage process, a considerable degree of lobbying occurred by the various interested parties, in an attempt to influence either the outcome of the investigations or the subsequent course of action decided upon. Moreover, considerable pressure tended to occur, even before a decision was taken as to whether or not to make a reference to the MMC. As a number of recent cases have shown, lobbying *against* a reference can represent a key step in justifying a proposed merger. By the same token, lobbying *for* a reference has tended to become an important weapon used by companies wishing to resist an unwelcome takeover, particularly where matters of public interest appear paramount.

Following the passage of the Competition Act 1998, the MMC was replaced (on 1 April 1999) by the **Competition Commission**, an independent public body. The chairperson (full-time) and members (part-time) of the Commission are appointed by the government following an open competition and – as in the case of the MMC – are drawn from a variety of backgrounds and initially serve for a period of eight years. Organised into a series of panels, the Commission is supported by a staff of about 150, who include administrators, specialists and individuals engaged in support services. Most of these are direct employees; the remainder are seconded from government departments.

The role of the Commission is to examine mergers and market situations referred to it by another authority, usually the Office of Fair Trading. It has no powers to conduct enquiries on its own initiative. Under the Enterprise Act 2002, the Commission has been given the responsibility for making decisions on competition questions and for making and implementing decisions on appropriate remedies. It also investigates references on the regulated sectors of the economy, including the privatised public utilities, the broadcasting and media businesses and the financial services sector.

The **Office of Fair Trading** was initially a non-ministerial government department headed until recently by a **Director General**, who was appointed by the Secretary of State for Trade and Industry. Under the Fair Trading Act 1973, the DGFT was given the responsibility of overseeing consumer affairs as well as competition policy and this included administering various pieces of consumer legislation, such as the Consumer Credit Act 1974 and the Estate Agents Act 1979. In carrying out his or her responsibilities in both these areas, the Director General was supported by a team of administrative, legal, economic and accountancy staff and had a Mergers Secretariat to co-ordinate the Office's work in this field.

With regard to competition policy, the OFT's duties were originally governed primarily by the Fair Trading Act and the Competition Act 1980; in addition, under the Restrictive Trade Practices Act 1976 the Director General had responsibility for bringing cases of restrictive practices before the Restrictive Practices Court. With the passage of the Competition Act 1998, the new prohibition regime has been applied and enforced by the DGFT, and the OFT was given additional resources to root out cartels and restrictive behaviour. The legislation gave the Director General considerable powers to investigate if he/she had a reasonable suspicion that either of the prohibitions was being infringed. Under certain circumstances the DGFT could also grant exemptions from the scope of the two prohibitions and could be called upon to defend her/his decisions before the Competition Commission.

Following the Enterprise Act 2002, the OFT has become a corporate body headed by a board which has replaced the role of the DGFT. Under the legislation, the OFT has been given a leading role in promoting competition and consumer interests and is now the main source of reference for mergers referred to the Competition Commission. According to the OFT website, the organisation has three main operational areas of responsibility: competition enforcement, consumer regulation enforcement, and markets and policy initiatives. Its Annual Plan – required under the 2002 Act – is a useful source of reference on the work of the OFT and on its key objectives.

Some illustrative cases of competition policy

Since it was established in 1948, the MMC/Competition Commission has produced hundreds of reports, covering a wide range of issues and affecting firms of different sizes in a variety of markets. At the outset most of its inquiries concerned monopolies – reflecting its initial role as the Monopolies Commission. In more recent times, its work has embraced not only mergers, which have tended to be its major preoccupation, but also nationalised industries and, more recently, the work of the privatised large utilities.

The examples below provide a good insight into the Commission's role in competition policy and its relationship with the Office of Fair Trading. Students wishing to investigate a particular case in more detail should consult the appropriate report, a full list of which can be obtained from the Commission's library in London or via its website (**www.competition-commission.org.uk**).

Nestlé, 1991

This concerned the claim that the Swiss-based foods group was using its monopoly on the supply of instant coffee in the United Kingdom to keep prices high. Concerned that the company was being slow to pass on to consumers the benefits of a fall in the price of raw coffee beans, the DGFT asked the MMC to investigate the instant coffee market. Following a nine-month investigation, the Commission concluded that, while the company supplied more than 47 per cent (by volume) of the United Kingdom's instant coffee, there was still effective competition in the market and a wide degree of consumer choice, with more than 200 brands available (in 1989) and the leading supermarkets stocking on average 30 brands. Despite the facts that Nestlé had higher levels of profitability than its main competitors, and that there was a tendency for branded coffees generally to respond less quickly than own brands to reductions in input prices, the Commission concluded that Nestlé's monopoly did not operate against the public interest. The DGFT indicated, however, that the operation of the soluble coffee market should be kept under review to ensure that it remained competitive.

British Gas, 1992

This involved two parallel references to the Commission by both the President of the Board of Trade (under the terms of the Fair Trading Act) and the Director General of Gas Supply (under the Gas Act 1986). The first asked the Commission to investigate the supply of gas through pipes to both tariff and non-tariff customers; the second to investigate the supply of gas conveyance and gas storage facilities. According to the Office of Fair Trading, very little competition existed in the gas industry, since 17 million domestic household customers had no alternative source of supply and BG's control over storage and transmission facilities inhibited true competition in the industrial market where, theoretically, industrial customers could buy from other suppliers. In the Commission's report published in August 1993, the MMC called for British Gas to lose its monopoly of supply to domestic households by no later than 2002 and for the privatised utility to be split into two separately owned companies.

Midland Bank, 1992

This concerned two bids for the Midland Bank, made by Lloyds Bank and the Hong Kong and Shanghai Banking Corporation, and illustrates the question of split jurisdiction between the United Kingdom and the EU. Lloyds' bid fell within the United Kingdom's jurisdiction and was referred to the MMC as raising potential competition issues – a course of action which caused Lloyds to abandon its proposed merger. In contrast, the HSBC bid was deemed to be of wider concern and was referred to the competition authorities in Brussels. Following clearance by the EU, the HSBC proceeded with its bid and this was accepted by Midland's shareholders.

Video games, 1995

This investigation concerned the supply of video games to the UK market which was dominated by two Japanese companies, Nintendo and Sega. The Commission found the existence of a monopoly situation which affected pricing and entry by new firms. It recommended the abolition of licence controls which allowed the two suppliers to charge excessive prices and the removal of restrictions on rental of games.

UK car prices, 1999–2002

After persistent claims that UK car prices were higher on average than prices in other European countries, the OFT called for a full-scale monopolies investigation into the relationship between car makers and dealerships. In its most recent report the Competition Commission found that the existing system operated against the public interest, particularly with regard to prices, choice and innovation (see e.g. **www.competition-commission.org.uk/reports/439cars**). It highlighted, in particular, the adverse effects of the selective and exclusive distribution system permitted by the block exemption within the EU (see case study below).

Morrison's takeover of Safeway, 2003

In March 2003 the Competition Commission was asked to look at the proposed acquisition of the supermarket chain Safeway by four other rival supermarket groups: Asda, William Morrison, Sainsbury's and Tesco. The key concern was whether the proposed acquisition would lead to a lessening of competition that would adversely affect the consumer. After a lengthy investigation of the likely competitive impact, if any, of the proposed mergers went ahead, the Commission recommended that Asda, Sainsbury's and Tesco be prohibited from acquiring the whole or any part of Safeway, while Morrison's bid could go ahead subject to the company divesting some Safeway stores in certain localities.

Supermarkets enquiry, 2006–8

A two-year enquiry by the Competition Commission into the major UK supermarkets basically concluded that consumers were getting a 'good deal' from the Big 4 supermarket chains. The investigation found evidence that the major grocery retailers at times exercised considerable power in their relationship with suppliers, but this issue was beyond the Commission's responsibilities, which are essentially to protect the interest of consumers. The Commission did, however, propose an enhanced code of practice to govern retailer/supplier relationships which would be overseen by an independent ombudsman.

Government and the labour market

Government involvement in the **labour market** has taken a variety of forms and its influence on market conditions can be direct or indirect and can operate at different spatial levels. Many of the government initiatives mentioned in Chapter 13, for example, seek to affect employment prospects in the regions or in local economies and thus clearly have labour market implications. Similarly, in its general management of the economy through fiscal and monetary means (see Chapter 5), the government will influence the overall demand for labour, which is derived from the demand for the products that labour produces. Some of that demand, of course, will come from the government itself, as a central provider of goods and services and hence a key employer of labour, and its attitude to pay settlements will affect wage levels throughout the public sector. This, in turn, can spill over to the wage bargaining process in the private sector and on occasions may even involve the use of statutory or voluntary restrictions on wage rises that invariably interfere with the operations of the free market (e.g. incomes policies).

While all of these areas would need to be considered in any detailed analysis of labour market policies, in the brief discussion below attention is focused on government initiatives to improve employment prospects and training opportunities for the unemployed, and on the government's efforts to curb the power of the trade unions. Both of these approaches are particularly pertinent to the discussion on how government has sought to improve the efficiency of markets as part of its supply-side approach to economic management – using, in this case, a combination of policy and legislation to achieve its objectives.

Curbing trade union power

As a major force in the labour market, representing the interests of millions of workers, trade unions have been seen as an obstacle to the operation of market forces and as a cause of high wage costs and low labour productivity in the United Kingdom. For almost 20 years after 1979, Conservative governments sought to curb the influence of the trade unions through legislative means, in the belief that more **labour market flexibility** would develop and that this would benefit businesses seeking to respond to competition and change. To assist further in this direction, the government – with the general support of industry – abolished the Wages Councils (which were set up to protect the interests of the lower-paid) and originally refused to participate in the Social Chapter of the Maastricht Treaty (which included a provision for works' councils and the principle of equal pay for male and female workers for equal work).

The government's step-by-step approach to reducing the influence of trade unions is demonstrated by the following legislative measures, enacted in the period 1980–93.

The Employment Act 1980

This Act gave employers legal remedies against secondary picketing and most other types of secondary action. It also provided for all new 'closed shops' to be approved by four-fifths of the workforce and for public funds to be made available to encourage unions to hold postal ballots.

The Employment Act 1982

This Act further tightened the law on closed shops and outlawed union-labour-only contracts. Employers were given legal remedies against 'political' strikes and trade unions were made liable for damages, if they instigated unlawful industrial action (e.g. 'secondary' action).

The Trade Union Act 1984

This Act sought to strengthen internal union democracy. Unions were required to hold a secret ballot every ten years if they wished to keep a political fund and union executives had to submit themselves for re-election by secret ballot every five years. In addition, pre-strike ballots were required if unions wished to retain their immunity from civil action for damages in the event of a strike.

The Employment Act 1988

This Act strengthened the rights of individual union members. Unions were banned from disciplining members who refused to support strike action; all senior union officials had to be elected by secret ballot; workers were permitted to apply for court orders instructing unions to repudiate industrial action organised without a secret ballot. Moreover strikes in defence of the closed shop lost all legal protection.

The Employment Act 1990

This Act made unions legally liable for 'wildcat' strikes called by shop stewards without a proper ballot. Pre-entry closed shops were banned and so individuals could not be refused a job for not belonging to a trade union prior to appointment.

Trade Union and Labour Relations (Consolidation) Act 1992

This Act consolidated previous legislation in the field of labour relations.

The Trade Union Reform and Employment Rights Act 1993

This Act essentially had two main purposes: first, to impose further restrictions on trade unions and trade union activity; second, to enact certain employment rights as a consequence of EU directives and case law. Under section 13, for example, employers are permitted to provide inducements to employees to opt out of collective bargaining or to leave a union, while section 17 introduces a requirement for industrial action ballots to be conducted fully by postal voting.

While there is no doubt that such legislation has altered the balance of power between employee and employer and has significantly weakened the power of the trade unions, this has been only one influence, and arguably not the most important. Apart from the fact that union membership has fallen significantly over the last decade, weakening their financial position and making them less able to sustain union action, the unions have at times had to operate in a market that has been severely affected by changes in the economic cycle. Gone are the days when governments aspired to full employment and were willing to use fiscal and monetary means to achieve this objective. In the new climate of less than full employment, the influence of organised labour in the economy has inevitably been reduced and has been replaced, to some degree, by the pursuit of individual self-interest.

As a postscript it is worth noting that since the election of a Labour government in 1997 there has been a kind of rehabilitation of the trade unions and an attempt by government to enshrine certain employment rights in law. Following the Employment Rights Act of 1996, other significant pieces of legislation have included the Employment Rights (Dispute Reduction) Act 1998, the National Minimum Wage Act 1998, the Working Time Regulations 1998, the Human Rights Act 1998, the Employment Relations Act 1999, the Employment Act 2002, the Employment Relations Act 2004, Work and Families Act 2006, the Employment Equality (Age) Regulations 2006 and the Disability Discrimination Act 2005.

Employment policies

Employment policies are targeted specifically at the unemployed and over recent decades have included a wide range of measures aimed at assisting individuals to prepare themselves for employment and to gain a job. Many of the schemes have been designed to give a limited amount of work experience and/or to improve vocational training, with increasing emphasis being given to the problem of skills shortages in the economy and to matching the needs of labour with the requirements of firms. Additionally, as the following examples illustrate, governments have sought to promote the idea of 'self-help' among the unemployed and to encourage the growth of self-employment, in the hope that an expanding small firms sector will generate a large number of jobs, to replace those lost in medium- and larger-sized enterprises.

- *Restart* – introduced in 1986 and requiring anyone drawing unemployment benefit for over six months to see a specialist counsellor to try to identify possible routes back into employment.
- *Youth Training (YT)* – replaced the Youth Training Scheme in 1990. Under this scheme any person under 18 who was unemployed was guaranteed a YT place (with some exceptions, e.g. students). It has been used to combine training and education and to allow individuals to acquire nationally recognised qualifications (e.g. NVQs).
- *Employment Training (ET)* – introduced in 1988 for long-term unemployed people and others with specific needs, including those returning to the labour market. It aimed to provide training in order to help individuals to acquire the skills needed to get jobs and vocational qualifications (or credits towards them).
- *Employment Action (EA)* – introduced in 1991 and designed to help the unemployed to maintain their skills and find employment. It provided opportunities for individuals to undertake community work and offered structured jobsearch support.
- *Training for Work (TfW)* – started in 1993 to replace ET and EA, combining the characteristics of both programmes.
- *Work Trials* – designed to give long-term unemployed people a chance to prove themselves to employers by working on a trial basis while receiving benefit.

The change in government in 1997 saw the introduction of the **New Deal**, a flagship scheme designed to get individuals claiming unemployment benefits off welfare and into work. Targeted initially at 18-24-year-olds, the scheme has now been extended to other categories of person (e.g. those over 25 and those over 50, lone parents, the disabled and partners). Funded from the windfall tax levied on the privatised utility companies, the New Deal is an attempt to reduce reliance on state benefits and to make work more attractive to groups often excluded from the labour force. Like other measures, including working families' tax credits and efforts to increase the numbers going into further and higher education, it is part of an attempt by government to improve the supply side of the economy.

Local schemes

Historically, local schemes have taken a variety of forms, including interest-free loans for individuals wishing to set up a local business (e.g. Sir Thomas Whyte Charity in Leicester), local training awards to stimulate interest among local employers or individuals (e.g. Bedfordshire TEC), programmes for groups with specific training needs such as women returners (e.g. Calderdale and Kirklees TEC) and partnerships with local companies to part-fund new training initiatives (e.g. Birmingham TEC's Skills Investment Programme). As a final comment it is important to note that the government's national training programme was initially run by a system of local **Training and Enterprise Councils (TECs)** which were responsible for providing training schemes for the unemployed and school leavers and for administering various business enterprise schemes. Funded by central government and run by a board of directors drawn predominantly from industry, the TECs (known as Local Enterprise Councils in Scotland) had control of the training funds for existing training programmes and were given the wider role of encouraging training and enterprise in the economy, including supporting initiatives aimed at promoting local economic development. To this end the TECs were expected to work closely with local employers in both the public and private sector and to improve the quality and effectiveness of training in their locality, by identifying priorities and needs within the local community. TECs were replaced by the **Learning and Skills Council (LSC)** in April 2001 which became responsible for all post-16 education and training, excluding higher education. The LSC operates through a network of local LSCs which deliver national priorities at a local level (N.B. LECs in Scotland still exist). The Council is scheduled to be wound up in 2010 and replaced by two other bodies.

Synopsis

In market-based economies, governments exercise considerable influence over the structure and functioning of markets, not only through their own economic activities but also through their legislative and policy preferences. Privatisation policy seeks to reduce the role of the state in the workings of the economy through the sale of government-owned assets, in the belief that this will improve the operation of the free market. Competition policy tends to focus on the use of legal and institutional changes to curb the growth of monopoly power and to regulate market behaviour in a manner felt to be conducive to the public interest.

In both these areas the focus of government attention is essentially on the supply side of the economy and this parallels its approach to the operation of the labour market. Through a variety of legislative and administrative changes, the government has sought to create a more 'flexible' market for labour through the introduction of initiatives on training and employment and through its attempts to curb the power of the trade unions through statutory means.

Summary of key points

- Competitive markets are thought to provide major advantages, particularly with regard to enhancing wealth creation, economic efficiency and consumer choice.

- Governments, through policy and legislation, can promote increased competition within the economy and its markets.

- Privatisation has become a global phenomenon and reflects the belief in official circles that competitive, private markets are a superior method of allocating economic resources.

- Privatisation in practice has both advantages and disadvantages.

- Competition policy is basically concerned with regulating market behaviour and with controlling potential abuses of market power.

- Governments in the UK and elsewhere use legislation and regulation to promote competition and have established institutional arrangements to implement and oversee their chosen policies.

- Through its membership of the EU, the UK is influenced by competition laws that have been adopted at Community level.

- Other forms of government intervention in markets include steps taken to improve the workings of the labour market and, in particular, to promote greater labour market flexibility.

- Key approaches in this area in the UK have included legislation to curb the power of the trade unions and the use of targeted employment policies designed to boost employment opportunities and generally improve the supply side of the economy.

case study   The end of the block exemption

As we have seen in the chapter, governments frequently use laws and regulations to promote competition within the marketplace in the belief that this has significant benefits for the consumer and for the economy generally. Such interventions occur not only at national level, but also in situations where governments work together to provide mutual benefits, as in the European Union's attempts to set up a 'Single Market' across the member states of the EU.

While few would deny that competitive markets have many benefits, the search for increased competition at national level and beyond can sometimes be restrained by the political realities of the situation, a point underlined by a previous decision of the EU authorities to allow a block exemption from the normal rules of competition in the EU car market. Under this system, motor manufacturers operating within the EU were permitted to create networks of selective and exclusive dealerships and to engage in certain other activities normally outlawed under the competition provisions of the single market. It was argued that the system of selective and exclusive distribution (SED) benefited consumers by providing them with a cradle-to-grave service, alongside what was said to be a highly competitive supply situation within the heavily branded global car market.

Introduced in 1995, and extended until the end of September 2002, the block exemption was highly criticised for its impact on the operation of the car market in Europe. Following a critical report by the UK competition authorities in April 2000, the EU published a review (in November 2000) of the workings of the existing arrangement for distributing and servicing cars, highlighting its adverse consequences for both consumers and retailers and signalling the need for change. Despite intensive lobbying by the major car manufacturers, and by some national governments, to maintain the current rules largely intact, the European Commission announced its intention of replacing the block exemption regulation when it expired in September, subject of course to consultation with interested parties.

In essence the Commission's proposals aimed to give dealers far more independence from suppliers by allowing them to solicit for business anywhere in the EU and to open showrooms wherever they want; they would also be able to sell cars supplied by different manufacturers under the same roof. The plan also sought to open up the aftersales market by breaking the tie which existed between sales and servicing. The proposal was that independent repairers would in future be able to get greater access to the necessary spare parts and technology, thereby encouraging new entrants to join the market with reduced initial investment costs.

While these proposals were broadly welcomed by groups representing consumers (e.g. the Consumer Association in the UK), some observers felt that the planned reforms did not go far enough to weaken the power of the suppliers over the market (see e.g. the editorial in the *Financial Times*, 11 January 2002). For instance it appeared to be the case that while manufacturers would be able to supply cars to supermarkets and other new retailers, they would not be required by law to do so, suggesting that a market free-for-all was highly unlikely to emerge in the foreseeable future. Equally the Commission's plans appeared to do little to protect dealers from threats to terminate their franchises should there be a dispute with the supplier.

In the event the old block exemption scheme expired at the end of September 2002 and the new rules began the next day. However, the majority of the provisions under the EC rules did not come into effect until the following October (2003) and the ban on 'location clauses' – which limit the geographical scope of dealer operations – only came into effect two years later. Since October 2005 dealers have been free to set up secondary sales outlets in other areas of the EU, as well as their own countries. This is expected to stengthen competition between dealers across the Single Market to the advantage of consumers (e.g. greater choice and reduced prices).

Current evidence suggests, however, that consumer decisions in future will be influenced more by considerations such as fuel efficiency and carbon impact than by the location of dealerships.

Case study questions

1 Can you suggest any reasons why the European Commission was willing to grant the block exemption in the first place, given that it ran counter to its proposals for a Single Market?

2 Why might the new reforms make cars cheaper for European consumers?

Review and discussion questions

1 Explain the paradox that government needs to intervene in the economy to allow markets to work more freely. What forms does this intervention take?

2 Why is privatisation felt to be a spur to greater efficiency in the major utilities? How would you measure such efficiency 'gains'?

3 In what ways might a government's policy on privatisation be related to its policy on competition?

4 Examine the basis of the previous government's attempts to reform the labour market. How far do you think its reforms have been successful?

Assignments

1 Draft a press release on behalf of the government explaining why it favoured turning Railtrack into a not-for-profit company. Indicate in your statement why the option to renationalise the company was rejected.

2 You are employed by a firm of professional lobbyists which has been commissioned by a group representing European consumer interests to lobby the European Commission over the labelling of food products (e.g. contents, origin, environmental aspects). Produce a report outlining the benefits of more informative labelling on food products within the EU.

Notes and references

1 Numerous books and articles exist on privatisation within the United Kingdom. An excellent starting-point for students wishing to study UK policy is G. C. Cook's *Privatisation in the 1980s and 1990s*, Hidcote Press, 1992.

2 The concept of 'market testing' has increasingly been applied to all parts of the public service, including the civil service, with some civil servants being required to compete with the private sector for their jobs.

3 For a more detailed assessment of the UK's privatisation experience, including a review of numerous studies over recent years, see the paper by Parker in the Further reading section below.

4 Cook, *op. cit.*, pp. 23–4.

5 In a sense, however, individuals invest indirectly in shares through their pension funds, insurance policies, unit trusts and bank accounts.

Further reading

Cook, G. C., *Privatisation in the 1980s and 1990s*, Hidcote Press, 1992.

Cook, M. and Farquharson, C., *Business Economics*, FT/Prentice Hall, 1998, esp. chs. 22 and 24.

Griffiths, A. and Wall, S. (eds), *Applied Economics*, 11th edition, Financial Times/Prentice Hall, 2007.

Guislain, P., *The Privatization Challenge: A Strategic, Legal and Institutional Analysis of International Experience*, The World Bank, 1997.

Livesey, F., 'Competition Policy' in Atkinson, B., Livesey, F. and Milward, B., *Applied Economics*, Macmillan, 1998.

Martin, S. and Parker, S., *The Impact of Privatisation: Ownership and Corporate Performance in the UK*, Routledge, 1997.

Parker, D., 'The UK's Privatisation Experiment: The passage of time permits a sober assessment', CESIFO Working Paper No 1126, 2004, available in electronic form from *www.cesifo.de*.

Potts, N., 'Privatisation: a false hope', *International Journal of Public Sector Management*, 12 (5), pp. 388–409, 1999.

Worthington, I., Britton, C. and Rees, A., *Economics for Business: Blending Theory and Practice*, 2nd edition, Financial Times/Prentice Hall, 2005.

web link

Web links and further questions are available on the website at:
www.pearsoned.co.uk/worthington

The global financial crisis

In economics the term 'market' basically means a situation where buyers and sellers come together to effect an exchange. Some markets have a physical manifestation (e.g. a local farmers' market), others do not (e.g. eBay). The essential point is that a market is an arrangement where a transaction takes place; this can occur at any spatial level from local to national through to international and global and under differing structural conditions (e.g. oligopoly, monopoly, monopsony etc.). Some markets can be relatively free from government control, while others may be heavily regulated and/or, in some cases, dominated by state intervention. How a market operates, and under what conditions, can, of course, vary both spatially and temporally and will differ in other terms including the degree of formality or complexity.

As we saw in Chapter 17, for much of the last 30 years political leaders across the globe have tended to favour an increased measure of state disengagement from economic activity and have embarked on programmes of privatisation and state deregulation in many sectors of their respective economies. In doing so governments have sought to improve economic efficiency (e.g. by making markets more competitive) and to encourage wealth creation for the benefit of individuals, businesses and governments alike. In this, as in other spheres, changes of this kind can bring benefits for the business community and can open up multiple opportunities for firms operating in the marketplace for their goods or services. By the same token, the process of change brings with it certain risks and threats, some of which may apply to the market as a whole and not just to the individual participants involved in buying and selling in a particular market.

An excellent contemporary example of the latter is the global financial crisis which gripped the world in 2008 and which resulted in action at both national and international levels (see below) in an attempt to stabilise the international financial system which was under serious threat of collapse. While it is very difficult to pinpoint any single cause for this crisis, many commentators are agreed that a contributory factor was the deregulation of financial markets in previous decades, which helped to encourage credit expansion and the emergence of new forms of complex and often highly risky financial instruments (e.g. collateralised debt obligations) that were traded globally between financial institutions. One area where this 'securitisation' of debt had a very significant impact was in the housing market in countries such as the United States and the UK, with lenders granting mortgages to some customers without necessarily confirming their ability to repay. Some of these loans (subsequently known as sub-prime mortgages) proved to be highly risky and when the US housing market declined in 2007, the problem and reach of the so called 'toxic' debt rapidly became apparent.

The mini case in Chapter 3 outlines how quickly the financial contagion spread, impacting on a wide range of financial institutions across the globe and on stock markets, currency markets and on the 'real' economies in many countries. Some of the key events are worth repeating here:

- October 2007 – Citigroup announced a multi-billion-dollar write-off of sub-prime mortgage losses.
- February 2008 – a run on Northern Rock in the UK ultimately resulted in part-nationalisation by the UK government.
- March 2008 – the collapse of the US investment bank Bear Stearns resulted in its takeover by its competitor JPMorgan which was underwritten by the US government.
- September 2008 – US mortgage giants Fanny Mae and Freddy Mac were taken into temporary public ownership (see Mini case, Chapter 17, 'Government to the rescue').
- September 2008 – Lehman Brothers (US) was declared bankrupt and allowed to collapse by the US government.
- September 2008 – Merrill Lynch was taken over by the Bank of America.
- September 2008 – Washington Mutual went into receivership following a bank run.

- September 2008 – Goldman Sachs and Morgan Stanley were pressured by the US government into changing their status from investment to deposit banks.
- September 2008 – plans were unveiled for the takeover of HBOS by Lloyds.
- September 2008 – Bradford and Bingley in the UK was nationalised.
- September 2008 – nationalisation of the Fortis Bank by the Luxembourg, Belgian and Dutch governments.
- September/October 2008 – the Icelandic government nationalises the country's three main banks: Giltnir, Landsbanki, Kaupthing.
- October 2008 – the commercial property loan giant Hypo Real Estate was bailed out by the German government.

In seeking to address the various problems that were both causes and effects of the global financial crisis, governments have intervened both unilaterally and collectively in a variety of ways. Among the key instruments used have been the following:

- Nationalisation or partial nationalisation of some financial institutions to guarantee their continued existence.
- Injections of hundreds of billions of dollars by central banks to recapitalise the international financial system.
- Temporary bans on short-selling of bank shares in order to prevent speculative pressures that could cause institutional collapse.

- Temporary suspension of competition rules to allow bank mergers/takeovers.
- Financial support from the International Monetary Fund for countries in severe difficulties, including Iceland, Hungary and the Ukraine.
- Government underwriting of bank assets (e.g. loans) and provision of short-term loans to increase inter-bank lending.
- Cuts in interest rates (e.g. in the US, UK, China, Sweden, Canada) to try to stimulate borrowing in order to offset recessionary pressures in the global economy.

What is particularly significant about the global financial crisis is the recognition that action by any one government alone is insufficient to address the problems that have emerged in this and related markets (e.g. the stock market; the foreign exchange market). Moreover, while it seems unlikely that national governments will wish to retain control of key financial institutions in the future, it seems equally unlikely that they will be prepared to allow largely unfettered market capitalism to shape the global financial system in the coming decades. Indeed, it may be that the lasting legacy of this crisis is not so much the gradual restructuring of financial institutions and markets, but the demise of the mystical belief in the ability of markets to deliver optimum outcomes that has dominated political and economic thinking and discourse for much of the last 30 years.

Part Five

CONCLUSION

18 Strategy and the changing environment

18 Strategy and the changing environment

David Orton and Ian Worthington

Business organisations operate within a changing and often uncertain environment. To ensure that corporate resources are used effectively in pursuit of organisational objectives, firms need ideally to examine the external influences upon them and, where possible, to anticipate the nature and extent of environmental change. The study and practice of strategic management and decision-making has provided a number of useful approaches in this area and has generated a variety of techniques for analysing the business environment. These techniques rely on the generation of data and information, much of which is in the public domain. Accessing this information has become significantly easier with improvements in computer technology and in collecting and collating material from both national and international sources.

Learning outcomes

Having read this chapter you should be able to:

● demonstrate the need to monitor the changing business environment

● explain broad approaches to environmental analysis

● analyse a range of qualitative and quantitative techniques used by business organisations as an aid to decision making

● access a variety of national and international sources of information and data useful to both students and practitioners of business

Key terms

Brainstorming	Porter's five-forces model	SWOT (or TOWS) analysis
Cross-impact matrix	of competition	The Delphi method
Environmental analysis	Scenario writing	Trend extrapolation
Environmental scanning	Strategic fit	Trend–impact analysis
PESTLE analysis	Strategic management	

Introduction

The purpose of strategy is to provide the future direction and objectives of the organisation and to identify and gather the resources necessary in order to achieve these objectives. A simplified and popular perspective of strategy views it as a series of chronological phases: strategic analysis, identification and selection of strategic choices and, finally, implementation. For many managers this begins with a consideration of the following questions;

- Where are we now?
- What is the situation we face?
- Where do we wish to be?
- Which factors in our environment may pose challenges or opportunities to us in the future?

Managers need to be keenly aware of their organisation's internal environment (where its strengths and weaknesses may lie), and also be able to diagnose their external environment. It can be argued that the successful strategies are those that best match the organisation's resources to the pressures and forces of the environment. In short, the organisation is seeking a **strategic fit** between the internal and external environments.

Kenneth Andrews, a Harvard Professor and acclaimed as one of the earliest and foremost thinkers in corporate strategy, believed that strategy could be prescribed and should adopt the following structure in its development and application within an organisation (see Figure 18.1).

Figure 18.1   Corporate strategy

Source: Adapted from Andrews, K. (1980) *The Concept of Corporate Strategy*.

This structure emphasises the importance of assessing environmental conditions and trends as a necessary first stage in the generation of organisational strategies. The external environment is examined with the objective of identifying opportunities and risks (commonly termed threats). At the same time, the organisation should also identify its own strengths and weaknesses, which result from analysing its own internal resources. The organisation may then bring together these two forms of analysis, external and internal, and seek to identify an optimal 'fit' or 'best match' between the two. This process led to the development of the popular **SWOT** tool, which will be explored later in this chapter.

The need to monitor environmental change

Every organisation, from the smallest sole trader to the largest multinational firm, whether public or private sector, ought ideally to continually monitor its environment in order to identify potential changes or the development of long-term trends that could affect the enterprise. For some organisations, the environment is likely to be relatively stable during the mid-term, as in the case of civil service departments, the emergency services and heavy manufacturing. That said, there will always exist the possibility of environmental shocks that can destabilise the *status quo*, such as acts of terrorism, financial scandals and, more recently, the effects of the global financial crisis (see 'International business in action').

In other organisations and industries, the environment may prove to be far more turbulent. The retail sector, especially the fast moving consumer goods sector (FMCG) and consumer electronics, experiences continual innovation in product development that both shapes and reflects changing consumer demand patterns as well as increasing competition through the bewildering proliferation of product choices and condensing of product life cycles. The markets for mobile phones and portable MP3 players are just two such examples, and of course, technological developments and technology transfer now permit the boundaries of these previously distinct markets to become blurred.

The nature of the environment, or at least the way it may be perceived by each organisation in terms of stability versus dynamism, may then reflect the actions and efforts of organisations with regard to engaging in external analysis.

For organisations that perceive their environment as turbulent, the impetus for thorough and formal external analysis may be high and efforts towards such analysis might be afforded a prominent role in formulating strategies. This, however, is sometimes not sufficient. Some organisations may see their environment as so chaotic and complex that they simply do not know where to start or what to consider. With an absence of direction and clarity, organisations may inadvertently enter into a phase of soporific stupor or inertia. Alternatively, for many organisations undertaking external analysis may seem too resource intensive, in terms of money, time and people and hence may not be an attractive proposition. The act of external analysis *per se* will not confer a competitive advantage for the organisation and therefore it can sometime become difficult to justify the initial resource commitment when the returns or rewards for doing so may be unknown or uncertain.

Equally, for organisations that may perceive their environment as relatively stable, the act of continual monitoring may seem inappropriate or even illogical. If the organisation believes that the external environment in the future is likely to share the same or broadly similar characteristics as the environment it has operated within in the past, then there is little incentive to engage in external analysis.

This attitude can be likened to the simple parable of the 'boiled frog syndrome'. A frog that is placed into a pot of boiling water will immediately jump out. If the frog is placed into a tepid pot of water, it will sit there contentedly. If that pot is then slowly heated up, the frog will continue to stay in the water, until it becomes too late. The frog is unable to identify incremental changes in its environment, given that its internal apparatus is geared towards sensing sudden changes instead.

An example of this 'boiled frog syndrome' can be seen with the American giant car manufacturer General Motors (GM). In 1998, GM bought the Hummer brand name, and the off-road vehicle became an icon for GM during the early part of the millennium as it was favoured by the celebrity and Hollywood set, including high-publicity owners such as David Beckham and Governor of California and former movie star Arnold Schwarzenegger. However, in recent times, sales of the Hummer car have fallen dramatically, as rising fuel prices and concern over its impact on the natural environment have made the vehicle increasingly unpopular with consumers. GM is currently seeking to sell the Hummer brand but is finding it difficult to find another car manufacturer that is seriously interested in purchasing the brand and continuing production of the vehicle.

Analysing the environment is therefore important for all organisations. To do nothing is at best foolish and at worst, potentially disastrous.

Analysing the business environment: broad approaches

Environmental analysis is the process of scanning the environment to identify changes or trends that have the potential to generate opportunities and threats to the organisation's current or future intended strategies. The form and means by which this **environmental scanning** may be operationalised within an organisation will vary from firm to firm and can be undertaken informally or using quite sophisticated analytical tools and techniques that may require significant employment of an organisation's resources.

Informal scanning may take the form of getting information about, and from, the organisation's customers, suppliers, rivals, consultants and pressure groups. Such information from customers could, for instance, be gathered through questionnaires, sample interviewing or from feedback from the organisation's own sales and customer service staff. In retail, it is not uncommon for shop staff within a town or shopping centre to visit local rival stores and shops to get information about the prices being charged and promotional activities of their competitors. All such informal activities, whilst relatively low cost to implement and generally lacking structure, should not be undervalued. Whilst neither elaborate nor sophisticated, for smaller organisations especially, such informal techniques can provide necessary local market information.

An example of such informal scanning is where a local independent music store sends out a staff member of its small team at the beginning of each week to check up on the prices being charged by the large music chain retailers within the town for popular CD albums. This ensures that the small independent record shop is able to price its products competitively and react quickly to any price changes or promotional activities by its competitors.

For many larger organisations, however, they may prefer a more systematic and formal means for scanning and analysing the environment. In broad terms, these more deliberate approaches to environmental analysis tend to focus on the firm's societal and task environments.

As discussed in Chapter 1, the societal and general environment (often termed the macroenvironment) is typically analysed through the lens of **PESTLE** analysis, which focuses attention on political, economic, socio-cultural, technological, legal and environmental and/or ethical issues. At this point, for the organisation a distinction can be drawn between environmental scanning and environmental analysis. The process of scanning is the identification of trends and changes, whilst analysis is the consideration of which trends and environmental changes will, or are likely to, impact on the organisation in terms of presenting new challenges and also opportunities. For example, a period of relatively high or rising interest rates may be of general concern, but it is how increases in interest rates may directly affect a firm's borrowing capacity, expansion or plans for further investment that is really of relevance to the organisation.

mini case   Multinational inward investment: a PESTLE analysis

In highly competitive markets businesses must be constantly alert to the challenges they face and ideally should attempt to gain some form of advantage over their main rivals. For some organisations this might mean investing in production and/or service facilities in other countries, either as a means of reducing costs (e.g. by exploiting cheaper sources of labour) or as a strategy for boosting demand (e.g. by developing new markets). Given that many industries could be described as 'footloose' (i.e. relatively free to locate anywhere), one key question facing organisational decision makers is *where* to invest: what are the relative merits of one country over another? One way of beginning to answer this question is to undertake a PESTLE analysis in order to provide useful information about the broad macro-environmental context against which the final decision has to be taken.

To illustrate how this might occur the hypothetical example in this mini case looks at how a major car manufacturer considering investing in a new greenfield facility in Eastern Europe might identify some of the key influences on the locational decision. Given that there is no definitive way in which to undertake an analysis of this kind, the approach adopted here is to highlight some of the key questions that are likely to be considered by those charged with the final decision on where to invest. For convenience these questions are presented in tabular form (Table 18.1). You should note that the allocation of questions to categories can be a matter of personal choice (e.g. is a government tax law *political* or *legal* or *economic*?); the important point is that the questions are asked, not which category they go in.

As Table 18.1 illustrates, a PESTLE analysis can provide a valuable insight into some of the potential risks and uncertainties of a locational decision and can encourage corporate decision makers to examine future as well as current circumstances in each of the alternative locations. By adding weightings to reflect the relative importance of the different factors to the final

▶

decision and building in some allowance for the perceived degree of risk, the analysis can become more sophisticated and hence a more useful tool that can be used by the organisation. While it is likely that an approach of this kind will often be used negatively (i.e. to rule out certain locations), the fact that a particular country looks a less favourable location than the alternatives does not necessarily mean it will not be chosen. It could be, for example, that other factors weigh heavily in the final choice of location and that the PESTLE analysis has more influence on the level and nature of the investment undertaken (e.g. a joint venture might be seen as preferable to a direct commitment of funds) rather than where it occurs.

Table 18.1 Locating a car plant: a PESTLE approach

Political
- How stable is the government now and in the future?
- Is the political regime favourable to foreign investment?
- Is membership of the EU planned and likely in the near future?

Economic
- Is there a favourable economic framework within which to engage in business?
- Is the economy likely to remain stable over the longer term?
- Is there a favourable business infrastructure?

Social
- How will the structure of the population impact upon the demand for the product and/or the supply of labour?
- Are economic conditions likely to provide increased market opportunities?
- What skills currently exist within the labour force?
- Are the welfare and educational systems supportive of the planned investment?

Technological
- What is the current state of technological advance?
- Is technology transfer feasible?
- Will the current (or future) infrastructure help or hinder the investment process?
- What facilities exist for technological training?

Legal
- Is the current legal framework likely to support or hinder business operations?
- Do the current (or planned) employment laws provide an advantage or disadvantage to the business?
- Do the current tax laws favour the organisation?

Ethical
- Are the ethical standards in a chosen location likely to affect the operations of the business favourably or unfavourably and/or the company's image?
- How will the organisation be affected by current (or planned) environmental standards and regulations?

Organisations can also analyse their task or competitive environment (frequently termed the microenvironment). Analysis of this kind focuses attention on external factors that are most proximal to the organisation, typically residing at the industry level. A number of models and frameworks have been designed that explore how industry-level factors influence organisational performance, with the best known being Harvard Professor Michael **Porter's five-forces framework** (1980). Porter argued that average industry profitability and therefore organisational performance was predominantly determined by five key industry characteristics:

- The intensity of incumbent rivalry.
- The threat of new entrants.
- The threat of substitutes.

- The power of buyers.
- The power of suppliers.

In very broad terms, the greater the power of each of these forces, the lower the profitability for competing organisations within the industry. The influence or power of each force will vary from industry to industry and therefore explain why some industries (e.g. pharmaceuticals) are inherently more profitable than others (e.g. airlines). An important additional component of Porter's work was his application of 'barriers to entry'. Whilst barriers to entry was not a new concept, Porter used it to demonstrate how their existence would determine the extent to which the stability of average profitability could be maintained. With barriers to entry high, the threat of new entrants would remain low, whilst low barriers to entry would encourage new firms to enter the industry and increase the level of rivalry and therefore reduce profitability. These barriers to entry have already been described in Chapter 15, but what is of relevance here is to recognise that an organisation's external analysis should not just be restricted to the consideration of the five forces but also needs to incorporate environmental factors that might influence the height of these barriers to entry.

An example of this was in the United States during October 2001. During that month there had been a series of terrorist attacks using the US postal system to deliver letters to American citizens that contained anthrax spores. The American government, assuming the worst and unaware of the potential scale of the threat, wished to procure treatments for exposure to anthrax for up to 12 million people. Treatment against anthrax was a patented drug called ciprofloxacin, which was sold under the brand name Cipro by the German pharmaceutical firm Bayer. The American government had significant concerns as to Bayer's ability to supply such large volumes of Cipro in an extremely short period of time and at a relatively high cost. The US Congress indicated its intention to disregard Bayer's patent and buy ciprofloxacin cheaper elsewhere. After a series of talks between US officials and Bayer, the pharmaceutical firm eventually maintained its patent but had to agree to a reduction in the contracted price from $1.83 to less than $1 a tablet.

The five-forces framework remains perhaps the most influential method for analysing an industry and understanding a firm's performance. Underpinning the framework is an acceptance that value and, ultimately, profit are distributed between these five forces, and the extent to which the firm can capture an increasing share of the profit is determined by its ability to reduce the power of these forces. Inherent within the framework is the notion that relationships between the five forces are competitive, with all organisations competing in what may be considered a 'zero-sum' game.

Whilst the five-forces framework therefore provides a useful means of exploring industry characteristics, it has not been beyond criticism. Brandenburger and Nalebuff, for example, in 1995 introduced their 'value net' framework. In many ways it is similar to Porter's five forces, in that it also identifies competitors, suppliers and customers as key industry characteristics but it also introduced a further component, that of 'complementors' (see Figure 18.2).

Figure 18.2   The concept of complementors

Source: Adapted from Brandenburger, A. and Nalebuff, B. (1995) 'The Right Game: Use Game Theory to Shape Strategy', *Harvard Business Review*, July–August, pp. 57–71.

For Brandenburger and Nalebuff, competing firms could also at times be complementors and in so doing could further add value (and, ultimately, profitability) to the industry. They argued that a complementor existed if the customer was to value an organisation's product more when they have another organisation's product.

This has led to a popular view that the five-forces framework should be extended to incorporate a sixth force, that of complementors; in short, in undertaking external analysis an organisation will need to consider both competition and cooperation, which has become known by the portmanteau term 'co-opetition' (see case study at the end of the chapter).

Techniques

Organisations may employ a range of techniques to assist them in analysing the external environment. Some of these techniques use statistical measures, such as the various forms of trend extrapolation and cross-impact matrices, whilst others, such as Delphi methods and scenario planning, use qualitative or narrative assessments. Some techniques for external analysis seek to predict likely future states or identify relationships between external variables, whilst others strive to illuminate possible future states. Furthermore, each tool presented below often focuses on different future time frames.

The value of the techniques will vary from organisation to organisation, and there is no hierarchy in terms of their quality. Each technique that will be explored within this chapter has both strengths and limitations. These methods of external analysis should not be considered as surrogates for each other, but rather whether the merits of a particular technique or techniques can help illuminate understanding of the external environment and aid the organisation in its identification of environmental opportunities and threats. The various techniques presented here also have differing resource requirements in terms of cost, labour and time, and therefore the organisation needs to find a balance between its desire for understanding and gaining insight into the environment and its willingness to commit resources to achieve such understanding. There is also the danger of paralysis – achieved through analysis. The organisation can never gain a complete appreciation of all external issues, and nor should it attempt to. Analysis by itself only has value once it is acted upon by the organisation in terms of designing new strategies to either take advantage of opportunities or mitigate environmental threats. A well thought through and considered strategy is desirable, but one that is well thought through, considered and implemented before those of the organisation's rivals is preferable.

> If you would like more details of the various techniques referred to in this section (e.g. SWOT, the cross-impact matrix, the Delphi technique) try typing these terms into Yahoo.

Trend extrapolation

As its name suggests, **trend extrapolation** is essentially a technique for predicting the future based on an analysis of the past. Implicit in this is the assumption that, in the short run at least, most factors tend to remain fairly constant and critical changes in the key variables are unlikely to occur. Accordingly, extending present trends into the future is seen as a useful means of anticipating forthcoming events and tends to be one of the techniques most frequently used by business organisations seeking a relatively simple and inexpensive means of forecasting.

At its simplest level, trend analysis tends to be used to predict changes over time (e.g. in the likely demand for a product), a process which can sometimes prove relatively accurate where there are sufficient historical data to allow seasonal and cyclical fluctuations to be taken into consideration. The analysis can also be refined to examine an observed relationship between one factor (e.g. sales) and another (e.g. levels of disposable income) and can even be extended to the simultaneous consideration of several variables felt to influence the subject under consideration (e.g. by using multiple regression techniques). In addition, techniques also exist to investigate causal or explanatory factors that link two or more time series together (e.g. statistical modelling techniques) and to consider the likely impact on forecasted trends of a range of factors, identified by analysts as likely both to occur and to have an effect on the predicted outcome. The latter technique is generally known as **trend–impact analysis** and is sometimes used by large companies in conjunction with other methods of forecasting, including the Delphi approach and opinion canvassing (see below).

The fundamental drawback in the use of trend analysis as a forecasting tool is that there is no guarantee that the trends identified from historic patterns will continue in the future; sudden discontinuities – such as the United Kingdom's decision to leave the ERM – can invalidate or undermine the existing assumptions on which a trend was predicted. In a majority of cases, trends are based on a series of patterns or relationships among a wide range of variables, a change in any one of which can drastically alter the future course of events. These variables are not always easy to identify and the interactions between them are not necessarily fully understood. Attempts to link a simple cause with a simple effect run the danger of underestimating the complexities of the business environment.

Scenario planning

Scenario planning is about undertaking a disciplined method for imagining and examining possible futures. It is not an attempt to predict the future, and indeed it would be typical for an organisation to generate between two and four generically different possible futures as an outcome of the scenario planning process. This technique often focuses on 'best case' and 'worst case' scenarios, although Royal Dutch Shell – the company most renowned for the use of scenario planning as a core component of its environmental analysis activities for over thirty years – has in its most recent scenarios (published in 2008) expressed a preference for one particular scenario case.

Scenario planning as a strategic tool can be traced back to the Rand Corporation in the early 1960s, and is often associated with the work of one of its employees, physicist and mathematician Herman Kahn. At the time of his research, the Cold War between the United States and the Soviet Union was at its peak. In 1962, the Cuban Missile Crisis brought the two Cold War Superpowers perhaps within only a matter of days of nuclear war, when US air force reconnaissance planes took aerial photographs of Soviet installations of nuclear bases on the island of Cuba, which would provide a direct nuclear threat to American soil.

Herman Kahn, in conjunction with the Rand Corporation, presented his text entitled 'On Thermonuclear War' in 1962, which argued against common views at the time that 'mutually assured destruction' would happen in a nuclear war. Instead, Kahn presented the view that, as with any other form of warfare, a nuclear war could be ultimately winnable and his text identified a range of scenarios by which this might be possible.

In business organisations, scenario planning seeks to consider the possible effects of, and interactions between, various external environmental forces on the future and to test the resiliency of specific strategies that the organisation may be considering, in such a scenario. Typically, scenario planning is most relevant to large organisations, as it is a resource-intensive technique and is most commonly found in industries considered to have highly dynamic, complex and uncertain environments and/or those industries that require heavy forward investment (e.g. energy companies).

The process of scenario planning normally begins with the organisation considering which key environmental trends to consider, and over what time period. Royal Dutch Shell has historically published scenarios on a three- to four-year cycle that project 20–25 years ahead. Its most recent scenarios consider the nature of the energy markets by 2050. General consensus, however, suggests that scenarios should ideally be looking at least ten years ahead. Once the key trends have been identified, organisational focus then moves to considering what external forces or developments are likely to have the greatest ability to shape the future, which could include such factors as regulatory policy and corporate social responsibility.

The following case of Royal Dutch Shell presents its latest scenarios looking towards the global energy markets in 2050.

mini case   Scenario planning at Shell – the global energy market in 2050

Royal Dutch Shell has utilised scenario planning as an integral part of its range of techniques for undertaking external analysis since the early 1970s (see Figure 18.3). Its first scenarios were developed in 1972 and were narrow in scope, concentrating on forecasts for economic growth and the impacts of a discontinuity or shortage of supply of oil on prices. Until this point, both economic growth and oil supply had shown high levels of consistent and predictable growth, and Royal Dutch Shell was interested in exploring a 'what if' scenario should oil supply become destabilised. This scenario became realised in October 1974, following the Yom Kippur War and subsequent Arab oil embargo on supply of oil to the United States and supporting governments of the state of Israel.

The realisation of Shell's first scenarios acted as a powerful argument for the continued investment in scenario planning, and Shell has continued to produce scenarios, typically on a three-year cycle, to the present day.

Initially, Shell's scenarios tended to focus narrowly on economic perspectives of oil demand and supply over a relatively short time horizon (3–5 years). The scenarios were presented as 'in-house' publications only, having been produced by the organisation's own strategic analysts. As Shell's experience, willingness to invest increasing resources and scenario planning skills matured, the scenarios gradually became more complex and broader in scope, incorporating both geo-political and geo-societal trends. The decade of the 1980s was characterised by Shell as being driven by what it termed 'transition', trends that would see the end of the Cold War, the beginning of the collapse of the former Soviet Block and increasing market liberisation. The 1990s would be one of continuing liberalisation, underpinned by powerful

Figure 18.3   Evolution of scenario planning at Royal Dutch Shell

1970s Methodology Development	1980s Integration into Corporate Strategy	1990s Focus on External Stakeholders	2000s Integration into Business Strategy
The rapids	**Transition**	**Tina: there is no alternative**	**People and Connections**
• Pioneering of scenarios to prepare the organization for uncertainty and change	• Broadly based global scenarios	• Scenarios involve external stakeholders & incorporate their views	• Global scenarios are used to develop focused scenarios on specific business initiatives
• Focus on energy markets (oil)	• Energy focus is combined with political and economic analysis	• Deeper analysis of social trends and environment change	• Scenarios are used systematically to test business strategy robustness
• Internal publication only	• Internal publication only	• Internal and external publication	• Internal and external publication
	• Workshop with business units	• Workshop with business units & externals	

forces for globalisation and technological innovation. So pervasive and dominant were these trends considered to be that Shell coined the expression 'TINA' (there is no alternative) to describe them. The evolution of the scope of Shell's scenarios is presented in Figure 18.3.

In 2005, Shell introduced three new scenarios that were looking ahead to 2025. These scenarios questioned for the first time the assumptions of its 'TINA' trends. The scenarios published – named 'Open Doors', 'Low Trust Globalisation' and 'Flags' – suggested that there might be a break on globalisation and market liberalisation. Shell drew upon the events of 9/11 and the financial scandal of Enron as examples of geo-political crises of security and trust. These environmental shocks could foreshadow a period of slowing international trade, as governments became more protective in their policies towards their own domestic industries and, specifically, energy resources. Additionally, there would be increased pressure on all organisations to be far more transparent and accountable towards society in all their business activities and disclosure of performance.

In early 2008, Shell published its latest scenarios, which consider the global energy markets in 2050. In the foreword of its published report, Shell's Chief Executive, Jeroen van der Veer states:

> Never before has humanity faced such a challenging outlook for energy and the planet. This can be summed up in five words: 'more energy, less carbon dioxide'.

Shell has identified three key trends that are likely to significantly alter the energy landscape. It has termed these its 'three hard truths':

● There will be a surge in energy demand (global requirements are predicted to double by 2050) especially resulting from the growth in economic activity from both China and India.
● Traditional energy sources are struggling to keep up with demand.
● Current and future projected uses of energy will continue to raise carbon dioxide emissions and other greenhouse gases with adverse effects on the environment.

Given the above trends, which when compared can be seen to create obvious tensions, Shell has characterised the possible future energy landscape as 'TANIA' (there are no ideal answers).

From these trends, two scenarios have been developed, one entitled 'Scramble', the other, 'Blueprints'.

In the scenario of 'Scramble', Shell suggests that events will continue to outpace action. For the next decade, people from all walks of life will join the debate about energy and climate change, but for governments, security of energy supply and fears of losing economic ground will shape decision making and policy. The primary focus will be on meeting the needs of global demand and there will be little in the way of consideration of investing in more efficient means of providing energy until traditional sources become critically depleted. In a 'Scramble' future, focus on addressing greenhouse gas emissions will receive scant attention much before around 2020, by when an increasing frequency of climate shocks will force governments to belatedly respond to the needs of the natural environment. Even then, Shell believes that such responses will be localised, with both governments and firms taking individual action, with little framework for a co-ordinated, considered global response. Although by 2050 greenhouse gas emissions will have been reduced, it is argued that the efforts may be seen as too little too late.

In 'Blueprints', groups of seemingly disconnected people (e.g. politicians, environmentalists, venture capitalists, farmers and businesses) all begin to recognise the profitable potential of finding solutions to the challenges of economic development, energy security and environmental pollution at the same time. These seemingly disparate groups begin to collaborate together in localised and regionalised areas, motivated by recognising the need to take action before it's forced upon them by circumstance.

These actions receive public support, which then transfers into public pressure on governments for change. Buildings are made more energy efficient, and there are government efforts to reduce greenhouse gas emissions and improve air quality. Participating governments will use a range of individualised, local initiatives and policy investments, from tax breaks to subsidies, mandates, and investment and support for new 'cleaner' technologies. Whilst governments begin to take a holistic view of the challenges posed, multinational firms find international investment decisions and strategies difficult to implement given the patchwork of government initiatives. These firms begin to pressure local, national and international authorities to harmonise approaches towards energy consumption, supply and environmental management.

With harmonisation comes widespread adoption of good efficiency practices. Trading schemes for carbon dioxide emissions' rights begin to cover a critical mass of industry sectors in a critical mass of countries and transport becomes 'greener' through growth in vehicle engine hybrids and, later, full-electric vehicles.

Royal Dutch Shell does not indicate which of the two scenarios is most likely, but suggests that both are plausible. Shell is keen to indicate its preference for the 'Blueprints' scenario, which is a break from tradition, as the organisation has previously always presented a neutral view towards it scenarios.

web link The Shell website (2008) can be found at: *www.shell.com*

Expert opinion: the Delphi method

To predict future developments or to build likely scenarios, some organisations turn to experts, an increasing number of whom work as consultants. These experts often operate as a group to produce an analysis which is presented to management in the form of a report or which emanates from a discursive technique known as **brainstorming**. Alternatively, the organisation may prefer to canvass the views of an anonymous panel of experts, using a technique known as the **Delphi method**, which was originally developed by the Rank Corporation in the United States to forecast likely military events.

In essence the Delphi approach involves eliciting opinions from a group of experts who operate individually, and anonymously, unaware of the other members of the group. Each expert is asked to respond to an initial set of questions and the answers are clarified and tabulated by a neutral investigator who uses them to generate a more refined set of questions that are then put to the experts. Following their replies, further revisions may occur and the respondents may be asked again to provide another set of predictions that take into account the information provided in the earlier replies. This process may continue for several rounds until a measure of convergence occurs between the views of the panel and a form of consensus is reached on likely future developments. As a technique the Delphi method tends to be expensive and time-consuming and there is no guarantee that a clear view will emerge. It can, however, be used to investigate any aspect of a firm's environment and to identify not only the effects of predicted changes, but also their causes, and this information may be incorporated into other forms of environmental analysis of both a qualitative and quantitative kind.

Cross-impact matrices

The **cross-impact matrix** provides a more complex means of assessing and forecasting environmental change than some of the other methods previously described. Under this approach, analysts identify a set of events that are forecast to occur within a given time period, and specify not only the expected timing of each event but also its probability of occurrence. Arranging these events in anticipated chronological order in rows and columns of a matrix (see Figure 18.4) permits attention to be focused on the interaction between the events and, in particular, on the extent to which one may influence the timing or likely occurrence of another.

As a means of predicting likely interactions between anticipated future developments, cross-impact analysis serves at least two significant purposes. First, it can be used to check the consistency of the various forecasts which go into it – such as the prediction of events and their relationships – given that inconsistencies will become apparent from an analysis of the results. Second, it provides a means of identifying events and trends that will have the greatest impact on subsequent developments, whether they be in individual segments of the environment or across a range of segments, as in the case of interactions between economic, technological, social and political factors.

SWOT or TOWS analysis

It is widely accepted that corporate performance is influenced by a combination of internal and external factors. These factors can be characterised as the organisation's internal 'strengths' and 'weaknesses' and its external 'opportunities' and 'threats'. Systematically analysing these factors as an aid to strategic decision making represents a form of situational analysis known commonly by the acronym **SWOT** (or **TOWS**).

Figure 18.4   A simple cross-impact matrix

Probability and timing	Event 1	Event 2	Event 3	Event 4	Event 5
Event 1 (probability/ timing)					
Event 2 (probability/ timing)					
Event 3 (probability/ timing)					
Event 4 (probability/ timing)					
Event 5 (probability/ timing)					

The starting-point for a SWOT analysis is usually a review of the organisation's internal strengths and weaknesses, which may be undertaken by management or by external consultants brought in to provide a more objective view. The identified factors which have been listed may then be given scores to indicate their importance, with the more significant issues receiving a larger score. This process is then repeated for the firm's external opportunities and threats in order to highlight those external factors which are likely to occur and which are expected to have an impact on the organisation's future position. The resultant SWOT grid can then be used to focus attention on the key environmental influences faced by the organisation and to consider how far current strategy is relevant to the changes taking place in the business environment.

It is worth pointing out that the analysis of opportunities and threats cannot be absolute, since what might at first appear to be an opportunity may not be so when viewed against the organisation's resources or its culture or the expectations of its stakeholders. Moreover, the true value of the SWOT approach lies not in the listing of influences but in their contribution to the formulation of appropriate organisation strategies. One means of focusing attention on the latter is to produce a SWOT (TOWS) matrix which matches the firm's opportunities and threats against its internal strengths and weaknesses (see Figure 18.5). The result is four sets of possible strategic alternatives – termed SO, ST, WO and WT strategies – which range from the positive exploitation of strengths in order to take advantage of opportunities to the essentially defensive strategy of minimising weaknesses and avoiding anticipated threats.

Figure 18.5 A SWOT matrix

	Strengths (S) List major organisational strengths (e.g. quality products)	Weaknesses (W) List major organisational weaknesses (e.g. poor distribution)
INTERNAL ASPECTS / EXTERNAL ASPECTS		
Opportunities (O) List major organisational opportunities (e.g. new markets)	SO strategies	WO strategies
Threats (T) List major organisational threats (e.g. competition)	ST strategies	WT strategies

Limitations to environmental analysis

The techniques described above represent some of the ways in which organisations can examine the changing business environment in an attempt to understand what changes are likely to occur, how these may affect the organisation and what responses would be appropriate in the circumstances. In short, the value of such analysis lies not only in the information provided but also in the process of gathering and evaluating it and in applying it to the task of strategic management.

Despite its potential value as a tool of decision-making, environmental analysis is not without its limitations and these need to be taken into account. For a start, analysing the business environment is not a precise science and does not eliminate uncertainty for an organisation, caused, for instance, by unanticipated events which do not follow the normal pattern. Nor should it be regarded by managers as a means of foretelling the future, allowing them to avoid their responsibilities as strategic planners and decision-makers by blaming problems on a deficiency in the application of a particular technique or on inaccuracies in the data provided.

Added to this, environmental analysis of itself is by no means a guarantee of organisational effectiveness, and can sometimes complicate the decision-making process by providing information which calls into question the intuitive feeling of experienced managers. The danger is that the analysis may become an end in itself and may obscure information and data coming from other sources, rather than being used in conjunction with them. Accordingly, its value in strategic thinking and strategic decision-making may not be exploited to its full potential and this may represent a lost opportunity to the organisation, as well as an inefficient and ineffective use of resources.

Sources of information

Researching the business environment can be a daunting task, given the extensive amount of information and statistical data available. To help in this direction the final section of this chapter outlines some of the key national and international information sources which are readily accessible to both students and businesses. While the list is by no means exhaustive, it gives a good indication of the wide range of assistance available to researchers and of the different formats in which information is published by government and non-government sources for different purposes. Much of this information is available in an electronic as well as a print format, with the latter a particularly good starting-point for students of business. The Internet is now an invaluable resource for business information.

Statistical sources

Statistical information is an important component of business research and students need to be aware of what is available, particularly as some data turn up in the most unexpected places. Three key guides in locating statistical information are:

1   *National Statistics – the official UK statistics site.* A portal to UK officially produced statistics. Some information is available on-line, at other times you will be referred to print publications, including the ones listed below (***www.statistics.gov.uk***).

2   *Sources of Unofficial UK Statistics.* Complied by David Mort, this book provides details of a large number of unofficial statistical publications from a wide variety of organisations (e.g. pressure groups, trade unions, professional associations).

3   *World Directory of Non-Official Statistical Sources.* Published by Euromonitor and a key guide to non-official sources in selected countries outside western Europe, the latter being covered by the *European Directory of Non-Official Statistical Sources*. The *Directory* concentrates particularly on sources dealing with consumer goods, consumer trends, key industries and national economic and business trends. It has a subject and a geographical index. Also available on the GMID web service.

Some of the main statistical sources are discussed below:

4   *Annual Abstract of Statistics.* Published by the ONS, this is an authoritative source of official statistics arranged under various headings, which include population, production, energy, transport, trade and public services. Figures usually cover a ten-year period and are presented in tabulated form. There is a detailed alphabetical index at the end. It is available to download at no charge from the National Statistics website (***www.statistics.gov.uk***).

5   *Consumer Europe.* Produced by Euromonitor and available on CD-ROM and via the Internet. This is a pan-European source of marketing statistics with the emphasis on consumer goods and consumer trends. The information examines the main product groups and includes predictions on future levels of consumption. It is split into two regions – 'Consumer Western Europe' and 'Consumer Eastern Europe'.

6   *Datastream.* A finance and economics on-line database, produced by Thomson Financial. Accounts for public companies around the world, as well as share prices and stock market indices are available. The economics databases cover a vast range of current and historical international economic series, including money supply, inflation and interest rates for 150 countries. Data are taken from many statistical sources, including OECD and the UK government, central banks and unofficial statistical sources.

7   *United Nations Economic Commission for Europe (UNECE).* Another source of European economic data can be found on the UNECE website (***www.unece.org/stats/Welcome.html***). Data on national accounts, labour figures, gender and transport statistics can be accessed for individual countries and compared with other European, North American or central Asian countries.

8   *Economic & Labour Market Review.* Merging *Economic Trends and Labour Market Trends* in January 2007, this is a monthly publication by the ONS and a key guide to the current economic indicators (e.g. prices, unemployment, trade interest rates and exchange rates) and labour market data.

9   *Economist Intelligence Unit.* Reviewing the business environment for selected countries, the EIU produce Country Reports for around 195 countries. A more in-depth look is offered by their Country Forecasts, providing macroeconomic projections for the world's largest economies. The Country Data reports provide economic indicators, forecasts and statistics for 150 countries. Available in print or on-line.

10 *Employment in Europe*. Contains an excellent overview of employment issues in Europe. Published annually by the European Commission, with a different focus in each issue.

11 *Europa World Year Book*. A Routledge publication available in print and on-line. An annual book which has an A–Z listing of all countries, not just European countries as the title suggests.

12 *Europe in Figures: Eurostat Yearbook*. A comprehensive and useful introduction to statistical data on the European Union and its Member States. The yearbook is also a useful alternative if overwhelmed by the Eurostat website. Background data and over 500 statistical tables, graphs and maps are presented. Areas covered include the economy, education, the labour market, industry and services, international trade, transport and the environment. The yearbook is free to download from the Eurostat website (***http://epp.eurostat.ec.europa.eu***) where the most up-to-date statistical tables can also be found.

13 *European Economic Statistics*. A broad overview of the economic developments of European Union Member States. Key areas covered include government finances, balance of payments, foreign trade and the labour market. Commentary is also offered on topical issues arising from the data. It is available to download from the Eurostat website (***http://epp.eurostat.ec.europa.eu***).

14 *European Marketing Data and Statistics*. An annual publication by Euromonitor providing statistical information on the countries of western and eastern Europe. The data cover a wide range of market aspects – including demographic trends, economic indicators, trade, consumer expenditure, retailing – and often show trends over a 21-year period. The information is provided primarily in a spreadsheet format and there is an alphabetical index.

15 *Expenditure and Food Survey*. This annual ONS publication merges the Family Expenditure Survey and the National Food Survey and is available on the ONS website (***www.statistics.gov.uk***). The ONS has overall responsibility for the EFS but DEFRA sponsors the food data. The publication is a survey of spending and other aspects of finance and data on food consumption presented in detailed charts and tables. The EFS is primarily used to provide information for the Retail Prices Index.

16 *Financial Statistics*. A monthly publication by the ONS on a wide range of financial aspects including the accounts of the public and non-public sectors of the economy. Figures cover the latest month or quarter together with those of previous years.

17 *General Household Survey*. A continuous sample survey produced by the ONS, based on the financial year of the general population. The survey spans a wide range of household-related aspects – including housing, health, education and employment – and is widely used as a source of background information for central government decisions on resource allocation. Since 1994 it has been renamed 'Living in Britain: Results of the General Household Survey'. NB: There was a break in the years 1997/8 and 1999/2000.

18 *International Marketing Data and Statistics (IMDAS)*. An international compendium of statistical information on the Americas, Asia, Africa and Oceania published annually by Euromonitor. Information on demographics, economic trends, finance, trade, consumer expenditure and many other areas usually covers a 21-year trend period, and an alphabetical index is provided. Available on CD-ROM – 'World Marketing Data and Statistics'. See also ***www.euromonitor.com***.

19 *Marketing Pocket Book*. Published by NTC Publications. An essential source of statistics and information. Published annually. Sister publications include *European Marketing Pocket Book* and *Retail Pocket Book*.

20 *Monthly Digest of Statistics*. The key source of current information on national income, output and expenditure, population, employment, trade, prices and a range of other areas. Previous as well as current data are provided. Published by ONS and available on-line.

21 *Annual Survey of Hours and Earnings*. Replacing the *New Earnings Survey* in 2004 ASHE presents detailed data in tables on earnings and hours paid for employees within industries, occupations and regions. It is free to download from the ONS website (*www.statistics.gov.uk*).

22 *National Income and Expenditure*. Now known as the *United Kingdom National Accounts* (or 'Blue Book'). Published annually by ONS, it contains data on domestic and national output, income and expenditure, and includes a sector-by-sector analysis. Figures often cover ten years or more and an alphabetical index is provided. Available on CD-ROM and on-line.

23 *OECD Economic Outlook*. A periodic assessment of economic trends, policies and prospects in OECD and non-member countries. Published twice a year, the Outlook includes articles as well as figures, tables, charts and short-term projections, and looks at developments on a country-by-country basis. Available for subscribers on the Internet.

24 *OECD Economic Surveys*. An annual publication by the OECD providing individual country reports of the world's advanced industrial economies. Very useful. Available on CD-ROM.

25 *Regional Trends*. An annual ONS publication providing a wide range of information on social, demographic and economic aspects of the United Kingdom's standard planning regions, together with some data on the sub-regions and on the EU. The guide includes a subject index. Available on the Internet via *www.statistics.gov.uk*.

26 *Social Trends*. Another annual ONS publication, in this case looking at different aspects of British society, including population, education, environment, housing, leisure and transport. It provides a more detailed analysis of data produced for the *Annual Abstract of Statistics* and includes a large number of charts and diagrams. Information often spans a 15–20-year period and an alphabetical subject index is included. Available on the Internet via *www.statistics.gov.uk*.

27 *United Kingdom Balance of Payments*. Known as the 'Pink Book'. It is a comprehensive guide to the United Kingdom's external trade performance and contains a wide range of statistics covering a ten-year period. Available on the Internet (see *Social Trends*).

28 *United Nations Statistical Yearbook*. Written in both English and French, the *Yearbook* is a detailed international comparative analysis of UN member countries. Data cover a wide variety of topics, including international finance, transport and communications, population, trade and wages, and a World Statistical Summary is provided at the beginning.

29 *World Economic Outlook*. Usually published twice a year by the International Monetary Fund (IMF); the focus is on the analysis and projections of global economic developments in the short and medium terms. It also considers current world economic policy issues. It is available in print and also as a free download from the IMF website (*www.imf.org*) where other useful statistics can be found.

Other useful statistical sources

1 Most government departments publish statistics on their own websites. Of particular interest is:

   (a) *Department for Business, Enterprise and Regulatory Reform*. The successor to the Department of Trade and Industry has a useful statistics webpage (*http://stats.berr.gov.uk*) with a wide variety of information, including SME statistics, UK competitiveness indicators, construction and energy statistics and regional data, such as economic performance indicators.

   (b) *Bank of England*. For the very latest information on the UK interest rates and inflation the Bank of England website is invaluable (*www.bankofengland.co.uk*). Other financial data is also available as well as full text publications on surveys and working papers.

2 *Eurostat*. The Statistical Office of the European Communities (Eurostat) is responsible for producing data for the European Union. There are numerous links to information on areas including general and regional statistics, demography, economic development and trade statistics. All are available to view on the Eurostat website (*http://epp.eurostat.ec.europa.eu*).

3 *UK Data Archive*. The UK Data Archive (University of Essex) is a specialist national resource containing the largest collection of accessible computer-readable data in the social sciences and humanities in the UK. Users must register; minimal charges apply for data delivery. Most of the large survey data can be accessed on-line free by academic researchers via MIMAS (see *www.data-archive.ac.uk*).

4 *MIMAS*. Based at the University of Manchester, this is another data centre which provides on-line access to census information, international data and large-scale survey information (e.g. OECD, IMF).

5 *Sources of further information*. By selecting a gateway site, you will often find links to just the information you need much more quickly than by just using Google.

   (a) *Business information on the Internet*. A gateway maintained by Karen Blakeman, including links to websites covering most aspects of business (see *www.rba.co.uk/sources/index.htm*).

   (b) *Useful UK Statistics sites from the University of Glasgow Library*. Very thorough summary (see *www.lib.gla.ac.uk/depts/mops/stats/statistics_on_internet.shtml*).

   (c) *Subject guide to statistics at Warwick*. Although this listing also includes specialist databases (which may not be available without payment) it is a very clear and comprehensive list (see *www2.warwick.ac.uk/services/library/main/tealea/socsciall/lawofficialpublications/statistics/websites2/*).

Information sources

Information on the different aspects of the business environment can be found in a variety of sources, including books, newspapers and periodicals. These often provide a wealth of contemporary data and commentary which can be located relatively easily in most cases, using specialist databases designed to assist the researcher. While an increasing amount of information is available on the Internet, the fastest and most reliable way of finding what you want tends to be to use newspapers and magazines, which are often available electronically (and which are loved by librarians!). In the last few years more and more abstracting databases have moved over to the Web, and now also offer the full text of articles, thereby reducing the amount of time it takes to research a topic. ProQuest (see below) can be used to trace information, but there are other alternatives (e.g. LexisNexis). It is even possible to customise your business databases to cover the most popular titles in a particular library. But remember, the situation tends to change on a regular basis, so you need to keep up to date. Some key sources in this area are discussed below:

1 *RDS Business & Industry*. Covers worldwide trade and business news, sourcing their information from journals, national and international newspapers and industry newsletters. It is available as an on-line subscription database.

2 *Ebsco*. Ebsco have a range of business databases including the *Business Source* range that offer full text articles and abstracts in the areas of business, economics and management.

3 *Newspaper Index*. A very useful website (***www.newspaperindex.com***) giving on-line access to newspapers from around the world. The main international quality newspapers are available here, as well as the Sunday papers. Where an English translated website is available, this is indicated.

4 *Emerald*. An Internet version of all the journals published by MCB University Press; includes some keys titles like the *European Journal of Marketing*. Also includes abstracts from many other journals in the *Emerald* reviews section.

5 *FT Intelligence*. This on-line subscription database combines a ten-year rolling archive of the *Financial Times* and Europe Intelligence Wire (formally known as FT McCarthy). Especially good for European financial and economic news, it is a good starting point when researching current events.

6 *General BusinessFile ASAP*. On-line database used in business research, covering a wide range of academic and trade journals.

7 *IMID/MICWeb*. Based on the holdings of the Institute of Management's book and journal article databases which form part of the largest collection of resources on management in Europe, focusing on all aspects of management theory and practice. MICWeb is updated monthly, as is the IMID CD-ROM. Business students can join the Institute of Management and have access to the library services.

8 *ProQuest*. ProQuest have a series of databases useful for business students. Particularly noteworthy is ABI/Inform. Though not as large as some other business databases, ABI/Inform is noted for the quality of its abstracting and information retrieval.

Other useful sources

1 *Bank of England Quarterly Bulletin*. An assessment of economic developments in the United Kingdom and the rest of the world. It includes articles and speeches, together with general commentary on the economy, and is available from the Bank of England website.

2 *Bank Reviews*. Quarterly publications by some of the leading clearing banks and often available free on request. These include *Barclays Economic Review* and *Lloyds Economic Bulletin*.

3 *Business Studies Update*. A very helpful source of discussion on contemporary business issues. Publication of this resource has been transferred from Hidcote Press to the Business School at the University of Lincoln. Released annually, it is free to download from the University of Lincoln website (*www.lincoln.ac.uk/lbs/resources/update)*.

4 *CBI Industrial Trends Survey*. A quarterly guide to the state of UK manufacturing industry based on questionnaire responses by businesses. It provides a useful insight into business prospects and an indicator to future changes.

5 *Company Annual Reports*. Available on request from all public companies and some private ones. Many are available on-line through company websites or from the following sites:

(a) *Annual Reports.com* offers free access to many popular American companies. Though you are unlikely to find some of the more obscure companies, this is still a useful resource (*www.annualreports.com*).

(b) *CAROL* is an on-line service offering direct links to the financial pages of listed companies in Europe and the USA. This is a practical site for company balance sheets, profit and loss statements and financial highlights. Annual reports are also available to registered users (see *www.carol.co.uk*).

(c) *Corporate information*. Gateway providing international coverage of company information including industry sector profiles, economic data and country and regional-specific searches (see *www.corporateinformation.com*).

(d) *Financial Times Annual Reports Service* (*http://ftcom.ar.wilink.com/asp/ P002_search_ENG.asp*). The site is sponsored by the participating companies which can be searched for by either name or sector. The requested reports can be delivered either on-line or by mail (in some instances). There is also an alerting service to notify users when a specified report is issued.

(e) *Wright research centre*. This site includes information on 18 000 companies in fifty countries. In many cases it includes ten years of financial data (see *www.wisi.com/ramainnew.htm*).

6 *Economics Update*. Another annual publication by Hidcote Press and designed to provide a review and discussion of contemporary issues relevant to students of economics and business.

7 *Ernst and Young's International Business Series*. Many are free to download from their website (*www.ey.com*). PriceWaterhouse Cooper produce a similar series also prefixed with the title 'Doing business in...' and are freely available from their website (*www.pwc.com*).

8 *European Business Review*. A pan-European journal published by MCB University Press. It includes articles, editorial comment, news reports and a discussion of recent publications. The journal also incorporates the *New European* which looks at the more cultural, political and environmental developments within Europe. Has CD-ROM and on-line facilities.

9 *European Journal of Marketing*. Another publication by MCB University Press, relevant particularly to students of international marketing. It includes abstracts in French, German and Spanish and offers an on-line service.

10 *Income Data Services*. A regular series of studies and reports on pay and other labour-market issues (e.g. teamworking, child care, redundancy), containing valuable up-to-date information and some statistical analysis. Available on the Internet via *www.incomesdata.co.uk*.

11 *Journal of Marketing.* A quarterly publication by the American Marketing Association and comprising articles together with recent book reviews in the field of marketing. Details of the journal and some sample articles can be found on the AMA website *www.marketingpower.com*.

12 *Kelly's Business Directory.* Marketed as a business-to-business supplier search engine, basic information is available free on their website (*www.kellysearch.co.uk*).

13 *Key British Enterprises.* A multi-volume compendium from Dun and Bradstreet giving details of Britain's top 50 000 companies. Companies are listed alphabetically and are also indexed by trade, product and geographical location. Available on the Internet via *www.dnb.co.uk*; also on CD-ROM.

14 *Kompass (United Kingdom).* A multi-volume directory with details on companies including products and services, industrial trade names and employee numbers. The Kompass website (*www.kompass.com*) allows a product or company search in 66 countries worldwide; basic information is free.

15 *Management Decision.* Published ten times a year by MCB University Press. Looks at management strategy and issues. Available on CD-ROM and on-line.

16 *Marketing.* A weekly source of facts and articles on various aspects of marketing, presented in a journalistic style. Available on the Internet via *www.haymarket.com/marketing/marketing_magazine/default.aspx*.

17 *Marketing Intelligence.* Also known as *Mintel Marketing Intelligence* and an invaluable source of information and statistics on a wide range of products. Reports cover market factors, trends, market share, the supply structure and consumer characteristics, and frequently include forecasts of future prospects. Available on-line via *www.mintel.co.uk*.

18 *Retail Price Index – Headline Rate.* A site maintained by Devon County Council giving a table with the RPI (headline rate), month by month for the last 30 years. Available at *www.devon.gov.uk/economyrpi.htm*.

19 *The Economist.* A standard reference source, published weekly and examining economic and political events throughout the world. It is an invaluable publication for business students and regularly contains features on specific business-related topics. It has a useful update on basic economic indicators. Available on the Internet via *www.economist.co.uk* or *www.economist.com*.

20 *WARC Advertising and Marketing Knowledge.* The World Advertising Research Centre's Advertising and Marketing Knowledge database is a vast collection of case studies and articles from authoritative sources. It covers all areas of advertising, marketing and media activity. The database also contains demographic information on a wide range of countries. Available at *www.warc.com*.

21 *Who Owns Whom.* An annual publication which identifies parent companies and their subsidiaries. It is a very useful source of information for examining the pattern of corporate ownership in the United Kingdom. Companion volumes are also available covering other parts of the world.

A final comment

When researching a business topic you are particularly recommended to use library catalogue sites, especially the British Library catalogue (*www.bl.uk*) and COPAC (*http://copac.ac.uk*), which is the combined catalogue of major British academic libraries. WorldCat (*www.worldcat.org*) is an integration of over 10 000 library catalogues from across the world, so WorldCat could be useful when searching for more obscure international business information. You might also want to check references on Internet bookshops sites such as Blackwell's (*http://bookshop.blackwell.co.uk/jsp/welcome.jsp*) or *Amazon.co.uk*. For older material *Abe.co.uk* is useful as they specialise in older, out of print books.

Synopsis

As the chapter has demonstrated, there is a need for business organisations to monitor the environment in which they exist and operate and, where possible, to anticipate changes which are likely to affect the enterprise. Rather than being an optional extra, environmental analysis and scanning should be seen as an intrinsic part of strategic management and should ideally provide data and information that are used to guide the decision-making process. Many of these data and much of the information already exist in published form and/or can be easily gathered from both literary and electronic sources on a national and international basis. Analysing them is also possible, using a range of techniques which have been developed by businesses and academics over a considerable number of years.

Summary of key points

- A firm's business environment changes over time.

- Firms need to consider and anticipate potential changes in their general and operational environments in order to take advantage of opportunities and/or minimise possible threats.

- Environmental analysis should be seen as a key part of the strategic management process; ideally it should form part of the basis on which corporate decisions are taken.

- Such analysis can occur at both a societal level (e.g. through PESTLE analysis) and at a task level (e.g. through industry-based approaches) and can involve the use of a wide variety of established techniques.

- Key techniques include trend extrapolation, scenario writing, the Delphi approach, cross-impact matrices and SWOT analysis.

- In researching the business environment, students and practitioners can utilise a wide range of information sources, many of which are relatively inexpensive and readily accessible.

- Accessing this information has been made considerably easier with improvements in information technology, especially the Internet.

case study

Co-opetition and the influence of the macroenvironment on industry analysis: the case of Sony Blu-ray

On 18 February 2008, Toshiba announced its withdrawal from the market of its HD-DVD range, leaving the path now clear for Sony and its Blu-ray DVDs to provide the sole standard for high definition or second generation DVDs.

The announcement brought to an end a near six-year format war between the rival giant organisations, which had resembled in many ways the format battle during the 1980s between Sony's Betamax and JVC's VHS.

At stake was a market that was worth nearly $25 billion a year.

Both Toshiba and Sony were intent on providing rival high definition DVDs to replace the existing DVD format which had first entered the market in late 1995. Back in 1993, Sony and Philips were developing a high density optical storage disk called the Multimedia Compact Disk (MMCD), whilst a consortium including Toshiba, JVC, Thomson, Pioneer, Mitsubishi, Matsushita, Hitachi, Pioneer and Time Warner was working on what it called the Super Density Disk (SDD). A format war was narrowly avoided after pressure from a number of computer manufacturers for the two camps to agree on a single standard. Ultimately, the SDD format won the day, and the DVD was subsequently introduced using much of the SDD technology.

The DVD proved hugely successful and sales of pre-recorded films now account for nearly 50 per cent of the total revenues of the Hollywood studios, although sales growth of DVDs has slowed dramatically as the product enters the maturity phase of its life cycle.

Sony first introduced its Blu-ray disk in 2002 at a trade show in Japan. The new Blu-ray disk had far more storage capacity than standard DVDs (25 or 50GB versus the 4.7GB of standard DVDs). This additional capacity would enable a Blu-ray DVD to contain not only far more material (for example, all three Lord of the Rings films and extras) on a single disk but also have far superior picture and sound quality. With the introduction of large flat screen LCD and plasma televisions, it was envisaged that DVDs with near cinematic audio and visual quality would be a natural complementor.

Meanwhile, Toshiba was developing its own HD-DVD format. Picture and sound quality would be virtually identical to the Blu-ray, but Toshiba was trusting that it would succeed over Sony as its production costs were significantly lower. The HD-DVD format built upon common production and manufacturing activities associated with the manufacture of standard DVDs.

Both disk formats were considered incompatible and both Sony and Toshiba realised that in order for either format to become the industry standard it would be necessary for both firms to enter into a series of collaborative arrangements with other organisations throughout the industry. The Hollywood studios and DVD player manufacturers would need to cooperate in order to compete.

In 2005, the Blu-ray Disk Association was formed; founding members included Sony, Pioneer Electronics, Sharp and Panasonic, along with Dell and Hewlett Packard, the two largest manufacturers of personal computers. Toshiba's rival HD-DVD format was supported by Sanyo, NEC and Microsoft. With both formats having dedicated DVD player manufacturers on board, focus then turned to two further critical industry sectors, the film studios and game consuls market.

In both areas, Sony had a distinct advantage. The Sony Corporation had owned the Columbia Tristar film studio since 1989, which was now the fourth largest Hollywood studio by box office revenue. Sony was also the market leader in sales of game consuls and was about to release the eagerly awaited PlayStation3 (PS3) in 2006. The PS3 would have an integrated Blu-ray DVD player.

The HD-DVD also had some significant supporters, most notably Bill Gates at Microsoft. In response to the challenge of the PlayStation3, Microsoft's Xbox360 would be compatible with the HD-DVD format, although 'gamers' would need to purchase a separate hard drive. The founder of Microsoft also had influence in Hollywood, as the co-owner of Dreamworks Animations, the sister company to Paramount Pictures.

By 2007, all but one of the major film studios had decided which DVD format they would support. Warner Bros, the largest studio, was the only one that was prepared to offer its films in both formats (see Table 18.2).

Table 18.2 The major film studios' choice of format

Studio	Market share by revenue	Format	
		HD-DVD	Blu-ray
Warner Bros/ New Line	19.7	✓	✓
Paramount	15.5	✓	
Disney/Buena Vista	14.0		✓
Sony/Columbia	12.9		✓
Universal	11.4	✓	
20th Century Fox	10.5		✓
Lionsgate	3.8		✓
MGM/UA	3.8		✓
Other	8.4		

Source: *The Economist*, 'Everything's gone Blu', 12 January 2008, p. 56.

With the battle for Hollywood's adoption of a favoured format for pre-recorded films finely balanced, the net result was confusion among the general public. Consumers had no idea which format would ultimately become the standard, and whilst the film studios would continue to sell new releases and their back catalogue in standard DVD, there seemed little logic in purchasing a dedicated high definition DVD player that would only be able to recognise one of the two new formats. Therefore, sales of both new format DVDs and DVD players remained negligible.

Sony's eventual victory was predominantly down to the success of its 2006 launched PS3. Globally, sales of PS3 since its introduction has risen to over 10.5 million and with the built-in Blu-ray player, the Blu-ray disk became the *de facto* standard. Toshiba's sales of HD-DVD players was languishing at nearer to 1 million, and the end was in sight when in late 2007 American retailers Wal-Mart and Best Buys, along with video rental firm Blockbuster, decided to cease orders of HD-DVDs due to low sales volumes. In January 2008, Warner Bros decided that it would also no longer have its films pre-recorded on the Toshiba format and would adopt exclusively the Blu-ray format. With minimal pre-recorded material now available on HD-DVD, and low purchase volumes of HD-DVD dedicated players, there was no alternative but for Toshiba to exit the market. The spoils of victory, however, cannot yet be savoured by Sony, for whilst the format war may be over, it now has to face a potentially far more significant threat as a result of technological change.

Technological developments in broadband speed and connectivity are now driving increasing demand for electronic distribution of content through downloading. Increasing bandwidth makes streaming and downloading of high definition video accessible to many. Whilst the Blu-ray DVD undoubtedly offers far enhanced viewing quality to standard DVDs, the drivers of customer demand now seem to be predicated upon convenience, speed and portability. MP3s, for example, are as popular, if not more so, than music CDs, despite the latter's superior audio quality. Meanwhile, media and IT firms, such as Apple and Netflix are making more and more video content available on-line with little or no compromise on quality.

How Sony, the Hollywood studios, Blu-ray player manufacturers and DVD retailers respond to the on-line challenge of digital distribution will ultimately determine if the DVD format war was a profitable strategy.

Case study questions

1 What in your view are the key environmental influences shaping corporate strategy in this industry?

2 What examples of co-opetition are evident in the case study?

Review and discussion questions

1 Discuss the costs and benefits to businesses of the introduction of a system for monitoring and analysing the changing external environment in which they operate.

2 To what extent do you agree with the proposition that only large firms should or can make use of the various techniques of environmental analysis?

3 Using a firm or organisation of your choice, attempt a 'SWOT' analysis. For example, can you apply such an analysis to the organisation in which you work or study?

4 Using the information sources discussed in the text, and any others with which you are familiar, provide a comparative analysis of consumer markets in at least eight leading European countries (including eastern Europe).

Assignments

1 You work for a medium-sized private company in the UK fashion industry (it can be on either the production or the retailing side). As a personal assistant to the managing director, your brief is to provide help and advice on various aspects of the firm's operations. You have recently become concerned about the lack of a system for monitoring changes in the business environment and have agreed to produce a report on the issue for the board of directors. In producing this report, you are required to identify both the costs and the benefits to the business of implementing a system of environmental scanning.

2 As a librarian in a college (or university) library, with responsibility for help and advice to students on business studies courses, you are frequently asked for guidance on how to access information and data on a particular company. Choosing any well-known company you wish, produce a diagrammatic representation (e.g. flow chart) of the steps you would advise students to undertake to get the information they require. At each step, indicate what type of information is available and how and from where it can be obtained.

Further reading

Brandenburger, A. and Nalebuff, B., 'The Right Game: Use Game Theory to Shape Strategy', *Harvard Business Review*, Jul–Aug, 1995, pp. 57–71.

Cook, M. and Farquharson, C., *Business Economics: Strategy and Applications*, Pitman, 1998.

Cooke, S. and Slack, N., *Making Management Decisions*, 2nd edition, Prentice Hall, 1991.

The Economist, 'There will be blood', 23 February 2008.

Edwards, C., 'RIP, HD-DVD', *Business Week*, 21 February 2008.

Fahey, L. and Narayanan, V. K., *Macroenvironmental Analysis for Strategic Management*, West Publishing, 1986.

Finlay, Paul. N., *Strategic Management: An Introduction to Business and Corporate Strategy*, Financial Times/Prentice Hall, 2000.

Grant, R. M., *Contemporary Strategy Analysis*, 6th edition, Blackwell Business, 2007.

Gupta, U. and Clarke, R., 'Theory and Applications of the Delphi Technique: A Bibliography (1975–1994)', *Technological Forecasting and Social Change*, Volume 53, 1996, pp. 185–211.

Jasmin, M. and Wolpin, S., 'Hollow victory for Blu-ray.' *Electronic Engineering Times*, 20 June 2008.

Johnson, G., Scholes, K. and Whittington, R., *Exploring Corporate Strategy*, 8th edition, Financial Times/Prentice Hall, 2008.

Proctor, T., 'Strategic marketing management for health management: cross impact matrix and TOWS', *Journal of Management in Medicine*, 14 (1), 2000, pp. 47–56.

Ringland, G., *Scenario Planning: Managing for the Future*, Wiley, 1998.

Rowe, G. and Wright, G., 'The Delphi Technique as a forecasting tool: issues and analysis', *International Journal of Forecasting*, Volume 15, 1999, pp. 353–375.

Snider, M., 'The DVD War', *Maclean's*, 10 January 2005.

Weihrich, H., 'Daimler-Benz's move towards the next century with the TOWS matrix', *European Business Review*, 93 (1), 1993, pp. 4–11.

Wheelen, T. L. and Hunger, J. D., *Strategic Management and Business Policy*, 11th edition, Pearson Education (US), 2008.

Worthington, I., Britton, C. and Rees, A., *Business Economics: Blending Theory and Practice*, 2nd edition, Financial Times/Prentice Hall, 2005, esp. Chapter 15.

web link

Web links and further questions are available on the website at:
www.pearsoned.co.uk/worthington

Glossary

Abnormal profits: profits over and above normal profits.

Accelerator effect: increases in investment spending as a result of changes in output or sales.

Acceptance: under contract law acceptance is the notion of legally agreeing to an offer that is made.

ACORN: an acronym for A Classification of Residential Neighbourhoods, a method of segmenting consumer markets.

Age structure: the proportions of a population in different age band.

Ageing population: the increase in the average age of a population.

Agent: a person or organisation who is authorised by another person or organisation to act on behalf of the latter.

Aggregate monetary demand: the total demand for goods and services in the economy.

Articles of Association: a document regulating the internal administration of a company including the rights of shareholders, the qualifications required of directors and rules relating to company rules, etc.

Assisted Area: an area qualifying for state aid under government regional policy.

Authoritarianism: the disposition to settle disputes through the enforcement of rules, regulations and orders by an established authority.

Average cost of production: total costs per unit of output.

Backbench MPs: ordinary members of Parliament who do not occupy a role in government or on the Opposition front bench.

Balance of payments: a record of the transactions between one country and the other countries with which it trades.

Balance of trade: the balance of the import and export of goods.

Barriers to entry: any barriers which prevent or inhibit the entry of firms into an industry or market.

Barriers to exit: any barriers which prevent or inhibit the exit of firms out of an industry or market.

Birth rate: usually measured by the number of live births per thousand of the population in a given year.

Black economy: unofficial economic activity beyond the gaze of the tax authorities.

Brainstorming: is normally taken to mean a discursive activity designed to generate ideas and solutions to problems.

Bureaucracy: an organisational form associated with hierarchy and a system of rules and procedures.

Bureaucrats: in government those who are official and permanent advisers to elected decision-makers, e.g. civil servants.

Business angels: informal investors in business organisations, especially smaller enterprises.

Business culture: the underlying attitudes and values of business organisations which affect their decisions and operations.

Business ethics: concerned with issues of 'right' and 'wrong' behaviour in a business context.

Business Link: an agency which provides advice and information to UK small businesses.

Business-to-Business (B2B) Commerce: The full spectrum of e-commerce that can occur between two business organisations, including supply management, procurement and purchasing, sale activities, payments, and service and support.

Business-to-Consumer (B2C) Commerce: The full spectrum of e-commerce business models, in which businesses sell to consumers.

Buyers' market: a market where there is excess supply of the product. This affords the buyer greater market power.

Buy-Side Marketplace: a marketplace where one organisation does all the buying.

Cabinet: in UK central government the core decision-making body comprising the Prime Minister and the other senior ministers responsible for formulating government policy and overseeing its implementation.

CAD: the use of computers in the design of products and processes.

Capacity: under contract law, capacity is the notion that a party to an offer is legally able to enter into a binding contract.

Capital: man-made assets which are capable of producing goods and services.

Capital account: a record of the international flows of money for investment purposes.

Capital market: the market for longer-term loanable funds.

Capital market flows: flows of money from private investors wishing to include foreign assets in their portfolios.

Capitalist economy: a politico-economic system based upon private property and the pursuit of private profit through entrepreneurial activity.

Cartel: a collection of firms acting together as one producer to exercise market power.

Case law: law established by previous judicial decisions, i.e. judicial precedent.

Central bank: a country's state or national bank, usually responsible for exercising control over the country's monetary system.

Centrally planned economy: an economy in which the state makes the major decisions over resource allocation.

Chamber of Commerce: a body representing the interests of smaller firms in a particular locality.

Checks and balances: in a democratic system the existence of social, economic and political arrangements which act as a constraint on the power of government.

Circular flow of income model: a simplified model of the economy which portrays economic activity as a flow of income and expenditures passing between households and firms in a circular motion.

City Action Teams: teams of individuals drawn from government, voluntary organisations, local community groups and businesses to tackle problems in inner city areas.

City Challenge: a scheme designed to concentrate resources in areas experiencing urban problems by establish cross-sector partnerships to bid for project funding.

City Grant: a system of grant-aid that was designed to support private sector capital projects in urban areas.

Civil servants: permanent officials appointed to advise government ministers and to implement government decisions. Also called bureaucrats.

Classical theories of organisation: theories of organisation which essentially focus on organisations as formal structures established to achieve certain objectives under the direction of management.

Coalition government: a government formed by representatives of two or more parties either by choice or following an election in which no single party wins a majority of the seats being contested.

Codes of practice: a code of conduct, usually drawn up voluntarily with the aid of a professional or trade association, which members of the trade or profession are expected to follow.

Collusion: co-operation between independent firms to modify their behaviour.

Common Agricultural Policy: a policy set up by the European Union to help the agricultural sector in Europe.

Common external tariff: a tariff payable on goods entering the European Union from non-member countries.

Common Market: a group of countries acting as one in terms of trade – there are no barriers to trade between members and a common external tariff for non-members.

Company: a corporate body recognised by law as having a legal identity separate from that of its members (i.e. shareholders).

Company directors: individuals appointed or elected by a company's shareholders to run the company and to represent their interest.

Competition Act 1998: a major piece of UK competition policy designed to bring UK law in line with EU law on issues of anti-competitive agreements and abuse of dominant market position.

Competition Commission: a public body replacing the UK Monopolies and Mergers Commission with responsibilities in the field of competition policy.

Competition policy: government policy aimed at promoting competition in the marketplace by regulating market behaviour and controlling potential abuses of market power by firms acting singly or in concert.

Competitive advantage: the sources of superior performance by an organisation.

Complements: products which are related to each other such that as the price of one goes up the demand for the other goes down, CD players and CDs as an example.

Concentration: a measure of the level of competition in an industry or market. Concentration can be measured by sales or employment.

Concentration ratio: a ratio which calculates the percentage of the total market accounted for by the largest firms.

Confederation of British Industry: a body formed to promote the interests of British industry and to represent its views in government circles in an attempt to influence government decisions.

Conglomerate integration: a merger or take-over between firms in different, unrelated industries.

Consideration: under contract law some right, interest, profit or benefit accruing to one party or some forbearance, detriment, loss or responsibility given, suffered, or undertaken by the other.

Consortium: an association or syndicate of business organisations normally established in order to undertake a major enterprise by polling resources and/or expertise.

Constitution: in the political sense it usually refers to a written statement or document identifying where formal political power resides in a country and the relationships between political institutions.

Consumer Prices Index: the new UK measure of inflation.

Consumer societies: a form of 'self-help' organisation set up to serve its members.

Consumer sovereignty: the notion that the pattern of supply and hence the allocation of resources in the economy is dictated by the demands of consumers.

Contestable market: a market where there are no barriers to entry or exit.

Contingency approaches: in organisational theory the idea that organisational design and management should adapt to the situation confronting an organisation.

Corporate image: essentially how an organisation is seen by its customers and other interested parties.

Corporate social responsibility: the idea that an organisation should be responsible for the effect its actions might have on the broader society.

Cost-benefit analysis: a technique which seeks to evaluate the social costs and benefits of an investment project as an aid to decision making.

Council: in local government, the central elected decision-making body.

Council of Ministers: the EUs ultimate decision-making body, also referred to as the Council of the European Union.

Criminal law: that branch of law which relates to a legal wrong, a breach of public duty punishable by the state on behalf of society.

Cross price elasticity: the responsiveness of quantity demanded of one product to changes in the price of other products.

Cross subsidisation: where profits from one market can be used to keep prices down in another market – common in multinationals.

Cross-impact matrix: a technique for evaluating and assessing environmental change based on an identification of events thought likely to occur including an indication of their sequencing and probability of occurrence.

Crowding out: the thesis that the use of funds by government for public expenditure denies the private sector access to those funds for entrepreneurial activity.

Cultural diversity: normally associated with countries which have a mixture of citizens of different racial and ethnic origins.

Culture: a complex set of values, norms , beliefs, attitudes, customs, systems and artefacts handed down from generation to generation.

Current account (Balance of Payments): a record of the international flows of money in exchange for goods and services.

Current balance (Balance of Payments): the balance of payments on the current account.

Customs: particular forms of behaviour which have come to be accepted as social norms within a specific community.

Customs Union: a union of countries which constitute a single customs territory (see common market above).

Cyclical unemployment: unemployment which results from downswings in the trade cycle.

Death rate: usually measured as the number of deaths per thousand of the population in a given year.

Debentures: long-term bonds or loans to the company on which it pays interest.

Decisions: within the EU, a decision that is binding on those states, companies or individuals to whom it is addressed.

Deficit (Balance of Payments): a situation where imports are greater than exports, so that there is an outflow of money from a country.

Deindustrialisation: a decline in the importance of manufacturing industry in the economy.

Delegated legislation: law made by a person or body to which Parliament has given limited powers of law-making.

Demand: the quantity of a product that buyers are willing and able to buy at every conceivable price level.

Demand Chain Management (DCM): the management of the organisation's activities related to its customers, distribution channels and markets.

Demand curve: a graph which shows the relationship between the price of a product and the quantity demanded of that product.

Democracy: literally government by the people. In practice democracy refers to the idea of elected government, based upon universal suffrage and regular, free and fair elections.

Demographic time bomb: the shortage of young people entering the labour force as a result of low birth rates 16 years earlier.

Demography: the study of populations.

Dependant Population: those non-working members of a population (e.g. pensioners, the young) who depend on the working population for various forms of support.

Derived demand: a demand for a product which is not required for its own sake but because it is used to produce another product.

Devaluation: a deliberate reduction in the exchange rate of a currency.

Directives: EU decisions which lay down compulsory objectives but which leave it to member states to translate them into national legislation.

Directorates General: major administrative and executive structures within the EU to administer and oversee EU policy.

Differentiation: making a product different in the minds of consumers – these differences may be real or imagined.

Digital products (services): products that are transformed to information that can be expressed digitally. Music, computer software and movies are examples of products that can be digitised and delivered electronically to buyers.

Direct controls: government policies designed to tackle specific economic problems such as the control of imports or wage inflation.

Direct democracy: where government decisions are based upon the expressed preference of the people, usually through a referendum.

Direct taxation: taxes imposed on income and wealth.

Director General of Fair Trading: in the UK the person responsible for overseeing consumer affairs and competition policy on behalf of the government.

Diseconomies of scale: increases in average costs of production which occur when an organisation grows in size (or scale). These mainly stem from the problems of managing large organisations.

Diversification: extending production into unrelated areas through development of new products or entry into unrelated markets.

Dividends: the distribution of part of the company's profit to its shareholders.

Divisional structure: an organisational form involving the splitting up of an organisation into a number of self-contained units or divisions, each of which operates as a profit centre.

Downsizing: a reduction in the size of the firm, normally through redundancy and/or delayering.

Eco-label: a system of labelling products so as to identify those which have a reduced impact on the environment.

Eco-Management and Audit Scheme (EMAS): a voluntary EU standard indicating a participating firm's level of environmental management.

Economic efficiency: efficiency in the use and allocation of resources.

Economic growth: a country's increase in national income (national output) over time.

Economic scarcity: a situation in which there are insufficient resources to satisfy all the actual and potential demands for those resources.

Economics: a social science concerned primarily with the production, distribution and consumption of goods and services under conditions of relative economic scarcity.

Economies of scale: reductions in average costs of production which occur when an organisation grows in size (or scale). These can stem from a variety of sources including technical, marketing and financial.

Educated workforce: a workforce which has the necessary level of education and training for a modern economy.

Effective Demand: demand for a product backed up by the willingness and ability to pay for that product.

Effective Supply: supply which firms are able and willing to make available to a market.

Elasticity: a measurement of the responsiveness of one variable (e.g. demand, supply) to a change in another variable (e.g. price, income).

Elasticity of demand: the responsiveness of quantity demanded of a product to changes in its price.

Elasticity of supply: the responsiveness of quantity supplied of a product to changes in its price.

Electoral system: a system for electing a country's or area's governing authority.

Electronic Business (*E-Business*): The exchange of products, services, or information, whether paid or unpaid, across electronic networks, at any stage within the value system (including the supply chain, the value chain, and the distribution chain). The term embraces activities such as servicing customers, and collaboration with partners.

Electronic Commerce (*E-Commerce*): *E-Commerce* covers a narrower sphere of activities than *E-Business*, and refers in particular to the process of electronic transactions involved in the exchange of products, services and information between a buyer and seller.

Electronic Customer Relationship Management (eCRM): software and management practices designed to serve the customer from order through delivery and after-sales service.

Electronic Data Interchange (EDI): the computer-to-computer exchange of structured data, sent in a form that allows for automatic processing with no manual intervention. This is usually carried out over specialist EDI networks.

Electronic Enterprise (*E-Enterprise*): An organisation that uses the Internet and/or WWW to execute some, or all, of its main business processes.

Electronic Fund Transfer (EFT): the process of exchanging account information electronically over private communications networks.

Electronic Markets (*E-Markets*): The business centre, where business transactions take place, is a network-based location, and not a physical location. This is sometimes referred to as the *marketspace*. The buyers, sellers and intermediaries are all situated at different locations. The electronic market handles all the necessary transactions, including the transfer of payments.

Electronic Point of Sale (EPOS): the application of electronic technology at the point-of sale.

Emerging economies: those developing economies which often have increasing levels of income and have considerable potential for future growth.

English Partnerships: a government development agency involved in reclaiming industrial sites for economic purposes.

Enterprise: the business unit or organisation as a whole.

Enterprise Grants: government grants designed to promote entrepreneurial activity.

Enterprise Zones: an experiment introduced by the UK government in the early 1980s to promote industrial and commercial activity within designated localities.

Entrepreneurship: often added as a fourth factor of production, it is the act of bringing together land, labour and capital in the production of goods and services.

Environmental analysis: consideration of which environmental trends and changes might impact upon the organisation in the future.

Environmental change: the predisposition of the business environment to undergo change rather than to remain static.

Environmental Management System: a formalised set of procedures designed to guide an organisation on how to control its impact on the natural environment.

Environmental scanning: the identification of trends and changes in an organisation's environment.

Equilibrium price: the price at which demand and supply are equal. It is the market clearing price.

Equity: the ordinary share capital of the company.

Establishment: parts or branches of an enterprise. Large enterprises like supermarkets are likely to have a number of branches or establishments.

European Commission: the EUs major bureaucratic arm responsible for implementing EU decisions, for proposing policies and legislation and for acting as guardian of the Treaties.

European Council: annual meetings of the President of the European Commission and the heads of government/state and foreign ministers of EU member states.

European Court of Justice: the major judicial body within the EU responsible for interpreting EU law.

European Economic Area: an organisation which consists of members of the EU and members of the European Free Trade Association.

European Monetary System: a system of fixed exchange rates for members of the EU.

European Parliament: the EUs elected decision-making body.

European Structural Funds: various financial support mechanisms within the EU to address structural problems within disadvantaged EU regions.

Excess demand: where market price is below equilibrium price and as a result demand exceeds supply.

Excess supply: where market price is above equilibrium price and as a result supply exceeds demand.

Exchange control: a limit on the quantity of currency that can be purchased.

Exchange rate: the price at which one currency exchanges for another currency.

Exchange rate mechanism: a system of fixed exchange rates.

Executive directors: company directors with responsibility for a division or functional area within an organisation.

Export subsidy: a payment made to the producers of goods and services for export.

External environment: the external context within which an organisation exists and operates.

External growth: growth in firm size which takes place through merger or take-over.

Externalities: the spill-over effects of economic activity that are over and above the private costs and benefits that occur.

Extranet: a Web-based network that connects an organisation's network to the networks of its business partners, selected customers, or suppliers.

Factor market: the market where factors of production are bought and sold.

Factor of production: a resource used in the production of goods and services in an economy – land, labour, capital and entrepreneurship.

Factory gate prices: literally the price of goods leaving an organisation which can be used as an indication of possible future inflationary pressures in the economy.

Family life cycle: the stages through which families can pass as they mature over time.

Federal system of government: a system of government in which decision-making authority is split between a central (i.e. federal) government and government at sub-national level.

Financial account (balance of payments): a record of the international flows from trade in financial assets.

Financial intermediaries: individuals or institutions which help to link borrowers to lenders in the financial system.

First mover advantage: in the context of E-business, an assumption that the deployment of the Internet would increase switching costs and create strong network effects, which would provide first movers with competitive advantages and robust profitability.

First-past-the-post system: a system of elections in which the winner in a given constituency is the person with a simple majority of the vote cast. Also called a plurality system.

Fiscal policy: government policy concerned with the taxing and spending decisions of government.

Five-forces model: an economic model used to characterise industries and markets. It says that these are formed by five forces acting upon them – current competition, potential competition, the power of buyers, the power of sellers and the power of suppliers.

Fixed capital: the investment in fixed physical assets within a firm – buildings, plant and machinery are examples.

Fixed exchange rate: where the exchange rate is determined by the government or some other authority.

Flexible firm: a firm which is organised in such a way that it distinguishes between core and peripheral activities as a cost saving measure.

Floating exchange rate: where the exchange rate is determined by the free market.

Foreign Direct Investment (FDI): the establishment of production facilities in overseas countries.

Formal structures: the intended or official structure within an organisation that represents the way it is intended to function.

Franchising: an agreement between two parties in which the one permits the other to market something in its possession according to an agreed format and under certain contractual conditions.

Free market: a market without restrictions on its operations.

Free market economy: an economic system in which resource allocation is determined by market forces.

Free trade: trade without barriers.

Free trade area: where members of an area abolish barriers to trade with other members, but maintain their own barriers against non-members.

Full employment: when all or virtually all the labour force in a country is employed in paid work.

Functional organisation: an organisational form based on the grouping of individuals by common purpose or function.

Functional specialisation: where individuals within an organisation specialise in particular tasks associated with a specific function such as marketing or production.

G7 nations: the Group of Seven leading industrial nations, namely USA, Japan, UK, France, Germany, Canada, Italy. The G8 incorporates Russia.

Gearing: the proportional relationship between a firm's debt capital and its equity capital.

General (or Contextual) environment: the broad external context in which an organisation exists and operates. It comprises the PESTLE factors.

Genetically modified (GM) foods: food products which have undergone some element of genetic modification.

Geo-Demographic Segmentation: segmentation of a market on the basis of geographical and demographic variables.

Geographical immobility: the inability to move between geographical locations.

Globalisation: the internationalisation of products and markets.

Golden share: a special retained share holding by government when privatising a state owned organisation that permits the government to exercise some control over future developments.

Government: the structures and processes within a given territory by which laws are made and put into effect.

Government departments: large, state bureaucratic agencies which play a key role in shaping and implementing government policy within their sphere of competence.

Government spending: spending by government on public goods and services. Also called public spending or public expenditure.

Gross domestic product: the value of total economic activity within an economy over a particular period of time.

Gross investment: the total amount of capital goods purchased by firms.

Headline inflation: the rate of inflation in the UK including the effect of mortgage interest payments. Known as RPI.

Hierarchy of Needs: Maslow's notion that human needs form a kind of hierarchy of importance.

Holding company: a company set up to maintain or gain control of one or more other companies by holding a majority of shares of these subsidiaries.

Homogeneous products: products which are regarded by consumers as identical to each other and therefore perfect substitutes.

Horizontal integration: a merger or take-over between competitor firms at the same stage of the production process.

House of Commons: the lower house of the UK Parliament with major responsibility for discussing and deciding on laws proposed by the government.

House of Lords: the upper house of the UK Parliament, currently with limited powers.

Human relations approach: an approach to the study of organisation and management which emphasises the importance of social and psychological factors in the workplace.

Human Resource Management: the management of people within an organisation, including the processes of selection, recruitment, performance evaluation, rewards and compensation and training and development.

Hyperglobalisation: where the world market is seen as a borderless global marketplace consisting of powerful multinational corporations and powerless nation states.

Immediate (or Operational) environment: the more immediate external influences on an organisation from its customers, competitors, suppliers and other stakeholder groups.

Immobility of labour: the inability of labour to move between geographical locations, jobs or occupations.

Import control: a control placed on the import of goods and services into a country. This could be in the form of a quota, a tariff or exchange controls.

Import Penetration: a measurement of the degree of importation relative to home demand.

Income elasticity: the responsiveness of quantity demanded to changes in household income.

Income flows: flows of income or expenditure in the economy between its constituent parts as a result of economic activity.

Indirect taxation: taxation imposed on consumption or spending.

Industrial concentration: the proportion of an industry which is dominated by large firms.

Industrial policies: loosely speaking any government policy designed to improve the performance of a country's industries.

Industrial structure: the combination of industries and sectors in an economy.

Inferior goods: goods where, as income rises, demand falls.

Inflation: an increase in the general level of prices within the economy which results in a fall in the value of money (i.e. in the purchasing power of a given nominal sum of money).

Information technology: the use of computer systems for storing, retrieving and communicating information.

Infrastructure: services considered to be essential to a developed economy, such as power and transport systems.

Injections: in the circular flow of income model, those major increases in spending over and above consumption which increase the level of income in the economy (e.g. export spending, investment spending, government spending).

Inner City Task Forces: small teams of civil servants and others established to promote economic development in inner city urban locations.

Innovation: the use of new ideas, methods or approaches.

Inputs: the resources which flow into the production process in order to produce outputs.

Intention to create legal relations: under contract law, the notion of an intent to enter into a contract that is recognised in law as being legally binding.

Interdependence: the idea of the interconnectedness of firm behaviour in an oligopoly market.

Interest rates: the price(s) of borrowed money.

Internal growth: growth in the firm which takes place from within.

Internationalisation: increased links between countries with respect to trade and the movement of resources.

Internet: a global network of computer networks that use a common protocol (TCP/IP) for communication.

Intranet: a network within a single organisation that enables access to company information using internet technology such as web browsers and email.

Investment: spending by firms on capital goods – physical productive assets.

Investment appraisal: the analysis of the costs and benefits of possible new investment projects with a view to deciding on the desirability of committing resources to them.

Invisible trade: the import and export of services.

J-curve effect: a curve which describes the effect of a devaluation of a currency on the balance of payments over time.

Joint venture: a jointly owned and independently incorporated business venture involving more than one organisation.

Judicial precedent: see 'Case law'.

Judiciary: the legal institutions within a country responsible for enacting and interpreting the law.

Keynesianism: broadly speaking the view that economic activity is predominantly shaped by demand.

Knowledge Management infrastructure: an infrastructure that provides an organisation with a framework for making knowledge available where it is required internally.

Labour: human resources.

Labour market: the market(s) in which wage levels are theoretically determined by the supply and demand for labour.

Labour market flexibility: the degree to which individuals in the labour market are able to respond to changing market demands.

Land: natural resources; resources which are not man-made, including the soil, air, seas, minerals, etc.

Law of demand: as the price of a product rises the quantity demanded will normally fall.

Law of supply: as the price of a product rises the quantity supplied will normally rise.

Leakages: in the circular flow of income model, those activities which potentially cause a reduction in spending on domestically produced products and hence on income flows in the economy (e.g. taxation, import spending, saving).

Learning curve effect: the idea that performance can be improved as a result of experience in carrying out a procedure or action.

Learning and Skills Council: a newly established body responsible for funding and planning education and training for over-16 year olds in England.

Legislation: laws made by the elected decision makers. Also called statute law and (in the UK) Acts of Parliament.

Legislature: a country's law-making body.

Licensing: a form of non-equity agreement in which one party (e.g. a firm) grants another party or parties (e.g. another firm) the right to use its intellectual property (e.g. patent, trade name) in return for certain considerations (e.g. royalty payments).

Life-cycle analysis: a technique for assessing the environmental impact of a product throughout its life cycle. Sometimes called 'cradle-to-grave' analysis.

Life-cycle model: a model of the changes in sales and profitability of a product over time. There are four phases – development, growth, maturity and decline.

Lifestyles: the way in which people live and spend their money.

Lobbies: groups of individuals actively seeking to influence decision makers.

Local Enterprise Agencies: companies limited by guarantee, typically set up as partnerships between the private sector and local authorities, to deliver business support services to clients.

Macroeconomic analysis: economic analysis concerned with interactions within the economy as a whole.

Macroeconomic environment: the broad economic influences which are part of the external environment within which firms exist and operate.

Management: the structures and processes involved in directing an organisation towards the achievement of its objectives.

Managing Director: the chief administrative or executive officer within a company who is responsible for ensuring that Board decisions are put into effect and who forms the key link between the Board of directors and the management team of senior executives.

Manifesto: a document setting out a political party's views and policy preferences when seeking election to government.

Manufacturing sector: the sector of the economy which produces manufactured products.

Market: a place where buyers and sellers are brought together.

Market failure: the notion that free markets sometimes deliver solutions which are not always socially or economically desirable.

Market mechanism: the interaction of demand and supply.

Market niche: a gap in a market which can be exploited by a firm by satisfying a need that is not currently being met.

Market Segmentation: breaking down a market into different segments on the basis of particular variables.

Market structure: the amount of competition that exists between producers in a market.

Market system: an economic system based on the operation of free markets.

Marketing: essentially those processes involved in finding out what customers want and supplying them with the product in a way which is profitable to the organisation.

Marketing concept: the idea that organisations should seek to satisfy consumer wants by adopting a customer-focused orientation.

Marketing mix: the set of controllable variables which a firm can use to try to influence the consumer's response.

Marketspace: the digital equivalent of a physical-world marketplace.

Mass Customisation: the ability to provide tailored products or services for individual customers or a group of similar customers, but retains the economies of scope and the capacity of mass marketing or production.

Matrix structure: an organisational form based on both functional specialisation and structures built round products, projects or programmes.

Memorandum of Association: a document setting out the name of a company, its legal status, the address of its registered office, its objects, the amount of nominal share capital and a number of other aspects of the firm's operations.

MEPs: directly elected members of the European Parliament.

Merger: the voluntary combination of two or more separate companies into one.

Merit goods: goods/services which the government feels to be of general benefit to the community and which are therefore often funded by the state (e.g. education).

Microeconomic analysis: economic analysis which focuses on economic decisions by both individuals and firms.

Minimum efficient scale: the level of production where all economies of scale have been reached by the firm.

Minimum wage: the specification of a minimum level for wage rates.

Ministers: individuals who occupy senior decision-making roles in government.

Monetarism: broadly speaking the view that the level of output and employment in the economy are supply determined.

Monetary aggregates: the different measures used to calculate the money stock.

Monetary policies: government policies concerned with the availability and/or price of credit within the economy.

Money market: the market for short-term funds.

Money stock: the quantity of money in existence in an economy as determined by which monetary aggregates are included in the calculation.

Monopolistic competition: a market structure where there are a large number of sellers producing a differentiated product.

Monopoly: a market structure where there is one dominant producer.

Monopsony: a market where there is a single buyer.

MOSAIC: a tool to assist with market segmentation designed by Experian.

MPs: Members of Parliament, elected representatives in UK national elections.

Multinational enterprise or corporation: an enterprise that operates in a number of countries and which has production or service capabilities outside the country of origin.

Multiplier effect: a measure of the effect on total national income of some component change in aggregate monetary demand.

National debt: the accumulated debt from borrowings by past and present governments.

Nationalised industry: a state owned and controlled industry.

Natural monopoly: a industry where production conditions (e.g. large economies of scale) mean that the least wasteful market structure is monopoly.

Natural population change: the difference between the birth rate and the death rate in a given population over a specific period of time.

Natural resources: resources which are not man-made (see 'Land' above).

Negademand: where the use of less resources produces negative demand for particular commodities.

Negotiated environment: the idea that the policy making environment in a democratic country is characterised by a bargaining process involving individuals, groups and government in shaping decisions.

Net investment: the level of investment after replacement investment has been taken out – it represents net additions to the capital stock.

Networking: the relationships that exist between organisations and the people within those organisations.

New Deal: a UK government programme aimed at tackling the problem of social exclusion.

Non-executive directors: directors in a company (usually part-time) without functional responsibility.

Non-price competition: the use of non-price factors to sell a product, e.g. advertising, branding or special offers.

Non-renewable resources: resources which cannot be replenished after use, such as oil and coal.

Normal goods: goods where, as income rises, demand falls.

Normal profits: the minimum profit required by the entrepreneur to stay in production.

NVQs: National Vocational Qualifications.

Occupational immobility: the inability of workers to move between different occupations.

Occupational structure: the proportions of the workforce in different occupational groups.

Offer: under contract law a declaration by the offeror that they intend to be legally bound by the terms stated in an offer if it is accepted by the offeree.

Office of Fair Trading: a non-ministerial government department responsible for consumer affairs in the UK.

Oligopoly: a market structure where there are a small number of large producers and a great deal of interdependence of decision making.

One-to-One marketing: a unique dialogue that occurs directly between an organisation and individual customers.

Open system: a system in interaction with the external environment.

Opportunity cost: the real cost of a decision expressed in terms of the value of the alternative courses of action which have been sacrificed.

Ordinary shares: or 'equity' are shares in a company which do not carry a fixed dividend. Dividends paid depend upon the performance of the company.

Organisation by product: an organisational form in which the division of work is determined by the product or service being provided.

Organisation chart: a diagram which seeks to portray the responsibilities and relationships within an organisation or part of an organisation.

Outputs: the goods or services or other results that derive from the production process.

Parliament: in the UK the supreme law-making body.

Parliamentary system of government: a system of government based on election to a parliament from whom the senior members of the political executive are chosen.

Participation rate: the proportion of the population that works.

Partnership: an unincorporated form of business organisation comprising two or more individuals working together for mutual benefit.

People: human resources or labour.

Perfect competition: a market structure in which there are many buyers and sellers all producing an identical product and where the degree of competition is very high.

Perfect knowledge: where all actors in a market have complete knowledge of everything in the market.

Perfect mobility: a situation where there are no barriers to movement – it can be applied to firms, consumers and workers.

PESTLE Analysis: analysis of the business environment which focuses on the political, economic, social, technological, legal and ethical influences on the firm.

Plebiscites: see referendums.

Political accountability: the idea that elected politicians are ultimately accountable for their actions and decisions to the people who elected them.

Political executive: the key elected decision-making part of government responsible for the formulation and implementation of government policy and legislation.

Political parties: voluntary groups of like-minded individuals who organise themselves to contest elections and to seek formal political office.

Political sovereignty: the legitimate authority given to an individual or group to make decisions affecting large numbers of people.

Politics: the processes which help to determine how conflicts are contained, modified, postponed or settled.

Polluter pays principle: the idea that the responsibility for resolving environmental problems rests with the person causing them.

Porter's Five-Forces model: see 'Five-forces model'.

Preference shares: shares in a company which carry a fixed dividend.

Presidential system of government: a system of government in which the head of government or chief executive is elected separately by the people and is not normally part of the elected legislature.

Pressure groups: voluntary groups of like-minded people who join together in order to seek to influence government decision makers. See also 'Lobbies'.

Price ceiling: a maximum price above which the price of the product is not allowed to rise.

Price competition: the use of changing prices to sell products.

Price controls: a control exercised over price which prevents the working of the market mechanism.

Price discrimination: the charging of different prices to different users for the same product.

Price elasticity of demand: the responsiveness of quantity demanded of a product to changes in its price.

Price floor: a minimum price below which the price of the product is not allowed to fall.

Price leadership: where one firm in an industry takes the lead in setting prices and other firms follow.

Price maker: a producer that has enough market power to influence price.

Price taker: a producer that has no power over price, as in perfect competition.

Price war: a situation where a reduction in price by one company is followed by reductions in price by other companies.

Primary Reference Groups: groups which have a direct and face-to-face influence on a person's attitudes and behaviour.

Primary sector: the part of an economy that deals with the extraction of raw materials, including agriculture and mining.

Prime Minister: the head of government and of the majority party in the UK Parliament.

Principal: under agency law, a person or organisation hiring an agent to act on their behalf.

Private law: law governing the relationship between individuals.

Private Limited Company: an incorporated business organisation restricted by its Articles of Association from any invitation to the general public to subscribe for its shares or debentures.

Privatisation: the process of transferring the ownership of state assets to the private sector.

Process innovation: the development of new approaches in the production process.

Product innovation: the development of new products.

Product market: the market where products are bought and sold.

Productivity: the relationship between input and output, for example labour productivity measures output per worker.

Professional lobbyist: a person or organisation paid to lobby on behalf of another person or organisation.

Profit: the payment or reward to the entrepreneur for bringing together the other factors of production.

Profit centre: a section or area of an organisation to which revenue can be traced and costs attributed so that profits (or losses) can be ascribed to that area.

Project team: a temporary form of organisational structure set up to carry out a particular task.

Proportional representation: a form of voting system in which the final result of a ballot more closely approximates the number of votes cast for a candidate or candidates than under a first-past-the-post system of voting.

Psychographic Segmentation: market segmentation on the basis of variables such as social class and lifestyles.

Public corporation: a state owned and controlled organisation set up to run a publicly owned enterprise.

Public goods: goods which must be supplied communally because they cannot be withheld from one individual without withholding them from all (e.g. national defence).

Public law: laws relating to the relationship between individuals and the state.

Public Limited Company (PLC): an incorporated form of business organisation which can invite the general public to subscribe for its shares and debentures.

Public sector net borrowing: the extent to which a government's annual expenditure on public goods and services exceeds it revenue from taxation and other sources of income.

Public sector organisations: organisations in the state sector of the economy.

Qualified majority vote (qmv): a voting system in which the outcome of a vote is determined by a previously agreed proportion of votes cast by the majority of voters.

Qualitative Control: controls on the quality of goods in international trade rather than quantity or price.

Quality of people: the quality of labour in a country, which is largely determined by the level of education and training.

Quota: a physical limitation on the level of imports.

Real cost: see 'Opportunity cost'.

Real flows: flows of good and services and resources in the economy as a result of economic activity.

Real interest rates: the true cost of borrowing allowing for inflation.

Real national income: the value of the national income having allowed for price inflation.

Recession: a downturn in economic activity, currently defined in the UK as two successive quarters of negative economic growth.

Recommendations and Opinions: EU statements which have no binding force but merely state the view of the institution which issues them.

Re-engineering: radical redesign of business processes.

Reference Groups: groups which influence a person's attitudes and behaviour.

Referendums: an example of direct democracy in which individuals are able to cast their vote for or against a proposal with the expectation that the majority view will prevail. Also called plebiscites.

Region: a geographical area possessing certain characteristics which help to differentiate it from surrounding areas thus permitting boundaries to be drawn around it.

Regional Chambers: bodies set up in the English regions to represent the various regional interests.

Regional Development Agencies: recently established agencies in the UK regions for designing and delivering integrated programmes of regional regeneration.

Regional Government Offices: the regionally-based offices of central UK government departments.

Regionalism: essentially the move towards regional trade agreements (e.g. NAFTA) in an age of globalisation.

Regional Selective Assistance: a discretionary form of government assistance to businesses under UK regional policy.

Regional trade agreements: trade agreements between countries within a given regional area.

Regulations: EU decisions which apply directly to all member states and which are legally binding without recourse to national parliaments.

Renewable resources: resources that can be replenished after use, such as fishing stocks and solar power.

Replacement investment: spending on capital goods which replace old and worn out capital goods.

Representative government: government chosen to represent the people through a system of democratic election.

Research and development: the introduction of and the development of new ideas.

Resource-based view: an approach to strategy which emphasises firm processes and suggests that superior firm performance is related to the accumulation of valuable resources and capabilities.

Resources: scarce inputs into the production process used to produce goods and services.

Retail Prices Index (RPI): a weighted index of a 'basket of consumer goods and services' used in the UK to calculate the rate of inflation.

Revaluation: a deliberate increase in the exchange rate of a currency.

Scenario writing: a technique of environmental analysis based on imagined future developments in the business environment.

Scientific management: an approach to organisation and management which essentially believes that scientific methods can be used to improve performance in the workplace.

Secondary Reference Groups: groups which tend to have a more indirect influence on a person's attitudes and behaviour.

Secondary sector: the part of an economy that includes industries which process raw materials, like manufacturing and construction.

Secretary of State: in UK government, the political head of a major government department.

Self-regulation: where the state allows organisations (e.g. businesses) to regulate themselves in certain areas (e.g. environmental performance).

Sellers' market: a market where there is excess demand for the product. This affords the seller greater market power.

Sell-Side Marketplace: a marketplace where one organisation does all the selling.

Separation of powers: where the three major functions of government are held by separate authorities.

Sex distribution of population: the balance of men and women in a population.

Shareholders: the owners (or members) of a limited company.

Single Market: a common market (see above). Often applied to the European Union.

Single Regeneration Budget: a scheme to bring together a number of programmes from different government departments aimed at simplifying and streamlining the assistance available for local regeneration.

Skill shortages: shortages which exists in certain skills (e.g. IT skills) and which at times can co-exist with unemployment.

Small firm: a firm which is small in terms of the number of people it employs or its turnover.

Smart Cards: physical cards that contain a memory chip that can be inserted into a smartcard reader before items can be purchased.

Social capital: capital that is owned by the community such as hospitals and schools.

Social Class: a system of grouping together people with a similar social status, based on variables such as income, education and occupation.

Social Mobility: the ability to move between different strata in society, for example different social classes.

Sole trader: an unincorporated form of business organisation owned by one individual. Also called a sole proprietorship.

Sovereignty: in a general sense, the power to influence events and decisions.

Specialisation: the tendency for countries to specialise in producing goods where they have a comparative advantage.

Speculation: the buying and selling of currencies in order to make a capital gain on any movements in exchange rates.

Stakeholders: anyone with an interest in an organisation and who is affected by and can affect its performance.

Standard Industrial Classification (SIC): the official classification of industries in the UK, it is based on the European classification – Nomenclature générale des activités économiquees dans les Communautés européennes (NACE).

State bank: see 'Central bank'.

Statute law: see 'Legislation'.

Sticky prices: this describes the phenomenon of rigid prices commonly found in oligopolistic markets.

Stock: the capital of a business entity.

Stock exchange: a market for second-hand securities.

Strategic alliance: a collaborative agreement between firms to achieve a common aim.

Strategic fit: the notion of achieving a match or fit between the organisation's internal and external environments in pursuit of its objectives.

Strategic management: the management of the organisation as a whole through strategic analysis, choice and implementation.

Structural unemployment: unemployment caused by a decline in a particular industry as a result of a long-term change in demand or technological conditions.

Structure-conduct-performance model: an economic model used to characterise industries and markets. It says that the structure of the market determines conduct which in turn determines performance.

Subcontracting: the outsourcing of part of the production process to another firm.

Sub-culture: groups of individuals within the broader culture who have shared value systems based on common experiences, origins and/or situations.

Subsidy: in the export field, government financial support for businesses involved in exporting.

Substitutes: products which are related to each other such that as the price of one goes up the demand for the other goes up, e.g. different brands of petrol.

Sub-systems: the component parts of a system.

Supply: the quantity of a product that sellers are willing and able to sell at every conceivable price level.

Supply chain management (SCM): the management of the organisation's activities related to its suppliers, and supply channels.

Supply curve: a graph which shows the relationship between the price of and the quantity supplied of a product.

Supreme Court: the ultimate judicial authority in interpreting the law under a written constitution.

Surplus (balance of payments): a situation where the value of exports is greater than the value of imports, so that there is an inflow of money into a country.

Sustainable development: an approach to economic growth and development which takes account of the social and environmental consequences.

SWOT (or TOWS) analysis: a technique for analysing a firm's internal strengths and weaknesses and its external opportunities and threats.

Systems approach: an approach to organisational analysis which portrays organisations as socio-technical systems interacting with their external environment.

Takeover: the acquisition of one company by another.

Tariff: a tax imposed on imported products.

Technological change: changes in the technology used in production – automation and computerisation are examples.

Technological unemployment: unemployment resulting from the replacement of labour by technology (e.g. robotics).

Technology: the sum of knowledge of the means and methods of producing goods and services.

Tertiary sector: the part of the economy devoted to the production of services.

The Delphi method: a technique of environmental analysis involving several iterations by expert observers of the business environment. Also called expert opinion.

Theory X and Y: the idea that management sees individuals in the workplace as either inherently lazy or committed to the organisation and seeking responsibility.

Theory Z: an approach to management which gives individuals a positive orientation towards an organisation as a result being of provided with a number of discernible benefits.

Third way: broadly speaking the notion of new progressivism in politics based on the traditions of social democracy as applied to the modern world.

Top-down approaches: the tendency for decisions to be determined by those in formal positions of authority.

Tort: a civil wrong other than a breach of contract or a breach of trust; a duty fixed by law on all persons.

Trade Associations: bodies formed to protect and assist members in the same industry.

Trade Union: organisations of workers which are designed to counteract and protect their members from the power of the employer.

Training and Enterprise Councils: a system set up by the UK government to run its national training programme. Now replaced by the Learning and Skills Council.

Transaction Cost Economics: a branch of economics which looks at the make or buy decision based on the relative costs of transactions.

Transfer pricing: internal pricing used in large organisations to transfer products (raw materials for example) between divisions.

Transformation system: a system by which inputs are converted into outputs.

Transformationalism: the idea that globalisation brings about changes both in the power of countries and companies and in national characteristics and culture.

Transnational corporation: an international organisation that does not have a national base.

Trend extrapolation: a technique for predicting the future based on an analysis of the past.

Trend–impact analysis: a technique of environmental analysis designed to examine the likely impact on forecasted trends of a range of variables.

Trust: an equitable obligation imposing on one or more persons a duty of dealing with property, over which they have no control, for the benefit of other persons who may enforce the obligation.

Trusted control protocol/Internet protocol (TCP/IP): the standard for passing of data packets on the Internet.

Underlying inflation: the rate of inflation excluding the effect of mortgage interest payments. In the UK known as RPIX.

Unitary system of government: a system of government in which sovereign power is vested in a single central authority.

Unlimited personal liability: in unincorporated business organisations the legal liability of the owner of the business for all the debts of the business.

Urban Development Corporations: independent government development agencies set up to oversee inner-city regeneration in designated areas.

Urban Regeneration Companies: specialist organisations set up in declining urban areas to lead and coordinate redevelopment and new investment.

VALS: an acronym for Values and Lifestyles, a form of psychographic segmentation developed by SRI International.

Value System: an interconnection of processes and activities within and among organisations that create benefits for intermediaries and end consumers.

Vertical integration: a merger or takeover between firms at different stages of the production process.

Virtual organisation: broadly speaking a loose web of freelance individuals or businesses who organise themselves to produce a specific consumer product. Also an organisation where the core operating company outsources most of its processes to a network of other companies.

Visible trade: the import and export of goods.

Wage rate: earnings per hour or per standard working week excluding overtime payments.

Wages: the payment made to people for their labour services.

Wages/prices inflationary spiral: a situation in which wage increases fuel inflation which in turn fuels further wage demands causing further inflation and so on.

Withdrawals: see 'Leakages'.

Workers' co-operatives: a business owned and controlled by the people who work in it and who co-operate for mutual benefit.

Workforce: the number of people able and eligible to work and offering themselves for work.

Working capital: the investment in a firm in capital used on a day-to-day basis such as raw materials; often called circulating capital.

Working week: the number of hours spent in work per week.

Index